Developing and Mastering the New Way of Thinking

Natalia I. Hughson, M.D.

University of Advancing Technology

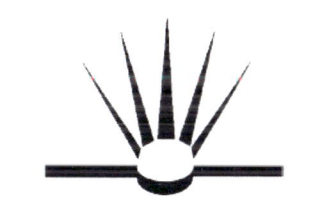

De Omnibus Publishing

Chandler, Arizona

Library of Congress Cataloging-in-Publication Data

Hughson, I. Natalia

Developing and mastering the new way of thinking / I. Natalia Hughson

365 p. cm

Includes bibliographical references and index.

ISBN 0-9787685-1-5

1. Cognitive psychology. I. Title.

Designer: Natalia I. Hughson, M.D.

Copyright © 2010 by De Omnibus Publishing Company. All rights reserved. Printed in the United States of America. This publication is protected by Copyright and permission should be obtained from the publisher priori to any prohibited reproduction, storage in a retrieval system, or transmission in any form or by any means, electronic, mechanical, photocopying, recording, or likewise.

De Omnibus Publishing Company
516 E. Tonto Dr.
Chandler, Arizona 85249

Deomnibus.com

480-375-0794

480-802-2018

602-383-8228

ISBN 0-9787685-1-5

Brief Contents

Preface		VII
Acknowledgment		IX
CHAPTER 1	**The Brain Is the Foundation of the Mind**	2
CHAPTER 2	**Learning and Thinking**	17
CHAPTER 3	**Developmental Aspect of Thinking**	43
CHAPTER 4	**How Self-Image Is Related to Thinking?**	68
CHAPTER 5	**What Is Intelligence?**	87
CHAPTER 6	**What Is Thinking?**	101
CHAPTER 7	**Modes of Thinking**	123
CHAPTER 8	**Creative Thinking**	251
CHAPTER 9	**Problem Solving**	283
CHAPTER 10	**What You Can Learn from Great Thinkers?**	309
Annotated Bibliography		339
References		345
Index		351

Contents

Preface VII

Acknowledgement IX

CHAPTER 1

The Brain Is the Foundation of the Mind   2

    Your Brain Structure and Functions in Short   2

    Brain Functions   2

    Interesting Facts about Brain   10

    Summary   11

EXERCISE 1.1. Creating MindMap   12

EXERCISE 1.2. Idea Quota   16

CHAPTER 2

Learning and Thinking   17

    Classical Conditioning   19

    What Is Operant Conditioning?   22

    What is Social Learning Theory?   23

    The 'What-Is-It?' Reaction   25

    Cognitive Learning   27

    How to Enhance Learning?   29

    Summary   31

TEST. Your Thinking and Learning Style   34

CHAPTER 3

Developmental Aspect of Thinking 43

The Nature of Early Brain Development 44

Stages of Thinking Development 46

Children Creativity 49

Gifted Children 51

Summary 57

TEST. Intelligence Test 57

CHAPTER 4

How Self-Image Is Related to Thinking? 68

What Is the Self-Concept? 68

Components of a Self-Concept 69

Self-Efficacy and Success 72

Self and Creativity 78

The Mature Personality 83

Summary 83

TEST. My Self Image (Winner and Losers) Check List 84

CHAPTER 5

What Is Intelligence? 87

Intelligence: History of Study 89

Gardner's Multiple Intelligences Theory 91

Sternberg's Theory 93

Interesting Facts 96

Summary 97

TEST. Multiple Intelligences Inventory 97

CHAPTER 6

What Is Thinking? 101

Human Reasoning 103

What is Thinking /Cognition? 107

Summary 110

EXERCISE 6.2. Recognition: What Is It? 112

EXERCISE 6.3. Concepts: Putting Things Together 112

EXERCISE 6.4. Judgment 118

EXERCISE 6.5. Problem Solving 119

CHAPTER 7

Modes of Thinking 121

Analogical Thinking 123

Symbolic Thinking 138

Analysis 147

Synthesis 156

Holistic Thinking 158

Systems Thinking 161

Dialectical Thinking 169

Integrative Thinking 173

Heuristic Thinking 178

Divergent Thinking 181

Convergent Thinking 189

Conscious Thinking 189

Unconscious Thinking 189

Critical Thinking 191

Deductive Thinking 202

Inductive Thinking 212

Abductive Thinking 218

The "Doubting Game" 219

The "Believing Game" 219

Automatic Thinking 225

v

Reversal Thinking 227

CHAPTER 8

Creative Thinking 251

Definitions of Creativity 253

You are more creative than you think 255

The Enemies of Ideas 263

Group Activities 274

CHAPTER 9

Problem Solving 283

Problems 285

Problem Solving and Decision Making 285

The Decision-Making Process 286

Behavioral Influence on Decision Making 290

Stages of Creative Process 291

Group Decision Making 293

Common Barriers to Problem Solving 295

How Solve Problems? 296

Summary 299

EXERCISE. 21 Steps of Synectic.

CHAPTER 10

What Can We Learn from Great People? 309

Failure and Greatness 311

The Key Elements of Maslow's Humanistic Perspective 312

Approaches to Giftedness 318

Primary Traits Related to Creativity 319

Histories of Creative People 322

Genius Productivity and Errors 329

Summary 333

TEST. Self-Actualization 334

Annotated Bibliography 339

References 345

Index 351

Preface

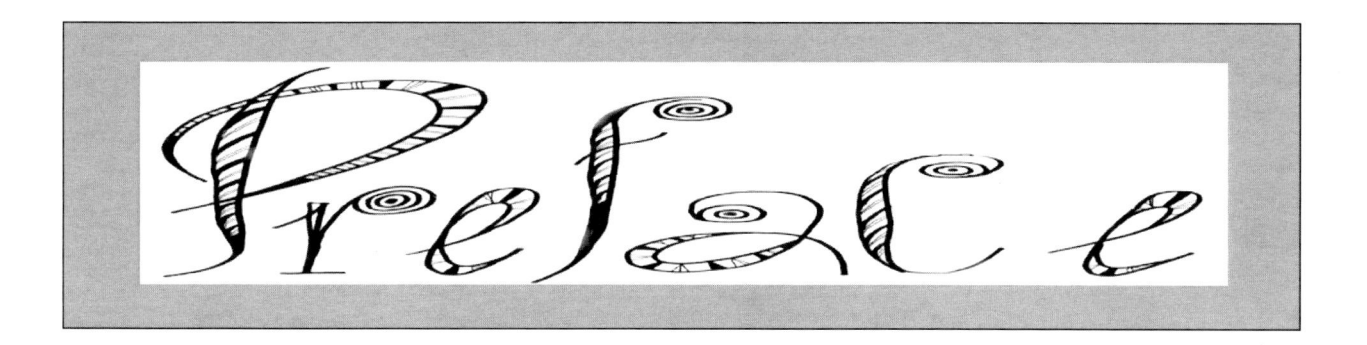

Right now you are reading and thinking. Think about it. What exactly is happening in your head? Can you figure it out? How does your brain works?

Learning to be a good thinker means acquiring several thinking abilities. In this book you will be introduced to 21 the most important, applicable, and widely useful modes of thinking. You will be encouraged to develop and strengthen them. By learning and applying the various concepts and techniques presented here, you will

- Understand how your brain works and learn to use it more effectively
- Think more clearly and creatively
- Solve problems and make decisions more effectively
- Comprehend more perceptively what is going on around you
- Free yourself from dogmatic thinking and mental rigidity
- Adjust yourself in the best way to a constantly changing world
- Learn from the lives of great thinkers and more.

Modern society is saturated with information, and that saturation is growing at an accelerating rate. The overflow of information presents people with two fundamental challenges: *filtering* information and *using* the information attended to in the most efficient way. These two fundamental challenges are composed of partially specified problems, that is, problems for which people usually do not have a full set of guidelines to solve. In real life, people seldom encounter a problem that is fully specified. Therefore, it is essential to learn how to solve partially specified problems. In most educational experiences, students face fully specified problems and are expected to learn the set of steps to solve them. This approach works in lower grades and in college introductory courses where we learn simple problems.

This book intends to teach skills necessary to confront and solve more difficult problems. When problem solver is able to recognize what is missing in partially specified problems and use the available information to span the gaps in those problems, he or she develops more professional skills and, the most practical of all, real-life skills. Learning thinking skills helps to meet the challenges of living in information-saturated society that is thirsty for talents and innovators.

Here are some of the features of the book:
- Numerous diagrams clarifying complex psychological concepts. We believe that when we can clearly illustrate any psychology concept, the majority of students can comprehend it. The diagrams provide visual aid to understanding of the text.
- Opportunities for readers to develop their own opinion. Readers become involved in this text because, chapter by chapter, they are working out their own position, borrowing knowledge from prominent psychologists and attacking arguments of opponents. It helps readers understand their own behavior and elaborate their own place in the social world.
- Lively chapter openings encouraging readers to read further. Every chapter begins with a study case, proverb, paradox, or some other attention-getting device. Such design intrigues and motivates readers for learning more about thinking under consideration.
- Thinking exercises. It is important for learners to develop various cognitive abilities while studying such a dynamic subject as thinking. Our exercises help readers to build their position on important cognitive issues.
- Chapter heads stated as question. This simple device makes it easy to evaluate reader's progress.
- In the text the key words and important concepts are highlighted.

- Text is accompanied by numerous illustrations, pictures, drawings, mind-maps, clipart, charts, and tables.

Each chapter includes:
1. Chapter Outline
2. Objectives
3. Creative thinking questions
4. Questions for discussion
5. Text
6. Summary
7. Numerous exercises that help you to improve your thinking.

Acknowledgments

Writing a textbook is a cooperative effort requiring the talents, knowledge, and energies of a large group of researchers, writers, scholars, and teachers. This book reflects the efforts of a large number of people.

We deeply appreciate the contribution of all those who have developed theoretical background and practical techniques and generated the most exciting ideas in the field of creative thinking. We would like to single out the following researchers and writers, each of whom has made this a better book:

Teresa M. Amabile, Ph.D.
Brandeis University
Silvano Arieti, M.D.
New York Medical College
Richard L. Anderson
Kansas City Art Institute
B. Armbuster,
J. Ayan,
F. Barron,
W. I. B. Beveridge, Ph.D.
University of Cambridge
J. Bier,
Max Black, Ph.D.
Johns Hopkins University
M. Boden,
E. De Bono,
Daniel J. Boorstin, Ph.D.
Librarian of Congress, the Preston and Sterling Morton Distinguished Service Professor of American History, University of Chicago
Bradley, R.
W. Lambert Brittain
Department of Human Development and Family Studies, Cornell University
M. Britton,
T. Brown,
L. Carey,

J. Carney,
Ernst Cassier, Ph.D.
Yale University
Delia Chairo,
University of Naples, Italy
D. Cohen, Ph.D.
L. Cooper, Ph.D.
Dennis Coon, Ph.D.
The University of Arizona
Mihaly Csikszentmichalyi, Ph.D.
Professor and chairman of the Department of Psychology at the University of Chicago
Irwin Edman, Ph.D.
Columbia University
Betty Edwards, Ph.D.
Professor in the Art Department at California State University
Eysenck, H. J., M.D.
Institute of Psychiatry, University of London
J. Flowers,
Howard Gardner, Ph.D.
Harvard University
M. Goetzel,
V. Goetzel,
T. Goetzel,
E. Gombrich,
J. Goodpaster,
J. Gilford, Ph.D.
R. Green,

Donald F. Gustafson, Ph.D.
University of Colorado
N. Herrmann,
D. Jablow Hershman,
Artist and novelist
Larry A. Hjelle, Ph.D.
State University of New York
S. Hibino, J
J. Ivancevich,
Gary R. Kirby,
G. Klein,
A. Koestler,
J. Lieb, M.D.
Psychiatrist
Rollo May, Ph.D.
Harvard University,
Princeton University,
Yale University,
University of California
M. Michalko,
P. Murray,
Stephen Nachmanovitch, Ph.D.
Violinist, composer, poet, teacher, and computer artist
G. Nadler,
L. Nichols,
Gerard I. Nierenberg,
President of the Negotiation Institute
Roger von Oech
Jane Piirto, Ph. D.
E. Raudsepp,

Nicholas Roukes, Ph. D.
University of Calgary, Canada
Ottone M. Riccio,
Boston Center for Adult Education
Potter, J, Ph D
University of California
Raymond Smullyan, Ph.D.
Professor of Philosophy at Indiana University
Dennis J. Sporre
B. Stein,
Storr, A
Sutton, R. I. Ph.D.
Stanford Engineering School
E. Torrance,
A. VanGundy,

CHAPTER 1

The Brain

Is the Foundation of the Mind

Thinking is a function of the brain. It is impossible to understand thinking processes without knowledge of the brain's structure and functions. Intelligence arises as the brain reasons, plans, and solves problems. The brain makes sense of the world by using all available information, including senses, emotions, instincts and remembered experiences. This chapter introduces you to what neuroscientists know about brain structure and functions.

LEARNING OBJECTIVES

After reading this chapter, you will be able to

1. Define functions of the nervous system
2. Describe and discuss anatomy of the Brain
3. Compare and contrast structure and functions of neurons and glial cells
4. Compare and contrast chemical and electrical neurotransmission
5. Demonstrate comprehension of the brain sections and their functions
6. Practice the brain functions through exercising your brain "muscles."

CHAPTER 1

Your Brain Structure and Functions in Short

Your brain is made up of hundreds of billions of cells. You might think of each of these cells as a musician in an orchestra. Each person in the orchestra plays notes that—in harmony with all of the sections in the orchestra—results in elaborate music.

The complex concerto that the orchestra's musicians play is—in this case—your own behavior patterns.

Your thoughts, actions, and senses (sight, smell, taste, touch, hearing) affect distinct sets of nerve cells and brain chemicals.

How It Works?

Patterns of chemical and electrical signals travel between the nerve cells in your brain.

Nerve cells (neurons) are the workhorses of the brain. Their fibers (**axons and dendrites**) form connections (**synapses**) with other nerve cells.

When a nerve cell is activated, it sends a low-level **electrical current** down its axon. This releases brain chemicals (**neurotransmitters**) that reach across the gaps between nerve cells and latch onto receptors.

Nerve cells that receive neurotransmitters then pass the signal along, like runners in a relay race. When you repeat experiences (for example, practicing a musical score), you reactivate the same nerve cell connections (synapses) over and over again.

After many repetitions, the synapse changes physically, making the connections more efficient and storing the experience or behavior in your long-term memory. Scientists believe that your **long-term memories** are actually stored—or "encoded"—in specific **synapse patterns** in your brain folds and ridges.

How Parts of Your Brain Relate to Function?

The part of your brains called the "frontal lobe of the cerebral cortex"—especially the so-called "prefrontal cortex"—is where important functions like **reasoning and planning** take place.

Other areas of your brain (the hippocampus, the amygdala, and neighboring structures in the temporal lobe) are connected to the cortex by complex nerve cell connections, which form the core of your **brain's memory-processing system**.

Let's go deeper into details about your brain.

Brain Functions

Human brain performs the following functions:

1. Using sensory receptors *monitors changes* occurring both inside and outside the body (sensory input)
2. It *processes and interprets* the sensory input and makes decision (integration)
3. It *affects a response* by activating muscles or glands (motor output).

Let's take a close look on each of those processes.

1. *Using sensory receptors monitors changes occurring both outside and inside the body* (sensory input)

   Outside the body. All experience is filtered by sensory systems. All sensory signals (e.g., sound, sight, taste, touch), in turn, initiate a cascade of cellular and molecular processes in the brain that alter neuronal neurochemistry, cytoarchitecture and, ultimately, brain structure and function. This process of creating some internal representation of the external world (i.e., information) depends upon the pattern, intensity and frequency of neuronal activity produced by sensing, processing and storing signals.

   Inside the body. There are other sensory mechanisms to tell the brain what is going on in the internal world – the physiological milieu of the body. For example, we have special sensory apparatus that tell the brain the concentration of oxygen in the blood; others sense the concentration of salts (too high and we become thirsty), or gases such as CO_2. These internal sensory apparatus, like the five senses for the external world, help the brain continuously monitor and act to keep you alive.

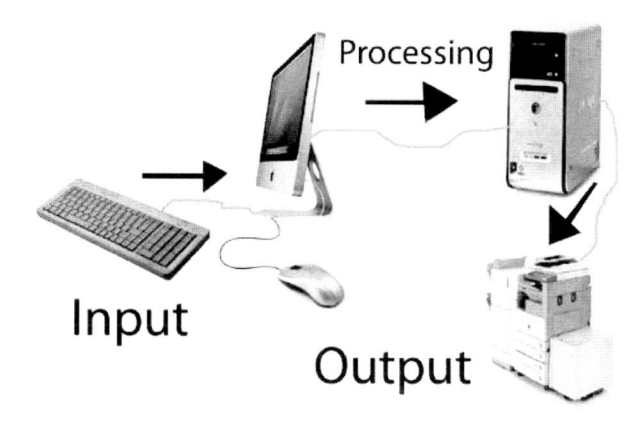

The Brain Is the Foundation of the Mind

Figure 1. Computer Processing the Information. Information enters the computer through key board and mouse (INPUT). It goes to the processor that has certain hardware and software (PROCESSING). It sends command to the printer (OUTPUT).

Your brain is not creative. It does not like to be surprised. All unknown or unfamiliar environmental cues are judged to be 'threatening' until proven otherwise.

Human's brain functions are very complex. You can compare it to the functions of computer. As a computer it has input (sensory organs), processor (brain), and output (muscles, internal organs).

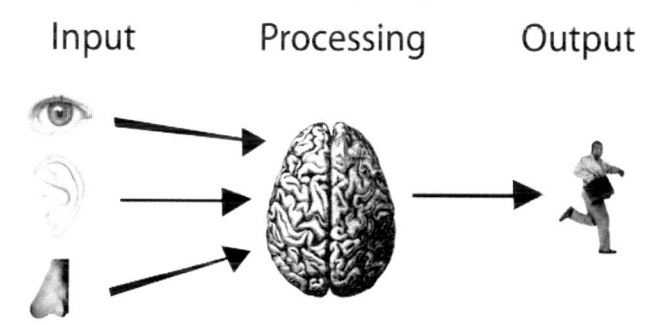

Figure 2. Brain Processing the Information. Sensory systems (vision, hearing, smell, taste, touch) receive information from the internal or external environment. Brain sorts it out, interprets it, and sends signals/commands to muscles or internal organs to respond to changing environment.

Innovation means something different. What is safe and comfortable becomes so through experience; something in the present moment matches the associated, stored 'memories' of previous safe, pleasing or rewarding experiences.

2. *It processes and interprets* the sensory input and makes decision (integration)

Once your sensory apparatus has translated physical or chemical information *from the outside* (or inside) world into neuronal activity, this set of signals travels up into the brain to be *processed*. Sensory information *from the external environment* (visual, auditory, tactile, olfactory, gustatory) and *the internal environment* (e.g., blood glucose, arterial pressure, CO_2 levels) enters the central nervous system at the level of the *brain stem and midbrain*. As this *primary sensory input* comes into the brain stem and midbrain, it is *matched against previously stored patterns* of activation and if unknown, or if associated with previous threat, the *brain will activate a set of responses* that are designed to help promote survival.

Throughout life, the brain is sensing, processing and storing patterns of neuronal activation (i.e., making memories) that correspond to various sights, sounds, smells, tastes, movements. Using various modes of *memory* (e.g., cognitive, emotional, motor) *the brain stores these patterns*, making *associations* between the multiple sensory stimuli that co-occur, *creating templates* of experience against which all future experience is *matched*.

In this regard, the brain is a *conservative organ*. Your brain is not creative. It does not like to be surprised. All unknown or unfamiliar environmental cues are judged to be 'threatening' until proven

3

otherwise. Novel stimuli focus attention, increase arousal and induce an alarm response until they can be ***proven neutral or safe. New patterns and cues that do not match the stored 'memories' of previous*** experience prime the stress-response systems in the brain. Once categorized as neutral, safe or threatening, these stored 'memories' are added to the catalogue of patterns, cues and associations against which subsequent environmental cues are matched.

Figure 3. Roger von Oech's Coffee Cup
Look at the picture. This is a coffee cup.
What is your first reaction?
What is going on in your mind?
How many negative thoughts your brain generated?
- It looks strange;
- It is not going to stand on a surface;
- Why it has handle on the bottom?

But what if this cup was designed for an airplane or a car?
What if you can stick it in the sand on the beach?
Because this cup doesn't look like the pattern that your brain has from previous experience, your mind sees it as nonsense.

Your brain is not creative. On the contrary. Your brain is very conservative. It is designed ***to recognize familiar patterns***. If something doesn't match patterns stored in your memory, brain rejects it. But everything creative SHOULDN'T match anything existing. Innovation means something different.

What is *safe and comfortable* becomes so through experience; something in the present moment matches the associated, stored 'memories' of previous safe, pleasing or rewarding experiences. In contrast, when the environment, internal or external, matches with stored neuronal patterns associated with a previous threatening experience, the brain's stress- response systems will be activated. Key signs of ***previous failure*** (i.e., you had previous bad experience with mathematics; you tried to compose music and failed; you studied drawing and was labeled of being an awful artist) result from these memories of 'fear' – storing elements of traumatic experience, making associations, generalizing and, later, triggering complex, multi-system responses (i.e., cognitive, emotional, motor, 'state') reflecting these 'memories'. This process of creating memories of fear occurs at multiple levels in the brain's hierarchical systems. It stops you from trying again to study mathematics, or composing music, or drawing.

As the neural signals ***from primary sensory systems*** (i.e., vision, hearing, taste, touch, smell) come into the ***brainstem***, a process of ***integrating*** the signals starts. At each level of the brain, ***further integration*** takes place so that by the time the signals from an event reach the ***thalamic nuclei***, there has been an integration that allows a more complex "*internal*" representation. ***Sensory integration*** – putting the sight, sound, smell and feel of an event together – is a crucial step in healthy thinking. There can be disruption of this capacity by even minor timing errors. If the signals coming from the neural systems responsible for hearing do not get into the thalamus and cortex in a synchronous way, there can be confusion, disorganization and abnormal functions. A tiny glimpse into this dysynchrony can be illustrated by the feeling you get when you watch a poorly dubbed foreign film – or if you watch TV with a tiny sound delay. The movements don't match with the sound – it is disorienting. Again, this can happen with fear alters the processing of incoming information – time seems suspended, sounds fade or accentuate, movement can seem in slow motion (anyone who has driven on ice and watched as their car slips towards someone else's bumper knows this feeling).

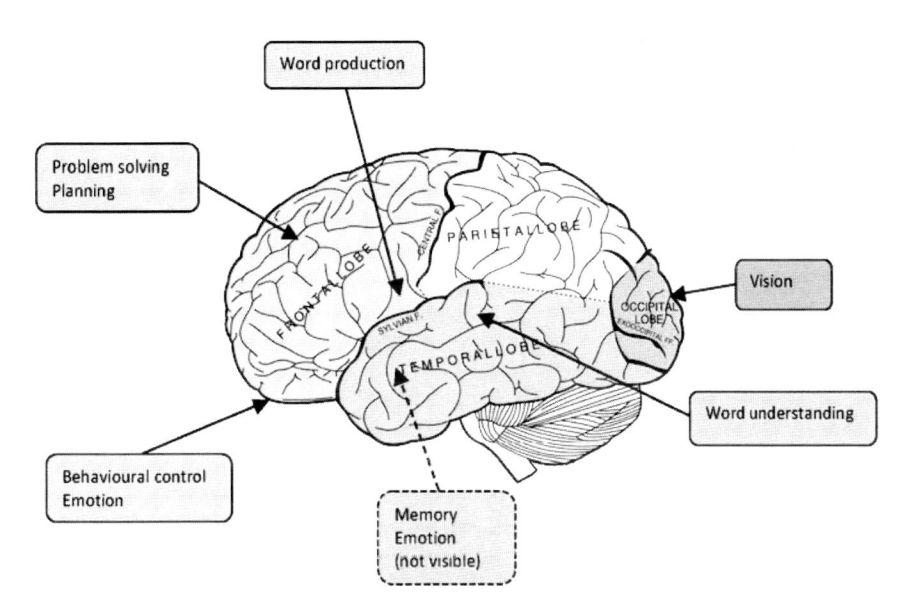

Figure 4. Brain's Organization. Certain areas of your brain are responsible for controlling certain functions of your body.

At each level of brain organization, the *incoming afferent signal is categorized*. By comparing the incoming signal with previously stored patterns, the brain can help categorize the incoming information. Sometimes this results in mistakes. For the war veteran, a loud firecracker can induce a startle response and anxiety even though he knows it is only a firecracker. That is because the incoming loud sound is categorized in the brainstem as being previously associated with threat and danger – and there is an immediate response – even before the signal can get to the cortex. At each level of processing that takes place, there is a categorization process. This immediate, localized processing and acting can be crucial for survival. Your brainstem and spinal cord will tell you to withdraw your hand from a fire even before your cortex knows that you have been burned.

Another key step in processing experience is in *organizing information*. Because the brain cannot possibly create a unique neural imprint or pattern of change to store every element of every experience, the brain stores 'template' patterns based upon the first set of organizing experiences. All future incoming input is matched against these stored templates and, if sufficiently different from the original pattern, the brain will make neural changes (i.e., create a memory) that reflects that tiny difference. Take the visual image of mother's face. To the infant, if no other face has ever been seen, the infant's brain will create some neural templates the basic features of a face – eyes, nose, mouth, expressions. And when baby first sees father – the neural templates for face are in place – only minor modifications need be stored.

Store: Inherent in the processing of information coming into the brain is the capacity to store elements of these incoming signals. At the heart of our survival neurobiology is the capacity to make and store internal representations of the external world – memory. The ability of the brain to create memories is due to the capacity of neurons and neural systems to change from one 'homeostatic' state to another. In response to a set of stimuli-induced (e.g., sensations) alterations in activity, neurons undergo molecular changes that reflect this activity. In a very real sense, unless the homeostatic dynamic of a neural system is altered by "use", it will not change – it will not make internal representations of the experience – it will not make memories. Neurons and neural systems change in a "use-dependent" fashion. Therefore, when

> At each level of brain organization, the incoming afferent signal is categorized.

> Because the brain cannot possibly create a unique neural imprint or pattern of change to store every element of every experience, the brain stores 'template' patterns based upon the first set of organizing experiences.

neural systems that have their homeostatic patterns of activation influenced by new or extreme patterns corresponding to new or extreme environmental situations, they will change their molecular neurophysiology, creating "memories."

This has important implications for understanding how we 'create' memories of traumatic experiences. For adults, most experiences have only a small component that is 'new' or unique. Typically, the majority of places, faces, words, sounds, smells, tastes in any given moment are familiar – the brain has sensed, processed and stored these *patterns* before. In these situations only some portions of the brain are 'activated' and processing outside of their homeostatic range. In the classroom, for example, a lecture may result in cortical activation but will cause little **new emotional, motor or arousal activity**. The result, hopefully, is new cognitive memories – storing the information from the lecture. Similarly, practicing piano may result in new cerebellar-basal ganglia-motor cortex activity and create 'motor' memories but have little effect on emotional or state-regulation areas of the brain.

> The brain mediates and controls the actions of the human body.

3. *It affects a response* by activating muscles or glands (motor output).

Act: Finally, the brain mediates and controls the actions of the human body. By regulating and directing the actions of the neuromuscular, autonomic, endocrine and immune systems the brain controls the actions of the human being. The neuronal pathways sending signals into a brain area are called ***afferent*** and those sending signals out are called ***efferent.*** The efferent pathways regulate the actions resulting from the process of sensing, processing and storage of incoming signals. Now this simple (and somewhat misleading) linear process is only a crude approximation of the key actions of the brain. Indeed, there are hundreds if not thousands of local and regional feedback loops in an open and interactive dynamic system (well beyond any mathematical models of complex systems yet developed).

> The neuronal pathways sending signals into a brain area are called *afferent* and those sending signals out are called *efferent.*

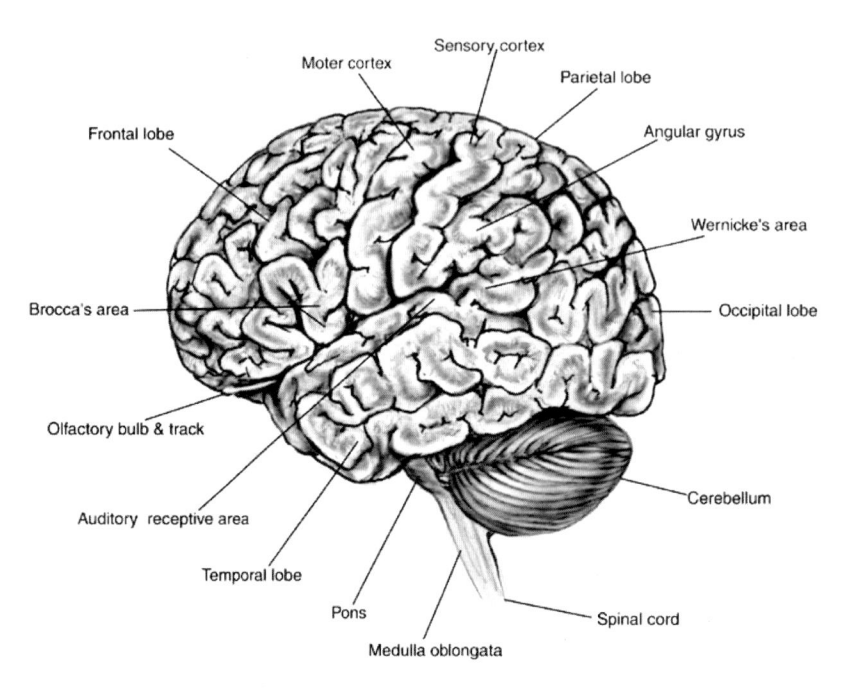

Figure 5. Brain's Functions. The brain has a hierarchical organization, from bottom to top, becoming more complex. The most complex part of the brain is the cortex when 50% of all neurons in the brain are within the outer ¼ inch of the surface of the cortex. When examining genetic homology across species, the frontal cortex (part of the neocortex) is the most "uniquely" human with only about 94 % homology with non-human primates while other cortical areas are 96 to 98 % homologous. It should be no surprise then that the most unique human properties are mediated by the cortex, especially, the frontal cortex.

Matching the hierarchical structure is a hierarchy of function. The simplest regulatory functions are mediated by the lower brainstem areas and the most complex by *the neocortex* (see figures above). The key to remember is that different brain areas and systems mediate different functions. This will be important when trying to understand the changes in emotional, behavioral and cognitive functioning that take place when someone is threatened.

Neurons: The basic structural units of the human brain are cells. The brain is comprised of two major types of specialized cells, neurons and glial cells.

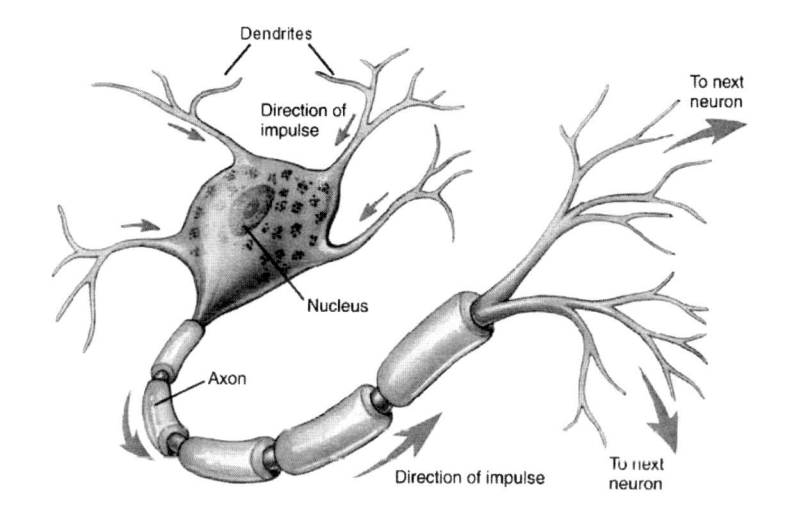

Figure 6. Neuron's Structure.

Neurons are cells specialized to *receive, store and transmit information* – the business of neurons is *communication*. All neurons have special structural features that allow neurons to 'communicate' - to receive, process, store and send 'information' that comes from their outside (extracellular) world (sound familiar?). Specialized structural and biochemical properties allow to receive a stream of chemical signals from other neurons, process these incoming 'messages', change their chemical interior in response to these signals (and thereby, store important 'information'), and then transmit the summed signals to other neurons. Chains of neurons embraced in continuous dialogue, continuous communication, create functional systems that allow the brain to mediate and control a host of remarkable activities.

The principle *of neural conduction* can be described by neural impulses and synaptic transmission. These are two complementary methods of conduction which neurons are capable of. The neural impulse is either on or off, whereas synaptic conduction –based on the transmission of chemicals– is gradual. This can be likened to digital and analogue signal conduction. A neuron fires an impulse when it is stimulated by chemical messages from connected neurons, or by pressure, heat, or light. This impulse, called action potential, is caused by the depolarisation of the membrane potential of an excitable cell. Normally an electrical potential exists between the inside and outside of the cell. When ion channels in the cell membrane open, the exchange of ionised elements through the open channels causes an electric discharge. This impulse travels through the cell membrane and the axon hillock down to the axon and is then carried away from the cell. It propagates through the body at a speed of 10-100 meter per second, depending on the type of axon. The impulse doesn't travel like an electrical signal, but rather through successive depolarisation of adjacent areas of the axon membrane, much like falling dominoes. During a very brief resting pause, the neuron pumps positively charged atoms back outside the membrane, after which the neuron is ready to fire again. This electrochemical process can be repeated 100 times per second.

The major functions of *glial cells*, however, appear to be "supportive" of the communication functions of neurons. To do so, there are several types of glial cells in the CNS. Some of them (oligodendroglia in the CNS and Schwann Cells in the periphery) form myelin sheaths, which are fat wrappings –like insulation - around axons that allow the axons to conduct information more rapidly. Other types of glial cells regulate the composition of extracellular fluids, complement neurons in certain metabolic activities, and participate in various humoral functions within the CNS. Glial cells provide crucial 'support' functions for neurons (e.g., guiding developing neurons to the 'right' places in the brain, storing extra energy for active neurons).

CHAPTER 1

Neurotransmission

Neurons and glial cells are the *'building blocks'* of brain structure, while **neuron-to-neuron communication** is the basic unit of **brain function**. Just imagine that the memory of your loved one's face or the capacity to create a new loving bond with another person is created by some dynamic pattern of synaptic activation. Synaptic transmission is different. Neurotransmission (or synaptic transmission) is communication between neurons as accomplished by the movement of chemicals or electrical signals across a synapse.

There *are two types of synapses*, electrical and chemical synapses. *Electrical synapses* couple neurons electrically via gap junctions. *Chemical synapses* work through the exchange of special chemicals called neurotransmitters. There are some 75 known neurotransmitters which amplify, relay, or modulate signals between neurons and other cells. These substances are produced by the soma, the chemical factory inside the neuron. The neurotransmitter molecules are usually packaged in spherical vesicles. These vesicles are conveyed through the axon towards the terminal buttons through special channels called microtubules, which are tiny pipelines running inside the axon. When a neural impulse reaches the knob-like terminals of the axon it triggers a biochemical cascade which causes the vesicles to fuse with the presynaptic membrane and release their neurotransmitters.

The neurotransmitter molecules then cross the synaptic gap from the presynaptic membrane to the postsynaptic membrane within 1/10,000th of a second. It is like a very brief rain shower of neurotransmitters. Receptors on the postsynaptic membrane bind the neurotransmitter molecules. For a very brief period, ion channels on the postsynaptic membrane open to allow ions to rush in or out. This causes the transmembrane potential of the receiver cell to change. There are two types of changes. Depolarisation causes an excitatory postsynaptic potential; hyperpolarisation causes an inhibitory potential.

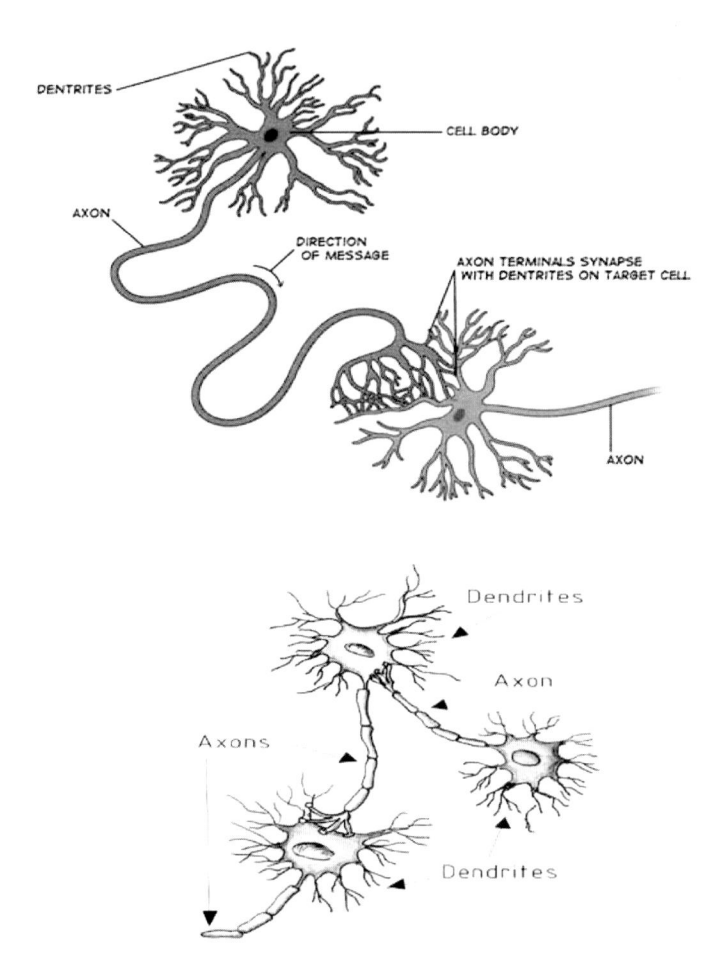

Figure 7. Neurons' Connections and Interactions.

This image represents a neural network. "Information" flows between the neurons through electrical or chemical synapses.
Chemical neurotransmission occurs at chemical synapses. In chemical neurotransmission, the presynaptic neuron and the postsynaptic neuron are separated by a small gap — the synaptic cleft. Although very small, typically on the order of a few nanometers (a billionth of a meter), the synaptic cleft creates a physical barrier for the electrical signal carried by one neuron to be transferred to another neuron. In electrical terms, the synaptic cleft would be considered a "short" in an electrical circuit. The function of neurotransmitter is to overcome this electrical short. It does so by acting like a chemical messenger, thereby linking the action potential of one neuron with a synaptic potential in another. How this occurs is illustrated in the following animation.

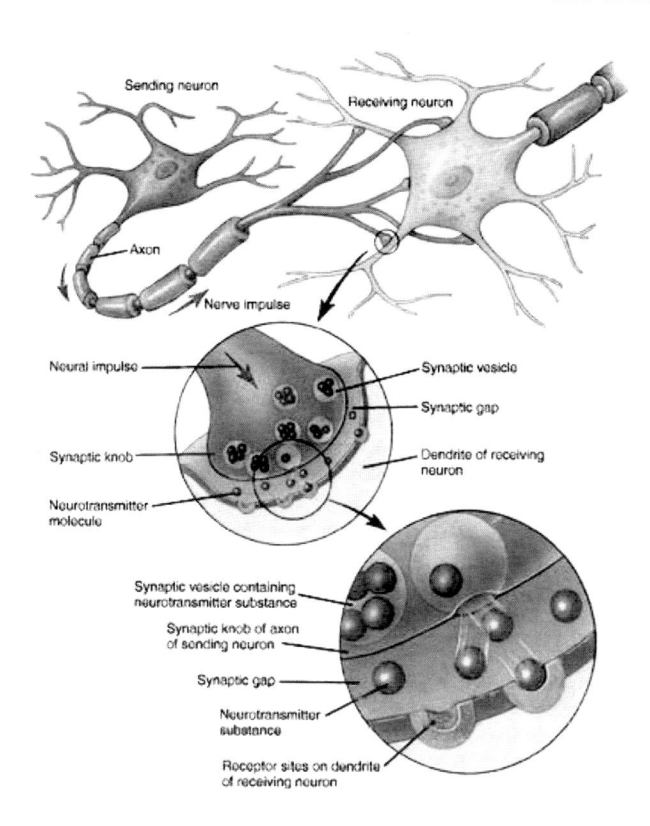

Figure 8. Synaptic Transmission.

At electrical synapses, two neurons are physically connected to one another through gap junctions. Gap junctions permit changes in the electrical properties of one neuron to effect the other, and vice versa, so the two neurons essentially behave as one. Electrical neurotransmission is communication between two neurons at electrical synapses.

Cerebral Cortex

This part of the brain is divided into four sections. 1. Occipital Lobe; 2. Temporal Lobe; 3. Parietal Lobe; and 4. Frontal Lobe. Functions such as hearing, vision, speech, and executive function are associated with these regions.
The *frontal lobe* performs four functions:

1. the initiation of voluntary movements.
2. the production of speech and written language.

The *prefrontal cortex* is involved in what may be described as personality, insight, and foresight.
Parietal lobe: The lateral surface of the parietal lobe is divided into three areas: the post-central gyrus, the superior parietal lobules, and the inferior parietal lobules.
The *parietal lobe* is associated with three functions:

1. the initial cortical processing of tactile and proprioceptive (sense of position) information.
2. the comprehension of language (Wernicke's Area).
3. the complex aspects of orientation of the individual in space and time.

The *temporal lobe* is associated in general with three functions:

1. processing the auditory signals
2. regulation of the emotional and visceral responses.
3. learning and memory recall.

Occipital lobe is exclusively concerned with visual functions.
Diencephalon
The diencephalon has four main substructures: thalamus, hypothalamus, epithalamus, and subthalamus. The thalamus is a nuclear mass of great importance in both sensory and motor systems. No sensory information, with the exception of olfactory information, reaches the cerebral cortex without prior processing in thalamic nuclei.

CHAPTER 1

The *hypothalamus* the major visceral control center of the brain.

Parietal Lobe
- Sense of touch (tactile senstation)
- Appreciation of form through touch (stereognosis)
- Response to internal stimuli (proprioception)
- Sensory combination and comprehension
- Some language and reading functions
- Some visual functions

Frontal Lobe
- Behavior
- Abstract thought
- Problem solving
- Attention
- Creative thought
- Some emotion
- Intellect
- Reflection
- Judgment
- Initiative
- Inhibition
- Coordination
- Generalized
- Some eye movements
- Sense of smell
- Muscle movements
- Skilled movements
- Some motor skills
- Physical reaction
- Libido (sexual urges)

Occipital Lobe
- Vision
- Reading

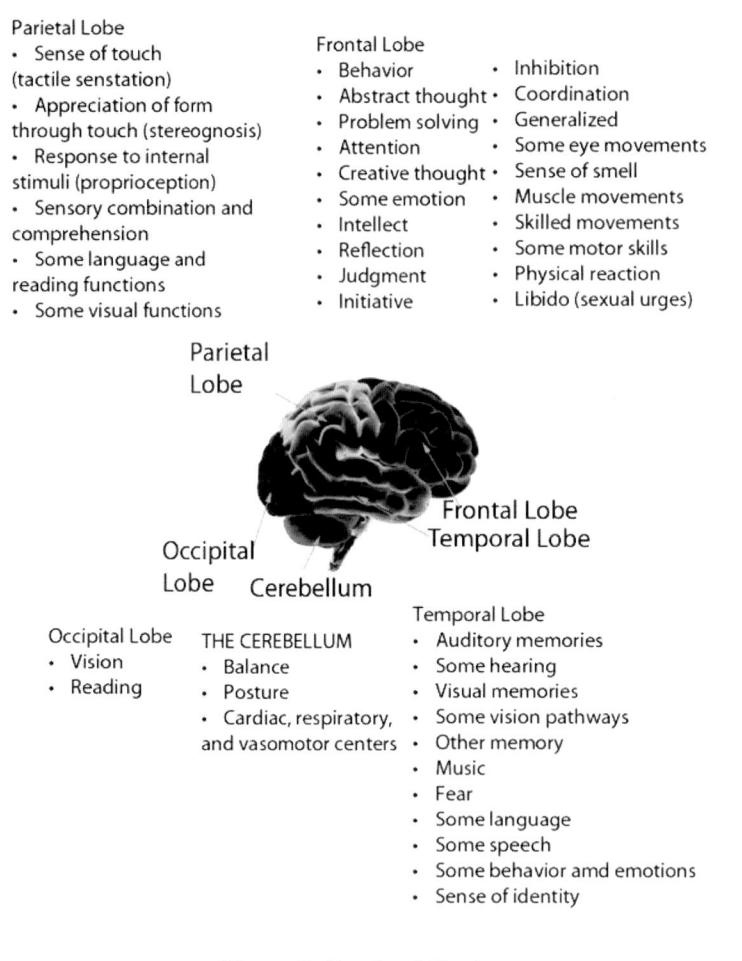

THE CEREBELLUM
- Balance
- Posture
- Cardiac, respiratory, and vasomotor centers

Temporal Lobe
- Auditory memories
- Some hearing
- Visual memories
- Some vision pathways
- Other memory
- Music
- Fear
- Some language
- Some speech
- Some behavior amd emotions
- Sense of identity

Figure 9. Cerebral Cortex.

INTERESTING FACTS ABOUT BRAIN

- The brain is a ***complex system*** of distinct elements that functions as a synergistic interconnected whole.
- The brain innately searches to ***construct meaning out of patterns*** and ***perceived regularities***.
- The functional organization of the brain can be ***altered by experience***.
- The brain utilizes ***two distinct memory systems***.
- Constructing new knowledge begins with the ***activation of prior knowledge***.
- The recall of information is maximized by ***utilizing multiple input modalities*** and methods of encoding.
- Human learning is a ***constructive process*** facilitated by the active manipulation of materials and ideas.
- The nature and quality of human learning and memory are closely tied to our ***emotional state***.
- Human learning is a process sensitive to ***social and cultural context***.
- Human learning is a process that requires periods of down time.

SUMMARY

1. The Brain Is the Foundation of the Mind. Intelligence arises as the brain reasons, plans, and solves problems. The brain makes sense of the world by using all available information, including senses, emotions, instincts and remembered experiences.
- Emotions are based on value judgments made by our brains and are manifested by feelings as basic as love and anger and as complex as empathy and hate.
- The brain learns from experiences and makes predictions about best actions in response to present and future challenges.
- Consciousness depends on normal activity of the brain.
- The Nervous System Controls and Responds to Body Functions and Directs Behavior. The brain is the body's most complex organ.
- There are a hundred billion neurons in the human brain, all of which are in use.
- Each neuron communicates with many other neurons to form circuits and share information.
- Proper nervous system function involves coordinated action of neurons in many brain regions.
- The nervous system influences and is influenced by all other body systems (e.g., cardiovascular, endocrine, gastrointestinal and immune systems).
- Humans have a complex nervous system that evolved from a simpler one.
- This complex organ can malfunction in many ways, leading to disorders that have an enormous social and economic impact.

2. Neurons communicate using both electrical and chemical signals.
- Sensory stimuli are converted into electrical signals.
- Action potentials are electrical signals carried along neurons.
- Synapses are chemical or electrical junctions that allow electrical signals to pass from neurons to other cells.
- Electrical signals in muscles cause contraction and movement.
- Changes in the amount of activity at a synapse can enhance or reduce its function.
- Communication between neurons is strengthened or weakened by an individual's activities, such as exercise, stress, and drug use.
- All perceptions, thoughts, and behaviors result from combinations of signals among neurons.

3. Nervous System Structure and Function Are Determined by Both Genes and Environment Throughout Life. Genetically determined circuits are the foundation of the nervous system. Who you are is the product of your genes or blueprint, contained in every one of your cells, and your environment, much of which comes from the rich contributions of your family and culture.
- Neuronal circuits are formed by genetic programs during embryonic development and modified through interactions with the internal and external environment.
- Sensory circuits (sight, touch, hearing, smell, taste) bring information to the nervous system, whereas motor circuits send information to muscles and glands.
- The simplest circuit is a reflex, in which a sensory stimulus directly triggers an immediate motor response.
- Complex responses occur when the brain integrates information from many brain circuits to generate a response.
- Simple and complex interactions among neurons take place on time scales ranging from milliseconds to months.
- The brain is organized to recognize sensations, initiate behaviors, and store and access memories that can last a lifetime.
- Life experiences change the nervous system.
- Differences in genes and environments make the brain of each animal unique.
- Most neurons are generated early in development and survive for life.
- Some injuries harm nerve cells, but the brain often recovers from stress, damage, or disease.
- Continuously challenging the brain with physical and mental activity helps maintain its structure and function — "use it or lose it."
- Peripheral neurons have greater ability to regrow after injury than neurons in the brain and spinal cord.
- Neuronal death is a natural part of development and aging.

CHAPTER 1

EXERCISES FOR YOUR BRAIN

EXERCISE 1. CREATE A MINDMAP FOR THIS CHAPTER.

Mindmapping

Mind maps are tools which help think and learn.

Mind maps were developed in the late 60s by Tony Buzan as a way of helping students make notes that used only key words and images. They are much quicker to make, and because of their visual quality much easier to remember and review.

The non-linear nature of mind maps makes it easy to link and cross-reference different elements of the map - which is why hypertext was developed for computers (again initially by a student wanting to make note-taking easier).

Disadvantages of traditional linear notes:

- Energy and time wasted writing down superfluous words.
- Other information may be missed while noting down one idea.
- Take longer to read and review.
- Associations and connections between key words and ideas not readily apparent.
- Attention wanders easily.
- Lack of color and other visual qualities handicap memory.
- Traditional notes aid forgetting not memory.

Advantages of Mind Maps

Mind maps work the way the brain works - which is not in nice neat lines.

Memory is naturally associative, not linear. Any idea probably has thousands of links in your mind. Mind maps allow associations and links to be recorded and reinforced. The mind remembers key words and images, not sentences -- try recalling just one sentence from memory! Mind maps use just key words and key images, allowing a lot more information to be put on a page. Because mind maps are more visual and depict associations between key words, they are much easier to recall than linear notes. (For example, although you may not have studied it in depth, see how much of the Home Mind Map of this site you can recall in your mind's eye.)

How to Do It?

Starting from the center of the page rather than top-left corner allows you to work out in all directions.

The organization of a mind map reflects the way your own brain organizes ideas.

Mind maps are easy to review. Regular review reinforces memory. Best is to try reviewing in your imagination first, then go back and check on those areas that were hazy.

We remember what stands out (where were you when John Lennon was shot?). Visual quality of mind maps allows you to make key points to stand out easily.

Uses of Mind Maps

Notes. Whenever information is being taken in, mind maps help organize it into a form that is easily assimilated by the brain and easily remembered. They can be used for noting anything -- books, lectures, meetings, interviews, phone conversations.

Recall. Whenever information is being retrieved from memory, mind maps allow ideas to be quickly noted as they occur, in an organized manner. There's no need to form sentences and write them out in full. They serve as quick and efficient means of review and so keep recall at a high level.

Creativity. Whenever you want to encourage creativity, mind maps liberate the mind from linear thinking, allowing new ideas to flow more rapidly. Think of every item in a mind map as the center of another mind map.

Problem solving. Whenever you are confronted by a problem -- professional or personal -- mind maps help you see all the issues and how they relate to each other. They also help others quickly get an overview of how you see different aspects of the situation, and their relative importance.

Planning. Whenever you are planning something, mind maps help you get all the relevant information down in one place and organize it easily. They can be used for planning any piece of writing from a letter to a screenplay to a book (I use a master map for the whole book, and a detailed sub-map for each chapter), or for planning a meeting, a day or a vacation.

Presentations. Whenever I speak I prepare a mind map for myself of the topic and its flow. This not only helps me organize the ideas coherently; the visual nature of the map means that I can read the whole thing

The Brain Is the Foundation of the Mind

How to Mind Map

- Use just key words, or wherever possible images.
- Start from the center of the page and work out.
- Make the center a clear and strong visual image that depicts the general theme of the map.
- Create sub-centers for sub-themes.
- Put key words **on** lines. This reinforces structure of notes.
- Print rather than write in script. It makes them more readable and memorable. Lower case is more visually distinctive (and better remembered) than upper case.
- Use color to depict themes, associations and to make things stand out.
- Anything that **stands out** on the page will stand out in your mind.
- Think three-dimensionally.
- Use arrows, icons or other visual aids to show links between different elements.
- Don't get stuck in one area. If you dry up in one area go to another branch.
- Put ideas down as they occur, wherever they fit. Don't judge or hold back.
- Break boundaries. If you run out of space, don't start a new sheet; paste more paper onto the map. (Break the 8x11 mentality.)
- Be creative. Creativity aids memory.
- Get involved. Have fun.

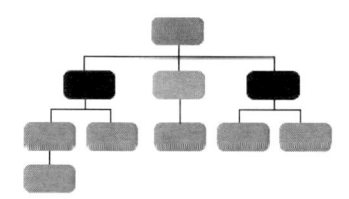

There is a variety of mind maps:

Classifying Information
Rules are used to group items by attributes that demonstrate relationships.
Essential Questions:
- What items are being organized?
- How can these items be placed together into groups that are alike or share common features?
- What rules apply to each group?
- What determines whether an item is included or excluded?
- How are the excluded items alike and different?
- How many different groups and rules are needed to organized your items?
Content Area Ideas:
- Reading: Organize books or readings into genres.
- Writing: Organize most and least important information.
- Science: Group items by common characteristics such as elements of the universe

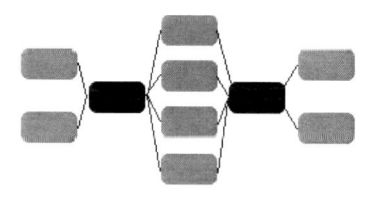

Comparing Information
Use a visual to compare two or more ideas.

Essential Questions:
- What are two (more more) important ideas, concepts, events, people, places, or things related to this topic or problem?
- How are they alike and different?
- What do they have in common?
- What do they not have in common?
Content Area Ideas:
- Reading: Compare the book with the movie.
- Reading: Compare characters, plots, or settings.
- Writing: Create similes and metaphors. Our library (family, playground, backyard, room) is ...
- Geography: Compare two cities, states/provinces, countries.
- Science: Compare two biomes, climates, issues
- Math: Compare and contrast two ways to solve a problem.

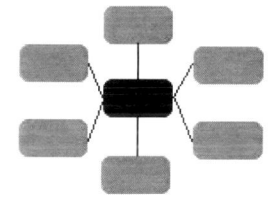

Describing Information
Create a visual description. Information is recorded to:

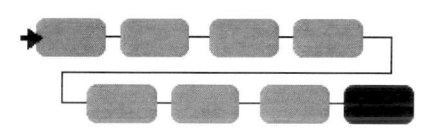

Sequencing Information
Visualize the sequence of activities.

•define subjects •generate ideas, topics, and questions •explore new topics •recall prior knowledge •reflect on interests Essential Questions: •What is the central idea, topic, word, problem, or question? •What are the key ideas related to this topic? •How are the ideas connected to each other? •What are questions related to your ideas? Content Area Ideas: •All: Create definitions of words, related words, examples •Literacy: Create a character map •Science: Materials needed in experiment •Social studies: Describe what makes an effective leader; list characteristics of a particular leader; provide examples Strategies: •Brainstorm: characteristics, similar ideas, examples, definitions, descriptive words, questions, steps. •Organize: right to left; left to right; top-down; branching; general to specific	Essential Questions: •What is the central process, procedure, cycle, or event? •How does the event begin and end? •What are the key events, phases, stages, or steps? •Is there a trigger, catalyst, or specific event that creates a causal relationship? •How are the series of elements related to each other? •Is the sequence linear or can it be recursive or branched? Content Area Ideas: •Reading: Retelling a story. •Writing: Journaling •Science: Steps in the scientific method •Science: Use PGeo Timeline Palm Software to explore geologic time scale. •Science: Track the history of radioactive decay at a specific location. Strategies: •Add to the steps as you follow the process yourself. •Brainstorm all of the step. Then put them in order

Thompson (1992) stresses that the proper problem articulation is the key point for problem resolution. Relatively simple step-by-step process to formulate problems helps to resolve this problem more effectively. Thompson's *Idea Mapping* is a five-minute exercise in word and idea association; it relies on keywords, colors, and graphics to form a nonlinear network of potential ideas and observations. It leads to spontaneous idea generation and a vast amount of visible information.

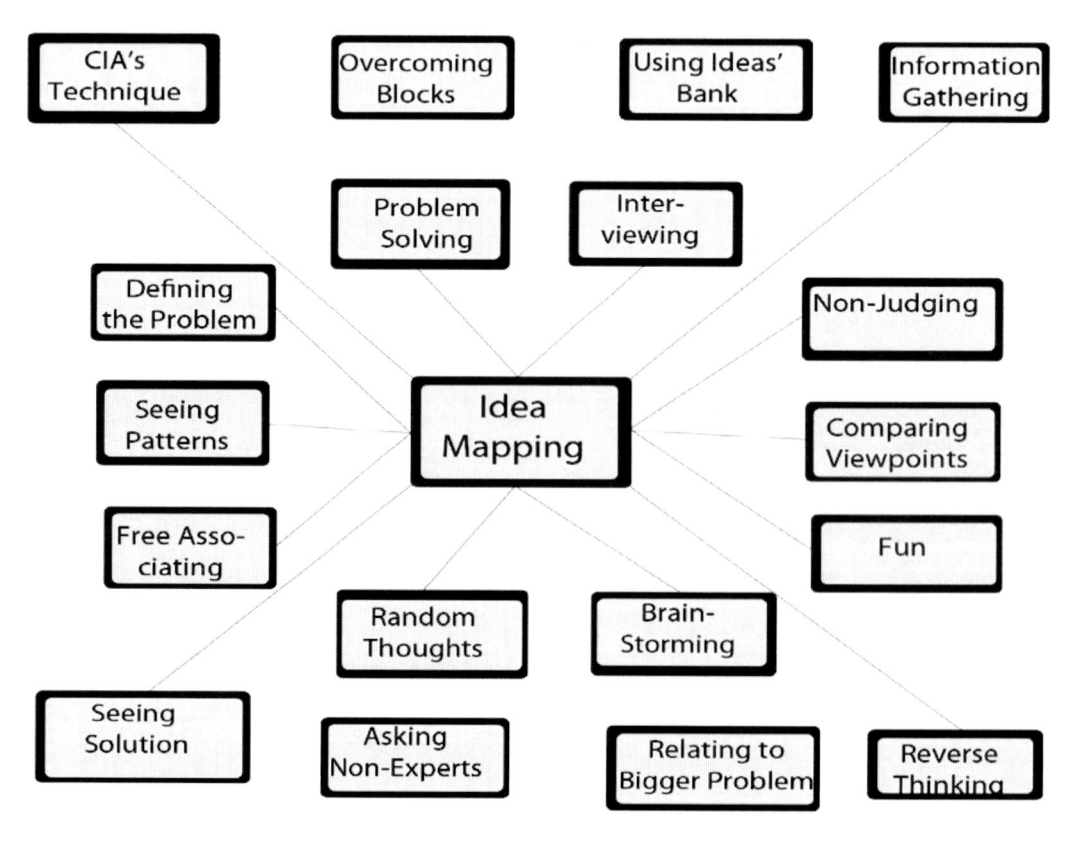

In order to create an Idea Map, you need to follow these steps:

1. State the problem.
2. Write in the center of your sheet a word or phrase that describes the essence of your problem and put a circle around it. Let's call that word the Trigger Word.
3. Now, without judging, fire away for two minutes and write down around this Trigger Word as many aspects of your problem as you can think of. Do not evaluate their quality; just keep firing.
4. See if any of the words are related to any of the others. If so, draw arrows between them, connecting your key thoughts. Build up as many associations as you like. Add more words as necessary.
5. Step back and look at your entire map to find three or four main concepts. Assign a geometric symbol to each of those main concepts and put that symbol around each of the words in the map that would be grouped under that concept. This process is called "clustering."
6. Now create a cluster outline. Put the three or four geometric symbols with main concepts written inside at the top of another sheet of paper. Then list the related words from the map below each symbol. Rank in an order that seems logical to you. A cluster outline for our Ideas Map is shown at the top of the next page.

"Ideas Maps facilitate problem solving by helping to define the problem. They place different viewpoints about the problem side by side in a graphic relationship which helps us see the questions we need to ask."

Example:

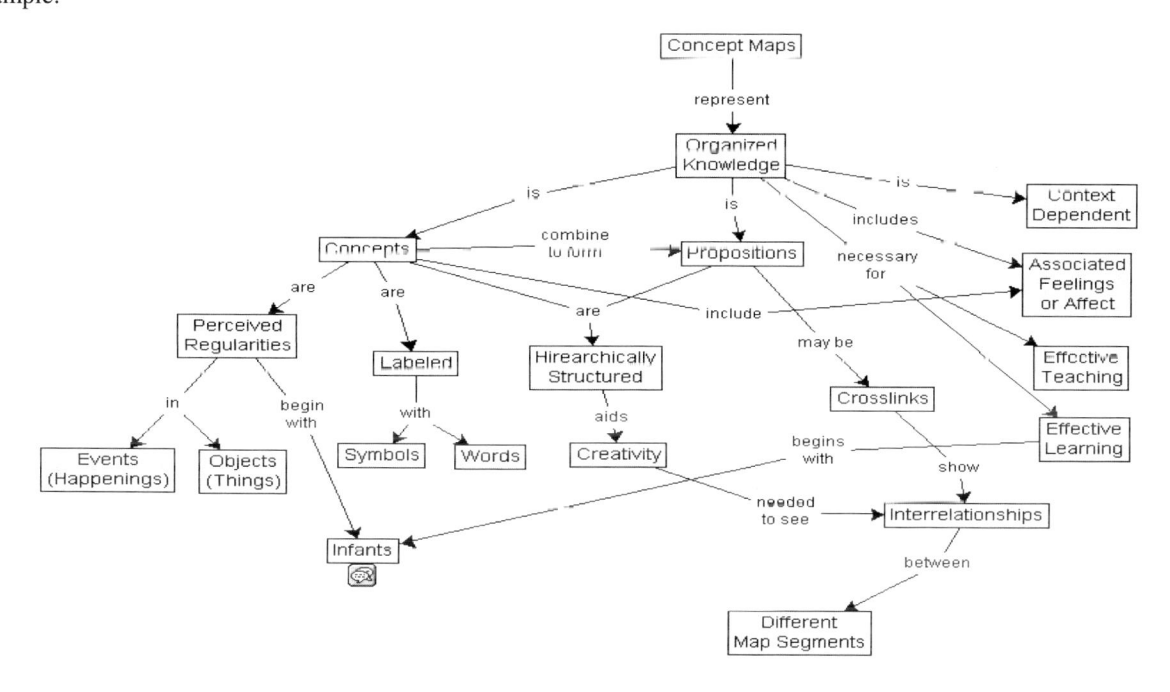

Thompson (1992) also suggested asking "Dumb Questions". He mentioned Aristotle's asking "When you ask a dumb questions, you get a smart answer."

1. Why have we always done it that way?
2. Does anyone actually look at that form?
3. Why do I have to sign this form?
4. Why can't I send a handwritten letter?
5. Why do I need a hard copy of this report?
6. Why do we need a committee to look into this?
7. What's a _____? (fill in the blank with any high-tech term used by a high-tech type).

The ideas come from asking questions and there are only six universal ones: What? Where? When? How? Why? Who? Asking these questions helps to tear a problem apart, organize and reorganize it:

1. What is it?
2. Where does it happen?
3. When does it happen?
4. How does it happen?
5. Why does it happen?
6. To whom does it happen? Who causes it to happen?

In order to get in the root of the problem, Thompson (1992) suggests the procedure of asking several times again and again "Why it happened?"

Exercise 1.2. Idea Quota

Thomas Edison held 1,093 patent. He was a great believer in exercising his mind and the minds of his workers and felt that without a **quota** he probably wouldn't have achieved very much. His personal **invention quota** was a minor invention every ten days and a major invention every six months. To Edison, an **idea quota** was the difference between eating beefsteak or a plateful of Black Beauty stew.

Give your mind a workout every day. **Set yourself an idea quota** for a challenge you are working on, such as five new ideas every day for a week. You'll find the first five are the hardest, but these will quickly trigger other ideas. The more ideas you come up with, the greater your chances of coming up with a winner.

Having a quota will force you to actively generate ideas and alternatives rather than waiting for them to occur to you. You will make an effort to fill the quota even if the ideas you come up with seem ridiculous or far-fetched. Having an idea quota does not stop you from generating more ideas than the quota, but it does ensure that you generate your minimum (Michalko, 1995).

Create an Idea Bank

- Use cards for each idea;
- Combine and re-combine them;
- Get a notebook. Have it always in your pocket.
- Use any free minute to come up with new idea. Record it immediately before you forget it;
- Reading books or newspaper, watching TV or video, try to find new ideas amidst somebody else's ones.

Chapter 2

Learning and Thinking

This chapter investigates different orientations to learning, memory and thinking. Exploring these diverse perspectives should help you think differently and more broadly about what learning means, how it happens, and how it changes your thinking.

LEARNING OBJECTIVES

After reading this chapter, you will be able to

1. Define learning and memory
2. Summarize the history of learning theory
3. Describe, compare and contrast the three major learning theories
4. Explain the differences between classical conditioning, operant conditioning, and social learning
5. Define your personal learning and thinking style.

QUESTIONS FOR DISCUSSIONS:

- Is learning a quantitative increase in knowledge? Learning means acquiring information or 'knowing a lot'.
- Is learning the same as memorizing? Is learning just storing information that can be reproduced?
- Is learning just acquiring facts, skills, and methods that can be retained and used when necessary?
- Does learning mean making sense or abstracting meaning? Does learning involve relating parts of the subject matter to each other and to the real world?
- Does learning mean interpreting and understanding reality in a different way? Learning involves comprehending the world by reinterpreting knowledge. (quoted in Ramsden 1992: 26)

CHAPTER 2

> Learning is "a relatively permanent change in behavior that results from practice" (Atkinson et al 1993). It also means changes in "capability" or even simple "knowledge" or "understanding", even if it is not manifest in behavior.

When people learn, they organize, shape, and strengthen their brains.

"Learned" behavior is ***not pre-programmed*** or wholly instinctive, even if an instinctual drive underpins it. Behavior can also change as a result of maturation—simple growing-up—without being totally learned. Think of the changing attitude of children and adolescents to opposite-sex peers. Whatever the case, there has to be interaction with the environment.

Humans are learning machines. From the day they are born—and even before—their brains are ready to capture any experiences and encode them into a web of nerve connections.

Human brain possesses ***plasticity*** that is a physical process. Gray matter can actually shrink or thicken; neural connections can be forged and refined or (conversely) weakened and severed. Changes in the physical brain manifest as changes in your ***thinking abilities***. For example, each time you learn a new dance step, it reflects a change in your physical brain: new "wires" (neural pathways) that give instructions to your body on how to perform the step. Each time you forget someone's name, it also reflects brain change— "wires" that once connected to the memory have been degraded, or even severed. As these examples show, changes in the brain can result in improved skills (a new dance step) or a weakening of skills (a forgotten name).

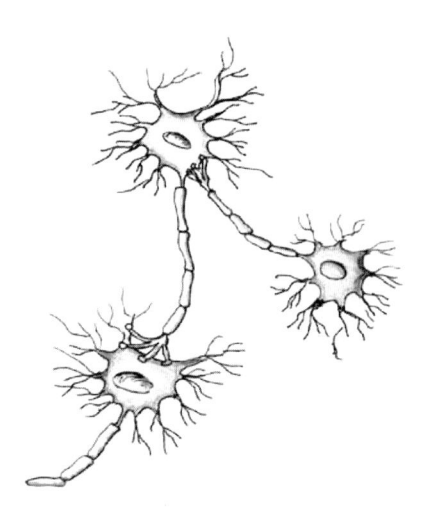

Figure 2.1. Neurons Connections.

Each of these cells is capable of making thousands of connections with others. These cells and connections are the nuts and bolts of the learning machine.

Recent brain research suggests that actively engaging brains in learning throughout life significantly affects how well people age. Let's explore what we mean by learning.

What Does "Learning" Mean?

To most of us, "learning" means an ***attempt to create a memory*** that lasts. Mastering new dance steps, learning foreign languages, or remembering acquaintances' names require brains to encode and store new information until you need it.

How much do you remember of what you learned in school?

Unless you have used skills from school in your day-to-day life, you may have trouble recalling the details. This is why brain researchers draw differences between learning and memory. They are closely linked—but they are not the same things.

Difference between Learning and Memory

Not all learning is transformed into lasting memories.

"Learning is how you acquire new information about the world, and memory is how you store that information over time," says Eric R. Kandel, M.D., vice chairman of The Dana Alliance for Brain Initiatives and recipient of the 2000 Nobel Prize in Physiology of Medicine for his work on the molecular basis of memory. "There is no memory without learning, but there is learning without memory."

For example, you may look up a telephone number and remember it just long enough to make your call. This is sometimes called "working memory." It requires learning—but not for the long haul.

There are three major learning theories: (1) Classical Conditioning; (2) Operant Conditioning; and (3) Social Learning Theory.

CLASSICAL CONDITIONING

Classical conditioning was discovered by Russian physiologist Ivan Pavlov. Classical conditioning is a learning process that occurs through **associations** between an environmental stimulus and a naturally occurring stimulus. In order to understand how classical conditioning works, it is important to be familiar with the basic principles of the process.

The Unconditioned Stimulus

The *unconditioned stimulus* is one that *unconditionally*, naturally, and automatically *triggers a response*. For example, when you smell one of your favorite foods, you may immediately feel very hungry. You may start to salivate; your stomach starts to produce digestive enzymes. In this example, the smell of the food is the unconditioned stimulus.

The Unconditioned Response

The *unconditioned response* is the *unlearned* response that occurs naturally in response to the *unconditioned stimulus*. In our example, the feeling of hunger in response to the smell of food is the unconditioned response.

The Conditioned Stimulus

The *conditioned stimulus* is previously neutral stimulus that, *after becoming associated with the unconditioned stimulus*, eventually comes to trigger a *conditioned response*. In our earlier example, suppose that when you smelled your favorite food, you also heard the sound of a whistle. While the whistle is unrelated to the smell of the food, if the sound of the whistle was paired multiple times with the smell, the sound would eventually trigger the conditioned response. In this case, the sound of the whistle is the conditioned stimulus.

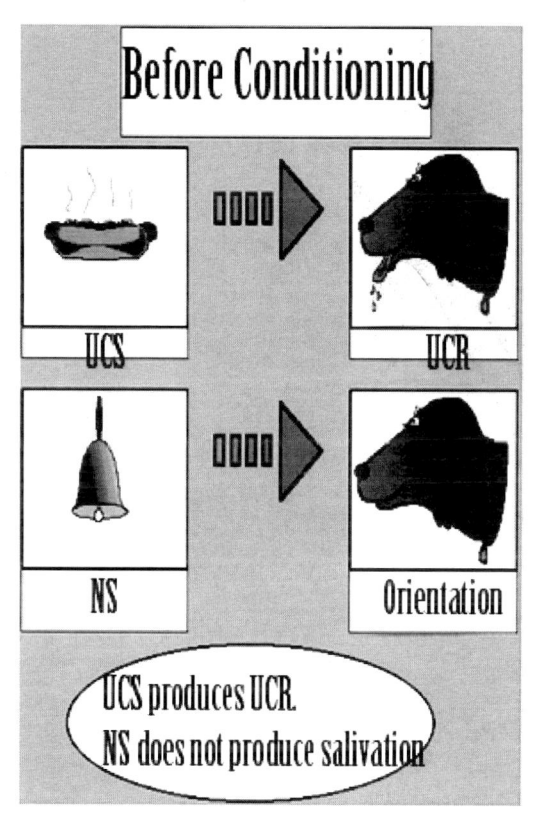

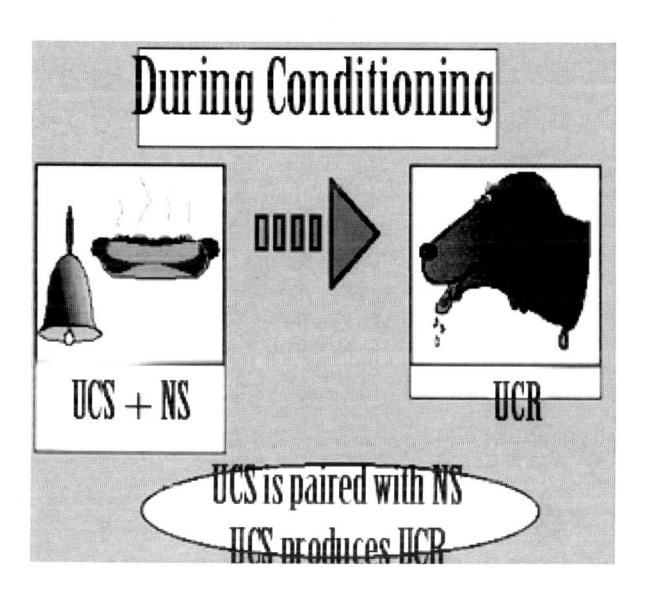

Figure 2.2. The *conditioned response* is *the learned response* to the previously *neutral stimulus*. In our example, the conditioned response would be feeling hungry when you heard the sound of the whistle.

After Conditioning

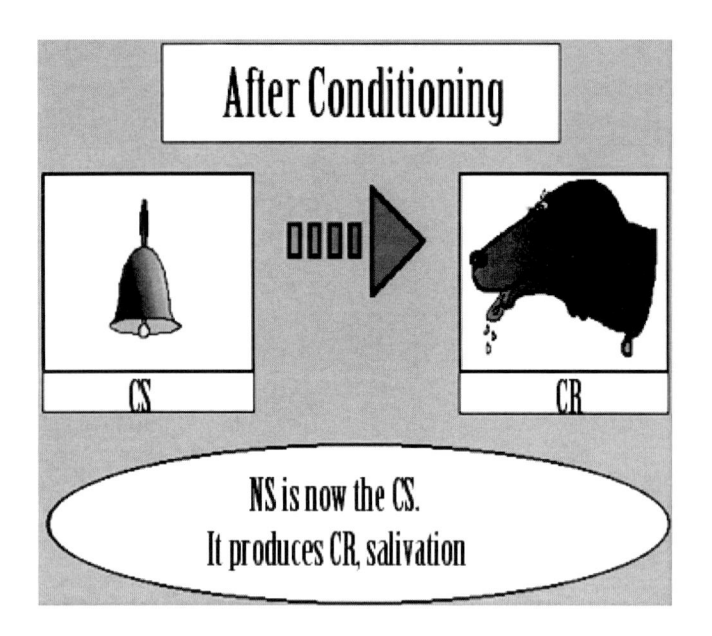

CS → CR

NS is now the CS. It produces CR, salivation

Elements of Classical Conditioning

1. Acquisition

During acquisition, or training, a *conditional response must be reinforced* (strengthened). Classical conditioning if reinforced when the CS is followed by, or paired with, an unconditioned stimulus. For Pavlov experiment the bell is the CS; salivating is the UR; and the meat powder is an unconditional stimulus. To reinforce salivating to the bell, we must link the bell with the meat powder.

Once a response is learned, it can bring about higher order conditioning. In this case, a well-learned CS is used to reinforce further learning. In other words, the CS has become strong enough to be used like an unconditioned stimulus. Many artists try to apply this effect by pairing images that evoke good feelings (such as people smiling and having fun) with pictures of their art. Obviously, they hope that you will learn, by association, to feel good when you see their art.

2. Expectancies

How does classical conditioning occur? Many psychologists believe it takes place as *we process information that might aid survival*. According to this informational view, learning occurs as we detect associations among events. This creates new mental expectancies, or expectation about how events are related.

Conditioned stimulus reliably precedes the unconditioned stimulus. Because it does, the CS predicts the US. During conditioning, the brain learns to expect that the US will follow the CS. As a result, the brain prepares the body to respond to the US. This expectancy, which was acquired during classical conditioning, changes people behavior.

3. Extinction and Spontaneous Recovery

If the US never again follows the CS, conditioning will *extinguish*. Let's return to the dog and the bell. If you ring the bell many times and do not follow it with food, the dog's expectancy that "bell precedes food" will weaken. As it does, the dog will lose her tendency to salivate when she hears the bell. As a result we see that classical conditioning can be weakened by removing reinforcement. This process is called extinction.

Several extinction sessions may be necessary to completely reverse conditioning. If the bell is rung until the dog quits responding, it might seem that extinction is complete. However, the dog will probably respond to the bell again on the following day, at least at first. The reappearance of a response following apparent extinction is called spontaneous recovery. It explains why people who have had terrifying automobile accidents may need many slow, calm rides before their fears extinguish.

4. Generalization

After conditioning, *other stimuli similar to the CS may also trigger a response*. This is called stimulus generalization. For example, we might find that the dog salivates to the sound of a ringing telephone or doorbell, even though they were never used as conditioning stimuli.

It is easy to see the value of stimulus generalization. Consider the child who burns her finger while playing with matches. Most likely, lighted matches will become conditioned fear stimuli for her. But will she fear only matches? Because of stimulus generalization, she should also have a healthy fear of flames from lighters, fireplaces, stoves, and so forth. It's fortunate that generalization extends learning to related situations. Otherwise, we would all be far less adaptable.

Stimulus generalization has limits. As stimuli become less like the original CS, responding decreases. If you condition a person to blink each time you play a particular note on a piano, blinking will decline as you play higher or lower notes. If the notes are much higher or lower, the person will not respond at all.

5. Discrimination

Suppose the dog is again conditioned with a bell as the CS. As an experiment, we occasionally sound a buzzer instead of the bell, but never follow it with the US (food). At first, the buzzer produces salivation (because of generalization). But after hearing the buzzer several times more, the dog will ***stop responding*** to it. The dog has now learned to discriminate, or respond differently, to the bell and the buzzer. In essence, the child's generalized response to the buzzer has extinguished.

Stimulus discrimination is the ability to respond differently to stimuli that initially seemed to be alike. For example, you might remember being able to tell, as a child, when your mother's or father's voice changed to it is you're-about-to-get-swatted tone. (Or the dreaded give-me-that-Game-Boy tone). Most children quickly learn to discriminate voice tones associated with pain from those associated with indifference, praise, or affection.

Many involuntary, autonomic nervous system responses ("fight-or-flight" reflexes) are linked to new stimuli and situation by classical conditioning.

Emotional Topic in Classical Conditioning

Classical conditioning ***depends on reflex responses***. As mentioned earlier, a reflex is a dependable, inborn stimulus-and-response connection. For example, your hand reflexively draws back from pain. Bright light causes the pupil of the eye to narrow. Various foods elicit salivation. Any of these reflexes, and others as well, can be associated with a new stimulus. At the very least, you have probably noticed how your mouth waters when you see or smell a bakery. Even pictures of food may make you salivate.

Of large importance, perhaps, are the more subtle ways that conditioning affects us. In addition to simple reflexes, more complex emotional, or "gut," responses may be linked to new stimuli. For instance, if your face reddened when you were punished as a child, you may blush now when you are embarrassed or ashamed.

One of the types of conditioning is prejudice.

Prejudice is a baseless and usually negative attitude toward members of a group. Common features of prejudice include negative feelings, stereotyped beliefs, and a tendency to discriminate against members of the group.

Vicarious, or Secondary, Conditioning

Conditioning also occurs ***indirectly***, which adds to its impact on our behavior. Let's say, for example, that you watch another person get a car accident. Each time, a signal light comes on before the accident occurred. Even if you don't receive pain or injury yourself, you will soon develop a CER to the light. Children who learn to fear thunder by watching their parents react to it have undergone similar conditioning.

Vicarious classical conditioning occurs when we learn to respond emotionally to a stimulus by observing another person's emotional reactions. Such secondary learning affects feelings in many situations. For example, "horror" movies filled with screaming actors probably add to fears of snakes, caves, spiders, heights, and other terrors.

The emotional attitudes people develop toward arts are probably not only conditioned by direct experiences, but vicariously as well. No one is born prejudiced; all attitudes are learned. Parents may do well to look in a mirror if they wonder how or where a child "picked up" a particular fear or emotional attitude.

Figure 2.3. Sexism is an example of prejudice.

Classical Conditioning in Everyday Life

In reality, people do not respond exactly like Pavlov's dogs. There are, however, numerous real-world applications for classical conditioning.

Many dog trainers use classical conditioning techniques to help people train their pets. These techniques are also useful in the treatment of phobias or anxiety problems.

Teachers are able to apply classical conditioning in the class by creating a positive classroom environment to help students overcome anxiety or fear. Pairing an anxiety-provoking situation, such as performing in front of a group, with pleasant surroundings helps the student learn new associations. Instead of feeling anxious and tense in these situations, the student will learn to stay relaxed and calm.

Many ***phobias*** that people experience are the results of conditioning. For example - "fear of bridges" - fear of bridges can develop from many different sources. For example, while a child rides in a car over a dilapidated bridge, his father makes jokes about the bridge collapsing and all of them falling into the river below. The father finds this funny and so decides to do it whenever they cross the bridge. Years later, the child has grown up and now is afraid to drive over any bridge. In this case, the fear of one bridge generalized to all bridges which now evoke fear.

Students may experience *fear of mathematics* or other sciences. Having troubles in high school (i.e., because of lack of interest, or unsuitable teaching, etc.) student become conditioned not even try to learn it again.

Advertising - modern advertising strategies evolved from John Watson's use of conditioning. The approach is to link an attractive US with a CS (the product being sold) so the consumer will feel positively toward the product just like they do with the US.

US → CS → CR/UR

attractive person → car → pleasant emotional response

You may use classical conditioning to *enhance your learning abilities*. Do something pleasant right before you start studying. For example, play your favorite music, go for a walk, or play your favorite game for couple of minutes.

WHAT IS OPERANT CONDITIONING?

Psychologist B.F. Skinner was the first to describe operant conditioning.

Operant conditioning (sometimes referred to as *instrumental conditioning*) is a method of *learning that occurs through rewards* and *punishments* for behavior. Through operant conditioning, an association is made between a behavior and a consequence for that behavior.

Operant conditioning was coined by behaviorist B.F. Skinner, which is why you may occasionally hear it referred to as Skinnerian conditioning. As a behaviorist, Skinner believed that internal thoughts and motivations could not be used to explain behavior. Instead, he suggested, we should look only at the external, observable causes of human behavior.

Skinner used the term operant to refer to any "active behavior that operates upon the environment to generate consequences" (1953). In other words, Skinner's theory explained how people acquire the range of learned behaviors they exhibit each and every day.

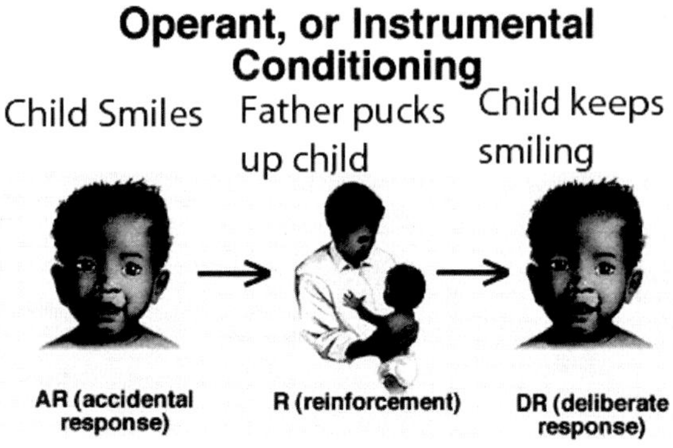

Examples of Operant Conditioning

Consider the case of children completing homework to earn a reward from a parent or teacher, or employees finishing projects to receive praise or promotions.

In these examples, the promise or possibility of rewards causes an increase in behavior, but operant conditioning can also be used to decrease a behavior. The removal of an undesirable outcome or the use of punishment can be used to decrease or prevent undesirable behaviors. For example, a child may be told they will lose recess privileges if they talk out of turn in class. This potential for punishment may lead to a decrease in disruptive behaviors.

Figure 2.4. Operant Conditioning.

Components of Operant Conditioning

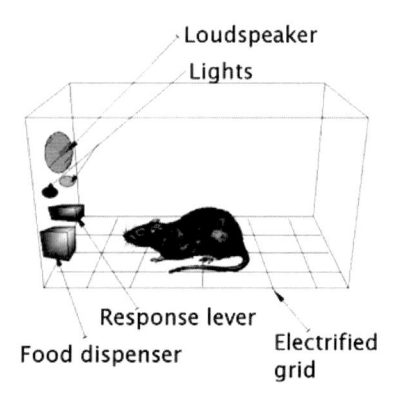

Some key concepts in operant conditioning:

A re-enforcer is any event that strengthens or increases the behavior it follows.

Operant Conditioning-trial and error learning; associating behavior with reward or punishment. Classical Conditioning-Associating a "neutral stimulus" with a "significant stimulus." Operant Conditioning is easy to remember. Just think about Skinner's box, and the mouse's repeated action of pressing the lever to get food. After pushing the lever for the first time (and every time after that), the mouse gets a piece of food. The mouse then learns to associate the act of pushing the lever with a reward.

There are two kinds of re-enforcers:

Positive Re-Enforcers	Negative Re-Enforcers
Positive re-enforcers are favorable events or outcomes that are presented after the behavior. In situations that reflect positive reinforcement, a response or behavior is strengthened by the addition of something, such as praise or a direct reward.	Negative re-enforcers involve the removal of an unfavorable events or outcomes after the display of a behavior. In these situations, a response is strengthened by the removal of something considered unpleasant.

Praise	Direct Reward	Positive Punishment	Negative Punishment
In its common usage, praise is the act of making positive statements about a person, object or idea, either in public or privately. Praise is typically, but not exclusively, earned relative to achievement and accomplishment.	• wages: a recompense for worthy acts or retribution for wrongdoing; "the wages of sin is death"; "virtue is its own reward" • payment made in return for a service rendered • honor: bestow honor or rewards upon; "Today we honor our soldiers"; "The scout was rewarded for courageous action" • an act performed to strengthen approved behavior	Positive punishment, sometimes referred to as punishment by application, involves the presentation of an unfavorable event or outcome in order to weaken the response it follows.	Negative punishment, also known as punishment by removal, occurs when an favorable event or outcome is removed after a behavior occurs.
In both of these cases of reinforcement, the behavior increases.		In both of these cases of punishment, the behavior decreases.	

WHAT IS SOCIAL LEARNING THEORY?

The social learning theory proposed by Albert Bandura has become perhaps the most influential theory of learning and development. Bandura believed that direct reinforcement could not account for all types of learning.

His theory added a social element, arguing that people can learn new information and behaviors by **watching other people**. Known as **observational learning** (or **modeling**), this type of learning can be used to explain a wide variety of behaviors.

CHAPTER 2
Basic Social Learning Concepts

Figure 2.5. People can learn through observation.

Observing parents' behavior (domestic violence)	Copying violence (bullying)	Joining gang

Observational Learning

In his famous "Bobo doll" studies, Bandura demonstrated that ***children*** learn and ***imitate*** behaviors they have observed in other people. The children in Bandura's studies observed an adult acting violently toward a Bobo doll. When the children were later allowed to play in a room with the Bobo doll, they began to imitate the aggressive actions they had previously observed.

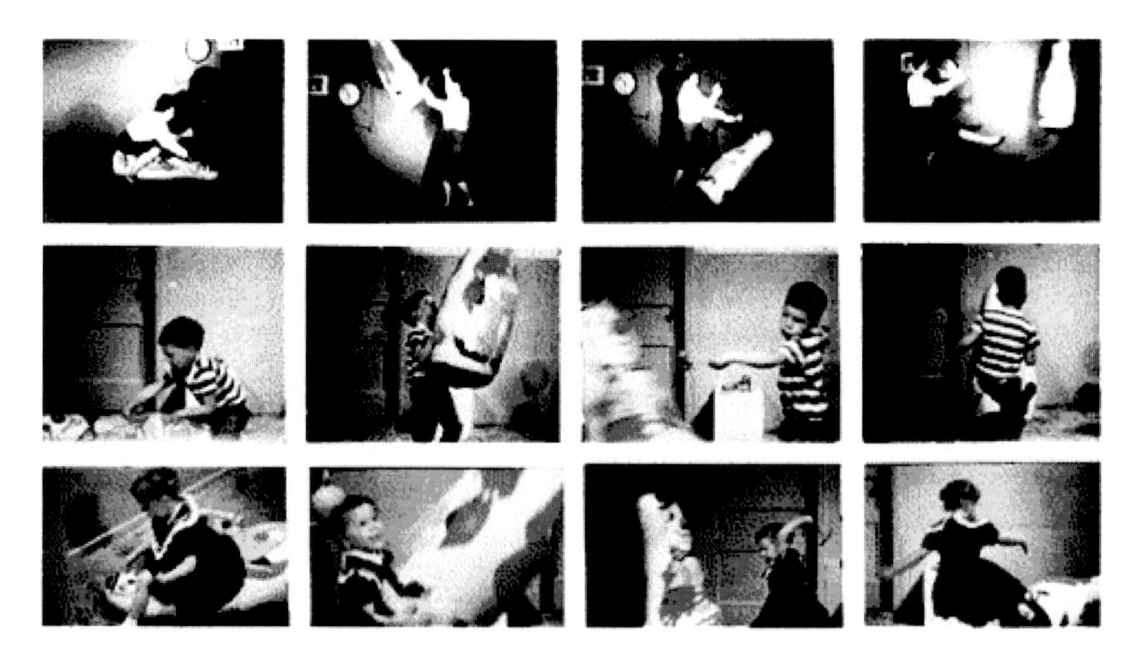

Figure 2.6. Bobo Doll Experiment. The children observed an adult acting violently toward a Bobo doll. When the children were later allowed to play in a room with the Bobo doll, they began to imitate the aggressive actions they had previously observed.

Bandura identified three basic models of observational learning:

    1. *A **live model**,* which involves an actual individual demonstrating or acting out a behavior.

  2. *A verbal instructional model*, which involves descriptions and explanations of a behavior.
  3. *A symbolic model*, which involves real or fictional characters displaying behaviors in books, films, television programs, or online media.
II. Mental states are important to learning.

Intrinsic Reinforcement

Bandura noted that external, environmental reinforcement was not the only factor to influence learning and behavior. He described intrinsic reinforcement as a form of internal reward, such as pride, satisfaction, and a sense of accomplishment. This emphasis on *internal thoughts* and cognitions helps connect learning theories to cognitive developmental theories. While many textbooks place social learning theory with behavioral theories, Bandura himself describes his approach as a 'social cognitive theory.'

III. Learning does not necessarily lead to a change in behavior.

While behaviorists believed that learning led to a permanent change in behavior, observational learning demonstrates that people can learn new information without demonstrating new behaviors.

The Modeling Process

Not all observed behaviors are effectively learned. Factors involving both the model and the learner can play a role in whether social learning is successful. Certain requirements and steps must also be followed. The following steps are involved in the observational learning and modeling process:

Attention:
In order to learn, you need to be paying attention. Anything that detracts your attention is going to have a negative effect on observational learning. If the model interesting or there is a novel aspect to the situation, you are far more likely to dedicate your full attention to learning.

Retention:
The ability to store information is also an important part of the learning process. Retention can be affected by a number of factors, but the ability to pull up information later and act on it is vital to observational learning.

Reproduction:
Once you have paid attention to the model and retained the information, it is time to actually perform the behavior you observed. Further practice of the learned behavior leads to improvement and skill advancement.

Motivation:
Finally, in order for observational learning to be successful, you have to be motivated to imitate the behavior that has been modeled. Reinforcement and punishment play an important role in motivation. While experiencing these motivators can be highly effective, so can observing other experience some type of reinforcement or punishment. For example, if you see another student rewarded with extra credit for being to class on time, you might start to show up a few minutes early each day

THE 'WHAT-IS-IT?' REACTION

  There are few things more effective in lowering a lecturer's self-evaluation than seeing the members of the audience, supposedly enraptured by his compelling rhetoric, turn their hands to attend to a door opening, someone leaving his seat, or virtually any other "trivial" stimulus that occurs.
  This mechanism for paying attention to novel environmental stimuli is called the *orienting reaction.* It has long been studied extensively by Russian researchers, but it was not until the 1950s that

American researchers began studying it. Curiosity and exploratory behavior are some of the more complex forms of it that have been extensively studied since then.

Curiosity plays important role in creativity. It is considered to be the first stage of discovery.

Many changes accompany the apparently simple turning toward the source of the novel stimulus. In general, they serve to increase the sensitivity of the organism to the incoming stimulus, so that he can discern where it is and mobilize for action if necessary. Components of the orienting reaction include:

1. **Increased sensitivity.** Auditory and visual thresholds are lowered, the pupil dilates to let in more light, and ability to discriminate between similar stimuli is increased.
2. **Specific skeletal muscle changes.** Depending the species, muscles that direct the sense organs operate to turn the head, focus the eyes, prick up the ears, and so on.
3. **General muscle changes.** Ongoing activities are suspended; general muscle tonus rises, and electrical activity in the muscles increases.
4. **Brain wave changes.** The pattern of the EEG is modified toward increased arousal, with fast, low-amplitude activity predominating.
5. **Visceral changes.** Blood vessels in the limbs constrict, while those in the head dilate. The galvanic skin response (GSR), a change in the electrical resistance of the skin occurs, breathing becomes deeper and slower, and (in man and some other animals) heart rate decreases. Thus the orienting reaction plays the dual role of maximizing sensitivity of informational input while simultaneously preparing the body for emergency.

Conditions that elicit orientation

There are three classes of stimuli which generate orienting reactions (Berlyne, 1960):

1. **Novel or complex stimuli.** Events which are different from those recently experienced or arranged in a novel sequence, creating "surprise," elicit orientation. Monkeys trained to find a banana under a cup showed marked orienting reactions when they found lettuce there. In addition, stimuli of moderate to high intensity elicit orientation, as do varicolored stimuli compared to monochromatic stimuli. Complex or incongruous figures are more likely to elicit orientation than are simple ones.
2. **Conflicting stimuli.** When an organism must make a difficult perceptual discrimination between similar stimulus events, one of which has been associated with positive consequences and the other with negative consequences, strong orienting reactions occur. A conflict between required motor responses or between required verbal responses can also result in orientation.
3. **Significant (signal) stimuli.** When a stimulus has acquired special significance for a subject, its presentation elicits orientation. Furthermore, it continues to elicit orientation even though it is repeated, is not novel, and produces no conflict. Your own name, "Watch out," and "Danger" (either seen or heard) are examples of a class of stimuli which continue to call forth the orienting reaction, whereas many non-significant stimuli that are presented equally often produce no reaction.

To Orient or to Habituate?

Virtually all stimuli have the power to evoke an *orienting reaction*, although those belonging to one of the three classes outlined above produce stronger, more enduring orienting reactions. There is obvious functional value in attending to and investigating stimuli which are novel, surprising, puzzling, or of biological or personal significance. If the environmental detection system is to be truly efficient, however, there must be some mechanism for "turning off" the orienting reaction once incoming stimuli have become familiar, understood, and expected and it is known that they do not signal anything of importance happening "out there."

Most stimuli cease to evoke an orienting reaction merely by being repeated in identical form. With such repetition the organism habituates to the stimulus, both physiologically and psychologically, and stops responding to it. It is as if a stimulus loses its existence once it stops carrying new or significant information of potential value to the organism. Thus, after ten to thirty stimulations, the generalized orienting reaction typically habituates.

Repeated stimulation by stimuli of even moderate intensity can produce drowsiness and eventually sleep (a fact you must have experienced while reading certain books or listening to

---

*This mechanism for paying attention to novel environmental stimuli is called the **orienting reaction**.*

Curiosity plays important role in creativity. It is considered to be the first stage of discovery.

canned large-hall lectures delivered in a droning monotone). It has been shown that many normal rested adults fall asleep after being exposed to only eight minutes of repetitive stimulation (Gastaut & Bert, 1961). Inducting sleep by "counting sheep" or inducing a hypnotic state of extreme relaxation by repeating a simple verbal formula both employ this principle of habituation. Both orientation and habituation are necessary for species survival, since each individual organism must learn what is going on in his particular environment before he can try to adapt to or control it. Although present in some form in all species, however, orienting is more pronounced among the more highly developed animals than among the simpler ones. In addition, since they are equipped to extract more information per stimulus exposure, higher animals also show more rapid habituation.

The importance of orientation for art perception and appreciation is indicated by the observation how human beings react on visual art, music, or poems when they are exposed to for the first time and after several times of exposure.

Dis-Habituation – Return of the Orienting Reaction

After habituation has occurred, the orienting response can be induced again if the stimulus input becomes distinguishably different – even if it includes the same elements but in an unusual or unexpected order.

Dis-habituation may occur with changes in the length, the pattern, or the "meaning" of the stimulus. This response to unexpected stimuli suggests that the incoming stimulus is constantly being compared to some expectancy on the part of the organism. Apparently the organism has associated all the characteristics of the original stimulus presentation as belonging to a particular pattern, and can instantly identify as "different" – and worth responding to – any variation in the pattern. Thus whereas orientation and habituation merely involve responses to change (or lack of change) in stimulus input, dis-habituation seems to give evidence of some primitive form of learning.

If dis-habituation does not occur when habituation has taken place and some element of the stimulus complex is altered, we can infer either that the change is too small to be detected or that the organism has not noticed the change that has taken place. This latter may mean simply that the organism did not perceive that particular element as part of the original stimulus complex.

Figure 2.7. Art Perception. In visual art, music, and literature people react on unusual or unexpected stimuli.

Information

Like classical conditioning, operant learning is based on information and expectancies. In operant conditioning, we learn to expect that a certain response will have a certain effect at certain times. From this point of view, a re-enforcer tells a person or an animal that a response was "right" and worth repeating.

Superstitious Behavior

Re-enforcers affect not only the response they follow, but also other responses that occur shortly before. This helps explain many human superstitions. If a golfer taps her club on the ground three times and then hits an unusually fine shot, what happens? The successful shot reinforces not only the correct swing but also the three taps. During operant training, animals often develop similar unnecessary responses.

Superstitious behavior is repeated because they appear to produce reinforcement, even though they are actually unnecessary. If you get the large half of a wishbone and have good fortune soon after, you may credit your luck to the wishbone. If you walk under a ladder and then break a leg, you may avoid ladders in the future.

COGNITIVE LEARNING

Even basic conditioning has "mental" elements. As a human, you can anticipate future reward or punishment and react accordingly. (You may wonder why this doesn't seem to work when a doctor or

CHAPTER 2

dentist says, "This won't hurt a bit." Here's why: They lie!) There is no doubt that human learning includes a large cognitive, or mental, dimension. As human, we are greatly affected by information, expectations, perceptions, mental images, and the like.

Cognitive learning refers to **understanding, knowing, anticipating**, or otherwise making use of information-rich higher mental processes. Cognitive learning *extends beyond basic conditioning* into the realms of **memory, thinking, problem solving, and language.**

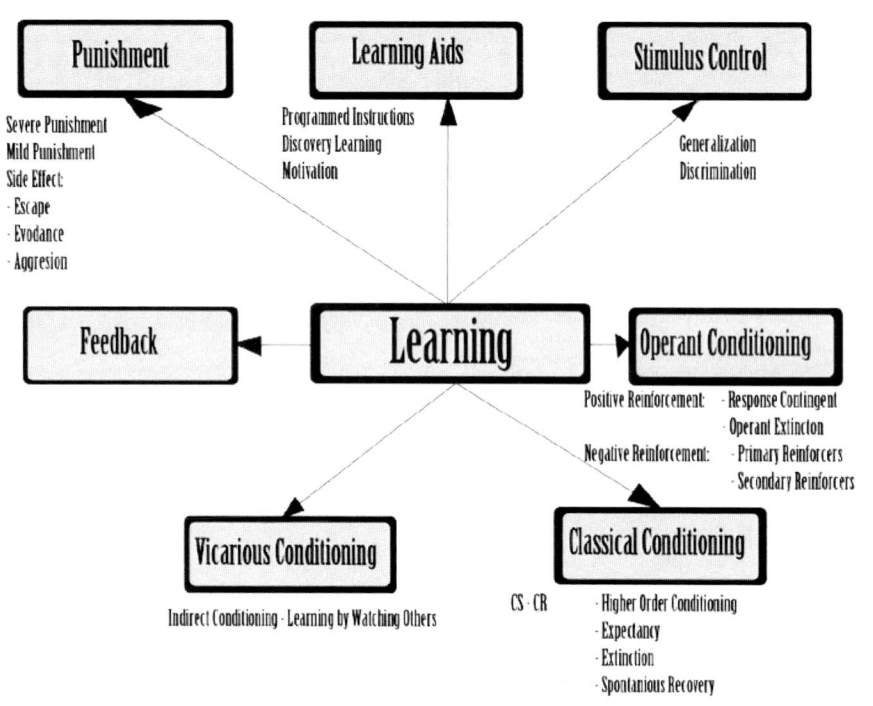

```
Punishment          Learning Aids        Stimulus Control
Severe Punishment   Programmed Instructions
Mild Punishment     Discovery Learning   Generalization
Side Effect:        Motivation           Discrimination
 - Escape
 - Evoidance
 - Aggresion

Feedback  ←——  Learning  ——→  Operant Conditioning
                                 Positive Reinforcement: - Response Contingent
                                                         - Operant Extinction
                              Negative Reinforcement:    - Primary Reinforcers
                                                         - Secondary Reinforcers

   Vicarious Conditioning        Classical Conditioning
Indirect Conditioning - Learning by Watching Others   CS - CR
                                       - Higher Order Conditioning
                                       - Expectancy
                                       - Extinction
                                       - Spontanious Recovery
```

Cognitive Maps

How are you oriented in the town you live in? You have simply learned to make a series of right and left turns to get from one point to another? It is far more likely that you have an overall mental picture of how the town is laid out. This cognitive map acts as a guide even when you must detour or take a new route. A cognitive map is an internal representation of an area, such as a maze, city, or campus.

Latent Learning

Cognitive learning is also revealed by latent or hidden learning. Latent learning occurs **without obvious reinforcement**. It remains unseen until reinforcement is provided. For example, two groups of rats were allowed to explore a maze. The animals in one group found food at the far end of the maze. Soon, they learned to rapidly make their way through the maze when released. Rats in the second group were unrewarded and showed no signs of learning. But later, when the "uneducated" rats were given food, they ran the maze as quickly as the rewarded group. Although there was no outward sign of it, the unrewarded animals had learned their way around the maze. Their learning, therefore, remained latent at first.

Just satisfying curiosity can be enough to reward learning. In humans latent learning is probably related to anticipating future reward. For example, if you give an attractive classmate a ride home, you may make mental notes about how to get to his or her house, even if a date is only a remote future possibility.

Discovery Learning

Much of what is meant by cognitive learning is summarized by the word understanding. Each of us has, at times, learned ideas by rote (repetition and memorization). Although rote learning is efficient, many psychologists believe that learning is more lasting and flexible when people discover facts and principles on their own. In discovery learning, skills are gained by insight and understanding instead of by rote.

Observational Learning

By observing someone who serves as an example a person may
Learn new responses;

Learn to carry out or avoid previously learned responses (depending on what happens to this person (model) for doing the same thing);

Learn a general rule that can be applied to various situations.

How to Enhance Learning?

Let us assume that you are teacher, parent, or trainer and you have a pocketful of reinforcements you want to dispense – if only the individual will make the correct response. What procedures can you use to elicit the first correct response, so that it can be reinforced and thus can be made to recur more frequently? This is a problem Pavlov never had because he was studying responses that could always be produced by careful presentation of the proper eliciting stimulus.

Each of these techniques has certain advantages and disadvantages, depending on whether only immediate results or more permanent, long-term ones are desired. Because some of the consequences of applying these techniques are unintentionally negative, especially in the long run, we must be judicious in deciding which fits the particular learning situation best.

Some of the means of getting the individual to make that first correct response so you can reinforce it are:
- Increasing motivation;
- Lowering restraints;
- Structuring the environment;
- Forcing;
- Providing a model;
- Giving instructions;
- Trial and error;
- Successive approximation or shaping.

1. Increasing motivation.

Prodding the individual into responding and emitting many responses increases the probability that one of them will be the correct one. For example, electrifying a grid will get the rat moving about, and in the process he may discover an escape route. Here necessity is the mother of invention. Threats and promises of future reward (called "incentive motivation") as well as deprivation states or noxious stimulation all may be successfully used to motivate action. There are, however, a number of potentially bad effects such motivators may have on the learning process.

Raising the level of motivation is not recommended if the individual does not have the response in his repertoire or does not have the ability to make it. For example, the mother who "won't love baby any more if baby soils his diapers" will have no effect on changing the bowel movements if the child does not have sphincter muscle control yet. She may, however, produce both feelings of inferiority and a long-lasting resentment in her child. Such a procedure can also lead to conflict if there is strong competing motivation. Finally, if the individual makes the response only because of the extrinsic motivation provided by avoidance of pain or anticipation of reward (perhaps a gold star or a dessert), he will be less likely to learn to value the task activity itself (studying or eating spinach).

2. Lowering restraints.

If the individual has already learned the skills involved in making the correct response, but does not emit it under motivating conditions, it may well be that the response is being inhibited or suppressed. Previously learned habits may be incompatible with emitting the desired response. The shy student who knows the answer will not ever get reinforced for it unless he raises his hand and says it out loud, but this he cannot do because he has learned that it is very painful to him to talk in class. Many males cannot express "tender" responses such as love or grief because prior learning has defined them as "unmasculine" responses. To get soldier to kill, or medical students to start to cut up a cadaver, techniques are used to lower learned restraints against such "antisocial" behavior.

Discovering what are the competing motives and weakening them, or finding out what reinforcers are maintaining the inhibitions on behavior and removing them, may help to induce the desired response. On the negative side, whatever is inhibiting the behavior in question may also be holding in check other behaviors which you would not want to be released.

3. Structuring the environment.

Suppose you want two competitive children to learn to cooperate with each other. One way to encourage this type of responding is to place them in an area containing toys which can be manipulated only by two or more children. You can make the behavior more likely by removing distracting, irrelevant stimuli, simplifying the environment, making the manipulandum stand out more than other features of the environment. The change from Thorndike's relatively complicated puzzle box to the simplicity of the Skinner box is an illustration of making the desired response more likely by structuring the environment to remove most other possibilities. Of course, learning to survive in only a relatively simple environment may leave the organism overwhelmed by the stimulus variety if it encounters a complex environment (as when the country inhabitant goes to the city).

4. Forcing

Often the most efficient method of getting out that first correct response is to assist its execution physically. You take the child's hand with the spoon full of unfamiliar food and direct it into his mouth. Then you reinforce his putting the food in his mouth (and hopefully swallowing it) with praise or whatever.

This rapid response elicitation technique probably has the worst long-term consequences for human learners, especially if they are involuntary or unwilling participants or if the individual using the technique is inept. Imagine how our shy student would feel toward the teacher who forced the response of answering in class by picking up his hand. Regardless of the size of the subsequent reinforcement for the response, this crude type of forcing would likely develop negative emotional responses toward the coercive agent of reinforcement, inculcate a sense of personal inadequacy, or lead the subject to make the correct response by rote without ever understanding the underlying principle.

5. Providing a model

"Repetez, s'il vous plait," says the French teacher, and the student attempts to imitate what she has said – both the content and manner of delivery. Observational learning or imitation of model is also valuable where the details of a complex motor task cannot be easily communicated in words – as, for example, tying one's shoelaces, or hitting a baseball. It is important in the social learning.

On the other hand, over-dependence on models (who usually are "authority figures") may limit the individual's own initiative, making him a conformist; it may also lead him to "pick up" a host of other responses made by the model. These may be responses correlated with the desired one, such as parents' speech habits, dialects, and so on, learned along with the language. Or they may be unrelated responses that just happen to be emitted with high frequency by the model, such as statements of prejudice against minority groups.

6. Giving instructions

"Do what I say, not what I do," distinguishes this approach from the previous one. The ability to use language can clearly facilitate some kind of learning and can greatly accelerate elicitation of the first correct response. In fact, verbal instructions can be used not only to outline how the response should be made, but also to provide a description of the happy consequences that such responding will bring. Complex sequences may be communicating delay of response, ways of using past learning and instructions for the future.

Naturally, following verbal instructions presupposes understanding them which is not always the case, as parent will testify who have tried in frustrating desperation to assemble a child's toy from the "easy-to-follow directions." Ambiguity in language skills, and the occasional difference between what is said and what is actually meant all may reduce the effectiveness of verbal instruction for many potential learners. On the other hand, overly explicit instructions can lead in the long run to a learned dependence on being told exactly what to do and how to do it – along with a loss of intellectual curiosity and a fear of taking risk.

7. Trial and error

This "sink or swim," survival-of-the-fittest method is peculiar in a number of ways. It is one of the least effective techniques for getting out that first correct response (in the absence of any other techniques), but it may have the most desirable long-term consequences when it works. It is a decidedly undemocratic, elitist approach, however, where many are called, but only a few are reinforced. For those who try and do succeed, the relative subjective reinforcement is greater when viewed in the perspective of all those who did not succeed. In addition, what is reinforced is not only the correct response, but the entire process of searching for a solution. In contrast, for the many whose trials end only in more errors, reinforcement for correct responding never comes, and the effort and curiosity involved in the behavior are likely to undergo experimental extinction. The vast wastefulness of over-reliance on such a general approach is evident in the failure of about half of all graduate students (who are bright and motivated) to complete the trial-and-error procedure of the doctoral dissertation.

8. Successive approximation or shaping

How would you get a pigeon to play Ping-Pong, or a rat to lift more than his body weight?

Learning and Thinking

For many behaviors which are complex and unlikely to occur in perfect form on the first trial, the criterion for reinforcement must be lowered. At the beginning, the "correct" response is any overt response which is an approximation of (bears some resemblance to) the final behavior desired or of one step in a desired sequence. Then, on successive trials, the response must be progressively more like the response wanted in order to earn reinforcement. Finally, these partial behaviors get shaped into the whole complex sequence. By the end of training, only the sequence is followed by reinforcement.

If done subtly, shaping can elicit the desired behavior without the individual's awareness that he is being conditioned. However, shaping can be a very time-consuming procedure, requiring much skill and patience on the part of the re-inforcer. For many behaviors, some of the other techniques we have discussed would elicit the correct terminal response more rapidly and effortlessly.

For example, if you have a human subject and wanted him to turn a page, it would be far simpler to say "Turn the page now" than to try, through reinforcement of successive approximations, to shape all the actions involved in page turning.

In many learning situation, the "teacher" (used in the broadest sense) should not only be aware of the various possible techniques but seriously consider both their immediate results and their possible long-term consequences.

Improve Your Personal Learning Skills

1. Chose a target behavior. Identify the activity you want to change.
2. Record a baseline. Record how much time you currently spend performing the target activity, or count the number of desired or undesired responses you make each day.
3. Establish goals. Remember the principle of shaping and set realistic goals for gradual improvement on each successive week. Set daily goals that add up to the weekly goal.
4. Choose reinforces. If you meet your daily goal, what reward will you allow yourself?
5. Record your progress. Keep accurate records of the amount of time spent each day on the desired activity or the number of times to make the desired responses.
6. Reward successes. If you meet your daily goal, collect your reward.
7. Adjust your plan as you learn more about your behavior. Overall progress will reinforce your attempts at self-management.

SUMMARY

1. Learning is "a relatively permanent change in behavior that results from practice" (Atkinson et al 1993). It also means changes in "capability" or even simple "knowledge" or "understanding", even if it is not manifest in behavior.
2. When people learn, they organize, shape, and strengthen their brains.
3. There are three major learning theories: (1) Classical Conditioning; (2) Operant Conditioning; and (3) Social Learning Theory
4. Classical conditioning is a learning process that occurs through associations between an environmental stimulus and a naturally occurring stimulus.
5. Operant conditioning (sometimes referred to as instrumental conditioning) is a method of learning that occurs through rewards and punishments for behavior. Through operant conditioning, an association is made between a behavior and a consequence for that behavior.
6. Social Learning Theory states that people can learn new information and behaviors by watching other people. Known as observational learning (or modeling), this type of learning can be used to explain a wide variety of behaviors.
7. Orientation Reaction is the ability to respond immediately to the novel stimuli. Three factors elicit orientation (Berlyne, 1960):
- Novel or complex stimuli. Events which are different from those recently experienced or arranged in a novel sequence, creating "surprise," elicit orientation.
- Conflicting stimuli. When an organism must make a difficult perceptual discrimination between similar stimulus events, one of which has been associated with positive consequences

and the other with negative consequences, strong orienting reactions occur. A conflict between required motor responses or between required verbal responses can also result in orientation.

- Significant (signal) stimuli. When a stimulus has acquired special significance for a subject, its presentation elicits orientation. Furthermore, it continues to elicit orientation even though it is repeated, is not novel, and produces no conflict. Your own name, "Watch out," and "Danger" (either seen or heard) are examples of a class of stimuli which continue to call forth the orienting reaction, whereas many non-significant stimuli that are presented equally often produce no reaction.

IMPROVING YOUR MEMORY AND LEARNING

1. **Focus your attention on the materials you are studying.** Attention is one of the major components of memory. In order for information to move from short-term memory into long-term memory, you need to actively attend to this information. Try to study in a place free of distractions such as television, music, and other diversions.

2. **Avoid cramming by establishing regular study sessions.** According to Bjork (2001), studying materials over a number of session's gives you the time you need to adequately process the information. Research has shown that students who study regularly remember the material far better that those did all of their studying in one marathon session.

3. **Structure and organize the information you are studying.** Researchers have found that information is organized in memory in related clusters. You can take advantage of this by structuring and organizing the materials you are studying. Try grouping similar concepts and terms together, or make an outline of your notes and textbook readings to help group related concepts.

4. **Utilize mnemonic devices to remember information.** Mnemonic devices are a technique often used by students to aid in recall. A mnemonic is simply a way to remember information. For example, you might associate a term you need to remember with a common item that you are very familiar with. The best mnemonics are those that utilize positive imagery, humor, or novelty. You might come up with a rhyme, song, or joke to help remember a specific segment of information.

5. **Elaborate and rehearse the information you are studying.** In order to recall information, you need to encode what you are studying into long-term memory. One of the most effective encoding techniques is known as elaborative rehearsal. An example of this technique would be to read the definition of a key term, study the definition of that term, and then read a more detailed description of what that term means. After repeating this process a few times, your recall of the information will be far better.

6. **Relate new information to things you already know.** When you are studying unfamiliar material, take the time to think about how this information relates to things that you already know. By establishing relationships between new ideas and previously existing memories, you can dramatically increase the likelihood of recalling the recently learned information.

7. **Visualize concepts to improve memory and recall.** Many people benefit greatly from visualizing the information they study. Pay attention to the photographs, charts, and other graphics in your textbooks. If you don't have visual cues to help, try creating your own. Draw charts or figures in the margins of your notes or use highlighters or pens in different colors to group related ideas in your written study materials.

8. **Teach new concepts to another person.** Research suggests that reading materials out loud significantly improves memory of the material. Educators and psychologists have also discovered that having students actually teach new concepts to others enhances understanding and recall. You can use this approach in your own study by teaching new concepts and information to a friend or study partner.

9. **Pay extra attention to difficult information.** Have you ever noticed how it's sometimes easier to remember information at the beginning or end of a chapter? Researchers have found that the position of information can play a role in recall, which is known as the serial position effect. While recalling middle information can be difficult, you can overcome this problem by spending extra time rehearsing this information or try restructuring the information so it will be easier to remember. When you come across an especially difficult concept, devote some extra time to memorizing the information.

10. **Vary your study routine.** Another great way to increase your recall is to occasionally change your study routine. If you are accustomed to studying in one specific location, try moving to a different spot to study. If you study in the evening, try to spend a few minutes each morning reviewing the information you studied the previous night. By adding an element of novelty to your study sessions, you can increase the effectiveness of your efforts and significantly improve your long-term recall.

11. **Keep Learning (and Practicing) New Things.** Learning and practicing new skills helps your brain retain new information. One sure-fire way to become a more effective learner is to simply keep learning. A 2004 Nature article reported that people who learned how to juggle increased the amount of gray matter in their occipital lobes, the area of the brain is associated with visual memory. When these individuals stopped practicing their new skill, this gray matter vanished. So if you are learning a new language, it is important to keep practicing the language in order to maintain the gains you have achieved. This "use-it-or-lose-it" phenomenon involves a brain process known as "pruning." Certain pathways in the brain are maintained, while other are eliminated. If you want the new information you just learned to stay put, keep practicing and rehearsing it.

12. **Learn in Multiple Ways.** Focus on learning in more than one way. Instead of just listening to a podcast, which involves auditory learning, find a way to rehearse the information both verbally and visually. This might involve describing what you learned to a friend, taking notes or drawing a mind map. By learning in more than one way, you're further cementing the knowledge in your mind. According to Judy Willis, "The more regions of the brain that store data about a subject, the more interconnection there is. This redundancy means students will have more opportunities to pull up all of those related bits of data from their multiple storage areas in response to a single cue. This cross-referencing of data means we have learned, rather than just memorized."

13. **Teach What You Have Learned to Another Person.** Teaching can improve your learning. Educators have long noted that one of the best ways to learn something is to teach it to someone else. Remember your seventh-grade presentation on Costa Rica? By teaching to the rest of the class, your teacher hoped you would gain even more from the assignment. You can apply the same principle today by sharing your newly learned skills and knowledge with others. Start by translating the information into your own words. This process alone helps solidify new knowledge in your brain. Next, find some way to share what you've learned. Some ideas include writing a blog post, creating a podcast or participating in a group discussion.

14. **Utilize Previous Learning to Promote New Learning.** Another great way to become a more effective learner is to use relational learning, which involves relating new information to things that you already know. For example, if you are learning about Romeo and Juliet, you might associate what you learn about the play with prior knowledge you have about Shakespeare, the historical period in which the author lived and other relevant information.

15. **Gain Practical Experience.** For many of us, learning typically involves reading textbooks, attending lectures or doing research in the library or on the Web. While seeing information and then writing it down is important, actually putting new knowledge and skills into practice can be one of the best ways to improve learning. If you are trying to acquire a new skill or ability, focus on gaining practical experience. If it is a sport or athletic skill, perform the activity on a regular basis. If you are learning a new language, practice speaking with another person and surround yourself with immersive experiences.

16. **Look Up Answers Rather Than Struggle to Remember**. Of course, learning isn't a perfect process. Sometimes, we forget the details of things that we have already learned. If you find yourself struggling to recall some tidbit of information, research suggests that you are better offer simply looking up the correct answer. One study found that the longer you spend trying to remember the answer, the more likely you will be to forget the answer again in the future. Why? Because these attempts to recall previously learned information actually results in learning the "error state" instead of the correct response.

17. **Understand How You Learn Best.** Another great strategy for improving your learning efficiency is to recognize your learning habits and styles. There are a number of different theories about learning styles, which can all help you gain a better understanding of how you learn best. Gardner's theory of multiple intelligences describes eight different types of intelligence that can help reveal your individual strengths. Looking at Carl Jung's learning style dimensions can also help you better see which learning strategies might work best for you.

18. **Use Testing to Boost Learning.** Testing can be more beneficial than studying alone. While it may seem that spending more time studying is one of the best ways to maximize learning, research has demonstrated that taking tests actually helps you better remember what you've learned,

CHAPTER 2

even if it wasn't covered on the test.3 The study revealed that students who studied and were then tested had better long-term recall of the materials, even on information that was not covered by the tests. Students who had extra time to study but were not tested had significantly lower recall of the materials.

19.   **Stop Multitasking.** Multitasking can hurt learning effectiveness For many years, it was thought that people who multitask, or perform more than one activity at once, had an edge over those who did not. However, research now suggests that multitasking can actually make learning less effective. In the study, participants lost significant amounts of time as they switched between multiple tasks and lost even more time as the tasks became increasingly complex.4 By switching from one activity to another, you will learn more slowly, become less efficient and make more errors. How can you avoid the dangers of multitasking? Start by focusing your attention on the task at hand and continue working for a predetermined amount of time.

TEST

Challenge reaction.

Person sees the situation as an opportunity for a bit of mental exercise, in addition to a problem in need of resolution.

Avoidance reaction.

Such person sees the situation as threatening, uncomfortable, and involving an unpleasant and defeating experience.

Thinking is a matter of *selecting, organizing and manipulating* information. Problems or situations that involve thinking call for *structure*, for *relationships* between facts, and for *chains* of reasoning that "makes sense" (Albrecht, 1987). When faced with a problem or decision that requires some kind of understanding and finding solution, how do you react? To what extent do you think of yourself as a creative person?

Research into practical thinking processes has shown that there are *two contrasting types of reactions* that many people have, with relatively few individuals falling in the middle. On the one hand, there is the *challenge reaction*. One person sees the situation as an opportunity for a bit of mental exercise, in addition to a problem in need of resolution. Just as a person who enjoys playing tennis responds positively to being handed a tennis racquet, so a person who enjoys clear, reasonable thought responds positively to being handed a situation that calls for comprehension.

At the other extreme, there is the *avoidance reaction*. Such person sees the situation as threatening, uncomfortable, and involving an unpleasant and defeating experience. He or she experiences what might be called the failure reflex, a snap-reaction feeling of dread, which originates in ancient experiences of having been defeated by situations similar to the one presenting itself. Just as the person who is in very poor physical condition tends to get negative feelings at the prospect of playing a round of tennis, so the person who has trouble with proper thinking tends to shudder at the anticipation of a round of reasonable thought.

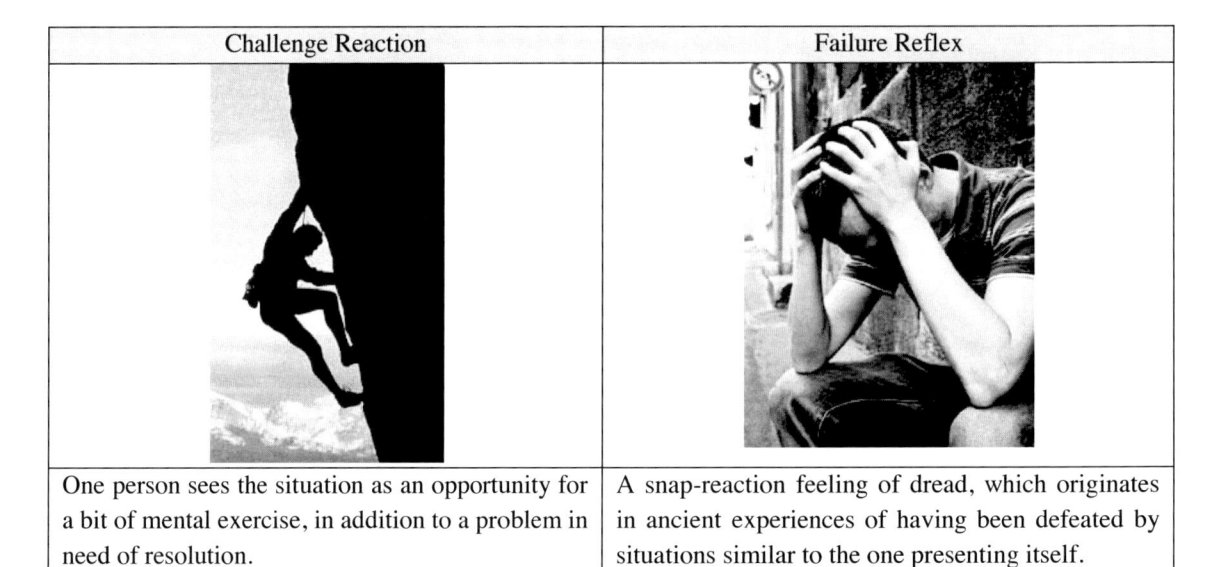

Challenge Reaction	Failure Reflex
One person sees the situation as an opportunity for a bit of mental exercise, in addition to a problem in need of resolution.	A snap-reaction feeling of dread, which originates in ancient experiences of having been defeated by situations similar to the one presenting itself.

What is a good thinker?

Good thinker usually is a good learner.

- Good thinkers prefer knowledge over information.
- Information is piecemeal and transitory.
- Information resides in the messages, while knowledge resides in a person's mind.
- Information gives something to a person to interpret, while knowledge reflects that which the person has already interpreted.
- Knowledge is structured and organized, and it has enduring significance.
- Good thinkers rarely finds value in simply memorizing facts, because they know that when they have memorized a list of facts, they have not created knowledge; all they have done is acquired a pile of 'info-bricks' and have not built anything with those materials.
- Good thinkers know that they must construct knowledge structures for themselves, so they must actively do something with the information they encounter. No one can give them these structures, and they cannot memorize them. They need to construct knowledge structures piece by piece so that those structures become the very context of how they think.
- Good thinkers are careful in determining the value of information, so they have few inaccurate facts in their knowledge structures.
- Good thinkers are well organized; they know how to process new information very quickly and catalog it in the proper place, so they can find it when they need to retrieve it.

The following test helps you to determine your personal style of thinking, learning and problem-solving (Potter, 2005). Those skills are characterized by four cognitive abilities:

- field dependence/independence
- crystallized intelligence
- fluid intelligence
- vertical thinking
- lateral thinking, and
- conceptual differentiation.

Field dependence/independence – is the ability to distinguish between the ***"signal"*** and the ***"noise"*** in any message. ***Noise*** is the ***chaos*** of symbols and images. Signal is the information that emerges from the chaos. People who are highly field-dependent get stuck in the field of chaos – ***seeing all details*** but missing the patterns and the "big picture", which is the signal. Field-independent people are able to sort quickly through the field to ***identify the important elements*** and ***ignore the distracting elements***.

For example, when they are watching a story during a television news show, field-independent people will be able to identify the key information – the who, what, when, where, and why of the story. They will quickly sort through what is said, the graphics, and the visuals to focus on the essence of the event being covered.

The field-dependence/independence construct was defined in Witkin's theory (Witkin, Moore, Goodenough, & Cox, 1977) of psychological differentiation—the pioneer work in the study of intellectual styles. The field dependent thinker is one who processes information globally. He or she is less analytical, not attentive to detail, and sees the perceptual field as a whole. This whole resists analysis or decomposition. The field independent person on the other hand can easily break the field down into its component parts. He or she is typically not influenced by the existing structure and can make choices independent of the perceptual field. Field dependent persons are more socially oriented and therefore they respond more to reward and punishment (Ferrell, 1971). They also need more explicit instructions when material to be learned is disorganized. They also are less able to synthesize and analyze (Frank & Davis, 1982).

> ***Field dependence /independence*** – is the ability to distinguish between the "signal" and the "noise" in any message.

CHAPTER 2

Thinking, Learning, Problem-Solving Styles	
FIELD-DEPENDENT	**FIELD-INDEPENDENT**
Perceives globally	Perceives analytically
Experiences in a global fashion, adheres to structures as given	Experiences in an articulate fashion, imposes structures of restrictions
Makes broad general distinctions among concepts, sees relationships	Makes specific concept distinctions, little overlap
Social orientation	Impersonal orientation
Learns material with social content best	Learns social material only as an intentional task
Attends best to material relevant to own experience	Interested in new concepts for their own sake
Requires externally defined goals and reinforcements	Has self-defined goals and reinforcements
Needs organization provided	Can self-structure situations
More affected by criticism	Less affected by criticism
Uses spectator approach for concept attainment	Uses hypothesis-testing approach to attain concepts

Fluid intelligence gives people the facility to challenge what is on the surface, to look deeper and broader, and to recognize new patterns. Fluid intelligence is the ability to find meaning in confusion and solve new problems.

Crystallized intelligence is the ability to memorize facts, to utilize previously acquired knowledge and experience. Highly developed crystallized intelligence allows a person to absorb the images, definitions, opinions, and agendas of others.

Vertical thinking is systematic, logical thinking that proceeds step by step in an orderly progression.

The lateral thinker jumps to a new position that might seem random and unconnected, then works backward and tries to construct a logical path between this new position and the starting point. Lateral thinkers are more intuitive and creative.

What is Fluid Intelligence? Psychologist Raymond Cattell (1971) first proposed the concepts of fluid and crystallized intelligence and further developed the theory with John Horn. The Cattell-Horn theory of fluid and crystallized intelligence suggests that intelligence is composed of a number of different abilities that interact and work together to produce overall individual intelligence.

Fluid intelligence gives people the facility to challenge what is on the surface, to look deeper and broader, and to recognize new patterns. Fluid intelligence is the ability to find meaning in confusion and solve new problems. It is the ability to draw inferences and understand the relationships of various concepts independent of acquired knowledge (Cavanaugh & Blanchard-Fields, 2006).

Cattell defined fluid intelligence as "...the ability to perceive relationships independent of previous specific practice or instruction concerning those relationships." Fluid intelligence is the ability to think and reason abstractly and solve problems. This ability is considered independent of learning, experience, and education. Examples of the use of fluid intelligence include solving puzzles and coming up with problem solving strategies.

What Is Crystallized Intelligence? Crystallized intelligence is the ability to memorize facts, to utilize previously acquired knowledge and experience. Highly developed crystallized intelligence allows a person to absorb the images, definitions, opinions, and agendas of others. Crystallized intelligence is learning from past experiences and learning. Situations that require crystallized intelligence include reading comprehension and vocabulary exams. This type of intelligence is based upon facts and rooted in experiences. This type of intelligence becomes stronger as you age and accumulate new knowledge and understanding.

Fluid vs. Crystallized Intelligence

According to Knox (1977), ". . . they constitute the global capacity to learn, reason, and solve problems that most people refer to as intelligence. Fluid and crystallized intelligence are complementary in that some learning tasks can be mastered mainly by exercising either fluid or crystallized intelligence" (p. 420).

Both types of intelligence are important for good thinking. People with strong crystalline intelligence can absorb and retain basic information, such as definitions, lists, dates, names, and other elements that can be memorized. People with strong fluid intelligence can creatively bridge the gaps of information in partially specified problems. When the two types of intelligences work together, they form a much more powerful thinking style.

Vertical thinking. People mostly are vertical thinkers. Vertical thinking is systematic, logical thinking that proceeds step by step in an orderly progression. A learner needs this type of thinking to learn basic information on any topic.

Lateral thinking, in contrast, does not proceed step by step. Instead, when confronted with a problem, the lateral thinker jumps to a new position that might seem random and unconnected, then works backward and tries to construct a logical path between this new position and the starting point. Lateral thinkers are more intuitive and creative. They reject the standard beginning points to solve

36

problems and instead begin with an intuitive guess, brainstorming, or proposed solution "out of the blue." The lateral thinkers work backward from innovative conclusions to the beginning of a problem. They tend to arrive at solutions that other thinkers would never imagine, because they are locked into a rigid form of thinking.

Few people have a natural aptitude for lateral thinking. But it is possible to develop such skills by practicing creative problem solving techniques that are abundant in this book.

Vertical Thinking	**Lateral Thinking**
Vertical thinking is selective	Lateral thinking is generative
Rightness is what matters in vertical thinking.	Richness is what matters in lateral thinking
Analytical	Provocative
Sequential	Lateral thinking can make jumps. One may jump ahead to a new point and then fill in the gap afterwards.
It may be necessary to be on top of the mountain in order to find the best way up. With vertical thinking one has to be correct at every step.	With lateral thinking one does not have to be.
With vertical thinking one uses the negative in order to block off certain pathways.	With lateral thinking there is no negative.
With vertical thinking one concentrates and excludes what is irrelevant.	With lateral thinking one welcomes chance intrusions.
With vertical thinking categories, classifications and labels are fixed.	With lateral thinking they are not.
Vertical thinking follows the most likely paths.	Lateral thinking explores the least likely.
Vertical thinking is a finite process.	Lateral thinking is a probabilistic one.
With lateral thinking there may not be any answer at all. With vertical thinking one uses information for its own sake in order to move forward to a solution.	With lateral thinking one uses information not for its own sake but provocatively in order to bring about repatterning.

Conceptual differentiation is the degree to which people group and classify things. Individuals who classify objects into a large number of mutually exclusive categories exhibit high conceptual differentiation. In contrast, people who use a small number of categories have low conceptual differentiation.

Related to the number of conceptual categories is category width. People who have few categories usually have broad categories so as to contain all types of messages. For example, if a person only has three categories for all media messages (e.g., news, ads, and entertainment), then each of these categories must contain a wide variety of messages. In contrast, someone who has a great many categories would divide media messages into thinner slices (e.g., breaking news, feature news, documentary, commercial ads, public service announcements, action/adventure shows, sitcoms, game shows, talk shows, cartoons, and reality shows).

Emotional/Motivational Qualities. Your thinking and learning style is composed of more than cognitive abilities. Three characteristics of emotional ability contribute to your thinking and learning style:

1. Emotional intelligence
2. Tolerance to ambiguity
3. Non-impulsiveness.

Emotional intelligence. Emotional intelligence (EI) refers to the ability to perceive, control, and evaluate emotions. Some researchers suggest that emotional intelligence can be learned and strengthened, while others claim it is an inborn characteristic.

Conceptual differentiation is the degree to which people group and classify things. Individuals who classify objects into a large number of mutually exclusive categories exhibit high conceptual differentiation.

Emotional intelligence (EI) refers to the ability to perceive, control, and evaluate emotions.

Understanding the Five Categories of Emotional Intelligence (EQ)

1. Self-awareness. The ability to recognize an emotion as it "happens" is the key to your EQ. Developing self-awareness requires tuning in to your true feelings. If you evaluate your emotions, you can manage them. The major elements of self-awareness are:

- Emotional awareness. Your ability to recognize your own emotions and their effects.
- Self-confidence. Sureness about your self-worth and capabilities.

2. Self-regulation. You often have little control over when you experience emotions. You can, however, have some say in how long an emotion will last by using a number of techniques to alleviate negative emotions such as anger, anxiety or depression. A few of these techniques include recasting a situation in a more positive light, taking a long walk and meditation or prayer. Self-regulation involves

- Self-control. Managing disruptive impulses.
- Trustworthiness. Maintaining standards of honesty and integrity.
- Conscientiousness. Taking responsibility for your own performance.
- Adaptability. Handling change with flexibility.
- Innovation. Being open to new ideas.

3. Motivation. To motivate yourself for any achievement requires clear goals and a positive attitude. Although you may have a predisposition to either a positive or a negative attitude, you can with effort and practice learn to think more positively. If you catch negative thoughts as they occur, you can reframe them in more positive terms—which will help you achieve your goals. Motivation is made up of

- Achievement drive. Your constant striving to improve or to meet a standard of excellence.
- Commitment. Aligning with the goals of the group or organization.
- Initiative. Readying yourself to act on opportunities.
- Optimism. Pursuing goals persistently despite obstacles and setbacks.

4. Empathy. The ability to recognize how people feel is important to success in your life and career. The more skillful you are at discerning the feelings behind others' signals the better you can control the signals you send them. An empathetic person excels at

- Service orientation. Anticipating, recognizing and meeting clients' needs.
- Developing others. Sensing what others need to progress and bolstering their abilities.
- Leveraging diversity. Cultivating opportunities through diverse people.
- Political awareness. Reading a group's emotional currents and power relationships.
- Understanding others. Discerning the feelings behind the needs and wants of others.

5. Social skills. The development of good interpersonal skills is tantamount to success in your life and career. In today's cyberculture all professional accountants can have immediate access to technical knowledge via computers. Thus, "people skills" are even more important now because you must possess a high EQ to better understand, empathize and negotiate with others in a global economy. Among the most useful skills are:

- Influence. Wielding effective persuasion tactics.
- Communication. Sending clear messages.
- Leadership. Inspiring and guiding groups and people.
- Change catalyst. Initiating or managing change.
- Conflict management. Understanding, negotiating and resolving disagreements.
- Building bonds. Nurturing instrumental relationships.
- Collaboration and cooperation. Working with others toward shared goals.

Since 1990, Peter Salovey and John D. Mayer have been the leading researchers on emotional intelligence. In their influential article "Emotional Intelligence," they defined emotional intelligence as, "the subset of social intelligence that involves the ability to monitor one's own and others' feelings and emotions, to discriminate among them and to use this information to guide one's thinking and actions" (1990).

People with stronger emotional intelligence have a well-developed sense of empathy; they are able to see the world from another person's perspective.

How well you do in your life and career is determined by both. IQ alone is not enough; EQ also matters. In fact, psychologists generally agree that among the ingredients for success, IQ counts for roughly 10% (at best 25%); the rest depends on everything else—including EQ. A study of Harvard graduates in business, law, medicine and teaching showed a negative or zero correlation between an IQ indicator (entrance exam scores) and subsequent career success. Three examples illustrate the importance of emotional competencies.

Tolerance to Ambiguity. The converse, ***ambiguity intolerance***, which was introduced in 1950 by Adorno. Norton (1975) defined it as a "tendency to perceive or interpret information marked by vague, incomplete, fragmented, multiple, probable, unstructured, uncertain, inconsistent, contrary, contradictory, or unclear meanings as actual or potential sources of psychological discomfort or threat." It allows you to perceive ambiguity in information and behavior in a neutral and open way.

Ambiguity tolerance is an important issue in personality development and education. In psychology and in management, levels of tolerance of ambiguity are **correlated with creativity**, risk aversion, psychological resilience, lifestyle, orientation towards diversity (cross-cultural communication, intercultural competence), and leadership style.

The converse, ***ambiguity intolerance*** (Norton, 1975) is a "tendency to perceive or interpret information marked by vague, incomplete, fragmented, multiple, probable, unstructured, uncertain, inconsistent, contrary, contradictory, or unclear meanings as actual or potential sources of psychological discomfort or threat."

In everyday life you are dealing with new situations and people. To prepare yourself for such situations, you have developed sets of expectation. What do you do when your expectations are not met and you are surprised? That depends on your level of tolerance for ambiguity (Potter, 2002).

Impulsiveness vs. Non-impulsiveness. Impulsiveness is the tendency ***to act spontaneously*** without too much thought. It demonstrates the ***level of control*** over one's behavior, feeling, and thoughts. Barratt identified three main aspects: motor (acting without thinking), cognitive (quick decisions), and non-planning (present orientation).

Some examples of impulsive behaviors include:

- Engaging in dangerous activities without considering possible consequences
- Difficulty waiting turns
- Calling out in class
- Intruding in on or interrupting conversations or games
- Blurting out answers before questions have been completed.

Tolerance to Ambiguity is defined as a tendency to perceive or interpret information marked by vague, incomplete, fragmented, multiple, probable, unstructured, uncertain, inconsistent, contrary, contradictory, or unclear meanings as actual or potential sources of psychological discomfort or threat.

Impulsiveness is the tendency to act spontaneously without too much thought. It demonstrates the level of control over one's behavior, feeling, and thoughts.

CHAPTER 2

For each of the 30 items below, decide whether the description fits you, then write the appropriate number from the following scale next to the item.

0 = Not at all like me 1 = A bit like me 2 = Like me 3 = Very much like me

___ 1. When I encounter a new idea in a course of study/in a book I am reading/in a discussion with friend, I like to analyze it in depth.

___ 2. The most important element in any course is a well-prepared teacher who can present the information clearly.

___ 3. I don't like memorizing lots of material.

___ 4. I like courses where we deal with a few topics but explore them in depth rather than curses where we cover many different topics but don't go into much depth on any one.

___ 5. I dislike tests where you're supposed to guess what the teacher wants.

___ 6. In many courses, I just can't get started.

___ 7. While the teacher is lecturing, I often find myself thinking beyond the points he or she is trying to make.

___ 8. It is important for teachers to hand out study guides before the test so I can know what I should study.

___ 9. When I have a difficult problem, I like to "cut to the chase" and make a quick decision rather than doing a lot of work that might not amount to anything.

___ 10. Not all ideas in a course/ in a book/ in a discussion are equally important. I like to decide for myself what is important more than I want my teacher or anybody else to make that decision for me.

___ 11. During the class, I try to write down everything the teacher says.

___ 12. My teachers usually lecture in a way that is hard to follow.

___ 13. I get excited by challenges; the harder the challenge, the more excited I get.

___ 14. I do not like the teacher to waste class time by getting off the track by telling irrelevant stories that won't be on the tests. Teachers should stick to the facts.

___ 15. If I do not understand the course material, I try not to worry about it.

___ 16. When I run into something that does not immediately make sense, I keep working with it and thinking about it until I really understand it.

___ 17. I think test questions should be taken directly from the class notes. It's not fair when the teacher surprises me with a test question over material we did not cover in class.

___ 18. I prefer that the teacher never call on me during class.

___ 19. The learning challenge I like the most is the task of trying to make order out of chaos.

___ 20. My confidence level in a course is highest when the course has a lot of well-organized facts that I can memorize easily.

___ 21. It is the teacher's job to motivate me to do my best work.

___ 22. I am the kind of person who likes to set my own goals for learning, even if they are very different from the teacher's goals in the course.

___ 23. When I am exposed to new information, I want my teacher to tell me what is most important.

___ 24. No matter how hard I work, I never seem to do as well as I would like.

___ 25. When my teachers give a reading assignment, I like it when they don't tell me what to look for in the reading; I like to determine what is important for myself.

___ 26. I hate courses where the instructor gives you lots of readings and you have to figure out what is important in those readings.

___ 27. If I don't learn much in a course, it is usually because the material was too hard.

___ 28. I am often frustrated in course when we don't examine something in enough depth to find out what is really going on.

___ 29. During the first class meeting, I want to get an accurate idea of how hard the course will be.

___ 30. When I get a low grade on a test or on an assignment, I feel frustrated and it is hard to shake that feeling.

Transfer the numbers you wrote on your questionnaire to the tabulation sheet below. Then sum the numbers down each of the three columns and write the totals at the bottom of the columns.

Learning and Thinking

1.	2.	3.
4.	5.	6.
7.	8.	9.
10.	11.	12.
13.	14.	15.
16.	17.	18.
19.	20.	21.
22.	23.	24.
25.	26.	27.
28.	29.	30.
TOTAL	TOTAL	TOTAL

Circle the largest number of the three totals. If that circled number is more that 25 and the other two totals are below 15 each, then the circled number indicates your dominant style. If no total is more than 20 and especially if all three totals are similar (within about 7 points of each other), then you likely do not have a dominant style – that is, you have a mix of all three.

The right-hand column contains items that indicate an information avoider style. In your number in this column is large relative to the numbers in the other two columns, and then you are likely to be an information avoider.

The middle column contains items that indicate an information consumer style. If your number in this column is large relative to the numbers in the other columns, then you are likely to think like a consumer.

The left-hand column contains items that indicate a strategic thinker's style. If your number in this column is large relative to the number in the other two columns, then you are lucky to have been born with many natural abilities that can make you a good learner.

Profile of the Information Avoider

Field dependence. Information avoiders have a lot of trouble discerning what is important in messages, so they miss the point of many messages and therefore would rather avoid them altogether.

Weak fluid intelligence. Information avoiders do not like the challenge of solving problems, preferring to let things work themselves out on their own. Also, they do not like trying to think of thing in new ways. An information avoiders make a decision quickly and resist reconsidering it, avoiding change.

Weak crystallized intelligence. Information avoiders find it difficult to memorize things, so they use lots of mnemonics to keep things in their shirt-term memory long enough to do well on tests of memorization.

Weak vertical and lateral thinking. Information avoiders resist the work required to reason systematically. While they may appear intuitive in their opinions and even wild in their generalizations, they do not do what good lateral thinker do, which is carefully check their intuitively constructed guesses against the facts in order to determine if those guesses are valid or useful.

Weak conceptual differentiation. Information avoiders tend to have few categories for information. Rather than working to acknowledge differences and create new categories, their attitude toward new information that does not fit into existing categories is either to ignore the information or simply throw the new information into the easiest category and justify it by saying "Whatever!"

Low emotional intelligence. When information avoiders feel negative emotions as they encounter information, they are not sure how to deal with these emotions other than to retreat. Thus, negative emotions from a barrier between them and the information.

Low tolerance to ambiguity. Information avoiders are quick to avoid messages that introduce uncertainty or complexity. Over time they narrow their exposure down to fewer messages so that they always stay with what is familiar and thereby protect themselves from having to expend more mental effort.

High impulsiveness. Information avoiders dislike uncertainty, so they make decisions as fast as they can. They feel that sacrificing accuracy is a small price to pay for escaping the negative emotions that characterize decision-making situations.

CHAPTER 2
Profile of the Consumer Knowledge Style

Field dependence. Consumers have a lot of trouble discerning what is important in messages. They need someone else to tell them what is important; for example, before each test they tend to ask for a study guide so the professor will tell them what is important, rather than feeling confident figuring this out for themselves.

Weak fluid intelligence. Consumers do not have a great deal of educational experience or positive reinforcement in problem solving or creative thinking. They believe that truth rests in the expertise of authorities, such as teachers and texts. They have low confidence that something they construct (a conclusion, opinion, or solution to a problem) on their own will be valued.

Strong crystallized intelligence. Consumers are successful at memorize lots of facts. To consumers, facts, not skills, are the commodities to be acquired in the supermarket of education.

Relatively strong vertical thinking. Consumers want to follow rules in order to move to a solution as efficiently as possible. They are skeptical of lateral thinking, because it is often not efficient in the short term. They are uncertain that any proposed solution will work. They prefer to have someone tell them the best solution method, and then vertically follow that path.

Relatively strong conceptual differentiation. Consumers absorb other people's category schemes, even if those schemes are very complex and contain many categories and sub-categories, but they typically are not good at constructing them for themselves.

Relatively good emotional intelligence. Consumers tend to use their emotions well to focus on material while they try to memorize it.

Low tolerance to ambiguity. Consumers are quick to avoid messages that introduce uncertainty or complexity. Over time they narrow their exposure down to fewer messages so that they always stay with what is familiar and thereby protect themselves from having to expend more mental effort.

Relatively good non- impulsiveness. Consumers want to achieve accuracy – but only up to a point. When the cost get too high, they switch to a criterion of efficiency, and this can lead to impulsive decisions. Consumers sometimes feel that sacrificing accuracy is a small price to pay for getting past the decision-making situation and on to other things.

Profile of the Strategic Thinker and Learner Style

Field dependence. Strategic learners have the ability to focus on the essence of messages and keep other details in the background. When encountering information, they quickly and accurately distinguish the signal from the noise.

Strong fluid intelligence. Strategic learners are able to find creative solutions to problems and innovative ways of organizing information. Highly developed fluid intelligence allows them to challenge what appears on the surface, to look deeper and broader, and to construct new patterns in areas where other people accept the old patterns.

Strong crystallized intelligence. Strategic learners have the ability to memorize lots of detail (short-term memory) as well as the ability to retain detail for long periods of time (long-term memory). Highly developed crystalline intelligence allows them to absorb the images, definitions, and opinions of others.

Strong vertical and lateral thinking. Strategic learners use both types of thinking. Most important, they know when to use one or the other.

Strong conceptual differentiation. Strategic learners are willing and able to construct many categories for information so that the differences and similarities across messages are apparent. When they encounter information that does not fit well into their categorization system, they are willing to create new categories for that information.

High emotional intelligence. Strategic learners have a great deal of understanding of their emotions, as well as the ability to control their emotions, especially in translating negative emotions into motivation toward goals.

High tolerance to ambiguity. New and complex messages energize strategic learners. They are willing to meet the challenge of creating order out of chaos

High non-impulsiveness. Strategic learners refrain from jumping to conclusions too quickly merely to have decisions completed, because they prefer accuracy in decision-making over efficiency. They can be impulsive when efficiency warrants it, but their typical approach to information is to reflect on it.

Chapter 3

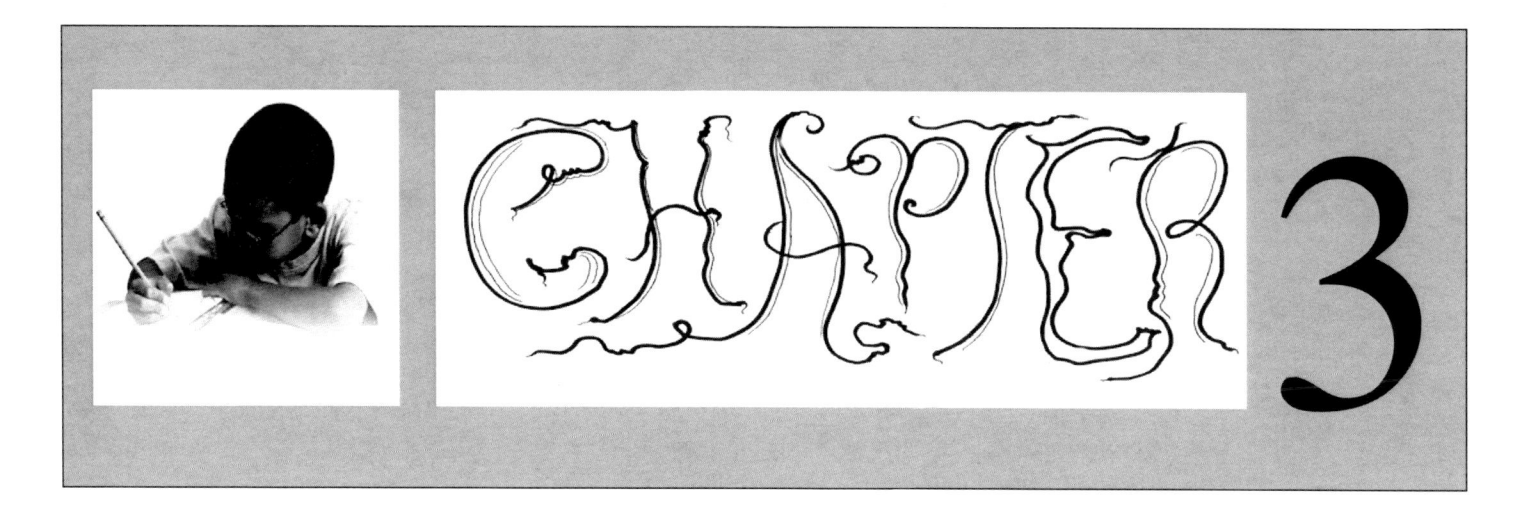

Developmental Aspect of Thinking

How mind develops? What is more important for intellectual development – heredity or environment? Nature or Nurture?

How geniuses are made? Or they are born being different from the rest of people? Are there any difference between girls and boys in their brains' functions?

Find the answers to those and other questions regarding thinking development in the following chapter.

LEARNING OBJECTIVES

After reading this chapter, you will be able to

1. Identify stages of child development
2. Be able to identify, describe and discuss stages of thinking development
3. Through discovery and research project be able to describe general characteristics of parents of highly creative people
4. Through discovery and research project be able to describe environment that stimulates child's creativity
5. Through discovery and research project be able to describe environment that stops child's creativity
6. Through discovery and research project be able to describe general characteristics of gifted children.
7. Define developmental psychology and name its principal focus.
8. Name and describe adaptive reflexes and intellectual capabilities of a neonate.
9. Discuss the concepts of maturation.
10. Understand the basic mechanisms of the transmission of heredity.
11. Explain what is meant by the nature-nurture controversy.
12. Understand the range and effects of maternal caretaking styles.
13. Compare theories of development.

CHAPTER 3

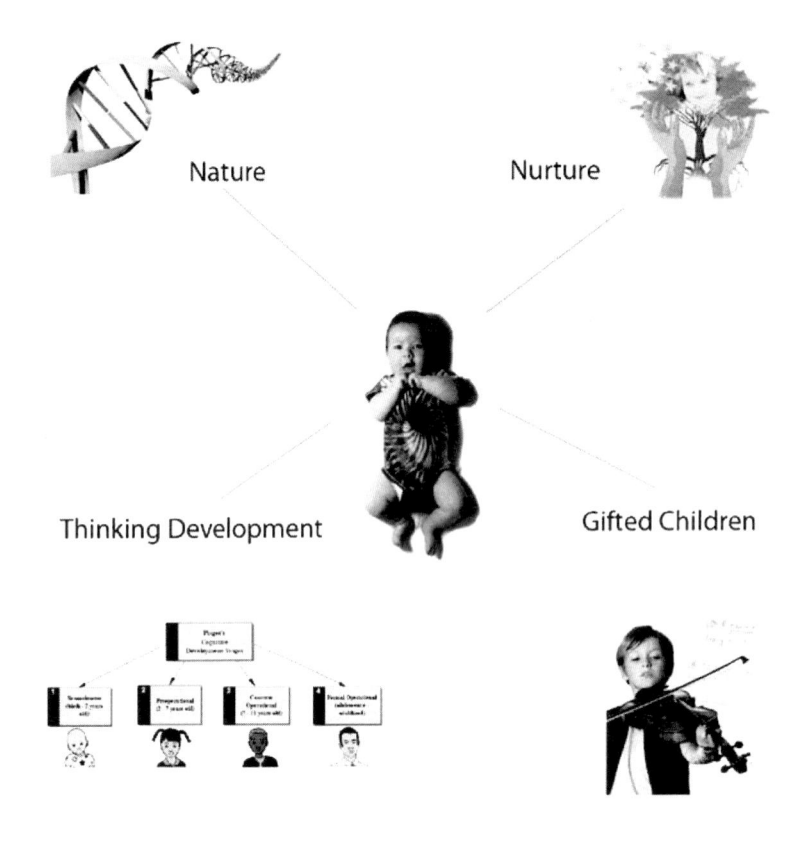

THE NATURE OF EARLY BRAIN DEVELOPMENT

At birth, the human brain is still ***preparing for full operation***. The brain's neurons exist mostly apart from one another. The brain's task for the first 3 years is to establish and reinforce connections with other neurons. These connections are formed when impulses are sent and received between neurons. Axons send messages and dendrites receive them. These connections form synapses.

Neurons mature when axons send messages and dendrites receive them to form synapses.

As a child develops, the ***synapses become more complex***, like a tree with more branches and limbs growing. During the first 3 years of life, the number of neurons stays the same and the number of synapses increases.

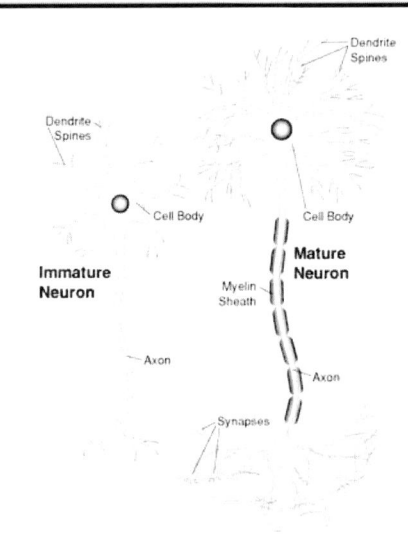

Figure 3. 1. Neurons mature when axons send messages and dendrites receive them to form synapses.

After age 3, the creation of synapses slows until about age 10.

Between birth and *age 3*, the brain creates **more synapses** than it needs. The synapses that are used a lot become a permanent part of the brain. The **synapses that are not used** frequently are **eliminated.** This is where experience plays an important role in wiring a young child's brain. Because we want children to succeed, we need to provide many positive social and learning opportunities so that the synapses associated with these experiences become permanent.

How the social and physical environments respond to infants and toddlers plays a big part in the creation of synapses. The child's experiences are the stimulation that sparks the activity between axons and dendrites and creates synapses.

Critical periods and sensitive periods: What is the difference?

Brain development research distinguishes between **sensitive periods** and **critical periods** of development. Understanding the difference is very important for recognizing what infants and toddlers need early in life. The information presented in this guide centers mostly on sensitive periods.

Critical periods represent a narrow window of time during which a **specific part of the body is most vulnerable to the absence of stimulation** or to environmental influences. Vision is a good example: Unless an infant sees light during the first 6 months, the nerves leading from the eye to the visual cortex of the brain that processes those signals will degenerate and die.

Prenatal development, the period before a baby is born, also includes critical periods. Remember the drug thalidomide and its effects on prenatal development? Women who took the drug between the 38th and 46th days of pregnancy gave birth to infants with deformed arms, or no arms, Women who took the drug between the 40th and 46th days of pregnancy gave birth to infants with deformed legs or no legs. Women who took the drug after the 50th day of pregnancy gave birth to babies with no birth defects or problems.

Sensitive periods are the broad windows of opportunity for certain types of learning. Sensitive periods represent a **less precise** and often **longer period** of time when **skills**, such as acquiring a second language, **are influenced**. But, if the opportunity for learning does not arise, these potential new skills are not lost forever. Individuals learn new languages at many different times in their lives.

The skills acquired during sensitive periods are those that some people are better at than others. They include the social, emotional and mental characteristics that make us interesting people. Individuals who work with children need to be aware of the sensitive period concept so that they can provide learning opportunities that benefit children in many ways. The early brain research highlights birth through age 3 as a sensitive period for development and learning in all areas.

The Nurture of Early Brain Development

Infants and toddlers learn about themselves and their world during *interactions with others*. Brain connections that lead to later success grow out of nurturant, supportive and predictable care. This type of caregiving fosters child curiosity, creativity and self-confidence. Young children need safety, love, conversation and a stimulating environment to develop and keep important synapses in the brain.

Caring for infants and toddlers is mostly about building relationships and making the most of everyday routines and experiences.

Learning with all five senses

During the first 3 years of life, children experience the world in a more complete way than children of any other age. The brain takes in the external world through its system of sight, hearing, smell, touch and taste. This means that infant social, emotional, cognitive, physical and language development are stimulated during multisensory experiences. Infants and toddlers need the opportunity to participate in a world filled with stimulating sights, sounds and people.

Create a multi-sensory environment

- *Experiment* with different smells in the classroom. Try scents like peppermint and cinnamon to keep children alert and lavender to calm them down.

The Creative Curriculum for Infants and Toddlers (Dombro, Colker and Dodge, 1997) says that during the first 3 years of life, infants and toddlers look to caregivers for answers to these questions:

- Do people respond to me?
- Can I depend on other people when I need them?
- Am I important to others?
- Am I competent?
- How should I behave?
- Do people enjoy being with me?
- What should I be afraid of?
- Is it safe for me to show how I feel?
- What things interest me?

- Remember that *lighting* affect alertness and responsiveness. Bright lights keep infants and toddlers alert; soft lights help infants and toddlers to calm down.
- Expose infants and toddlers to *colors* that stimulate the brain. Use colors like pale yellow, beige, and offwhite to create a calm learning environment; use bright colors such as red, orange, and yellow to encourage creativity and excitement.
- Use quiet and soft *music* to calm infants and toddlers and rhythmic music to get them excited about moving.
- Create a *texture book* or board that includes swatches of *different fabrics* for infants and toddlers to feel.
- *Describe* the foods and drinks that you serve infants and toddlers and use words that are associated with flavor and texture ("oranges are sweet and juicy;" "lemon yogurt is a little sour and creamy").

Thinking and Feelings

Before children are able to talk, emotional expressions are the language of relationships. Research shows that infants' positive and negative emotions, and caregivers' sensitive responsiveness to them, can help early brain development. For example, shared positive emotion between a caregiver and an infant, such as laughter and smiling, engages brain activity in good ways and promotes feelings of security. Also, when interactions are accompanied by lots of emotion, they are more readily remembered and recalled.

STAGES OF THINKING DEVELOPMENT

Stage One: The Unreflective Thinker
Stage Two: The Challenged Thinker
Stage Three: The Beginning Thinker
Stage Four: The Practicing Thinker
Stage Five: The Advanced Thinker
Stage Six: The Master Thinker

Skill in Thinking: Unreflective thinkers may have developed a variety of skills in thinking without being aware of them. However, these skills are inconsistently applied because of the lack of self-monitoring of thought. Prejudices and misconceptions often undermine the quality of thought of the unreflective thinker.

Figure 3. 2. Piaget's Stages of Thinking Development

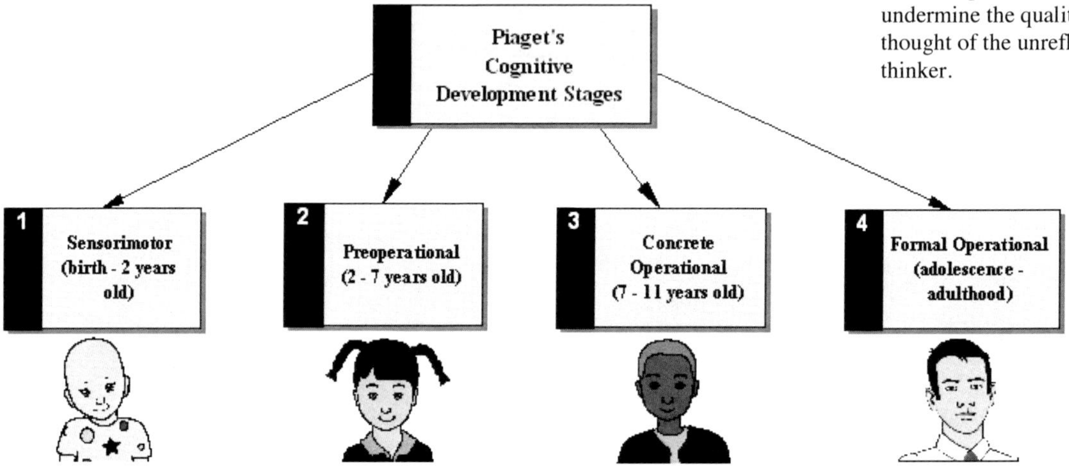

Piaget's Cognitive Development Stages

1. Sensorimotor (birth - 2 years old)
2. Preoperational (2 - 7 years old)
3. Concrete Operational (7 - 11 years old)
4. Formal Operational (adolescence - adulthood)

Stage One: The Unreflective Thinker

Defining Feature: Unreflective thinkers are largely unaware of the determining role that thinking is playing in their lives and of the many ways that problems in thinking are causing problems in their lives. Unreflective thinkers lack the ability to explicitly assess their thinking and improve it thereby.

Knowledge of Thinking: Unreflective thinkers lack the knowledge that high quality thinking requires regular practice in taking thinking apart, accurately assessing it, and actively improving it. In fact, unreflective thinkers are largely unaware of thinking as such, hence fail to recognize thinking as involving concepts, assumptions, inferences, implications, points of view, etc. Unreflective thinkers are largely unaware of the appropriate standards for the assessment of thinking: clarity, accuracy, precision, relevance, logicalness, etc.

Stage Two: The Challenged Thinker

Defining Features: Thinkers move to the "challenged" stage when they become initially aware of the determining role that thinking is playing in their lives, and of the fact that problems in their thinking are causing them serious and significant problems.

Principal Challenge: To become initially aware of the determining role of thinking in one's life and of basic problems that come from poor thinking.

Knowledge of Thinking: Challenged thinkers, unlike unreflective thinkers are becoming aware of thinking as such. They are becoming aware, at some level, that high quality thinking requires deliberate reflective thinking about thinking (in order to improve thinking). They recognize that their thinking is often flawed, although they are not able to identify many of these flaws. Challenged thinkers may develop an initial awareness of thinking as involving concepts, assumptions, inferences, implications, points of view, etc., and as involving standards for the assessment of thinking: clarity, accuracy, precision, relevance, logicalness, etc., though they have only an initial grasp of these standards and what it would take to internalize them. Challenged thinkers also develop some understanding of the role of self-deception in thinking, though their understanding is limited. At this stage the thinker develops some reflective awareness of how thinking operates for good or ill.

Stage Three: The Beginning Thinker

Defining Feature: Those who move to the beginning thinker stage are actively taking up the challenge to begin to take explicit command of their thinking across multiple domains of their lives. Thinkers at this stage recognize that they have basic problems in their thinking and make initial attempts to better understand how they can take charge of and improve it. Based on this initial understanding, beginning thinkers begin to modify some of their thinking, but have limited insight into deeper levels of the trouble inherent in their thinking. Most importantly, they lack a systematic plan for improving their thinking, hence their efforts are hit and miss.

Principal Challenge: To begin to see the importance of developing as a thinker. To begin to seek ways to develop as a thinker and to make an intellectual commitment to that end.

Knowledge of Thinking: Beginning thinkers, unlike challenged thinkers are becoming aware not only of thinking as such, but also of the role in thinking of concepts, assumptions, inferences, implications, points of view, etc. Beginning thinkers are also at some beginning stage of recognizing not only that there are standards for the assessment of thinking: clarity, accuracy, precision, relevance, logicalness, etc., but also that one needs to internalize them and thus begin using them deliberately in thinking. They have a beginning understanding of the role of egocentric thinking in human life.

Relevant Intellectual Traits: The key intellectual trait required at this stage is some degree of intellectual humility in beginning to recognize the problems inherent in thinking. In addition, thinkers must have some degree of intellectual confidence in reason, a trait which provides the impetus to take up the challenge and begin the process of active development as critical thinkers, despite limited understanding of what it means to do high quality reasoning. In addition, beginning thinkers have enough intellectual perseverance to struggle with serious problems in thinking while yet lacking a clear solution to those problems (in other words, at this stage thinkers are recognizing more and more problems in their thinking but have not yet discovered how to systematize their efforts to solve them).

Stage Four: The Practicing Thinker

Defining Feature: Thinkers at this stage have a sense of the habits they need to develop to take charge of their thinking. They not only recognize that problems exist in their thinking, but they also recognize the need to attack these problems globally and systematically. Based on their sense of the need to practice regularly, they are actively analyzing their thinking in a number of domains. However, since practicing thinkers are only beginning to approach the improvement of their thinking in a systematic way,

---

Skill in Thinking: Most challenged thinkers have very limited skills in thinking. However like unreflective thinkers, they may have developed a variety of skills in thinking without being aware of them, and these skills may (ironically) serve as barriers to development. At this stage thinkers with some implicit critical thinking abilities may more easily deceive themselves into believing that their thinking is better than it actually is, making it more difficult to recognize the problems inherent in poor thinking.

Skill in Thinking: Beginning thinkers are able to appreciate a critique of their powers of thought. Beginning thinkers have enough skill in thinking to begin to monitor their own thoughts, though as "beginners" they are sporadic in that monitoring. They are beginning to recognize egocentric thinking in themselves and others.

Relevant Intellectual Trait: The fundamental intellectual trait at this stage is intellectual humility, in order to see that problems are inherent in one's thinking. *Skill in Thinking:* Practicing thinkers have enough skill in thinking to critique their own plan for systematic practice, and to construct a realistic critique of their powers of thought. Furthermore, practicing thinkers have enough skill to begin to regularly monitor their own thoughts. Thus they can effectively articulate the strengths and weaknesses in their thinking.

they still have limited insight into deeper levels of thought, and thus into deeper levels of the problems embedded in thinking.

Principal Challenge: To begin to develop awareness of the need for systematic practice in thinking.

Knowledge of Thinking: Practicing thinkers, unlike beginning thinkers are becoming knowledgeable of what it would take to systematically monitor the role in their thinking of concepts, assumptions, inferences, implications, points of view, etc. Practicing thinkers are also becoming knowledgeable of what it would take to regularly assess their thinking for clarity, accuracy, precision, relevance, logicalness, etc. Practicing thinkers recognize the need for systematicity of critical thinking and deep internalization into habits. They clearly recognize the natural tendency of the human mind to engage in egocentric thinking and self-deception.

Relevant Intellectual Traits: The key intellectual trait required to move to this stage is intellectual perseverance. This characteristic provides the impetus for developing a realistic plan for systematic practice (with a view to taking greater command of one's thinking). Furthermore, thinkers at this stage have the intellectual humility required to realize that thinking in all the domains of their lives must be subject to scrutiny, as they begin to approach the improvement of their thinking in a systematic way.

Stage Five: The Advanced Thinker

Defining Feature: Thinkers at this stage have now established good habits of thought which are "paying off." Based on these habits, advanced thinkers not only actively analyze their thinking in all the significant domains of their lives, but also have significant insight into problems at deeper levels of thought. While advanced thinkers are able to think well across the important dimensions of their lives, they are not yet able to think at a consistently high level across all of these dimensions. Advanced thinkers have good general command over their egocentric nature. They continually strive to be fair-minded. Of course, they sometimes lapse into egocentrism and reason in a one-sided way.

Principal Challenge: To begin to develop depth of understanding not only of the need for systematic practice in thinking, but also insight into deep levels of problems in thought: consistent recognition, for example, of egocentric and sociocentric thought in one's thinking, ability to identify areas of significant ignorance and prejudice, and ability to actually develop new fundamental habits of thought based on deep values to which one has committed oneself.

Knowledge of Thinking: Advanced thinkers are actively and successfully engaged in systematically monitoring the role in their thinking of concepts, assumptions, inferences, implications, points of view, etc., and hence have excellent knowledge of that enterprise. Advanced thinkers are also knowledgeable of what it takes to regularly assess their thinking for clarity, accuracy, precision, relevance, logicalness, etc. Advanced thinkers value the deep and systematic internalization of critical thinking into their daily habits. Advanced thinkers have keen insight into the role of egocentrism and sociocentrism in thinking, as well as the relationship between thoughts, feelings and desires.

They have a deep understanding of the powerful role that thinking plays in the quality of their lives. They understand that egocentric thinking will always play a role in their thinking, but that they can control the power that egocentrism has over their thinking and their lives.

Relevant Intellectual Traits: The key intellectual trait required at this stage is a high degree of intellectual humility in recognizing egocentric and sociocentric thought in one's life as well as areas of significant ignorance and prejudice. In addition the thinker at this level needs: a) the intellectual insight and perseverance to actually develop new fundamental habits of thought based on deep values to which one has committed oneself, b) the intellectual integrity to recognize areas of inconsistency and contradiction in one's life, c) the intellectual empathy necessary to put oneself in the place of others in order to genuinely understand them, d) the intellectual courage to face and fairly address ideas, beliefs, or viewpoints toward which one has strong negative emotions, e) the fair-mindedness necessary to approach all viewpoints without prejudice, without reference to one's own feelings or vested interests. In the advanced thinker these traits are emerging, but may not be manifested at the highest level or in the deepest dimensions of thought.

Stage Six: The Master Thinker

Defining Feature: Master thinkers not only have systematically taken charge of their thinking, but are also continually monitoring, revising, and re-thinking strategies for continual improvement of their

---

Skill in Thinking: Advanced thinkers regularly critique their own plan for systematic practice, and improve it thereby. Practicing thinkers regularly monitor their own thoughts. They insightfully articulate the strengths and weaknesses in their thinking. They possess outstanding knowledge of the qualities of their thinking. Advanced thinkers are consistently able to identify when their thinking is driven by their native egocentrism; and they effectively use a number of strategies to reduce the power of their egocentric thoughts.

thinking. They have deeply internalized the basic skills of thought, so that critical thinking is, for them, both conscious and highly intuitive. As Piaget would put it, they regularly raise their thinking to the level of conscious realization. Through extensive experience and practice in engaging in self-assessment, master thinkers are not only actively analyzing their thinking in all the significant domains of their lives, but are also continually developing new insights into problems at deeper levels of thought. Master thinkers are deeply committed to fair-minded thinking, and have a high level of, but not perfect, control over their egocentric nature.

Principal Challenge: To make the highest levels of critical thinking intuitive in every domain of one's life. To internalize highly effective critical thinking in an interdisciplinary and practical way.

Knowledge of Thinking: Master thinkers are not only actively and successfully engaged in systematically monitoring the role in their thinking of concepts, assumptions, inferences, implications, points of view, etc., but are also regularly improving that practice. Master thinkers have not only a high degree of knowledge of thinking, but a high degree of practical insight as well. Master thinkers intuitively assess their thinking for clarity, accuracy, precision, relevance, logicalness, etc. Master thinkers have deep insights into the systematic internalization of critical thinking into their habits. Master thinkers deeply understand the role that egocentric and sociocentric thinking plays in the lives of human beings, as well as the complex relationship between thoughts, emotions, drives and behavior.

Relevant Intellectual Traits: Naturally inherent in master thinkers are all the essential intellectual characteristics, deeply integrated. Master thinkers have a high degree of intellectual humility, intellectual integrity, intellectual perseverance, intellectual courage, intellectual empathy, intellectual autonomy, intellectual responsibility and fair-mindedness. Egocentric and sociocentric thought is quite uncommon in the master thinker, especially with respect to matters of importance. There is a high degree of integration of basic values, beliefs, desires, emotions, and action.

Skill in Thinking: Master thinkers regularly, effectively, and insightfully critique their own use of thinking in their lives, and improve it thereby. Master thinkers consistently monitor their own thoughts. They effectively and insightfully articulate the strengths and weaknesses inherent in their thinking. Their knowledge of the qualities of their thinking is outstanding. Although, as humans they know they will always be fallible (because they must always battle their egocentrism, to some extent), they consistently perform effectively in every domain of their lives.

CHILDREN CREATIVITY

Children have a lot of special talents to offer. Their pursuit of novelty and wonder is both a cause and an effect - a gift of the life fully lived and one of the things that makes life worth living. Anyone who knows children can tell you that they do the following:

- *Children follow their interests.* If a kid is bored, you know it. None of this polite interest stuff the rest of us get stuck in. What they like, they do, and this teaches them that following what they like makes them happy - so they do it some more.
- *Children seek out and risk experimenting with new things.* If kids are confronted with something unfamiliar, they will take a chance and try it out. They prod and poke it, smell it, look at it from all angles, try using it in different ways, look to see what you think about it. We adults, by contrast, slap a label on it, say, "I know what that is," and dismiss it. What we're really saying is, "I know what I already know about that, and there's nothing more worth knowing," which is almost never true of anything or anyone.
- *Children pay attention to their own rhythms.* We grownups tend to drive ourselves until something's done, or until a certain hour strikes, but children do things when they feel like it. Children honor dreams and daydreams. Children pay attention to, talk about, and follow up on their dreams and fantasies. They may draw pictures they saw in their dreams, conduct conversations with dream characters, and try to recreate something experienced in dreams and day dreams. These are all creative acts. Moreover, they are important.
- *Children consider mistakes as information, rather than as something unsuccessful.* "That's a way it doesn't work. I wonder how else it doesn't work?"
- *Children play.* Kids make a game out of everything. Their essential business is play, so to speak. They delight in spoofing each other, parents, and personalities. They love to mimic, pretend, wrestle, hide and seek, surprise, play practical jokes. They love to laugh, tell secrets, devise stories of goblins and fairies and giants and monsters and heroes.

Parents of Less Creative Children (Amabile, 1972)
Attitudes These Parents Have
- I teach my child that in one way or another punishment will find him when he is bad.

- I do not allow my child to get angry with me.
- I try to keep my child away from children or families who have different ideas or values from our own.
- I believe that a child should be seen and not heard.
- I feel my child is a bit of a disappointment to me. I do not allow my child to question my decisions.

What These Parents Did When Trying to Teach Their Child a Task
- Tended to overstructure the tasks.
- Tended to control the tasks.
- Tended to provide specific solutions to the tasks.
- Were hostile in the situation.
- Were critical of the child; rejected the child's ideas and suggestions.
- Appeared ashamed of the child, lacked pride in the child.
- Got into a power struggle with the child; parent and child competed.
- Gave up and retreated from difficulties; failed to cope.
- Pressured the child to work at the tasks.
- Were impatient with the child.

Parents of Highly Creative Children (Amabile, 1972)

Attitudes These Parents Have
- I respect my child's opinions and encourage him to express them.
- I feel a child should have time to think, daydream, and even loaf.
- I let my child make many decisions for herself.
- My child and I have warm, intimate times together.
- I encourage my child to be curious, to explore and question things.
- I make sure my child knows I appreciate what he or she tries or accomplishes.

What These Parents Did When Trying to Teach Their Child a Task
- Encouraged the child.
- Were warm and supportive.
- Reacted to the child in an ego-enhancing manner.
- Appeared to enjoy the situation.
- Derived pleasure from being with the child.
- Were supportive and encouraging of the child.
- Praised the child.
- Were able to establish a good working relationship with the child.
- Encouraged the child to proceed independently.

GIFTED CHILDREN

Gifted and talented is another widely-used phrase with lots of potential for misunderstanding. It can sound elitist and imply that creativity is an entirely inherited "gift" which is immutable. Yet there is no evidence to support this. Wouldn't it make more sense to talk about "highly creative" or "highly achieving" people? This would allow for the possibility that high levels of performance are something to which everyone can aspire.

Do high IQ scores in childhood predict later ability? To directly answer this question, Lewis Terman selected 1,500 children with IQs of 140 or more. Terman followed this gifted group (the "Termites" as he called them) into adulthood and found that they were generally quite successful. Far more than average completed college, earned advanced degree, and held professional positions. The gifted group produced dozens of books, thousands of scientific articles, and hundreds of short stories and other publications

Some of gifted committed crimes, were unemployed, or were poorly adjusted. **High IQ reveals potential.** It does not guarantee success. Marilyn vos Savantm with an IQ of 230, has contributed little to science, literature, or art. Nobel prize-winning physicist Richard Feynman, whom many regarded as a genius, had an IQ of 122 (Michalko, 1998). Only 2 people out of 100 score above 130 on IQ tests. These bright individuals are usually described as "gifted." Less than 1/2 of one percent of the population scores above 140. These people are certainly gifted or perhaps even "geniuses." Some psychologists reserve the term genius for people who are exceptionally creative.

(Terman & Oden, 1959). IQ scores are not generally good predictors of real-world success. However, when scores are in the gifted range, the likelihood of outstanding achievement does seem to be higher (Shurkin, 1992).

Most of the successful Termites had **educated parents** who placed a high value on learning and **encouraged their children** to do the same. They also possessed **intellectual determination**. That is, they had a desire to know, to excel, and to persevere. The most successful gifted persons tend to be more persistent and motivated to learn.

There are a lot of people walking around with high IQs who have learned and accomplished very little. Talents most often blossom when they are combined with support, encouragement, education, and effort.

Genetic Theory

The common notion of hereditary or genetic versus environmental factors is much oversimplified. The genes do indeed provide for the transmission of hereditary qualities, but they do not determine an individual's height, or intelligence, or creativity. They are predispositions, whose effects develop differently in different environments; that is, they interact with environmental conditions or experiences and produce not a fixed effect but a certain "range of reaction." Nature and nurture are not opposed factors but are complementary to each other. Sometimes also the genes control or modify the environment by choosing books to read and other intellectual activities (Vernon, 1989).

Why should a feature of human behavior that is seemingly so critical to the advancement of the species be restricted to so small a segment of the species? The tendency of the human species is to resist change, both genetically and socio-culturally. To let up on the biological brakes that regulate extraordinary creativity might threaten the delicate adaptational balance of the species. This would tend to explain the otherwise inexplicable eruption of creativity at isolated moments in history, each moment being separated by at least as long a period of adjustment. This line of reasoning implies that there is some biological or genetic underpinning to extraordinary creativity. It has been argued, in this regard, that an entire epoch of human inspiration and talent, the golden age of Athens, was attributable to genetics (Darlington, 1969). The forces of heredity alone contrived to initiate (and conclude) that remarkable period of intellectual development. Darlington may actually be correct, but it is all speculation.

There is no way of determining the influence of Athenian genes independent of the current zeitgeist. Indeed, it has been argued that the achievements of Periclean (Pericles was the ruler who saved Athens from the Persians, still later accomplished great public works, then destroyed Athens in a senseless war with Sparta) Athens were attributed to "the peace of mind allowed by good government... [and] intellectual freedom and the consequent encouragement to entertain new ideas, and new art forms" (Pickering, 1974, p. 276). In sum, evidence supporting higher rates of illness in the biological parents or offspring of gifted subjects may imply a diathesis for that illness and suggest nothing about the possibility coincidental appearance of creativity (Vernon, 1989).

Predictability from Early Childhood to Adulthood

Early signs of giftedness are not always purely "intellectual." Giftedness can be either the possession of a high IQ or special talents or aptitudes. The following signs may reveal that a child is gifted (Alvino, 1996):

- A tendency to seek out *older children* and *adults;*
- An early fascination with *explanations* and *problem solving;*
- *Talking* in complete sentences as early as *2 or 3 years of age;*
- An unusually *good memory;*
- Precocious *talent* in art, music, or number skills;
- An *early interest* in *books,* along with early *reading* (often by age 3);
- Showing of *kindness, understanding, and cooperation* toward others.

This list goes beyond straight "academic" intelligence. Children may be gifted in ways other than having a high IQ. If artistic talent, mechanical aptitude, musical aptitude, athletic potential, and so on, were considered, 19 out of 20 children could be labeled as having a special "gift" of some sort. Limiting giftedness to high IQ can shortchange children with special talents or potentials. This is especially true of ethnic minority children, who may be the victims of subtle biases in standardized intelligence tests. These children, as well as children with physical disabilities, are less likely to be recognized as gifted.

Weeisberg and Springer (Mooney and Razik, 1967) chose 50 of the most creative and gifted children out of 400 in the Cincinnati schools and gave them tests and interviews. The five highest judgment categories (all significant at the 5 percent level) following the interview were:

- Strength of self-image
- Ease of early recall
- Humor
- Availability of oedipal anxiety
- Uneven ego development.

Whelan (1965) used a theoretical key of seven scales with the following correlations with creativity:

- Energy: few illnesses, avid reader, early physical development, good grades, active in organizations
- Autonomy: values privacy, independent, early to leave home
- Confidence
- Openness to new experience
- Preference for complexity
- Lack of close emotional ties
- Permissive value structure.

Often the genes do not manifest their full effects until puberty. Certainly, measures of intelligence show big fluctuations from infancy until later childhood, though there are fairly high correlations between 12-year and early adult IQs, and even more consistence from then on until old age. Even physical attributes are to some extent modifiable by environmental conditions conducive to good or poor health; and mental attributes are likely to be much more liable.

Creative scientists and artists have to acquire a great deal of knowledge and skills to be creative with in the adolescent and early adult periods. Also, at least in the arts, it may be that the emotional maturity and drive necessary to creative production do not develop until late adolescence (with rare exceptions).

Welsh (1967) used an adjective check list on Governor's School students which indicated that high creative adolescents are independent, nonconforming individuals who have change and variety in environment and also have active heterosexual interests.

Gender Differences

Considering the virtually complete agreement of American social and differential psychologists on the cultural origins of differences between males and females in abilities, interests, attitudes, and personality, it may seem odd to cite sex differences in creativity as giving strong evidence of genetic factors. In secondary schools and colleges (in Western countries) far fewer girls than boys opt for science and mathematics courses (Maccoby & Jacklin, 1974).

Sometimes, too, the total number of female science students increases, but the number of males increases even more, so that the female proportion actually drops. The discrepancy is greatest in high-level employment, with extremely few women reaching full professorships in the natural sciences. The numbers of science publications by women also lag greatly behind those of men. Also women are more often employed as teachers than as research workers.

What is more surprising that the number of highly creative women in most of the arts is about as low as in the sciences. This is true in music and the visual arts, including sculpture and architecture. However, there are many well-known female writers (though few poets). Probably there are more women than men in decorative and applied arts. The situation is very different, too, among performers. In music and drama, there is probably little difference in the totals of men and women, but in ballet dancing, women are clearly in the majority.

There can be doubt that, in Western cultures, there are different pressures on boys or men and girls or women to engage in different toys from girls, for example, bricks or cars as against dolls, cuddly animals, and books. Boys are encouraged to engage in physical activities and are expected to be more aggressive, girls are expected to be quieter, more conformist, and to express themselves more in verbal that in motor actions. The educational system of Western society have accepted the same stereotyping, and often it is the influence of the teachers that deters girls from taking advanced mathematics and science courses and concentrating more in the arts, humanities, or domestic training. Girls themselves accept these differences, and a majority of them aspire to marriage or to a limited range of jobs, such as teachers, secretaries, hairdressers, or nurses, which they can readily abandon for marriage.

Fox et al. (1980) noted that the proportions of mathematically or scientifically inclined girls vary considerable from one high school to another, presumably because some schools have higher quality staff, or different traditions. Single-sex schools for girls tend to produce more scientists than mixed sex, because their students are less affected by fear of competition with boys. Most girls in ordinary mixed schools show some degree of "fear of success." That is, they prefer not to get higher marks or appear to be better achievers than boys, because this makes them less attractive as potential marital partners.

There are large numbers of girls who reject these stereotypes and aim to become scientists or eventually to succeed in business careers. Some of them marry and bring up children as well. But these rebels against convention are a minority, and they may undergo considerable emotional stress as a result. Helson (1967) and Barron (1969) give descriptions of the difficulties of women mathematicians in pursuing their careers.

It is possible to make a case for certain biological sex differences, particularly those that are responsible for aggression, exploration, and initiative in males, and nurturance in females; and these traits might well underlie spatial, mechanical, and technological talents, even predisposing to scientific inclinations in males, and verbal and domestic inclinations in females. It is hardly possible to prove this, when social-environmental influences are so strong. But it is entirely implausible that human society should approve of females becoming highly talented performers of music, dance, and drama, and even allowing them to become creative writers, while, at the same time, disapproving of their becoming musical composers or painters.

Creative Environment

Even the most abstract mind is affected by the environment created by the relationship of that mind with its own body. Nietzsche suffered from arthritis, tuberculosis and tertiary syphilis. No one is immune to the impressions that invade through their senses from the outside world. Beethoven was deaf when he wrote his glorious ninth.

Somerset Maugham suffered from a stutter and gave a character in Of Human Bondage a clubfoot. Creative people may seem to disregard their environment and work happily in even the most dreary, dark, and deep surroundings: Michelangelo struggled to control his work while on a scaffold below the Sistine ceiling, the Curies freezing in their shabby Parisian lab, and an infinitude of poets scribbling away in less than pleasant rooms or anarchists and political types formulating their ideas in gulags or prison cells. But, in reality the space-time context in which creative persons live has consequences that often go unnoticed.

The right surroundings are important in its acceptance; therefore, it is not surprising that creative individuals tend to migrate toward centers of vital activity, where their work has the chance of succeeding. From time immemorial artists, poets, scholars, and scientists have sought out places of natural beauty expecting to be inspired by the majestic peaks or the thundering sea. But, in the last analysis, what sets creative individuals apart is that *regardless of whether the conditions in which they find themselves are luxurious or miserable, they manage to give their surroundings a personal pattern* that echoes the rhythm of their thoughts and habits of action. Within this environment of their own making, they can forget the rest of the world and concentrate on pursuing the Muse (a mythological non-existent goddess – actually it's where the word music comes from), who inspires creativity. Personally, this writer has always chosen to create a home environment full of art, music, books, and interesting things than to go to New York to write or to Paris to paint. Personally, I hated the majestic Rockies and have never been able to afford the live near the seashore.

In sciences and in the arts, in business and in politics, location matters almost as much as in buying real estate. The closer one is to the major research laboratories, journals, departments, institutes, and conference centers, the easier it is for a new voice to be heard and appreciated. At the same time, there is a downside to being near the centers of power.

Being in the Right Place

For someone to say that the great centers of learning and commerce have always acted as magnets for ambitious individuals who wanted to leave their mark on the culture, may be a mistake. It might be like saying that everyone who goes to Washington, D.C. wants to be a good public servant. Perhaps deep throat was right in *All of the President's Men* when he said, "Follow the money." That is exactly what they did, from the Middle Ages onward, master craftsmen traveled all over Europe to build cathedrals and palaces, attracted now by the wealth of one city, then by that of another. The stone-masons of Milan, Italy built fortresses for Teutonic knights in Poland; The Architects and painters of Venice went to decorate the courts of the Tsars of Russia. Even Leonardo, that shining example of creativity, kept serving one master after another depending on whether a Duke, Pope, or King could best finance his dream.

It could have been a *creative impulse*. It might be hard to prove that Van Gogh did it for the money. If he did, he was in the wrong business. What few things he was able to sell, sold for something less than a dollar. Today, however, he has 3 paintings that are in the top ten all time high-priced list for paintings. Personal observations would say that this writer was more stimulated in his graduate program in philosophy than any other time, but one cannot stay in school forever.

The place where one lives is important for *three main reasons*. *The first* is that one must be in position to access the domain in which one plans to work. Information is not distributed evenly in space but has been clumped in diffcrent geographical nodes. In the past, when the diffusion of information was slower, one might go to MIT to study physics, to Cambridge because Russell and Wittgenstein were there or Heidelberg for the dueling scar. Even with our dazzling electronic means for exchanging information, Paris is still the best place for an aspiring artist to find out firsthand what's happening in the art world, what future trends other artists are talking about now. But, Paris is not the best place to learn creative writing or etching, and one can learn things about heart bypass surgery in Pittsburg that one cannot learn anywhere else.

There is a hospital in Pittsburg that does 80 quadruple bypasses per day. If you want to be a heart surgeon, that is the place to be. The Cleveland Clinic has a world famous burn ward. Pittsburg may be more famous for heart surgery than steel these days because the U. S. gets the majority of their steel from Japan. What might be a greater center for art or industry during one age may become a center for health care or recreation. Atlantic City once was a haven for family vacations. There was the beach, the boardwalk, the world famous Steel Pier with its diving horse. Now it is a cluster of neon casino besieged or surrounded by an urban slum.

People often moved to places where information of interest was stored. Sometimes it is not the person who chooses the place to further his or her knowledge: Frank Lloyd Wright was saying 30 years ago that it is no longer necessary. MIT will soon have all of its courses online and free for anyone who wants to take them for no credit. The opportunities for learning that a place offers capture the person's interest on the other hand they may be interested in becoming a chef because they were born in Paris. It is a two way street, and sometimes the strengths of a geographical area shape the people. The Internet is shrinking the world at a dizzying rate.

The second reason why a place may help creativity is that fresh inspiration is not evenly distributed by location. Certain environments have a greater concentration of contacts and provide more excitement and a greater stimulation of ideas; therefore, they prompt the person who is already inclined to break away from conventions to experiment with innovation and originality than if he or she had continued to live in their own home town where things were more conservative, more repressive setting.

The young artists who were drawn to Paris from all over the world at the end of the nineteenth century lived in a stimulating atmosphere where new ideas, new expressions, and new ways of living constantly bumped up against one another and called brought about further novelty. I recently saw a documentary on the 50s in New York City. It was a time and a place that was about books and literature. Jack Kerouac, Allen Ginzberg, Pierre Salinger and others read, discussed and wrote.

For theoretical scientists the stimulation of colleagues in neighboring offices is indispensable. Bell Laboratories is a wonderful example. Bell Labs now Lucent has registered a patent a day ever since they opened their doors in 1925 and have more than 25,000 patents as a result including the transistor and the superconductor. Edison may have stimulated himself with nearly 900 patents of his own. Einstein worked in a patent office in his native land before leaving to escape fascism. He reviewed new ideas everyday perhaps these ideas made it possible for him to develop his own novel and revolutionary insights. Science, even more than art, is a collective enterprise where information grows much faster in "hot spots" where the thought of one person builds on the ideas of others. And then there are places that inhibit the generation of novelty. According to some, universities are too committed to their primary function, which is the preservation of knowledge, to be very good at stimulating creativity.

Finally, access to the field is not evenly distributed in space. The centers that facilitate the realization of novel ideas are not necessarily the ones where the information is stored or where the stimulation is greatest. Often sudden availability of money at a certain place attracts artists or scientists to an otherwise infertile environment, and that place becomes, at least for a while, one of the centers of the field. John D. Rockefeller borrowed a thousand dollars from his father and went to Cleveland to seek his fortune. Still later, when in the 1890s William R. Harper was able to convince John D. Rockefeller, flush with dollars made in the oil fields, to part with a few million to start a university in the cornfields south of Chicago, he almost immediately attracted a number of leading scholars from the Northeast who flocked to the wilderness and established a great center of research and scholarship.

Eighty years later the same phenomenon repeated itself farther west, when oil money made it possible for the University of Texas to attract a new generation of intellectual leaders to Austin. Oil is just one source of financial lure hat greases the movement of academic fields from one place to another. After luminaries settle down in a particular place, it becomes difficult for young people with similar interests to resist their attraction.

Inspiring Environments

The belief that the ***physical environment*** deeply affects our ***thoughts*** and ***feelings is*** held in many cultures. The Chinese sages chose to write their poetry on dainty island pavilions or craggy gazebos. The Hindu Brahmins retreated to the forest to discover the reality hidden behind illusory appearances. Christian monks were so good at selecting the most beautiful natural spots that in many European countries it is a inescapable conclusion that a hill or plain particularly worth seeing must have a convent or monastery built upon it.

There is no evidence – and probably there never will be – to prove that a delightful surrounding will induce creativity. The island peoples of Polynesia are not as technologically advanced as people from harsher climates. Perhaps their location caused them to be peaceful and simply enjoy life's bounty.

> It is true that inspiration does not come only in locations sanctioned by the board of tourism. As Samuel Johnson said, nothing focuses the mind as sharply as the news that one will be executed in a few days. Life-threatening conditions, like the beauties of nature, push the mind to think about what is essential. Other things being equal; however, it would seem that a serene landscape is a preferable source of inspiration.

However, the Eskimos who were forced to carve out a more subsistence living is not especially advanced. Perhaps because of too harsh of a climate although I think that people from so called more advanced civilizations might have difficulty surviving that hostile environment.

Certainly a great number of creative works of music, art, philosophy, and science were composed in unusually beautiful sites. But would not the same works have issued forth even if their authors had been confined to a steamy urban alley or a sterile suburban spread? One cannot answer that question without a controlled experiment, and given the fact that creative works are by definition unique, it is difficult to see how a controlled experiment could ever be performed.

However, accounts by creative individuals strongly suggest that their thought processes are not indifferent to the physical environment. But the relationship is not one of simple causality. A great view does not act like a silver bullet, embedding a new idea in the mind. Rather, what seems to happen is that when persons with prepared minds find themselves in beautiful settings, they are more likely to find new connections among ideas, new perspectives on issues they are dealing with.

Perhaps Gauguin had properly prepared himself when he went to Tahiti. He also brought the perspective of another civilization. But it was essential to have a "prepared mind." What this means is that unless one enters the situation with some deeply felt question and the symbolic skills necessary to answer it, nothing much as likely to happen. It was the formulation rather than the solution of the problem that mattered most.

How one spends time in a beautiful natural setting seems to matter as well. Just sitting and watching is fine, but taking a leisurely walk seems to be even better. The Greek philosophers had settled on the peripatetic method – they preferred to discuss ideas while walking up and down in the courtyard of the academy or in the olive groves around the city of Athens.

When ordinary people are signaled with an electronic pager at random times of the day and asked to rate how creative they feel, they tend to report the highest levels of creativity when walking, driving, or swimming; in other words, when involved in a semiautomatic activity that takes up a certain amount of attention, while leaving some of it free to make connections among ideas below the threshold of conscious intentionality. Devoting full attention to a problem is not the best recipe for having creative thoughts.

When we think intentionally, thoughts are forced to follow a linear, logical – hence predictable – direction. But when attention is focused on the view during a walk, part of the brain is left free to pursue associations that normally are nor made. This mental activity takes place backstage, so to speak; we become aware of it only occasionally. Because these thoughts are not in the center of attention, they are left to develop on their own.

There is no needs to direct them, to criticize them prematurely, to make them do hard work. And of course it is just this freedom and playfulness that makes it possible for leisurely thinking to come up with original formulations and solutions. For as soon as we get a connection that feels right, it will jump into our awareness. The compelling combination may appear as we are lying in bed half asleep, or while shaving in the bathroom, or during a walk in the woods. At that moment the novel idea seems like a voice from heaven, the key to our problems. Later on as we try to fit it into "reality," that original thought may turn out to have been trivial and naïve. Much hard work goes into evaluation, explanation and expansion is necessary before brilliant flashes of insight can be acknowledged and put to use. But without them, creativity would not be what it is.

Centers of creativity
- Athens in its heyday;
- The Arab cities of the tenth century;
- Florence in the Renaissance;
- Venice in the fifteenth century;
- Paris, London, and Vienna in the nineteenth,
- New York in the twentieth

Creating Creative Environments

While novel and beautiful surroundings might be the catalyst for a moment of insight, the other phases of the creative process – such as preparation and evaluation – seem to benefit more from familiar, comfortable settings, even if these are often no better than the compositions for string quartets, Johann Sebastian Bach did not travel far from his native Thuringia, and Marcel Proust wrote his masterpiece in a dark cork-lined study. Albert Einstein needed only a kitchen table in his modest lodgings in Berne to set down the theory of relativity.

Of course, we do not know whether Bach, Liszt, Chopin, and Einstein may not have been inspired at some time in their lives by a sublime sight and spent the rest of their lives expanding upon the inspiration thus obtained. Occasionally a single experience of awe provides the fuel for a lifetime of creative work. For this writer the Grand Canyon and Niagara Falls were awe inspiring, but they have not resulted in much productivity for "…your humble narrator…." to borrow a phrase from the central figure in Anthony Burgess' Clockworks Orange.

While a complicated, stimulating environment is useful for providing new insights, a more routine and everyday setting may be indicated for pursuing the bulk of the creative endeavor – the much longer periods of preparation that must precede the flash of insight, and the equally long periods of evaluation and explanation that follow. Do surroundings matter during these stages of the creative process?

Here it may be useful to make a distinction between the macro-environment, the social, cultural, and institutional context in which a person lives, and the microenvironment, the immediate setting in which a person works. In term of the broader context, it goes without saying that a certain amount of surplus wealth never hurts.

They tended to be at the crossroads of cultures, where information from different traditions was exchanged and synthesized. They were also center of social change, often driven by conflicts between ethnic, economic, or social groups. W. Edwards Deming said that he personally knew 9 Nobel laureates. They had the following in common; all of their physical needs were met without them having to work and aside from that they could do whatever they wanted to do all day every day.

Not only states but also institutions can foster the development of creative ideas. The Bell Research Laboratories have become legendary because of their ability to nurture important new ideas. Every university or think tank hopes to be the place that attracts future celebrities. Successful environments of this type provide freedom of action and stimulation of ideas, coupled with a respectful and nurturing attitude toward potential geniuses, who have notoriously fragile egos and need lots of tender, loving care.

Most of us cannot do a great deal about the macro-environment. There is not that much we can do about the wealth of the society we live in, or even about the institutions in which we work. We can, however, gain control over the immediate environment and transform it so that is enhances personal creativity. On this score, there is much to learn from creative individuals, who generally take great pains to ensure that they can work in easy and uninterrupted concentration. How this is done varies greatly depending on the person's temperament and style of work. The important thing, however, is to have a special space tailor-made to one's own needs, where one feels comfortable and in control.

Just furnishing one's house in a certain way does not miraculously make one's life more creative. The causal connections are, as usual, more complicated. The person who creates a more unique home environment is likely to be more original to begin with. Yet having a home that reinforces one's individuality cannot but help increase the chances that one will act out one's uniqueness.

SUMMARY

1. At birth, the human brain is still preparing for full operation. The brain's neurons exist mostly apart from one another. The brain's task for the first 3 years is to establish and reinforce connections with other neurons. These connections are formed when impulses are sent and received between neurons. Axons send messages and dendrites receive them. These connections form synapses.

2. There are six stages of thinking development:
    - **Stage One:** The Unreflective Thinker
    - **Stage Two:** The Challenged Thinker
    - **Stage Three:** The Beginning Thinker
    - **Stage Four:** The Practicing Thinker
    - **Stage Five:** The Advanced Thinker
    - **Stage Six:** The Master Thinker

3. Environmental influences are the most important for thinking and creativity development.

4. The following signs may reveal that a child is gifted (Alvino, 1996):
    - A tendency to seek out older children and adults;
    - An early fascination with explanations and problem solving;

Talking in complete sentences as early as 2 or 3 years of age;
    - An unusually good memory;
    - Precocious talent in art, music, or number skills.

Intelligence Test

Do you want to know your IQ? Take the following test. Please remember, that there is no accurate measurement of intelligence. If you miss certain questions, go back and try to figure out the right answers.

This test is a modification of Raven's intelligence test.

Instruction

In the big window there is missing piece. Below the big window there are several figures. One of them fit to the pattern/algorithm presented. Write down the number of the missing figure in the blank:

Set I	Your Answer	Set II	Your Answer	Set II	Your Answer	Set II	Your Answer
1		1		13		25	
2		2		14		26	
3		3		15		27	
4		4		16		28	
5		5		17		29	
6		6		18		30	
7		7		19		31	
8		8		20		32	
9		9		21		33	
10		10		22		34	
11		11		23		35	
12		12		24		36	

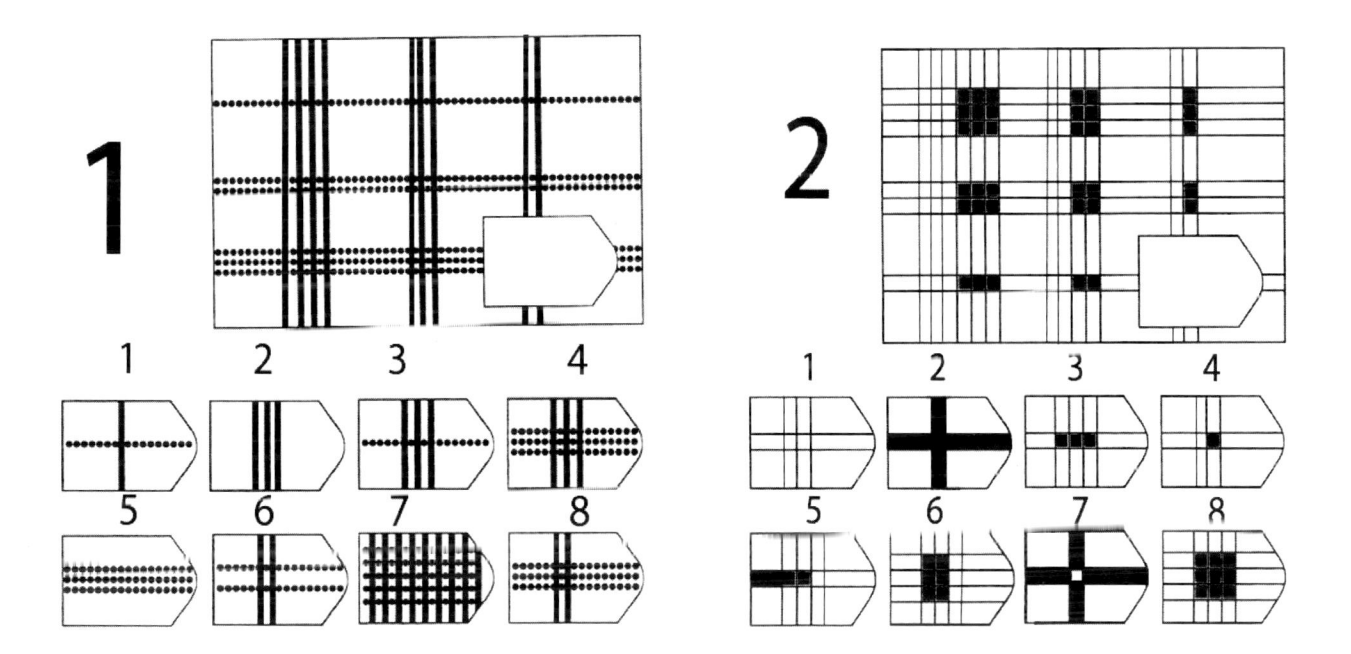

57

CHAPTER 3

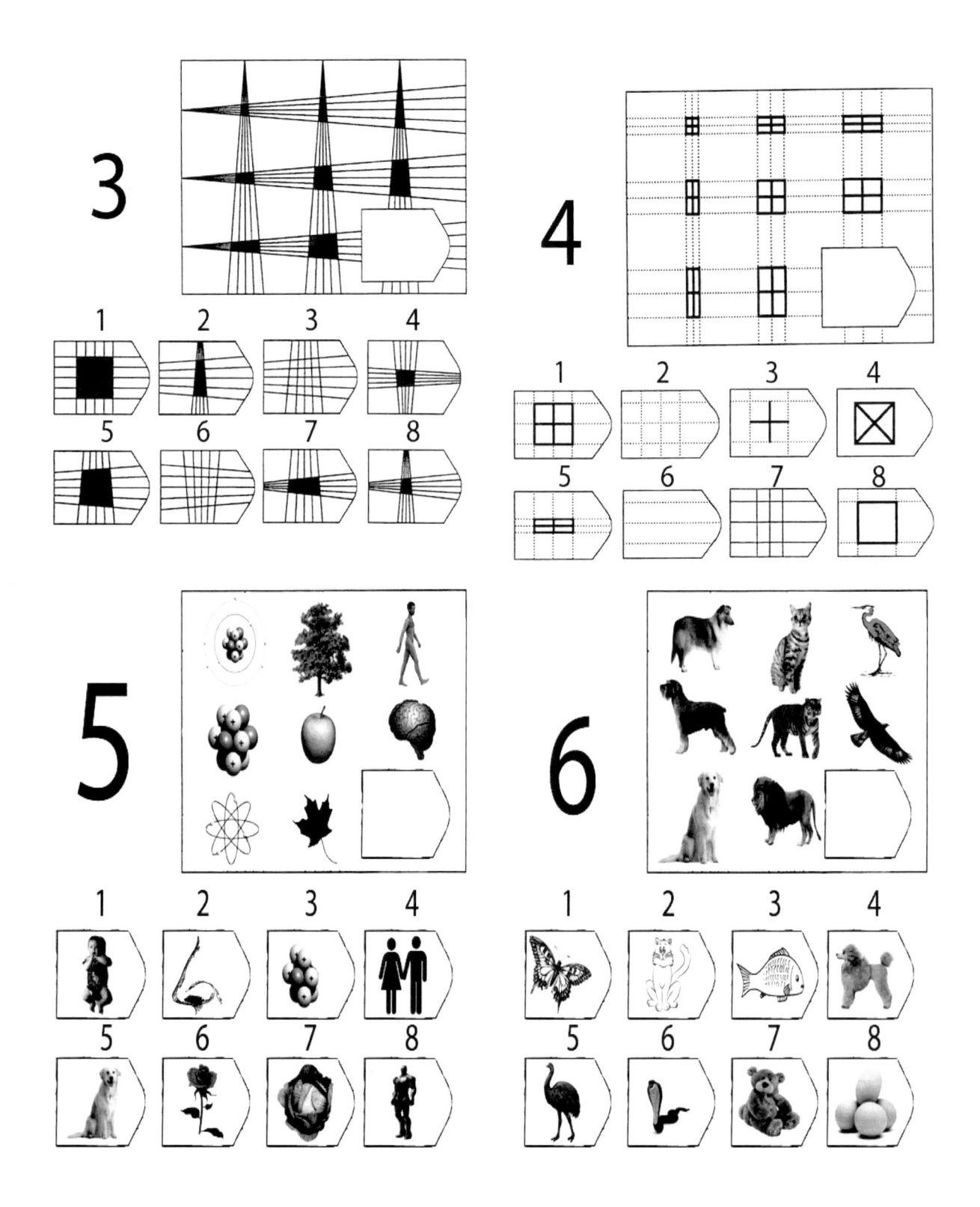

58

Developmental Aspect of Thinking

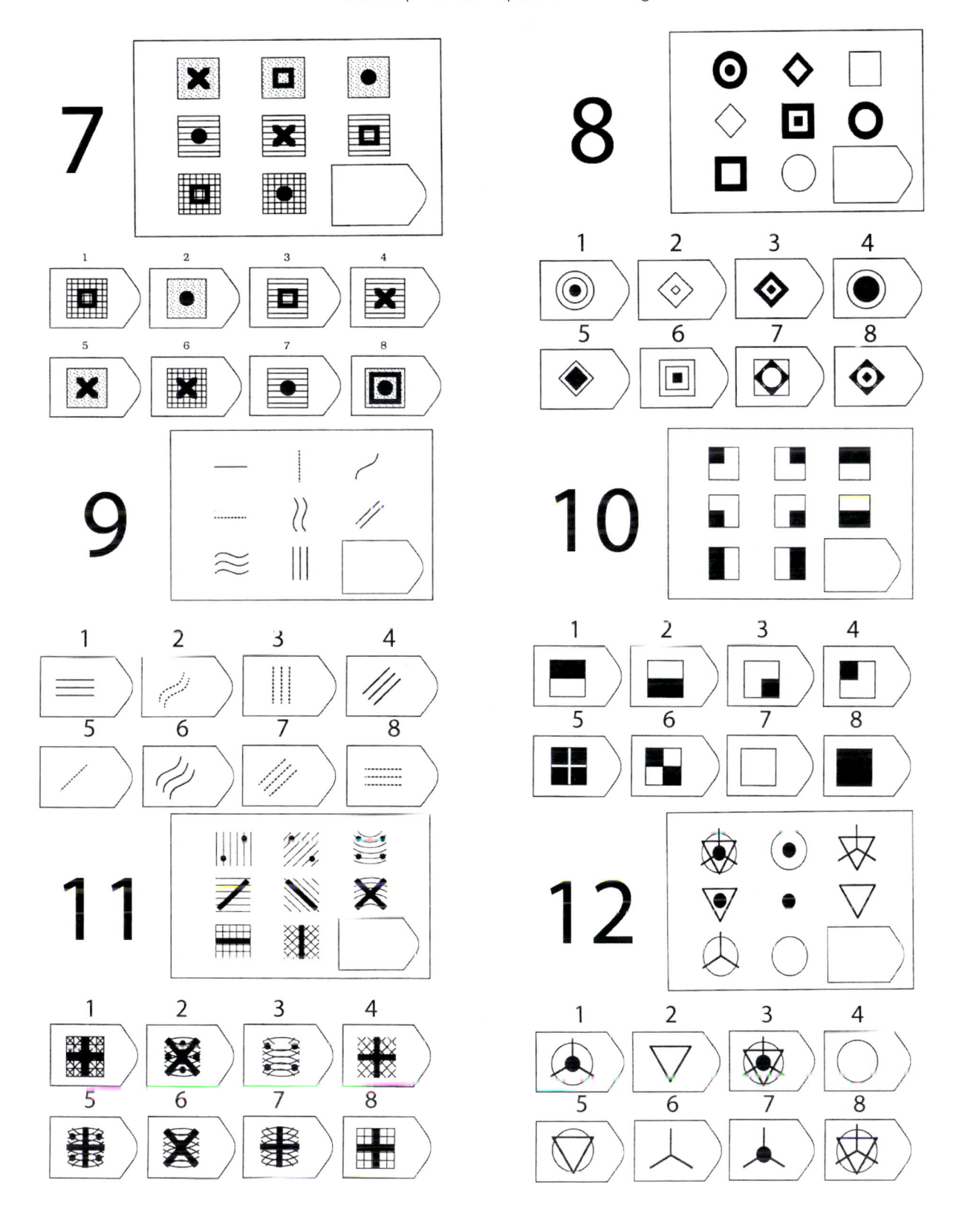

CHAPTER 3

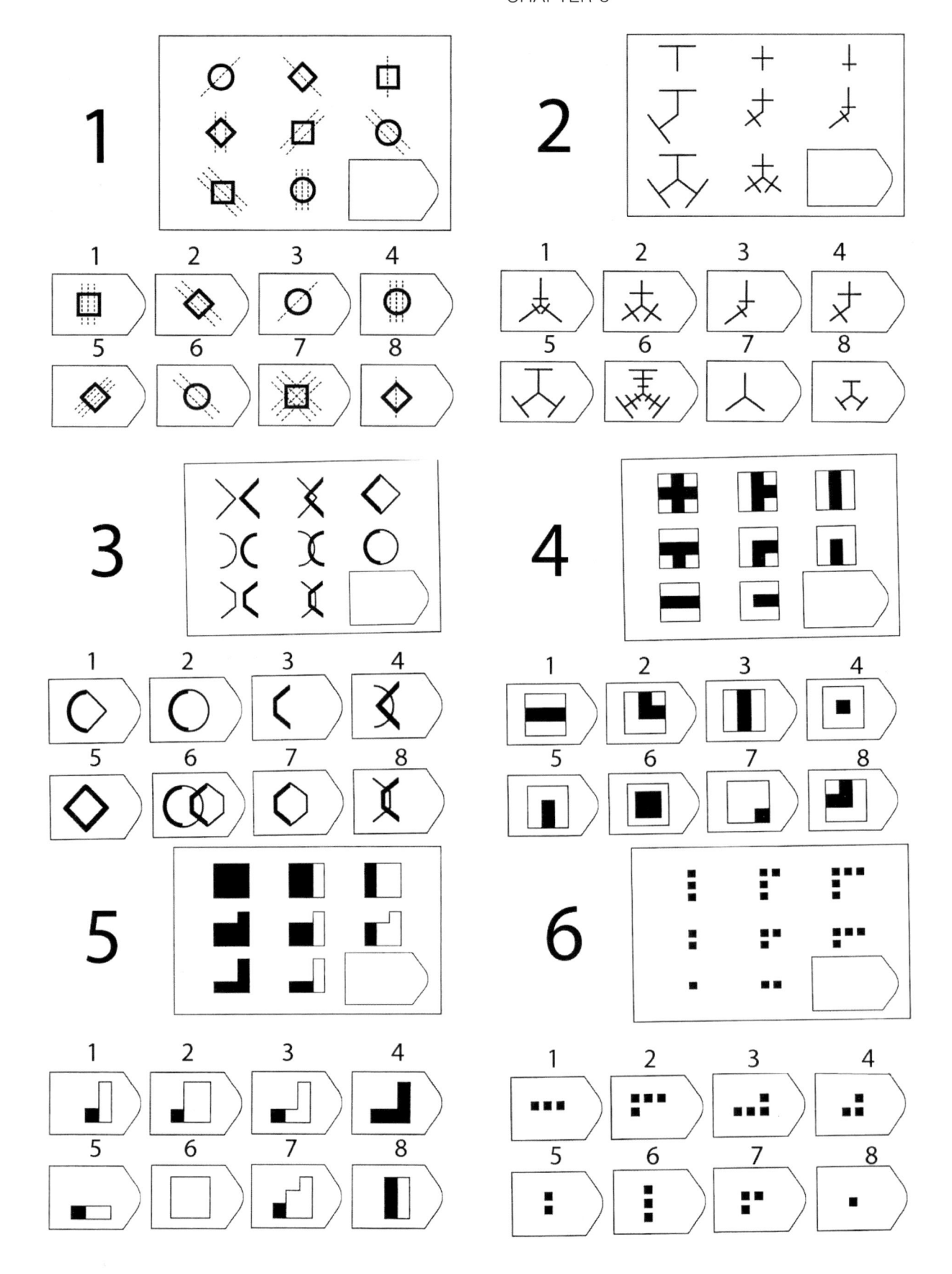

Developmental Aspect of Thinking

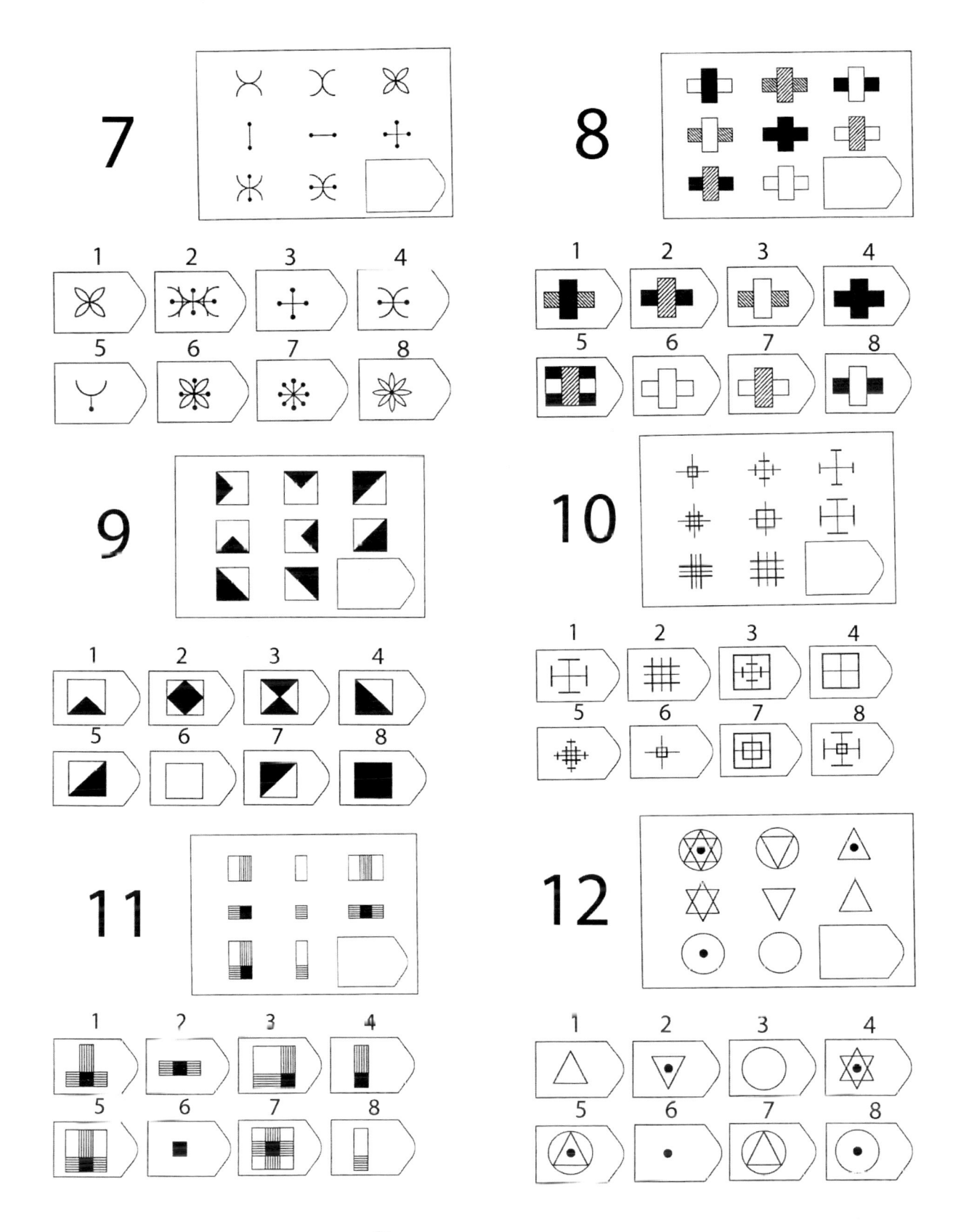

CHAPTER 3

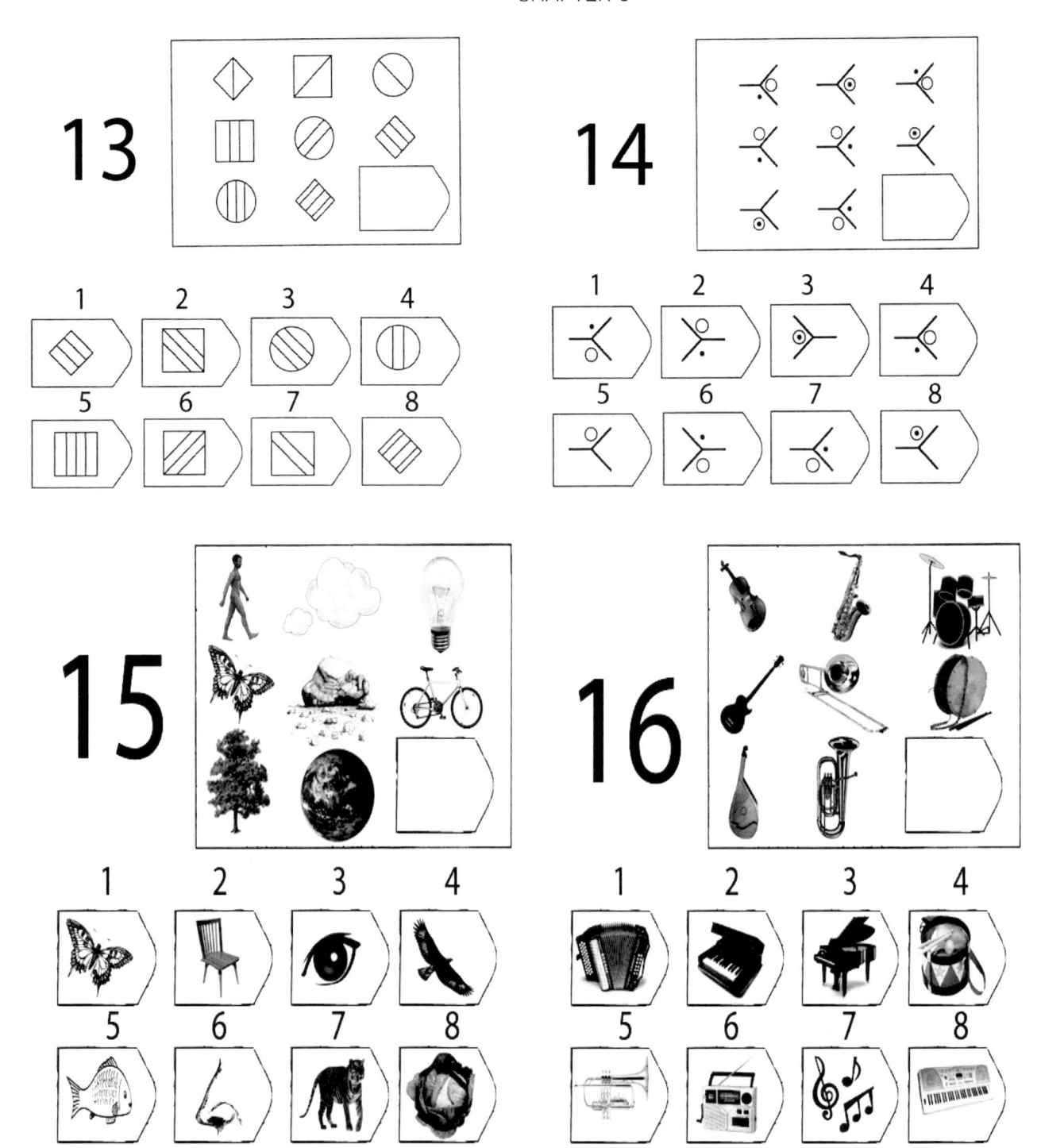

Developmental Aspect of Thinking

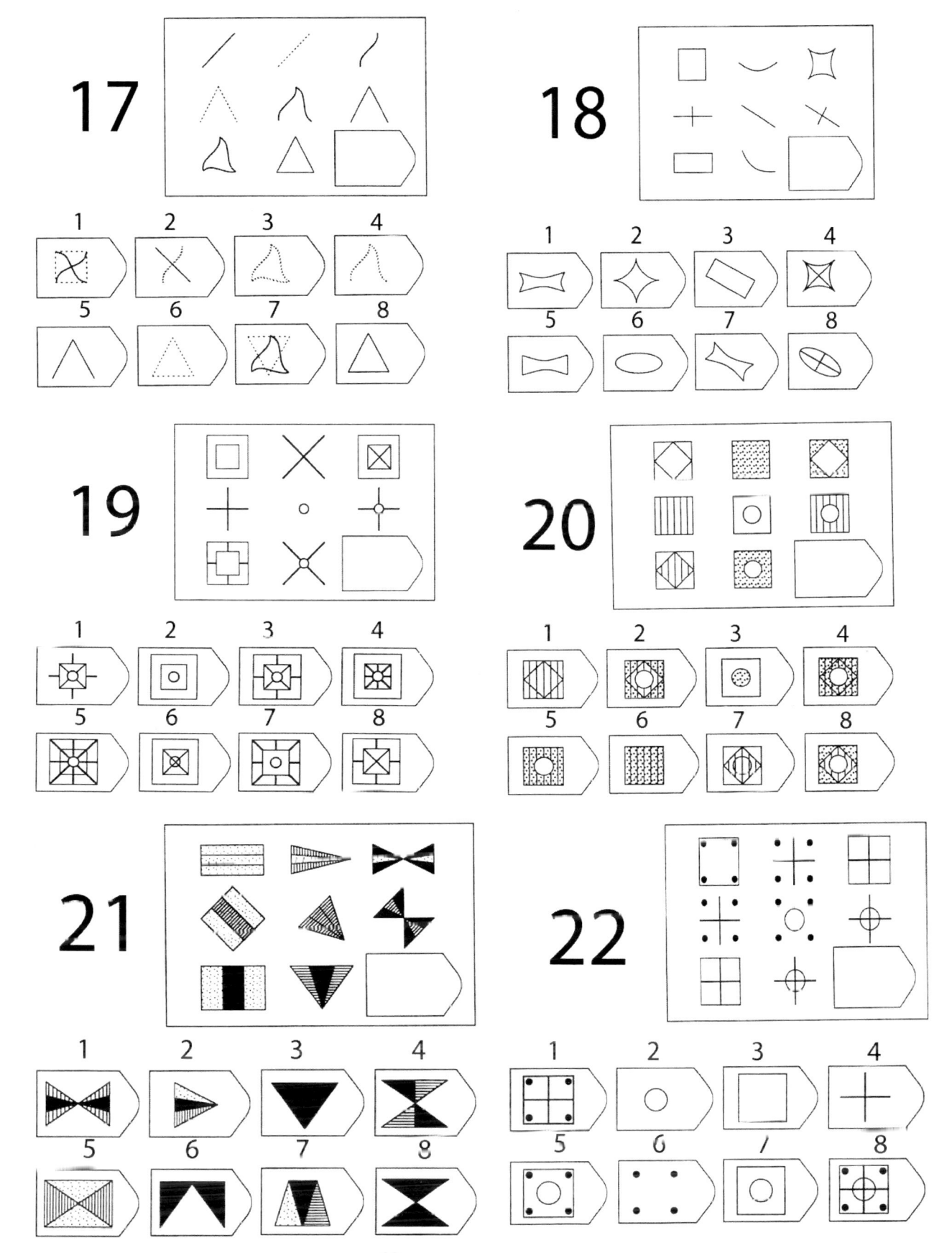

CHAPTER 3

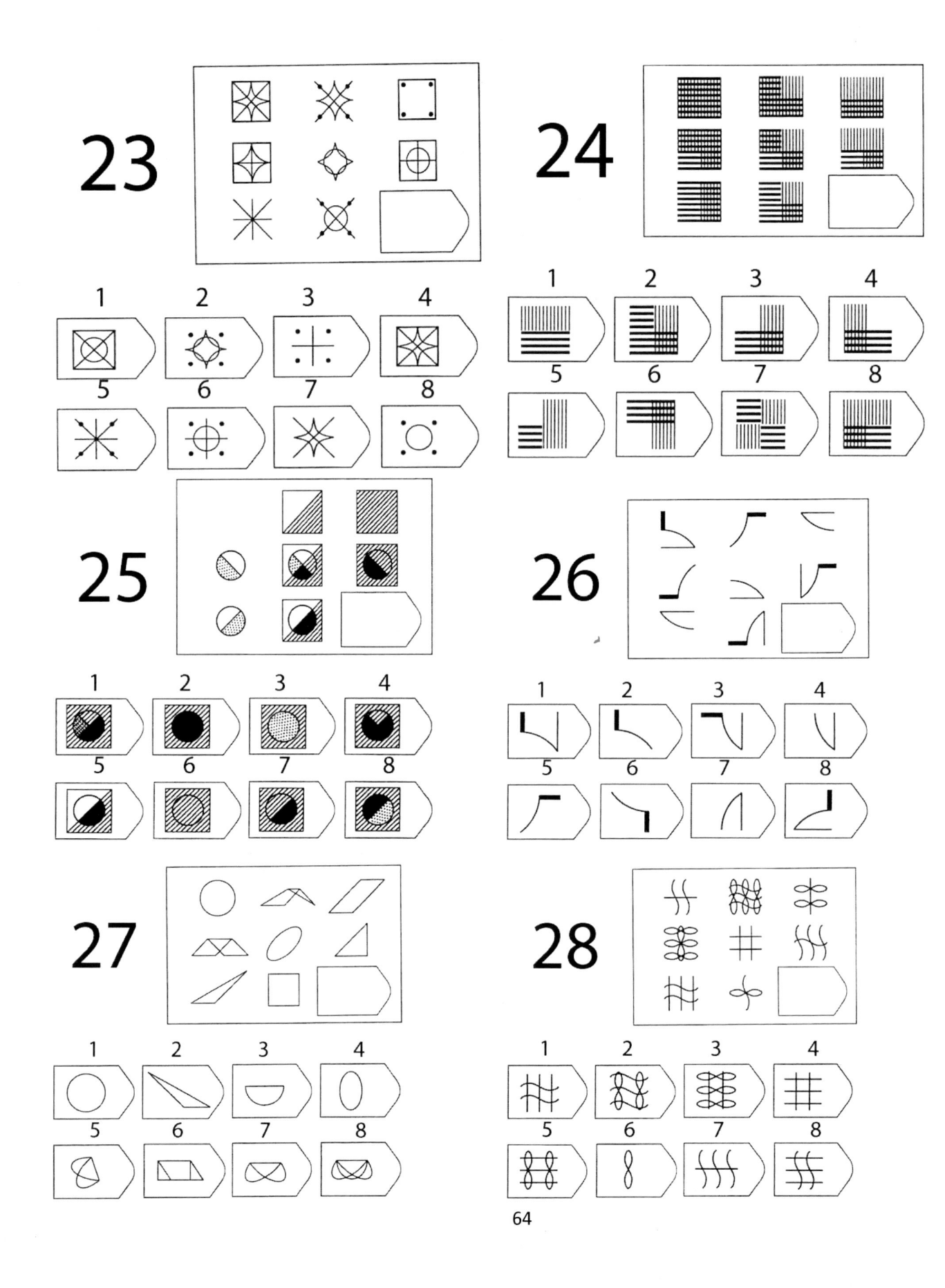

23

24

25

26

27

28

64

Developmental Aspect of Thinking

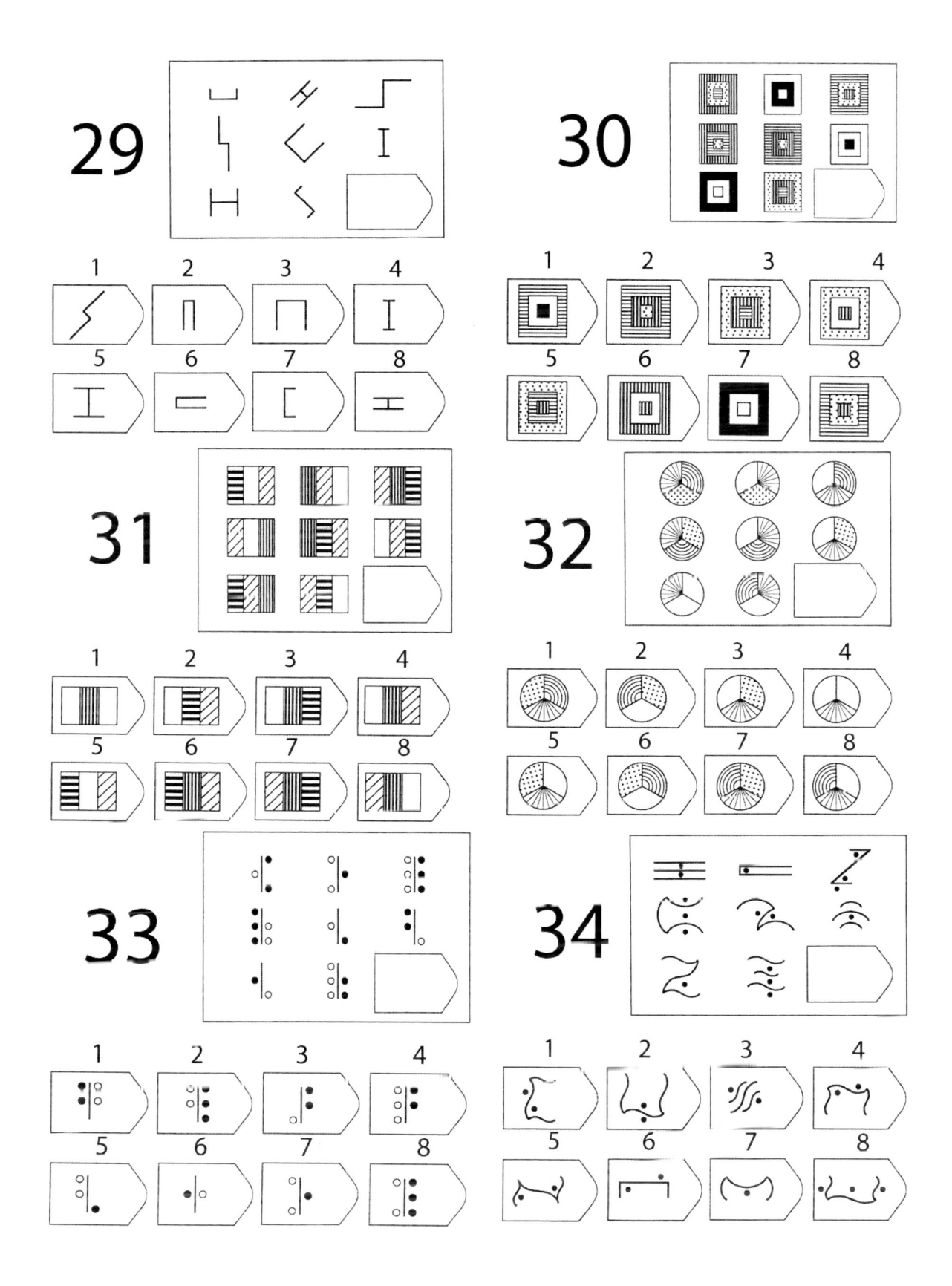

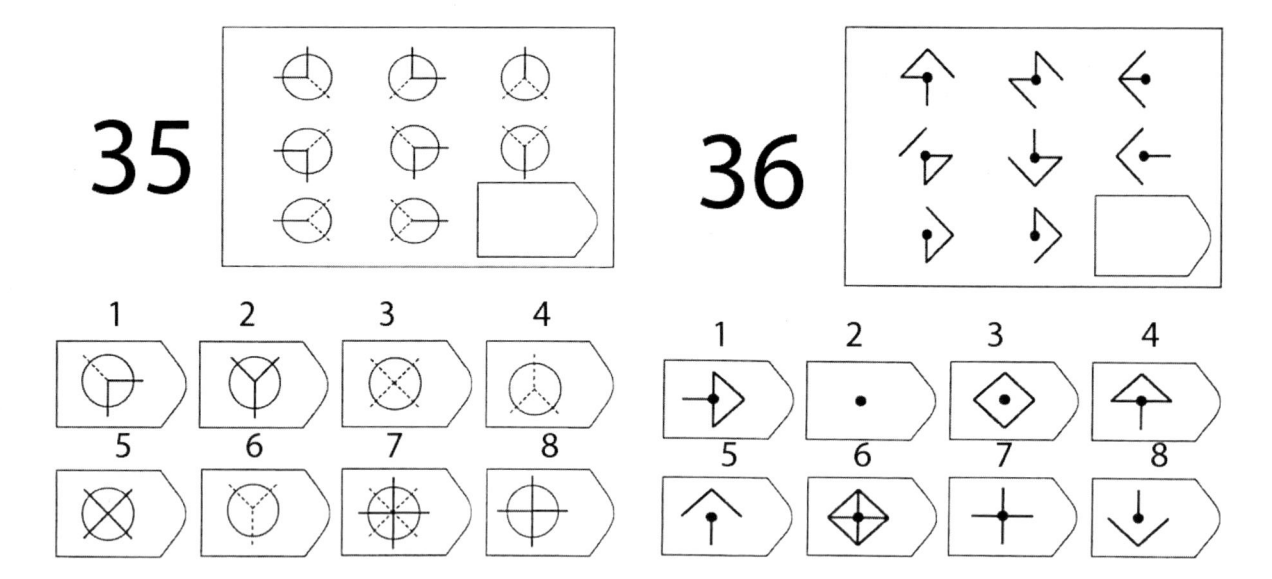

Now compare your answer with the right ones.

Set I	Right Answer	Set II	Right Answer	Set II	Right Answer	Set II	Right Answer
1	8	1	5	13	2	25	7
2	4	2	1	14	1	26	2
3	5	3	7	15	2	27	7
4	1	4	4	16	4	28	5
5	2	5	3	17	6	29	6
6	5	6	1	18	7	30	5
7	6	7	6	19	3	31	4
8	3	8	1	20	8	32	8
9	7	9	8	21	8	33	5
10	8	10	4	22	7	34	1
11	7	11	5	23	6	35	3
12	6	12	6	24	3	36	2

Calculate the percent of your right answers:
48 x 100 : (number of your right answers) = _____ %
Find the percent in the following table. Against the percent there is the IQ.

IQ	Percentile Rank	IQ	Percentile Rank	IQ	Percentile Rank	IQ	Percentile Rank
135	99.0	126	95.8	117	87.1	108	70.2
134	98.8	125	95.2	116	85.8	107	68.1
133	98.6	124	94.5	115	84.1	106	65.5
132	98.3	123	93.7	114	82.4	105	62.9
131	98.1	122	92.9	113	80.8	104	60.6
130	97.7	121	91.9	112	78.8	103	57.9
129	97.3	120	90.8	111	76.7	102	55.2
128	96.9	119	89.8	110	74.9	101	52.8
127	96.4	118	88.5	109	72.6	100	50.0

CHAPTER 4

How Self-Image Is Related to Thinking?

Do you know yourself? How have you built your self-image? What factors are important in the process of self-understanding?
This chapter leads you through the journey of self-discovery exploring the relationship between your self-image, thinking, and success.

LEARNING OBJECTIVES

After reading this chapter, you will be able to

1. Define Self-Concept
2. Identify the component of Self-Concept
3. Compare and contrast theories of Self
4. Be able to describe and discuss a Boundary-Maintaining System
5. Define and describe Cognitive Self
6. Define and describe Emotive Self
7. Describe and analyze your Self-Concept.

Create your self-image map:

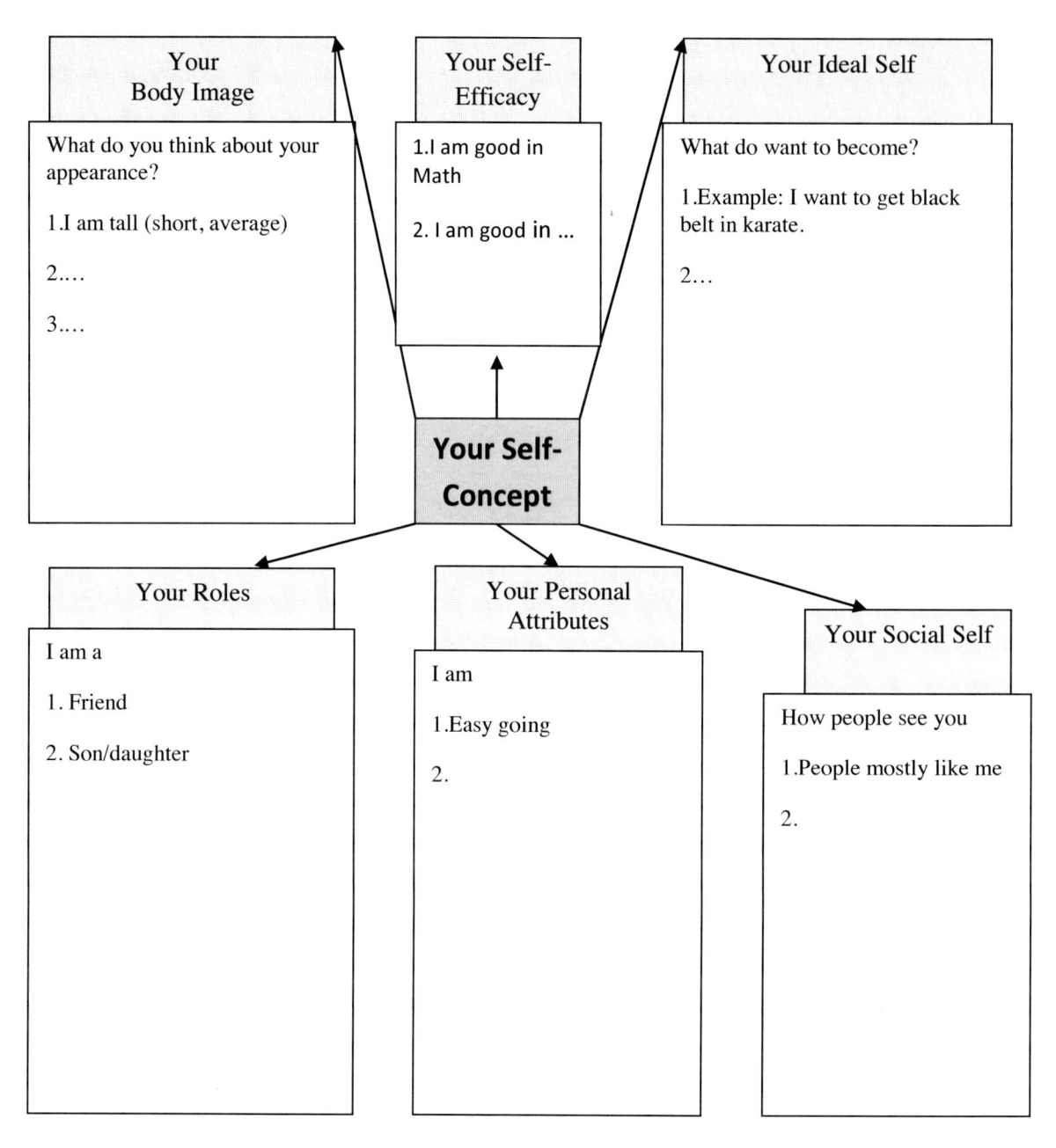

Your Body Image

What do you think about your appearance?

1. I am tall (short, average)
2. ...
3. ...

Your Self-Efficacy

1. I am good in Math
2. I am good in ...

Your Ideal Self

What do want to become?

1. Example: I want to get black belt in karate.
2. ...

Your Self-Concept

Your Roles

I am a
1. Friend
2. Son/daughter

Your Personal Attributes

I am
1. Easy going
2.

Your Social Self

How people see you
1. People mostly like me
2.

WHAT IS THE SELF-CONCEPT?

Carl Rogers (1959) referred to the self as an organized and consistent set of perceptions of the characteristics of "I" or "me" as well as the perceptions of the relationships of this "I" to other people. Thus, although Rogers stresses the internal knowledge that it is at least partially formed through our interactions with others.

The concept of self has had a tangled history that in part may account for its fuzziness. It belongs to the domain of philosophy as well as psychology. Adam Smith originally spoke of society as a mirror in which individuals could see themselves as spectators of their own behavior and who therefore could acquire knowledge about themselves. William James and Charles Horton Cooley, in elaborating on this concept, stressed that individuals develop a self-feeling based on how they think they appear to other people. This has been termed the social self or the reflected self and implicit in this construct is the assumption that people develop their sense of self out of their ongoing interactions with other people.

How Self-Image Is Related to Thinking

Definition:

The self-concept is the accumulation of knowledge about the self, such as beliefs regarding personality traits, physical characteristics, abilities, values, goals, and roles. Beginning in infancy, children acquire and organize information about themselves as a way to enable them to understand the relation between the self and their social world. This developmental process is a direct consequence of children's emerging cognitive skills and their social relationships with both family and peers. During early childhood, children's self-concepts are less differentiated and are centered on concrete characteristics, such as physical attributes, possessions, and skills. During middle childhood, the self-concept becomes more integrated and differentiated as the child engages in social comparison and more clearly perceives the self as consisting of internal, psychological characteristics. Throughout later childhood and adolescence, the self-concept becomes more abstract, complex, and hierarchically organized into cognitive mental representations or self-schemas, which direct the processing of self-relevant information.

The self is a complex process of gaining self awareness. You develop a concept of who you are through your interactions with others.

This view is expressed in pragmatic philosophy in the works of William James and George Herbert Mead, among others.

Self-concept is the totality of an individual's thoughts and feelings having reference to himself/herself as an object (Hawkins, 1982). Basically, self-concept is how you see yourself, and how you feel about yourselves.

Self-concept can be described as "an image shaped by the very person holding the image" (Hong, 1978).

In order to let others know what "image" we are portraying, we buy and use products that reflect our image.

COMPONENTS OF A SELF-CONCEPT

It is composed of
- your *social character* or abilities
- your *physical appearance* and your body image
- your *thinking*

Your ***self-concept*** can change because you see and understand things differently depending on your feelings, beliefs and attitude. Self awareness is a two way process as your feelings and beliefs affect your self-concept and the opposite is also true.

Your self-concept is your understanding of unchanging characteristics you have:

1. *Social*
   - are you sociable?
   - are you shy?
   - are you confident?
2. *Physical*
   - are you tall?
   - are you fat?
   - are you handsome?
3. *Psychological*
   - are you pessimistic or optimistic?
   - are you a happy?
   - can you make decisions easily?

Your self concept is just one factor among many that have an impact on your self esteem and self confidence.

Self-Concept: The collection of an individual's thoughts, feelings, and beliefs about him/herself. An individual's internal representation of who s/he is.

Self: while this term is sometimes used interchangeably with "Self-Concept" the self refers to the agent - the active doer who has thoughts, feelings, and beliefs. The self-concept is different because it is the sum of the thoughts, feelings, and beliefs that the person has about him/herself.

Self-Views: Self-perceptions in specific domains, (e.g. your thoughts, feelings, and beliefs about who you are as a student). The sum of all your self-views is then your Self-Concept.

Self Esteem: The feelings of worth one has about oneself as a whole.
Affect for Specific **Self-Views**: The feelings of worth one has about oneself in a particular role.

CHAPTER 4

There are **four basic dimensions** to self-concept that create motives for your actions. These dimensions include

The "Schema" organization: A schema is a network of inter-associated representations that are stored in memory. You use the schema idea to think about self-views and how they are organized.

- **Actual self-concept.** Actual self-concept is the perception of "who I am now" (Hawkins et al. 430). This is a realistic perception of one's self. For example, I am a college student. This is a real perception of myself and is what I portray to others. One's actual self-concept can include social status, age, gender, etc. Most people can describe how they see themselves in their present state.
- **Ideal self-concept.** Ideal self-concept is one's perception of who they would like to be (Hawkins et al., 1988). Many Americans are constantly in pursuit of bettering themselves whether it is through their income, education, occupation, etc. Most Americans aspire to have an ideal life and they sometimes purchase products that make them feel closer to their ideal self-concept. Individuals use their ideal self-concept to compare the value of their actual self (Hong, 1996). People essentially want their actual self to have similar characteristics to their ideal self. If these two self-concepts are not close in relationship, then an individual will attempt to achieve their ideal self-concept. One may purchase products to achieve their ideal self-concept. For example, a person may want to be wealthy. They may not make enough money to be considered upper class, yet they aspire to be. This person may buy certain things that make them feel more similar to the upper class. By buying an item that is known to be affordable by the upper class, this individual may feel closer to their ideal self-concept. They may choose to by a Lexus car, which symbolizes the finest in automobiles and is affordable to the wealthy.

You develop a healthy self-concept through self-assessment, planning, and effort. You acquire the necessary life skills that can help you take on the challenges that life presents and you integrate them with your knowledge and experience.

- **Private self-concept.** "This is how I am or would like to be to myself" is what is termed private self-concept (Hawkins et al. 430). Private self-concept can be how you believe that you act as a person such as friendly, creative, or adventurous.
- **Social self-concept** (Hawkins, 1982). These self-concepts are perceptions that we have of ourselves that help us to develop reasons for certain behavior. In the first major theory of social learning, Julian B. Rotter (1998) claimed that the expected outcome of an action and the value we place on that outcome determine much of our behavior. For example, people whose positive self-concept leads them to believe they will succeed at a task are likely to behave in ways that ultimately lead to success, while those who expect failure are much more likely to bring it about through their own actions. In a general theory of personality he developed subsequently with two colleagues, Rotter designated variables based on the ways that individuals habitually think about their experiences. One of the most important was I-E, which distinguished "internals," who think of themselves as controlling events, from "externals," who view events as largely outside their control. Internal-external orientation has been found to affect a variety of behaviors and attitudes.

When you maintain a solid self-concept nothing can rattle you or take you off your stride. Nobody can put you down. You are self-confident and assured because you know that you are able to handle the adversities and challenges that come your way.

What constitutes a *healthy self-concept*?
- The ability *to know yourself*; to be able to assess your strengths, weaknesses, talents and potential.
- The ability *to love and accept yourself* as you are; knowing that you can improve and develop any aspects of yourself that you choose.
- The ability *to be honest with yourself* and be true to who you are and what you value.
- The ability *to take responsibility* for your choices and actions.

Self-Concept Formation

Four Components of Self-Concept
- Body Image
- Role Performance
- Personal Identity
- Self-Esteem

Body Image
How a person perceives the size, appearance, and functioning of their body and parts - the physical self

How Self-Image Is Related to Thinking

- Develops from attitudes and responses
- Individual exploration
- Culture and Society

Alterations in Body Image
- Actual or Potential
- Create anxiety
- Illness, Loss of Limbs, Threat

Where it comes from:

1) THE REACTION OF OTHERS. If people admire you, flatter you, seek out your company, listen attentively and share your values and ideas you tend to develop a positive self-image. If they avoid you, neglect you, tell you things about yourself that you don't want to hear you develop a negative self-image. Two types of others are critical in the development of the self. The significant other refers to people who are important to you, whose opinions matter. The generalized other refers to a conception of the community, group, or any organized system of roles (e.g., a baseball team) that are used as a point of reference from which to view the self.

The importance of others in the formation of self-concepts is captured in Cooley's (1902) influential concept, the *looking-glass self*. Cooley proposed that to some extent individuals see themselves as they think others see them. Self-conceptions and self-feelings (e.g., pride or shame) are a consequence of how people imagine others perceive and evaluate them. This process is called *reflected appraisals* and is the main process emphasized in the development of the self.

Personality: View others hold of us, according to Adler & Rodman (G&C, p. 25) -- outward appearance or self presentation.

2) COMPARISON WITH OTHERS. If the people we compare ourselves with (our reference group) appear to be more successful, happier, richer, better looking than ourselves we tend to develop a negative self image BUT if they are less successful than us our image will be positive.

Self awareness: The degree to which your own vision of your self, or your self concept, matches the self others see.

3) SOCIAL ROLES. Some social roles carry prestige e.g. doctor, airline pilot, TV presenter, premiership footballer and this promotes self-esteem. Other roles carry stigma. E.g., prisoner, mental hospital patient, refuse collector or unemployed person. The content of self-concepts reflects the content and organization of society. This is evident with regard to the roles that are internalized as role-identities (e.g., father, student).

Roles, as behavioral expectations associated with a status within a set of relationships, constitute a major link between social and personal organization. Sheldon Stryker (1980) proposes that differential commitment to various role-identities provides much of the structure and organization of self-concepts. To the extent that individuals are committed to a particular role identity, they are motivated to act according to their conception of the identity and to maintain and protect it, because their role performance implicates their self-esteem. Much of socialization, particularly during childhood, involves learning social roles and associated values, attitudes, and beliefs. Initially this takes place in the family, then in larger arenas (e.g., peer groups, school, work settings) of the individual's social world. The role identities formed early in life, such as gender and filial identities, remain some of the most important throughout life. Yet socialization is lifelong and individuals assume various role identities throughout their life course.

Socialization is not a passive process of learning roles and conforming to other's expectations. The self is highly active and selective, having a major influence on its environment and itself. When people play roles, role-making often is as evident as is learning roles. In role-making, individuals actively construct, interpret, and uniquely express their roles. When they perceive an incongruity between a role imposed on them and some valued aspect of their self-conception, they may distance themselves from a role, which is the disassociation of self from role. A pervasive theme in this literature is that the self actively engages in its own development, a process that may be unpredictable.

4) IDENTIFICATION. Roles aren't just "out there." They also become part of your personality i.e. your identity with the position you occupy, the roles you play and the groups you belong to.

Worldview or "frame of reference": your view of life, the universe, and your place in the universe; influences how you understand yourself.

High Self-Esteem
i.e. you have a positive view of ourselves. This tends to lead to
- **Confidence** in your own abilities
- **Self acceptance**
- Not worrying about **what others think**
- **Optimism**

SELF-EFFICACY AND SUCCESS

Often people <u>underestimate</u> chances of success because

- Previous successes & failures
- Messages from others
- Successes & failures observed in others
- Successes & failures observed in the group

Definition

Better to <u>overestimate</u>: more likely to try AND SUCCEED (Bandura, 1994).

Self efficacy is defined as a person's belief that he/she can successfully execute a behavior required to produce a given result.

Self-efficacy refers to an individual's convictions and beliefs about his or her abilities to mobilize
- **COGNITIVE** (learned by awareness, understood)
- **MOTIVATIONAL** (desire held an expectancy and belief that it will be realized)
- **BEHAVIORAL** (change to gain results)

facilities needed to successfully execute <u>a specific task</u> <u>within a given context.</u>

Self efficacy is defined as a person's belief that he/she can successfully execute a behavior required to produce a given result.

Bandura's theory (1977) proposed that **behavioral changes could be mediated through self efficacy.** Locke's theory (1968) proposed that **specific, difficult goals produced higher levels of performance.**

1) Before people select their choices and initiate their effort, people tend to:
   - weigh
   - evaluate
   - integrate information about their perceived capabilities.
2) Expectations of personal efficacy determine whether an individual's coping behavior will be:
   - initiated
   - how much task-related effort will be expended
   - how long that effort will be sustained despite disconfirming evidence.
3) Especially relevant to human performance in organizations is that:
   - people who perceive themselves as highly efficacious will activate sufficient effort which, if well executed, produces successful outcomes.
   - people who perceive low self-efficacy are likely to cease their efforts prematurely and fail on the task.

Self-Efficacy Dimensions

1) The M*agnitude* of Self-Efficacy. Expectations which refers to the <u>level of task difficulty</u> that a person believes he or she is capable of executing.

2) The *Strength* of Self-Efficacy. Expectations which refers to whether the judgment about magnitude is

– <u>strong</u> (perseverance in coping efforts despite disconfirming experiences [obstacles]), or

– <u>weak</u> (easily questioned in the face of difficulty).

Example. Ask yourself, can you lift a chair? You have no doubt that you can. Why you are so sure? Because
1. You did it before and succeeded (positive previous personal experience).
2. You observed others doing it and succeeded (positive social observation).
3. Somebody told you that this is possible to lift a chair (persuasion).

If I ask you: "Can you lift your car?" Your first reaction is to answer "No." But what if there is a person under the car and you need to save his or her life? (motivation). What if you call tow truck? Or ask people to help you to lift a car?

A strong sense of efficacy enhances human accomplishment and personal well-being in many ways. People with **high assurance** in their capabilities approach **difficult tasks as challenges** to be mastered rather than as threats to be avoided. Such an efficacious outlook fosters intrinsic interest and deep engrossment in activities. *They set themselves challenging goals* and maintain strong commitment to them. They **heighten and sustain their efforts** in the face of failure. They *quickly recover* their sense of efficacy *after failures* or setbacks. They *attribute failure to insufficient effort* or deficient knowledge and skills which are acquirable. They **approach threatening situations with assurance** that they can exercise control over them. Such an efficacious outlook produces *personal accomplishments*, *reduces stress* and *lowers vulnerability to depression*.

In contrast, people who doubt their capabilities shy away from difficult tasks which they view as *personal threats*. They **have low aspirations** and **weak commitment** to the goals they choose to pursue. When faced with difficult tasks, they *dwell on their personal deficiencies*, on the obstacles they will encounter, and all kinds of adverse outcomes rather than concentrate on how to perform successfully. They *slacken their efforts* and *give up quickly* in the face of difficulties. They are *slow to recover* their sense of efficacy following failure or setbacks. Because they view insufficient performance as deficient aptitude it does not require much failure for them to lose faith in their capabilities. They fall easy victim *to stress and depression*.

Sources of Self-Efficacy

People's beliefs about their efficacy can be developed by *four main sources of influence*. The most effective way of creating a strong sense of efficacy is *through mastery experiences*. Successes build a robust belief in one's personal efficacy. Failures undermine it, especially if failures occur before a sense of efficacy is firmly established.

If people experience only easy successes they come to expect quick results and are easily discouraged by failure. A resilient sense of efficacy requires *experience in overcoming obstacles through perseverant effort*. Some setbacks and difficulties in human pursuits serve a useful purpose in teaching that success usually requires sustained effort. After people become convinced they have what it takes to succeed, they persevere in the face of adversity and quickly rebound from setbacks. By sticking it out through tough times, they emerge stronger from adversity.

The second way of creating and strengthening self-beliefs of efficacy is *through the vicarious experiences provided by social models*. Seeing people similar to oneself succeed by sustained effort raises observers' beliefs that they too possess the capabilities to master comparable activities required to succeed. By the same token, observing others' fail despite high effort lowers observers' judgments of their own efficacy and undermines their efforts. The impact of modeling on perceived self-efficacy is strongly influenced by perceived similarity to the models. The greater the assumed similarity the more persuasive are the models' successes and failures. If people see the models as very different from themselves their perceived self-efficacy is not much influenced by the models' behavior and the results its produces.

Modeling influences do more than provide a social standard against which to judge one's own capabilities. People seek proficient models who possess the competencies to which they aspire. Through their behavior and expressed ways of thinking, competent models transmit knowledge and teach observers effective skills and strategies for managing environmental demands. Acquisition of better means raises perceived self-efficacy.

Social persuasion is a third way of strengthening people's beliefs that they have what it takes to succeed. People who are persuaded verbally that they possess the capabilities to master given activities are likely to mobilize greater effort and sustain it than if they harbor self-doubts and dwell on personal

---

A strong sense of efficacy enhances human accomplishment and personal well-being in many ways. People with high assurance in their capabilities approach difficult tasks as challenges to be mastered rather than as threats to be avoided.

Sources of Self-Efficacy:

1. Previous success
2. Modeling influence
3. Social persuasion

deficiencies when problems arise. To the extent that persuasive boosts in perceived self-efficacy lead people to try hard enough to succeed, they promote development of skills and a sense of personal efficacy.

Efficacy-Activated Processes

Much research has been conducted on the four major psychological processes through which self-beliefs of efficacy affect human functioning.

A. Cognitive Processes

Personal goal setting is influenced by self-appraisal of capabilities. The stronger the perceived self-efficacy, the higher the goal challenges people set for themselves and the firmer is their commitment to them.

Most courses of action are initially organized in thought. People's beliefs in their efficacy shape the types of anticipatory scenarios they construct and rehearse. Those who have a high sense of efficacy, visualize success scenarios that provide positive guides and supports for performance. Those who doubt their efficacy, visualize failure scenarios and dwell on the many things that can go wrong. It is difficult to achieve much while fighting self-doubt. A major function of thought is to enable people to predict events and to develop ways to control those that affect their lives. Such skills require effective cognitive processing of information that contains many ambiguities and uncertainties. In learning predictive and regulative rules people must draw on their knowledge to construct options, to weight and integrate predictive factors, to test and revise their judgments against the immediate and distal results of their actions, and to remember which factors they had tested and how well they had worked.

B. Motivational Processes

There are three different forms of cognitive motivators around which different theories have been built. They include causal attributions, outcome expectancies, and cognized goals. The corresponding theories are attribution theory, expectancy-value theory and goal theory, respectively. Self-efficacy beliefs operate in each of these types of cognitive motivation. Self-efficacy beliefs influence causal attributions. People who regard themselves as highly efficacious attribute their failures to insufficient effort, those who regard themselves as inefficacious attribute their failures to low ability. Causal attributions affect motivation, performance and affective reactions mainly through beliefs of self-efficacy.

In expectancy-value theory, motivation is regulated by the expectation that a given course of behavior will produce certain outcomes and the value of those outcomes. But people act on their beliefs about what they can do, as well as on their beliefs about the likely outcomes of performance. The motivating influence of outcome expectancies is thus partly governed by self-beliefs of efficacy. There are countless attractive options people do not pursue because they judge they lack the capabilities for them. The predictiveness of expectancy-value theory is enhanced by including the influence of perceived self-efficacy.

The capacity to exercise self-influence by goal challenges and evaluative reaction to one's own attainments provides a major cognitive mechanism of motivation. A large body of evidence shows that explicit, challenging goals enhance and sustain motivation. Goals operate largely through self-influence processes rather than regulate motivation and action directly. Motivation based on goal setting involves a cognitive comparison process. By making self-satisfaction conditional on matching adopted goals, people give direction to their behavior and create incentives to persist in their efforts until they fulfill their goals. They seek self-satisfaction from fulfilling valued goals and are prompted to intensify their efforts by discontent with substandard performances.

Motivation based on goals or personal standards is governed by three types of self influences. They include self-satisfying and self-dissatisfying reactions to one's performance, perceived self-efficacy for goal attainment, and readjustment of personal goals based on one's progress.

C. Affective Processes

People's beliefs in their coping capabilities affect how much stress and depression they experience in threatening or difficult situations, as well as their level of motivation. Perceived self-efficacy to exercise control over stressors plays a central role in anxiety arousal. People who believe they can exercise control over threats do not conjure up disturbing thought patterns. But those who believe they

---

It requires a **strong sense of efficacy** to remain task oriented in the face of pressing situational demands, failures and setbacks that have significant repercussions. When people are faced with the tasks of managing difficult environmental demands under taxing circumstances, those who are beset by self-doubts about their efficacy become more and more erratic in their analytic thinking, lower their aspirations and the quality of their performance deteriorates. In contrast, those who maintain a resilient sense of efficacy set themselves challenging goals and use good analytic thinking which pays off in performance accomplishments.

Self-efficacy beliefs contribute to motivation in several ways: They determine the goals people set for themselves; how much effort they expend; how long they persevere in the face of difficulties; and their resilience to failures. When faced with obstacles and failures people who harbor self-doubts about their capabilities slacken their efforts or give up quickly. Those who have a strong belief in their capabilities exert greater effort when they fail to master the challenge. Strong perseverance contributes to performance accomplishments.

cannot manage threats experience high anxiety arousal. They dwell on their coping deficiencies. They view many aspects of their environment as fraught with danger. They magnify the severity of possible threats and worry about things that rarely happen. Through such inefficacious thinking they distress themselves and impair their level of functioning. Perceived coping self-efficacy regulates avoidance behavior as well as anxiety arousal. The stronger the sense of self-efficacy the bolder people are in taking on taxing and threatening activities.

Anxiety arousal is affected not only by perceived coping efficacy but by perceived efficacy to control disturbing thoughts. Both perceived coping self-efficacy and thought control efficacy operate jointly to reduce anxiety and avoidant behavior.

D. Selection Processes

Beliefs of personal efficacy can shape the course lives take by influencing they types of activities and environments people choose. People avoid activities and situations they believe exceed their coping capabilities. But they readily undertake challenging activities and select situations they judge themselves capable of handling. By the choices they make, people cultivate different competencies, interests and social networks that determine life courses. Any factor that influences choice behavior can profoundly affect the direction of personal development. This is because the social influences operating in selected environments continue to promote certain competencies, values, and interests long after the efficacy decisional determinant has rendered its inaugurating effect.

Adaptive Benefits of Optimistic Self-Beliefs of Efficacy

Human accomplishments and positive well-being require an optimistic sense of personal efficacy. This is because ordinary social realities are strewn with difficulties. They are full of impediments, adversities, setbacks, frustrations, and inequities. People must have a robust sense of personal efficacy to sustain the perseverant effort needed to succeed. In pursuits strewn with obstacles, realists either forsake them, abort their efforts prematurely when difficulties arise or become cynical about the prospects of effecting significant changes.

It is widely believed that misjudgment breeds personal problems. Certainly, gross miscalculation can get one into trouble. However, the functional value of accurate self-appraisal depends on the nature of the activity. Activities in which mistakes can produce costly or injurious consequences call for accurate self-appraisal of capabilities. It is a different matter where difficult accomplishments can produce substantial personal and social benefits and the costs involve one's time, effort, and expendable resources. People with a high sense of efficacy have the staying power to endure the obstacles and setbacks that characterize difficult undertakings.

When people err in their self-appraisal they tend to overestimate their capabilities. This is a benefit rather than a cognitive failing to be eradicated. If efficacy beliefs always reflected only what people can do routinely they would rarely fail but they would not set aspirations beyond their immediate reach nor mount the extra effort needed to surpass their ordinary performances.

People who experience much distress have been compared in their skills and beliefs in their capabilities with those who do not suffer from such problems. The findings show that it is often the normal people who are distorters of reality. But they display self-enhancing biases and distort in the positive direction. People who are socially anxious or prone to depression are often just as socially skilled as those who do not suffer from such problems. But the normal ones believe they are much more adept than they really are. The nondepressed people also have a stronger belief that they exercise some control over situations.

Social reformers strongly believe that they can mobilize the collective effort needed to bring social change. Although their beliefs are rarely fully realized they sustain reform efforts that achieve important gains. Were social reformers to be entirely realistic about the prospects of transforming social systems they would either forego the endeavor or fall easy victim to discouragement. Realists may adapt well to existing realities. But those with a tenacious self-efficacy are likely to change those realities.

Theories and technologies that are ahead of their time usually suffer repeated rejections. The rocket pioneer, Robert Goddard, was bitterly rejected by his scientific peers on the grounds that rocket propulsion would not work in the rarefied atmosphere of outer space. Because of the cold reception given to innovations, the time between conception and technical realization is discouragingly long.

Career choice and development is but one example of the power of self-efficacy beliefs to affect the course of life paths through choice-related processes. The higher the level of people's perceived self-efficacy the wider the range of career options they seriously consider, the greater their interest in them, and the better they prepare themselves educationally for the occupational pursuits they choose and the greater is their success.

Innovative achievements also require a resilient sense of efficacy. Innovations require heavy investment of effort over a long period with uncertain results. Moreover, innovations that clash with existing preferences and practices meet with negative social reactions. It is, therefore, not surprising that one rarely finds realists in the ranks of innovators and great achievers.

Rejections should not be accepted too readily as indicants of personal failings. To do so is self-limiting.

Development and Exercise of Self-Efficacy over the Lifespan

Different periods of life present certain types of competency demands for successful functioning. These normative changes in required competencies with age do not represent lock-step stages through which everyone must inevitably pass. There are many pathways through life and, at any given period, people vary substantially in how efficaciously they manage their lives. The sections that follow provide a brief analysis of the characteristic developmental changes in the nature and scope of perceived self-efficacy over the course of the lifespan.

A. Origins of a Sense of Personal Agency

The newborn comes without any sense of self. Infants exploratory experiences in which they see themselves produce effects by their actions provide the initial basis for developing a sense of efficacy. Shaking a rattle produces predictable sounds, energetic kicks shake their cribs, and screams bring adults. By repeatedly observing that environmental events occur with action, but not in its absence, infants learn that actions produce effects. Infants who experience success in controlling environmental events become more attentive to their own behavior and more competent in learning new efficacious responses, than are infants for whom the same environmental events occur regardless of how they behave.

Development of a sense of personal efficacy requires more than simply producing effects by actions. Those actions must be perceived as part of oneself. The self becomes differentiated from others through dissimilar experience. If feeding oneself brings comfort, whereas seeing others feed themselves has no similar effect, one's own activity becomes distinct from all other persons. As infants begin to mature those around them refer to them and treat them as distinct persons. Based on growing personal and social experiences they eventually form a symbolic representation of themselves as a distinct self.

B. Familial Sources of Self-Efficacy

Young children must gain self-knowledge of their capabilities in broadening areas of functioning. They have to develop, appraise and test their physical capabilities, their social competencies, their linguistic skills, and their cognitive skills for comprehending and managing the many situations they encounter daily. Development of sensorimotor capabilities greatly expands the infants' exploratory environment and the means for acting upon it. These early exploratory and play activities, which occupy much of children's waking hours, provide opportunities for enlarging their repertoire of basic skills and sense of efficacy.

Successful experiences in the exercise of personal control are central to the early development of social and cognitive competence. Parents who are responsive to their infants' behavior, and who create opportunities for efficacious actions by providing an enriched physical environment and permitting freedom of movement for exploration, have infants who are accelerated in their social and cognitive development . Parental responsiveness increases cognitive competence, and infants' expanded capabilities elicit greater parental responsiveness in a two-way influence. Development of language provides children with the symbolic means to reflect on their experiences and what others tell them about their capabilities and, thus, to expand their self-knowledge of what they can and cannot do.

The initial efficacy experiences are centered in the family. But as the growing child's social world rapidly expands, peers become increasingly important in children's developing self-knowledge of their capabilities. It is in the context of peer relations that social comparison comes strongly into play. At first, the closest comparative age-mates are siblings. Families differ in number of siblings, how far apart in age they are, and in their sex distribution. Different family structures, as reflected in family size, birth order, and sibling constellation patterns, create different social comparisons for judging one's personal efficacy. Younger siblings find themselves in the unfavorable position of judging their capabilities in relation to older siblings who may be several years advanced in their development.

C. Broadening of Self-Efficacy Through Peer Influences

Children's efficacy-testing experiences change substantially as they move increasingly into the larger community. It is in peer relationships that they broaden self-knowledge of their capabilities. Peers serve several important efficacy functions. Those who are most experienced and competent provide models of efficacious styles of thinking and behavior. A vast amount of social learning occurs among peers. In addition, age-mates provide highly informative comparisons for judging and verifying one's self-efficacy. Children are, therefore, especially sensitive to their relative standing among the peers in activities that determine prestige and popularity.

Peers are neither homogeneous nor selected indiscriminately. Children tend to choose peers who share similar interests and values. Selective peer association will promote self-efficacy in directions of mutual interest, leaving other potentialities underdeveloped. Because peers serve as a major influence in the development and validation of self-efficacy, disrupted or impoverished peer relationships can adversely affect the growth of personal efficacy. A low sense of social efficacy can, in turn, create internal obstacles to favorable peer relationships. Thus, children who regard themselves as socially inefficacious withdraw socially, perceive low acceptance by their peers and have a low sense of self-worth. There are some forms of behavior where a high sense of efficacy may be socially alienating rather than socially affiliating. For example, children who readily resort to aggression perceive themselves as highly efficacious in getting things they want by aggressive means.

D. School as an Agency for Cultivating Cognitive Self-Efficacy

During the crucial formative period of children's lives, the school functions as the primary setting for the cultivation and social validation of cognitive competencies. School is the place where children develop the cognitive competencies and acquire the knowledge and problem-solving skills essential for participating effectively in the larger society. Here their knowledge and thinking skills are continually tested, evaluated, and socially compared. As children master cognitive skills, they develop a growing sense of their intellectual efficacy. Many social factors, apart from the formal instruction, such as peer modeling of cognitive skills, social comparison with the performances of other students, motivational enhancement through goals and positive incentives, and teachers interpretations of children's successes and failures in ways that reflect favorably or unfavorably on their ability also affect children's judgments of their intellectual efficacy.

The task of creating learning environments conducive to development of cognitive skills rests heavily on the talents and self-efficacy of teachers. Those who are have a high sense of efficacy about their teaching capabilities can motivate their students and enhance their cognitive development. Teachers who have a low sense of instructional efficacy favor a custodial orientation that relies heavily on negative sanctions to get students to study.

Students' belief in their capabilities to master academic activities affects their aspirations, their level of interest in academic activities, and their academic accomplishments. There are a number of school practices that, for the less talented or ill prepared, tend to convert instructional experiences into education in inefficacy. These include lock step sequences of instruction, which lose many children along the way; ability groupings which further diminish the perceived self-efficacy of those cast in the lower ranks; and competitive practices where many are doomed to failure for the success of a relative few.

E. Growth of Self-Efficacy through Transitional Experiences of Adolescence

Each period of development brings with it new challenges for coping efficacy. As adolescents approach the demands of adulthood, they must learn to assume full responsibility for themselves in almost every dimension of life. This requires mastering many new skills and the ways of adult society. Learning how to deal with pubertal changes, emotionally invested partnerships and sexuality becomes a matter of considerable importance. The task of choosing what lifework to pursue also looms large during this period. These are but a few of the areas in which new competencies and self-beliefs of efficacy have to be developed.

With growing independence during adolescence some experimentation with risky behavior is not all that uncommon. Adolescents expand and strengthen their sense of efficacy by learning how to deal successfully with potentially troublesome matters in which they are unpracticed as well as with advantageous life events. Insulation from problematic situations leaves one ill-prepared to cope with potential difficulties. Whether adolescents forsake risky activities or become chronically enmeshed in them is determined by the interplay of personal competencies, self-management efficacy and the prevailing influences in their lives.

Impoverished hazardous environments present especially harsh realities with minimal resources and social supports for culturally-valued pursuits, but extensive modeling, incentives and social supports for transgressive styles of behavior. Such environments severely tax the coping efficacy of youth enmeshed in them to make it through adolescence in ways that do not irreversibly foreclose many beneficial life paths.

F. Self-Efficacy Concerns of Adulthood

Young adulthood is a period when people have to learn to cope with many new demands arising from lasting partnerships, marital relationships, parenthood, and occupational careers. As in earlier mastery tasks, a firm sense of self-efficacy is an important contributor to the attainment of further competencies and success. Those who enter adulthood poorly equipped with skills and plagued by self-doubts find many aspects of their adult life stressful and depressing.

Beginning a productive vocational career poses a major transitional challenge in early adulthood. There are a number of ways in which self-efficacy beliefs contribute to career development and success in vocational pursuits. In preparatory phases, people's perceived self-efficacy partly determines how well they develop the basic cognitive, self-management and interpersonal skills on which occupational careers are founded. As noted earlier, beliefs concerning one's capabilities are influential determinants of the vocational life paths that are chosen.

It is one thing to get started in an occupational pursuit, it is another thing to do well and advance in it. Psychosocial skills contribute more heavily to career success than do occupational technical skills. Development of coping capabilities and skills in managing one's motivation, emotional states and thought processes increases perceived self-regulatory efficacy. The higher the sense of self-regulatory efficacy the better the occupational functioning. Rapid technological changes in the modern workplace are placing an increasing premium on higher problem-solving skills and resilient self-efficacy to cope effectively with job displacements and restructuring of vocational activities.

The transition to parenthood suddenly thrusts young adults into the expanded role of both parent and spouse. They now not only have to deal with the ever-changing challenges of raising children but to manage interdependent relationships within a family system and social links to many extrafamilial social systems including educational, recreational, medical, and caregiving facilities. Parents who are secure in their parenting efficacy shepherd their children adequately through the various phases of development without serious problems or severe strain on the marital relationship. But it can be a trying period for those who lack a sense of efficacy to manage the expanded familial demands. They are highly vulnerable to stress and depression.

By the middle years, people settle into established routines that stabilize their sense of personal efficacy in the major areas of functioning. However, the stability is a shaky one because life does not remain static. Rapid technological and social changes constantly require adaptations calling for self-reappraisals of capabilities. In their occupations, the middle-aged find themselves pressured by younger challengers. Situations in which people must compete for promotions, status, and even work itself, force constant self-appraisals of capabilities by means of social comparison with younger competitors.

G. Reappraisals of Self-Efficacy with Advancing Age

Major life changes in later years are brought about by retirement, relocation, and loss of friends or spouses. Such changes place demands on interpersonal skills to cultivate new social relationships that can contribute to positive functioning and personal well-being. Perceived social inefficacy increases older person's vulnerability to stress and depression both directly and indirectly by impeding development of social supports which serve as a buffer against life stressors.

SELF AND CREATIVITY

People differ in how they are creative and how they express their creativity. They differ in their interests, values, and needs, in how they process reality, observations, problems, and how they arrive at new combinations of phenomena. Commonsense observation confirms this, but it does not explain why the differences exist.

Thinking, feeling, sensation, and intuition are the functional types. Extraversion and introversion are the attitudinal orientations.

Adolescence has often been characterized as a period of psychosocial turmoil. While no period of life is ever free of problems, contrary to the stereotype of "storm and stress," most adolescents negotiate the important transitions of this period without undue disturbance or discord. However, youngsters who enter adolescence beset by a disabling sense of inefficacy transport their vulnerability to distress and debility to the new environmental demands. The ease with which the transition from childhood to the demands of adulthood is made similarly depends on the strength of personal efficacy built up through prior mastery experiences.

How Self-Image Is Related to Thinking

In trying to understand personality as the origin of your creative style, the functional type offers the crucial key – it gives the personality its particular direction, its stamp and flavor, while the attitudinal orientation describes the direction of creative energy.

According to Jung, there are two ways of perceiving: sensing, by which we become aware of thing directly through our five senses, and intuition, by which we comprehend ideas and associations indirectly, through the unconscious. Although everyone makes use of both ways of perceiving, for a particular individual one always predominates and is preferred.

Two ways of judging are by thinking, a logical process that attempts to be objective and impersonal, and by feeling, a process of appreciation that is subjective and personal.

Extravert, Introvert, or Somewhere Between

The introvert's main interests are in the inner world of personal or subjective events, concepts and ideas, and the extravert's are in the outer world of people and things. Therefore, when circumstances permit, the introvert prefers to direct perception and judgment upon ideas, whereas the extravert likes to direct both outwardly.

No one, of course, is exclusively one or the other. Most introverts can innovatively deal with the world about them when necessary, and extraverts can often deal effectively with ideas. But the introvert does his best work inside his head, in reflection, and the extravert does his best work externally, in action. In other case the preference for either introversion or extraversion remains, like a natural right- or left-handedness.

People usually underrate the value and strength of their primary functional and attitudinal direction.

Because these are so natural to them, they erroneously believe that everyone else is also similarly capable, and so do not truly appreciate their unique personality, capacities, and gifts for expressing creativity. For example, creative extraverts generate lots of ideas about events "out there," while the other is creative about things "in here."

Discover the type and source of your creativity as you uniquely experience and express it. Check twelve characteristics from the list below that describe you best as the personality you think you are.

There are eight personality types that Jung conceptualizes:

1. Extraverted thinking
2. Introverted thinking
3. Extraverted feeling
4. Introverted feeling
5. Extraverted sensing
6. Introverted sensing
7. Extraverted intuitive
8. Introverted intuitive

Dominant	dependable	easygoing	disciplines
curious	tactful	modest	imaginative
energetic	sensitive	involved	determined
sincere	analytical	bold	realistic
quick	committed	diplomatic	systematic
confident	enthusiastic	practical	warm
efficient	agreeable	cheerful	controlled
perceptive	adaptable	patient	decisive
persevering	considerate	objective	intellectual
friendly	organized	independent	logical
observant	mature	stable	conscientious
understanding	creative	loyal	soft-spoken
stimulating	factual	quiet	responsible
painstaking	reliable	ingenious	frank
persistent	cooperative	open-minded	thoughtful
clear thinking	reserved	idealistic	intelligent
forward-looking	persuasive	calm	

Answer

The following are the characteristics that are usually checked by the different types. Remember that there are no pure classifications and your self-perception may span several different categories, adding individuality and variety to your creative style.

Extraverted thinking	Introverted thinking	Extraverted intuitive	Introverted intuitive	Extraverted sensing	Introverted sensing	Extraverted feeling	Introverted feeling
dominant practical bold disciplined objective analytical conscientious logical decisive energetic confident responsible determined	analytical independent quiet disciplined curious adaptable clear thinking intellectual organized logical persistent efficient thoughtful	innovative enthusiastic imaginative confident persistent involved stimulating perceptive persuasive forward-looking mature serious energetic	creative persevering ingenious understanding soft-spoken reserved intelligent sincere observant determined patient persistent frank	realistic factual persuasive openminded easygoing tolerant efficient quick calm considerate tactful diplomatic friendly	dependable stable thorough factual systematic painstaking persevering reliable practical objective serious-minded effective conservative	friendly tactful warm cooperative enthusiastic cheerful agreeable understanding considerate loyal idealistic sympathetic gracious	modest cooperative sincere loyal understanding tolerant sensitive sympathetic committed independent controlled soft-spoken patient

The descriptions that follow analyze the eight basic types of creative personalities previously mentioned. Each type's creative style is described.

Extraverted-Thinking Type – "But the facts are…"

The extraverted-thinking type likes to take charge of things and run the whole show.

A disciplined thinker, this person respects objectivity, well-thought-out plans, and orderly procedures. Being strongly analytical and objectively critical, he or she is unlikely to be creative about, or persuaded by, anything but clear reasoning and logic. According to him, everyone's focus should be governed strictly by logic, and he is his own stern task-maker in this respect. He likes innovation that involves facts, figures, and concrete matters.

He enjoys manipulating the real world, and is unstinting in his efforts to act upon and implement his ideas. He likes to make decisions, is good at organizing plans and projects, and enjoys interplay with others. If his creative plans are carried out half-heartedly, he is capable of losing his temper. He tends to demand recognition of his performance by others, and believes that his approach to innovation and decision making is the only right one. Being strong-willed, he can intimidate people with ease and without feelings of guilt.

Introverted-Thinking Type – "I'll have to give it some further thought."

The introverted-thinking person prefers to analyze rather than control. He or she is good at creatively organizing ideas and facts, rather than people and situations. When absorbed in analysis or creative problem-solving, he remains markedly independent of external circumstances. He shows great perseverance and can easily work uninterruptedly on one novel idea for a long time, frequently to the exclusion of almost everything else.

Outwardly quiet, reserved, and sometimes withdraw, he can be detachedly curious about what is going on, and can be adaptable as long as his inner ruling principles are not violated. Although confident in the realm of ideas, this person requires time to arrive at decisions requiring action and implementation. He is ideally suited to working out the difficulties underlying a complex problem. Others can then do the implementing.

His or her major shortcoming is difficulty in communicating. The introverted-thinking type can state his creative ideas and solutions clearly and exactly, but keeps them so exact, abstract, and complicated that others frequently find it difficult to follow him.

Extraverted-Intuitive Type – "I have a hunch."

The extraverted-intuitive man or woman is the ebulliently enthusiastic innovator. Possessing a great deal of imagination, he or she constantly perceives new possibilities or new ways of doing things. This person is happiest dreaming up and initiating new ideas, and, by getting others involved, usually carries them out.

He is confident of the worth of his ideas, tireless in problem solving, and shows great ingenuity in tackling the difficulties or snags encountered. Having patience and stick-to-itiveness with complicated situations, this person can almost always be relied upon to discover creative solutions that work. He gets so involved in ideas that he thinks of little else.

Another of his positive attributes is the ability to animate, stimulate, and persuade others to accept his ideas. His perceptive and empathetic understanding of people enables him to win ready support.

His biggest problem is his aversion to uninspired routine, and he can hardly force himself to attend to humdrum details or projects alien to his major interests. Even his pet projects begin to pall and lose their challenge with time. What will happen next is more significant to him than what is happening in the here-and-now. As a result, he is happiest and most productive with a variety of creative challenges. Other individuals can then do the implementing once the major problems are solved.

Introverted-Intuitive Type – "Silence – genius at work."

The person is conventionally recognized as the true creator. He or she completely trusts intuitive insights. Complex and ambiguous problems stimulate him, and he sees many possibilities in situations that appear to others as "closed."

He tends to drive his associates as intensely as his own ideas drive him, and he backs up his creative insights with determination. He likes to have his ideas worked out, applied and accepted, and will spend any amount of time and effort to achieve this goal.

His Achilles' heel is his single-minded concentration and abhorrence of compromise. At times he seems so blinded by the value of his ideas and plans that he fails to see the conditions, circumstances, or other counter-forces that should be taken into account.

This person is effective in situation where boldly ingenious creativity is needed. Although his boldness may be of great value, reality-check is mandatory.

He creates in bursts of energy powered by excitement and enthusiasm, and feels smothered in routine full of small details. Where he may be lacking most is in judgment. He cannot comfortably listen to outside judgment or criticism of his ideas and insights, and is, at times, in danger of ignoring the real world. Nor always having the power to shape his ideas into effective action, he may appear to others as an impractical genius or crank, or simply a dreamer who indulges in fruitless fantasy.

He is little involved with others and needs minimal companionship.

Extraverted-Sensing Type – "The right tool for the right job."

This person is an adaptable realist who is keenly attuned to the concrete, the actual, and the factual. He always knows what the facts are because he notices, absorbs, and remembers more of them than anyone else around. There is a sort of effortless economy in the way he tackles concrete situations. Coupled with the ability to see and consider the needs of the moment is his resourcefulness in implementing plans and projects without delay.

Being a perceptive person, the extraverted-sensing type searches for the satisfying creative solution, instead of trying to impose any "should" or "ought" of his own; and his associates usually accept the unique compromises he arrives at. He tends to be open-minded, easygoing, unprejudiced, and tolerant of almost everyone. He knows how to manage conflict and is good at easing a tense situation or pulling warring factions together to bring a new creative idea into function.

CHAPTER 4

Introverted-Sensing Type – "The real meaning is not what it seems."

This person is very dependable. Like his extraverted-sensing counterpart, he also handles facts with ease, and can absorb, remember, and use a tremendous number of them. Everything for him has to be clearly stated and put on a factual basis before he attacks the issue.

He reacts to facts and problems in an individualistic way, but what he actually does about them is usually sound and valid. This is because he senses the deeper aspect of things. In his creative problem-solving he is thorough, painstaking, and systematic. He is patient with detail and routine and his persevering attitude has a stabilizing effect on others around him.

This person does not leap impulsively into projects, but once involved, it is difficult to distract, discourage, or stop him; and he is unstinting in the effort and time he expends. Unless circumstances convince him that he is on a wrong track, he will persist.

His practical judgment, memory for detail, and conservative bent make him consistent and reliable. He can always be counted on to cite cases to support his ideas. Responsibilities of maintenance and implementation are ideally suited for him.

His shortcoming is that he cannot readily empathize with needs that diverge radically from what he perceives are the needs of a situation, and he is apt to dismiss them out of hand. In his interpersonal relationships this person tends to be impersonal and rather passive. He accepts others as long as they don't try to interfere with what he is producing.

Extraverted-Feeling Type – "The more the merrier."

This person radiates good fellowship and is sensitive to emotional atmosphere. In relationships with others, he or she tends to be friendly, tactful, and sympathetic. Since his sense of security and well-being derives from the warmth of others, he can become quite upset by any display of indifference. Other people constitute the source for his creative inspirations.

The obvious forte of this type of person is in situations that deal with people, and he does his best creative thinking when talking with others. He is good at greeting people and often enjoys long telephone conversations, during which he gets many of his ideas. For him to be brief and businesslike requires special effort.

Since this person has to be constantly involved and interacting with others to be inspired, he tends to be impatient with long, slow situations or complicated procedures, especially when these require solitary absorption. His other shortcoming is tending to jump to conclusions and acting upon assumptions which may be wide of the mark.

He is drawn to those having similar creative traits and interests, and can be insensitive or blind to conflict and potentially explosive interpersonal situations, because of his strong desire to ignore unpleasant feelings and disharmony.

Introverted Feeling Type – "Still waters run deep."

This person has as much wealth of feeling as the feeling extravert, but he or she focuses more deeply on fewer things and has greater inner intensity. He, like the feeling extravert, puts duty and obligations first, but is more strongly guided by inner-directed values in the search for creative ideas and solutions.

He can be understanding, tolerant, and sensitive to other people's feelings as long as his deepest values and convictions are not challenged or threatened. He prefers to be left alone when problem solving, and has little need to impress, change, or persuade others.

The main problem of this person is that he tends to be overly sensitive and vulnerable to criticism and frequently suffers from a sense of inadequacy, even though he may be just as creative as the other types.

He exhibits practiced control of feelings, and his true motives generally remain concealed and secret. He is able to suppress negative feelings and judgments in an attempt to keep unpleasant situations at a distance.

THE MATURE PERSONALITY (ALLPORT, 1961)

Allport (1961) believed that the emergence of personal maturity is a continuous and lifelong process of becoming. He also saw a qualitative difference between the mature and the immature or neurotic personality. The behavior of mature persons is functionally autonomous and is motivated by conscious processes. In contrast, the behavior of immature persons is dominated by unconscious motives stemming from childhood experiences. According to Allport, the psychologically mature adult is characterized by six attributes:

1. The mature person has a *widely extended sense of self*. Truly mature persons can get "outside" of themselves. They actively participate in work, family and social relationships, hobbies, political and religious issues, or whatever else they experience as valuable. Each activity required authentic ego involvement and commitment resulting in some direction to life. For Allport, self-love is a prominent factor in everyone's life, but it need not dominate the person's life-style.

2. The mature person has a *capacity for warm social interactions*. There are two kinds of interpersonal warmth subsumed under this criterion – intimacy and compassion. The intimate aspect of warmth is seen in a person's capacity to show deep love for family and close friends unencumbered by possessive and jealous feelings. Compassion is reflected in a person's ability to tolerate differences (concerning values or attitudes) between the self and others, which allows the person to show profound respect and appreciation for the human condition and a sense of kinship with all people.

3. The mature person demonstrates *emotional security and self-acceptance*. Mature adults have a positive image of themselves and are thus able to tolerate frustrating or irritating events as well as their own shortcomings without becoming inwardly bitter or hostile. They also deal with their emotional states (e.g., depression, anger, guilt) in such a way that they do not interfere with the well-being of the others. For example, if they are having a bad day, the do not fly off the handle at the first person they see. Furthermore, they express their beliefs and feelings with consideration for those of others.

4. The mature person demonstrates *realistic perception, skills, and assignments*. Healthy people see things as they are, not as they wish them to be. They are in direct contact with reality; they do not continually distort it perceptually to fit their needs and fantasies. Moreover, healthy people possess appropriate skills for their work, provisionally setting aside personal desires and impulses while a task takes precedence.

5. The mature person demonstrates *self-insight and humor*. Socrates observed that there is one paramount rule for achieving the good life: "Know thyself." Allport called this "self-objectification." By it, he meant that mature adults have an accurate picture of their own strengths and weaknesses. Humor is an important ingredient in self-insight because it prevents pompous self-glorification and just plane phoniness.

6. The mature person has a *unifying philosophy of life*. Mature adults can "put it all together" with a clear, consistent, and systematic way of seeing meaning in their lives. Allport noted that people do not have to be an Aristotle in order to comprehend life's purpose in terms of an intelligible theory. Instead, they simply need a value system that will present them with a dominant goal or theme that makes their lives meaningful. Different people may develop different central values around which their lives will purposefully revolve. They may choose the pursuit of truth, social welfare, religion, or whatever – there is no one best value or philosophy in Allport's opinion.

SUMMARY

1. Self-Concept: The collection of an individual's thoughts, feelings, and beliefs about him/herself. An individual's internal representation of who s/he is.

2. Self: while this term is sometimes used interchangeably with "Self-Concept" the self refers to the agent - the active doer who has thoughts, feelings, and beliefs. The self-concept is different because it is the sum of the thoughts, feelings, and beliefs that the person has about him/herself.

3. Self-Views: Self-perceptions in specific domains, (e.g. your thoughts, feelings, and beliefs about who you are as a student). The sum of all your self-views is then your Self-Concept.

4. Self Esteem: The feelings of worth one has about oneself as a whole. Self-Concept Formation

5. Four Components of Self-Concept
   - Body Image
   - Role Performance
   - Personal Identity
   - Self-Esteem

6. Factors that influence the self-concept formation:
   - THE REACTION OF OTHERS. If people admire you, flatter you, seek out your company, listen attentively and share your values and ideas you tend to develop a positive self-image. If they avoid you, neglect you, tell you things about yourself that you don't want to hear you develop a negative self-image.
   - COMPARISON WITH OTHERS. If the people we compare ourselves with (our reference group) appear to be more successful, happier, richer, better looking than ourselves we tend to develop a negative self image BUT if they are less successful than us our image will be positive.
   - SOCIAL ROLES. Some social roles carry prestige e.g. doctor, airline pilot, TV presenter, premiership footballer and this promotes self-esteem. Other roles carry stigma. E.g., prisoner, mental hospital patient, refuses collector or unemployed person. The content of self-concepts reflects the content and organization of society. This is evident with regard to the roles that are internalized as role-identities (e.g., father, student).
   - IDENTIFICATION. Roles aren't just "out there." They also become part of your personality i.e. your identity with the position you occupy, the roles you play and the groups you belong to. Self efficacy is defined as a person's belief that he/she can successfully execute a behavior required to produce a given result.

7. Self-efficacy refers to an individual's convictions and beliefs about his or her abilities to mobilize
   - COGNITIVE (learned by awareness, understood)
   - MOTIVATIONAL (desire held an expectancy and belief that it will be realized)
   - BEHAVIORAL (change to gain results)

   facilities needed to successfully execute a specific task within a given context.

My Self Image (Winner and Losers) Check List

In the following list of statements, use a tick mark against those that fit to your self image. Use a cross mark against those that do not fit. Use a question mark against statements that you are unsure about. Don't stay on a question for long time. Answer each question quickly.

How Self-Image Is Related to Thinking

1. I like myself
2. I am afraid of or hurt by others
3. People can trust me
4. I usually say the right things
5. I feel bad about myself
6. I am fearful of the future
7. I depend on others for ideas
8. I use my talents entirely
9. I think for my self
10. I know my feelings
11. I don't understand myself
12. I manage time well
13. People avoid me
14. I am not interested in community problems
15. I enjoy work
16. I enjoy Nature I don't enjoy work
17. I trust myself
18. I usually say the wrong things
19. I am not happy with my gender
20. I am discouraged about life
21. I don't like to be around people
22. I have not developed my talents
23. I am happy with my gender
24. I often do the wrong things
25. I am involved in solving the community problems
26. People like to be around me
27. I am competent on the job
28. I enjoy life
29. I don't like myself.

Winners

Now that you have taken the self-check test mentioned above, check your responses by tallying them with the winner traits given below. Everyone is born to win. You too can be a winner. Start changing for better.

A winner:

1. Loves and accepts him/herself
2. Values his/her uniqueness
3. Wants to and tries to improve himself
4. Is responsible for their behavior
5. People can trust him/her
6. Tries to achieve
7. Thinks positive
8. Feels confident about his abilities to achieve
9. Uses his talents
10. Faces challenges
11. Does not play helpless or the blaming games
12. Has purposes or goals and takes steps to achieve them
13. Uses his/her time well
14. Thinks for himself
15. Knows and expresses his/her feelings
16. Cares for other people
17. Can get and give affection
18. Has good friends
19. Enjoy work, play and life

How Self-Image Is Related to Thinking

    20. Does not hurt other people
    21. Winners sometimes lose and they also make mistakes but they learn from their mistakes.

Losers
A loser:

    1. Does not like and value him/herself
    2. Feels unsure of him/herself and his/her capabilities
    3. …

Finish this list.

CHAPTER 5

What Is Intelligence?

Are you smart? How smart are you? How psychologists measure "smartness" (intelligence)? Is intelligence a stable quality? Can you change your intelligence? Is intelligence related to success?

LEARNING OBJECTIVES

After reading this chapter, you will be able to

1. Define intelligence
2. Describe, discuss, compare and contrast intelligence tests
3. Compare and contrast seven intelligences (Gardner)
4. Distinguish the components of intelligence
5. Measure your personal intelligence.

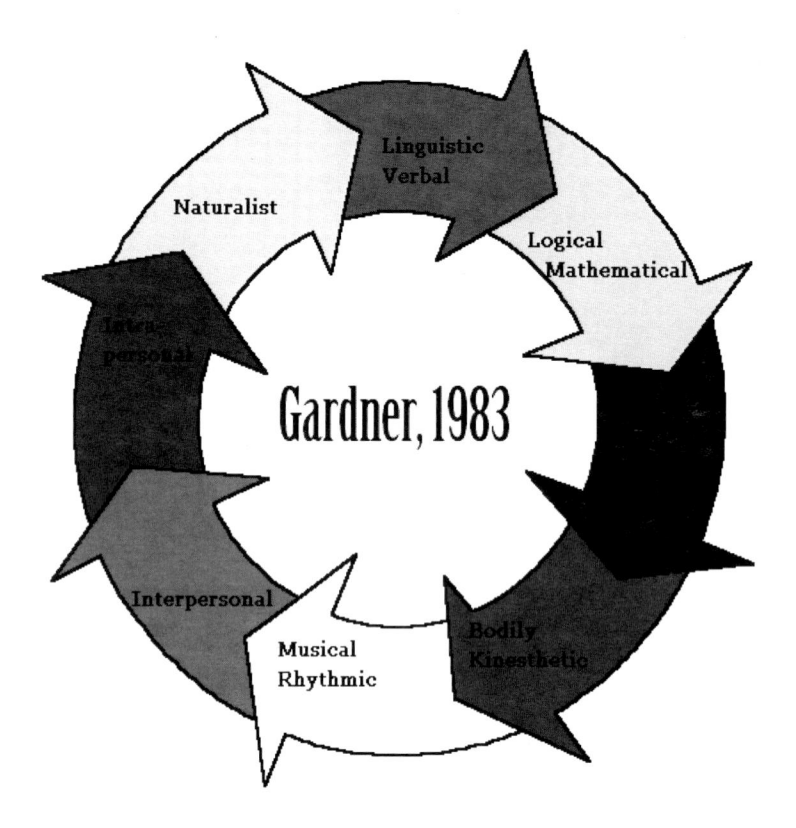

Trials, temptations, disappointments -- all these are helps instead of hindrances, if one uses them rightly. They not only test the fibre of a character, but strengthen it. Every conquered temptation represents a new fund of moral energy. Every trial endured and weathered in the right spirit makes a soul nobler and stronger than it was before.
~ James Buckham

Aim at the sun and you may not reach it; but your arrow will fly far higher than if you had aimed at an object on a level with yourself.
~ F. Hawes

The characteristic of genuine heroism is its persistency. All men have wandering impulses, fits and starts of generosity. But when you have resolved to be great, abide by yourself, and do not try to reconcile yourself with the world. The heroic cannot be common, nor the common heroic.
~ Ralph Waldo Emerson

"We find greatest joy, not in getting, but in expressing what we are... Men do not really live for honors or for pay; their gladness is not the taking and holding, but in doing, the striving, the building, the living. It is a higher joy to teach than to be taught. It is good to get justice, but better to do it; fun to have things but more to make them. The happy man is he who lives the life of love, not for the honors it may bring, but for the life itself."
~ R.J. Baughan

That only which we have within, can we see without. If we meet no Gods, it is because we harbor none. If there is a grandeur in you, you will find grandeur in porters and sweeps.
~ Ralph Waldo Emerson

What Is Intelligence?
INTELLIGENCE: HISTORY OF STUDY

IQ is often measured because it correlates well with success in a variety of life events. People with high IQs generally finish a higher level of education, have bigger incomes, do better at their jobs, have lower violent crime rates and have better health. It should be noted that IQ seems to be independent of self-assessed levels of happiness. E. G. Boring, a well-known Harvard psychologist in the 1920's defined intelligence as *whatever intelligence tests measure*. Wechsler, one of the most influential researchers in the area of intelligence defined it as *the global capacity of a person to act purposefully, to think rationally, and to deal effectively with his/her environment*. Many modern psychology textbooks would accept a working definition of intelligence as *the general ability to perform cognitive tasks*. Others might favor a more behaviorally-oriented definition such as *the capacity to learn from experience* or *the capacity to adapt to one's environment*. Sternberg has combined these two viewpoints into the following: *Intelligence is the cognitive ability of an individual to learn from experience, to reason well, to remember important information, and to cope with the demands of daily living*.

Intelligence is composed of three main elements:

1. Practical problem-solving ability

2. Verbal ability

3. Social Skills

Measuring Intelligence

There are numerous intelligence tests. The first IQ test was originated by Alfred Binet (1857-1911) to measure, objectively, comprehension, reasoning, and judgment. Binet was motivated by a powerful enthusiasm for the emerging discipline of psychology and a desire to overcome the cultural and class prejudices of late nineteenth-century France in the assessment of children's academic potential. Although the traditional concept of IQ was a breakthrough at the time of its formulation, contemporary research shows that it suffers from two significant flaws. To understand IQ (Intelligence Quotient), you should first have an idea about what intelligence is. IQ scores reflect general capacity for performing intellectual tasks, such as solving verbal and mathematical problems.

The average IQ score is 100. The standard deviation of IQ scores is 15. So, this means:
- 50% of people have IQ scores between 90 and 110
- 2.5% of people are very superior in intelligence (over 130)
- 2.5% of people are mentally deficient / impaired / retarded (under 70)
- 0.5% of people are near genius or genius (over 140).

There have been various classification systems for IQ.
Terman's classification was (6):

IQ Range	Classification
140 and over	Genius or near genius
120-140	Very superior intelligence
110-120	Superior intelligence
90-110	Normal or average intelligence
80-90	Dullness
70-80	Borderline deficiency
Below 70	Definite feeble-mindedness

Although it is hard to overstate geniuses brilliance, recent scientific research reveals that people usually underestimated their potential for learning and creativity (Gelb, 1998). Ninety-five percent of what we know about the capabilities of the human brain has been learned in the last twenty years. Schools, universities, and corporations are only beginning to apply this emerging understanding of human potential.

High IQ and Genius IQ

Wechsler thought that it would be much more legitimate to base his classifications on the Probable Error (PE) so his classification was (6):

Classification	IQ Limits	Percent Included
Very Superior	128 and over	2.2
Superior	120-127	6.7
Bright Normal	111-119	16.1
Average	91-110	50
Dull Normal	80-90	16.1
Borderline	66-79	6.7
Defective	65 and below	2.2

Genius IQ is generally considered to begin around 140 to 145, representing ~.25% of the population (1 in 400). Here is a rough guide:

115-124 - Above average (e.g., university students)
125-134 - Gifted (e.g., post-graduate students)
135-144 - Highly gifted (e.g., intellectuals)
145-154 - Genius (e.g., professors)
155-164 - Genius (e.g., Nobel Prize winners)
165-179 - High genius
180-200 - Highest genius
>200 – "Unmeasurable genius"
(Terman wrote the Stanford-Binet test (1), which has a SD of 16.)

Mental deficiency is now generally called mental retardation. The following is the currently used classification of retardation in the USA (5):

IQ Range	Classification
50-69	Mild
35-49	Moderate
20-34	Severe
below 20	Profound

Moreover, "educable mentally retarded" is roughly equivalent to mild mental retardation, and "trainable" mentally retarded is roughly equivalent to moderate (5). The DSM now requires an assessment of a person's adaptive functioning as an additional criterion for labeling someone retarded. IQ is not enough. Maybe the same sort of thing should be done for labeling somebody a genius.

The Highest IQs On Record	
People Still Alive	**From the Past**
• Physicist / Engineer Kim Ung-yong has a verified IQ of 210 • Bouncer Christopher Michael Langan has a verified IQ of 195 • Engineer Philip Emeagwali is alleged to have an IQ of 190 • World Chess Champion Garry Kasparov is alleged to have an IQ of 190 • Author Marilyn Vos Savant has a verified IQ of 186 • Actor James Woods is alleged to have an IQ of 180 • Politician John H. Sununu is alleged to have an IQ of 180 • Prime Minister Benjamin Netanyahu is alleged to have an IQ of 180 • Mathematician Andrew Wiles is alleged to have an IQ of 170 • World Chess Champion Judith Polgar is alleged to have an IQ of 170 • Chess Grandmaster Robert Byrne is alleged to have an IQ of 170 • Mathematician / Physicist Stephen W. Hawking is alleged to have an IQ of over 160 • Microsoft Founder Paul Allen is alleged to have an IQ of over 160 • Actress Sharon Stone is alleged to have an IQ of 154	• 190 - Ludwig Wittgenstein • 190 - Sir Isaac Newton • 190 - François-Marie Arouet (Voltaire) • 180 - Leonardo da Vinci • 180 - David Hume • 180 - Buonarroti Michelangelo • 179 - Johann Wolfgang von Goethe • 176 - Emanuel Swedenborg • 176 - Gottfried Wilhelm von Leibniz • 175 - Johannes Kepler • 175 - Edmund Spenser • 175 - Baruch Spinoza • 174 - John Stuart Mill • 171 - Blaise Pascal • 170 - Michael Faraday • 170 - George Frederic Handel • 170 - Antoine Lavoisier • 170 - Martin Luther • 165 - Galileo Galilei • 165 - Charlotte Brontë • 165 - Johann Sebastian Bach • 165 - Thomas Hobbes • 165 - Carl Linnaeus • 165 - John Locke • 165 - Joseph Priestley • 165 - Ludwig van Beethoven • 165 - Samuel Johnson • 162 - René Descartes • 160 - Albert Einstein • 160 - Robert Boyle • 160 - Benjamin Franklin • 159 - Immanuel Kant • 156 - Linus Carl Pauling

The first flaw is the idea that intelligence is fixed at birth and immutable. Although individuals are endowed genetically with more or less talent in a given area, researchers such as Buzan, Machado, Wenger, and many others, have shown that IQ scores can be raised significantly through appropriate training.

What Is Intelligence?

The second weakness in the commonly held concept of intelligence is the idea that the verbal and mathematical reasoning skills measured by IQ tests (and SATs) are the *sine qua nons* of intelligence. This narrow view of intelligence has been thoroughly demystified by contemporary psychological research. In his modern classic, *Frames of Mind* (1983), psychologist Howard Gardner and his colleagues catalogued twenty-five different subintelligences).

GARDNER'S MULTIPLE INTELLIGENCES THEORY

Criteria for Establishing Distinct Intelligences:

1. Isolation by brain damage
2. The existence of individuals with exceptional talent
3. A distinct developmental history
4. An evolutionary history
5. A set of core operations
6. Experimental evidence
7. Encoding in a symbol system

Definition: A human intellectual competence must entail a set of skills of problem solving - enabling the individual to resolve genuine problems or difficulties that he or she encounters and, when appropriate, to create an effective product--and must also entail the potential for finding or creating problems - thereby laying the groundwork for the acquisition of new knowledge (Gardner, 1983, p. 62).

	Gardner's Multiple Intelligences (Seven Original Plus 1 Additional)	
Symbol Analyst Intelligences	**Verbal-Linguistic**	
	Core element: ability to make a rapid conversion from a physical representation of stimuli (i.e., letters and/or other verbal symbols) to higher-level codes; ability to manipulate information in activated memory	Examples: William Shakespeare, Emily Dickinsin, Jorge Luis Borges
	Logical-mathematical	
	Core element: ability to generalize from specific experiences and form new, more abstract concepts and rules; ability to reason quickly and well; ability to reason quantitatively	Examples: Stephen Hawking, Isaac Newton, Marie Curie
Non-canonical (normally described) Intelligences	**Musical**	
	Core elements: translate written symbols into pitch, rhythm, timbre	Examples: Mozart, George Gershwin, Ella Fitzgerald
	Spatial-Mechanical	
	Core element: ability to visualize and mentally rotate a stimulus or stimulus array	Examples: Mickelangelo, Georgia O'Keefe, Bickminster Fuller
	Bodily-Kinesthetic	
	Core element: control of one's bodily motions and capacity to handle objects skillfully	Examples: Morihei Ueshiba, Muhammad Ali, F. M. Alexander
	Naturalist	
	Core element: ability to discern differences in the living environment	Examples: Charles Darwin, Carl Linney, Luis Paster
Personal Intelligences	**Interpersonal-Social**	
	Core element: ability to notice and make distinctions among other individuals and, in particular, among their moods, temperaments, motivations, and intentions	Examples: Nelson Mandela, Mahatma Gandhi, Queen Elizabeth 1
	Intrapersonal (Self-knowledge)	
		Examples: Victor Frankl, Thich Nhat Hanh, Mother Teresa.

The more detailed diagram below expands the detail for the original seven intelligences shown above, and also suggests ideas for applying the model and underpinning theories, so as to optimize thinking and learning.

Intelligence Type	Description	Typical Roles	Related Tasks, Activities or Tests	Preferred Learning Style Clues
Linguistic	**words and language**, written and spoken; retention, interpretation and explanation of ideas and information via language, understands relationship between communication and meaning	writers, lawyers, journalists, speakers, trainers, copy-writers, English teachers, poets, editors, linguists, translators, PR consultants, media consultants, TV and radio presenters, voice-over artistes	write a set of instructions; speak on a subject; edit a written piece or work; write a speech; commentate on an event; apply positive or negative 'spin' to a story	words and language
Logical-Mathematical	**logical thinking**, detecting patterns, scientific reasoning and deduction; analyze problems, perform mathematical calculations, understands cause and effect relationship towards a tangible outcome or result	scientists, engineers, computer experts, accountants, statisticians, researchers, analysts, traders, bankers bookmakers, insurance brokers, negotiators, deal-makers, trouble-shooters, directors	perform a mental arithmetic calculation; create a process to measure something difficult; analyze how a machine works; create a process; devise a strategy to achieve an aim; assess the value of a business or a proposition	numbers and logic
Musical	**musical ability**, awareness, appreciation and use of sound; recognition of tonal and rhythmic patterns, understands relationship between sound and feeling	musicians, singers, composers, DJ's, music producers, piano tuners, acoustic engineers, entertainers, party-planners, environment and noise advisors, voice coaches	perform a musical piece; sing a song; review a musical work; coach someone to play a musical instrument; specify mood music for telephone systems and receptions	music, sounds, rhythm
Bodily-Kinesthetic	**body movement control**, manual dexterity, physical agility and balance; eye and body coordination	dancers, demonstrators, actors, sports-people, soldiers, fire-fighters, PTI's, performance artistes; osteopaths, fishermen, drivers, crafts-people; gardeners, chefs, healers, adventurers	juggle; demonstrate a sports technique; flip a beer-mat; create a mime to explain something; toss a pancake; fly a kite; coach workplace posture, assess work-station ergonomics	physical experience and movement, touch and feel
Spatial-Visual	**visual and spatial perception**; interpretation and creation of visual images; pictorial imagination and expression; understands relationship between images and meanings, and between space and effect	artists, designers, cartoonists, story-boarders, architects, photographers, sculptors, town-planners, visionaries, inventors, engineers, cosmetics and beauty consultants	design a costume; interpret a painting; create a room layout; create a corporate logo; design a building; pack a suitcase or the boot of a car	pictures, shapes, images, 3D space
Interpersonal	**perception of other people's feelings**; ability to relate to others; interpretation of behavior and communications; understands the relationships between people and their situations, including other people	therapists, HR professionals, leaders, counselors, politicians, educators, sales-people, clergy, psychologists, teachers, doctors, healers, advertising, coaches professionals, mentors; (clear association between this type of intelligence and what is now termed 'Emotional Intelligence'.	interpret moods from facial expressions; demonstrate feelings through body language; affect the feelings of others in a planned way; coach or counsel another person	human contact, communications, cooperation, teamwork
Intrapersonal	**self-awareness**, personal cognizance, personal objectivity, the capability to understand oneself, one's relationship to others and the world, and one's own need for, and reaction to change	anyone who is self-aware and involved in the process of changing personal thoughts, beliefs and behavior in relation to their situation, other people, their purpose and aims; there is a similarity to Maslow's Self-Actualization level, association between this type of intelligence and 'Emotional Intelligence'	consider and decide one's own aims and personal changes required to achieve them (not necessarily reveal this to others); consider one's own 'Johari Window', and decide options for development; consider and decide one's own position in relation to the Emotional Intelligence model	self-reflection, self-discovery

What Is Intelligence?

Another way to group these intelligences is:

- Symbol manipulation - Linguistic, Logical-mathematical, and Musical
- Person-related - Interpersonal, Intrapersonal, and Existential
- Object-related - Spatial, Bodily-kinesthetic, and Naturalist

The theory of multiple intelligences is now accepted widely and when combined with the realization that intelligence can be developed throughout life, offers a powerful inspiration for aspiring Renaissance men and women.

Contemporary psychological research has revealed startling truths about the extent of human potential. Human brain:
- is more flexible and multidimensional than any supercomputer
- can learn seven facts per second, every second, for the rest of one's life and still have plenty of room left to learn more
- will improve with age if one uses it properly
- is unique. Of the six billion people currently living and the more than ninety billion people who have ever lived, there has never been anyone identical (except identical twins)
- is capable of making a virtually unlimited number of synaptic connections or potential patterns of thought.

Sternberg believes that intelligence is comprised of three separate, though interrelated abilities: analytical, creative, and practical.

	Abilities of Intelligence
Analytical	try to solve familiar problems by using strategies that manipulate the elements of a problem or the relationship among the elements (e.g., comparing, analyzing)
Creative	try to solve new kinds of problems that require us to think about the problem and its elements in a new way (e.g., inventing, designing)
Practical	try to solve problems that apply what we know to everyday contexts (e.g., applying, using)

STERNBERG'S THEORY

Sternberg hypothesizes that intelligence relates to, and is demonstrated in, three different aspects: (1) the internal world of information processing, (2) experience and past learning, and (3) the external world of adapting to, shaping and selecting real-world environments.

The components of intelligence describes the structure of cognitive processes that are used to adapt to, shape, or select real-world environments.

	Components of Intelligence (Internal World)
Metacomponents	higher-order mental processes used in planning, monitoring, and evaluating performance of a task; these are "executive" functions guide the use of other components
Performance components	mental processes used in the performance of a task; probably best measured by current intelligence tests
Knowledge-Acquisition components	mental processes used in learning

CHAPTER 5

Intelligence is demonstrated in two complimentary ways: a person's ability to deal with novelty or new aspects on one's environment and how quickly one makes new information processing automatic.

Intelligence and Prior Knowledge (Experience and Past Learning)	
Dealing with Novelty	intelligence is the ability to learn and think within new conceptual systems, which can then be brought to bear upon already existing knowledge
Automatizing Information Processing	complex verbal, mathematical, and other tasks can feasibly be executed only because many of the operations involved in their performance have been automatized

Intelligence is not only one's ability to adapt to one's environment; it also includes changing that environment or selecting a new one.

Dealing With Real-world Contexts (External World)	
Adapting to	Sometimes one displays one's intelligence by demonstrating an ability to adapt to the situation or context one finds oneself in. This is the primary aspect of intelligence that is considered by psychometricians, learning theorists, and other cognitivists such as Piaget
Shaping	Sometimes it is necessary to demonstrate one's intelligence by shaping or changing the environment so that it better meets one's needs. Vygotsky and dynamical systems theorists focus on this aspect of intelligence.
Selecting	There are times when it is necessary to demonstrate one's intelligence by selecting an alternate environment or context within which to live and work. Not all environments should be adapted to and some are not worth trying to change.

One of the most important parts of Sternberg's work on intelligence is his Adaptive Behavior Checklist. Because he considers intelligence as a set of skills, each of the behaviors on the checklist is considered modifiable.

Which of these have we been working on in this class?

Which of these have you worked on in other college-level courses?

Which of these do you work on in classes you teach?

What Is Intelligence?

	Sternberg's Adaptive Behavior Checklist
Practical Problem-Solving Ability	• Reasons logically and well • Identifies connections among ideas • Sees all aspects of a problem • Keeps an open mind and responds thoughtfully to others' ideas • Sizes up situations well • Gets to the heart of problems • Interprets information accurately • Makes good decisions • Goes to original sources for basic information • Poses problems in an optimal way • Is a good source of ideas • Perceives implied assumptions and conclusions • Deals with problems resourcefully
Verbal Ability	• Speaks clearly and articulately and is verbally fluent • Converses well • Is knowledgeable about a particular area of subject matter • Studies hard • Reads widely with high comprehension • Writes without difficulty • Sets aside time for reading • Displays good vocabulary
Social Competence	• Accepts others for what they are • Admits mistakes • Displays interest in the world at large • Is on time for appointments • Has social conscience • Thinks before speaking and doing • Makes fair judgments • Assesses well the relevance of information to a problem at hand • Is sensitive to other people's needs and desires • Displays interest in the immediate environment

Sternberg recognizes that intelligence is only one explanation of why some people succeed and why others do not. These reasons have been arranged in terms of Huitt's (2003) Systems Model of Human Behavior.

What are some benefits of this arrangement with respect to helping you learn and remember these reasons?

Do you agree with the classification scheme?

How would you modify it?

CHAPTER 5

Sternberg's Beliefs About Why Intelligent People Fail	
Cognitive-Oriented Reasons	• Distractibility and lack of concentration • Spreading oneself too thin or too thick • Inability or unwillingness to see the forest for the trees • Lack of balance between critical, analytic thinking and creative, synthetic thinking • Using the wrong abilities
Affective/Socially-Oriented Reasons	• Misattribution of blame • Fear of failure • Excessive self-pity • Excessive dependency • Wallowing in personal difficulties • Too little or too much self-confidence
Conative/Volitionally- Oriented Reasons	• Failure to initiate • Lack of motivation • Lack of perseverance and perseveration • Inability to complete tasks and to follow through • Lack of impulse control • Inability to translate thought into action • Procrastination • Lack of product orientation • Inability to delay gratification

Interesting Facts

- Alfred Binet launched the field of psychological testing. He was asked by the French minister of public education to develop a test that could be used to identify children who would have difficulty in school so that they could be given special instruction. The Stanford-Binet intelligence scale which is still in use today was developed in 1916 when Lewis Terman, a psychologist from Stanford university, translated into English and revised the tasks created by Binet and his collaborator Theodore Simon in 1904.
- The most commonly used IQ tests for adults and children were developed by David Wechsler (1896-1981). Building on Binet's pioneering work the Wechsler scales came to embody the psychometric assessment of intelligence. The Stanford-Binet and the Wechsler Series tests are standardized tests, which have to be individually administered and interpreted by a trained psychologist. A slew of group tests which purport to measure intelligence were also created for mass, easy administration in a variety of educational, occupational and military contexts. Furthermore, tests similar to IQ tests, such as the SAT and GRE, are widely used for selection and evaluation within the education system.
- In 1904 the British psychologist Charles Spearman proposed the existence of a general intelligence factor, g. He based this theory on a statistical technique which he invented, called factor analysis. Since its introduction, the factor g has been the cornerstone of psychometric models of intelligence. Furthermore, Spearman's g has often been used by researchers and theoreticians to make the case for the genetic basis of intelligence and to downplay the importance of environmental influences.
- The nature versus nurture debate in the context of the study of human intelligence is by far the most viciously contested aspect of this field. This is the case because psychometric IQ tests have been misused to label certain ethnic and racial groups as superior or inferior based on the belief that these tests measure genetically based, non-modifiable aspects of human performance. This strong genetic determinism view is also used for the promotion of the neoconservative political agenda calling for the abolition of affirmative action, as well as early intervention programs such as Head Start, which attempt to compensate for detrimental environmental factors experienced by certain groups within society. Even worse, genetic determinism of intelligence serves the eugenics movement, which argues for genetic selection to produce superior human beings.
- An additional important controversy surrounds the issue of the validity of IQ tests. That is, do such tests measure what they were intended to measure, namely, human intelligence. Prominent current researchers of human intelligence, such as Robert Sternberg and Howard Gardner, argue that IQ tests measure only a very narrow aspect of human intellectual performance. Such researchers also highlight the crucial importance of considering the cultural context for a proper evaluation of performance. Recently, Mayer & Salovey and Goleman argued for a further extension of the concept of intelligence to include emotional intelligence.

SUMMARY

1. Intelligence is composed of three main elements: practical-problem solving ability, verbal ability and social skill.

2. The first IQ test was originated by Alfred Binet (1857-1911) to measure, objectively, comprehension, reasoning.

3. IQ scores reflect general capacity for performing intellectual tasks, such as solving verbal and mathematical problems. The average IQ score is 100. The standard deviation of IQ scores is 15.

4. Gardner (1983) developed theory of multiple intelligence that includes linguistic, logical-mathematical, musical, bodily-kinesthetic, spatial-visual, interpersonal, and intrapersonal intelligences.

5. Only 2 people out of 100 score above 130 on IQ tests. These bright individuals are usually described as "gifted." Less than one-half of one percent of the population scores above 140.

MULTIPLE INTELLIGENCES INVENTORY (Walter McKenzie, 1999)

Part I

Complete each section by placing a "1" next to each statement you feel accurately describes you. If you do not identify with a statement, leave the space provided blank. Then total the column in each section.

Section 1

_____ I enjoy categorizing things by common traits
_____ Ecological issues are important to me
_____ Classification helps me make sense of new data
_____ I enjoy working in a garden
_____ I believe preserving our National Parks is important
_____ Putting things in hierarchies makes sense to me
_____ Animals are important in my life
_____ My home has a recycling system in place
_____ I enjoy studying biology, botany and/or zoology
_____ I pick up on subtle differences in meaning

_____ TOTAL for Section 1

Section 2

_____ I easily pick up on patterns
_____ I focus in on noise and sounds
_____ Moving to a beat is easy for me
_____ I enjoy making music
_____ I respond to the cadence of poetry
_____ I remember things by putting them in a rhyme
_____ Concentration is difficult for me if there is background noise

_____ Listening to sounds in nature can be very relaxing
_____ Musicals are more engaging to me than dramatic plays
_____ Remembering song lyrics is easy for me

_____ TOTAL for Section 2

Section 3

_____ I am known for being neat and orderly
_____ Step-by-step directions are a big help
_____ Problem solving comes easily to me
_____ I get easily frustrated with disorganized people
_____ I can complete calculations quickly in my head
_____ Logic puzzles are fun
_____ I can't begin an assignment until I have all my "ducks in a row"
_____ Structure is a good thing
_____ I enjoy troubleshooting something that isn't working properly
_____ Things have to make sense to me or I am dissatisfied

_____ TOTAL for Section 3

Section 4

_____ It is important to see my role in the "big picture" of things
_____ I enjoy discussing questions about life
_____ Religion is important to me
_____ I enjoy viewing art work
_____ Relaxation and meditation exercises are rewarding to me
_____ I like traveling to visit inspiring places
_____ I enjoy reading philosophers
_____ Learning new things is easier when I see their real world application
_____ I wonder if there are other forms of intelligent life in the universe
_____ It is important for me to feel connected to people, ideas and beliefs

_____ TOTAL for Section 4

Section 5

_____ I learn best interacting with others
_____ I enjoy informal chat and serious discussion
_____ The more the merrier
_____ I often serve as a leader among peers and colleagues
_____ I value relationships more than ideas or accomplishments
_____ Study groups are very productive for me
_____ I am a "team player"
_____ Friends are important to me
_____ I belong to more than three clubs or organizations
_____ I dislike working alone

_____ TOTAL for Section 5

Section 6

_____ I learn by doing
_____ I enjoy making things with my hands

What Is Intelligence?

_____ Sports are a part of my life
_____ I use gestures and non-verbal cues when I communicate
_____ Demonstrating is better than explaining
_____ I love to dance
_____ I like working with tools
_____ Inactivity can make me more tired than being very busy
_____ Hands-on activities are fun
_____ I live an active lifestyle

_____ TOTAL for Section 6

Section 7

_____ Foreign languages interest me
_____ I enjoy reading books, magazines and web sites
_____ I keep a journal
_____ Word puzzles like crosswords or jumbles are enjoyable
_____ Taking notes helps me remember and understand
_____ I faithfully contact friends through letters and/or e-mail
_____ It is easy for me to explain my ideas to others
_____ I write for pleasure
_____ Puns, anagrams and spoonerisms are fun
_____ I enjoy public speaking and participating in debates

_____ TOTAL for Section 7

Section 8

_____ My attitude effects how I learn
_____ I like to be involved in causes that help others
_____ I am keenly aware of my moral beliefs
_____ I learn best when I have an emotional attachment to the subject
_____ Fairness is important to me
_____ Social justice issues interest me
_____ Working alone can be just as productive as working in a group
_____ I need to know why I should do something before I agree to do it
_____ When I believe in something I give more effort towards it
_____ I am willing to protest or sign a petition to right a wrong

_____ TOTAL for Section 8

Section 9

_____ Rearranging a room and redecorating are fun for me
_____ I enjoy creating my own works of art
_____ I remember better using graphic organizers
_____ I enjoy all kinds of entertainment media
_____ Charts, graphs and tables help me interpret data
_____ A music video can make me more interested in a song
_____ I can recall things as mental pictures
_____ I am good at reading maps and blueprints
_____ Three dimensional puzzles are fun
_____ I can visualize ideas in my mind

_____ TOTAL for Section 9

Part II

Now carry forward your total from each section and multiply by 10 below:

Section	Total Forward	Multiply	Score
1		X10	
2		X10	
3		X10	
4		X10	
5		X10	
6		X10	
7		X10	
8		X10	
9		X10	

Part III

Now plot your scores on the bar graph provided:

	Sec 1	Sec 2	Sec 3	Sec 4	Sec 5	Sec 6	Sec 7	Sec 8	Sec 9
100									
90									
80									
70									
60									
50									
40									
30									
20									
10									
0									

Part IV

Key:

Section 1 – This reflects your Naturalist strength
Section 2 – This suggests your Musical strength
Section 3 – This indicates your Logical strength
Section 4 – This illustrates your Existential strength
Section 5 – This shows your Interpersonal strength
Section 6 – This tells your Kinesthetic strength
Section 7 – This indicates your Verbal strength
Section 8 – This reflects your Intrapersonal strength
Section 9 – This suggests your Visual strength

Remember:

- Everyone has all the intelligences!
- You can strengthen each intelligence!
- This inventory is meant as a snapshot in time - it can change!
- MI is meant to empower, not label learners!

What Is Thinking?

This chapter is not going to teach you how to think. You already know how to do it. You are thinking right now while reading this book. The main goal of this chapter is to help you understand how you can think better by becoming a great thinker.

LEARNING OBJECTIVES

1. After reading this chapter, you will be able to
2. Define cognition and thinking
3. Identify various cognitive processes
4. Compare and contrast different forms of thinking
5. Define and discuss basic components of thinking
6. Identify factors that may improve thinking skills
7. Practice thinking skills.

Thinking Taxonomy

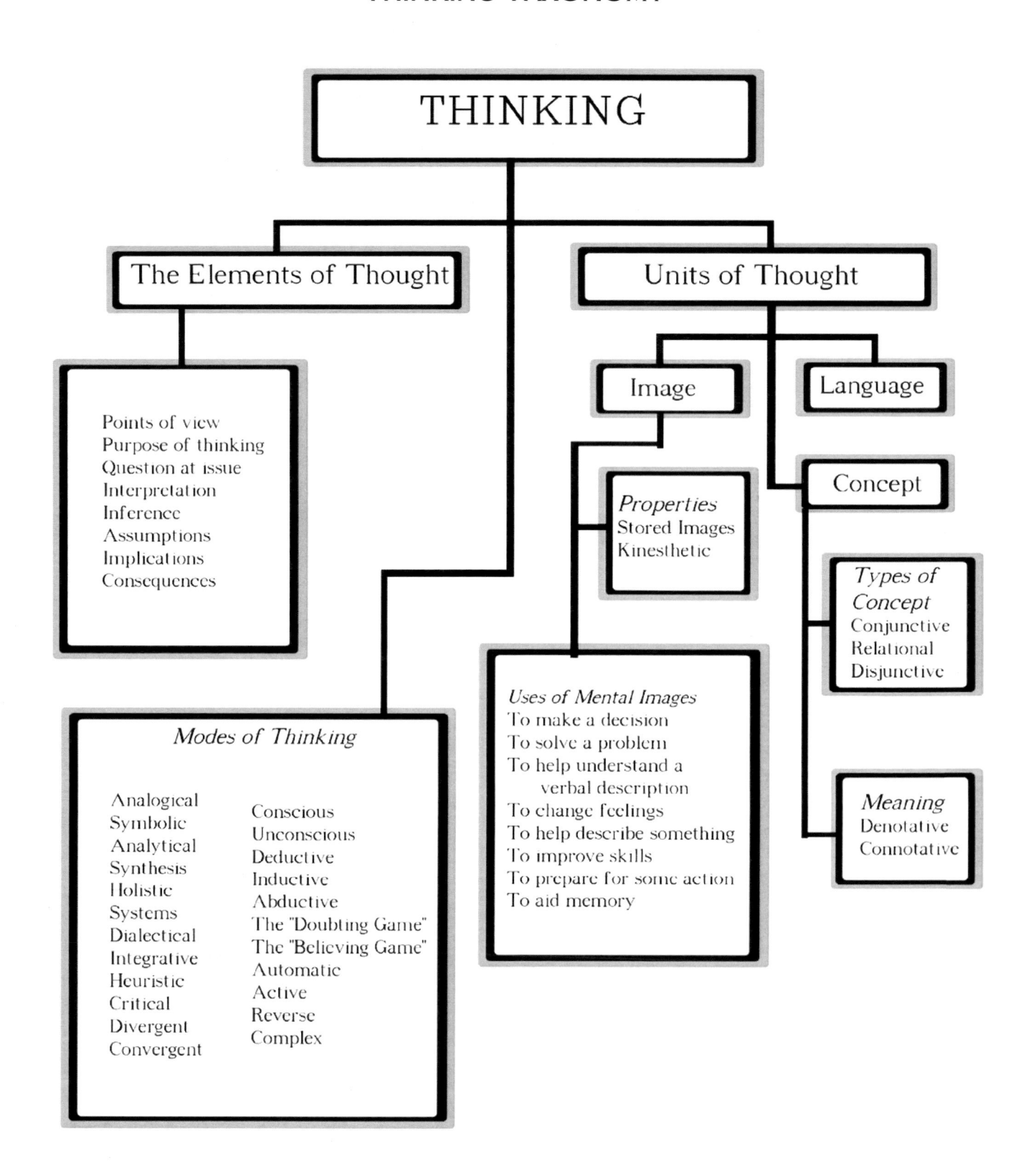

THINKING

The Elements of Thought

Points of view
Purpose of thinking
Question at issue
Interpretation
Inference
Assumptions
Implications
Consequences

Modes of Thinking

Analogical	Conscious
Symbolic	Unconscious
Analytical	Deductive
Synthesis	Inductive
Holistic	Abductive
Systems	The "Doubting Game"
Dialectical	The "Believing Game"
Integrative	Automatic
Heuristic	Active
Critical	Reverse
Divergent	Complex
Convergent	

Units of Thought

Image

Properties
Stored Images
Kinesthetic

Uses of Mental Images
To make a decision
To solve a problem
To help understand a verbal description
To change feelings
To help describe something
To improve skills
To prepare for some action
To aid memory

Language

Concept

Types of Concept
Conjunctive
Relational
Disjunctive

Meaning
Denotative
Connotative

What Is Thinking?
HUMAN REASONING

Figure 6.1. A Model of Human Reasoning

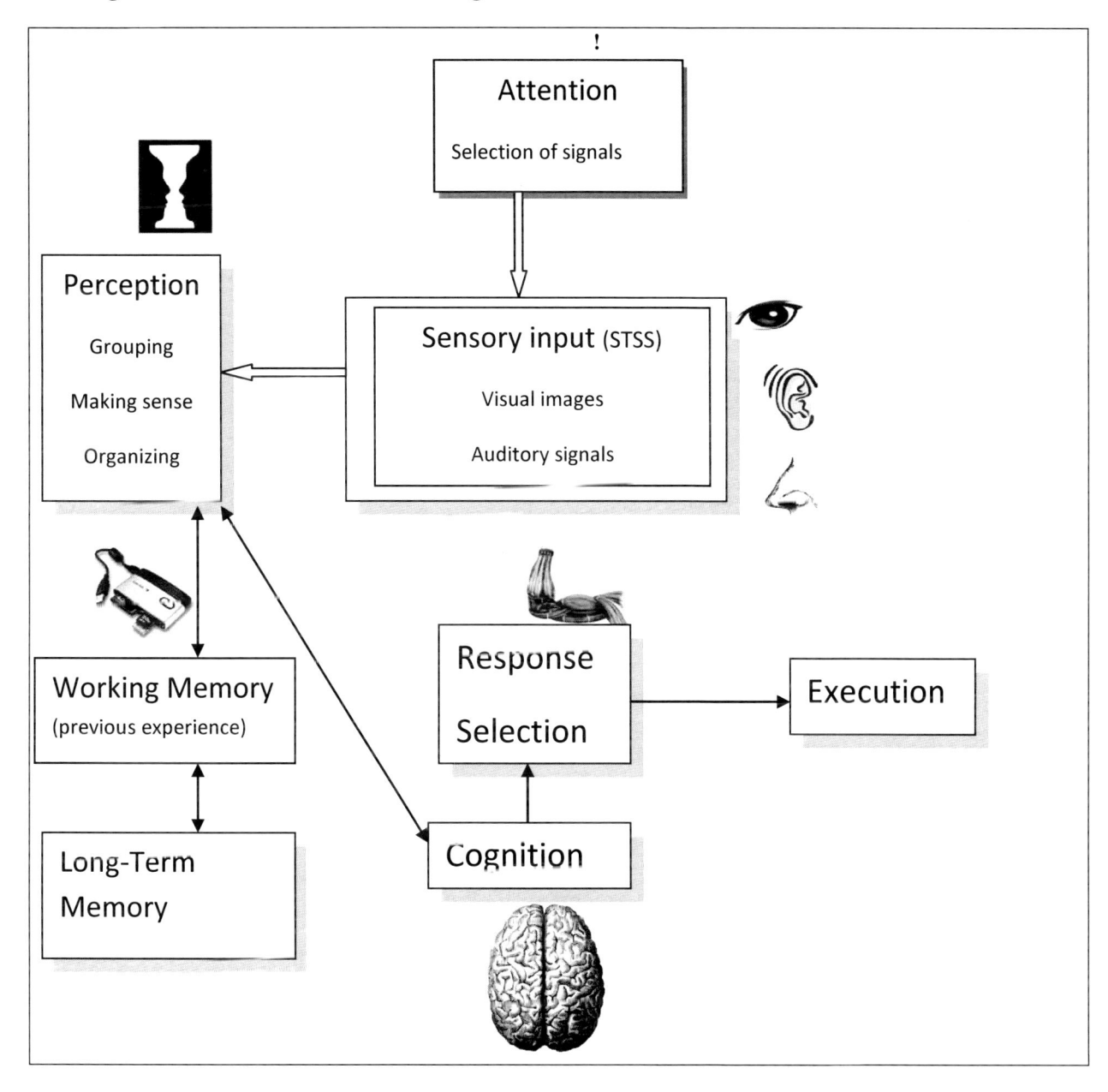

```
                          Attention
                      Selection of signals
                              │
                              ▼
   Perception            Sensory input (STSS)
   Grouping       ◄──
   Making sense            Visual images
   Organizing             Auditory signals


                           Response
   Working Memory          Selection      ──►   Execution
   (previous experience)      ▲
          ▲                   │
          ▼                Cognition
   Long-Term
   Memory
```

Human reasoning includes various operations such as daydreaming, visualizing, planning, etc. One of the most important part of reasoning is information processing. It may start by an environmental input or by the person's voluntary intention to act. The following figure demonstrates stages of the information processing.

CHAPTER 6

Attention. The first property or component of the model is attention, represented by a supply of mental resources. Many mental operations are not carried out automatically but require the **selective application** of these limited resources. At the top of the figure, we see attention selectively allocated to channels of sensory material to process (selective attention). For **visual information**, this limited resource is foveal vision, which can be (through eye movements) directed to different channels in the environment.

Like **top-down perceptual processing**, this scanning process is often driven by past experience – knowing where to look when. But this experience may also be the cause of errors.

The selective application of limited attentional resources is much broader than its application to scanning. Indeed, when, for example, student has many tasks to perform – listening to teacher's lecture, taking lecture notes, and trying to play computer game at the same time – he or she must select a strategy for dividing attention or allocating resources between these different tasks or mental operations. When the total attention demand of these tasks is excessive, one task or the other must suffer.

Sensory processing Information and events in the environment must gain **access to the brain**. Thus, the student, for example, must see or hear the teacher before any response can be made to teacher's command. Properties of both visual and auditory receptors (as well as those of the other senses) have a tremendous impact on the quality of information that reaches the brain. For example, the low visual or auditory quality of the material presented in class degrades student's ability to understand and retain the information.

As shown in Figure 6.2., all **sensory systems** have an **associated short-term sensory store** (STSS) that resides within the brain.

This is a temporary mechanism for prolonging the representation of the raw stimulus evidence for durations as short as around one half second (visual STSS), to as long as 2-4 seconds (auditory STSS). Thus, for example, if the teacher asks students to write down the statement: "Crocodile is swimming in the pond" students continue to "hear" the command to initiate a particular action (e.g., moving pen around the paper to create a text) for a few seconds after the teacher's voice had finished delivering the message. Hence, even if student was distracted at the moment of message delivery, he or she could still recover its contents for a few seconds after.

Figure 6.2. The teacher asks students to write down the statement: "Crocodile

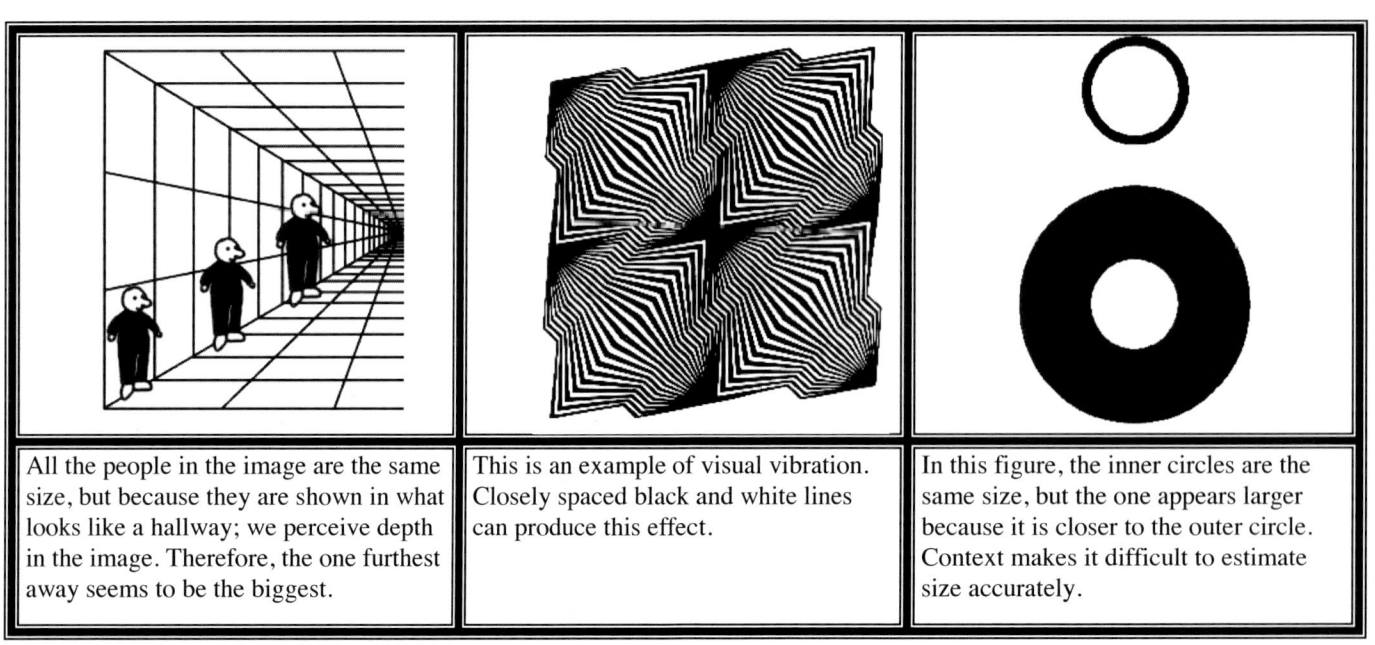

Perception. Perceptions vary from person to person. Different people perceive different things about the same situation. But more than that, we assign different meanings to what we perceive. And the meanings might change for a certain person. One might change one's perspective or simply make things mean something else.

Human perception is pretty accurate. It should be. Otherwise, people wouldn't be able to survive. But there is such phenomenon like illusions.

| All the people in the image are the same size, but because they are shown in what looks like a hallway; we perceive depth in the image. Therefore, the one furthest away seems to be the biggest. | This is an example of visual vibration. Closely spaced black and white lines can produce this effect. | In this figure, the inner circles are the same size, but the one appears larger because it is closer to the outer circle. Context makes it difficult to estimate size accurately. |

104

What Is Thinking?

Human perception is not just mirroring reality. It follows certain rules of organization.

Gestalt Laws of Perceptual Organization

1. **The Law of Proximity:** Stimulus elements that are closed together tend to be perceived as a group
2. **The Law of Similarity:** Similar stimuli tend to be grouped, this tendency can even dominate grouping due to proximity
3. **The Law of Closure:** Stimuli tend to be grouped into complete figures
4. **The Law of Good Continuation:** Stimuli tend to be grouped as to minimize change or discontinuity
5. **The Law of Symmetry:** Regions bound by symmetrical boarders tend to be perceived as coherent figures
6. **The Law Simplicity:** Ambiguous stimuli tend to be resolved in favor of the simplest.

The Law of Figure/Ground	The Law of Proximity	The Law of Similarity	The Law of Symmetry	The Law of Closure	The Law of Good Continuation
	O O O O O O O O O O O O	O X O X O O X O X O O X O X O O X O X O			
We have a tendency to perceive one aspect of a composition as the figure or foreground and the other as the ground or background. With many images that use this law the way in which we see two images is to just change our attitude and to look at another aspect of it.	Stimulus elements that are closed together tend to be perceived as a group.	Similar stimuli tend to be grouped, this tendency can even dominate grouping due to proximity.	Regions bound by symmetrical boarders tend to be perceived as coherent figures.	We tend to ignore gaps and complete contour line. In the image above there are no triangles or circles, but our mind fills in the missing information to create familiar shapes and images.	Stimuli tend to be grouped as to minimize change or discontinuity.

    Sensory processing is necessary but ***not sufficient*** for effective performance. Raw sensory data relayed to the brain (and perhaps preserved in a sensory store) must be interpreted, or given meaning, through the stage of perception. Thus, teacher's voice heard by the student is not an intense sound but conveys the meaningful message "write down the sentence." It is role of perception to decode this meaning from the raw sensory data. Perceptual processing has two important features. First, it generally proceeds automatically and rapidly (requiring little attention). Second, it is driven both by sensory input (which we call bottom-up processing) and by inputs from long-term memory about what events are expected (which we call top-down processing).

    The speed and relative automaticity of perception is what distinguishes it from the cognitive process. Thus, when the student reads the phrase "Crocodile is flying over the ocean" written on a whiteboard, it is a perceptual operation. When, instead, he must infer that the sentence has conflicting information, the operation is a cognitive one, requiring more time and mental effort. Of course the distinction between perceptual and cognitive operations is not always clear-cut; the two represent endpoints on a continuum.

    Perception is partially determined by an analysis of the stimulus or environmental input, relayed from the sensory receptors by the sensory or "lower" channels of neural information. Hence, this aspect

Figure 6.3. This is a perceptual operation

Imagination - traditionally, the mental capacity for experiencing, constructing, or manipulating 'mental imagery' (quasi-perceptual experience). Imagination is also regarded as responsible for fantasy, inventiveness, idiosyncrasy, and creative, original, and insightful thought in general, and, sometimes, for a much wider range of mental activities dealing with the non-actual, such as supposing, pretending, 'seeing as', thinking of possibilities, and even being mistaken.

of processing is often termed bottom-up perceptual processing. However, *when sensory evidence is poor, perception* may be *driven* heavily buy *expectations* based on past experience, an influence known as top-down processing. This past experience is stored in long-term memory. ***Bottom-up*** and ***top-down processing*** usually work ***harmoniously*** together, supporting rapid and accurate perceptual work. However, sometimes unfamiliar circumstances remove the ability to use past experience, leading bottom-up processing to do nearly all the work. Alternatively, poor sensory quality sometimes forces the perceiver to use top-down expectancies. If such expectancies are wrong, perceptual errors can occur. Thus, the quality of bottom-up evidence regarding the road ahead was poor for the driver's accident. Our driver relied on his expectations (that traffic ahead on a freeway moves forward) to perceive the vehicle in front to be moving. In this case the perception was wrong, and the near collision resulted.

Cognition and Memory. As noted above, the boundary between perception and cognition is sometimes blurred because both may provide similar implications for action. However, the important distinction is that cognitive operations generally require greater time, mental effort, or attention. This is because such cognitive operations as rehearsal, reasoning, or image transformation are carried out by using what is called working memory, a vulnerable, temporary store of activated information. Working memory would be involved in each of the following cognitive operations: when the student reads the sentences written on a whiteboard; mentally assesses the accuracy of both sentences; when he or she rehearses the known characteristics of crocodiles; when he or she plans the optimal way to correct the sentence. The key features of all of these operations are that they are conscious activities which transform or retain information, and that they are resource limited. That is, each is highly vulnerable to disruption when attentional resources are diverted to other mental activities.

Here are the mental processes which go on in learning or in any type of memory task (Gagné, 1985):

1. Receptance of information
- Receptors (eyes, ears, nose, skin, or taste buds) receive stimuli from the environment and generate patterns of neural impulses.

2. Selective perception
- The neural impulses are sent to a sensory register, a mechanism in the brain which receives them, rejects those which are irrelevant (like background noise), and selects features which need to be given attention.

3. Short term storage
- The selected impulses are then sent to short-term memory and are kept temporarily as auditory, articulatory, or visual images.

4. Semantic encoding
- If a decision is made that they should be kept more permanently, they are encoded semantically.

5. Long term storage
- The item is then placed in long-term memory.
- When the item is needed again, a retrieval process is initiated:

6. Retrieval
- Search
- A search is conducted in long-term memory.
- When the information is found, it is retrieved.

7. Response organization
- The information is sent to a response generator, another mechanism which organizes a suitable response.

8. Performance
- The response generator sends the signal to effectors, body parts such as the hands or eyes, which carry out the action.

9. Feedback and reinforcement
The mind observes the effect of its performance and prepares itself to repeat the process as appropriate in answer to the response perceived.

Stages
Here are
- the stages or internal processes that take place in information processing
- their corresponding instructional events (Instructional events are any activities during which learning takes place), and
- examples of actions that might cause the process to take place.

Response Selection and Execution. The understanding of a situation, achieved through perception and augmented by cognitive transformations, often triggers an action – the selection of a response. However, when student reached a decision on how to correct statement, a good deal of cognition was required. When he or she just wrote down the right sentence this response involved little or no cognition.

The selection of a response or choice of an action is quite distinct from its execution, the latter requiring the coordination of the muscles for controlled motion, to assure that the chosen goal is correctly obtained. Thus, student correctly selected the action to correct the wrong sentence, but he or she may execute the action poorly by overcorrecting, making grammar error, and ultimately failing the assignment.

Feedback. The feedback loop indicates that actions are directly sensed by the human or, if those actions influence the situation with which the human is interacting will be observable sooner or later. The presence of the feedback loop has two implications. First, its presence emphasizes that the "flow" of information can be initiated at any point. Thus, a student's decision to correct the wrong sentence is not driven by a perceived environmental event, but rather by a cognitive motivation to receive a good grade for an assignment.

The feedback loop is important for establishing that the intended goal was achieved. Second, the feedback loop emphasizes that in many real-world tasks, such as learning, driving, walking, or navigating through a computer information database, the flow of information is continuous, thus, it is just as appropriate to say that "action causes perception" as it is say that perception causes action.

A critical factor that influences the extent of this closed-loop interactivity is the delay of the situation in responding to human actions. For steering vehicles, this delay is typically short. The driver immediately perceives the change caused by turning the wheel, and hence, special properties of closed-loop dynamic systems must be considered in examining human performance.

However, for some actions like the student's decision to follow the command of the teacher to write down or correct the sentence, it may be several minutes before the implications of that decision are realized.

The sensitivity level is higher for simultaneous tasks than for successive tasks. A sensitivity decrement occurs for successive tasks at high event rates but does not occur at low event rates, or for simultaneous tasks at either rate.

The sensitivity decrement is eliminated when observers are highly practiced so that the task becomes automatic, rather than controlled.

A sensitivity increment (i.e., improvement with time on watch) sometimes occurs in simultaneous paradigms with cognitive (familiar) but not sensory stimuli.

Factors Affecting Sensitivity Level and Sensitivity Decrement

The following factors affect sensitivity in a vigilance task:
- ***Sensitivity decreases***, and the sensitivity decrement increases, as a target's signal strength is reduced, which occurs when the intensity or duration of a target is reduced or otherwise made more similar to non-target events.
- ***Sensitivity decreases*** when there is uncertainty about the time or location at which the target signal will appear. This uncertainty is particularly great if there are long intervals between signals.

For inspection tasks, which have defined non-target events, the sensitivity level decreases and the decrement increases when the event rate is increased. Event rate is defined as the number of events per unit time; an example of increasing the event rate would be speeding up the conveyer belt in an inspection situation.

WHAT IS THINKING / COGNITION?

Thinking takes many forms, including

1. Daydreaming,
2. Problem solving, and
3. Reasoning (to name but a few).

Stated more formally, thinking, or cognition, refers to mentally processing information.

Studying thinking is similar to figuring out how a computer works. But in cognitive psychology (the study of human information processing) the "computer hardware" is the brain, and thinking is the "software or program instructions" that we seek to understand.

CHAPTER 6

The Elements of Thought (modified from Paul & Elder, 2001)

1. **Points of view:** frame of reference, perspective, orientation
2. **Purpose of the thinking:** goal, objective
3. **Question at issue:** data, facts, observations, experiences
4. **Interpretation and inference:** conclusions, solutions
5. **Concepts:** theories, definitions, axioms, laws, principles, rules, modes
6. **Assumptions:** presupposition, taking for granted
7. **Implications and consequences**

Some Basic Units of Thought

Thinking is an internal representation (mental expression) of a problem or situation.
Basic units of thought:

    I. images,
    II. concepts, and
    III. language, or symbols.

The three basic units can be defined in this way:

Thinking involves

1. Attention,
2. Pattern recognition,
3. Memory,
4. Decision-making,
5. Intuition,
6. Knowledge, and more.

    i. **Image:** Most often, a mental representation that has picture-like qualities; a visual likeness or icon. For example world class players only use the Stauton design with the traditional horse and bishop. No civil war figures or carved onyx Aztec shapes. Bobby Fisher refused to play one man with a non-standard set.

    ii. **Concept:** A generalized idea representing a class of related objects or events. This might be an opening like the King's Indian or The StoenWall or the rules for the middle and end game.

    iii. **Language:** Words or symbols, and rules for combining them that are used for thinking and communication. This might be something like en passant, castle to the king side, or check.

I. Mental Imagery

Ninety-seven percent (97%) of all people have visual images, and ninety-two percent (92%) have auditory images. Over fifty-percent (50%) have imagery that includes movement, touch, taste, smell, and pain. Some people have a rare form of imagery called synesthesia. For these individuals, images cross normal sensory barriers.

Common Uses of Mental Images

Mental images are most frequently used for the following purposes:

1. To make a decision or solve a problem. Examples: Choosing what clothes to wear; figuring out how to arrange furniture in a room.
2. To help understand a verbal description. Examples: Mentally picturing what a person is talking about, picturing a scene described in a novel
3. To change feelings. Examples: Thinking of pleasant images to get out of a bad mood; imagining oneself as thin to help stay on a diet.
4. To help explain or describe something. Examples: Visualizing a scene at a party to describe it to a friend.
5. To improve a skill or to prepare for some action. Examples: Using images to improve a swimming stroke; mentally rehearsing how you will ask for a raise.
6. To aid memory. Example: Picturing Mr. Cook wearing a chef's hat, so you can remember his name.

Properties of Mental Images

It can be seen that mental images of objects can be moved about as needed.

What Is Thinking?

II. Concepts

A concept is an idea that represents a class of objects or events. Concepts are powerful tools because they allow us to think more abstractly, free from distracting details.

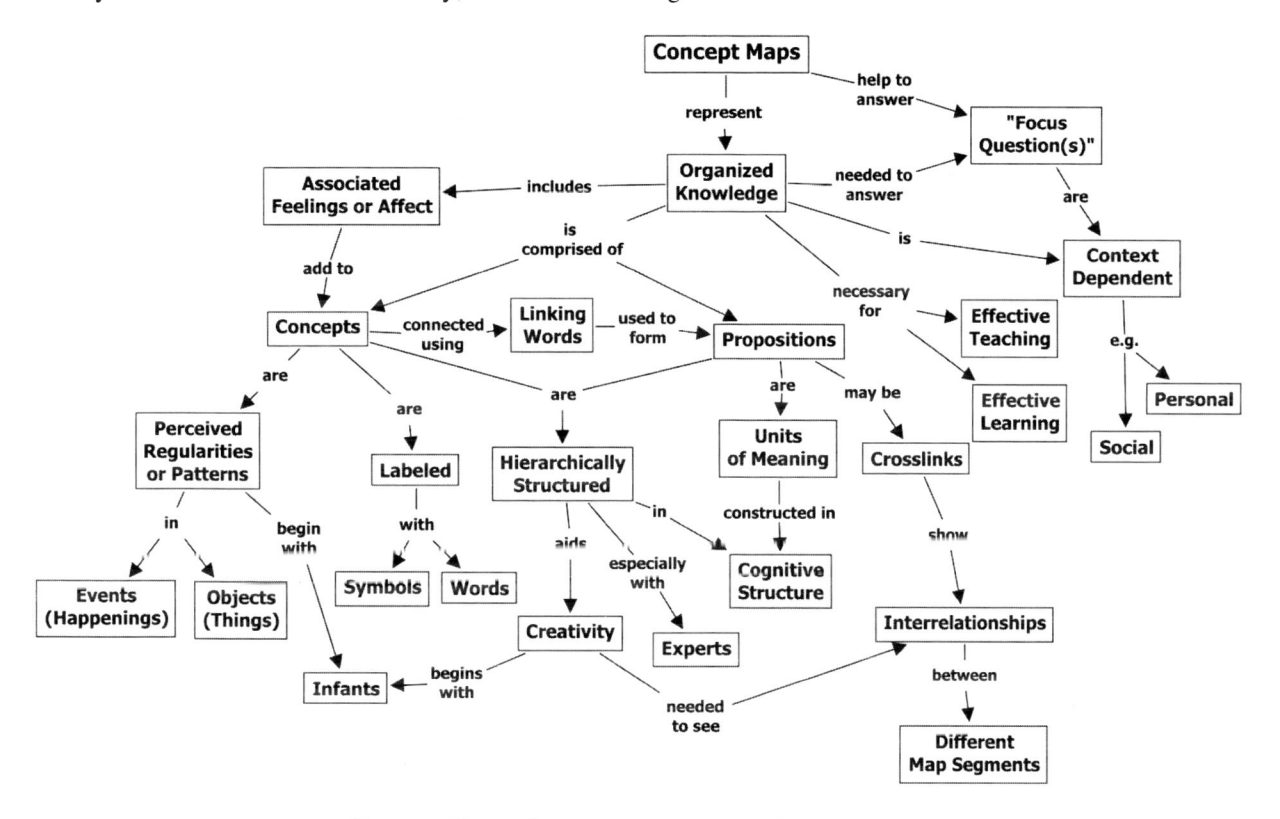

[Concept map diagram: "Concept Maps" represent "Organized Knowledge"; help to answer "Focus Question(s)" which are Context Dependent (e.g., Personal, Social); Organized Knowledge includes Associated Feelings or Affect (add to Concepts), is comprised of Concepts and Propositions, is necessary for Effective Teaching and Effective Learning. Concepts are connected using Linking Words (used to form Propositions), are Perceived Regularities or Patterns (in Events (Happenings), Objects (Things)), are Labeled with Symbols, Words (begin with Infants). Propositions are Hierarchically Structured (aids Creativity, especially with Experts), are Units of Meaning constructed in Cognitive Structure, may be Crosslinks (show Interrelationships between Different Map Segments, needed to see Creativity).]

a. Concept Formation

Concept formation is the process of classifying information into meaningful categories. At its most basic, concept formation is based on experience with positive and negative instances (examples that belong, or do not belong, to the concept class).

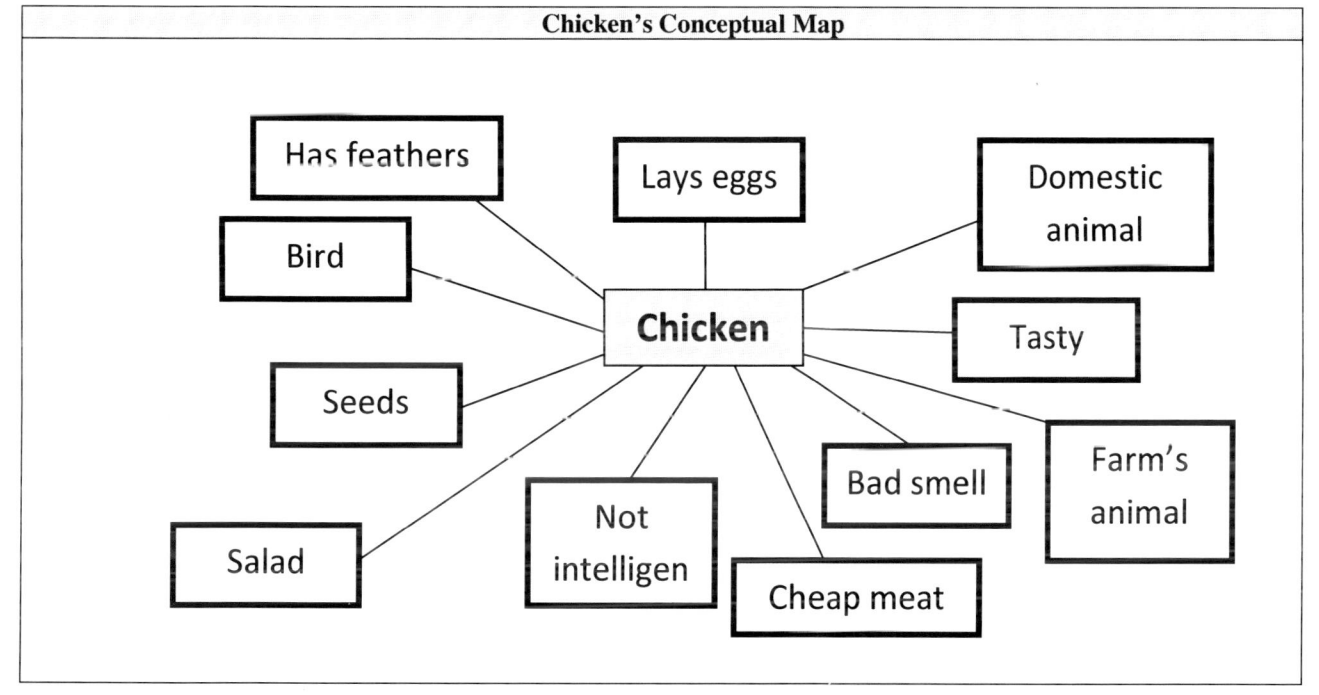

Chicken's Conceptual Map

[Diagram showing "Chicken" connected to: Has feathers, Lays eggs, Domestic animal, Bird, Tasty, Seeds, Farm's animal, Bad smell, Salad, Not intelligen, Cheap meat]

b. Types of Concepts

- ***Conjunctive concepts*** are defined by the presence of two or more features. In other words, these are "and" concepts: To belong to the concept class, an item must have "this feature and this feature and this feature." For example, a motorcycle must have two wheels and an engine and handlebars.
- ***Relational concepts*** are based on how an object relates to something else, or how its features relate to one another. All of the following are relational concepts: Larger, above, left, north, and upside down. Another example is sister, which is defined as "a female considered in her relation to another person having the same parents."
- ***Disjunctive concepts*** refer to objects that have at least one of several possible features. These are "either/or" concepts. To belong, an item must have "this feature or that feature or another feature." For example, in baseball, a strike is either a swing and a miss or a pitch down the middle or a foul ball. The either/or quality of disjunctive concepts makes them hard to learn.

c. Prototypes

When you think of the concept bird, do you make a mental list o features that birds have? Probably not. In addition to rules and features, we use prototypes, or ideal models, to identify concepts. A robin, for instance, is a model bird; an ostrich is not. In other words, some items are better examples of a concept than others are.

Concepts have two types of meaning.

1) ***The denotative meaning*** of a word or concept is its exact definition.

2) ***The connotative meaning*** is its emotional or personal meaning. The denotative meaning of the word naked (having no clothes) is the same for a nudist as it is for a movie censor, but we could expect their connotations to differ. Such meanings can influence how we think about important issues. For example, the term enhanced radiation device has a more positive connotation than neutron bomb does.

III. Language

Thinking sometimes takes place without language. Everyone has searched for a word to express an idea that exists as a vague image or feeling. Nevertheless, most thinking leans heavily on language, because it allows the world to be encoded (translated) into symbols that are easy to manipulate.

The study of meaning in words and language is known as semantics. It is here that the link between language and thought becomes most evident. Suppose, on an intelligence test, you were asked to circle the word that does not belong in this series:

Skyscraper cathedral temple prayer

If you circle prayer, you answered as most people do. Now try another problem, again circling the odd item:

Cathedral prayer temple skyscraper

Had you seen only this question, you probably would have circled skyscraper. Reordering the words subtly changes their meaning.

Successful Thinking

Successful thinking is that mode of thinking – about any subject, content, problem, or event – in which the thinker constantly develops and improves the quality of his or her thinking by skillfully taking charge of the structure inherent in thinking and imposing intellectual standards upon them.

As a result of proper thinking individual can achieve the following attributes:

1. He or she would be able to raise the vital questions and problems, formulating them clearly and precisely;
2. Gather and assess relevant information, using abstractions to interpret it effectively;
3. Come to well-reasoned conclusion and solutions.

SUMMARY

1. Human reasoning includes various operations such as daydreaming, visualizing, planning, etc. One of the most important part of reasoning is information processing.

What Is Thinking?

2. Here are the mental processes which go on in learning or in any type of memory task (Gagné, 1985):
   - Receptance of information
   - Selective perception
   - Short term storage
   - Semantic encoding
   - Long term storage
   - Retrieval
   - Response organization
   - Performance
   - Feedback and reinforcement

3. Thinking includes the three basic units:
   - **Image:** Most often, a mental representation that has picture-like qualities; a visual likeness or icon. For example world class players only use the Stauton design with the traditional horse and bishop. No civil war figures or carved onyx Aztec shapes. Bobby Fisher refused to play one man with a non-standard set.
   - **Concept**: A generalized idea representing a class of related objects or events. This might be an opening like the King's Indian or The Stonewall or the rules for the middle and end game.
   - **Language:** Words or symbols, and rules for combining them that are used for thinking and communication. This might be something like en passant, castle to the king side, or check.

CHAPTER 6

PRACTICING THINKING

Intelligence, according to De Bono (1995), is like horsepower of a car. A powerful car has the potential to drive at high speeds. But one can have a powerful car and drive it badly. Someone with a less powerful car may be a better driver. Like the horsepower of a car, intelligence is just a potential. Thinking is the driving skill with which each individual drives his or her intelligence. Anyone can develop a high degree of skill in thinking if he or she wants to do so. That means making some effort.

Edward De Bono (1995) stated that some people believe that thinking is just a matter of intelligence. They assume that if person is born with a high IQ, then he or she can think, and if not, then it is just too bad. This is complete nonsense. Many highly intelligent people are bad thinkers. They know how to defend their point of view, but that is all. Many people with lower IQ are much better thinkers.

The following exercises are designed to help you to practice each aspect of thinking.

Step 1: Recognition: What is it?

The Purpose of the Exercise

People get through life by dealing with the things they know. Most things are labeled and classified (De Bono, 1995). Once the label is in place, people know what to do with that thing. They eat bread, drink milk, use a bus to travel. When someone takes an apple out of the box labeled "apples," then he or she expects that apple to taste just as apples should taste. Once the label is clearly attached to the box, then person knows immediately what he or she getting out of the box. He or she doesn't need to recognize the thing all over again. He or she just trusts the label on the box. This is a very powerful system.

The easy part is getting something out of a labeled box. The more difficult part is the knowing which box to put something into. Does it go here or does it go there?

It is possible that one might be able to make a guess at what something is. However, if the item in question is completely unfamiliar to person, then he or she needs an explanation about the nature of a subject.

People get home by following the roads they know. They get through every day life by dealing with the things they know. It would be useful if everything were labeled, if everything gets its name. In fact, most things are labeled, but the labels are supplied in people's minds.

Create your own labels or names. Once the label is in place, you know what to do with that thing.

Identify the following items:

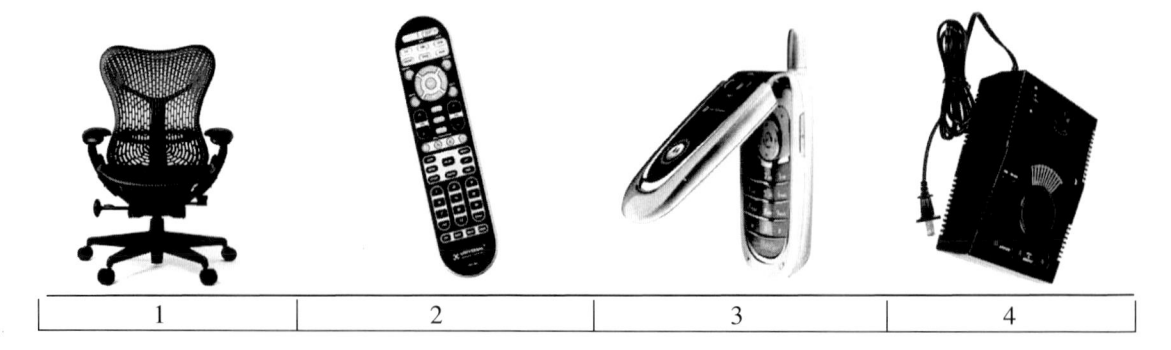

| 1 | 2 | 3 | 4 |

While looking on those pictures, what was going on in your mind? Your brain tried to find patterns stored in your memory. What if there is unfamiliar object? Brain still tries to find something similar. Your brain is guessing.

Step 2: Concepts: Putting Things into Groups

Human mind is experienced in recognizing and linking two items that are similar. This exercise can help you to develop analogical and analytical thinking.

What Is Thinking?

Can you recognize the following items? Sure, you can. All four items are watches. But each of them looks different. How you know that they are watches? Because you know "the watch" concept. You know the main features of watch. You have 'the watch' pattern stored in your memory.

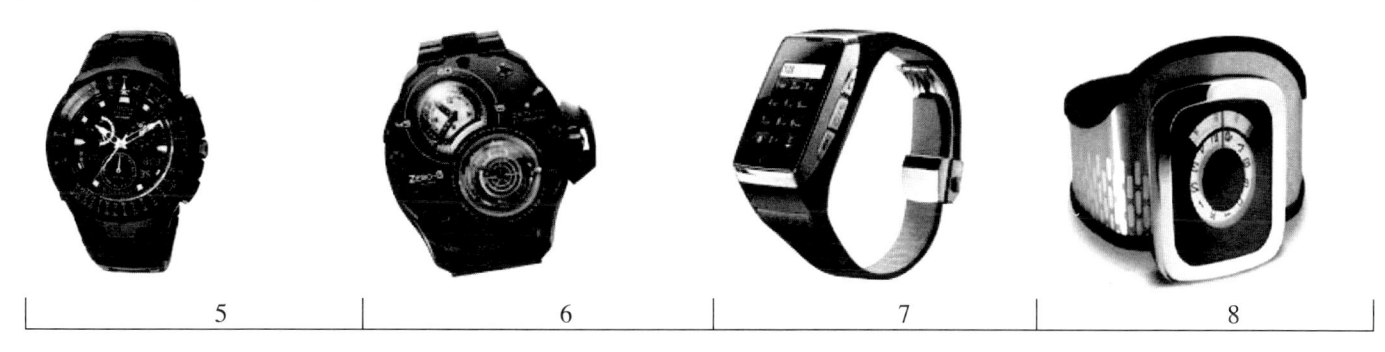

| 5 | 6 | 7 | 8 |

Look at the following four items. Can you recognize it? All four items are chairs. Some of them have a very unusual design. But you know the concept of chair. That is why you are able to recognize chair even if it has a very fancy design.

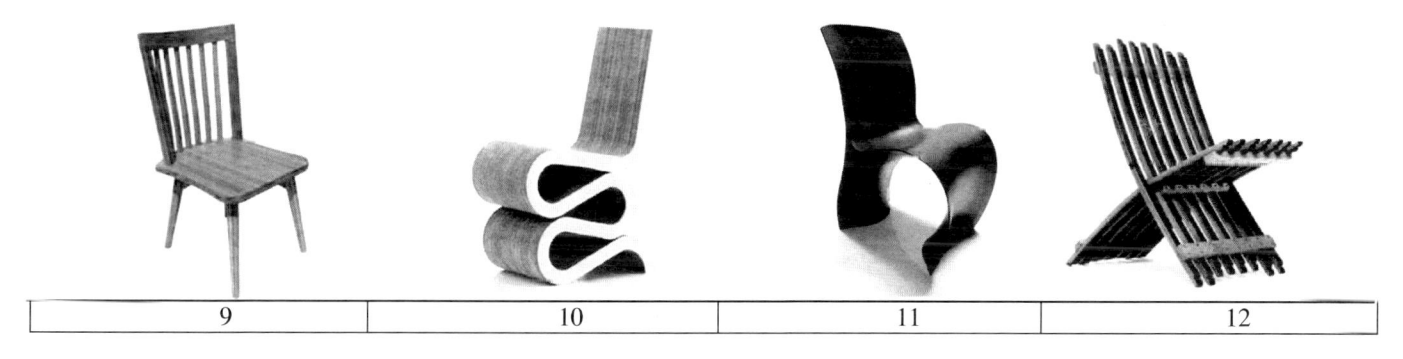

| 9 | 10 | 11 | 12 |

What about more complex concepts? Such as love. Are you able to distinguish love from non-love, from friendship, or from liking? Think about it.

Instructions:

Things around us are different. We use them for various purposes. At the same time they have something in common. Look at them. Study carefully the following items. As you can see, there are eight distinct and separate items. Can you divide the featured items into two clearly differentiated groups, each numbering four items? Use any basis that you like to create two groups.

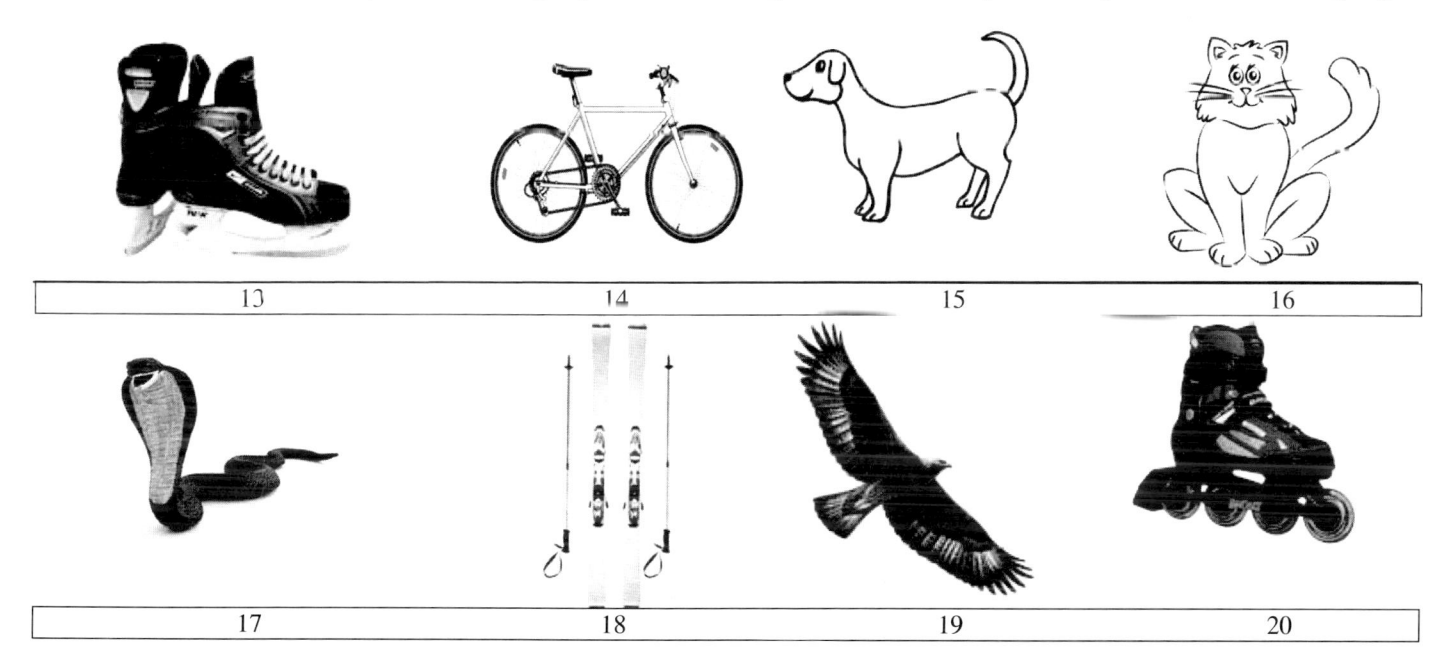

| 13 | 14 | 15 | 16 |

| 17 | 18 | 19 | 20 |

113

CHAPTER 6

Example:

1. 15, 16, 17, and 19 are animals.
2. 15 and 16 are drawings
3. Continue this list:
4. _____
5. _____
6. _____
7. _____
8. _____
9. _____

As soon as you are asked to put items into pairs, you need to look for something that two items have in common. In the above exercise, a skates are very different from a bicycle. Yet both skates and bicycle are sport devices. Dog and cat are pets. Snake and eagle are wild animals. Skates and ski are for winter sport, while bicycle and rollerblades can be used at any season. These are just some of the possible grouping that you might have thought of. You might have decided on your grouping on a totally different basis.

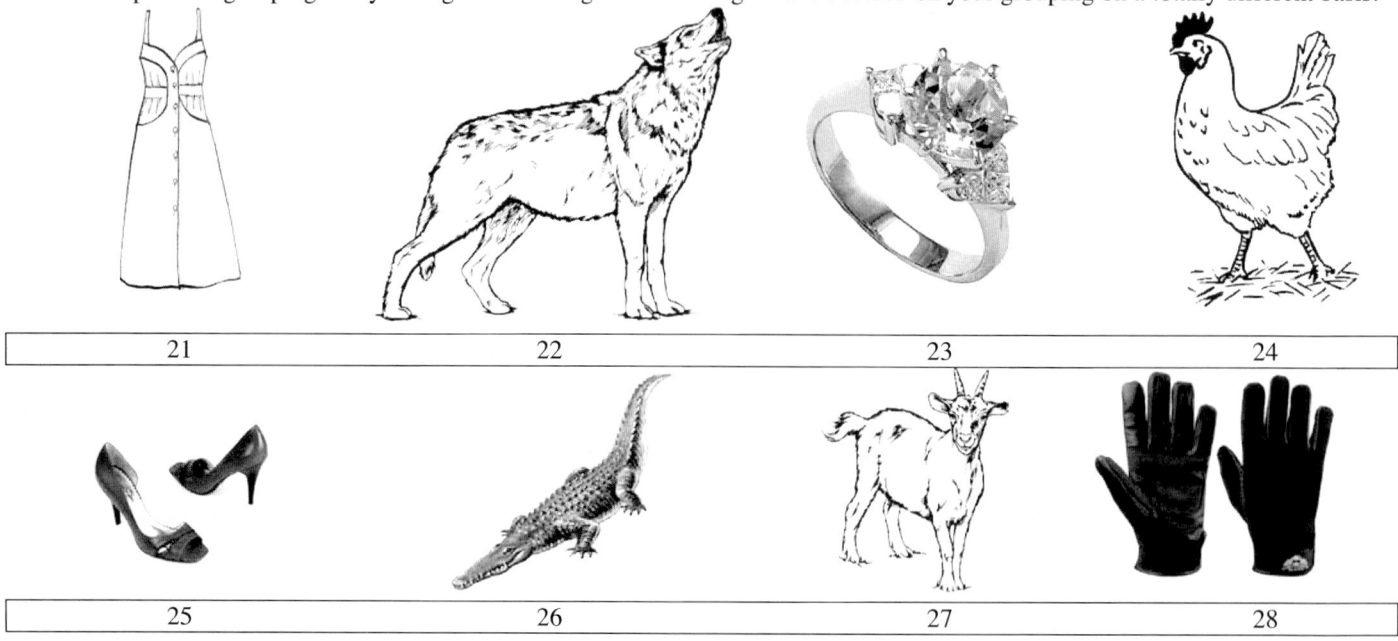

21	22	23	24

25	26	27	28

In the above exercise, you might decide that dress, ring, shoes, and gloves can be grouped together on the basis that they all are part of the outfit. Hen, goat, crocodile, and wolf are animals. Thinking more, you might decide that hen and goat are farm animals. Crocodile and wolf are wild animals.

Now it is your turn:

1. _____
2. _____
3. _____
4. _____
5. _____
6. _____
7. _____
8. _____
9. _____

Do your own thinking before you move further.

What Is Thinking?

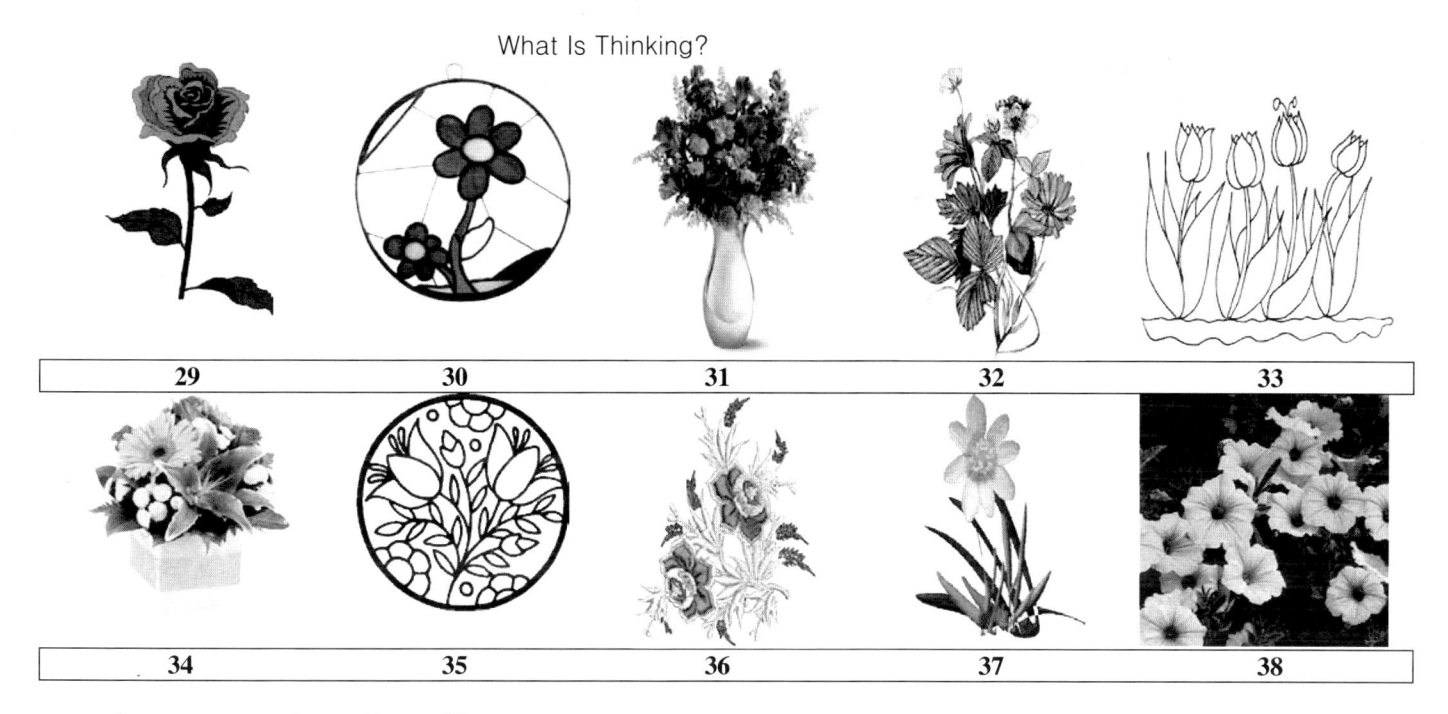

| 29 | 30 | 31 | 32 | 33 |
| 34 | 35 | 36 | 37 | 38 |

Can you arrange the ten kinds of flowers shown above into pairs?

1. _____
2. _____
3. _____
4. _____
5. _____
6. _____
7. _____
8. _____
9. _____

It can be easy to group items on the basis of a broad concept. It is more difficult to recognize the narrower concepts involved.

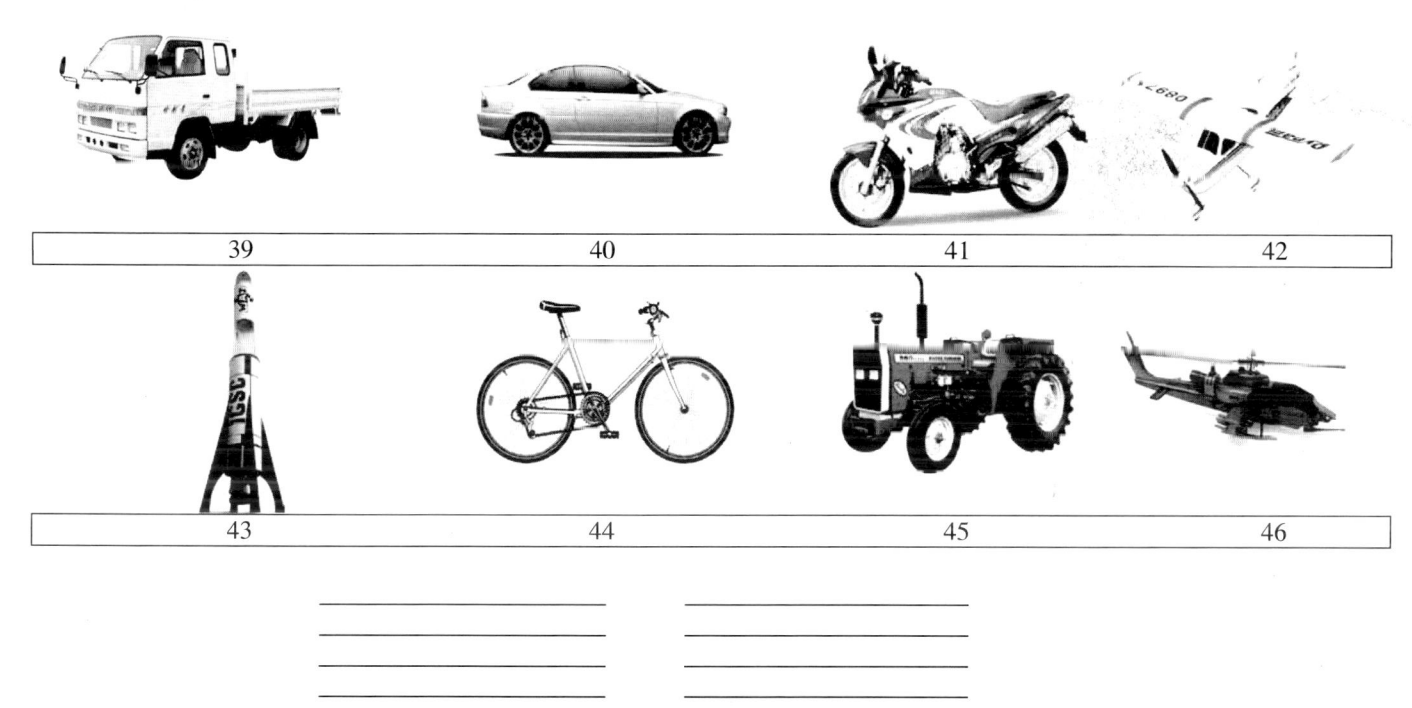

| 39 | 40 | 41 | 42 |
| 43 | 44 | 45 | 46 |

_____   _____
_____   _____
_____   _____
_____   _____

CHAPTER 6

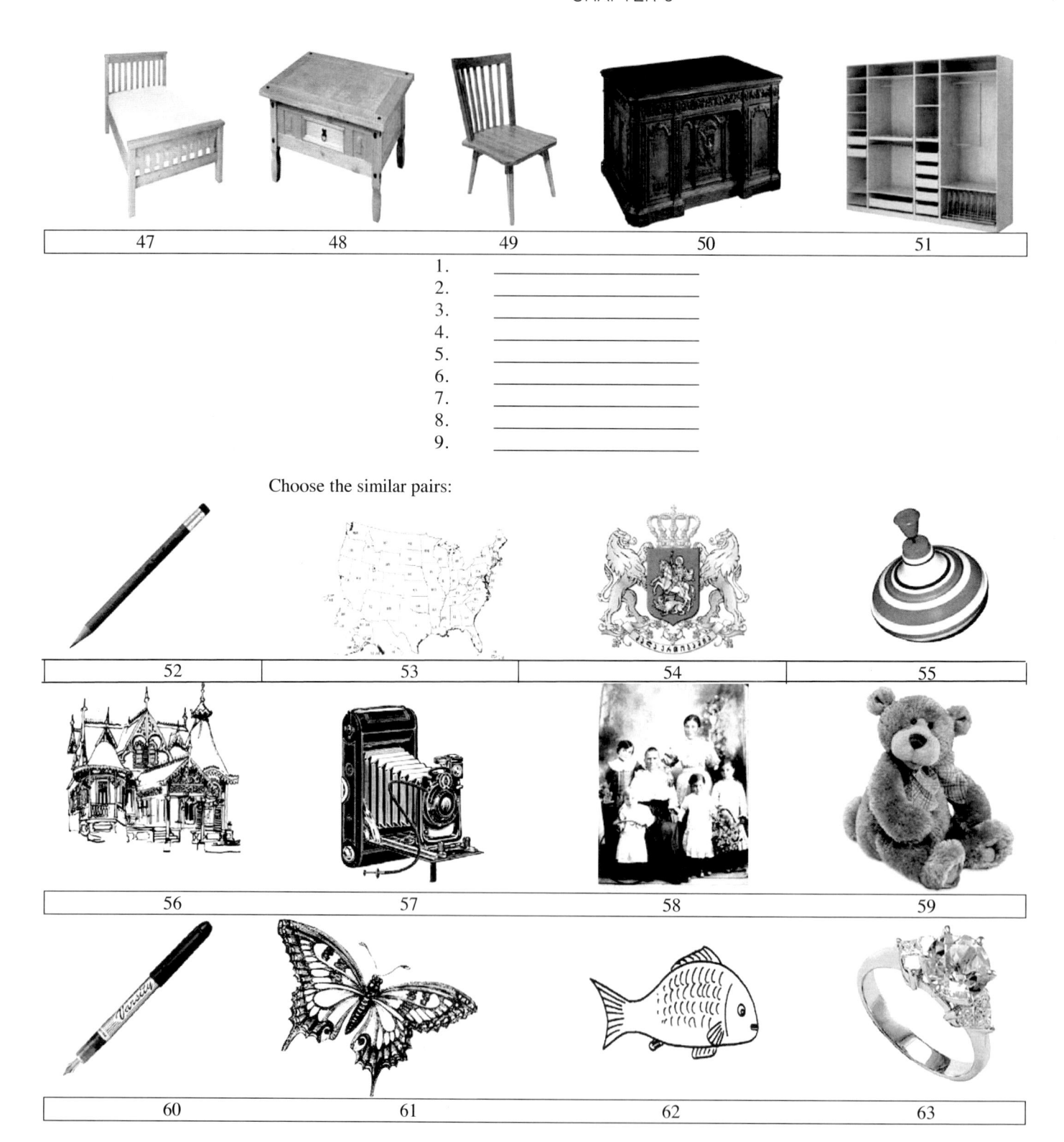

| 47 | 48 | 49 | 50 | 51 |

1. _____
2. _____
3. _____
4. _____
5. _____
6. _____
7. _____
8. _____
9. _____

Choose the similar pairs:

| 52 | 53 | 54 | 55 |

| 56 | 57 | 58 | 59 |

| 60 | 61 | 62 | 63 |

Possible answers:
1. Butterfly and fish are living creatures.
2. Teddy bear and humming top are toys.
3. Pen and pencil are tools for writing.
4. Photo camera and picture are machine and its product.
5. House and map. House location.
6. Emblems and ring are indicators of social status.

116

What Is Thinking?

Continue this list:

1. _____
2. _____
3. _____
4. _____
5. _____
6. _____
7. _____
8. _____
9. _____

Among the five things shown below, one does not belong. Which one of the five is least like the other four?

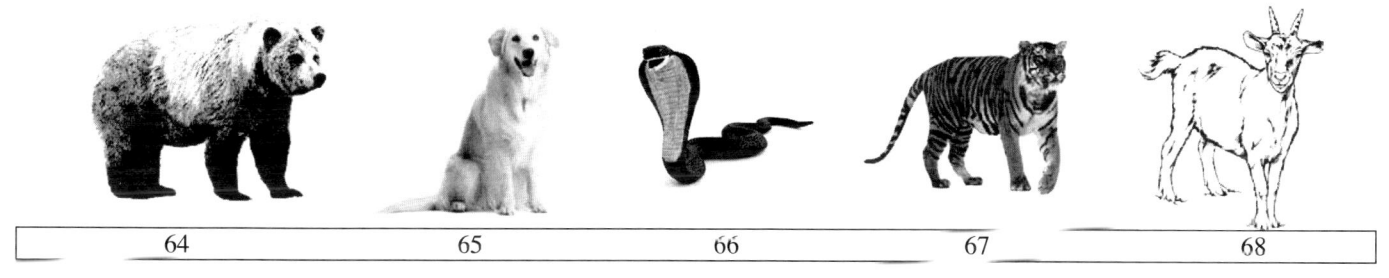

| 64 | 65 | 66 | 67 | 68 |

Possible answer is SNAKE (66). All the others have legs; the others are mammals.

| 69 | 70 | 71 | 72 | 73 |

The answer is APPLE. The others are vegetables.

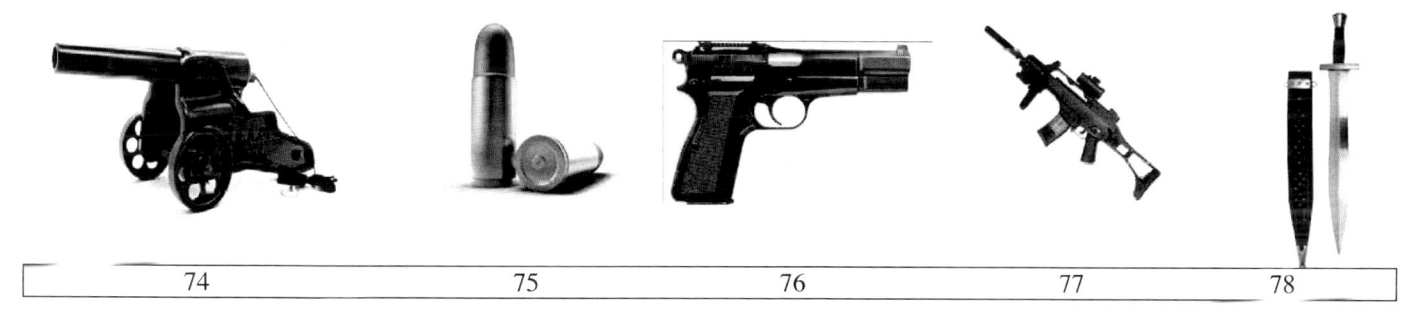

| 74 | 75 | 76 | 77 | 78 |

The answer is BULLET. The others are weapons.

CHAPTER 6

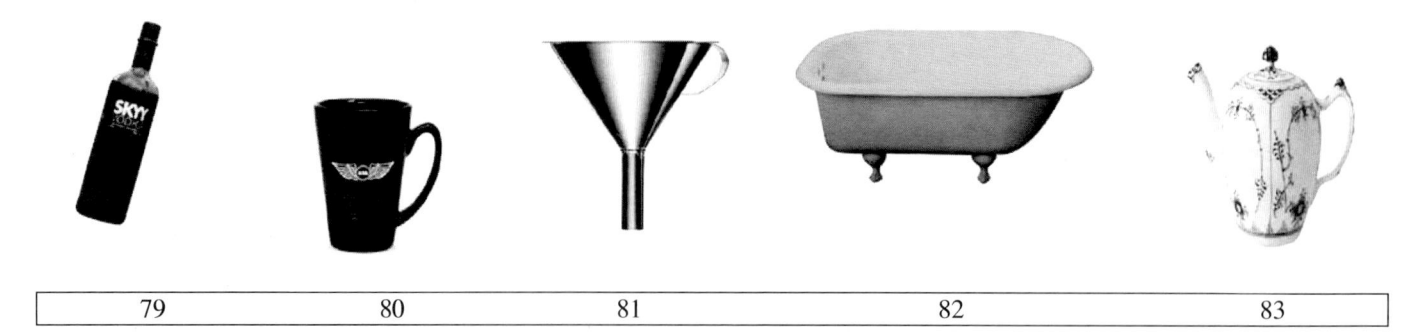

| 79 | 80 | 81 | 82 | 83 |

The answer is FUNNEL. The others hold liquids. They are containers.

The answer is KANGAROO. The others walk on 4 legs.

Step 3. Judgment

In some way, judgment is the most fundamental operation of human thinking. People have their ideas of how things should be. They then judge whether something matches this idea. Recognition is based on judgment. They see an unusual-looking cat or dog. Does this match mental picture of a cat or dog? Or does it challenge it? Experience gives people mental pictures of how things work and what happens under different circumstances. People then judge whether their actions are "right" depending upon whether these actions fit their mental pictures. There are rules in playing any game. There are traffic rules. There are rules of law. There are rules of grammar and rules of mathematics. People judge whether something is "right" depending on whether it follows or matches those rules.

Instruction:

Describe the following picture. What is going on? What is it? Where does it happen? How does it happen? Why does it happen? To whom does it happen? Who causes it to happen? What is wrong about it?

118

What Is Thinking?

Opposite

Write down the antonym (opposite meaning) in space provided:

Tall – short	Generous –	Nasty –	Familiar –	Joy –
Dark –	Early –	Haughty –	Friendly –	Sunset –
Clean –	Death –	Naïve –	Buy –	Disciple –
Rage –	Dry –	Comfortable –	Deny –	Remember –
Rare –	Smart –	Hazy –	Close –	Love –
Raw –	Creative –	Hazard –	Confession –	Good –
Close –	Smile –	Approval –	Trust –	Deep –
Hesitation –	Incidence –	Arrival –	Anxiety –	Light –
Achievement –	Rational –	Advantage –	Arousal –	Poor –
Peace –	Ironical –	Coward –	Knowledge –	Moist –

Step 4. Problem Solving

A problem is a gap between existing situation and desirable situation. A problem is usually some difficulty or thing that people want to overcome or be rid of. The term "problem" can also be used when people are trying to achieve some task, though in many cases "design" or "task achieving" are more appropriate.

When the course of action toward a desired objective is not easy or routine, then people have a problem.

The traditional method for problem solving is to find the cause of the problem and then to seek to remove that cause.

Fluency, Flexibility, and Originality

(Modified interesting ideas from Springboards to Creative Thinking by Patricia Tyler Muncy)

1. If you have a robot, what would you program it to do? List many interesting ideas. How many ideas you can come up with? _____

2. 50 imaginative fantastic excuses for not having your project done. The excuses can range from very believable to ridiculously unbelievable.

_____

3. Your office is a mess! Your boss is standing there with a scowl on his face wanting some explanation of why it looks like a disaster. Think up many highly imaginative, tall tale explanations of how your office got to be so messy.

_____

4. Sell that Haunted House! Imagine you are a Realtor with a haunted house to sell! Think of a number of clever "sales pitches" you can use. Example: "This haunted house represents a unique business opportunity! Yu can charge admission for guided tours of the house with guaranteed ghost appearances! This is an excellent buy for the investor who wants to get rich quick! _____

5. Super Gum. The president of the largest chewing gum factory in the world has asked you to develop some new and very unusual types of gum. Help him with at least 18 of your own unique ideas! Example: (1) Thinking Gum: It stimulates the brain and helps you remember better! (2) Freckle-Removing Gum: Chew a pack a day and freckles go away! (3) Vitamin containing gum. _____

6. So, That Is Woobly! What is Woobly? Is it a machine of some type? Is it a creature? Is it a product? Is it a piece of furniture? Draw your interpretation of a Woobly and describe its characteristics in as much detail as possible.

_____

7. A Wonderful Suitcase! Imagine that you have the most unusual magical suitcase! Begin listing at least 30 wild and unusual things it can do.

_____

CHAPTER 6

8. Super House of the Future! What would a house of the future be like? How would it be heated and cooled? What new, undreamed-of labour-saving conveniences would it have? Design your own Super House of the Future. _____

9. A Parrot with a Big Mouth! Imagine you have a parrot that talks too much. And that parrot's big mouth has created some pretty big problems for you and your family! Think of at least 20 different things that your parrot has said that have caused lots of trouble. Example: He told my boss that I said she was getting fat and should go on a diet! _____

10. Name that product. Much careful thought goes into the name of a new product. The name, if well chosen, can really give a boost to sales. Imagine you are the new product manager of the six new products below. You must think of a good marketable name for each one. Example: (1) A new soup; (2) A new toothpaste; (3) A new candy bar. _____

11. Unfinished Pictures: Each box below contains some lines of an unfinished picture. What could these unfinished pictures be? Use your imagination! List 10 things the picture could be if it were finished. Then select one of the possibilities for each unfinished picture and add lines to complete each.

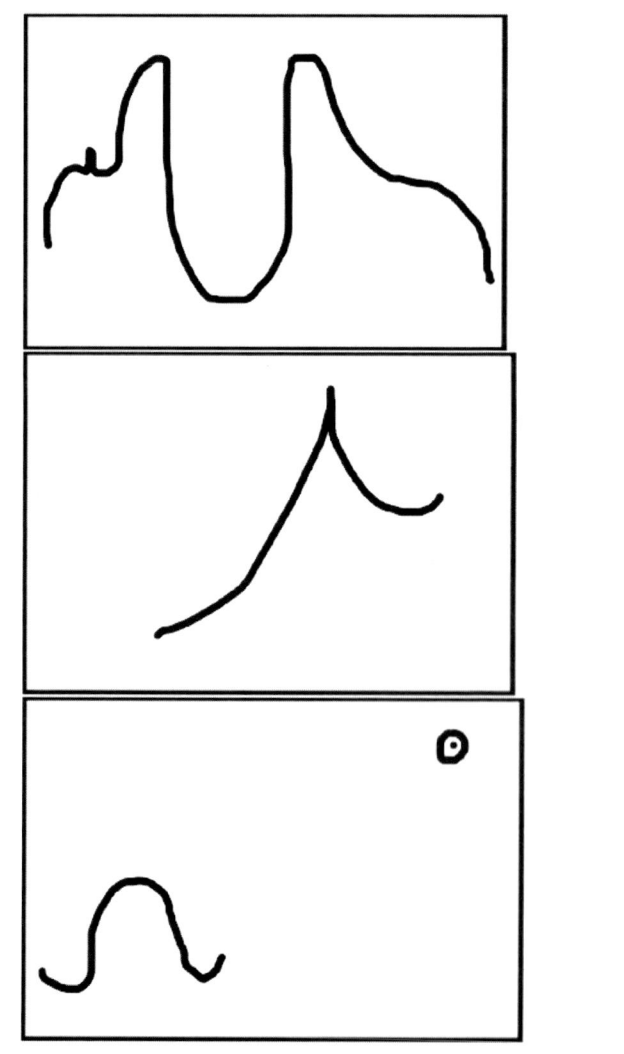

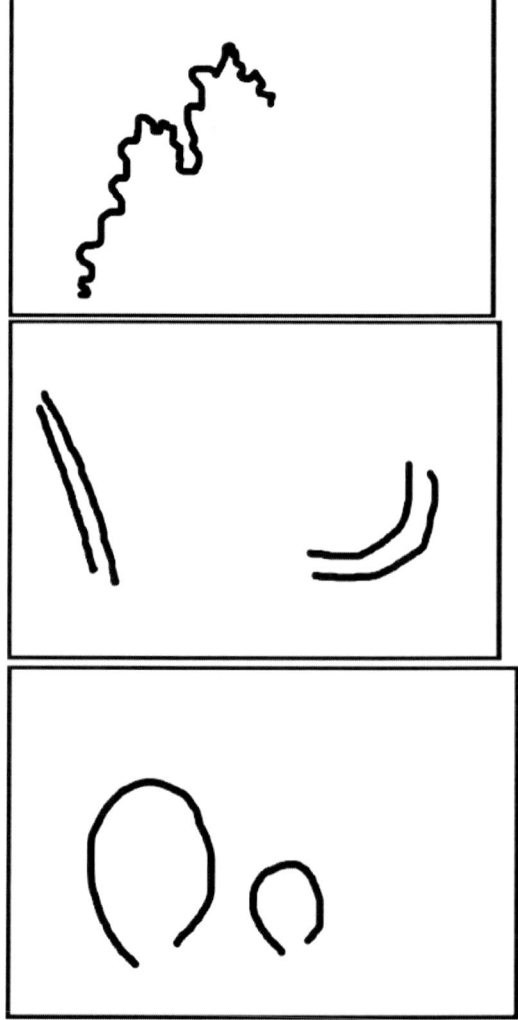

CHAPTER 7

Modes of Thinking

How brain processes the information? What is the most effective way to think and solve problems? How improve thinking process?

LEARNING OBJECTIVES

After reading this chapter, you will be able to

Define, describe, compare and contrast 21 modes of thinking:

1. Analogical Thinking
2. Symbolic Thinking
3. Analysis
4. Synthesis
5. Holistic
6. Systems
7. Dialectical
8. Integrative
9. Heuristic
10. Critical
11. Divergent
12. Convergent
13. Conscious
14. Unconscious
15. Deductive
16. Inductive
17. Abductive
18. The "Doubting Game"
19. The "Believing Game"
20. Automatic
21. Active.

QUESTIONS FOR DISCUSSION

1. What is the difference between various modes of thinking?
2. Is there the best mode of thinking?
3. Can thinking be improved?
4. Are we born with some preferences for certain mode of thinking?

Prologue

Previous sections demonstrated how information finds its way into and out of human system and how it is stored. Finally, it needs to be processed and manipulated. This is perhaps the area which is most complex and which separates humans from other animals. While they also receive and store information, there is little evidence to suggest that they can use it in quite the same way as humans. Similarly, artificial intelligence has produced machines that can see (albeit in a limited way) and store information. But their ability to use that information is limited to small domains.

Humans, on the other hand, are able to use information to reason and solve problems, and indeed do these activities when the information is partial or unavailable. Human thought is conscious and self-aware: while a person may not always be able to identify the process he or she uses, e or she can identify the products to these processes, his or her thoughts. In addition, people are able to think about things of which they have no experience, and solve problems that they have never seen before. How is this done?

Thinking can require different amount of knowledge. Some thinking activities are very direct and the knowledge required is constrained. Others require vast amounts of knowledge from different domains. For example, performing a subtraction calculation requires a relatively small amount of knowledge, from a constrained domain, whereas understanding newspaper headlines demands knowledge of politics, social structures, public figures and world events.

In this section multiple modes of thinking are presented: reasoning and problem solving. In practice these are not completely distinct since the activity of solving a problem may well involve all of them. However, the distinction is a common one and is helpful in clarifying the processes involved.

MODES OF THINKING

There are 21 different modes of thinking identified by various researchers.
1. Analogical Thinking
2. Symbolic Thinking
3. Analysis
4. Synthesis
5. Holistic
6. Systems
7. Dialectical
8. Integrative
9. Heuristic
10. Divergent
11. Convergent
12. Conscious
13. Unconscious
14. Critical
15. Deductive
16. Inductive
17. Abductive
18. The "Doubting Game"
19. The "Believing Game"
20. Automatic
21. Reversal.

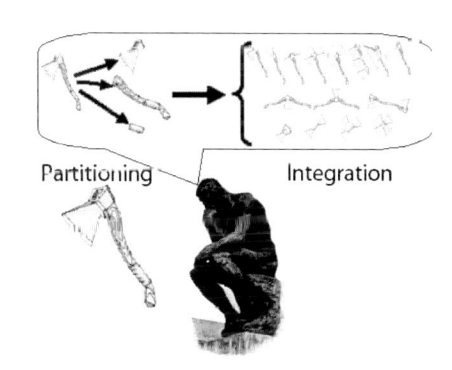

1. ANALOGICAL THINKING

Analogical thinking is *taking ideas from one context and applying them to another context* to produce a new idea (used in music composition, cartoons, science and inventions, literature, movie-making, television, Broadway, architecture, clothes design, etc.)

123

CHAPTER 7

Analogical thinking can be a conscious technique if you deliberately ask questions like these:

"What else is like this?"

"What have others done?"

"Where can I find an idea?"

"What ideas can I modify to fit my problem?"

It is the ***foundation for discovery*** and ***invention.*** The most common creative process is analogical thinking - the transfer of an idea from one context to a new one. Perhaps 80 percent of creative ideas are rooted in analogical thinking, and examples abound in every field of human creativity.

In *music*, Aaron Copeland's Appalachian Spring was based on the Quaker folk tune, Simple Gifts. You may know that the U.S. national anthem Star Spangled Banner originated as an English drinking song. And the Broadway musical *Cats* was based on T. S. Eliot's Book of *Practical Cats*.

Political cartoonists and creators of cartoon strips continually borrow ideas from movies, television commercials, the Bible, children's stories, and the headlines. Remember the caricature of Ronald Reagan, Ronbo? Did you notice the caption by cartoonist Gary Larson: "Moses as a kid," under a boy who was raising his arms to part the milk in his glass? Many movies, from Gone with the Wind to The Ten Commandments, derive from historical or Biblical themes.

We also see analogical thinking in the ***mechanical realm***. The irreplaceable fastener ***Velcro*** was inspired by the obnoxious cocklebur. Gutenberg's printing press was a combination of the stamper used for minting coins and a wine press. Eli Whitney was inspired to invent the cotton gin after watching a cat pluck at a chicken through a fence. The resulting paw full of feathers apparently reminded him of cotton fibers.

One technique is asking how nature has solved a similar problem. ***Pringles Potato Chips*** were conceived via the analogy of wet leaves--which stack compactly and do not destroy themselves. Darwin reversed the situation, using a human solution to explain a natural phenomenon: His origin of species explanation stemmed from selective cattle breeding practices.

Finally, virtually every architect and designer keeps stacks of books and magazines filled with ideas waiting to be adopted.

But you need not sit back and wait for analogous connections to appear by themselves.

Analogy can be used to make ***predictions***, provide ***explanations***, and restructure our ***knowledge***. Analogy is also used to ***influence public opinion***, ***fight battles***, win ***wars***, start and finish ***relationships***, and ***advertise*** laundry detergent. Analogies are also ubiquitous in ***science***. Because analogy use is so common, and such an essential part of human existence, there has been much research in Cognitive Science on the nature of analogy - many experiments have been conducted and computational models proposed.

Analogical thought can serve the purpose of setting forth an explanation by the correspondence of elements in ***known situations*** with those in fully understood situations. Scientific discovery processes are often aided by analogical thought. In political, economic, and intellectual movements, analogies are widely used in argumentation and persuasion. Analogies in the form of expressive metaphors and similes are prevalent in classical literature and everyday language.

A theory of analogical thinking and a ***computational model*** of the theory have been developed by Holyoak and Thagard (1989).

Every one holds ***many beliefs***. By and large, we hope that our beliefs are not irrational or unreasonable. And the more strongly we hold a set of beliefs, the stronger we hope that they are not irrational. Consistency is the minimum requirement of rationality. If we have a set of beliefs which are at odds with each other, rationality demands us to revise them so that the whole set becomes internally consistent. Most of us hold some beliefs on moral/ethical issues (e.g., such as whether suicide is morally wrong, or whether someone should be denied of the opportunity of education just because of his/her sex or skin color). Consistency plays one of the most important roles in moral reasoning (indeed reasoning of any kind). So if we do hold some moral beliefs, we should at least make sure that those beliefs are consistent with each other (putting aside for the moment the further question whether those beliefs are also true).

Analogical arguments are very often used in ***moral reasoning*** (i.e., reasoning about moral issues), and they often help us think about the consistency of our moral outlook (i.e., the set of moral beliefs we hold). The basic idea of analogical arguments in moral reasoning is: treat similar case similarly. For example, suppose we are already convinced that action X (e.g., slapping a human baby for fun) is morally wrong. Also suppose we are convinced that action Y (e.g., lashing a dog for fun) is similar to X in many aspects relevant to deciding whether or not the action is morally wrong (e.g., both actions are infliction of pain on innocent beings, both are voluntary, and both are motivated by trivial self-interests, namely fun). Then, to be consistent, we should also think that Y is morally wrong to a similar extent to which X is wrong.

In short, an ***analogical argument*** in ethics employs a presumably uncontroversial case X, to which we are supposed to agree to give a certain verdict, and a controversial case Y, to which we disagree about what verdict to give. The purpose of an analogical argument is to settle the controversy of Y, by comparing it with Y (which may be either a real case or a fictional case). What an analogical argument does is (1) to show that X and Y are analogous to each other (i.e., similar in many relevant aspects), and then (2) to point out that for the sake of consistency, the controversial case Y should receive a verdict similar to the one given to the uncontroversial case X. Analogical arguments in ethics often take the following basic form:

P1. Action X is morally wrong/permissible/unblamable/right/virtuous/etc. [Presumably uncontroversial verdict for X]
P2. Actions X and Y are analogous to each other. [Analogy between X and Y]
C. Action Y is morally wrong/permissible/unblamable/right/virtuous/etc. [From P1 & P2] Or
P1. State-of-affairs X is morally good/bad/neutral. [Presumably uncontroversial verdict for X]
P2. States-of-affairs X and Y are analogous to each other. [Analogy between X and Y]
C. State-of-affairs Y is morally good/bad/neutral. [From P1 & P2]

Analogy is property of **higher order thought** because it requires **fluency** – lots of ideas – and **integration** across multiple representations.

Analogy can also be thought of as *flexible pattern recognition*, the process involved in critical thinking and deduction, inference, and solutions by insight.

Analogical thinking - *dealing with a new situation by adapting a similar familiar situation*.

Many scientific discoveries were made based upon analogies.

Analogies and metaphors can ***make new and unfamiliar concepts more meaningful*** to students by connecting what they know to what they are learning. According to the National Research Council (2000) the effective use of metaphors and analogies is an important ***educational strategy***. Interestingly, even the concept of learning itself is described by numerous metaphors (e.g., planting flowers, switching on a light bulb, peeling an onion, a quest, etc.). In teaching, using either analogy or metaphor allows the instructor to relate a potentially unfamiliar idea with that which is familiar. For many instructors the objective for doing so is to transform a foreign concept to one that may be more recognizable to the student. Interestingly, the Greek root of metaphor is "metapherein," meaning to transfer; such as when one attempts to transfer the understanding or experience of one thing by relating it in terms of another.

Pedagogical use of analogy and metaphor can enhance learning and retention, but they must have a high degree of resonance for the listener. Students must be able to recognize the meaning that is being conveyed and its relevance to the issue at hand. Metaphors or analogies must be based on something that is familiar to the student. Glynn and Takahashi (1998) indicate that instructional use of analogies and metaphors must be utilized carefully, as incorrect use or a failure to appreciate the preconceptions that students may possess can lead to greater rather than less confusion. To be most effective, an analogy or metaphor must transfer ideas from a familiar concept to one that is less familiar or unknown. According to Bowers (1993) the metaphorical relationship must be clear and accurate—possessing face validity. Properly used, metaphors and analogies can provide a type of shorthand to help define the intangible or abstract. However, the process of selecting appropriate analogies or metaphors is necessarily constrained by the understanding or perceptions of learners. Teachers must ensure that the coherence of the metaphor is accurate and clear; if not, the intended effect of greater understanding of the topic or issue can be lost (Earle, 1995). An analogy works best when the concept being taught is new. If the student already has some understanding of the topic, it may be better to build on the already available framework. Use analogies only if the concept is hard to grasp. Analogies *take time to set up and explain*. If the concept is simple, a straightforward explanation may be quicker and will not open the student to possible misconceptions from misapplication of the analogy.

- Make sure the student understands the analog. If the students do not even understand the analog, it would not help in the understanding of the target concept.
- Explain the specific similarities. Simply stating the analogy does not focus the learners' attention on how it is similar.
- Be aware of misconceptions the analogy may leave. Ruhl warns that one of the greatest hazards of teaching by analogy is that the student may transfer inappropriate knowledge from the analog to the target and leave with misconceptions. Analogies can hinder as well as help learning. When stretched too far, analogies lead to misconceptions: "An analogy is like a car. If you take it too far, it breaks down."

When using analogies, one has to go through the following steps:
- Introduce the target concept (e.g. the DNA molecule). Review the analog concept (e.g. a long, twisted 'ladder').
- Identify relevant features of target and analog (e.g. the two side handles of the ladder contain sugar and phosphate units; the 'rungs' are made of pairs of chemicals called bases).
- Map similarities (e.g. 'side handles of the ladder' and DNA backbone; 'rungs' and bases).

Analogical Thinking is the transfer of an idea from one context to a new one.

Analogical thought can serve the purpose of setting forth an explanation by the correspondence of elements in known situations with those in fully understood situations.

Analogical thinking is the brain's ability to apply things it already knows to something it does not. Analogical thinking allows us to learn new things quickly by comparing them to what we already know. Analogical thinking is the most common type of thought process in the brain.

- Indicate where analogy breaks down (e.g. a ladder is rigid; a DNA molecule can open up and be replicated).
- Draw conclusions (e.g. about the structure and function of DNA or about mutations occurring at the bases).

Example: Protein synthesis process looks like the process of building a house.
Questions:
This problem looks like…
My knowledge of Psychology (Biology, other disciplines) can be applied to this subject …
Where this phenomenon can be applied outside of this discipline?

Analogy Organizer	
New Concept Bird Migration	**Familiar Concept** Vacation
Similarities	Differences
• Birds and humans are in need of rest while traveling. Coastal wetlands are important to bird migration; rest stops are important to people driving long distances. • Both birds and people travel from cold climates to warm climates. • Birds and some people return to the same general area year after year. • Some birds migrate during daylight. Some people travel during the day. • Travel routes that both people and birds use are usually well established. • Bad weather is a hazard for both people and birds.	• Ponds and marshes provide food and shelter for traveling birds. Rest areas, hotels, and gas stations provide food, rest, comfort, and fuel for traveling people. • Hazards include predators and buildings for birds, but malfunctioning transportation is a hazard for people. • Migration is instinctual, vacationing is planned. • Some people vacation to a colder climate. When birds migrate it is always to a warmer climate.
Categories of Comparison	
Dependence on rest Travel to warm locations Methods and hazards of travel Return to original location	

Archimedes' Principle of Buoyancy

The Law: According to Archimedes' principle, a body wholly or partially submerged in liquid is buoyed up by a force equal to the weight of the displaced liquid. This buoyant force depends on the density of the liquid and the volume of the object, but not its shape.

The Famous Legend behind the Law:
One day, King Hieron II of Syracuse, Sicily, wanted to find out whether his wreath-shaped crown was actually made from pure gold. He called upon Archimedes to find out (without damaging the crown, say by melting it down). Roman architect and engineer Marcus Vitruvius wrote:

While Archimedes was turning the problem over, he chanced to come to the place of bathing, and there, as he was sitting down in the tub, he noticed that the amount of water which flowed over the tub was equal to the amount by which his body was immersed. This showed him means of solving the problem … In his joy, he leapt out of the tub and, rushing naked toward his home, he cried out with a loud voice that he had found what he sought.

Archimedes was able to obtain the exact volume of the crown by dunking it in water and measuring the displaced water. He then took the weight of the crown and divided it by its volume to get the density of the crown, which turned out to be between that of gold and silver. Archimedes was thus able to show that the wreath was not made out of pure gold (and the royal goldsmith was executed).

Modern scholars suggest that this story was bogus, as it would be unlikely that Archimedes had measuring equipment with sufficient accuracy to detect the difference (plus, he hated to bathe).

Modes of Thinking

The law seems simple, but it is actually not intuitive that objects with equal volume experience the same buoyant force when held under water: cubes made of cork and lead would experience the same buoyant force, yet would have completely different behavior. This is because the different ratios of buoyant force to object weights.

Archimedes' Principle of Buoyancy has many applications, including determining the pressure of a liquid as a function of depth. It helps us understand how floatation works and is one of the founding principles of hydrostatics.

The Man behind the Law:

Archimedes of Syracuse (287-212 B.C.) was a Greek geometer and is often regarded as one of the greatest mathematicians and scientists who ever lived.
Here are a few things about Archimedes you may not know:
- Plutarch wrote that Archimedes was so obsessed with math that his servants had to force him to bathe, and that while they scrubbed him, he continued to draw geometrical figures on his body!
- Archimedes invented a machine called the Archimedean screw to pump water.
- He also invented a "death ray" weapon using a set of mirrors that focused sunlight on Roman ships, setting them on fire. After many scientists discounted the story as false, David Wallace of MIT actually did the experiment: He had his students build an oak replica of a Roman ship and focused sunlight on it using 127 mirrored tiles from a distance of 30 meters. After ten minutes of exposure, the ship burst into flames!
- When the Romans captured Syracuse in 212 B.C., a Roman soldier came upon the mathematician who was studying a mathematical diagram drawn in the sand. Archimedes was annoyed by the soldier's interruption, and said "Don't disturb my circles" before he was killed. Moral of the story: don't piss off a Roman soldier!

Examples
1. Finding a good job is like walking on hot sand
People try and get across the sand as fast as possible so that they don't get burned. Could we design a database to make finding peoples ideal jobs a faster and pain free process?
1. Top end computers are like sponges in water
Sponges soak up large amounts of liquid, Is there a device we could make that would keep computers from soaking up so much energy and run more efficiently?
2. Teaching a child is like reading a book
Books inspire people and provoke the imagination, could we make a lesson plan that would inspire children in such a way as well as provoke their imagination?
3. Producing a game is like a ballet.
Ballets are well timed and choreographed; do we need to organize our production team so that it is timed out more effectively?
4. Prices negations are like playing poker
Playing pokers is more skill then luck, it's about being able to read the person and the situation, can we instruct our salesmen to be effective at reading people?
5. Running a store is like a cool breeze
A cool gentle breeze calms people down and cheers them up, if we use a combination of fans and air-conditioning to simulate such a breeze on people entering our store can we but them in a better mood to buy our products?
6. Customer service is like good hat
People expect hats to be comfortable and to fit them, can we assign one customer service representative for small groups of people so that the customer will feel more comfortable interacting with the same person?
7. Writing music is like a chugging a energy drink
When someone chugs an energy drink they get a rush. Can we write a song that will stimulate that same region of the brain?
8. Patching software is like a crafting a sword

Examples of using analogies:

Parables

Case-based reasoning

Military planning

Legal reasoning

Politics

Mind as a computer

Metaphor in language

Inventions such as velcro, the telephone, and Windows

Analogical thinking involves *four stages*:

1. A target problem (new situation) needs to be solved.

2. Retrieval of a source problem (familiar situation) from memory.

3. Comparison of the similar features of the target problem and the source problem.

4. Adapting the source problem to produce a solution to the target problem.

CHAPTER 7

A finished sword is well balanced and works for a very long time as long as it is maintained well, if we work in multiplatform code into the software can we make the software better balanced and longer lasting?

9. Group meetings are like homeruns

Homeruns are an exciting and meaningful part of baseball. Can we make our meetings an exciting and meaningful part of our business plan by changing the locations of our meetings.

According to the National Research Council (2000) the effective use of metaphors and analogies is an important *educational strategy*. Interestingly, even the concept of learning itself is described by numerous metaphors (e.g., planting flowers, switching on a light bulb, peeling an onion, a quest, etc.). In teaching, using either analogy or metaphor allows the instructor to relate a potentially unfamiliar idea with that which is familiar. For many instructors the objective for doing so is to transform a foreign concept to one that may be more recognizable to the student. Interestingly, the Greek root of metaphor is "metapherein," meaning to transfer; such as when one attempts to transfer the understanding or experience of one thing by relating it in terms of another.

The tumor problem (Duncker, 1945):

A doctor wants to destroy a tumor inside a patient's body without damaging the surrounding healthy tissue. There is a device for delivering rays that can destroy the tumor, but at the intensity needed these rays also destroy the surrounding healthy tissue. What should the doctor do?

The fortress story (Gick & Holyoak, 1980) helps subjects solve the tumor problem.

Without hearing the fortress story, about 10% of college students solve the tumor problem.

After hearing the fortress story, about 75% of college students solve the tumor problem.

Similarity between the target and the source problem helps people notice and use the source problem as an analogy for the target problem.

For example, mentioning that two ray machines are available makes the tumor problem structurally similar to the fortress story, and easier to solve (Holyoak & Koh, 1987).

Finding Useful Analogs

Note: Source analogs that are "structurally similar" to target analogs are more useful than those that are superficially similar.

Fortress Story (source) Tumor Problem (target)
cause: powerful (army)
damage (army, country side)
cause: divided (army)
preserve (country side)
cause: converged (army)
destroy (dictator)
cause: powerful (rays)
damage (rays, healthy tissue)
cause: ?
preserve (healthy tissue)
cause: ?
destroy (tumor)

The Fortress Story is a useful source analog for the Tumor Problem because the relations in the two situations align perfectly: powerful, damage, preserve, and destroy.

What features do the target and source share?

How can we modify the source to solve the target?

Situations that merely have overlap in terms of objects, concepts, or arguments are less useful because they do not overlap in causal relations.

For example, a story about a doctor who surgically removes a patient's tumor that was caused by exposure to radiation shares the same objects as our Tumor Problem (doctor, patient, tumor, radiation), but does not align 'structurally' with the Tumor problem.

The sentences below are false when we consider only the literal meaning, but they may be true when we consider the metaphorical meaning.

- This job is a jail.
- It's Etna in here.
- Jack is a tiger in union meanings.

In each case, what is the source analog and what is the target analog?

Metaphorical Meaning

We can distinguish two types of meaning.

1.literal meaning – meaning that is based on the standard meanings of words and how they are combined into a sentence

2.metaphorical meaning – meaning that is based on superficial or structural similarities between objects or situations

We often use sentences to convey a metaphoric meaning rather than a literal meaning.

Type of Analogies:

1.superficial similarity - the extent to which two objects, subjects, phenomena, or situations involve the same concepts or arguments

2.structural similarity - the extent to which two objects, subjects, phenomena, or situations involve the same composition, relations, or predicates

3.functional similarity - the extent to which two objects, subjects, phenomena, or situations involve the same way of accomplishing specific goals.

Modes of Thinking

What are the similarities between the objects or situations that are being compared?

Why doesn't the following sentence convey the same metaphorical meaning as sentence 1 above?

   This job is a zebra.

Analogy in Language

People cannot help producing analogical (metaphorical) interpretations (Glucksberg & Keysar, 1990).

Decide whether each of the following sentences is literally true:
1. Some desks are junkyards.
2. Some desks are roads.

Despite the fact that both sentences are literally false, subjects take longer to make these judgments for #1 than for #2.

These results suggest that people impose a metaphorical interpretation on a sentence when it makes sense to do so, even when they are instructed to interpret it only literally.

Glucksberg & Keysar (1980) conclude that metaphorical interpretation is normal, not a special process that occurs only when literal interpretation doesn't work.

Brainstorming

The granddaddy creative technique, brainstorming, was the brainchild of Alex Osborn, co-founder of a major advertising agency. The procedure is simple and familiar. First you devise wild - even preposterous - ideas, and jot down every one. But the key is this: save the criticism and evaluation until this process is completed. Osborn tells us, with disarming logic, that we cannot simultaneously be creative and critical. Furthermore, he adds, wild ideas can often be "tamed" into workable solutions.

Although most people consider brainstorming a group technique, you can brainstorm by yourself as well as before a large audience. But the recommended small group, with 10 or 12 members, is usually suitable to a variety of situations. Brainstorming, I'd say, has survived for half a century because it works.

Attribute Listing

While brainstorming is a general procedure, attribute listing is a specific idea-finding technique (one that could even be used while brainstorming). You identify the key characteristics, or attributes, of the product or process in question. Then you think up ways to change, modify, or improve each attribute (in design engineering this is called the substitution method).

Almost anyone can "disassemble" a product into its attributes and then think of modifications for most of them. For example, a can of soda has these attributes: size, shape, color, color pattern, decorative theme, material, possible uses after modification, other audiences for the product if modified. Can you invent alterations for each of these attributes? Fran Stryker supplied himself with plots for Lone Ranger radio and television episodes for a couple of decades by modifying these characteristics: characters, goals, obstacles, and outcomes.

Morphological Synthesis

Morphological synthesis is a simple elaboration of attribute listing. After completing the list of attributes, list changes in one attribute (such as "products") along the horizontal axis, and list changes in a second attribute (such as "markets") along the vertical axis. Idea combinations, or syntheses, will appear in the intersections, or cells, of the table. Morphological synthesis will force you to look at many surprising combinations.

Idea Checklists

Have you ever consulted a telephone directory or a supplier's catalog as a "checklist" of resources or ideas for solving problems? You may not know that checklists have been written expressly to solve problems creatively. The best known is Osborn's "73 Idea Spurring Questions."

Of course, none of these techniques is guaranteed to solve your research problems. But they can help you find ideas without forcing you to wait for an uncooperative muse.

Analogical Thinking Every Day

Many parents know that *young children* take comfort in getting a kiss on an injury to "make it better." Little Aaron, aged 24 months, would routinely come to his mother saying things like, "I bump my head. Kiss it." But one morning, for the first time ever, the tables turned. While his mother was dressing him, she realized she had a bruise on her hand. Without really thinking she said, "Ow, my hand hurts."

Osborn's 73 Idea Spurring Questions

Put to other uses?

New ways to use as is?

Other uses if modified? Modify?

New twist?

Change meaning, color, motion, sound, form?

Other changes?

Magnify?

What to add?

Greater frequency?

Longer?

Extra value?

Duplicate?

Multiply?

Exaggerate?

Minify?

What to subtract?

Condensed?

Miniature?

Lighter?

Split up?

Understate?

Rearrange?

Interchange components?

Other sequence?

Change schedule?

Combine?

How about a blend, an assortment?

Combine units?

Combine purposes?

Combine appeals?

Aaron immediately responded, "I kiss it." His mother then put her hand in front of Aaron's face and received a kiss from him.

Aaron's reaction provides a small example of thinking by analogy: trying to reason and learn about a new situation (the target analog) by relating it to a more familiar situation (the source analog) that can be viewed as structurally parallel. Aaron's source is the knowledge that when he had been hurt in the past, his mother's kiss had made it better; this source is now evoked by the target situation of his mother's bruised hand (the access or retrieval step in analogy use). The child goes on to find the correspondences between the source and target (mapping step). Note that he does not simply use the superficial mapping of his mother to herself (if he had, he would have simply told mom to kiss her own hand!). Rather, Aaron maps his mother to himself (for she is now the injured one), and himself to her. Based on these mappings, he finds a solution to the target problem: his kiss will ease her pain (inference step). Although we don't know for sure, it is quite possible that Aaron's use of analogy also led him to learn something more general, a kind of abstraction of the commonalities shared by the source and target (learning step). Roughly, he may have induced a schema or rule along the lines, "If a person is injured, a kiss from a loved one will ease the pain." Our description of Aaron as analogizing from treatment of his own injury to treatment of his mother's assumes that he had not previously formed this general rule.

Aaron at age two had an analogical mind. The remarkable thing about this example of a child's reasoning is that it is not especially exceptional. Analogical thinking can be traced from these early phylogenetic and ontogenetic beginnings to an extraordinarily diverse range of uses by human adults, including generation of metaphors for the self, decision making in politics, business and law, and scientific discovery (Holyoak & Thagard, 1989, 1995). The multiconstraint theory assumes that people's use of analogy is guided by a number of general constraints that jointly encourage coherence in analogical thinking. We will first describe these constraints in qualitative terms, illustrating them with examples from psychological studies. We will then survey additional examples of naturalistic uses of analogy that can be understood in terms of the constraints. Finally, we will discuss approaches to implementing the multiconstraint theory in computational models that simulate the human analogical mind. (For a more thorough discussion of these issues see Holyoak & Thagard (1995).)

Young children, before they enter school, without any specialized tutoring from their parents or elders, develop a capacity for analogical thinking (e.g., Gentner, 1977; Goswami & Brown, 1989; Inagaki & Hatano, 1987; Holyoak, Junn, & Billman, 1984). The analogical mind is simply the mind of a normal human being. Indeed, to a limited but impressive degree, it is the mind of at least a few other primates, most notably chimpanzees that have received extensive training in symbol manipulation (Gillan, Premack & Woodruff, 1981).

Similarity, Structure, Purpose

Three broad classes of constraints form the basis of the ***multiconstraint theory***. Each of these constraints can be illustrated with young Aaron's analogy.

First, the analogy is guided to some extent by **direct similarity of the elements involved**. We noted that Aaron did not simply map his mother to herself (which would have maximized one local similarity between mapped objects). However, the analogy clearly depended on similarity of key relations between objects: the source and target both involve an injury sustained by a loved one. In general, similarity of concepts at any level of abstraction contributes to analogical thinking, particularly in the initial access step (e.g., Keane, 1986; Ross, 1989; Seifert, McKoon, Abelson, & Ratcliff, 1986).

Second, the analogy is guided by a pressure to identify consistent **structural parallels** between the roles in the source and target domain (Gentner, 1983). The key structural constraint underlying analogical mapping and inference is a pressure to establish an isomorphism -- a set of consistent, one-to-one correspondences -- between the elements of the source and target. Thus once Aaron had decided to place the source and target "injuries" into correspondence (based on similarity of relations), structural consistency required that the person injured in the source (child) be mapped onto the person injured in the target (mother), because each is playing the same relational role. In this case the constraint of maintaining consistent correspondences apparently dominated the rival similarity constraint, which by itself would encourage mapping the mother to herself. In the subsequent inference stage, consistency further required that it be the child in the target (now mapped to mother in the source) who provides the soothing kiss.

Third, the constraint of purpose implies that analogical thinking is **guided by the reasoner's goals** - what the analogy is intended to achieve. Why did Aaron even consider the analogy with the kissing ritual? It appears that his mother's expression of pain gave rise to the goal of alleviating it; this goal in turn caused the child's attention to focus on those aspects of the target situation that were relevant to achieving a solution. Once his attention was biased so as to favor goal-relevant aspects of the situation, Aaron was led to access source analogs involving injuries, rather than (for example) earlier instances of being dressed by his mother.

These three kinds of constraints - similarity, structure, and purpose - do not operate like rigid rules dictating the interpretation of analogies. Instead they function more like the various pressures that guide an architect engaged in creative design, with some forces converging, others in opposition, and their constant interplay pressing toward some satisfying compromise that is internally coherent. When we describe computational models of analogy, we will suggest how such local contradictions between constraints can be resolved by a process of constraint satisfaction. First, however, we will briefly review some examples of experimental tests that reveal the operation of the constraints in the analogical thinking of college students.

Here are some of the ***metaphors*** used by people recovering from severe ***psychological trauma***:
- I am a time bomb ticking, ready to explode.
- I feel like I am caught up in a tornado.
- I am a rabbit stuck in the glare of headlights who can't move.
- My life is like a rerun of a movie that won't stop.
- I feel like I'm in a cave and can't get out.
- Home is like a pressure cooker.
- I am a robot with no feelings.

All of these examples involve analogical mappings from a familiar situation to the situation of the patient. Meichenbaum (1994, p. 115) describes how changes in metaphors used by clients can mark improvements in their conditions. Recovering trauma victims ***replace metaphors*** such as those in the list in the previous paragraph by metaphors such as the following:
- One door closes and another opens.
- I want to be the author of my own stories.
- Get back in the driver's seat.
- Put a new coin in my juke box and play a new tune.
- I want to move out of whirlpools and into still waters.

The use of these hopeful metaphors for clients' problems suggests that people can map themselves to persons or situations in ways that suggest solutions to personal problems. Recognition of patients' changing metaphors can therefore be a useful part of Jane's clinical practice. There is as yet no experimental evidence that metaphor change plays a causal role in the patients' improvements, but clinical observations of patients suggest that metaphor change is an integral part of healing, not just a reflection of emotional states before and after treatment.

Analogy and Metaphor

Whether you are teaching someone else something new or trying to learn something yourself or trying to solve a problem, one of the best ways for doing that is to compare the unfamiliar, unknown, or problematic with something familiar and understandable. This is the method of analogy, to find a familiar thing or process that seems somewhat like the idea or problem to be clarified.

In creative thinking, analogies are used for their suggestive qualities, to see what ideas they can break loose, and especially for helping to examine the problem better. By searching for several points of similarity between the analogy and the problem, new aspects of the problem are revealed and new approaches arise.

Example problem: *Devise a better way to find your way driving through the fog. Analogy: This is like a nearsighted person finding his way around. How does he do that? feels with his hands, looks at the ground, uses glasses, waves a cane, asks directions.*

Ideas: *feel around--a radar system or fog lights or other feelers, uses glasses--develop a vision enhancing device, such as night light amplification, looks at ground--develop system for car to follow a track on the ground.*

Another analogy for the same problem: *This is like a traveler in a strange country trying to find his way to a particular location. Use direction signs, radio stations with tourist broadcasts. The traveler goes slow, asks directions, uses guidebook and perhaps foreign language dictionary. What is similar in the problem?*

Ideas: *direction signs--put signs or lights along the side of fog shrouded roads, asks directions--an electronic query system in the car?*

A metaphor is a comparison between two unlike things, in which one thing is identified with the other. In problem solving, the use of metaphor helps to break out of a stereotyped or obvious view. Again, similarities between these two essentially unlike things are looked for.

For example: *This problem is a real doughnut. My work schedule is a tree or barbed wire fence or brick wall or flowerpot.*

Hmm. My work schedule is a flowerpot, and right now there are too many flowers in it and not enough water. So I need more water or fewer flowers if I want healthy blossoms. I had been thinking in terms of fewer flowers (fewer things to do), but now I see that if I use more water (get some help and support), then I can do the same amount of work without suffering.

There is still some good thinking in traditional metaphors, like society as a ship, hierarchies as a great chain, and so on. For example, "History's not my cup of tea." Well, what is your cup of tea? What do you really like? A subject that's hot, sweet, strong, clear, weak, brimming over, aromatic, mixed with cream, flavored with honey or orange blossoms? What are the corresponding realities to each part of the metaphor? Strong equals weighty, technical, and concrete? Or orange blossom equals improved with esthetics, etc. But new metaphors are often the most revealing. So discover your own.

Try It Yourself
Analogy and Metaphor. Think of a good, original analogy or metaphor for one of the following and the trace at least four similarities. Describe the similarities in complete sentences.

1. studying
2. driving a car
3. solving problems
4. using a computer
5. education
6. love
7. painting

Trigger Concepts

A trigger concept (or idea seed or random seed) is an idea creating technique operated by bringing an unrelated idea into the problem and forcing connections or similarities between the two.

Example problem: *improve TV programming*
Trigger concept: *road*
Questions of association: *How is TV programming like a road? (a journey, dangerous curves, linear progress--would better continuity improve TV? scenery makes roads interesting); Does TV programming have a road in it? (bumpy, rough, leading astray); What do roads do? They take you somewhere. Does TV programming take you somewhere? Could improved programming do this better? More location filming? More programs from abroad? Programs that take viewers on intellectual journey? What are roads like? ribbons, tourist havens between the scenery, the route to something else, a path toward real life. What about TV programs that are the route to something else, like happiness, education, thinking, art, escape*

Another Example Problem: *How can we individualize mass education so that students receive as much personal attention and instruction as possible?*
Trigger concept: *Hatmaker*
Ideas: *put it on your head, iron each one out, custom made hats, custom made heads, custom made textbooks or information (computer generated?), hatboxes of knowledge, students choose a boxful of information to master, multiple hats like multiple disciplines, one hat at a time, one subject at a time? one student at a time? meet twenty students for fifteen minutes each*

As strange as the trigger concept method may sound at first, it can work quite well. And, oddly enough, any random seed will be fruitful if you are patient and energetic.

For example, *in his book,* The Care and Feeding of Ideas, *James Adams gives the following problem and random seed as an exercise: "Assume that you have been hired as a consultant by a restaurant that is having business problems. See how many ways you can think of to improve the business of the restaurant using the concept of a runover dead cat."*
What are the possibilities here? *Cat guts, catgut, tennis racket--make the restaurant a sports club like place or decorate it with a sports theme (The Avon River Rowing Club?), or install game machines (video) or put in a giant screen TV and show football games on Monday nights. Flat cat, tire tread marks, artsy in the avant garde area--add to the restaurant an art gallery with modern art on the walls, put in chrome and glass and high tech furnishings. Decorated dining plus art sales. Who killed the cat? Offer surprise menu items that guests won't know what they are until the food arrives. Cats, catsup, the Catsup Supper Club--a burger place. The cat was greased, hit--did the Mafia do it? Is the cat run over repeatedly? Build repeat business by giving a free meal, drink, gift after nine (cat's lives) visits.*

That's my list, and you can see that what Adams suggests is true: "One of the underlying theories of creativity techniques is that wild ideas are valuable because the normal forces of life will tend to convert them rapidly into practicality."

Final Example Problem: *Get a friend who is behind in his payments to the store to catch up and pay regularly.*

Modes of Thinking

Trigger concept: *Potato*
Ideas: *feed him, peel him, slice him up--divide his payments into smaller pieces, as in every week, and send in the monthly payment made up from that. fry him when he doesn't pay, plant him in the ground. salt him--give him some "flavorful" incentive to pay, as in some gift or verbal reward. Baked potato, butter and sour cream. Potato eyes--growth--convince him his credit rating will grow and be valuable to him if he pays regularly.*

Some useful questions to ask that will help you connect your trigger concept to your idea include these:
A. How is the problem or idea like the trigger concept?
B. Does the problem have the trigger concept in it?
C. What does the concept do?
D. What is the concept like?
E. What is it not like?
F. What does the concept suggest?

Try It Yourself

Trigger Concepts. Choose one of the following items and use its assigned trigger concept to stimulate ideas for improving the item. On the first part of a page, write down the ideas and associations that first occur to you when using the trigger concept. Then on the last part of the page, list at least five improvements, each described in a sentence or two, that resulted from your thinking.
   1. improve an automatic dishwasher using the trigger concept of a stone.
   2. improve a toy store using the trigger concept of hair
   3. improve a library using the trigger concept of candy

PRACTICING ANALOGICAL AND ANALYTICAL THINKING

Exercise 1.1. Similarity. What the following things have in common?

1. Apple, plum, orange, pear, apricot. _____
2. Poetry, literature, painting, music, architecture. _____
3. Physics, chemistry, biology, psychology, astronomy. _____
4. Perception, memory, thinking, emotions, attention. _____
5. France, Canada, Russia, Germany, Italy. _____
6. White, yellow, red, green, black. _____

What about the following list? It is more difficult to find similarities for them:

| What the following things have in common? ||||
Objects/Phenomena	List similar attributes	List similarities in structure	List similarities in functions
7. Light bulb and a book			
8. Computer and the brain			
9. Love and education			
10. Poetry and a soap			
11. Marker and rain			
12. Hurricane and scissors			
13. Cat and bulldozer			

CHAPTER 7

Exercise 1.2. Enter the appropriate word based upon the sample provided

Tree	Flower	Feeling	Bird	Metal	Furniture
Oak	?	?	?	?	?
1.2.1	1.2.1.1	1.2.1.2	1.2.1.3	1.2.1.4	1.2.1.5
Stone	Glass	Wood	Smoke	Sun	Milk
Hard	?	?	?	?	?
1.2.2	1.2.2.1	1.2.2.2	1.2.2.3	1.2.2.4	1.2.2.5
Boat	Airplane	Train	Sledge	Ski	Skates
Water	?	?	?	?	?
1.2.3	1.2.3.1	1.2.3.2	1.2.3.3	1.2.3.4	1.2.3.5
Writer	Artist	Scientist	Composer	Politician	Actor
Novel	?	?	?	?	?
1.2.4	1.2.4.1	1.2.4.2	1.2.4.3	1.2.4.4	1.2.4.5
Animal	Fish	Insect	Plant	Bird	Virus
Deer	?	?	?	?	?
1.2.5	1.2.5.1	1.2.5.2	1.2.5.3	1.2.5.4	1.2.5.5
Bacteria	Earthquake	Evolution	Knowledge	Wisdom	Creativity
Disease	?	?	?	?	?
1.2.6	1.2.6.1	1.2.6.2	1.2.6.3	1.2.6.4	1.2.6.5
Rain	Frost	Sunlight	Darkness	Disease	Distance
Umbrella	?	?	?	?	?
1.2.7	1.2.7.1	1.2.7.2	1.2.7.3	1.2.7.4	1.2.7.5

Exercise 1.3. Which word doesn't belong to the rest of three words?
1. Touch, taste, hear, smile, see.
2. Stocking, dress, shoe, purse, hat.
3. Copper, iron, brass, tin, lead.
4. Tree, branch, leaf, root, fruit.
5. Ham, liver, salmon, pork, beef.
6. Inch, mile, acre, yard, foot.

Exercise 1.4. Which one of the five makes the best comparison?

1. Brother is to sister as nice is to: MOTHER –AUNT – UNCLE – NEPHEW. _____
2. Milk is to glass as letter is to: STAMP – PEN – ENVELOPE – BOOK – MAIL. _____
L3.IVE is to EVIL as 5232 is to: 2225 – 3322 – 2325 – 3225 – 5223. _____
4. Tree is to ground as chimney is to: SMOKE – BRICK – SKY – GARAGE – HOUSE. _____
5. CAACCAC is to 3113313 as CACAACAC is to: 1333311 – 1313133 – 31311313 – 3313133 – 3131311_____
6. Belt is to buckle as shoe is to: SOCK – TOE – FOOT – LACE – SOLE_____
7. Finger is to hand as leaf is to: TREE – BRANCH – BLOSSOM – TWIG – BARK_____
8. Foot is to knee as hand is to: FINGER = ALBOW – TOE – LEG – ARM_____
9. Water is to ice as milk is to: HONEY – CHEESE – CEREAL – COFFEE – COOKIE. _____

Exercise 1.5.

Items	List one THE MANE (the most important, the principal) difference between two things	List one THE MANE (the most important, the principal) similarity between two things
EXAMPLE: Bird and an airplane	Bird is living creature while airplane is not.	Both can fly
1. Light bulb and the sun		
2. A rock and a brick		
3. Wood and plastic		
4. A pocket and a suitcase		
5. A necklace and a flower bed		
6. Football and chess		
7. Creativity and friendship		

Modes of Thinking

Exercise 1.6.

To think analogically, take a problem or idea or thing and consider:
1. What else is like this?
2. What have others done?
3. What could we copy?
4. What has worked before?
5. What would professionals do?

Direct Analogy:
Think of ways that related problems have been solved.
Examples: Sir March Isumbard Brunel solving the problem of underwater construction by watching a shipworm tunnel into a timber, and of Alexander Graham Bell inventing the telephone receiver on the model of the human ear.
Technique: Observe nature & ask; How have animals, birds, flowers, insects, worms, snakes and so on solved similar problems?

Personal Analogy:
Make yourself part of the problem to imaginatively create a new perspective.
Examples: What would you be if you were a dazzling dinner for important guests. Think of yourself as an extremely efficient floor mop. If you were a checkbook, how would you keep from getting lost?

Fantasy Analogy:
Think of a fantastic, far-fetched perhaps ideal solution, which can lead to creative yet practical solutions.
Examples: How can we make a carriage propel itself - car? How can we make a perfect drain, which can eat up bones or waste - disposal? How can we make an oven clean itself, a freezer defrost itself, a motor tell us what's wrong?

Symbolic Analogy:
requires applying an imaginary comparison of the problem to something else
Example: a vision of a snake swallowing its own tail gave the Dutch physicist Kekule a key insight into the benzene molecule.
Technique: Try to think of a two-word self-contradictory title or oxymoron for a particular problem, which will stimulate ideas (e.g. gentle toughness, simply complex)

Now try it yourself:

1. What animal typifies your concept of freedom? (Direct Analogy) _____

2. Put yourself in the place of the animal you have chosen. Be the thing! Describe what makes you feel and act with so much freedom (Personal Analogy). _____

3. Sum up your description of the animal you chose by listing the "free" and "unfree" parts of you animal life.
Free: _____
Unfree: _____

4. Express each of these parts of your life in a single word. Put together these two words and refine them into a poetic, compressed conflict phrase. _____

5. Circle the phrase you like best. You could write an essay about freedom in your thinking journal. Use any material you may have developed in this exercise. _____

Synectics Method (William J.J. Gorden)
- Derived from the Greek word synecticos meaning "understanding together that which is apparently different" (Gunter, Estes & Schwab, 2003, p. 135)
- a creative thinking technique where two seemingly unrelated things are compared

CHAPTER 7

– an approach to solving problems based on the creative thinking of a group of people from different areas of experience and knowledge

Synectic Exercises:

1. What animal is like a bass guitar? Why? _____
2. How is a jar of paste like a school bell? _____
3. Which is stronger, a brick wall or a young tree? Why? _____
4. Which is heaviest, a boulder or a sad heart? Why? _____
5. What color is sadness? Why? _____
6. In what ways can coolness be seen? _____
7. In what ways can softness be heard? _____
8. What is another sound like a dog's bark? _____
9. How is life like a flashlight battery? _____
10. Which grows faster, your confidence or an oak tree? _____
11. What could have given a cave dweller the idea for a spear? What was the connection? _____
12. A parachute is like what animal? Why? _____
13. Why is a calendar like a mirror? _____
14. What would it be like to be inside a lemon? _____
15. If you were a pencil, how would it feel to get sharpened? To get chewed on? To get worn down to a stub? _____
16. When you are happy you are like a _____
17. When you are busy, you are like a _____
18. How is someone who steals like a hungry shark? _____
19. How is Shirley-the-Shoplifter like a good case of the measles? _____
20. How is vandalizing like sticking your finger in a light socket? _____
21. How is a friendly, helpful person like a hot fudge sundae? _____
22. How is a good education like a good dream? _____
23. How is an iceberg like a creative idea? _____
24. If a classroom were a lawn, what would the weeds be? How do the weeds affect the rest of the classroom? _____

Modes of Thinking

Answers

Exercise 1.1
- 1.1.1 Fruits
- 1.1.2 The arts
- 1.1.3 Sciences
- 1.1.4 Components of human behaviour
- 1.1.5 Countries
- 1.1.6 Colours

Exercise 1.2
1.2.1. Rose, love, eagle, iron, table
1.2.2. Fragile, hard, gaseous, bright, liquid
1.2.3. Air, track, snow, snow, ice
1.2.4. Painting, discovery, music, war (peace), movie
1.2.5. Salmon, mosquito, grape, owl, HIV
1.2.6. Ruins, new species, comprehension, understanding, new product
1.2.7. Coat, tent, light, drug, vehicle.

Exercise 1.3
1.3.1. SMILE. The others are senses; smile is a facial expression
1.3.2. PURSE. The others are all articles of clothing that are worn.
1.3.3. BRASS. The others are simple metals; brass is an alloy (a combination of two metals).
1.3.4. TREE. The others are parts of the tree.
1.3.5. SALMON. The others are meats; salmon is a fish.
1.3.6. ACRE. Acre measures area; the others measure distance.

Exercise 1.4
1.4.1. NEPHEW. Brother and sister, and niece and nephew are all opposites.
1.4.2. ENVELOPE. Milk goes into glass, just as a letter goes into an envelope.
1.4.3. 2325. EVIL is the reverse spelling of LIVE; the reverse of 5232 is 2325.
1.4.4. HOUSE. A tree comes up out of the ground, just as a chimney comes up out of house.
1.4.5. 31311313. Substitute numbers for letters; C = 3 and A = 1.
1.4.6. LACE. You buckle a belt, just as you lace your shoes.
1.4.7. TWIG. Finger is an appendage of the hand, just as a leaf is an appendage of a twig.
1.4.8. ELBOW. Foot is attached to leg and knee a joint in the leg. Hand is attached to arm and elbow is a joint in the arm.
1.4.9. CHEESE. Water changes into ice and milk changes into cheese.

Exercise 1.5
1.5.1. Light bulb is manmade while the sun is a natural object. Both are sources of light.
1.5.2. Rock is a natural object while a brick is a manmade one. Both could be construction's materials.
1.5.3. Wood is a product of living plants while plastic is a manmade material. Both could be used as material for production or construction.
1.5.4. A pocket is a part of the clothes while a suitcase is an independent object. Both are containers.
1.5.5. A necklace is a piece of jewellery while a flower bed is a part of a landscape. Both serve as beautifiers.
1.5.6. Football requires active movements of multiple players while chess is a table game for two players. Both are sports.
1.5.7. Creativity is a human quality while friendship is one type of close relationships. Both are abstract concepts.

Now try to create your own exercise similar to the above exercises.

CHAPTER 7
2. Symbolic Thinking

Figure 7.1. Symbols of the World Religions.

Symbolic thinking plays significant role in human thinking. ***It enables symbols to be in place of words/thoughts***. It is a foundation of language. It allows for the translation of a feeling by some means.

A quantum leap (metaphorically speaking) occurred in neural development when the human brain acquired the capacity to think with symbols. A symbol is ***any kind of percept that stands for or represents something else***. All words are symbols although symbols are not limited to words or to visual or aural percepts. Symbols can represent ***events and objects*** (real or imagined) in far places and distant times. ***Scientists*** can use symbols (including mathematical symbols) to gain and record knowledge of our world. Novelists use symbols to create fantasy worlds for escape, entertainment, and moral instruction. ***Historians*** use symbols to study the past. Philosophers use symbols to examine fundamental beliefs. ***Psychologists*** use symbols to analyze and predict behavior. ***Religious concepts***, such as a concept of God and human moral values would not be possible without symbolic thinking.

People learn to convert percepts into symbols by association. When a symbol (a word, for example) is synchronically associated with an object, humans can learn to mentally equate the word with the object and can thus think about the object whether or not it is present. Children develop the capability for symbolic thinking and communication at an early age.

Historical Review

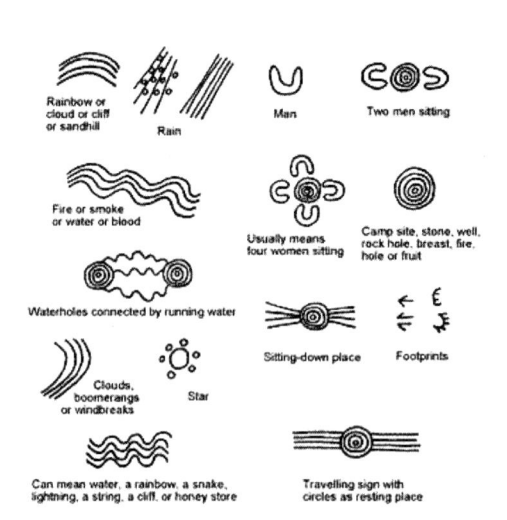

Figure 7.2. Ancient Aboriginal Symbols.

The earliest symbolic thinking started some 100,000 years ago when Red Ochre was buried with bodies for ritual burial.

The swastika is an ancient symbol that has been used for over 3,000 years. (That even predates the ancient Egyptian symbol, the Ankh!) Artifacts such as pottery and coins from ancient Troy show that the swastika was a commonly used symbol as far back as 1000 BCE.

Different cultures have different names for the same symbol:
- China - wan
- England - fylfot
- Germany - Hakenkreuz
- Greece - tetraskelion and gammadion
- India - swastika

The word "swastika" comes from the Sanskrit svastika – "su" meaning "good," "asti" meaning "to be," and "ka" as a suffix. Until the Nazis used this symbol, the swastika was used by many cultures throughout the past 3,000 years to represent life, sun, power, strength, and good luck. In *Mein Kampf*, Hitler described the Nazis' new flag: "In red we see the social idea of the movement, in white the nationalistic idea, in the swastika the mission of the struggle for the victory of the Aryan man, and, by the same token, the victory of the idea of creative work, which as such always has been and always will be anti-Semitic."

Over the years the swastika has actually been a symbol for good for a much longer amount of time.

History and events can change the way people view an image and the feelings that are associated with it.

Figure 7.3. The swastika is an ancient symbol that has been used for over 3,000 years.

138

Language

All languages use symbols. Symbols represent sounds.
Some languages are comprised entirely of symbols.

The discipline of *semiotics* has been studied in one form or another since before the time of Socrates. Indeed, some have argued that what sets the human species apart from other animals is our ability to adroitly use and manipulate symbols. Semiotics is highly relevant to the entire area of promotional strategy in creativity because it is throughout the use of various symbols or signs that artists communicate their massages to people.

New artifacts found in Tanzania's Serengeti National Park offer some of the strongest evidence yet that symbolic thinking developed in humans earlier than once thought. The artifacts were excavated from a site in the Loiyangalani River Valley, and they are the first of their kind found in East Africa.

Scientists presented the new findings at the Society of Paleoanthropology meeting in March 2004. Curtis Marean of ASU's Institute of Human Origins and J.C. Thompson from the Anthropology Department at ASU were among the presenters.

The findings include ochre pencils, bone artifacts, fish bones, mammal bones, and two ostrich eggshell beads. Other ostrich eggshell fragments found on the site could represent debris from bead making. The artifacts have not yet been dated using advanced dating techniques. However, Marean says that they were found alongside an assembly of Middle Stone Age tools.

Scientists define "behavioral modernity" as the ability to think abstractly and to create culture and art. Until recently, they believed that such modern behavior developed first in Eurasia. Human art and sophisticated artifacts found at various Eurasian sites have been dated to about 35,000 years ago.

Marean says that the Middle Stone Age in East Africa lasted from approximately 280,000 years ago to about 45,000 years ago. This is much earlier than what paleoanthropologists had considered the accepted beginning of symbolic thought.

"Some of the artifacts, in particular the ostrich eggshell beads, are rare or unprecedented in the Middle Stone Age," Marean explains. "Beads were not previously believed to be present in the Middle Stone Age. Nothing like this has been published in Africa."

The researchers see the beads as significant indicators of human cultural modernity because beads are clearly decorative. They say that decoration strongly implies abstract or symbolic thinking. The methods used to produce ostrich shell beads are also significantly more sophisticated than any techniques used to produce the tools generally found in the Middle Stone Age.—Diane Boudreau

Figure 7.4. Some languages are comprised entirely of symbols.

Figure 7.5. Symbols today.

Kinds of Symbolism

The survey of different epochs of civilization discloses great differences in their attitude towards symbolism (Whitehead, 1959). For example, during the medieval period in Europe symbolism seemed to dominate men's imaginations. Architecture was symbolical, ceremonial was symbolical, heraldry was symbolical. With the Reformation a reaction set in. Men tried to dispense with symbols as "found things, vainly invented," and concentrate on their direct apprehension of the ultimate facts.

But such symbolism is on the fringe of life. It has an unessential element in its constitution. The very fact that it can be acquired in one epoch and discarded in another epoch testifies to its superficial nature.

There are deeper types of symbolism, in a same artificial, and yet such that we could not get on without them. *Language,* written or spoken, is such a symbolism. The mere sound of a word, or its shape on paper, is indifferent. The word is a symbol, and it's meaning is constituted by the ideas, images, and emotions, which it raises in the mind of the hearer.

There is also another sort of language, purely written language, which is constituted by the mathematical symbols of the science of algebra. In some ways, these symbols are different to those of

Colored shapes are symbols for some elements in our experience, and when we see the colored shapes we adjust our actions towards those other elements. This symbolism from our senses to the bodies symbolized is often mistaken. A cunning adjustment of lights and mirrors may completely deceive us; and even when we are not deceived, we only save ourselves by an effort. Symbolism from sense-presentation to physical bodies is the most natural and widespread of all symbolic modes. It is not a mere tropism, or automatic turning towards, because both men and puppies often disregard chairs when they see them. Also a tulip which turns to the light has probably the very minimum of sense-presentation. Sense-perception is mainly a characteristic of more advanced organisms; whereas all organisms have experience of causal efficacy whereby their functioning is conditioned by their environment.

ordinary language, because the manipulation of the algebraical symbols does your reasoning for you, provided that you keep to the algebraic rules. This is not the case with ordinary language. You can never forget the meaning of language, and trust to mere syntax to help you out. In any case, language and algebra seem to exemplify more fundamental types of symbolism than do the Cathedrals of Medieval Europe.

Symbolism and Perception

There is still another symbolism more fundamental than any of the foregoing types. We look up and see a *colored shape* in front of us, and we say, - there is a chair. But what we have seen is the mere colored shape. Perhaps an artist might not have jumped to the notion of a chair. He might have stopped at the mere contemplation of a beautiful color and a beautiful shape. But those of us who are not artists are very prone, especially if we are tired, to pass straight from the perception of the colored shape to the enjoyment of the chair, in some way of use, or of emotion, or of thought. We can easily explain this passage by reference to a train of difficult logical inference, whereby, having regard to our previous experiences of various shapes and various colors, we draw the probable conclusion that we are in the presence of a chair.

The transition from a colored shape to the notion of an object which can be used for all sorts of purposes which have nothing to do with color, seems to be a very natural one; and we –men and puppy dogs – require careful training if we are to refrain from acting upon it.

Fallibility of Symbolism

There is one great difference between symbolism and direct knowledge. Direct experience is infallible. What you have experienced, you have experienced. But symbolism is very fallible, in the sense that it may induce actions, feelings, emotions, and beliefs about things that are mere notions without that exemplification in the world which the symbolism leads us to presuppose. Symbolism is an essential factor in the way we function as the result of our direct knowledge. Successful high-grade organisms are only possible, on the condition that their symbolic functioning is usually justified so far as important issues are concerned. But the errors of mankind equally spring from symbolism. It is the task of reason to understand and purge the symbols on which humanity depends.

An adequate account of human mentality requires an explanation of the following:
1. How we can know truly;
2. How we can err;
3. How we can critically distinguish truth from error.

Such an explanation requires that we distinguish that type of mental functioning which by its nature yields immediate acquaintance with fact, from that type of functioning which is only trustworthy by reason of its satisfaction of certain criteria provided by the first type of functioning.

Whitehead (1959) recognized two types of functioning:
1. Direct recognition
2. Symbolic reference.

All human symbolism, however superficial it may seem, is ultimately to be reduced to trains of this fundamental symbolic reference, trains which finally connect percepts in alternative modes of direct recognition.

Definition of Symbolism

The human mind is functioning *symbolically* when some components of its experience *elicit consciousness, beliefs, emotions, and usages,* respecting other components of its experience.

The former set of components is the "symbols," and the latter set constitute the "meaning" of the symbols. The organic functioning whereby there is transition from the symbol to the meaning will be called "symbolic reference."

This symbolic reference is the active synthetic element contributed by the nature of the percipients. It requires a ground founded on some community between the natures of symbol and meaning. But such a common element in the two natures does not of itself necessitate symbolic reference, nor does it decide which shall be symbol and which shall be meaning, nor does it secure that the symbolic reference shall be immune from producing errors and disasters for the percipient. We must conceive perception in the light of a primary phase in the self-production of an occasion of actual existence.

Modes of Thinking

Our *perception* of the external world includes *familiar immediate presentation* of the contemporary world, by means of *our projection* of our immediate sensations, determining for us characteristics of the contemporary physical entities. This type is the experience of the immediate world around us, a world decorated by sense-data dependent on the immediate stated of relevant parts of our own bodies.

The color and the spatial perspective are abstract elements, characterizing the concrete way in which the object enters into our experience.

The German philosopher **Ernst Cassirer** in his *An Essay on Man* (1981, p. 36) wrote: "In the boundless multiplicity and variety of mythical images, of religious dogmas, of linguistic forms, of works of art, philosophical thought reveals the unity of the general function by which all these creations are held together. Myth, religion, art, language, even science, is now looked upon as so many variations on a common theme – and it is the task of philosophy to make this theme audible and understandable."

Thus, in Cassirer's view, our **construction of reality** was based upon the availability of a vast collection of mental conceptions or symbolic forms. The efforts of human beings to capture their experiences, and to express them in forms which can effectively communicate, depended upon am amalgam of these symbolic conceptions or forms.

This embracing of symbols ran counter to many philosophical ideas prevalent during the early part of the century. To begin with, the notion that myth, imagination, and other forms of "imprecision" or "ignorance" ought to be treated with the same seriousness as mathematics or science was abhorrent to many philosophers reared in the Descartes-Leibniz-Kant tradition.

But Cassirer's thought appeared even more revolutionary to those committed to empiricism. Rather than presupposing a reality independent of symbolic forms, Cassirer claimed that our reality was created by symbolic forms, that language in fact constitutes rather than reflects reality. Contrary to a Lockean and Humean view, perception and meaning are not causally determined by or obtained from the objects in the external world, rather, meanings arise from within and are brought to bear upon the flux of objects and experiences.

Cassirer's conception challenged the establishment's philosophical view in yet another respect. Rather than there being a basic set of categories such as space, time, and number, which were apprehended by all human beings in the same way, one now encountered a far more complex state of affairs. Within each symbolic form there would be particular embodiments of space, time, and number, as well as particular forms of expression of these conceptions.

In place of the absoluteness of space, time, and number, Cassier substituted a far more pluralistic and relativistic picture reflecting different types and levels of symbolization.

And so, Cassirer, symbols were not simply tools or mechanisms of thought. They were the functioning of thought itself, vital creative forms of activity, our sole ways of "making" reality and synthesizing the world. It proves impossible to think of symbolizing activity apart from human imagination and creativity: man lives in a symbolic universe. And in the process of symbolic activity, human beings inevitably engage in meaning-making, in imaginative problem-solving, and in equally creative problem production.

From a philosophical anthropological perspective, which takes human consciousness as a point of departure, man might well be thought of as animal symbolicum. Cassirer (1981, p. 54) described the peculiar world of this symbolic animal:

"Physical reality seems to recede in proportion as man's symbolic activity advances. Instead of dealing with the things themselves, man is, in a sense, constantly conversing with himself. He has so enveloped himself in linguistic forms, in artistic images, and mythical symbolic or religious rights, that he cannot see or know anything except by the interposition of this artificial medium. He lives in the midst of imaginary emotions, in hopes and fears, in illusions and disillusions, in his fantasies and dreams."

The human mind, fortified with symbols, comes to re-create the physical world in its own symbolic image.

Symbols: Its Meaning and Effect on Creative Process

Signs and symbols are *simplified representation of human experience*. They *elicit consistent responses* because of *prior experience* of the same stimuli. Signs, in the more general sense of the word, are *indicators* and can be the *form or sounds, colors, words or events*. A rustle in the woods, for example, may be interpreted as a sign of impending danger, a black cloud as a sign of a coming storm, smoke as a sign of fire, and so on. Aside from this classification, another category is graphic signs, which are symbolic representations created and used solely for visual communication. As words are signs of thought, so, too, are visual images signs of conception.

Our dependence on symbols is extensive. Virtually our entire daily life pattern is spent going from one circle of symbols to another.

Contingencies, Creativity, and Symbols

There are two kinds of requirements for describing the creative process. One kind may be designated as contingencies, a category that includes everything external to the creative person. A human being cannot originate new things out of nothing. Proudhon said that each of us stands on the shoulders of our predecessors. Einstein himself would not have been able to develop his Theory of relativity without Alfred North Whitehead and Bertrand Russell's Principia Mathematica. People must be exposed. They

CHAPTER 7

must be exposed to an environment that provides them with cultural opportunities as well as stimulates them in a variety of ways, and they must have available some physical material such as a pen, a pencil, paper, a compass, a brush, a stone, a canvas, some object for scientific study, and so on. Maybe these correlate to Maslow's hierarchy of need at the minimum they need certain physical things. Obviously realistic contingencies are necessary not just for creativity but for every form of life.

The second requirement is much more specific. It refers to the psychological life of the individual, to anything that can be included under the category of imagination and amorphous cognition.

Imagination is the capacity of the mind to produce or reproduce several symbolic functions while in a state of consciousness, of wakefulness, without any deliberate effort to organize these functions. In other words, first of all, dreams are arbitrarily excluded. Secondly, whatever is unconscious is excluded, including such things as unconscious images. What is left are conscious images, ideas, sequences of words, sentences, and feelings, just as they occur. Imagination is related to what is called "free association" in psychoanalysis. However, free association refers predominantly to what is expressed in words, whereas imagination can assume nonverbal forms. Imagination excludes all that which cannot assume or has not yet assumed a form, verbal or nonverbal. A part of what is excluded is *amorphous cognition*.

And imagination itself is only prerequisite for or an antecedent to creativity. Subsequent elaborations of imaginations are necessary for creativity.

Symbols are very important concept in *imagination*. The characteristic of being symbolic is the main feature that distinguishes some human psychological functions from those of other animals, and is at the basis of creativity. Other animals too, exhibit cognitive processes, including such functions as learning, memory, and intelligence. They learn to respond in special ways to stimuli and to generalize their responses to all stimuli that belong in given categories.

> Evidence suggests that the image stream literally never ceases. Even when your mind is preoccupied with problem solving, conversation, or other tasks, the sensory mechanisms of your mind continue to generate imaginary sights, smells, sounds, tastes, and feelings. Many of these images consist of memories that are triggered by random associations. Others are echoes or reinforcements of your conscious thoughts at the moment (Wenger and Poe, 1995).

Some animals can reason, dream, and seem all too human from time to time. However, the conventional wisdom seems to believe that their responses depend entirely on their perceptions, on what is immediately given. They do not have to resort to their imagination and to elaborations thereof, except perhaps in rudimentary forms. In the conditioned reflex, too, an animal responds to the immediately given. For instance, in the Pavlov experiment, a dog learned to respond to the sound of a bell as he would respond to the sight of powdered meat. He learned that food would arrive after the buzz, so that he began to salivate and was already prepared for food at the sound of bell. The bell becomes a sign of incoming food. But a sign is not yet a symbol. It is true that it stands for something else (such as the buzz standing for food), but it stands for something that is about to be present and/or may be already a part of the present total situation. For instance, a cloud may be a sign of an incoming storm, of which it is a part; a certain rash on the skin may be a sign of chicken pox, of which disease it is a part, a condition.

> A symbol is a representative of something else, even when that "something else" is completely absent.

Men, too, use signs; but they also use symbols. In ordinary life, the most common symbol is the word. For instance, your friend Claire may not be with you; as a matter of fact, she may be living in New Jersey. But when you say the word "Claire," we all know that we are speaking about that particular friend. The word stands for that person; it is a symbol of her. Symbols are also generally used in association. If I am on top of Pike's Peak near Colorado Springs and I say, "the beautiful view," the person who hears me has a definite knowledge of what the sound "beautiful" stands for and what the sound "view" stands for. In ordinary language, however, we select words and put them in special orders for special purposes, whereas when we resort only to our imagination, we allow words to occur freely as in free association. The creative process differs from the ordinary functions of the mind insofar as it uses many kinds of symbols. It also uses the symbols in different contexts or proportions, so that these new, different contexts and proportions themselves become symbols of things never before symbolized or else symbolized previously in different ways. Some of these symbolic processes are primitive and belong to what Freud called the primary process. Others are high-level symbols and belong to what Freud called the secondary process.

Semiotics

The investigation of symbols and their meanings is called *semiotics*. This field of study originated in the desire to *analyze how people obtain meaning from signs*, or the **words, gestures, pictures, products, and logos** used to communicate information from one person to another.

Even nonverbal sounds can communicate meaning. For example, Harley-Davidson attempted in 1995 to trademark the distinctive sound made by its motorcycles. The guttural growl of Harley bikes has been compared to a growling animal saying "potato-potato-potato." According to a spokesperson for the company, "A lot of owners tell us they buy a Harley just for sound." Semiotics is also highly useful for gaining an experiential perspective in different fields of human activity. In order to understand how people emotionally react to symbols in the environment, one must know the shared meanings of various signs.

Semiotics has relevance to a number of creativity areas - consider the Freudian symbolism in visual art, music, writing, science, and leadership; symbols used to express one's self-concept, and signs employed in cross-cultural communications. Researchers working in this field emphasize that meaning is partly determined by cultural context. Thus a sign may have entirely different meanings in two different cultures. For instance, animals are frequently paired with products in the United States because Americans admire and cherish many animals. In some Asian cultures, however, animals are viewed negatively.

The *decoding of symbols* occurs in the comprehension stage of information processing. Artists, writers, musicians must be alert to the use of symbols and how their target auditory will interpret them. Indeed, art is some kind of modern substitute for myth and ritual and, directly or indirectly, uses semiotics (the science of signs) to invest creative product with meaning for a culture.

We learn the meaning of signs in our culture fairly early in life through acculturation. It seems that preschoolers have only a minimal ability to recognize the social implications of artistic choices. By the second grade, however, children are capable of making inferences about symbolic signs of art and music.

Semiotics is particularly applicable to brand positioning. For example, colleges and universities are currently working hard to refine – in some cases, to change – their logos and mascots. According to the university trade publication The Chronicle of Higher Education, universities are attempting to "Create a catchy symbol that paints a thousand words about the college and entices people to buy shirts and notebooks bearing the emblem." To helping to position a university, logos can bring a university millions of dollars, either directly through the sale of T-shirts, hats, and other memorabilia, or indirectly through the licensing of the logo to vendors.

Semiotics and the study of symbols are fascinating areas of study for artists. Ideas from this field will appear throughout this chapter.

Symbolic Thinking and the Arts

Appreciation of the fine arts is based more on perceptual processes than symbolic thinking. **Great art** presents us with sights and sounds that satisfy our **emotional needs** to experience harmony and perceive beauty. We also experience intellectual satisfaction from an **intuitive recognition** of the **highly complex systematized composition** of the art. (This is related to Ruskin's pathetic fallacy.) We respond to art in immediate real time, primarily via the distance receptors of sights and sounds. Even poetry and literature, although communicated by symbols, are appreciated as events or images taking place in imagined real time. Although animals sometimes appear to appreciate colors, forms, and sounds, their responses are probably associated more with food and sex than with aesthetic appreciation. Thus, the appreciation of art is a very advanced human capability that differs from symbolic thinking.

Symbols in Music

Langers' (1978) account of the significance of music. Langer rightly sensed that music was a symbolic system but that it did not directly communicate either reference (for example, the sound of waves) or feelings (for example, the composer's own sense of happiness or anger). She proposed that what music presented was the "forms of feelings" – the **tensions, ambiguities, contrasts, and conflicts** that permeate our feeling life but do not lend themselves to description in words or logical formulas. The composer presents in spaced tones his knowledge of the whole of human feeling life, and such non-articulate symbols constitute the appeal and mystery of music. In a passage that conveys the seductive appeal as well as the maddening ambiguity of her prose, the philosopher suggests:

"The real power of music lies in the fact that it can be "true" the life of feeling in a way that language cannot, for its significant forms have that ambivalence of content which words cannot have... Music is revealing where words are obscuring, because it can have not only content, but a transients play of contents. It can articulate feelings without becoming wedded to them.... The assignment of meaning is a shifting, kaleidoscopic play, probably below the threshold of consciousness, certainly outside the pale of discursive thinking. The imagination that responds to music is personal and associative and logical, tinged with affect, tinged with bodily rhythm, tinged with dream, but concerned with a wealth of formulations for its wealth of wordless knowledge, its whole knowledge of emotional and organic experience, of vital impulse, balance, conflict, the ways of living and dying and feeling. Because no

---

Symbols and signs are used to communicate meaning to others. A theoretical frame-work has been proposed for explaining how signs function as communications. This paradigm is called semiosis analysis. Semiosis analysis involves identifying an object, a sign, and an interpretant. The object is the thing whose meaning is to be communicated (e.g., a painting, a piece of music, a poetry); the sign is the symbol or set of symbols used to communicate the meaning of the object; and the interpretant if a person's reaction to and meaning derived from the sign.

assignment of meaning is conventional, none is permanent beyond the sound that passes, yet the brief association was a flash of understanding. The lasting effect is, like the first effect of speech on the development of the mind, to make things conceivable rather than to store up propositions."

Taking music as the prototype of the arts, Langer suggested that this knowledge of feeling life constitutes the perennial attraction of artistic symbols, herein lie the reasons we treasure those statements and works that top the logical empiricist have no meaning at all.

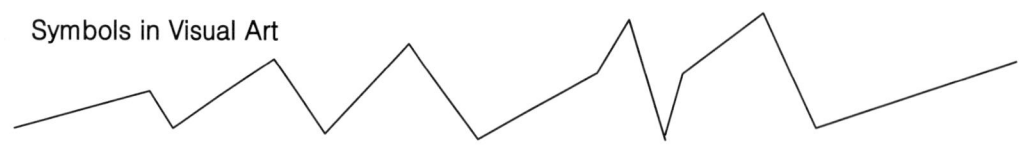

Symbols in Visual Art

With this squiggle, a simple zigzag line on a piece of paper Gardner (1982) showed the role of symbols in the arts. *Is it symbol*? An artistic symbol? And if it attains the status of an artistic symbol, what is its worth?

According to the philosopher Nelson Goodman (1969), the status of this squiggle depends entirely on how one chooses to construe it. If the squiggle stands for something – say a month-long record of the Dow Jones stock average – then it is functioning as a symbol. If it is part of a painting – say, the outline of a mountain range in a drawing by Hokusai – then it is functioning as an artistic symbol. The way in which one "reads" the squiggle depends upon the setting in which it is encountered, the graphic context which surrounds it, and the particular "mind set" of the viewer. And the determination of whether the symbol – be it taken from the artist's atelier or from the marketplace – is an effective one turns out to be the most challenging question of all.

The analysis begins with the recognition that there are ***different kinds of symbols*** and ***symbol systems***. Goodman then introduces his concept of a notational system – a symbol system that satisfies various syntactic and semantic criteria. Notationality is an ideal, and nearly all symbol systems in actual use violate at least one of the precise criteria of notationality. Still, it is possible to classify symbol systems according to the degree to which they approximate or deviate from notationality.

Such a classification reveals, for example, the Western musical notation basically fulfills the semantic and syntactic requirements of a notational system. Consistent with the rigorous demands of a notational system, it proves possible to go from the notation to the performed work and back again to the notation. Ordinary language fulfills the syntactic requirements in that one can recognize each of the constituent elements (words) and how they can be combined (syntax), but language does not fulfill the semantic requirements of notationality because the meaning universe of language is chock-full of ambiguity, redundancy, and other necessarily blurring features. Finally, such art forms as painting and sculpture violate all criteria of notationality. One cannot ascertain what the constituent elements are (there are no equivalents to words or notes in paintings), or how they might conceivably be combined, or what the elements of the work (or the work as a whole) stand for or represent. Painting is filled with multiple meanings at every possible level.

Figure 7.6. Guernica by Pablo Picasso.

Picasso's painting commemorates a small Basque village bombed by German forces in April 1937 during the Spanish Civil War. The painter, in desolate black, white and grey, depicts a nightmarish scene of men, women, children and animals under bombardment. The twisted, writhing forms include images of a screaming mother holding a dead child, a corpse with wide-open eyes and a gored horse.

Goodman turns his focus next to the question of how symbols function, how they in fact symbolize. Here again he acknowledges that symbols can stand for or denote objects, he goes on beyond common consensus or recognize other equally important but relatively neglected modes of symbolization.

Goodman devotes special attention to the fact that symbols can exemplify various properties. We can gain a feeling for these functions by considering a work of music. Strictly speaking, a work of music does not represent or denote anything in the world. As Stravinsky (among others) insisted, music is, by its very essence, powerless to convey specific meanings. On the other hand, it is clear that music had available to it considerable communicative powers. A work of music may literally exemplify certain properties, such as speed or loudness, and may in the process illuminate the same aspects in our own daily experience. Far more tellingly, music can metaphorically exemplify or "express" numerous other properties, such as gaiety, anger, conflict, passion, pride, and pomp and circumstance. Of course those properties cannot be literally exhibited by music: pride is a property of persons, pomp of events. But music functions symbolically by metaphorically recreating those properties through the use of such resources as mode, rhythm, and timbre.

Similar analytic tools can be brought to bear on works in the visual arts. To return for a moment to our opening squiggle, this meager line can denote elements ranging form an electrocardiogram to a road on a map, but if, for example, it is part of a painting, it can also express or exemplify certain properties. Our line can literally exemplify angularity or unevenness but it can also metaphorically express conflict, ambivalence, and other properties ordinarily associated with selves or situations.

In indicating some of the ways in which symbols can function, we approach the core of Goodman's assertions about art. Whether symbols function as artistic symbols depends upon which of the properties of the symbol one attends to. If, for example, one construes our squiggle simply as the Dow Jones average and pays attention only to the relative height on the ordinate of each of the points, then the symbol is only functioning in the denotational manner. Literal or metaphorical exemplificatory powers are irrelevant. If, on the other hand, the same squiggle is apprehended as a mountain range in a Hokusai drawing, one then focuses on an entirely different set of symbolic properties. Over and beyond the strictly denotational aspects of the mountain range (whether it is high or low, jagged or smooth, has two or three peaks), one notes literal exemplificatory properties (for example, its blackness) and its expressive properties (its gracefulness or grandeur). One attends as well to other properties of aesthetic symbols, such as the repleteness of the rendering – the fact that every detail, every nuance of the line contributes to the overall impact of the work. To the extent that these properties are noted and function in a significant manner in the work, that work is being constructed as an artistic symbol.

> People learn to convert percepts into symbols by association. When a symbol (a word, for example) is synchronically associated with an object, humans can learn to mentally equate the word with the object and can thus think about the object whether or not it is present.
> Children develop the capability for symbolic thinking and communication at an early age.

Graphic Signs

A graphic sign is a surrogate mark used as an abbreviation for a known meaning; it is a figure presented technically as devices designed by an artist (the sender), directed to the spectator (the receiver), and, owing to their peculiar properties and context, able to evoke in the receiver a definite thought, image, notion or judgment about an object other than itself.

Graphic signs, therefore, are visual notations, symbolic systems made up of a set of marks, signs, figure or characters. Graphic signs are created specifically to convey complex information, ideas, feelings and emotions in simple, understandable terms.

Signs can be divided into two categories:

1. ***Iconic.*** An icon is an image or representation. Iconic signs are those which resemble the object they represent. For example, a realistic drawing or a photograph is an iconic sign.
2. ***Conventional.*** Signature, signet ring, monogram or birth certificate are conventional signs. Symbolically, each of these in its own way identifies a person.

Art images often lie somewhere between (or incorporate both) iconic and conventional signs. (Roukes, 1988).

A quantum leap (metaphorically speaking) occurred in neural development when the human brain acquired the capacity to think with symbols. A symbol is any kind of percept that stands for or represents something else. All words are symbols although symbols are not limited to words or to visual or aural percepts. Symbols can represent events and objects (real or imagined) in far places and distant times. Scientists can use symbols (including mathematical symbols) to gain and record knowledge of our world. Novelists use symbols to create fantasy worlds for escape, entertainment, and moral instruction. Historians use symbols to study the past. Philosophers use symbols to examine fundamental beliefs. Psychologists use symbols to analyze and predict behavior. Religious concepts, such as a concept of God and our moral values would not be possible without symbolic thinking.

CHAPTER 7

Play and Symbolic Thinking

Playfulness is related to symbolic thinking although there are important differences. Both play and symbolic thinking require us to assume an "as-if" mental set. Play and symbolic thinking allow us to practice and develop skills in a pretend situation that does not have serious consequences while we are learning ("don't feel bad - it was only a game"). However, in play, the "as-if" applies only to the immediate situation. Symbolic thinking can occur independently of the situation we are in. The whole person is involved in play - motivations, emotions, and actions. Symbolic thinking is a mental activity that may or may not involve other parts of our personality. (However, symbolic thinking can be used playfully as with jokes and puns.) Play promotes social relationships and is restorative and re-creational. Symbolic thinking helps us analyze and mentally construct models for learning, thinking, planning, and experimenting.

PRACTICING SYMBOLIC THINKING

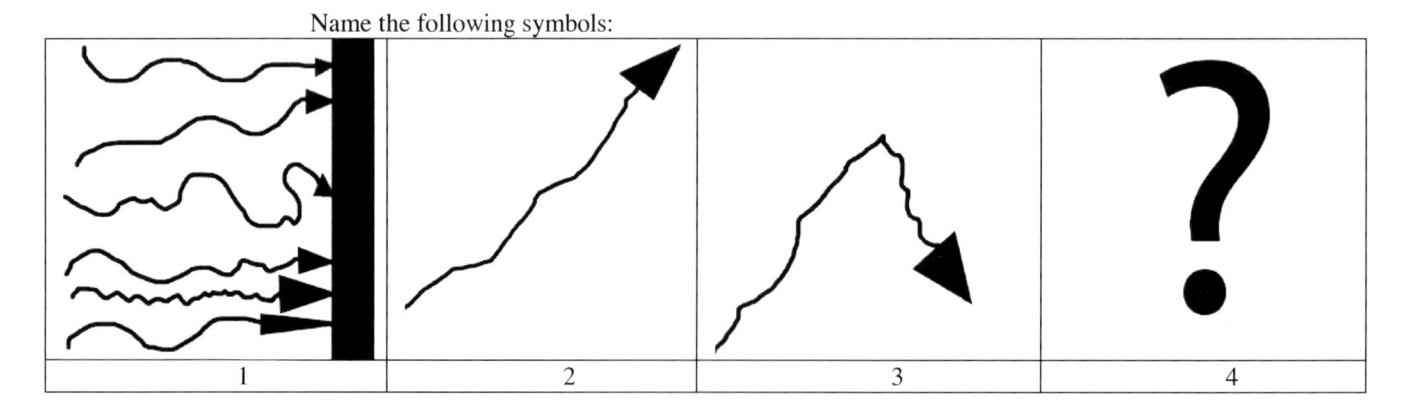

Name the following symbols:

1	2	3	4

Draw the symbols for each word:
1. Advertising
2. Argument
3. Block
4. Depression
5. Envy
6. Gratitude
7. Happiness
8. Initiative
9. Life
10. Luxury
11. Marriage
12. A pessimist
13. A politician
14. Procrastination
15. Progress
16. Reality
17. Self-evident

Answers:
 2.1. Resistance
 2.2. Development
 2.3. Puzzle
 2.4. Failure

3. ANALYSIS

Analysis is *the ability to break down a situation, issue, or problem into its intricate pieces in a systematic way*, or trace its *implications,* in order to achieve a higher level of *understanding and meaning*. Analysis *dissects* a whole into its *component parts*. It seeks to discover the *characteristics of those parts* and their *relationship* to each other and to the whole. The analytic approach is *microscopic*. It is the basis of the **Research Approach**.

Human mind is not capable to comprehend immediately complex phenomenon. It needs to be 'disassembled,' taking apart, divided into sections or sub-sections in order to be understood. Any and every course is divided into topic and sub-topics.

Analysis is one of the most fundamental processes of human thinking. In every field, analysis is a key activity. Many things in the world are quite complicated. Most things that people know are quite simple. So they have to break down the complicated matters into the simple things that are familiar and make judgement. Success in thinking often depends on success in analysis. But there *are two big dangers* Too many people are taught to believe that analysis and judgment are enough. They are not. Creativity and possibilities are the driving forces of progress. The other danger is that the behaviour of a complex system cannot be detected in the behaviour of its parts. If you chop an animal into pieces, you no longer have a functioning animal.

Analytical thinking answers the 'What is this?' question and is
- The ability to **scrutinize and break down facts and thoughts** into their strengths and weaknesses.
- Developing the capacity to think in a thoughtful, discerning way, to solve problems, analyze data, and recall and use information.
- Analytical thinking is **focused**, sharp, linear, deals with one thing at a time, is deconstructive, contains no perspective, is subject to disorientation, is brain centered, and tends to the abstract.
- Analytical thinking is efficient in the following conditions – sufficient time, relatively static conditions, and a clear differentiation between the observer and the observed.
- It is best suited for dealing with complexities, and works best where there are established criteria for the analysis (for example, rules of law). It is necessary when an explanation is required, seeks the best option, and can be taught in the classroom to beginners.

Analytical thinking means:
- *Objectivity is the key.* You must present reliable evidence, hard facts, and logical conclusions to convince an examiner that you have properly evaluated a given situation.
- *Inconsistent, missing, unsupported, or irrelevant information* – as well as plain untruths – will indicate *poor judgment* on your part, and may even raise suspicions of vested interest or dubious motivation.
- *Rationality* is an essential tool for developing reasoned arguments.

Analytical Problem Solving is recommended if...
- You are continuously "fire fighting" and "solving" the same quality problems without ever getting to the root cause
- You want a fast, efficient, standardized approach to results focused root cause determination and resolution
- You want to get in front of problems and keep them from occurring
- Your organization seems to swing between crazy, off-the-wall ideas which aren't really possible or "the same old thing"
- Some problems need a whole new solution - not just a tweak or refinement to existing processes.

Analytical Skills
- Ask questions: Who, what, when, where, why, how?

Look closer at Escher's art, and you will see how a complex pattern can be created from surprisingly few simple shapes.

Skilled analytical thinking requires you to **methodically break down problems**, ideas, or arguments into their constituent parts in order to explain why they are 'the way they are." Whether you agree with what's being suggested isn't the point. Analytical thinking demands an **unprejudiced and unbiased** approach – including accepting the possibility that you may be wrong. Considering every viewpoint helps to achieve balance of thought.

CHAPTER 7

To test for analytical skills one might be asked to look for inconsistencies in an advertisement, put a series of events in the proper order, or critically read an essay. Usually standardized tests and interviews include an analytical section that requires the examination to use their logic to pick apart a problem and come up with a solution.

- Look beneath the surface.
- Establish the validity of any assumptions surrounding the main issues.
- Investigate the credibility of those advancing certain arguments if required.
- Are emotional or subjective factors at play?
- What are the strengths and weaknesses of the points of view being expressed?
- Would these apply in all situations and if not, what allowances would have to be made?
- Leave no stone unturned.

Skills Demonstrated:
- seeing patterns
- organization of parts
- recognition of hidden meanings
- identification of components.

Analytical skill is the ***ability to visualize, articulate, and solve complex problems*** and concepts, and make decisions that make sense based on available information. Such skills include demonstration of the ability to apply logical thinking to gathering and analyzing information, designing and testing solutions to problems, and formulating plans.

There is no question that analytical skills are essential, other skills are equally required. For instance in systems analysis the systems analyst should focus on four set of analytical skills: systems thinking, organizational knowledge, problem identification, and problem analyzing and solving.

Question Cues: analyze, separate, order, explain, connect, classify, arrange, divide, compare, select, explain, infer.

Figure 7.7. Human Comprehension.

Human brain is not capable to comprehend immediately complex issue. How you learn computer? You learn first its components to understand the whole. First, you need to take it apart. The same is true for any new subject that you are learning. It is taking apart, separated to several topics. Each topic is divided into subtopics. This is the way of learning.

Analytical thinking shows that most of what we take to be clear in our minds is little more than an unexamined acceptance of the language with which we describe our superficial understanding of our EXPERIENCES as opposed to the reality beyond our sense data.

We are taught, "The pencil is yellow." The pencil is, in fact, not yellow if we mean by "yellow" that the color of the pencil is the same as the sensation of yellow that we are experiencing.

The pencil only *appears* to be yellow.

A simple lesson in elementary science verifies this claim.

In simplistic explanation, the "yellow" is "in our heads." The object, i.e., the paint on the pencil, has the potential (the disposition) to cause only the "yellow" magnetic-impulse frequency to be reflected from the object into the rods and cones of our optic-nerve system exciting the electrons which send a "message" to the brain creating a sensation of yellow.

This example in itself is not earth shaking.

Who really cares what the color of the pencil really is so long as it works as a tool?

A fair question indeed!

But we are interested in understanding the world and whether claims about more serious matters are true, such as:

Does a personal god exist?

What was the origin of the universe?

148

Modes of Thinking

Is there life after death?

Does mathematics really describe the physical world?

Obviously, then, the need to learn how to deal with such questions as, "What color is the pencil?" becomes a serious matter.

The analytical thinker is aware not only that concepts are given their meanings in terms of their relationship to each other but also of the limitations of those meanings.

To use a simple example viewed as a problem of science: I am at rest as I sit in my chair. The "educated" person knows that I am moving at approximately 1000 miles per hour around the "axis" of the earth, 18 miles a second around the sun, and 250 miles a second around the center of our galaxy, not to mention the movements of the Sun within the galaxy and the galaxy itself.

The astronauts, repairing the Hubble telescope are "at rest" relative to the telescope but, are moving five miles a second over our heads.

The analytical thinker comparing those motions in his mind's eye comes to understand, assuming the scientific data to be accurate, that even those motions may be deceptive in their interpretations depending on, among other things, their relative positions in space.

After all, as Einstein has shown, the astronauts overhead may be "at rest" and we, all the inhabitants on Earth, may be moving at 18,000 miles an hour beneath them.

Children in the pre-high school grades are taught times tables and other mathematical concepts by rote.

If, as they reach the higher grades, they have not been taught that mathematics is a form of deductive logic, and that mathematical concepts, i.e., numbers, points, lines, planes, etc., do not actually describe the physical world, then the teachers, the colleges, and universities are not teaching the students to think analytically.

Mathematical concepts have no physically existential status.

The teacher is not asking the student such questions as:

What is a number?

Do numbers, in fact, exist?

Would there be numbers if intelligent beings did not exist?

Does conceiving the idea of numbers bring them into existence?

What does "exist" mean in the claim, "Numbers, i.e., mathematical concepts, exist (autonomously?)?"

Why, when a mathematician says, "There are as many points on an infinitely small leg of a Pythagorean right triangle as there are on its infinitely long hypotenuse," should it be accepted as true when common sense would strongly suggest otherwise?

If a teacher does not explain to his students (as in the case of teaching times tables) that "a point has no dimensions" (to cite one definition), is equivalent to saying it is nothing; i.e.; it is only an idea (i.e.; there are as many ideas on the small leg as there are on the long hypotenuse), then he is not teaching the student to think analytically.

The same kind of examination of ideas (*a la* Socrates) applies to all kinds of language: mathematical, scientific, theistic, ordinary - to cite only a few - with which we make claims to having truth and knowledge.

We must never accept language at face value.

There are certain PRINCIPLES, rules, facts, information we must be aware of.

Otherwise, it is impossible to become an analytical thinker sufficient to protecting ourselves against the abuse of language that is and will be foisted upon us all our lives.

To the degree that one examines language and defines terms and distinguishes between DESCRIPTIVE and PRESCRIPTIVE statements, he is well on the road to becoming an analytical thinker and, hence, a clear and critical thinker.

Attribute Analysis

Attribute analysis is the process of breaking down a problem, idea, or thing into attributes or component parts and then thinking about the attributes rather than the thing itself.

For example, let's say you work for a ball bearing manufacturer and you discover that a flaw in one of the machines has caused the production of 800 million slightly out-of-round ball bearings. You could ask, "What can I do with 800 million slightly out-of-round ball bearings?" and, of course, a few things come to mind, like sling shot ammo and kid's marbles. But you could also break the ball bearings down into attributes, such as roundish, heavy, metal, smooth, shiny, hard, magnetizable. Then you could ask, "What can I do with 800 million heavy things?" or "What can I do with 800 million shiny things?"

Further, you can *focus on each identified attribute* and ask questions about it, like this:
- *What can heavy things be used for?* paperweights, ship ballast, podium anchors, tree stands, scale weights, and so on.
- *What can be done with metal things?* conduct electricity, magnetize them, melt them, make tools with them.

Then, each of these attributes can be addressed, either directly, or through further attribute analysis. For example, take "poor economic judgment." What are the attributes of that? Some possibilities: buying low quality items, buying smaller packages at higher price per ounce, wasteful spending habits, tendency to "blow a wad" on payday, inefficient food buying (expensive rather than quantity or health considerations), lack of market competition (and hence higher prices), lack of ability to budget, tendency to use money for non food items like alcohol, inability to calculate price per ounce, etc. to determine greatest economy

Discovering attributes can be aided by the use of checklists. For example:

Physical: color, weight, material, speed, odor, size, structure, taste

Psychological: appearance, symbolism, emotive ("happy smell of detergent")

Functional: intended uses, applications, how it does what it does

People: who's involved

Miscellaneous: cost, reputation, origin, class it belongs to, definition

> *Example problem:* How can we read and remember better? First, what are the attributes of reading and remembering?

Possibilities: books, repetition, visualization, understanding (comprehension), quantity of material and number of details, length of time desired to remember (short or long or permanent)

What are the attributes of visualization? ... Solution: draw pictures of what you read.

What are the attributes of understanding? ... Simplify text by rewriting it or summaries of it into your own words.

> *Another problem:* What are the uses for a yellow pencil? What are the attributes?
> *Possibilities:* yellow paint, hexagonal, pointed, rubber end, metal ring, wood, graphite rod, long and stick-like shape

What are the attributes of wood? burns, floats, electrical insulator, nailable, paintable, gluable, structural component, soaks up liquid slowly, can be sanded or carved

Morphological Analysis

Morphological analysis builds upon attribute analysis by *generating alternatives for each attribute*, thereby producing new possibilities.

The rules are simple:
    A. List the attributes of the problem, object, or situation as you would in a standard attribute analysis.
    B. Under each attribute, list all the alternatives you can think of.
    C. Choose an alternative from each column at random and assemble the choices into a possibility for a new idea. Repeat the choosing and assembly many times.

> *Example problem: Develop a better bandaid.*

Sidebar:

To solve the problem of poverty, ask, what are the attributes of poverty
Some answers: people, crime, lack of food, lack of goods, large families, psychological lacks, low self esteem, welfare, lack of jobs, lack of job skills, lack of value-rich upbringing, lack of education, lack of motivation, poor economic judgment (poor buying skills), poor quality housing, poor quality transportation.

Attribute analysis is sometimes described as a smashing technique, because it smashes our fixed and frozen collection of thoughts about a problem or idea. This is accomplished by refocusing onto something belonging to the problem but more general or abstract or more specific and concrete. Often, attribute analysis is another way of recognizing that a given problem is really a collection of interrelated smaller problems. And often it is a way of perceiving the variables that make up a situation or thing in a way that allows us to change one or more and improve the whole thing.

Modes of Thinking

What are the current attributes of a bandaid? In the table below the attributes are listed in the first row and alternates are listed under each attribute:

stick on	flesh colored	plastic	rectangular	gauzed
magnetic	red or green	cloth	round	medicated
tie on	flower pattern	paper	triangular	cellulose
glue on	transparent	Tyvek	octagon	sawdust
paint on	black	metal	square	plastishred
velcro	words (ouch)	wood	trapezoid	plastic
clamp on	stripes	rubber	animals	cotton

Example problem: Improve the textbook
What are the current attributes of a textbook?

size/shape	binding	cover	pages	type	pictures
small	perfect	hardback	large	Roman	photos
large	sewn	paper	small	varied	drawings
long	spiral	plastic	glossy	color	color
round	left	none	thick	highlighted	holograms
micro	top	thin	large	vertical	U-draw

Try It Yourself

Morphological Analysis. Use morphological analysis to improve or solve one of the following. List at least six attributes and at least six alternatives for each. Then choose one set that forms a practical, useful improvement.

- improve a bus
- improve a telephone
- solve flat tires
- improve a chair
- solve the problem of low participation in recycling efforts
- improve a shoe
- improve the game of basketball

Try It Yourself

Morphological Analysis. Use morphological analysis to improve or solve one of the following. List at least six attributes and at least six alternatives for each. Then choose one set that forms a practical, useful improvement.

Improve a cell phone

Size/shape	material	type	capacity	feelings/prestige	What else?

Invent a new toy

CHAPTER 7

Manipulative Verbs. Taking a hint from Osborn's questions above, some creative thinkers have asked, Why not use a large list of action verbs to stimulate creative thinking? And that is just what manipulative verbs are all about. The list could be very long; here we have just a few. You can make your own list if you like. Choose one of the verbs and think about how it can be applied to your idea or problem.

For example: The problem is to improve a table. The verb is inflate. What does that suggest? Make the table larger, floating, made of inflated vinyl, thick top and legs, high price to cater to upscale consumers, air vents in table to blow out cool or heated air or to suck in smoke from cigarettes. And so on. Here are a few verbs to begin with:

freeze	crush	rotate
heat	bend	transpose
melt	paint	display
loosen	stretch	submerge
twist	repeat	automate

Checklists

A checklist is a standard collection of items (things, verbs, questions, approaches, attributes) used to remind the creative thinker of possible ways to approach a problem or shape a solution. When running through a typical checklist, the creative thinker might ask, "Have I taken this into account? How might I change or use this aspect? What effect will this attribute have on my problem or solution or idea?"

Here are a few checklists, which you should supplement with your own customized ones, developed for your particular problem, or the kind of work your do. You might also locate or develop some additional general lists like these:

Aristotle's Categories

1. Substance or essence. What is it and what makes it unique or individual?

2. Quantity or magnitude. How many, how much, what degree?

3. Relation. Rank, comparison, derivation.

4. Quality. Value, attributes, shape, habits.

5. Action. What is it doing or does it do?

6. Affection. Reputation, attitudes toward.

7. Place. Where is it?

8. Time. When? (now? historical? future?)

9. Position. Sitting, standing, displayed, hidden

10. State. Planned, broken, untried, changing.

I. The Five Senses

1. **Touch.** Feeling, texture, pressure, temperature, vibration.
2. **Taste.** Flavor, sweet/salt/bitter.
3. **Smell.** Aroma, odor.
4. **Sound.** Hearing, speech, noise, music.
5. **Sight.** Vision, brightness, color, movement, symbol.

II. Human Needs

1. **Physical Comfort.** Food, clothing, shelter, warmth, health.
2. **Emotional Comfort.** Safety, security, freedom from fear, love.
3. **Social Comfort.** Fellowship, friendship, group activity.
4. **Psychological Comfort.** Self-esteem, praise, recognition, power, self-determination, life control.
5. **Spiritual Comfort.** Belief structure, cosmic organizing principle.
   (Note: some needs cross boundaries. These include: pleasure, recreation, activity.)

III. Physical Attributes

1. **Shape.**
2. **Color.**
3. **Texture.**
4. **Material.**
5. **Weight.**
6. **Hardness/Softness.**
7. **Flexibility.**
8. **Stability.** (rolls, evaporates, decomposes, discolors, etc.)
9. **Usefulness.** (edible, tool, esthetic, etc.)
10. **State.** (powdered, melted, carved, painted, etc.)

152

IV. General Comments

Customized checklists should be developed for individual problems or ideas when several factors must be considered. Listing each condition to be met or part to be covered will assure that none are overlooked. The mind can attend to only about seven items at one time; more than that will have to be recalled from memory, either by force of will or through a checklist. Checklists help enormously in keeping the idea maker or problem solver alert to multiple aspects of the issue at hand.

A checklist of available tools used in your ordinary work can also be helpful. These lists might be called availability reminders. An electrician might have a list (or even a board with samples) of the various kinds of wires and fasteners available. A student might have a list of common reference tools, outlining styles, and information storage methods (like writing, drawing, typing, voice and video recording, model building, memorizing, and so forth). These checklists simply save the mental effort required to bring up what's available when that list gets longer than six or seven.

Try It Yourself

Use one or more of the concepts in this article to respond to one of the following challenges. List the concept(s) you chose to use, and describe how you used it. Then list your suggested names.

Product Name. The KellMills Cereal Company has just created a new breakfast cereal made from formed wheat chunks. Instead of targeting this cereal either to the children's or adult's market, the company would like to target it toward young adults in the 13-19 year-old range. Your task is to think of ten possible names for this product and then to choose one of these names. Explain in a few sentences why the name is appropriate and appealing, and then in a paragraph sketch out a possible advertising campaign or advertisement that will appeal to the targeted group.

You may want to design the look of the cereal box also as part of the advertisement.

Company Name. A new company has been formed through the merger of two conglomerates, AXA Inc. and Flubco Industries. The new company now makes food items (bread, cake mix, cereal, soup), household products (light bulbs, telephones, dishwashing detergent), and original equipment for manufacturers (automobile mufflers and shock absorbers).

Your task is to create a new name for this company that will be attractive, memorable, and distinctive, and if possible, reflect the kinds of products the company makes and the market it serves. Suggest ten possible names and then choose one that seems to be the best. In a few sentences explain why this is the best choice.

Finally, generate a motto to go with the new name. (For example, "Flubco--Our light bulbs are a bright idea.")

PRACTICING ANALYSIS

Exercise 1. Content Analysis

This technique represents a combination of analytical and analogical thinking.

John Naisbitt, author of *Megatrends* and chairman of the Washington, D. C. - based Naisbitt Group, has been very successful in employing a method of trend spotting called "content analysis." He adapted this notion from methods used in a book he read about the Civil War. The historian who wrote the book, in turn, adapted content analysis from an article he had read about the CIA's intelligence-gathering methods. The CIA patterned it after method was used by the Allies in World War II. Allied forces discovered the strategic value of reading newspapers smuggled out of small German towns. These papers sometimes carried useful stories on fuel, food, and other items. Similarly, a small group of Swiss intelligence officers were able to figure out German troop movements by reading social pages to see where famous German officers were mentioned.

Here is how to do your own content analysis while working on your creative project or solving a problem:

Keep in mind your problem. For example:
You want to design a new household product. Having this in your mind, you

- Scan your junk mail before you discard it. What trends in advertising, marketing, new products, and new values can you discern?

- Let your junk mail collect for a month or two before scanning it. Patterns and trends are more readily apparent, because you can see the repetitive nature of emerging trends;

- When you are on the road, read the local newspapers and shopping news giveaways. What inferences can you make about the local economy? Is it growing or declining? What new business opportunities do you see? What opportunities are transferable to your home town? What are the area's values, attitudes, and lifestyles?

- Actively observe popular magazines and books, go to movies, and listen to popular songs. What are people interested in? What values and lifestyles are portrayed? Who are the popular heroes? Why are they heroes?

- Think about how your job has changed. What is in your basket as compared with its contents this time last years? Has the corporate emphasis changed? Do you have more paperwork or less? More meetings or fewer? Where is the company heading? Talk to the people you work with for clues to the ways work attitudes, values, and commitments are changing;

- Attend as many business conferences, seminars, and lectures as you can;

- Listen to a different radio station every week to get a variety of perspectives. Who is the market for the station? What are they addressing? Who listens? Who advertises? Why?

- Make it a practice to scan the week's television schedule, and then tape the programs that interest you. When you are in the mood for television, watch the taped programs instead of whatever is on.

Your own content analysis will be infinitely more valuable to you than any of the available services, some of which charge clients $25,000 a year to provide them with this type of information. When you perceive trends and patterns of interest, begin to pump your mind for ideas, opportunities, and business possibilities. Look for connections and relationships between your content analysis and your business challenges.

Using Citations

"The two most engaging powers of an author are to make new things familiar, familiar things new."

William Thackeray

Quotations help you think of ways to make familiar things new. That's an essential ingredient of creative thinking - taking what appears to be known and applying some unique twist to it. Quotations do this by forcing you to consider angles you might otherwise have overlooked.

Here are the steps for using quotations:

1. Read a list of quotations from various authors covering different topics. Two of the best reference books are Bartlett's Familiar Quotations and Edward's Dictionary of Thoughts.

2. Select one of the quotations and think about its meaning. Free associate if you wish and write down whatever comes to mind.

3. Select another quotation and repeat step 2 until you have generated as many ideas as you can. (Don't be discouraged if not all quotations spark ideas. That's not the purpose of this exercise. If even one quotation triggers one good idea, then it was worth the effort.)

4. Collect your own quotations and thoughts from books, biographies, the Bible, the Talmud, newspapers, magazines, cartoons, movies, and television. You can categorize them according to subject, or randomly.

Several books on quotations are available in your local library or bookstore (or perhaps even your own bookshelf). You may want to select quotations that pertain to your problem topic.

Examples:

"He who walks with butter on his head should not walk in the sun."

"Don't hitch a horse and an ox to the same wagon."

"One coin in a bottle rattles; the bottle filled with coins makes the noise."

"Woe to him who makes the door before he has a house or builds a gate and has no yard."

"If two logs are dry and one is wet, the kindling of the two will kindle the wet one, too."

"Just as wheat is not without straw, so no dream is without some nonsense."

"Ruling the big country is like cooking small fish." - Lao Tsu

"Where the telescope ends, the microscope begins. Which of the two has the grander view?" - Victor Hugo

" There are two way to spread the light, to be the candle or the mirror that reflects it." - Edith Wharton

"God is geometrician." - Plato

Modes of Thinking

"Handle your tools without mittens; remember that the cat in gloves catches no mice." - Ben Franklin

"The perfection of art is to conceal art." - Quintilian

"Not only strike while the iron is hot, but make it hot by striking." - Oliver Cromwell

"And I must find every changing shape, to find expression." - T. S. Eliot

"When you eliminated the impossible, whatever remains, however improbable, must be the truth." - Arthur Conan Doyle

Clichés, Proverbs, and Maxims

A friend in need is a friend indeed.
A penny saved is a penny earned.
A rolling stone gathers no moss.
A stitch in time saves nine.
Absence makes the heart grow fonder.
Actions speak louder than words.
All roads lead to Rome.
All that glitters is not gold.
All work and no play makes Jack a dull boy.
An ounce of prevention is worth a pound of cure.
Beggars can't be choosers.
Better late than never.
Better safe than sorry. Big oaks from little acorns grow.
Don't bite off more than you can chew.
Don't borrow from Peter to pay Paul.
Don't burn a candle at both ends.
Don't put all your eggs into one basket.
Don't rock the boat.
Early to bed and early to rise makes a man healthy, wealthy, and wise.
Every cloud has a silver lining.
Experience is the best teacher.
Familiarity breeds contempt.
Fools rush in where angels fear to tread.
For every drop of rain that falls, a flower grows.
Forewarned is forearmed.
Go ahead, make my day!
Good fences make good neighbors.
He who hesitates is losty.

He who tends a fig tree will eat its fruit.
His bark is worse than his bite.
It never rains but it pours.
It takes two to tango.
It's easier to catch files with honey than with vinegar.
Jack of all trades, master of none.
Keep your nose to the grindstone.
Look before you leap.
Loose lips sink ships.
Misery loves company.
Neither a borrower nor a lender be.
Nothing ventured nothing gained.
Out of sight, out of mind.
People who live in glass houses shouldn't throw stones.
Rome wasn't built in a day.
Seeing is believing.
Something must be seen to be believed.
Stone walls do not a prison make.
The early bird gets the worm.
The grass is always greener on the other side of the fence.
The meek shall inherit the earth.
The pen is mightier than the sword.
Too many cooks spoil the broth.
Two heads are better than one.
Two's company and three's a crowd.
Where there's smoke there's fire.
You can lead a horse to water, but you can't make him drink.
You can't judge a book by its cover.
You're barking up the wrong tree.

Now try it yourself.
Your task is to design a new children toy.
Go through your junk mail, use citations, clichés, and proverbs. What ideas come to your mind while doing it?

_____ _____ _____

Exercise 3.2.
Instruction
Find the right number:
1. 196 (25) 324; 325 (?) 137 _____
2. 12 (56) 16; 17 (?) 21 _____
3. 148 (110) 368; 243 (?) 397 _____
4. 18 – 10 – 6 – 4 – ? _____

Answers:
1. 21. 1 + 9 + 6 + 3 + 2 + 4 = 25
2. 76. (12 + 16) X 2 = 56; (17 + 21) X 2 = 76
3. 77. (368 – 148) : 2 = 110; (397 – 243) : 2 = 77
4. (18 + 2) : 2 = 10; (10 + 2) : 2 + 6; (6 + 2) : 2 = 4; (4 + 2) : 2 = 3

CHAPTER 7

4. SYNTHESIS THINKING

The term **synthesis** (from the ancient Greek σύνθεσις σύν "with" and θέσις "placing") is used in many fields, usually to mean a process which combines together two or more pre-existing elements resulting in the formation of something new.

Synthesis is the combination of ideas into a complex whole. Synthesis puts together parts into a whole. The purpose of synthesis is to achieve a construct that satisfies a goal. Synthesis is the mode of thinking that is the kernel of the process of design. In this sense, it is reasoning that proceeds from statements concerning the purpose of a new artifact to statements about its form and use. Whereas analysis can be an enemy of vision, synthesis is supposed to be its ally.

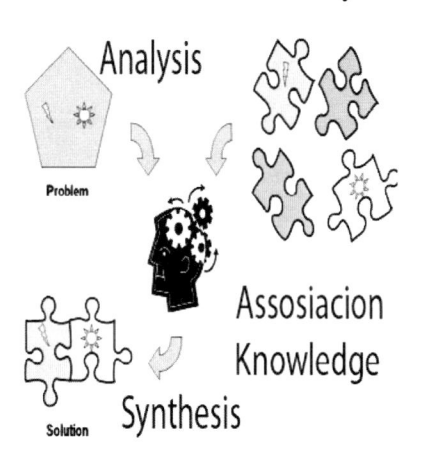

- Synthesis thinking is a method of thinking which relies **taking existing concepts** and **ideas** and then **creating new notions** or understanding from by **combining** them in new or unique ways.
- Synthesis thinking allows for **further understanding** with topic that are unfamiliar to a person. An example of synthetic thinking to gain understanding would be where when **exposed to a new object** a person **compares** that object to things that look like it or act like it and **derives an understanding** of the object from that or **finds a new way** to use the object that may have been previously overlooked.

Skills Demonstrated
- use old ideas to create new ones
- generalize from given facts
- relate knowledge from several areas
- predict, draw conclusions

Question Cues: combine, integrate, modify, rearrange, substitute, plan, create, design, invent, what if?, compose, formulate, prepare, generalize, rewrite.

Whenever you report to a friend the things several other friends have said about a film or CD you engage in synthesis. People synthesize information naturally to help others see the connections between things they learn. For example, you have probably stored up a mental data bank of the various things you've heard about particular professors. If your data bank contains several negative comments, you might synthesize that information and use it to help you decide not to take a class from that particular professor. Synthesis is related to but not the same as classification, division, or comparison and contrast. Instead of attending to categories or finding similarities and differences, synthesizing sources is a matter of pulling them together into some kind of harmony. Synthesis searches for links between materials for the purpose of constructing a thesis or theory.

Common words and phrases related to Synthesis Thinking
- What if …?
- Combine
- Adapt
- Integrate
- Invent
- Incorporate
- Generalize
- How can we improve …?

PRACTICING SYNTHESIS THINKING

Exercise 4.1. **What if**

- you were the only person in the world?

- no one ever had to work?
- murder were declared legal?
- nothing ever changed?
- everyone had to work 20 hours a day?
- all money were destroyed?
- everyone spoke without thinking?
- all your friends turned into enemies?
- all our wishes were satisfied?
- there were no armies?
- all babies were grown in testtubes?
- marriage were prohibited?
- you felt like a different person every other day?
- all sports were outlawed?
- no one ever felt guilty or ashamed?
- everyone loved his brother as himself?
- everyone failed at everything he or she ever tried?
- everyone did exactly what he or she felt like?

What-Iffing. A major block to creativity for many of us is the mind's fierce grasp on reality. This very factor that keeps us sane also keeps us from thinking beyond what we know to be true. What-iffing is a tool for releasing the mind, for delivering us from being blocked by reality.

In its simplest form, what-iffing involves describing an imagined action or solution and then examining the probable associated facts, consequences, or events. Instead of quickly saying, "That sounds dumb," or "That would never work," and leaving our criticism vague, we trace as exactly as our reasonable minds can generate the specific implications or consequences of the newly imagined fact.

For example, what if automobiles were all owned by the government and everybody had a key and could use any car that was handy? Consequences: Parking lot size could be reduced. There would probably be more car pooling with strangers. If cars were maintained by the government, too, some would be in better shape than now, but others would be in worse shape--no pride in personal ownership. On sunny days cars would be plentiful, but on rainy days, you might get stuck at the shopping center. Cars that broke down would be abandoned. You couldn't lock things in your car. You'd never know if the car you drove to a location (like the movie theater at night) would be there when you got out.

Another example might be to ask, "What if we do nothing about the problem?" Then seek as accurately as possible the consequences.

On another level, what-iffing allows us to create a completely new reality, to establish a new chain of being or relationships, to change the unchangeable in hope of generating a new perspective on a problem or a new idea.

For example: What if rocks were soft? We could put big ones in our houses like pillows to lean on in the living room. We could use them like 'medicine balls" to toss to each other for exercise. We could line roads with piles of rocks to keep cars from damage when control was lost on dangerous corners. We could jump off high buildings onto rock piles. Crushed rock pits could be used to jump into by athletes. On the other hand, rock grinding wheels wouldn't work anymore. Concrete, made of rock, would be soft. A cinderblock cell would be a padded cell.

Another example: What if we could see odors? You'd know the source of the bad smell in the kitchen--a plant, garbage disposal, wastebasket, old food in the refrigerator. You could see the perfume as it wafted off the girl wearing it--a visible "come on." Since we can see farther than we can smell, you could see who had an orange or banana or Limburger cheese sandwich in his lunch bag from across the room. Visible odors could be socially embarrassing in ways not necessary to detail.

Whether or not the "seeing odors" thought suggests the invention of an odor detecting device, a super sniffer like the ones used by the U.S. military to sniff out enemy soldiers, a main benefit of practicing what-iffing is to train the mind to explore unreality or imagined reality, to think about, for a few minutes, the necessary, logical consequences or facts needed to support such a change in real things. Too often when someone gets a new idea, little attempt is made to think about its logical consequences for a few minutes.

For example, we have heard some people say that the United States should legalize drugs like cocaine because then the pushers and organized crime couldn't make money and would stop pushing them and the drug problem would go away. Okay, what if drugs were legal? Would they be legal for everyone, even children? Well, no, you'd have to be 18 to buy them. But then wouldn't the pushers concentrate on selling drugs to those under 18 instead of to adults, which would be a worse situation than we have now? Or, would adults stop using cocaine if it were legal and cheap? Or would it be legal and expensive? And so on.

As I said, too often we simply stop thinking altogether when something contrary to fact comes across our minds or else we think about it in the most illogical and impractical way. When we ask, "What if the sky were green?" the response we tend to get, either from others or from ourselves, is, "Well, the sky isn't green, so why think about it?" But if nothing else, thinking about it is good practice at logical thinking.

In more practical terms, though, thinking about what does not exist is about the only way we have of eventually making it exist. In other words, the first step to implementing a new reality is to imagine it.

Notice when you mention a "what if" to your friends, their reaction will probably be to laugh and change the subject, or to laugh and suggest one funny consequence. There is little attempt to trace probable consequences thoroughly, to outline a full set of associated realities. By not doing so, we are in danger of cutting off many new ideas.

Try It Yourself

What If. Choose one of the questions below and then trace the reasonable and logical consequences that would follow. You might be sure to think of both good and bad (and perhaps indifferent) consequences. List or describe (in a sentence or two each) at least ten consequences.

1. What if anyone could set up as a doctor?
2. What if each home could run the television only one hour a day?
3. What if a citizen could serve only one term in one office during a lifetime?
4. What if gasoline grew on trees and was a renewable resource?
5. What if exams and grades were abolished in college?
6. What if our pets could talk?
7. What if gasoline cost $25 a gallon?
8. What if we never had to sleep?
9. What if we could read other people's minds (and they could read ours)?
10. What if all marriages were automatically cancelled by the state every three years?
11. What if everybody looked almost exactly alike?
12. What if clocks and watches didn't exist and daylight lasted six months?

Create a list of one dozen or more "fantasy questions"

1. _____
2. _____
3. _____
4. _____
5. _____
6. _____
7. _____
8. _____

Ask several people to answer your questions.

5. HOLISTIC THINKING

Holism (from ὅλος holos, a Greek word meaning all, entire, total) is the idea that **all the properties of a given system** (biological, chemical, social, economic, mental, linguistic, etc.) **cannot be determined or explained by the sum of its component parts alone.** Instead, the system as a whole determines in an important way how the parts behave.

The general principle of holism was concisely summarized by Aristotle in the Metaphysics: *"**The whole is more than the sum of its parts.**"*

Reductionism is sometimes seen as the ***opposite of holism***. Reductionism in science says that a complex system can be explained by reduction to its fundamental parts. Essentially, chemistry is reducible to physics, biology is reducible to chemistry and physics, psychology and sociology are reducible to biology, etc. Some other proponents of reductionism, however, think that holism is the opposite only of greedy reductionism.

Modes of Thinking

Holistic thinking deals with wholes rather than parts. The basic idea is pretty straightforward. Imagine you are trying to decide what to plant in a new garden, and you choose all sorts of plants and shrubs which you like. You can't just go on buying individual plants without, sooner or later, coming to some view of the whole of the garden, otherwise you'll have too many things for one part of the garden and not enough for another, or you may chose plants unsuited to the conditions, or that shade out each other.

Imagine, to take another example, that you are a member of a group which isn't working well. Much of its meetings are taken up with people defending themselves against real (or imaginary) criticisms and talking at cross purposes. Somehow, unimportant decisions are debated for hours and big ones go through on the nod. Everybody leaves the meeting feeling drained, but also feeling that not much has been achieved. If you wanted to understand why this was so, you could start by looking at each person individually – does he or she have the qualities which are needed to work in this group? You could list them one by one, and decide, in relation to each individual, whether or not that person was contributing to the problems. You might even decide that one person was really unsuited to the task, get them removed from the group and expect all to be well. The chances are that it wouldn't. Your way of thinking about this problem, by looking at the parts, overlooks the relationships between the people, and these are crucial to what is going on. And, when you think about it, the same is true if you look first at the relationships between two of the members, and then at relationships between another two and so on.

It is the interplay of all the relationships between all the members which is one of the major factors making the group function as it does. The behavior of the group emerges from the interactions of the whole, and can't be predicted by looking separately at the behavior of each of the parts.

So the basic idea of holistic thinking is that *you need to think about wholes rather than just about parts*. The problem with this idea is that it isn't always clear what is a whole and what is a part. A person is a whole, but he or she will be a part of a group, such as a family or workgroup. And that group, which is a whole, is a part of a larger group, such as a community or organization. So all of them seem to be both parts and wholes at the same time. Similarly, a fish is a whole, but it won't survive long unless it remains part of the pond in which it lives; and the pond is part of an ecological system and so on. So it looks as if, whatever you decide to think about, it is bound to be a whole! That is true: but what matters in practice is the way you go about trying to understand a phenomenon, or tackle a situation. One way is to start by breaking things up into separate bits, and then tackle each bit separately and draw inferences or take actions based on your understanding of these parts; if this doesn't seem to work, then the next step is often to break things into even smaller bits. As we saw earlier, this is the reductionist approach that has underpinned most scientific and technological activity. The holistic approach starts by looking at the nature and behavior of the whole you are concerned with, and if this doesn't yield results, the next step will be to look at the bigger whole of which it forms a part. In other words, the two approaches go in different directions.

But this seems to raise another problem, which is: How do you look at wholes? You'll never understand the whole of the behavior of a group or a pond, let alone a society or an ecological system. Isn't it simply impossible to think holistically? The answer to that question needs a short discussion. Because the brain is bombarded by information collected all the time by the senses, it has to order or structure it in some way. In this process the brain selects some pieces of information as important and ignores others, and the information it retains is fitted into pre-existing categories. People tend to remember incidents which confirm their view of the world. If I think someone is trying to do me down, I will notice and remember things she does which seem to confirm that view – even to the point of distorting what is really happening. She may be making overtures of friendship, but I will probably interpret them as part of a cunning plot. It is much simpler and easier to interpret what happens as confirming what I think, than to rethink and re-assess every belief I have all the time. In other words, like everyone else, my thoughts simplify the mass of ideas and information I receive into some familiar patterns. In fact, all ways of thinking simplify, because full knowledge and understanding of reality is impossible. So holistic thinking is bound to simplify wholes; what is interesting is how it does it.

Philosophers and scientists have recognized the need for holistic approach. The study of whole systems has been developing during the second half of the 20th century under such headings as general systems theory and systems sciences. Interdisciplinary research, cybernetics, operations research, systems analysis, are all disciplines engaged in understanding problems in a holistic way.

Not an easy task: "*...everything in the universe is connected to everything else... and if each relation helps to determine the nature of the thing that is related, then everything is what it is because everything else is what it is. This is perhaps rather confusing, and sounds metaphysical. But the resulting thought is important: the totality of what exists is an integrated system, and anything split off from the*

Holistic thinking is based on the following *assumptions*:

The whole is more than the sum of the parts;

The whole determines the nature of the parts; The parts cannot be understood if considered in isolation from the whole;

The parts are dynamically interrelated or interdependent.

Why is Holistic Thinking Important?

It hosts of various forms of knowledge:

- Social
- Economic
- Health
- Science
- Psychology
- Education
- Arts

CHAPTER 7

totality and considered separately is incomplete. In practice, we have to split things off and consider them separately, but we shall have to be extremely careful how we do it.

"We cannot bring everything into consideration and somehow must determine the boundaries of the problem in hand. Again, in practice, the scientist needs to enlarge the scope of her study in every dimension until the factors she is bringing in seem to make no tangible difference to the answers she is getting. At the very least, this process is going to take her outside the apparent problem area by one step in every direction" (Stafford Beer, Decision and Control, 1996).

What is holistic thought?

Dealing with wholes requires specific methodologies. The kinds of methods required emerge from the qualities natural to whole systems. General Systems Theory and the Systems Sciences mark humans' developing ability to study phenomena in a holistic way.

The internet, with its ability to interconnect individual thinkers and form a world-wide problem-solving community, is a powerful tool and promises a quantum step towards co-evolving an integrated view of knowledge -- a view corresponding more closely to the holistic nature of reality. With the press of a button we can visit, join, or participate in the endeavors of knowledge-communities anywhere in the world. Examples are *Principia Cybernetica, Union of International Associations, Rainbow Tribes, True Democracy, Global Justice Movement*.

The best model that illustrates the holistic thinking can be a regular solid with twelve 'corners' and 20 triangular sides -- an icosahedrons. The thirty 'edges' then naturally integrate the subjects into a holistic object.

The subjects are not separate disciplines but are composed of the other disciplines, being facets or sub categories of the one chosen to be the dominant focus of attention at any one time. The twelve-ness, though arbitrary, proposes a useful convention:

Twelve subject facets give an enumeration where the classes are not meaninglessly general, yet, are not too numerous to clutter the representation with too much detail. Resolution of finer details can be easily achieved by subdividing the facets and/or combining separate facets or their sub-divisions.

The mandala can also represents 'faculties' of a new type of learning circle. The vision is to attract for every facet a group of enthusiast-specialists--ideally twelve for each facet - in love with chosen fields of study and life application.

Some connections are more obvious than others. For example, politics, economics and science can easily be seen as related (although economists may try to deny the relevance of such relationships), while the significance of education and health issues being contributory facets to economics may not be so easy to appreciate at first. But this is the essence of new thinking about knowledge. We could call this new view vertical or in-depth thinking as an advancement on the dominant mode that call be called "flat" thinking which can only see the obvious surface layer of complex phenomena.

PRACTICING HOLISTIC THINKING

Shortly describe the following phenomena:
1. Globalization_____
2. Change _____
3. Harmony _____
4. Unity _____
5. Dependence _____

160

Modes of Thinking

6. SYSTEMS THINKING

General Systems Theory, an alternative to the analytical-mechanical conceptual schemes, arose in response to the need to investigate and understand living, open systems. It urged people to "look at all factors" or perspectives; but it still tends toward the dissection and decomposition of Conventional Thinking. Systems thinking is closely allied with holistic thinking.

Systems thinking offers you a powerful new perspective, a specialized language, and a set of tools that you can use to address the most stubborn problems in your everyday life and work. Systems thinking is a way of understanding reality that emphasizes the *relationships among a system's parts*, rather than the parts themselves. Based on a field of study known as system dynamics, systems thinking has a practical value that rests on a solid theoretical foundation.

Why Is Systems Thinking Important?

Why is systems thinking valuable? Because it can help you design smart, *enduring solutions to problems*. In its simplest sense, systems thinking gives you a more accurate picture of reality, so that you can work with a system's natural forces in order to achieve the results you desire. It also encourages you to think about problems and solutions with an eye toward the *long view*—for example, how might a particular solution you're considering play out over the long run? And what *unintended consequences* might it have? Finally, systems thinking is founded on some basic, universal principles that you will begin to detect in all arenas of life once you learn to recognize them.

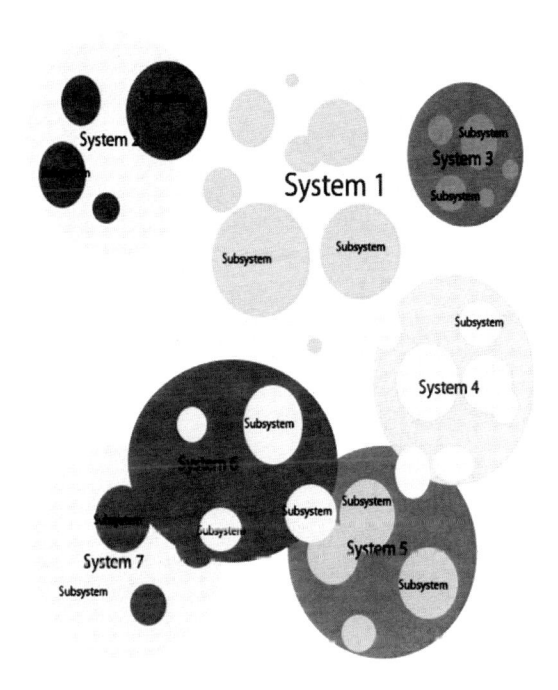

Figure 6.1. Systems' Interrelations and Interdependence.

What Are Systems?

What exactly is a system? *A system is a **group of interacting, interrelated, and interdependent components that form a complex and unified whole**.* Systems are everywhere—for example, the HR department in your organization, the circulatory system in your body, the predator/prey relationships in nature, the ignition system in your car, and so on. Ecological systems and human social systems are living systems; human-made systems such as cars and washing machines are nonliving systems. Most systems thinkers focus their attention on living systems, especially human social systems. However, many systems thinkers are also interested in how human social systems affect the larger ecological systems in our planet.

From the Latin and Greek, the term "system" meant **to combine**, to set up, to place together.

A **sub-system** is a system which is part of another system. In this case we are talking about different levels of system's organization. For example, human body is composed of several organ systems such as cardio-vascular, pulmonary, digestive, reproductive, nervous, endocrine, integumentary, muscular, skeletal, lymphatic, and urinary systems. This is a systemic level of human body's organization. You can go deeper into tissue level that gives you picture of human body's tissues such as connective, muscular, nervous, and epithelial tissue structure and functions.

You may go deeper to the cellular level of human body's organization. Or even deeper to the molecular level.

Systems have several defining characteristics:
- **Every system has a purpose within a larger system.** Example: The purpose of the HR department in your organization is to hire competent people for the organization.
- **All of a system's parts must be present for the system to carry out its purpose optimally.** Example: The HR system in your organization consists of people, equipment, and processes. If you removed any one of these components, this system could no longer function.

161

CHAPTER 7

Looking at the world through a systems thinking "lens" is so powerful: It lets you actually make the world a better place.

- **A system's parts must be arranged in a specific way for the system to carry out its purpose.** Example: If you rearranged the reporting relationships in your HR department so that the head of new-product development reported to the entry-level lab technician, the department would likely have trouble carrying out its purpose.
- **Systems change in response to feedback.** The word feedback plays a central role in systems thinking. Feedback is information that returns to its original transmitter such that it influences that transmitter's subsequent actions. Example: Suppose you turn too sharply while driving your car around a curve. Visual cues (you see a mailbox rushing toward you) would tell you that you were turning too sharply. These cues constitute feedback that prompts you to change what you're doing (jerk the steering wheel in the other direction somewhat) so you can put your car back on course.
- **Systems maintain their stability by making adjustments based on feedback.** Example: Your body temperature generally hovers around 98.6 degrees Fahrenheit. If you get too hot, your body produces sweat, which cools you back down.

Systems Thinking as a Perspective: Events, Patterns, or System?

Systems thinking is a perspective because it helps us see the events and patterns in our lives in a new light—and respond to them in higher leverage ways. For example, suppose a fire breaks out in your town. This is an **event**. If you respond to it simply by putting the fire out, you're reacting. (That is, you have done nothing to prevent new fires.) If you respond by putting out the fire and studying where fires tend to break out in your town, you'd be paying attention to **patterns**. For example, you might notice that certain neighborhoods seem to suffer more fires than others. If you locate more fire stations in those areas, you're adapting. (You still haven't done anything to prevent new fires.) Now suppose you look for the **systems**—such as smoke-detector distribution and building materials used—that influence the patterns of neighborhood-fire outbreaks. If you build new fire-alarm systems and establish fire and safety codes, you're creating change. Finally, you're doing something to prevent new fires!

Systems Thinking as a Special Language

As a language, systems thinking has unique qualities that help you communicate with others about the many systems around and within us:
- It emphasizes wholes rather than parts, and stresses the role of interconnections—including the role we each play in the systems at work in our lives.
- It emphasizes circular feedback (for example, A leads to B, which leads to C, which leads back to A) rather than linear cause and effect (A leads to B, which leads to C, which leads to D, . . . and so on).
- It contains special terminology that describes system behavior, such as reinforcing process (a feedback flow that generates exponential growth or collapse) and balancing process (a feedback flow that controls change and helps a system maintain stability).

Systems Thinking as a Set of Tools

The field of systems thinking has generated a broad array of tools that let you (1) graphically depict your understanding of a particular system's structure and behavior, (2) communicate with others about your understandings, and (3) design high-leverage interventions for problematic system behavior.

These tools include causal loops, behavior over time graphs, stock and flow diagrams, and systems archetypes—all of which let you depict your understanding of a system—to computer simulation models and management "flight simulators," which help you to test the potential impact of your interventions.

Types of Systems

There are three types of systems:
- An **open system** can be influenced by events outside of the declared boundaries of a system.
- A **closed system** is self-contained: outside events can have no influence upon the system. In practice many things are a mixture of the two. For example a prison is a closed

Modes of Thinking

system because the prisoners can't get out, and the wardens spend most of their time at the prison. However it is also an open system, because it depends on outside factors and the prisoners and wardens do go outside.
- **Dynamic systems** have components or flows or both, that change over time.

An **open system** may refer to more than one thing:
- In the **physical sciences**, an **open system (system theory)** is a system that matter or energy can **flow into and/or out** of, in contrast to a closed system, which no energy or matter may enter or leave.
- In **computing**, an **open system (computing)** is a computer operating system that provides **interoperability, portability or both**, particularly Unix systems.
- In **management science**, an **open system (system theory)** is a system that **takes in** (raw materials, capital, skilled labor) and **converts them into goods and services** (via machinery, human skills) that are sent back to that environment, where they are bought by customers.
- Contrarily a **closed system** is self contained, does not interact with its external environment and risks to experience entropy.

In practice many things are a **mixture of the two**. For example, a government is a closed system when it seeks to maintain confidentiality. However, it is open when it seeks advice and accepts universal voter input and petitions.

A **dynamical system** is a concept in mathematics where a fixed rule describes the **time dependence** of a point in a geometrical space. **The mathematical models** used to describe the swinging of a clock pendulum, the flow of water in a pipe, or the number of fish each spring in a lake are examples of dynamical systems. A dynamical system has a *state* determined by a collection of real *numbers*. Small **changes in the state** of the system correspond to small **changes in the numbers**. The numbers are also the coordinates of a geometrical space—a manifold. The *evolution rule* of the dynamical system is a fixed rule that describes what **future states** follow from the current state. The rule is **deterministic**: for a given time interval only one future state follows from the current state.

Another distinction is the relation of physical systems to conceptual systems.
- Physical systems are systems of matter and energy.
- Conceptual systems are made up of ideas. Conceptual systems generally exist to aid in the accomplishment of specific goals or may be used to model physical system.

An open system can be influenced by events outside of the declared boundaries of the system. A **closed system** is self-contained: outside events are separated from the system. The total **energy of the system stays the same**; there is no input or output of energy, just **transference** within.

Dynamic systems have components and/or flows that change over time.

Comparative Characteristics of Physical and Conceptual Systems

Physical Systems	Conceptual Systems
Examples of Systems' Entities	
• an atom • a human being • the solar system • a factory • a machine	• a family • an economy • a religion • a government • a college
Components and Subsystems	
• atoms in a molecule • organs in a human body	• sectors of business • industries in an economy
Preferred State	
• atomic Hydrogen prefers to be molecular Hydrogen • Iron metallic prefers to be iron oxide (rust)	• firm prefers to be profitable • human being prefers to be physiologically and psychologically healthy

CHAPTER 7

All societal systems of a certain order and level of integration, including educational system, share certain basic principles of organization and functional interaction that demonstrate common patterns that raise fundamental questions:

1. ***Genesis:*** how certain system evolved, and what were the prerequisite conditions for such occurrence in the social history?
2. ***Dynamics:*** how do systems change evolutionarily with the function of time?
3. ***Sociocybernetics:*** how do systems transmit themselves through time in terms of their informational capacities?
4. ***Systematics:*** how do systems become integrated and increasingly diverse and complex over time?
5. ***Globalization:*** how does integration of certain systems of various nations constitute a single global educational system that interacts and actively reshapes the societal environment and forms its own contexts?
6. ***Network:*** how do different systems co-exist together in complex interactions and create mutual social environments that influence their development?

According to Bailey (1994), successful modeling of a complex social system requires special attention to the following problems:

1. An adequate ***definition*** of the system
2. An adequate ***specification of the boundaries*** for the system as a whole, for systems components, and for subsystems (if any) and their components.
3. An adequate ***measure of system state*** and adequate operationalization of such a measure
4. The attainment of ***isomorphism between the theoretical systems model*** and the ***actual operating***, empirical, complex system
5. The selection of a suitable ***set of explanatory variables*** out of almost infinite number that could be identified in a complex social system
6. An adequate understanding of the ***relationship among the components*** of the system and between each component, and the whole, to overcome the problem of unwitting displacement of scope
7. An adequate ***analysis of both micro and macro levels*** and their interrelationships to solve or avoid problems such as reductionism and emergence
8. A recognition of the ***needs*** of individuals and subgroups within the system and of the systems as a whole
9. An adequate ***defense against the critics*** that the systems analysis is an inappropriate organic or mechanical analogy
10. The ***recognition of individual, subgroup, and systems goals*** and an understanding of how they are attained
11. An understanding of the ***role of matter - energy*** and information in ongoing system functioning
12. An adequate ***diachronic analysis*** of the system, to understand ***change over time***
13. The adequate ***explanation and prediction*** (including verification) of salient aspects of the complex system via the social systems model.

An open, complex, and adaptive system interacts with its environment, drawing certain inputs from the environment and converting it to outputs that are offered to the environment. The attainment of its preferred state is dependent on the efficiency with which it accomplishes its goals. It posses the following characteristics:

- A system is defined by its properties
- A system is a physical and/or conceptual entity composed of interrelated and interacting parts existing in the environment with which it may also interact
- The system has a preferred state
- The parts of the system may in turn be systems themselves
- A perfectly adaptive system can respond to any change or contingency in the environment
- All systems lie somewhere between non-adaptive and perfectly adaptive systems.
- In order to continue existing, any open system in a dynamic environment must adapt

- Cognitive systems have certain parts that are capable of thought. A single human being is a simple example of a cognitive system
- Cognitive systems are aware of their existence. More than this, they are to a greater or lesser extent aware of the relationship between the system and the environment
- Higher level cognitive systems will also attempt to change the environment to a state more suited to the system's preferred state.

According to Luhmann (1995), autopoietic systems produce their own basic elements; they are self-organizing insofar as they create their own boundaries and internal structures; they are self-referential insofar as their elements refer to the system itself; and they are closed systems insofar as they do not deal directly with their environments, but rather with representations of their environments.

Double contingency refers to the fact that every communication must consider the way in which it will be received. In Luhmann's view, social structures (e.g., roles and norms) make it more likely that communications will be understood by both sender and receiver. Social structures also give communications some continuity over time. Double contingency thus provides much of the impetus for the evolution of social systems.

A complex adaptive system, Buckley (1998) said, must include four basic mechanisms.

1. Some degree of "plasticity" and "irritability" *vis-a-vis* its environment such that it carries on a constant interchange with environmental events, acting on and reacting to it.
2. Some source of variety, to act as a potential pool of adaptive variability to meet the problem of mapping new or more detailed variety and constraints in a changing environment.
3. A set of selective criteria or mechanisms against which the "variety pool" may be shifted into those variations in the organization or system that more closely map the environment and those that does not.
4. An arrangement for preserving and/or propagating these "successful" mappings.

Any social system must deal with the variety in its environment. In addition to its structure maintaining features, it requires a structure elaborating and changing feature. As a result, in considering the term "steady-state", Buckley (1998, p. 47) said, it must "... not be identified with a particular structure of the system." In order to maintain a steady-state, the system must be capable of changing its structure. In describing these mechanisms Buckley uses the term "morphogenesis."

Modular versus Monolithic Structure of Complex Adaptive Systems

Patterns infuse the universe at all levels of organization. Patterns are also the realm of education with common themes that recur over and over in fundamentally different systems and subsystems.

Modularity is defined through a process that starts by **recognizing patterns** or events that **repeat at some scale of observation**. "The way we partition an object in order to study it determines our perception of its modularity" (Callebaut, 2005, P. 181).

This section of the chapter is devoted to making sense of modularity as a recognizable, observable feature in complex systems.

Simon's (1994) characterization of modularity in dynamical systems describes **subsystems** as having dynamics that are **approximately independent** of those of other subsystems (in the short term). This fits with the general intuition that modules must, by definition, be approximately independent. In the evolution of complex systems, such modularity may enable subsystems to be modified and adapted independently of other subsystems, whereas in a nonmodular system, modifications to one part of the system may result in deleterious side effects elsewhere in the system. But this notion of modularity and its effect on evolvability is not well quantified and is rather simplistic. In particular, modularity need not imply that intermodule dependences are weak or unimportant.

In dynamical systems this is acknowledged by Simon's suggestion that, in the long term, the dynamical behaviors of subsystems do interact with one another, albeit in an "aggregate" manner—but this kind of **intermodule interaction** is omitted in models of modularity for **evolvability**. In this brief discussion we seek to unify notions of modularity in **dynamical systems** with notions of how modularity

Society is an autopoietic system. Luhmann (1995) believes that the most basic element of society is communication, and anything that is not communication is part of a society's environment (e.g., biological and psychic systems). Both psychic and social systems — which are environments for each other — rely on meaning. In Luhmann's theory, meaning is comprehensible because of contingency. In other words, meaning emerges only because a specific action is different from other possible actions.

affects evolvability. This leads to a quantifiable measure of modularity and a different understanding of its effect on evolvability.

In summary, basic properties of modules include:

> Modules are *clusters of components* that interact with their environment as a *single unit*. They provide the most widespread means of coping with complexity, in both natural and artificial systems.

1. There is **structural and functional overlap across modules**, but on average **each module is unique** both in set of structures and in functions.
2. Modules are **often repeated** and conserved in different and similar context.
3. There is **strong connectivity within**, and **weak connectivity among modules**. Different modules are semiautonomous during both development and evolution.
4. Modules vary and **change over time**.
5. Modules exist at a **variety of levels**.

A module is *a set of some disassembly* and/or non-disassembly components or parts. It usually is used not only in supporting or carrying out the same function, but also in decreasing the complexity of a system in maintenance. Traditionally, the module form of a system is created according to either the function requirements or the desing considerations. It is determined mainly depending on the individual condition of systems in designing, and has no concrete and scientific approach to progress system modularity. (TSAI, Y-T.; WANG, K-S.; LO S-P., 2003).

> Modularity is a general systems concept: it is a continuum describing the degree to which a system can be separated and recombined, and it refers to both the tightness of coupling between elements and the degree to which the rules of the system enable (or prohibit) the mixing and matching of components' capabilities (Winther, 2005).

Modularity can *increase exponentially the number of possible task organization configurations achievable* from a given set of requirements and capabilities, greatly increasing the flexibility of education systems. According to Rasmussen and Niles (2005), nature proved early on that in complex systems, modular designs are the ones that survive and thrive. An important contributor to this success is the critical reliability advantage of fault tolerance, in which a modular system can shift operation from failed modules to healthy ones while repairs are made.

Why the modular, multi-celled design in biological world prevails over the entrenched monolithic design? Borrowing idea of modular design from living systems and applying it to educational systems may increases their

- *Ability to scale and grow.* System growth, both in size and in addition of new capabilities, could be accomplished simply by adding new modules that could interact with existing ones using standard interfaces.
- *Simplification of the process of duplication.* Duplicating a number of smaller, less complex modules is easier, faster, and more reliable than duplicating a single complicated one.
- *Ability to specialize the function of modules.* Delegation and specialization of module tasks provides the same effectiveness and efficiencies inherent in teamwork. Drawing parallel with living systems, in the early multi-celled organisms, one kind of cell could be for locomotion, another kind for protection, another kind for sensing food, and so on.
- *Rapid adaptation to the constantly changing environment.* By adding, subtracting, or modifying modules, incremental design changes could be more quickly tried and either adopted or rejected.
- *Fault tolerance.* With modules redundancy, individual module could fail without degrading the system, allowing for concurrent module repair without system downtime (disintegration or degradation of educational system in this case).
- *Enhanced Performance.* Modularity enables the delivery of up-to-the-minute information and quick interactive response time for heavy user loads.
- *High Efficiency.* Less load and memory usage per server connection is required, resulting in higher performance and better efficiency of the server, which, in turn, translates into more users per server.
- *Uncomplicated Administration.* Installation and administration of the application is simple, saving the administrator time and effort, while giving end-users easy and secure access to the information they need.
- *Fully Customizable.* Modular education is fully customizable so as to cater to the different needs and requirements of various educational institutions.
- *Version Upgrades.* By providing regular version upgrades to introduce new technical and functional information, as well as latest statutory requirements that may arise from time to time, organizations can be assured that the application will never become obsolete, both technically and functionally.

Modularity can be approached from several angles.

    I.   Structural and functional modules

Callebaut (2005) suggested that it is useful to distinguish modularity of structure from modularity of process. Module is a unit that is a component part of a larger system and yet possessed of its own structural and/or functional identity (Moss, 2001, p. 91). Modules are internally integrated and relatively independent from other modules. They must persist as identifiable units for long enough time spans, and they must be more or less identical, repetitive, and reusable 'building blocks' of larger wholes and/or different systems (Muller and Newman, 2003).

    II.   Goal-directed modules. Goal-directed are characterized by plasticity and persistence. Such systems do not always achieve their goals, but they do show persistence when obstacles are put in their way, and they also exhibit plasticity in that they tend to have multi-le ways of achieving their end state (Brandon, 2005).

PRACTICING SYSTEM THINKING

Exercise 1

This simple exercise is one of the examples of systems thinking, and the concept of the cause-effect of interrelationships of various systems.

Here is the scenario:

You have to complete assignment for Psychology class. You procrastinated. Instead of completing assignment, you have found a good resource on-line and copied it (plagiarism). You submitted it and got a good grade.

What can you write down about this decision? It seems like a very benign choice, and most people at this point do not have much to say.

    1. The first step is to describe how the decision can affect you.

    2. The next step is to describe how the decision affects the rest of the world around you - not only those you directly affect, but those beyond you. To do this the flows from you to the endpoint needs to be mapped out. Along the flows all of the people (essentially the fishbone of each action) that make the action happen have to be added. That includes: your fellow students, faculty, your family, and your friends. Once that is developed, you look at the decision and see who will and who will not benefit from the choice (keep in mind the Butterfly Effect).

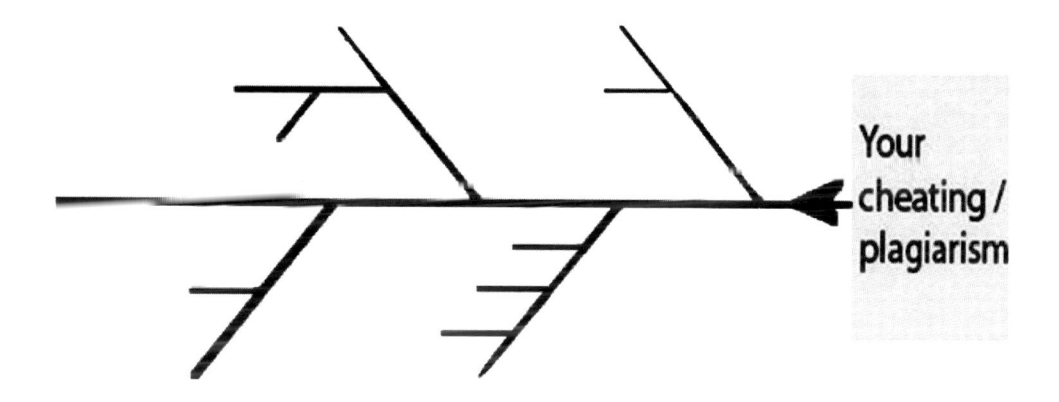

CHAPTER 7

Exercise 2. The Inspiration by Chaos (Think about 'Chaos Theory')

Chaos is a state of extreme confusion and disorder.

In physics chaos is a dynamical system that is extremely sensitive to its initial conditions.

Chaotic systems – such as raging waterfalls, boiling water, churning weather patterns, dancing fire, and runaway stock markets – all have the peculiar ability to leap almost instantly from one state to another upon the tiniest stimulus. One minute, all is calm. The next minute, a tornado has formed. One second, the snow lies quietly on the mountainside. The next second, a thundering avalanche rolls down the slope.

Da Vinci's Technique

Imagine rectangular tray containing a rubber bag partially filled with oil. A steel marble dropped onto the bag's surface gradually sinks to the bottom, pushing the surface of the rubber bag before it. When the marble comes to rest, it is in the center of a depression. Drop a second marble and it will roll down the contour and come to rest against the first one. The second marble is *active;* it does not stay where it has been put down, but follows the slope created by the first one. All subsequent marbles will roll toward the first marble, forming a cluster.

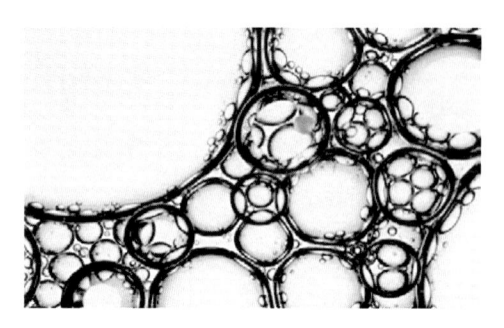

Figure 7.1. Oil in Water. Inspiration by chaos.

Albert Einstein observed that:

"The words of the language, as they are written or spoken, do not seem to play any role in my mechanism of thought. The psychical entities which seem to serve as elements in thought are certain signs and more or less clear images which can be voluntarily reproduced and combined."

In the same way, an active mind allows incoming information to organize itself into a new cluster, giving rise to new perspectives and new ideas. One good way to originate new clusters of information is through pictures. In the beginning, humans communicated with pictures. The alphabet evolved from the various pictographic techniques; however, this does not mean that verbal thinking is more advanced.

Leonardo da Vinci's technique for getting ideas was to close his eyes, relax totally, and cover a sheet of paper with random lines and scribbles. He would then open the eyes and look for images and patterns, objects, faces, or events in the scribble. Many of his inventions came forth unbeckoned from this random scribbling.

Scribbling allows you to put your abstract ideas into a tangible form. Imagine yourself flying over your challenge in an airplane to get a clear overview. While in the air, sketch what you see below you. Sketch as many alternative concepts as you think you see. You are your own audience; therefore, you can draw or sketch freely without worrying about what anyone will think. Sketching is a way of talking to yourself. Thomas Edison made hundreds of sketches and doodles about the light bulb, most of which are undesipherable to anyone but Edison.

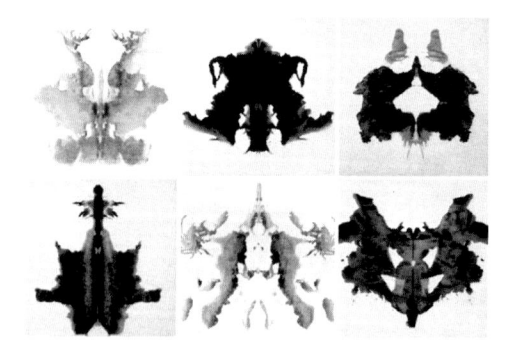

Figure 7.2. Rorschach's Test is a projective test that uses bilaterally symmetrical inkblots. Ambiguous images illicit individual interpretation of blots that supposed to reveal individual's hidden complexes and psychological problems. It may be also inspirational.

Modes of Thinking

Graphic ideation (sketching, doodling, or drawing) is complementary to verbal ideation and can help you muster up new ideas.

Step 1	Step 2	Step 3	Step 4
Randomly put dots and circles on a piece of paper. They look like stars and planets on a sky.	Start connecting them.	Keep connecting them.	Now it looks like a nice design.

7. DIALECTICAL THINKING

Broadly defined, Dialectic (Greek: διαλεκτική) is an *exchange of propositions* (theses) and *counter-propositions* (antitheses) *resulting in a synthesis of the opposing assertions*, or at least a qualitative transformation in the direction of the dialogue. The synthesis can be viewed as a solution to a problem or merely a resolving stage in an unending cycle of dialectical evolution. The dialectic begins with the awareness of a potential split, a denial of the established convention. It assumed polarity, a conflict between two defined positions. It is undertaken to settle a dispute.

History

Dialectics is a form of thought which goes back a long way. In the West, Heraclitus in Ancient Greece was aware of it, and in the East, there are a number of thinkers who practiced it. The Tao-Te-Ching is a good example of dialectical writing.

It is one of the three original liberal arts or trivium (the other members are rhetoric and grammar) in Western culture.

In ancient and medieval times, both rhetoric and dialectic were understood to aim at being persuasive (through dialogue). The aim of the dialectical method, often known as dialectic or dialectics, is to try to resolve the disagreement through rational discussion.

One of the most famous contributor to dialectic was German philosopher **Hegel**.

Georg Wilhelm Friedrich Hegel (August 27, 1770–November 14, 1831) was born in Stuttgart, Württemberg, in present-day southwest Germany. His influence has been widespread on writers of widely varying positions,) He is best known for attempting to elaborate a comprehensive and systematic ontology from a logical starting point

Hegel's dialectic was most often characterized as a three-step process of "Thesis, antithesis, synthesis", namely, that a "thesis" (e.g. the French Revolution) would cause the creation of its "antithesis" (e.g. the Reign of Terror that followed), and would eventually result in a "synthesis" (e.g. the Constitutional state of free citizens).

Hegel's dialectic, which he usually presented in a threefold manner, was vulgarized by Heinrich Moritz Chalybäus as comprising three dialectical stages of development: a thesis, giving rise to its reaction, an antithesis which contradicts or negates the thesis, and the tension between the two being resolved by means of a synthesis. Hegel rarely used these terms himself. In the Logic, for instance, Hegel describes a dialectic of existence: first, existence must be posited as pure Being; but pure Being, upon

There are *two ways* of dialectic:

1. One way — *the Socratic method* — is to show that a given hypothesis (with other admissions) leads to a contradiction; thus, forcing the withdrawal of the hypothesis as a candidate for truth.

2. Another way of *trying to resolve a disagreement* is by *denying* some presupposition of the contending thesis and antithesis; thereby moving to a third (syn)thesis.

Figure 8.1. Yin-Yang Symbol.

A good symbol for three dialectic's processes is the Yin-Yang symbol of Taoism. The *interdependence of opposites* is shown in each half being defined by the contours of the other. *The interpenetration of opposites* is expressed by having a black spot in the innermost center of the white area, and a white spot in the innermost center of the black area. The *unity of opposites* is shown by the circle surrounding the symbol, which expresses total unity and unbroken serenity in and through all the seeming opposition. It is, after all, one symbol.

examination, is found to be indistinguishable from Nothing. When it is realized that what is coming into being is, at the same time, also returning to nothing (consider life: old organisms die as new organisms are created or born), both Being and Nothing are united as Becoming.

What Is Dialectic?

The *first characteristic* of dialectical thinking is that it places all the emphasis on *change*. Instead of talking about static structures, it talks about process and movement. Hence it is in line with all those philosophies which say – "Let's not be deceived by what it is now as we perceive it – let's not pretend we can fix it and label it and turn it into something stiff and immutable - let's look instead at how it changes." Hence it denies much of the usefulness of formal logic, which starts from the proposition that "A is A", and is nothing but A. For dialectics the corresponding proposition is "A is not simply A". This is even true for things, but much more obviously true for people.

But the *second characteristic*, which sets it apart from any philosophy which emphasizes smooth continuous change or progress, is that *it states that the way change takes place is through conflict and opposition.* Dialectics is always looking for the contradictions within people or situations as the main guide to what is going on and what is likely to happen. There are in fact three main propositions which are put forward about opposites and contradictions.

The interdependence of opposites

This is the easiest thing to see: **opposites depend on one another**. It wouldn't make sense to talk about darkness if there were no such thing as light. I really start to understand my love at the moment when I permit myself up understand my hate. In practice, each member of a polar opposition seems to need the other to make it what it is.

The interpenetration of opposites

Here we see that opposites can be found **within each other**. Just because light is relative to darkness, there is some light in every darkness, and some darkness in every light. There is some hate in every love, and some love in every hate. If we look into one thing hard enough, we can always find its opposite right there. To see this frees us from the "either-or" which can be so oppressive and so stuck.

The unity of opposites

So far we have been talking about *relative opposites*. But dialectics goes on to say that if we take an opposite to its very ultimate extreme, and make it absolute, it actually turns into its opposite. Thus if we make darkness absolute, we are blind - we can't see anything. And if we make light absolute, we are equally blind and unable to see. In psychology, the equivalent of this is to idealize something. So if we take love to its extreme, and idealize it, we get morbid dependence, where our whole existence depends completely on the other person. And if we take hate to its extreme, and idealize it, we get morbid counterdependence, where our whole existence again depends completely on the other person. This appreciation of paradox is one of the strengths of the dialectical approach, which makes it superior to linear logic.

The lessons of the dialectic are hard ones. It tells us that any value we have, if held to in a one-sided way, will become an illusion. We shall try to take it as excluding its opposite, but really it will include it. And if we take it to its extreme, and idealize it, it will turn into its opposite. So peace and love, cosmic harmony, the pursuit of happiness and all the rest are doomed, if held to in this exclusive way.

The only values which will be truly stable and coherent are those which include opposition rather than excluding it. And all such values appear to be nonsense, because they must contain paradoxes. "Self-actualization" is one such value, because the concept of the self is self-contradictory, paradoxical and absurd. The self is intensely personal and completely impersonal at one and the same time. It is the lowest of the low and the highest of the high at the same time. And this is why, when we contact the self in a peak experience, our description of what happened is invariably a paradoxical one.

There is a logic of paradox, which enables the intellect to handle it without getting fazed, and its name is the dialectic. It is complex because it involves holding the spring doors of the mind open - hence it often tries to say everything at once. But it shows how we do not have to give up in the face of paradox and abandon the intellect as a hopeless case.

Three Laws of Dialectic

1. The Law of the Unity (Interpenetration) of Opposites;
2. The Law of Transformation of Quantity into Quality;
3. The Law of the Negation of the Negation

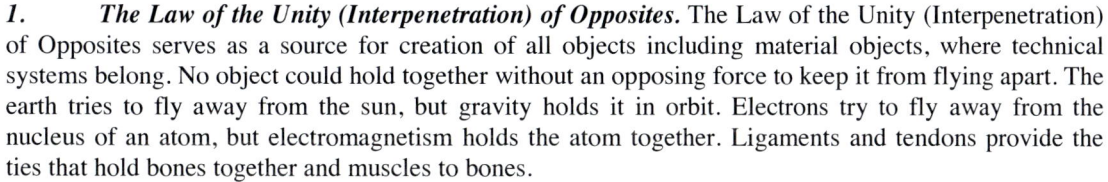

1. ***The Law of the Unity (Interpenetration) of Opposites.*** The Law of the Unity (Interpenetration) of Opposites serves as a source for creation of all objects including material objects, where technical systems belong. No object could hold together without an opposing force to keep it from flying apart. The earth tries to fly away from the sun, but gravity holds it in orbit. Electrons try to fly away from the nucleus of an atom, but electromagnetism holds the atom together. Ligaments and tendons provide the ties that hold bones together and muscles to bones.

Like material objects, the process of change needs opposing forces. Change needs a driving force to push it ahead, otherwise everything stays put. A billiard ball only moves when hit with a pool cue or another ball. We eat when our hunger tells us to. A car won't move if it's engine won't start. To win in fair elections candidates need more votes than their opponents.

Engels, drawing from the philosopher, Hegel, called this law the "interpenetration of opposites"; Hegel often referred to the "unity of opposites." This may sound contradictory, but it is easy to understand. It's like the saying, "It takes two to tango.' There is no game if one side quits. There is no atom if the electrons fly away. The whole needs all of its parts to be a whole.

To fully appreciate something, a person often has to be aware of both sides of it.

The most creative people have to ability see things this way as well as many dialectic traits in their personality such as: being smart and yet naïve, combination of playfulness and discipline, both extraverted and introverted, humble and proud, rebellious and conservative, passionate about their work and still objective as well.

Example:
- The direct opposite of light is darkness and vice versa
- One cannot exist without the other; without a concept of what darkness is, there can be no concept of light
- Each is not absolute; there is darkness in light and light in darkness because if either was pure then it would leave you blind to what's really there

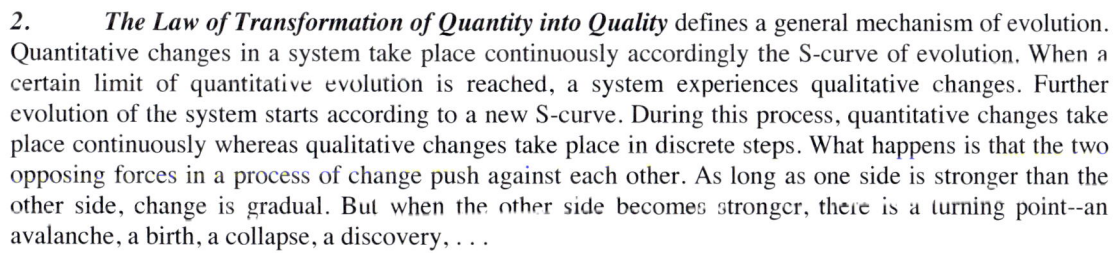

2. ***The Law of Transformation of Quantity into Quality*** defines a general mechanism of evolution. Quantitative changes in a system take place continuously accordingly the S-curve of evolution. When a certain limit of quantitative evolution is reached, a system experiences qualitative changes. Further evolution of the system starts according to a new S-curve. During this process, quantitative changes take place continuously whereas qualitative changes take place in discrete steps. What happens is that the two opposing forces in a process of change push against each other. As long as one side is stronger than the other side, change is gradual. But when the other side becomes stronger, there is a turning point--an avalanche, a birth, a collapse, a discovery, . . .

Physicist Michio Kaku gives a detailed example of this process in his book Hyperspace. He follows the turning points or stages in the heating of an ice cube.

Engels called this the law of the transformation of quantity into quality. Quantitative change is the gradual build-up of one opposing force. Qualitative change takes place when that opposite becomes dominant.

This law is powerful in describing the stages of development of anything. A person's life follows these quantitative/qualitative changes. Likewise human history, or the history of a particular place, has gone through many stages. The tool of dialectics is so powerful that Michio Kaku describes the history of the universe for its first 10 billion years by a series of dialectical stages, using only 250 words.

Using the same approach it is possible to trace the history of the universe right up to the present by identifying the key turning points.

3. ***An essence of the Law of the Negation of the Negation*** is that a process of progressive evolution consists of a series of relative repetitions, as if going through the same phases again and again. However, each repetition takes place at a higher level of evolution by using new elements, materials, and technologies. We can say, that in this case we have a spiral-shaped evolution. For example, fashion

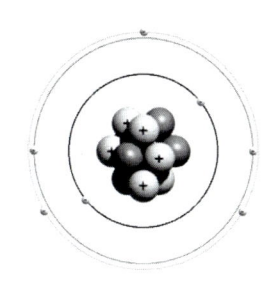

Figure 8.1. Atom is composed of positively charged protons and negatively charged electrons.

Figure 8.2. Computer code is created of two opposite entities: 1 and 0.

Figure 8.3. Melting ice. Gradually increasing temperature eventually reaches a critical point when ice turns into water.

design is the most obvious example of spiral-shaped evolution. Many changes are cyclical - first one side dominates, then the other - as in day/night, breathing in/breathing out, one opposite then another. Dialectics argues that these cycles do not come back exactly to where they started; they don't make a perfect circle. Instead, change is evolutionary, moving in a spiral.

Maybe the changes are tiny, so we think nothing is really different--it's true that we hardly change in a measurable way with every breath. But we can see that many cycles do come around to a different place - children are not the same as their parents, even if they are a lot alike. People go to school and learn; when they return home, they are no longer the same. And, like it or not, you are a bit older with every breath.

Engels, again following Hegel, called this law "negation of negation". This sounds complicated, but, as Engels said, it is going on all the time. What happens is that first one side overcomes its opposite--this is the first negation. This marks a turning point as in Engels' 2nd law. Next, the new side is once again overcome by the first side. This is negation of negation.

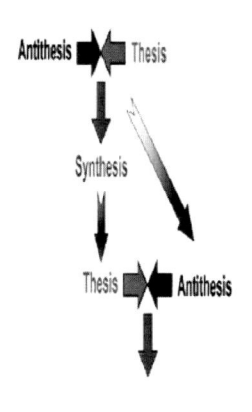

Figure 8.3. Negation of Negation.

Some Applications of the Dialectic

How does one actually use dialectical thinking in everyday life? Some say that dialectics is not for everyday life at all - it has to do with "ideas of the horizon" where we are dealing with concepts that are at the very limits of human thought. For everyday life, they say, formal logic is good enough. But I think humanistic psychology has shown us that you can use dialectical thinking even for walking, or driving, or eating, or playing tennis, or any other everyday activity.

TAKE NOTHING FOR GRANTED

This is one of the most important principles of humanistic psychology. All the time one is questioning the fixed categories, the rigid "should", the congealed knowledge that stops one seeing the world. Our beliefs are the greatest obstacle to clear perception, and the more we can unfocus from them, the more we can let in.

SPONTANEITY

Again a crucial concept, which dialectical thinking makes easy to understand and easy to do, intellectually, emotionally and intuitively. Spontaneity is obviously a paradoxical quality, which you can only aim at by letting go.

TRANSFORMATION OF QUALITY INTO QUANTITY

This important idea states that by simply adding things, we can eventually arrive at something quite different. In therapy, going intensively into one side of a conflict often brings us more vividly into the other; and if we push the whole conflict hard enough and far enough, a whole new vision may appear.

BREAKING PATTERNS

So the main practical application of the dialectic is in breaking fixed patterns of thought and behavior. Every time you adopt a regular pattern of washing, dressing, eating and so on, you are avoiding reality. But if awareness of these activities increases, the amount of play involved in them is also likely to increase. Taking responsibility for our actions is choosing our life, and this usually feels good. You can be responsible and playful at the same time, and this is one of the paradoxes in which dialectics delights.

Modes of Thinking

PRACTICING DIALECTICAL THINKING

Based upon your knowledge of the history, try to predict the future of the following phenomena:

	The future change
Language	
Games	
Movies	
TV	

8. INTEGRATIVE THINKING

Integrative thinking frames differences and problems so that practitioners and group participants focus on **what is to be gained**, rather than what is to be lost, by following a particular path of action. It further emphasizes that the identified gains can be accomplished only by working together.

Integrative Thinking is *the ability to face constructively the tension of opposing models* and instead of choosing one at the expense of the other, *to generate a creative resolution of the tension in the form of a new model* that contains elements of the individual models, but is superior to each.

Integrative thinkers **build models** rather than choose between them. Their models include consideration of numerous variables — customers, employees, competitors, capabilities, cost structures, industry evolution, and regulatory environment — not just a subset of the above. Their models capture the complicated, multi-faceted and multidirectional causal relationships between the key variables in any problem. Integrative thinkers consider the problem as a whole, rather than breaking it down and farming out the parts. Finally, they creatively *resolve tensions* without making costly trade-offs, turning challenges into opportunities.

Steps in Decision Making Process

1. Salience
2. Causality
3. Architecture
4. Resolution

1) In this first step we decide what **features are relevant to our decision.** We ask ourselves questions such as: What do we choose to **pay attention to**, and what not?

2) This is the second step. (Cause and Effect) In this step some of the question we might ask ourselves are: How do we make sense of what we see? What sort of relations do we believe exists between the various pieces of the puzzle?

3) During this third step an overall mental model is constructed based on what we got from the previous two steps.

4) This is the final step. Based on our reasoning of the three last steps, what will our **decision** be?

CHAPTER 7

Cause and Effect

Causality is the ***relationship between an event*** (the cause) and a ***second event*** (the effect), where the second event is a direct consequence of the first.

The philosophical treatment of causality extends over millennia. In the Western philosophical tradition, discussion stretches back at least to Aristotle, and the topic remains a staple in contemporary philosophy. Aristotle distinguished between accidental (cause preceding effect) and essential causality (one event seen in two ways). Aristotle's example of essential causality is a builder building a house. This single event can be analyzed into the builder building (cause) and the house being built (effect). Aristotle also had a theory that answered the question "why?" 4 different ways. The first was material cause, next was formal cause, then efficient cause, and lastly was final cause. These rules are known as "Aristotle's four causes."

> Though cause and effect are typically related to events, candidates include objects, processes, properties, variables, facts, and states of affairs; characterizing the causal relationship can be the subject of much debate.

Confusing Cause and Effect

Confusing Cause and Effect is a fallacy that has the following general form:
A and B regularly occur together.
Therefore A is the cause of B.
This fallacy requires that there is not, in fact, a common cause that actually causes both A and B.

> In order to determine that the fallacy has been committed, it must be shown that the causal conclusion has not been adequately supported and that the person committing the fallacy has confused the actual cause with the effect.

This ***fallacy*** is committed **when a person assumes that one event must cause another just because the events occur together.** More formally, this fallacy involves drawing the conclusion that A is the cause of B simply because A and B are in regular conjunction (and there is not a common cause that is actually the cause of A and B). The mistake being made is that the causal conclusion is being drawn without adequate justification.

In some cases it will be evident that the fallacy is being committed. For example, a person might claim that an illness was caused by a person getting a fever. In this case, it would be quite clear that the fever was caused by illness and not the other way around. In other cases, the fallacy is not always evident. One factor that makes causal reasoning quite difficult is that it is not always evident what is the cause and what is the effect. For example, a problem child might be the cause of the parents being short tempered or the short temper of the parents might be the cause of the child being problematic. The difficulty is increased by the fact that some situations might involve feedback. For example, the parents' temper might cause the child to become problematic and the child's behavior could worsen the parents' temper. In such cases it could be rather difficult to sort out what caused what in the first place.

Showing that the fallacy has been committed will typically involve determining the actual cause and the actual effect. In some cases, as noted above, this can be quite easy. In other cases it will be difficult. In some cases, it might be almost impossible. Another thing that makes causal reasoning difficult is that people often have very different conceptions of cause and, in some cases, the issues are clouded by emotions and ideologies. For example, people often claim violence on TV and in movies must be censored because it causes people to like violence. Other people claim that there is violence on TV and in movies because people like violence. In this case, it is not obvious what the cause really is and the issue is clouded by the fact that emotions often run high on this issue.

While causal reasoning can be difficult, many errors can be avoided with due care and careful testing procedures. This is due to the fact that the fallacy arises because the conclusion is drawn without due care. One way to avoid the fallacy is to pay careful attention to the temporal sequence of events. Since (outside of Star Trek), effects do not generally precede their causes, if A occurs after B, then A cannot be the cause of B. However, these methods go beyond the scope of this program.

All causal fallacies involve an error in causal reasoning. However, this fallacy differs from the other causal fallacies in terms of the error in reasoning being made. In the case of a Post Hoc fallacy, the error is that a person is accepting that A is the cause of B simply because A occurs before B. In the case of the Fallacy of Ignoring a Common Cause A is taken to be the cause of B when there is, in fact, a third factor that is the cause of both A and B. For more information, see the relevant entries in this program.

Examples of Confusing Cause and Effect

1. Just imagine that you have no knowledge of your car's engine. You are just driving your car every day without even thinking about its mechanics. One morning your car didn't start.

I are trying to find out the cause of engine's failure. You start thinking: "Every morning I was having glass of milk for breakfast. Today I didn't have milk. That is why my car didn't start." You had a glass of milk. You tried your car again. Somehow your car started. Now you are completely certain that drinking milk is important for the proper function of your car. You may even develop a theory that 'proves' the relationship between milk and car's engine.

2. Bill and Joe are having a debate about music and moral decay:

Bill: 'It seems clear to me that this new music is causing the youth to become corrupt."

Joe: "What do you mean?"

Bill: "This rap stuff is always telling the kids to kill cops, do drugs, and abuse women. That is all bad and the kids today shouldn't be doing that sort of stuff. We ought to ban that music!"

Joe: "So, you think that getting rid of the rap music would solve the drug, violence and sexism problems in the US?"

Bill: "Well, it wouldn't get rid of it all, but it would take care of a lot of it.'

Joe: 'Don't you think that most of the rap singers sing about that sort of stuff because that is what is really going on these days? I mean, people often sing about the conditions of their time, just like the people did in the sixties. But then I suppose that you think that people were against the war and into drugs just because they listened to Dylan and Baez."

Bill: "Well..."

Joe: "Well, it seems to me that the main cause of the content of the rap music is the pre-existing social conditions. If there weren't all these problems, the rap singers probably wouldn't be singing about them. I also think that if the social conditions were great, kids could listen to the music all day and not be affected."

Bill: "Well, I still think the rap music causes the problems. You can't argue against the fact that social ills really picked up at the same time rap music got started."

3. It is claimed by some people that severe illness is caused by depression and anger. After all, people who are severely ill are very often depressed and angry. Thus, it follows that the cause of severe illness actually is the depression and anger. So, a good and cheerful attitude is key to staying healthy.

4. Bill sets out several plates with bread on them. After a couple days, he notices that the bread has mold growing all over it. Bill concludes that the mold was produced by the bread going bad. When Bill tells his mother about his experiment, she tells him that the mold was the cause of the bread going bad and that he better clean up the mess if he wants to get his allowance this week.

Interpretations, Evaluations and Rules

There are countless ways of looking at life - how can you know which help and which hinder? Fortunately, there are some guidelines. It is probably most useful to start by learning how to recognize irrational thinking.

Why bother with problem thoughts? This is what distinguishes 'rational' from so-called 'positive' thinking: instead of rushing to tell yourself positive ideas, you first uncover and dispute the irrational ones. Otherwise, they remain untouched - and thus able to disturb you in the future.

In everyday life, events and circumstances trigger two levels of thinking: interpreting and evaluating. First, we attempt to interpret things in some way. That is, we make guesses or inferences about what is 'going on' - what we think has happened, is happening or will happen. Interpretations are statements of 'fact' (or at least what we think are the facts - they can be true or false). Second, we evaluate the situation and predict the consequences.

What does irrational mean? To describe a belief as irrational is to say:

- It distorts reality (it is a misinterpretation of what is happening); or it involves some illogical ways of evaluating yourself, others and the world around you - awfulising, discomfort-intolerance, demanding, and people-rating.
- It blocks you from achieving your goals and purposes.
- It creates extreme emotions which persist, and which distress and immobilize.
- It leads to behaviors that harm yourself, others and your life in general.

Here are some more examples to show the differences between *events, interpretations and evaluations*:

Event/Situation	Interpretation	Evaluation
Son won't do his homework.	He'll end up uneducated.	This would make me a failure as a parent.
Saw crash, one car had a young driver.	The young driver was at fault	These people shouldn't be allowed on the road.
Woke up feeling anxious.	There's too much pressure at work.	I can't stand it, so I'll have to take the day off.
Saw a cake.	That cake would be delicious.	I must have it.
He was really angry.	I caused it.	I'm a bitch.
Read that violent crime is on the increase.	The US is going to the dogs.	The government should reinforce the death penalty.

What to look for

We are concerned mainly with the irrational beliefs, the ones that cause our problems.

These are of three kinds

(1) interpretations, (2) evaluations and (3) general rules.

Interpretations

Irrational interpretations consist of distortions of reality: <u>black-and-white thinking</u>, <u>filtering</u>, <u>overgeneralising</u>, <u>mind-reading</u>, <u>fortune-telling</u>, <u>emotional reasoning</u> and <u>personalizing</u>. Interpretations are usually conscious, though not always.

Evaluations

Irrational evaluations consist of :

       1. <u>awfulising</u>: seeing something as awful, horrific, catastrophic or the like;
       2. <u>discomfort-intolerance</u>: defining something as 'unbearable' or 'intolerable' (also known as 'discomfort-intolerance');
       3. <u>demanding</u>: using 'shoulds' or 'musts'; and
       4. <u>people-rating</u>: labeling or evaluating your total self (or someone else's).

Evaluations/personal meanings are sometimes conscious but more often are beneath awareness. You uncover them by asking yourself, 'If my interpretation is true, how do I evaluate what is going on?' or, 'What does it mean to me?' Let us say, for example, your interpretation of news reports is that people are getting more violent. How do you evaluate this? What does it mean to you? You could evaluate it as 'terrible' (awfulising), 'intolerable' (can't-stand-it-itis), as meaning that the people concerned should be locked up (demanding), or as proving that they are 'animals' (people-rating).

Rules

Rules are the ***underlying beliefs that guide how we react to life***. What specific events mean to you (how you evaluate them) depends on the general rules you apply. The examples given earlier reflect general rules such as:

'If I fail at something important to me, this proves I'm a failure and therefore not worthwhile.'

'People should always behave correctly, and must be condemned and punished when they don't.'

'It's easier to avoid responsibilities than to face them.'

'I must have whatever I want and I can't stand the discomfort of being deprived.'

'I am responsible for other people's feelings, so I deserve to be condemned if I do anything that hurts or upsets them.'

'Violent people do not deserve to live.'

Note that an evaluation/personal meaning is a general rule applied to a specific situation. For example:

Interpretation: The young driver was at fault.

Evaluation: These kids should not be allowed on the road.

General rule: People should always behave correctly and must be punished when they don't.

Irrational beliefs	Rational alternatives
I need love and approval from those significant to me, and I must avoid disapproval from any source.	Love, approval and respect from others are all good things - but they are not absolute necessities for my survival. And while I dislike disapproval, it is uncomfortable - not catastrophic; I can stand it - as I have many times before. Better that I learn to accept myself, independently of what others think of me.
People should always do the right thing. When they behave obnoxiously, unfairly or selfishly, they must be blamed and punished.	It's unfortunate that people sometimes do bad things. But humans aren't yet perfect, and upsetting myself won't change that reality.
My unhappiness is caused by things outside my control, so there's little I can do to feel any better.	Many external factors are outside my control. But it is my thoughts (not the externals) which cause my feelings - and I can learn to control my thoughts.
I must worry about things that could be dangerous, unpleasant or frightening, otherwise they might happen.	Worrying about things that might go wrong will not stop them happening. It will, though, ensure I get upset and disturbed right now!
I can be happier by avoiding life's difficulties, unpleasantnesses and responsibilities.	Avoiding problems is only easier in the short term - putting things off can make them worse later on. It also gives me more time to worry about them!
Events in my past are the cause of my problems, and they continue to influence my feelings and behaviors now.	The past can't influence me now. My current beliefs cause my reactions. I may have learned these beliefs in the past, but I can choose to analyze and change them in the present.

Rational thinking: in touch with the real world

Rational thinking presents a vivid contrast to its illogical opposite:

- It is based on reality. It emphasizes seeing things as they really are, keeping them in perspective, preferring rather than demanding, and self-acceptance.
- It helps you achieve your goals and purposes.
- It creates emotions you can handle.
- It helps you behave in ways which promote your aims and survival.

People view themselves and the world around them on three levels:

1. interpretations,
2. evaluations/personal meanings,
3. underlying rules.

CHAPTER 7

PRACTICING INTEGRATIVE THINKING

Think about your future success. What factors contribute to it? What is already accomplished? What are you planning to accomplish?

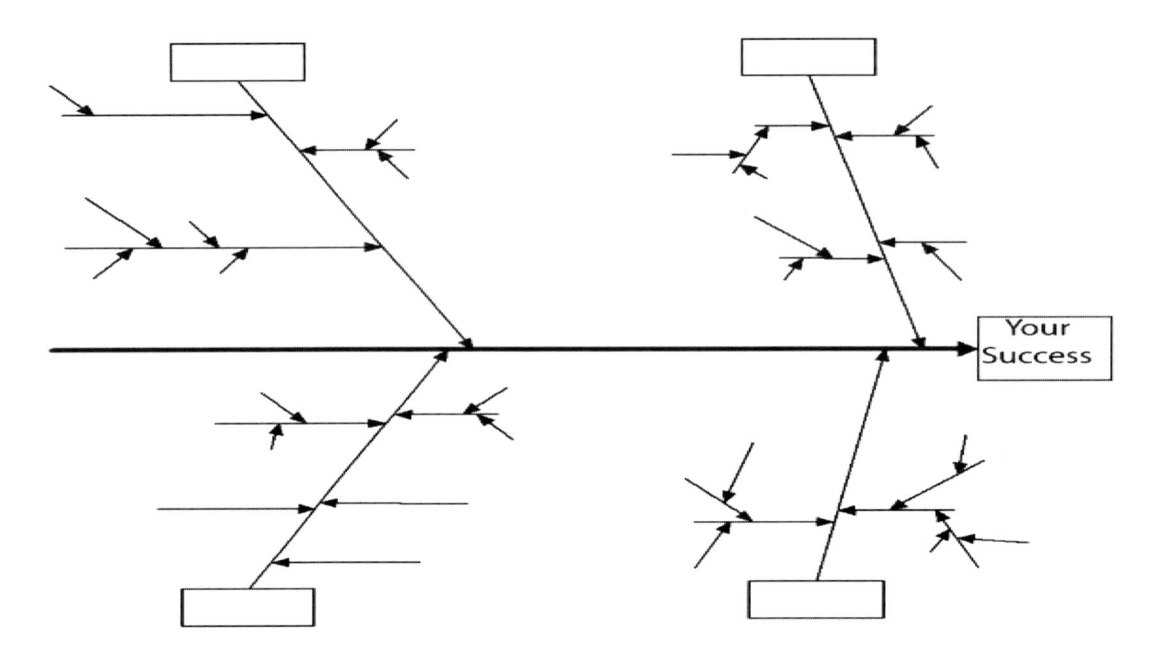

9. HEURISTIC THINKING

> Heuristic are *intuitive responses*, based on past experience. They are the "various learned shortcuts" that humans tend to apply in stressful or complex decision-making situations. Heuristic thinking proceeds "off-the-cuff." It is founded on "intuition as distilled experience."

Heuristic are *intuitive responses*, based on past experience. They are the "various learned shortcuts" that humans tend to apply in stressful or complex decision-making situations. Heuristic thinking proceeds "off-the-cuff." It is founded on "intuition as distilled experience."

Heuristic thinking is an important faculty of our mind that is extremely resourceful when it comes to problem-solving questions. It is a process of approximation starting with an initial pattern of thought and gradually assimilating to a target pattern that constitutes an insight into the subject matter at hand. The whole process leads to a holistic or interlaced knowledge.

We often experience in our daily application of thinking, that, after pondering upon a problem for quite some time, we suddenly and inadvertently hit upon the right solution or the brilliant answer to our initial question. This process involves Heuristic Thinking.

Heuristic Thinking always ***starts from an initial unresolved, unanswered, unknown or undecided situation***, so called "initial pattern." This ***initial pattern*** is the question or the problem to be solved or answered. Take for example a philosophical problem like the identity problem. If a philosopher embarks on a research inquiry to find an answer to this ancient problem, she has already set the initial pattern in her thought. The initial pattern alone is not sufficient, however. With merely this pattern, we would never obtain any answer, because the incipient cause for searching an answer does not suffice to attain an answer, too. The answer must already be implicitly inherent in our mind. This still latent and potential pattern is called "target pattern."

The process of heuristic thinking is therefore a ***gradual approximation to the target pattern by converging and merging the initial and the target pattern into a whole and complementary pattern***, consisting of the question and the answer. This convergence is called "knowledge." As soon as I can say that I know something, my initial and ignorant pattern has converged with the knowing target pattern and

178

thereby resolved my unknown ego with the knowing mind in the background. The "foreground mind" (Individual Mind -Exonoesis) with its imperfect memory system has merged with some part of the "background mind" (Universal Mind -Hyponoesis) that is all-knowing and contains all possibilities and potentialities of the universe.

This process of approximation to the target pattern proceeds circumstantially (Lat. circumstare = stand around), circumambiently (Lat. circum-ambire = to go around) or circumferentially (Lat. cirum-ferre = carry around), that is from all sides, surrounding the target pattern, encircling it more and more, until having become united with the core of the target pattern, the point of absolute knowledge. Absolute insofar, as this knowledge is independent of our sensual perception and other empirical data, but can a priori be discovered in the mind itself. This point of knowledge is the central insight into a matter, a situation. It is sometimes the anticipation of the Great Chain of Being, the interrelatedness of all things, the deepest comprehension of the universe, inexpressible in words.

However, there remains a serious question: when do I know, that I have found the right answer, that I arrived at the point of knowledge? The evidence and self-certainty of this insight and knowledge comes from the process of convergence. As soon as the initial pattern fits or matches the target pattern, both of them constitute a totality, a whole. Both patterns are complementary pieces of one whole, and only the whole is complete and this whole can be called knowledge, or absolute knowledge. Both, the question and the answer, the problem and its solution are part of the knowledge pattern, that is itself holistic and always comprises both parts, the initial and the target pattern. They belong together.

One might object that this would mean, there's only one answer to a question. Not necessarily. There need not be only one solution to a problem, because the **solution pattern depends on the problem pattern,** and problems can be set up in variegated ways, with subtle differences in their propositions. The meaning inherent in a proposition of a problem and the meaning thought of by the author of that proposition, implicates always the complementary variant part as the solution. If the structure of the initial pattern, say, emphasizes more the logical side of a problem, the answer would also be of a logical kind, because the questioner unconsciously expects that sort of answer. She believes that only a logical answer is the correct one. There are thus structural variants of convergent patterns, that is, differentiation in semantic structure, in meaning.

This process of Heuristic Thinking can be called the **ordinary heuristic thinking**. There is also an *extraordinary heuristic* mode of thinking. If we try to abstract from the subjectivity of the question by not expecting, consciously and unconsciously, a certain answer, we would be able to hit upon a completely "new" answer. This openness of mind can rarely be found amongst modern thinkers. Normally, this neutral mode of heuristic thinking demands a great discipline and objectivity that could only be found in a human being who has transcended her individuality.

Follow Your Hunches

One of the most dramatic and useful forms of creative problem-solving is hunch or intuition. Many artists and scientists regard it as the key to creativity. Inventors of great note depended strongly on intuition for their creative insights. Thomas Edison, for example, was unusually prolific in generating useful hunches which when tested turned out to be right. He had learned to completely trust the feeling of certainty accompanying his intuitions. Similarly, Einstein said, "I believe in intuition and inspiration.... At times I feel certain while not knowing the reason." In most of his work, Einstein did not take the slow, painful, linear step-by-step process to solution, but relied instead on "feeling" his way to the right solution.

Intuitive ability is not restricted to geniuses or individuals with special talents. We all possess this capacity, but most of us have been conditioned by education and environment to neglect, repress, and distrust our intuitions. This is frequently implied in phrases such as "It was only a hunch," or, "I'm not going to play any hunches," or "It's just a woman's intuition."

Since intuition, as a way of knowing, is crucial to creativity, you would do well to liberate and develop this latent ability. The following guidelines are presented to help you along.

- Determine first *how strong your intuitive ability is*. Start keeping a record of the intuitive hunches, flashes of insight, and images that come to you spontaneously and check later whether they had any validity.
- *Motivate yourself* to develop your intuitive abilities and believe in them.
- *Set aside one time every day* to tune in to your intuitive awareness and feelings.
- *Learn to relax* from physical and emotional stress. Tenseness prevents intuitive insights from rising to your conscious awareness.

"If you train yourself to listen to your intuition and to follow its bidding, you will greatly increase your percentage of success in life."

Harold Sherman

- Meditative practices and reverie provide a direct pipeline to intuitive thinking. Excessive, unrelenting activity blocks intuitive awareness.
- Openness and sensitivity to both inner and outer reality enrich the fund of experiential information, which in turn expands intuitive knowing.
- Learning to trust the validity of your subjective experiences, impressions, and judgments helps you to develop trust and confidence in your intuitions.
- Do not confuse intuitive thinking with other modes of thought or emotion which are intimately personal, biased, wishful, or prejudicial. You must constantly analyze your thinking to separate genuine intuitive grains from emotional chaff.
- Realize that intuitive thinking is a perfectly normal function of the brain. It probably is not related to clairvoyance, mystical precognition, or similar phenomena.
- Intuition is used to its greatest advantage in solving problems that involve many complex, interrelated factors. When you have many variables, logical reasoning or quantitative techniques are frequently inadequate for synthesizing all the elements into a coherent whole. The intuitive mode, by comparison, utilizes multiple processing to carry out a work of creative synthesis.

The important thing is to recognize the value of the intuitive hunch when it occurs. Don't brush it aside or dismiss it as something irrational or unnatural. Use and act upon it, for it can be your springboard to successfully attaining your desired goals in life.

Answer
Follow Your Hunches

As a "mental shortcut," intuition has been responsible for the dramatic success stories of many prominent inventors and businessmen. One classic case is that Dr. Edwin H. Land, president of Polaroid Corporation and inventor of the Polaroid camera. His original invention net with stiff resistance from his associates. Extensive market research indicated that there would be little or no demand for the camera; it would be too expensive to be sold as a toy and not up to the standards demanded of a fine camera. Fortunately, Dr. Land's intuition prevailed and he became the central figure in one of the all-time success stories in business.

Another prominent industrialist who sustained a hunch with great courage is George I. Long, then president of Ampex Corporation. Right after the war, when the television boom started, Long "guessed" that a product permitting the transcriptions of TV programs for distribution and rebroadcast would tap a huge potential market. Several other firms had considered the idea and had conducted preliminary research. But they all felt that the technical difficulties were too great and were dubious about the potential market value of the product. Ampex at that time considered itself too small to tackle the problem, but so strong was George :one's hunch about the success of such a product that the company risked the costly development project anyway. The decision was fortunate – the hunch paid off. The result was videotape, which established Ampex as a leader in the industry.

Intuitive versus Analytical Modes

Further clarification can be obtained by comparing intuitive thinking to the analytical mode of thinking. Dr. Jerome S. Bruner compares the two this way: "Analytic thinking characteristically proceeds a step at a time. Steps are explicit and usually can be adequately reported by the thinker to another individual. Such thinking proceeds with relatively full awareness of the information and operations involved....

"Intuitive thinking usually does not advance in careful, well-defined steps. Indeed, it tends to involve maneuvers based seemingly on an implicit perception of the total problem. The thinker arrives at an answer, which may be right or wrong, with little if any awareness of the process by which he reached it. He rarely can provide an adequate account of how he obtained his answer, and may be unaware of just what aspects of the problem situation he was responding to."

Professor George Turin of the University of California, Berkeley, states that the following elements are involved in an "intuitive approach" to problem solving:

- The ability to know how to attack a problem without quite being sure how you know
- The ability to relate a problem in one field to seemingly different problems in other fields
- The ability to recognize what is peripheral and what is central, without having understood the problem fully
- The ability to know in advance the general nature of the solution
- The ability to recognize when a solution must be right, first because "it feels right"

What is Intuition?

Although any single definition of intuitive thinking is almost certain to be incomprehensive, the process can be defined "operationally."

It is a form of reasoning in which the weighing and balancing of evidence is carried out unconsciously.

Intuition and Creativity

Is there experimental evidence that a high correlation exists between intuitive ability and creativity?

In an extensive study, Dr. Donald W. MacKinnon and his associates at the University of California tested hundreds of creative and "noncreative" subjects in a number of fields. One of the tests used was the Myers-Briggs Type Indicator, which distinguishes between two cognitive orientations – sense perception and intuitive perception. The person who favors sense perception is "inclined to focus upon his immediate sensory experience." He or she concentrates on the sensory attributes of the experience and centers the attention on existing facts as they are given. In contrast, the intuitive-perceptive person "immediately and instinctively perceives the deeper meanings and possibilities inherent in situations and ideas which he experiences." He is "ever alert to links and bridges between what is present and that which is not yet thought of." He focuses habitually upon what may be, rather than upon what is.

On this test, over 90 per cent of the creative subjects showed a marked preference for intuition. In the case of the less creative or "noncreative" individuals, the percentage preference for intuition was considerable lower. Dr. MacKinnon concludes: "It is not that this finding is surprising. One would not expect creative persons to be stimulus-and-object bound, but instead, ever alert to the as-yet-not realized. It is rather the magnitude of the preference for intuitive perception that is so striking among highly creative persons."

When are Hunches Valid?

Hunches can be validated only when acted upon and proven right or wrong. There are, however, some subjective clues used by people who believe in the intuitive hunch. They know, for example, that one characteristic of a valid hunch is the adherence to a keen sense of value. The hunch arrives brimming with positive feeling and a sense of certainty.

The person is sure, at the moment the hunch occurs, that he has grasped the core of the problem and has found the best alternative for solution. Doubt and uncertainty about the validity of the solution may occur later. But an individual who trust his intuitive judgment seldom abandons it because of later doubts.

Sense of Compulsion
An intuitive hunch is often accompanied by a sense of immediacy that recurrently invades a person's consciousness. When engaged in some other activity, he often becomes distracted. He feels compelled to return to the implementation of the intuitive hunch, even though the time or occasion for considering it is not propitious. Thus, the intuitive hunch sometimes has the earmarks of compulsion. And it is usually wise to heed this compulsion.

10. DIVERGENT THINKING

As originally defined by Guilford in 1950, *divergent thinking refers to an individual's ability to generate multiple potential solutions to a problem.* It is typically measured by presenting individuals with an open-ended stimulus problem to which they are required to generate as many solutions, ideas, concepts, and approaches as possible. The greater number of alternatives generated results in a greater probability of a better, more creative solution.

Divergent Thinking is the opposite of convergent thinking. It allows creative thinking; it allows you to expand your mind. There are many possible answers, unlike convergent thinking, which only allows one. For example, "Name as many things you can that are hot."

Strategies of Divergent Thinking

The goal of divergent thinking is to generate many different ideas about a topic in a short period of time. It involves breaking a topic down into its various component parts in order to gain insight about the various aspects of the topic. Divergent thinking typically occurs in a spontaneous, free-flowing manner, such that the ideas are generated in a random, unorganized fashion. Following divergent thinking, the ideas and information will be organized using convergent thinking, i.e., putting the various ideas back together in some organized, structured way.

Figure 10.1. Divergent Thinking. Generating multiple solutions for the same problem considering all of them being right.

To begin brainstorming potential topics, it is often helpful to engage in self analysis and topic analysis.

Self Analysis

Ask the following questions to help brainstorm a list of potential topics.

- How do I spend my time? What are my activities during a normal day?

CHAPTER 7

Topic Analysis

Ask the following questions to help narrow and refine a broad topic into a specific, focused one. Substitute your topic for the word "something."

- How would you describe something?
- What are the causes of something?
- What are the effects of something?
- What is important about something?
- What are the smaller parts that comprise something?
- How has something changed? Why are those changes important?
- What is known and unknown about something?
- What category of ideas or objects does something belong to?
- Is something good or bad? Why?
- What suggestions or recommendations would you make about something?
- What are the different aspects of something you can think of?

- What do I know about? What are my areas of expertise? What am I studying in school?
- What do I like? What are my hobbies? What are my interests?
- What bothers me? What would I like to change in my world or life?
- What are my strongest beliefs, values and philosophies?

TECHNIQUES TO STIMULATE DIVERGENT THINKING

1. Keeping a Journal. Journals are an effective way to record ideas that one thinks of spontaneously. By carrying a journal, one can create a collection of thoughts on various subjects that later become a source book of ideas. People often have insights at unusual times and places. By keeping a journal, one can capture these ideas and use them later when developing and organizing materials in the prewriting stage.

2. Freewriting. When free-writing, a person will focus on one particular topic and write non-stop about it for a short period of time. The idea is to write down whatever comes to mind about the topic, without stopping to proofread or revise the writing. This can help generate a variety of thoughts about a topic in a short period of time, which can later be restructured or organized following some pattern of arrangement.

3. Mind or Subject Mapping. Mind or subject mapping involves putting brainstormed ideas in the form of a visual map or picture that that shows the relationships among these ideas. One starts with a central idea or topic, then draws branches off the main topic which represent different parts or aspects of the main topic. This creates a visual image or "map" of the topic which the writer can use to develop the topic further. For example, a topic may have four different branches (sub-topics), and each of those four branches may have two branches of its own (sub-topics of the sub-topic) *Note* this includes both divergent and convergent thinking.

4. Brainstorming. Alex Osborn, advertising writer of the fifties and sixties, has contributed many very powerful creative thinking techniques. Brainstorming is probably the best known and certainly one of the most powerful. For a fuller treatment, see his book, Applied Imagination.

Brainstorming is an idea generating technique. Its main goal is **to separate idea generation process from idea evaluation.** Normally, right hemisphere of the brain generates idea. The left hemisphere immediately evaluates idea by comparing it to previous experience. If idea is innovative and does not fit to existing pattern, left brain kills such idea.

Basic Guidelines for Brainstorming

Brainstorming is useful for attacking specific (rather than general) problems and where a collection of good, fresh, new ideas (rather than judgment or decision analysis) are needed.

For example, a specific problem like how to mark the content of pipes (water, steam, etc.) would lend itself to brainstorming much better than a general problem like how the educational system can be improved. Note, though, that even general problems can be submitted to brainstorming with success.

Brainstorming can take place either individually or in a group of two to ten, with four to seven being ideal.

1. Suspend judgment. This is the most important rule. When ideas are brought forth, no critical comments are allowed. All ideas are written down. Evaluation is to be reserved for later. We have been trained to be so instantly analytic, practical, convergent in our thinking that this step is very difficult to observe, but it is crucial. To create and criticize at the same time is like watering and pouring weed killer onto seedlings at the same time.

2. Think freely. Freewheeling, wild thoughts are fine. Impossible and unthinkable ideas are fine. In fact, in every session, there should be several ideas so bizarre that they make the group laugh. Remember that practical ideas very often come from silly, impractical, impossible ones. By permitting yourself to think outside the boundaries of ordinary, normal thought, brilliant new solutions can arise. Some "wild" ideas turn out to be practical, too.

For example, when the subway was being dug under Victoria station in London, water began seeping in. What are the ways to remedy this? Pumps, steel or concrete liners? The solution: freeze it. Horizontal holes were drilled into the wet soil and liquid nitrogen was pumped in, freezing the water until the tunnel could be dug and cemented.

We've already talked about gold plating electrical contacts. In another example, it's a fact that electric generators can produce more power if the windings can be kept cool. How would you cool them? Fans, air conditioned rooms? How about a wild idea? Make the electric windings out of copper pipe *instead of wire and pump helium through them. That is what's actually done in some plants, doubling the output of the generators.*

3. Tag on. Improve, modify, build on the ideas of others. What's good about the idea just suggested? How can it be made to work? What changes would make it better or even wilder? This is sometimes called piggybacking, hitchhiking, or ping ponging. Use another's idea as stimulation for your own improvement or variation. As we noted earlier, changing just one aspect of an unworkable solution can sometimes make it a great solution.

Example problem: How can we get more students at our school? Brainstorm idea: Pay them to come here. That sounds unworkable, but what about modifying it? Pay them with something other than money--like an emotional, spiritual, or intellectual reward or even a practical value-added reward like better networking or job contacts?

5. **Quantity of ideas is important.** Concentrate on generating a large stock of ideas so that later on they can be sifted through. There are two reasons for desiring a large quantity. First, the obvious, usual, stale, unworkable ideas seem to come to mind first, so that the first, say, 20 or 25 ideas are probably not going to be fresh and creative. Second, the larger your list of possibilities, the more you will have to choose from, adapt, or combine. Some brainstormers aim for a fixed number, like 50 or 100 ideas before quitting the session.

Practical Methodology

1. Choose a recorder. Someone must be put in charge of writing down all the ideas. Preferably, the ideas should be written on a board or butcher papered walls so that the whole brainstorming group can see them. Lacking this, ideas should be put down on paper. In an ideal session, the recorder should be a non participant in the brainstorming session, since it's hard to be thoughtful and creative and write down everything at the same time. But in small sessions, the recorder is usually a participant, too.

For a one-person brainstorming session, using an idea map on a large piece of paper is useful.

2. Organize the chaos. For groups of more than three or four, have a moderator to choose who will offer an idea next, so that several people don't speak at once. The moderator should prefer those with ideas that tag onto previous ideas, then those with new ideas. If necessary the moderator will also remind members of the group not to inject evaluation into the session (in case a member tsks, sneers, says, "Oh, come on," and so forth).

3. Keep the session relaxed and playful. The creative juices flow best when participants are relaxed and enjoying themselves and feeling free to be silly or playful. Eat popcorn or pizza or ice cream or make paper airplanes or doodles while you work, even if the problem itself is deadly serious like cancer or child abuse. Don't keep reminding everyone that "this is a serious problem" or "that was a tasteless joke."

As an aid to relaxation and stimulation to creativity, it is often useful to begin with a ten-minute warm-up session, where an imaginary problem is tackled. Thinking about the imaginary problem loosens people up and puts them into a playful mood. Then the real problem at hand can be turned to. Some imaginary problem topics might include these:

- how to heat a house more efficiently
- how to light a house with a single light bulb
- how to improve your travel from home to work
- inventing a new game for the Olympics
- how to improve institutional food without increasing its cost

4. Limit the session. A typical session should be limited to about fifteen or twenty minutes. Longer than that tends to become dragging. You should probably not go beyond thirty minutes, though thirty is the "ideal" length recommended by Alex Osborn.

5. Make copies. After the session, neaten up the list and make copies for each member of the session. No attempt should be made to put the list in any particular order.

6. Add and evaluate. The next day (not the same day) the group should meet again. First, ideas thought of since the previous session should be shared (entered on the photocopied lists). Then the group should evaluate each of the ideas and develop the most promising ones for practical application.

During the evaluation session, wild ideas are converted to practical ones or used to suggest realistic solutions. The emphasis is now on analysis and real world issues. Some brainstormers divide the ideas found to be useful into three lists:

    A.   *Ideas of immediate usefulness.* These are the ideas you will be able to use right now.

B. Areas for further exploration. These are ideas that need to be researched, followed up, thought about, discussed more fully, and so on.

C. New approaches to the problem. These are ideas that suggest new ways of looking at the situation.

Note here that evaluation does not take place on the same day as the brainstorming session. This fact keeps the idea session looser (no fear that evaluation is coming soon) and allows incubation time for more ideas and time for thinking about the ones suggested.

Variations

1. Stop and Go. For stop and go brainstorming, ideas are generated for three to five minutes. Then the group is silent (and thinking) for three to five minutes. Then ideas are given out for another three to five. This pattern alternates for the entire session.

2. Sequencing. In this technique, the moderator goes in order from one member of the group to the next in turn or sequence. Each member gives whatever ideas he then has, and they are written down. If a member has no ideas, he just says, "Pass," and the next member responds. This movement in turn or around the table continues throughout the session. (Sequencing has been said to nearly double the number of ideas generated in a brainstorming session.)

Try It Yourself

Brainstorming. Choose one of the following problems for a brainstorming session. Generate at least 35 ideas for solving the problem. Then distill this list into at least three practical, effective ideas.

1. A new snack food
2. How to keep rowdy children quiet on a schoolbus
3. How to get more tourists into the United States
4. How compatible people can meet each other for romance
5. How to reduce hospital costs
6. How to reduce airport congestion and delays
7. A name for a new laundry detergent
8. How to keep your car keys safe at the beach
9. A new toy
10. A new electronic consumer product

Idea Generating Questions

Asking questions to stimulate curiosity and creativity has proven helpful for all kinds of endeavors, whether problem solving, product development, inventing, or communication. A written list of mind-stimulating questions is useful because it reminds us of approaches and possibilities that we otherwise would not have in mind. Yes, it is sometimes possible to be creative in a thorough and even orderly way.

The Journalistic Six

These are the six key questions that journalism students are taught to answer somewhere in their news articles to make sure that they have covered the whole story. For creative thinkers, these questions stimulate thinking about the idea in question and allow approaches to it from various angles.

1. Who? (Actor or Agent) Who is involved? What are the people aspects of the problem? Who did it, will do it? Who uses it, wants it? Who will benefit, will be injured, will be included, will be excluded?

2. What? (Act) What should happen? What is it? What was done, ought to be done, was not done? What will be done if X happens? What went or could go wrong? What resulted in success?

3. When? (Time or Timing) When will, did, should this occur or be performed? Can it be hurried or delayed? Is a sooner or later time be preferable? When should the time be if X happens?

4. Where? (Scene or Source) Where did, will, should this occur or be performed? Where else is a possibility? Where else did the same thing happen, should the same thing happen? Are other places affected, endangered, protected, aided by this location? Effect of this location on actors, actions?

5. Why? (Purpose) Why was or is this done, avoided, permitted? Why should it be done, avoided, permitted? Why did or should actor do it? Different for another actor, act, time, place? Why that particular action, rule, idea, solution, problem, disaster, and not another? Why that actor, time, location, and not another?

6. How? (Agency or Method) How was it, could it be, should it be done, prevented, destroyed, made, improved, altered? How can it be described, understood? How did beginning lead to conclusion?

Modes of Thinking

Historical Examination

These questions are especially useful for generating ideas for improving something (the evolutionary approach), but they also help to break thinking out of the evolutionary mode and put it into the revolutionary mode by returning the thinker to the origin and purpose of the idea or solution. By returning to the roots of the problem, a new vision can be created.

1. Essence. What is it? object, concept? What is it made of? What is its real, elementary nature? What are its parts? What is it like, unlike? (Similes and metaphors help in understanding abstractions). What is it related to? What are its various kinds, facets, shades? What is it a part of? Which part of it is unusual or outstanding? In what forms does it appear? Is it typical or atypical of its kind? What is it not? What is it opposed to? How is it different? What makes it different?

2. Origin. Where did it come from? How was it made or conceived or developed? What caused it? If an idea, how did it arise? Are its origins meaningful now? What makes it spread or multiply or gain adherents? What was the reason behind it? Is the reason still valid or useful? Why? Why not? Is it still needed? What influences it? Does it change? Can it, should it be changed, strengthened, eliminated? What could have prevented, delayed, encouraged it?

3. Purpose. What does it do? How does it work? What is its purpose? Is the purpose fulfilled? Better than by its predecessor? Can it, should it be improved? Is it helpful or harmful in intent? What are its implications; what does it lead to? Does it have obvious or hidden consequences? Does it have more than one purpose? What are its immediate effects and its long-term effects? Is its actual function the same as the original purpose intended by its originator? Can it be put to other uses?

4. Import. What is its overall significance? What is its significance to man, environment, civilization, happiness, virtue, safety, comfort, etc.? How is it important? Is it a key element in life, civilization, local area, one man's existence? Is it necessary? Is it desirable?

5. Reputation. What do you think about it? What are your underlying assumptions? What do others think about it? Do you find consensus, division? Is it good, bad, helpful, harmful in fact or in the opinion of others? Can you resolve any differences between truth and opinion, intent, and actuality, pro and con members? What weaknesses are commonly identified? Are there obvious areas of desired change or improvement or elimination?

PRACTICING DIVERGENT THINKING

1. **Uses For.** This is a simple technique that can be used for mental stimulation or practical application, depending on what you have in mind at the time. It is an excellent tool for breaking you out of a functionally fixated mindset. To use this technique, think of an item or object, usually a common one like a brick, toothpick, pencil, or bucket, and set the task of thinking of all the possible uses for that object, without regard to what the object is normally used for, what it is named, or how it is usually thought of.

Sometimes a time limit, like three to five minutes, is given. Other times a quantity limit, like 25 to 100 is given. All the techniques of idea generation are used, from checklist to attribute analysis to random stimulation.

For example: What are the possible uses for a brick?

Ideas: *doorstop, boat anchor, build a wall, build a walk, ballast, sanding block, powder and make dye, put on white background and make a sign (red letters), nut cracker, shoes, straightedge, red chalk, stop signal (use something green like a cucumber for go), heat reservoir, leaf press, paper weight, step stool, target for shooting, children's toys, scale weight standard, distance standard, definition of red, water holder (soaked), tamper, pattern maker (in soft material), pendulum weight, bell clapper, roofing material (crushed).*

Another example: What are the possible uses for a steak knife?

Ideas: *hot pad, planter stick or prop, hole digger, popsicle stick, bubble wand (through hole in handle), flipping tool or spring, hammer, gun sight, fishing weight/float, compass (magnetize the steel), plumb*

CHAPTER 7

bob, drill, can opener, carving tool, electrical (knife) switch or other electrical conductor use, awl, measuring device (two knives long and three knives wide), shim, design maker in wet plaster (serrated edge), writing instrument (dip in ink), all cutting and chopping uses, guitar pick, branding or soldering device (get red hot first), ice climbing aid (hook or glue to boots with part of blade down into ground)

Try It Yourself

Uses For. Choose one of the items below and think of at least 25 original uses for it. (That is, you cannot list things that the item is already used for.) The uses can be fanciful, but should at least approach practicality. Describe each use in a sentence or two.

Example: *Uses for a steak knife.*
1. *Drill a hole in the tip and use it as a "knife switch" to turn electricity on and off.*
2. *Use the wood or plastic handles of two or three to make a hot pad for serving casseroles or soup in hot containers.*
3. *Use it to measure a spot for a new sofa, so when you go to the store you will know how many "steak knife units" long your new sofa can be.*
4. *Use it to drill holes in plasterboard walls.*

a cardboard box	a towel
a nail	a sheet of paper
a spoon	a fan
a roll of adding machine paper	a ball point pen
the yellow pages	an inner tube
a candle	three feet of Scotch tape
popsicle sticks	a plastic drinking glass
a toothpick	a marble
old newspapers	ball bearings that aren't round
worn out automobile tires	non-returnable soda bottles
tons of broken rubber bands)	pencils

Versa Tarp. You have been hired by Acme Manufacturing to write an advertising brochure for its new product, Versa Tarp. The product is an 8 by 10 foot plastic tarp with the usual spaced grommets and reinforcing. (You can see tarps like this at most hardware stores.) In the brochure, Acme wants you to list as many good, practical uses for this tarp as you can, to show just how versatile it is. List at least 25 practical uses, with explanations if necessary. Drawings would be good, too.

Hole Punch. Redwood Mills, Incorporated is a manufacturer of paper. A principal product of theirs is three-hole punch notebook paper for schools. A byproduct of making this paper is tons and tons of punched paper holes. You have been hired to suggest as many uses for these punched pieces of paper as possible. Be imaginative and practical. Think of at least 25 uses.

Steamer. The Heiss manufacturing company of Germany has been making a steam-producing home appliance, designed to be used to steam milk in the making of cappuccino. Unfortunately for the company, its competitors now incorporate a steam maker right into the cappuccino maker, so that a steamer-only design no longer sells. You have been hired by a liquidator company that has acquired 40,000 of these steamers to write an advertising brochure, describing as many practical uses for this steamer as you can. Your basic task is to think of what steam can be used for. Describe at least 25 good uses, with any necessary explanations or drawings.

2. Improvements to. "Improvements to" is the counterpart of "uses for." Whereas "uses for" concentrates on using a given item, often unchanged, for multiple purposes different from the item's original purpose, the "improvements to" technique focuses on altering an item to enhance its original, given purpose. The item in question can be any of several kinds and is not limited to objects.

A. Objects. The first and most obvious "thing" to improve is an object, usually something common that most people would never think of changing. The classic, textbook example item is the coffee cup. Suggested improvements have included things like

- multiple handles
- anti skid
- anti tip over
- anti spill (lids)
- built-in heater
- decorations
- wheels
- tea bag holder on side
- insulated
- self brewing
- self cleaning

and so forth. The improvements ideally should move away from obvious bolt-on things, however. For example, in the problem, "Think of several ways to improve books," the first things that come to mind might be the addition or repair ones like

- better binding
- lighter weight
- lower cost
- clearer type
- more color pictures
- better indexes

but we might also think about more imaginative improvements like

- books that read themselves (talk to you)
- books with three dimensional pictures
- books with multiple reading paths
- books that explain their hard parts (better glosses?)
- books that project on the wall so you don't have to hold them

B. Places, Institutions, Things. In addition to the object, a second kind of thing that improvements for can be applied to is a place, institution, or thing. For example, list ten ways to improve a college, or a marriage, or a shopping mall, or the local church, or the road system, or communications channels (telephone, TV, radio). Improvements to these areas require more thoughtful and elaborate proposals, often involving improvements in attitudes, beliefs, behavior, relationships, or other non-tangible things, as well as changes in physical technology. A piece of wood and a tube of glue are no longer sufficient to effect improvement.

C. Ideas. A third area of improvement is even more removed from wood and glue: the improvement of ideas or abstractions. How can we improve art or the writing of history or the application of personal values to our actions?

In all of these cases, problem exploration (an exploration and articulation of needs) is usually the first step. What is there about a coffee cup that is deficient or that could be made better? What about shopping malls do you (and most people) dislike? How is the bulk of recorded or taught history insufficient or imperfect--what keeps it from being described as excellent?

Again, remember the constructive discontent philosophy. The coffee cup, the local church, the college, art, all may be really good and suitable and "satisfactory" in what they do; to look for ways to improve them should not imply condemnation or rejection. This "either it's fine or it's bad" attitude often gets in the way of thinking calmly about improvements. In personal relationships, romantic or supervisor/employee, in techniques and policies, whenever someone suggests an improvement, the typical response is, "So what's so terrible about it now?" Be sensitive, therefore, to the ego needs of the human element involved in improving things. Don't rush into the cafeteria and declare that you are there to make the putrid food edible at last--think of the people who make it now. Don't rush up to your boss and declare that you are about to reveal why his management style stinks. Don't call your best friend and offer to reform her disgusting and selfish personality.

CHAPTER 7

Try It Yourself

Improvements To. Choose one of the following and think of at least ten practical ways it can be improved. Describe each improvement in a sentence or two (why is it an improvement?) and supply any needed drawings.

pencil	calculator	spoon
paper	postal system	tires
lighting in a room	desk	controlling a car
museums	dating	spelling rules
court system	telephone	ball-point pen
textbook	hamburgers	telephone book
flashlight	bicycle	postage stamp
hair dryer	bus	window shades

You will probably want to submit drawings with this project to show what your improvements will look like.

An Idea List of Ways to Improve Something

- Simplify--remove complexity
- Apply to new use
- Automate
- Reduce Cost
- Make easier to use, understand
- Reduce fear to own, use
- Make safer
- Give more performance, capacity
- Make faster, less waiting
- Provide more durability, reliability
- Give better appearance
- Create more acceptance by others
- Add features, functions
- Integrate functions
- Make more flexible, versatile
- Make lighter weight--or heavier
- Make smaller--or larger
- Make more powerful
- Reduce or eliminate drawbacks, bad side effects
- Make more elegant
- Give better shape, design, style
- Provide better sensory appeal (taste, feel, look, smell, sound)
- Provide better psychological appeal (understandable, acceptable)
- Provide better emotional appeal (happy, warm, satisfying, enjoyable, fun, likable, "neat")
- Aim toward ideal rather than immediate goals
- Give larger capacity
- Make portable
- Make self-cleaning, easy to clean
- Make more accurate
- Make quieter

Note: Remember that some of the major problems in modern living are too much noise, too much information, too many decisions, too much complexity, together with a general lack of quality and reliability. Intelligent addressing of these problems in connection with your idea should produce welcome improvements to it.

11. Convergent

Convergent thinking is based on knowledge and experience and focuses on an answer, a solution. It is used when solving problems such as long-division and calculating income tax. Convergent thinking techniques eliminate uncertainty, simplify complexity, and enhance decision-making ability.

There is only "one right answer." Convergent thinking is the very opposite of divergent thinking. Convergent thinking is not considered "bad," but it is not always considered "good." Convergent thinking questions are like, "What is 2+2?" or "Where is the Empire State Building located?"

Convergent thinking does not let you expand your mind, as divergent thinking does. But, convergent thinking has its good points, too. It allows people to gain a good education necessary for jobs in their future. We need to know where things are, how to do things, etc. If we didn't know any of those essential things for life, we would probably be a bunch of walking, brainless people! So, in a way, convergent thinking is good, but not always the best.

There is only one right answer or solution for a problem.

Convergent thinking asks:
1. What's going on?
2. Why is this happening?

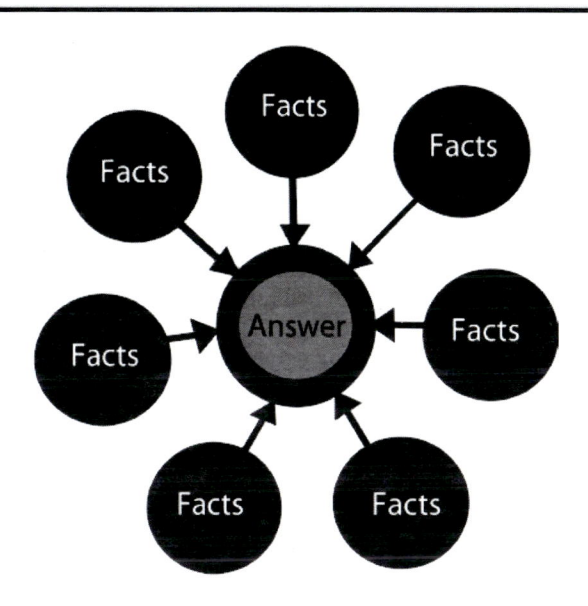

Figure 11.1. Convergent Thinking. Thinking "inside of the box." Before you learn how to think "outside of the box," you need to learn what is inside of the box. You need to acquire knowledge and skills before you start to create.

12. Conscious

Conscious thinking is regimented. It deals with abstractions of reality. It proceeds in "real" time, receiving information both from the senses and from memory. Conscious thinking is linear and single-channel. It is occupied by one topic until it switches to another. Conscious thinking prefers complete information and is limited by the nature of the information processing involved.

13. Unconscious

Unconscious thinking is uninhibited, faster and more flexible than conscious. It is better able to deal with uncertainty and able to operate in non-linear, multi-channel modes. It is powerful in discovery, invention, innovation, and accommodation to change. Incorporating previous experience to foster new insights, unconscious thinking is the well-spring of intuition and the foundation of the elusive quality known as "judgment." Unconscious thinking fosters creativity by allowing unconscious ideas and associations to flow into consciousness, thereby providing a basis for the integration and redirection of thought.

Conscious versus Subconscious

In each of us there is **an underworld of the mind.** Occasionally, for one reason or another, our conscious level is moved to probe this place, to try to pull some of its stored matter to the surface. At other times, bits and pieces float upward of their own accord, assuming vague shapes in beginning light. Most often, this subterranean material remains in its own darkness, protecting itself from the probing light of the conscious mind; attempts to reveal such material require effort and patience.

Individual, who is willing to create and makes use of material from the subconscious part of the mind learns that the impulse to create originates from the same area. **The conflicting desires to express**

CHAPTER 7

An individual's memory store occupies both parts of the mind. Parts of this store sink into the subconscious and are more resistant to recall. They lie hidden until some trigger – a sound, view, word, or feeling – reactivates them and makes them accessible once more to the conscious level of the mind. Other parts of the memory lie fairly close to the surface and are easier to recall. Creative individual makes use of both states of memory.

and to repress, the revelations that filter through our censor and make themselves known to us accompany the creative effort. The result of the artistic process, the work itself, is rarely shaped and organized by the subconscious. From the exuberant outpouring of its origin, your work is shaped into a manifest form through the sobering influences of the conscious mind and the application of poetic skills – skills learned and practiced during your apprenticeship. In a way, this critical process illuminates the ideas emerging from that darker side of the mind.

It is not unusual to experience difficulty in facing some of these things about ourselves that have been coaxed from our deeper recesses. If we can keep fears in check, we will learn to deal with these alarming facets of nature and to direct them toward contributing to creative output.

Consider your subconscious a dimly lit storehouse whose contents are being continually sorted, rearranged, catalogued, and suggested for your consideration. Make yourself receptive to these offerings, and you will be able to draw on this rich extensive inventory. And the data become yours to shape and transform into a work of art. Protect yourself, however, from mere spillage. Invariably, the material furnished from this deep place is *raw*; it needs *to be made into art* by the application of your creative skills.

From the time of our conception until our death, everything we experience or learn becomes an item in memory. Each item is continually processed and stored. Its retrieval, when and if retrieval becomes necessary, is conditioned by our emotional state and attitude at the time of retrieval, which is influenced, in turn, by the degree of urgency that inspires the desire to retrieve.

Creative person frequently forces or encourages it.

Conscious	**Unconscious**
The conscious mind is sequential. It likes logical order. The conscious mind is linear thinking. It thinks in terms of cause-effect. The conscious mind is logical. It likes things to make sense – have a reason.	The unconscious mind processes simultaneously. It multitasks. The unconscious mind makes associations and connections between many thoughts, ideas and feelings. The unconscious mind is intuitive and can make associations of information easily.
The conscious mind does your intellectual thinking. Is responsible for your self-talk. Your conscious mind is associated with the waking, thinking state. The conscious can voluntarily move parts of your body. Your conscious mind is only aware of the now.	Your unconscious mind does your perceiving and feeling. The unconscious mind is associated with the dreaming (including day dreaming), reflecting, meditating and sleeping state. The unconscious can involuntarily move parts of your body. Your unconscious mind is unlimited in time and space. It holds all your memories and future constructs.
The conscious mind is deliberate. The conscious mind is verbal (including self-talk). The conscious mind is the place of cognitive learning and understandings.	The unconscious mind is automatic. The unconscious mind is nonverbal (feeling). The unconscious mind is the place of experiential learning.
Your conscious mind uses intellect to come up with logical solutions for problems. Your conscious mind will tell you when your right because the facts line up. The conscious mind seeks understanding of problems and reasons that if it understands them, it can make them go away.	Your unconscious mind can access internal resources from memories of experiences, linking them all together - creating a resourceful state. Your unconscious mind will tell you when you are right because it will feel right. Your unconscious mind decides what it will do about it. It can forget (amnesia), distort (make false associations) or break connections (get over it).

How your subconscious helps solve problems? When you start to chart a problem, you are not only putting it on paper, you're also sending a message to your subconscious mind. You are, in effect, telling it to get busy with the problem even after your conscious mind has turned to other matters.

Because it is indeed subconscious, we're not aware of all that is going on in this "hidden" mind that each of us has. Nor are we aware of its great power to help resolve our problems. And certainly most people don't know how to tap this tremendous mental resource.

Here are some things you should know **about subconscious**:
- **It is subject to suggestions.** This means it will accept almost any thought you give it. Unlike your conscious mind, it is not controlled by reason, so it doesn't argue with what you tell it. If, for example, you repeatedly say to yourself, "I am a multimillionaire," your subconscious will believe it even though your conscious mind knows it's not true;
- Your brain stores enough information to fill 90,000,000 books. Somewhere, buried in all that information, are the **solutions to nearly every problem you are likely to face.** Unfortunately, only a small portion of this data is readily available to your conscious mind;
- **When you are stumped by a problem, you can "tell" your subconscious that somewhere within the depths of your mind there are ideas that will lead to a workable solution.** Then, as you go about your other business, your subconscious will search through your memory for ideas and events matching the current circumstances. It will present to your conscious mind information that you would never recalled otherwise.

14. CRITICAL THINKING

De omnibus dubitandum (Lat.) – doubt about everything

Ability to challenge your personal believes. Critical thinking can be defined as rationally deciding what to do or believe in a particular context. It is conscious, directed, controlled thinking, in which each link in a chain of reason is closely scrutinized to assess the validity of each inference. It is committed to accuracy and strives for logic and control.

What role critical thinking plays in creativity process?

There are several issues:

1. Critical thinking presupposes an *array of intellectual abilities*, including the following: the ability to identify, analyze, and evaluate the following:

   a) Goals, needs, and purposes;

   b) Problems and issues,

   c) Information, events, and experience,

   d) Inferences, interpretations, and judgments,

   e) Ideas, concepts, and theories,

   f) Assumptions and presuppositions,

   g) Implications and consequences,

   h) Points of view, frames of reference, and world views

2. Critical thinking presupposes a *commitment to rigorous intellectual standards*, including: clarity, accuracy, precision, relevance, depth, breadth, logicalness, and significance.

3. Critical thinking helps to develop *special skills of a critical thinker*. For this purpose one must manifest specific intellectual traits, including: intellectual humility, intellectual perseverance, intellectual integrity, fairmindedness, etc.

4. Critical thinking is *not a "natural" concomitant* of human thought, but a special, disciplined, acquirement.

Human thinking, in its "natural" state, is often egocentric, socio-centric, one-sided, prejudiced, and self-deluded. Critical thinking helps to eliminate these human "attributes" and make process of reasoning more objective. Different disciplines (such as physics, chemistry, mathematics, sociology, anthropology, etc.) represent forms of critical thought only so, far as they manifest a commitment to rigorous intellectual standards. Critical thinking is not the "possession" of any discipline, though presupposed by all of them.

Critical thinking does not define a particular "belief" system, but rather a manner of acquiring or holding a belief system (i.e., critically or uncritically; e.g., one can be a critical or uncritical conservative, a critical or uncritical liberal, etc.)

Critical Thinking Elements

There are two essential dimensions of thinking. They need to be able to identify the "parts" of their thinking, and they need to be able to assess their use of these parts of thinking, as follows:

All reasoning has a purpose.
All reasoning is an attempt to figure something out, to settle some question, to solve some problem.
All reasoning is based on assumptions.
All reasoning is done from some point of view.
All reasoning is based on data, information, and evidence.
All reasoning is expressed through, and shaped by, concepts and ideas.
All reasoning contains inferences by which we draw conclusions and give meaning to data.
All reasoning leads somewhere, has implications and consequences.

How to improve reasoning abilities?
There are some helpful guidelines:

1. All reasoning has a purpose.
- Take time to state your purpose clearly.
- Distinguish your purpose from related purposes.
- Check periodically to be sure you are still on target.
- Choose significant and realistic purposes.

2. All reasoning is an attempt to understand something, to state something, or to solve a problem.
- Take time to clearly and precisely state the question at issue.
- Express the question in several ways to clarify its meaning and scope.
- Break the question into sub questions.
- Identify if the question has one right answer, is a matter of opinion, or requires reasoning from more than one point of view.

3. All reasoning is based on assumptions.
- Clearly identify your assumptions and determine whether they are justifiable.
- Consider how your assumptions are shaping your point of view.

4. All reasoning is done from some point of view.
- Identify your point of view.
- Seek other points of view and identify their strengths as well as weaknesses.
- Strive to be fair-minded in evaluating all points of view.

5. All reasoning is based on information and evidence.
- Restrict your claims to those supported by the data you have.
- Search for information that opposes your position as well as information that supports it.
- Make sure that all information used is clear, accurate, and relevant to the question at issue.
- Make sure you have gathered sufficient
- information.

6. All reasoning is expressed through, and shaped by, concepts and ideas.
- Identify key concepts and explain them clearly.
- Consider alternative concepts or alternative definitions to concepts.
- Make sure you are using concepts with care and precision.

7. All reasoning contains inferences or interpretations, by which we draw conclusions and give meaning to data.
- Infer only what the evidence implies.

- Check inferences for their consistency with each other.
- Identify assumptions which lead you to your inferences.

8. All reasoning leads somewhere or has implications and consequences.
- Trace the implications and consequences that follow from your reasoning.
- Search for negative as well as positive implications.
- Consider all possible consequences.

Critical Thinking Standards

Universal intellectual standards are standards which must be applied to thinking whenever one is interested in checking the quality of reasoning about a problem, issue, or situation. Thinking critically entails having command of these standards. While there are a number of universal standards, the following are the most significant:

CLARITY:
Could you elaborate further on that point?
Could you express that point in another way?
Could you give me an illustration?
Could you give me an example?

Clarity is the gateway standard. If a statement is unclear, we cannot determine whether it is accurate or relevant. In fact, we cannot tell anything about it because we don't yet know what it is saying. For example, the question, "What can be done about the education system in America?" is unclear. In order to address the question adequately, we would need to have a clearer understanding of what the person asking the question is considering the "problem" to be. A clearer question might be "What can educators do to ensure that students learn the skills and abilities which help them function successfully on the job and in their daily decision-making?"

ACCURACY:
Is that really true?
How could we check that?
How could we find out if that is true?
A statement can be clear but not accurate, as in "Most dogs are over 300 pounds in weight."

PRECISION:
Could you give more details?
Could you be more specific?
A statement can be both clear and accurate, but not precise, as in "Jack is overweight." (We don't know how overweight Jack is, one pound or 500 pounds.)

RELEVANCE:
How is that connected to the question?
How does that bear on the issue?
A statement can be clear, accurate, and precise, but not relevant to the question at issue. For example, students often think that the amount of effort they put into a course should be used in raising their grade in a course. Often, however, the "effort" does not measure the quality of student learning, and when this is so, effort is irrelevant to their appropriate grade.

DEPTH:
How does your answer address the complexities in the question?
How are you taking into account the problems in the question?
Is that dealing with the most significant factors?
A statement can be clear, accurate, precise, and relevant, but superficial (that is, lack depth). For example, the statement "Just say No" which is often used to discourage children and teens fro using drugs, is clear, accurate, precise, and relevant. Nevertheless, it lacks depth because it treats an extremely complex issue, the pervasive problem of drug use among young people, superficially. It fails to deal with the complexities of the issue.

BREADTH:
Do we need to consider another point of view?
Is there another way to look at this question?
What would this look like from a conservative standpoint?
What would this look like from the point of view of...?

A line of reasoning may be clear accurate, precise, relevant, and deep, but lack breadth (as in an argument from either the conservative or liberal standpoint which gets deeply into an issue, but only recognizes the insights of one side of the question.)

LOGIC:
Does this really make sense?
Does that follow from what you said?
How does that follow?
But before you implied this and now you are saying that; how can both be true?

When we think, we bring a variety of thoughts together into some order. When the combination of thoughts are mutually supporting and make sense in combination, the thinking is "logical." When the combination is not mutually supporting, is contradictory in some sense, or does not "make sense," the combination is not logical.

Critical Thinking Traits

Intellectual Humility:
Having a consciousness of the limits of one's knowledge, including sensitivity to circumstances in which one's native egocentrism is likely to function self-deceptively; sensitivity to bias, prejudice and limitations of one's viewpoint. Intellectual humility depends on recognizing that one should not claim more than one actually knows. It does not imply spinelessness or submissiveness. It implies the lack of intellectual pretentiousness, boastfulness, or conceit, combined with insight into the logical foundations, or lack of such foundations, of one's beliefs.

Intellectual Courage:
Having a consciousness of the need to face and fairly address ideas, beliefs or viewpoints toward which we have strong negative emotions and to which we have not given a serious hearing. This courage is connected with the recognition that ideas considered dangerous or absurd are sometimes rationally justified (in whole or in part) and that conclusions and beliefs inculcated in us are sometimes false or misleading. To determine for ourselves which is which, we must not passively and uncritically "accept" what we have "learned." Intellectual courage comes into play here, because inevitably we will come to see some truth in some ideas considered dangerous and absurd, and distortion or falsity in some ideas strongly held in our social group. We need courage to be true to our own thinking in such circumstances. The penalties for non-conformity can be severe.

Intellectual Empathy:
Having a consciousness of the need to imaginatively put oneself in the place of others in order to genuinely understand them that requires the consciousness of our egocentric tendency to identify truth with our immediate perceptions of long-standing thought or belief. This trait correlates with the ability to reconstruct accurately the viewpoints and reasoning of others and to reason from premises, assumptions, and ideas other than our own. This trait also correlates with the willingness to remember occasions when we were wrong in the past despite an intense conviction that we were right, and with the ability to imagine our being similarly deceived in a case-at-hand.

Intellectual Integrity:
Recognition of the need to be true to one's own thinking; to be consistent in the intellectual standards one applies; to hold one's self to the same rigorous standards of evidence and proof to which one holds one's antagonists; to practice what one advocates for others; and to honestly admit discrepancies and inconsistencies in one's own thought and action.

Intellectual Perseverance:
Having a consciousness of the need to use intellectual insights and truths in spite of difficulties, obstacles, and frustrations; firm adherence to rational principles despite the irrational opposition of others; a sense of the need to struggle with confusion and unsettled questions over an extended period of time to achieve deeper understanding or insight.

Faith in Reason:
Confidence that, in the long run, one's own higher interests and those of humankind at large will be best served by giving the freest play to reason, by encouraging people to come to their own conclusions by developing their own rational faculties; faith that, with proper encouragement and cultivation, people can learn to think for themselves, to form rational vie points, draw reasonable conclusions, think coherently and logically, persuade each other by reason and become reasonable persons, despite the deep-seated obstacles in the native character of the human mind and in society as we know it.

Fairmindedness:
Having a consciousness of the need to treat all viewpoints alike, without reference to one's own feelings or vested interests, or the feelings or vested interests of one's friends, community or nation; implies adherence to intellectual standards without reference to one's own advantage or the advantage of one's group.

The Field of Critical Thinking: Where Do We Go From Here?

Certainly, the disciplines of physics, chemistry, biology, astronomy, geology, and mathematics are, as intellectual constructs, monuments to critical thought in action. Yet no one lives within these disciplines. Human life, real human life, is inescapably multi-dimensional. Our actual lives are—at a minimum—historical, political, economic, sociological, and personal in nature. No one can avoid being influenced subconsciously in his or her thinking by the following factors:

1. Culture/society (European, American, African, Asian);
2. Point in time (in some century in some year);
3. Some particular place (in the country, in the city, in the North or South, East or West);
4. Particular beliefs that their parents posses (about the family, personal relationships, marriage, obedience, religion, politics, schooling, etc.);
5. Various associations with people and groups with particular norms of behavior, viewpoints, values, beliefs, prejudices, and taboos.

Some of this thinking is highly charged emotionally, positively or negatively, profoundly influencing human sense of self, world view, emotional, and intellectual life. The result is that it is perfectly possible for a person to be, at one and the same time, a distinguished physicist or mathematician and an irrational, narrow-minded, self-deceived person. Everyone's actual life is, in the first instance, heavily shaped by such forces as culture, society, parents, and peers, and only secondarily shaped by such forces as specialized academic or professional training. Schooling seldom plays, or ever has played, a significant role in enabling individuals to recognize, analyze, or assess, let alone reconstitute, the thoughts, emotions, and desires that deeply abide within them. For all but the most exceptional individuals, thinking scientifically or mathematically represents a secondary part of their lives. What is more, there appears to be no convincing evidence that rationality is pre-dominant in the personal, or even in the professional lives, of scientists and mathematicians.

> Fair-minded critical thinking represents a fundamental and deep-seated need for all persons in all settings. Its absence in human decision-making accounts for most large-scale human problems. At present most, if not all, human cultures and groups, function as if their basic patterns of thought and behavior, their principal modes of decision-making, their fundamental intellectual values, were already infused with critical thinking. In fact, however, no human culture or group can reasonably be accepted as an exemplar of critical thinking in action. The most arguable exceptions are the hard sciences and mathematics.

PRACTICING CRITICAL AND CREATIVE THINKING

Leonardo Da Vinci, The Geniuses' Genius: Open Up Vast New Tracts Of Unlimited Brain Power With The Leonardo Da Vinci Techniques!

Leonardo da Vinci (1452-1519) was voted the ultimate genius in a poll of geniuses. It placed him above Einstein, Aristotle, Shakespeare and any other genius you care to name. What made this illegitimate son of a notary and a peasant girl grow to become one of the world's most famous artists and a scientist who was way "ahead of his time?"

Well, foremost, he had an insatiable desire for new discoveries and knowledge. He wanted to know everything and he kept detailed records of what he observed. He even called himself a "Disciple of Experience" meaning that he learnt from life by experiencing, experimenting and observing.

Leonardo studied birds and recorded his observations in the "Codex on the Flight of Birds." It wasn't until the 20th Century that the details he recorded were confirmed by high-speed photography! How's that for really looking closely at something!

Here are the 7 Dynamite Da Vinci "Noggin Knockers" to bash the boring out of your brain and replace it with Unadulterated Brilliance!

Da Vinci Brain Bomb Number 1: CURIOSITY

Curiosity may have killed the cat but it can make the cat-owner rich as King Solomon himself!

Curiosity is the driving force of learning and development. Just as lust drives us to procreate and expand the species, curiosity drives us to learn and expand the mind. Knowledge is a tool of survival. We are built to be curious because in life you have to learn quick or die!

But hot damn! We get most of the curiosity beaten, trampled and squashed out of us as we grow up and go to training "school". Most schools treat kids like Bonsai trees: stifle the roots, shape with wires into the correct shape, and cut back unwanted growth.

I was lucky enough to live with my grandparents as a child and my grandfather John was a fine exemplar of curiosity. My grandmother Eileen called him a "nosey old so-and-so" as he peered out of the window at what the neighbors were doing, or hung over the fence asking probing questions about their lives and business.

But John was a curious man. A man who could turn his hand to any skill from building, carpentry, decorating, welding, motor mechanics, electrical maintenance, engineering to running bars and hotels, book keeping, legal correspondence, and awesome people skills. I never really fathomed the limits of my granddad's abilities and he was an awesome role model in many areas.

He told me: "Never be afraid to ask questions. If you want to get learn about anything, you've got to ask, otherwise how will you find out!"

On the practical level, that also meant being willing to try something. If you want to find out how to do something, just start doing it. "Make lots of mistakes," he said. "If you are willing to make lots of mistakes at the beginning, you'll learn what you need to know in the end!"

If your curiosity has gone comatose, the best way to kick-start it is to find a kid. Have one if necessary!! Kid's are curiosity on legs. They ask the most off-planet questions that will really stump you and force you to question your universe again!

The fundamental toolkit of journalists and children is comprised of who, what, where, why, when and how. Children ask those questions harder and faster than Larry King interviewing in quicksand.

'Why is the sky blue?'; "Why was I born?"; "What do stars twinkle?"; 'When are you going to die?'; 'Who is God?'; 'How come that man is homeless and we don't help him?'; 'Where do babies come from?"

They get all the good ones going. Rat-a-tat-tat it's like a questioning tommy gun on Valentine's day!

Now you take your average curious kid, and then think what Leonardo da Vinci was like as a kid. Here's someone who was equally advanced in all the 7 intelligences outlined by Howard Gardner, the Harvard Professor of Education. You can just imagine the effect on his teachers.

They were banging their heads against the walls trying to keep up with the awkward probing questions that Leonardo threw at them. Giorgio Vasari, the first ever Art Historian, related that Leonardo "caused continuous doubts for the master who taught him and often confounded him."

What about you? Can you ask confounding questions?

Take Rudyard Kipling's six honest serving men and apply them to the creative challenge areas in your life. Under each of the six, form as many questions as you can about the area you are focusing on. Do as many "what" questions as you can. Then do the same for the whys, whens, hows, wheres and whos! Try to ask the questions that have never been asked before.

You've got to challenge yourself to wake up and observe this world anew. We are fed a mind-numbing diet of sound bites that quash curiosity. Break out of that. Get curious about the world again. This awesome creation is so replete with mysteries and magical phenomena that we have yet to work out and understand. What part will you play in probing the universe for new understanding, and improved ways of living our lives?

Leonardo has been described as the man who "wouldn't take 'Yes' for an answer."

Don't you love that! That is ultimate curiosity! Pushing past the accepted answers to question-question-question!

Is this really the right way to do it? Could this be stifling orders? Would it be better if... ? Challenge what you know. Make it stand up to the test of truth. A little knowledge is a dangerous thing. Great

---

The child you have is God's revenge (gift!) against your ignorance.

"I keep six honest serving men, they taught me all I knew: their names are What and Why and When and How and Where and Who."

~ Rudyard Kipling

discoveries are walled in by incomplete knowledge. Take a sledge hammer to the text book tradition and blast through it. Fortunes are often found just the other side of the accepted way of doing things.

Look at life as a hunt for treasure. Everywhere you go there are clues to where the treasure is buried. But you've got to sift and probe, be alert and aware, watch and question everything. When you do that, you will find the treasure. I know it.

Curiosity Exercise:

I. Write down 100 questions. They can be anything from "How can I become rich?" to "Does the Universe have an edge and if so what is beyond it?" Just write down all the questions that come to mind, all the things that you would love to know the answers to. Don't stop until you've got 100.

Look through the questions and notice if any dominant themes emerge. Are there any areas of life that you seem most concerned with? Such as money, work, relationships, love, or health?

II. Pick your top 10 questions. The ones that seem the most important to you. You don't have to answer them right now. It's enough that you have organized them and know that they are important to you.

Use the "Top 10 questions" technique on any area of your life where you are looking for improvements. It'll focus you on what's really important in that area. And the see-sawing effect of different angled questions will hone your mind and produce the innovative ideas and insights that you need.

III. Ask your friends or family members to answer your questions:

- _____
- _____
- _____
- _____
- _____
- _____
- _____
- _____
- _____

Da Vinci Brain Bomb Number 2: TEST EVERYTHING

You learn from books such as this. But you learn nothing until you test present knowledge and experience it for yourself. Scientists constantly have to challenge accepted knowledge. Even when it comes from geniuses... We progress forwards by standing on the shoulders of giants, but sometimes you have to give those giants a good kick in the bollocks to make sure that they are still up to the job!

Knowledge is not a static thing. It actually pulses as it grows larger and larger. Knowledge is expanded by exceptional individuals, and contracts slightly when they die. Those unique people push through the accepted envelope of knowledge and discover more beyond that. They push the envelope to a new dimension. But that new dimension is never the limit of knowledge; it is only ever the currently accepted limit.

To discover the limits of accepted knowledge, you have to question it and test it in your own experience. Knowledge opens up as you focus upon a subject. Just as the Universe opens up as you focus upon it. We are creators after all... And we create new knowledge to the limits of our creativity.

While creativity involves imagination, testing definitely requires objectivity and the swift-kick-to-the-balls of reality!

The reality checks come in the form of our errors, mistakes and cock-ups. Love your failures, for they are the foundations on which new empires are built. Everybody knows about Edison and his 10,000 attempts to invent the light bulb. The 9,999 times he got it wrong gave him the feedback he needed to get it right on the 10,000th attempt.

We are biofeedback learning machines. We try. We fail. We learn. We adjust and try again. And again. And again.

And then we succeed.

Leonardo knew, based on his own experiments and experience, that most conventional wisdom is inherently flawed and limited. It was for this reason that he strongly resisted imitating anyone. This is a great clue for genius wanna-bes. Be yourself.

You were born to be the genius that YOU are - you are not here to be Einstein, Jim Carrey, Madonna, or Mother Theresa. You can certainly learn from other geniuses and sometimes it's highly beneficial to wear other people's heads (or walk in their moccasins), but YOU are the genius the world wants to see. Not another Elvis impersonator.

Think for yourself and question authority ... those are the watch words that Leonardo advised. Do you think that he was right to recommend that? Test it and see.

Da Vinci Brain Bomb Number 3: NURTURE YOUR SENSES

As mentioned earlier, Leonardo Da Vinci had amazing visual abilities - I mean, he really did have the eyes of a hawk! You may not be an artist, and your work may not call upon your eyesight and appreciation of light and color, but developing your sight is a skill that will benefit you in many ways.

Learning to really look at something is... a magical experience. When you observe something closely, and follow it moment by moment, you disengage from the stream of consciousness. A great stillness and profundity comes over you. The chattering mind drops away. By focusing on something, it is as though you are being brought into focus.

As you become still, a kind of tectonic movement occurs inside. You can almost sense invisible plates of ancient psychic energy shifting and opening in your mind. New awareness floods in. It's a powerful way to access your super mind.

The most powerful response occurs when you observe yourself that closely. It is then that you experience what the late philosopher Krishnamurti described simply as an "otherness". And that is a very beautiful experience for you to have.

Cultivating your senses ties in with testing things in your own experience. I said previously that knowledge expands as you focus on a subject. Well, the primary vehicles for learning about anything are our senses. If you can develop your ability to really look at something ... you will see things that most people miss. That is a genius trait.

Similarly, if you can learn to really listen to the sounds of people's voices, the way in which they say things, you will deduce things that others miss. Listen to music and penetrate into it. Let the sounds fill you and become you. Become saturated by sounds and let them enter you like teachers. Pay attention to every nuance, every lilt of a melody, the rises and falls in timbre, pitch and meaning.

If you are able, listen to birdsong ... let it fill you. Become empty and just let the sound be there fully. There are few things that will make your heart soar as standing in a stream of song from a blackbird. One fine summer's day, I was cycling through the countryside. I saw a black bird perched in the hedge. I turned to look at it as I free-wheeled by and was hit full force by its song. It went straight into my heart and laid down a marker in that moment. A marker which said, I'm fully alive and life is joyous and wonderful right this instant.

I like to think that the work we are doing here is about learning to lay down a lot more of those kind of markers. Moments of sheer intensity and beauty. You will get those as you develop your awareness, as you look, listen, feel, taste, smell and live with full present-moment intensity.

Leonardo, across the centuries, admonishes us to NOT be like the average human who "looks without seeing, listens without hearing, touches without feeling, eats without tasting, moves without physical awareness, inhales without awareness of odor or fragrance, and talks without thinking."

If life slides by in a blur of insignificance, that is stupid. If you capture moments and make them special, that is smart.

Once gone, gone forever. Savor your quota of time.

Sensitivity Exercises:

For Sight:
Get some colored pencils. Do some Mandalay and patterns. Notice which colors work together. Become aware of colors in your environment. Which ones go together? What are your favorite colors?
Look up into the sky at least once a day and towards the far horizon.
Describe a room or a scene as accurately as possible.
Practice doodling and drawing. Sketch people's faces.
Look for the subtle clues to people's moods and feelings reflected in their eyes and skin.
Become more aware of great photography, artwork and paintings. What's great about them?
Watch movies as though you were the cameraman. What do you appreciate about the different angles, lighting, and presentation in each scene?

Modes of Thinking

If you have any kind of visual impairment that can be treated ... duh, get it treated!

Consider what it would be like to be blind. Give yourself the "contrast" of thinking how blessed you are in being able to see. Appreciation and gratitude sharpen the senses wonderfully. Wear a blindfold for an hour and then slowly remove it and notice the effects.

For Hearing:

Get some earplugs! Put them in for a few minutes a day. Refresh your ears.

Pause in the midst of your daily life and just listen. Just become aware of all the different sounds that you can hear. Sort through the melee of sound in the city to identify as many unique sounds as you can.

Really sit down with headphones and listen to your favorite songs. Don't sing along. Just listen. Try to hear the sounds in the track as purely as possible. Let them be. Let them emerge as they wish to and you just follow along.

Expand your musical tastes. Listen to classical music. If you've never listened to it before... keep going until you find a piece that you respond to. It takes a mental shift if you've lived till now on rock and roll, hip hop, rap or country music. And for all you classic buffs, sample the delights of modern music and get jaggy with the best of MTV. And don't forget there is a whole planet of different cultural music to explore. All part of the riches in your abundant universe, so do take time to enjoy them. That's what you are here for!

Go out into nature. Listen. Let it teach you.

For Touch:

Interrupt the unconscious movement of your day. Become aware of the sensations of your body. Feel the clothes on your skin, feel the texture and hardness of the chair you are sitting on. Feel the movement of the air through your nostrils and around you.

Go into a clothes shop and feel the clothes. If you were buying on touch alone, what outfit would you choose?

When you hug someone, really feel what it is like to be body to body. Feel the pressure of your hands on their back and vice versa and the emotional warmth conveyed.

Give massages and get massages. Oh sheer bliss!

Enjoy textures... stone, wood, marble, silk, skin.

For Feeling:

When you go into a building, feel the atmosphere. How does it feel?

Before you join a group or a meeting, send your feelings out (mentally) to that situation. What do you sense about it.

Learn to play your feelings like a keyboard. You can create emotions as readily as you choose. Act happy and you are happy. Act sad and you are sad. Decide to feel what you want to feel and you will feel it.

Emotions can be intensified or lessened. Play with increasing your sense of excitement, of joy, of bliss. Breathe deep and powerfully into your good feelings and imagine turning up the intensity dial. Bigger! Better! More and More Pleasure!

When you want something, feel what it would be like to have it. Intensify that feeling. Mix it with gratitude. Let the pleasure live in you. Keep at it and you will get what you want in reality too.

For Taste:

Fast for a few hours. When you are good and hungry, take a raison. Look at it in your hand and then slowly put it in your mouth and close your eyes. Do everything super slow. Notice everything as it hits your tongue. Don't chew it yet. See how long you can go just tasting... your mouth should water with anticipation as you continue to roll it on your tongue, sucking and tasting the sweetness of that raison. When you start to chew it be aware of everything that you do.

Buy as many different fruits as you can find ... have a fruit feast one Sunday morning ... let each wonderful fresh fruit work its magic on your tongue.

If you drink alcohol, learn about wine tasting and practice it yourself. Learn the terms and invent your own too. Describe what you taste in the wine in terms of other things you have experienced.

Avoid junk food like the plague.

Use herbs and spices and intrigue your taste buds!

Taste your lover all over!

For Smell:
Oh the sweetness of roses. Stand and smell the roses and get high on life.
Notice how smells trigger memories.
Learn to recognize people by their scent. This doesn't mean you have to go round sniffing your pal's ass. Just the general aroma and perhaps the perfume or cologne they wear!
Spend a minute smelling your breakfast, lunch, dinner before you eat it. That act a lone will trigger all kinds of beneficial biological responses!
Aromatherapy - get some oils. Sandalwood is my personal favorite. And rose. What do you like?

Mixing Your Senses:
Play with your senses. What color would the smell of apple pie be? If ruby red was a sound, what sound would it be? What would the drone of a builder's drill taste like? What visual image would represent the way you feel when you eat pizza? What does bliss smell like? How bright is the feeling of horniness? What do you hear when you are touching silk? If blue could talk, what sort of voice would it have?
Learn to describe one sense in terms of the others. This is called Synesthesia.
Da Vinci Brain Bomb Number 4: LOVE MYSTERY, PARADOX & AMBIGUITY
Einstein introduced us to the astounding idea that everything is relative. There is no absolute Truth that we have been able to nail to the wall. There is only true for now, or true under certain specific circumstances, or true according to whom is watching.

If you are an explorer, as I know you are, you will have been faced with paradox and ambiguity throughout your life. This is most obvious for any of you exploring religious or spiritual ideas as you quest for the Truth. You will find yourself in the dichotomy of sustaining a perception of yourself as a universal being with causal powers and as an all too human animal, a biological disposable organism being inhabited by Life and used to further the gene pool.

You can experience yourself as the most magnificent creation at one moment and a mere particle of cosmic dust at the next. What a kicker!

Your Universe Awaits…

Life is full of mystery. And meaning is relative to where our attention and focus is put. Quantum Theorists are creating the universe in the image of their own ideas and theories. And then finding that the universe mutates to fit the next theory. In a spiral of expanding knowledge, it seems we can only ever hope for a more inclusive "model" of reality. Never the real thing.

And yet the next big idea always feels or seems like the real thing… until someone pushes the envelope a bit further and says, "But guys…" at which point all the black hats groan and start building the pyre around the stake!

Leonardo embraced mystery. He loved puzzles, riddles and visual paradoxes. He developed special painting techniques, chemical processes, to imbue his paintings with a hazy, mysterious quality suggestive of many layers of meaning that Life holds.

Whaddya Mean?

Develop your appreciation of irony by looking for opposite meanings in people's statements and actions. This is startlingly obvious in politics with all its bloated posturing and platitude mongering. Mr Sleazy Politician has his picture taken with a few babies and speaks in passionate, concerned tones about how he will help children when he is voted into office. You hear and see his outer message, but can you hear the real message?

The entertainment industry is full of peacocks fanning their tails and wanting to buff their images to dazzling saint-like dimensions. They say all the right words, and make the right faces. But you can hear the real message, can't you? "Love me! Like me! Buy my records! See my movie! Don't let me fall from grace!"

The Shadow Messages
Look for the shadow message behind every circumstance and message. We can only recognize something by contrast with its opposite. And like Siamese twins light and dark, good and evil, black and white, up and down, left and right are always joined at the hip. There is always a relationship and you get to interpret that relationship along a very broad spectrum.

Listen to what people say to you. Notice what you understand them to mean by their statements. Then ask yourself, "What else could they have meant? Why did they say that? What is going on inside them really? What do they want from me? Are they conscious of what they are saying to me? Are they saying this with awareness or are they mouthing something parrot fashion?"

Modes of Thinking

Observe the way people respond to what you say. Ask yourself, "Have I made my true meaning clear? Does he really understand what I intended to say? What could he have misunderstood about what I said? How could I say that differently? Do I really mean what I said? What's a better way of saying that?" In NLP, there is a presupposition that states: The meaning of your communication is the response you get. That means that the responsibility of communicating something so that people understand it is yours alone.

I say, I say, I say

Ambiguity in language is so vast. You say: I sat on a chair. That seems clear enough, doesn't it? But did you sit upright on the edge of the chair? Did you slouch at the back of the chair? Did you perch on the arm of the chair? Did you sprawl sideways and hang your legs off the side? Did you sit because you were tired? Or because you were told to? Or because you fainted and landed on the chair? Was the chair made of wood? Metal? Baked beans glued together with horse hoof glue? What color was the chair? How did it feel? Was it soft, hard, scratchy, shiny, smelly? Was it on the floor? Stuck to a wall? In a room? At the top of a mountain? On the dark side of the moon? What do you mean by chair? Could you possibly mean a member of a family called Chair? Little Jenny Chair? When you say "I" do you really mean you, yourself, or are you referring to someone or something else that you are calling "I"?

Language is full of layers of meaning. The map is not the territory. We have a limited number of words to describe an unlimited number of experiences. So we ascribe words to generalized and universalized meanings. And somehow we generally muddle by, but the confusion we cause each other is obvious in the society we live in. You only have to look at your family life!

Absolutely, I disagree…

Generalizing is a real snake in the grass and one to watch cause it keeps biting you on the ass! Look at when you use absolutes such as, "always", "never", "totally", "must" and "never". These types of words limit your world, and demonstrate an intolerance for ambiguity.

Beware of generalizing negative feelings with absolutes: "I always get depressed when the skies are grey!"… No actually you don't. You may have some moments when you are depressed. But as they point out in the Japanese therapy called Naikan, you only ever experience one moment at a time right now. And our feelings change moment by moment. You cannot have an endless succession of depressed moments. You have a rich variety of feelings throughout any particular day, some of which may be moments of feeling depressed. But you may also feel moments of amusement, anger, joy, fascination, dreaminess, intensity, shock, fun, wonder, love, boredom, hate, comfort, enjoyment and more on the great spectrum of emotions.

Curiosity k-k-konfounded the cat!

Like Leonardo, as you explore life and expand your knowledge, you will be equally confounded, confused, mystified and befuddled by Life. As a great mind once said, "The more I know, the more I realize that I don't know."

You will be constantly faced by situations in which there is no right answer. You will see that complete opposite answers are equally true. And you must be BIG ENOUGH and ballsy enough to handle that!

The mind is a playground for the genius that you are. It's a wild forest full of adventures in which you will lose yourself many times. Just know that you are the adventurer. That it is here for you to play in. And do play with it. Have fun and laugh a lot – it's the best response to confusion and challenging times. One of the key defining characteristics of geniuses is their sense of humor. How can you not laugh when Life is so completely twisted!

Dive into the whirlpool – feel the fizz of confusion!

Life is one big Jacuzzi with multiple meanings bubbling together. Get in there and enjoy the fizz. Soak it up! Give yourself a context to enjoy life. Give yourself a whole armory of contexts with which to enjoy life. Infinite possibilities! What greater freedom than that?

Here's some totally turned-on tips and ideas to help you play with paradox, mystery and I ambiguity!

1. Buy your very favorite food (e.g. strawberry ice-cream) and buy the food that you hate (eg. tuna chunks)! Eat some of the food that you hate and really hate it. Now eat some of the food that you love – oh God, how good does that taste now?! Take a break for a minute. Now, eat some of the food that you hate as though you love it. Really relish every sensation of that food. What can you love about it? Let's say you hate the taste of tuna. Put a spoonful of tuna in your mouth and love that fishy taste like you are a cat. Imagine this is the greatest treat in the world. Imagine you are starving. Try fasting for a few days and then see how good that tuna starts to look. What if Regis came along and offered you a million dollars just to eat and enjoy a mouthful of tuna? What if your child was ill and you could save her life by

eating a spoonful of tuna? What if, every time you ate tuna you got incredibly aroused and had the most mind-blowing, knee-knocking orgasm? Would you like tuna then? What about that strawberry ice cream that you love so much? What if I told you that a recent study demonstrated that strawberry ice cream was inhabited by 30 different parasites? Still taste as good? There is an awful lot of pus in milk, isn't there? What if I force feed you strawberry ice cream until you are sick, would you want another helping? Enjoyment is context dependent. That context includes environment, knowledge, past experiences, social consensus, conditions of punishment or reward and anything else you care to come up with!

2. Who do you fancy? Does Britney Spears get you hard as the Rock of Gibraltar? Do you go all of a quiver when Ben Affleck moseys onto the screen? Who do you think is hot, sexy, beautiful or handsome? Really study that person and others like him or her. What is it about them that makes them sexy, handsome or incredibly pretty? Search for the elusive quality of beauty. Then look at the dawgs! Who do you detest? Who makes your stomach turn? Who repulses you? Who do you think is uglier than your butt-hole spitting excrement? Really look at those people. Entertain them in your consciousness, so that you can really observe them as they are. Leonardo da Vinci used to throw special parties for the ugliest, most deformed and most hideous people that he could find. He would feed them and tank them up with alcohol and then entertain them with joke after joke. Their deformed faces would crease with laughter becoming even more hideous in the candlelight. Leonardo would study their faces with incredible interest, and when they left he would stay up all night sketching their faces. Without ugliness we wouldn't know what beauty was. Without beauty we wouldn't know what ugliness is. To a baby, an ugly mother is beautiful and fascinating. To a blind person, perhaps, a man's deformed face is interesting and characterful. Did you ever notice how ugly some supermodels can look when they wear that stoney, superbitch look? Did you ever notice how beautiful an ugly person looks when they look lovingly at their child?

3. To be finished ... a very Da Vincian trait! If you can't wait to learn more about Leonardo's amazing genius techniques, I suggest you run screaming with hysterical delight to your nearest bookstore and purchase a copy of "How To think Like Leonardo Da Vinci" by Michael Gelb. It is superb.

LOGICAL THINKING

Thinking logically and identifying reasoning fallacies in one's own and in others' thinking is the heart of critical thinking.

Reasoning

Reasoning is a process by which we use the knowledge we have to draw conclusions or infer something new about the domain of interest.

There are a number of different types of reasoning:

- deductive,
- inductive, and
- abductive.

We use each of these types of reasoning in everyday life, but they differ in significant ways.

15. DEDUCTIVE THINKING

Deductive reasoning *derives the logically necessary conclusion from the given premises*. Deductive thinking is the kind of reasoning that *begins with two or more premises* and *derives a conclusion* that *must follow from those premises*. The basic form of deductive thinking is the syllogism. An example of a syllogism follows:

All squares have four sides.
This figure is a square.
Therefore, this figure has four sides.

Usually our thinking is not as formal as this but takes on a shorter form: "Because a square has four sides and this figure has also four sides, it is a square." To understand the logic behind our shortened thought, we need to understand the structure that supports it: the syllogism. A syllogism is a three-step form of reasoning which has two premises and a conclusion. (Premises are statements that serve as the basis or ground of a conclusion.) Not all syllogisms are alike. We will look at three types: the categorical, the hypothetical, and the disjunctive (Kirby,1999).

Categorical Syllogisms

The *classic example* of a categorical syllogism comes from the philosopher Socrates. Updated for gender, it goes as follows:

MAJOR	- All human beings are mortal.
MINOR	- Ann is human being.
CONCLUSION	- Therefore, Ann is mortal.

We can see that *categorical syllogisms* categorize. In the example above "human beings" are put in the "mortal" category. "Ann" is the "human being" category. And in the last statement "Ann" is in the "mortal" category. If the first line of the syllogism above read, "some human beings are mortal," then only some human beings would be in the "mortal" category.

A categorical syllogism is a form of **argument that contains statements** (called *categorical propositions*) that either **affirm or deny** that a *subject is a member of a certain class* (category) or *has a certain property*. For example, "Toby is a cat" is a categorical statement because it affirms that Toby (the subject) is a member of a class of animals called "cats" (Kirby, 1999).

"Toby is brown" affirms that Toby has a property of brownness. Similarly, "Toby is not a cat" and "Toby is not brown" are categorical statements because they deny that Toby has the property of brownness and that Toby belongs to a class of animals called "cats." All valid syllogisms must have at least one affirmative premise.

In the *standard form* of a categorical syllogism, the *major premise* always appears first. It contains the *"major" term* (in this case "mortal"), which is *the term that appears as the predicate in the conclusion*:

MAJOR	- All human beings are mortal.
MINOR	- Ann is a human being.
CONCLUSION	- Therefore, Ann is mortal.

What is a predicate? It is simply *the property* or class being assigned to the subject in the last line. In our example above, *the subject* in the last line is Ann, and the property of Ann is that she is "mortal." If a syllogism concluded with the words "Robert is intelligent," then *"intelligent"* would be *the predicate* because in this sentence it is the property of the subject, "Robert." "Intelligent" is also the major term and would appear in the first (or major) premise:

MAJOR	- Our faculty are intelligent.
MINOR	- Kerry is one of our faculty.
CONCLUSION	- Therefore, Kerry is intelligent.

Let's look at the other parts of the syllogism and see how they combine to form a valid argument. The minor premise introduces the minor term (in our examples, "Ann" and "Kerry").

MAJOR	- All human beings are mortal.
MINOR	- Ann is a human being.
CONCLUSION	- Therefore, Ann is mortal.

MAJOR	- Our faculty are intelligent.
MINOR	- Kerry is one of our faculty.
CONCLUSION	- Therefore, Kerry is intelligent.

CHAPTER 7

The *minor premise* makes a *connection* between the *minor term* and the *major term*. It makes this connection through the "middle term," which then disappears in the conclusion:

MAJOR	- All human beings are mortal.
MINOR	- Ann is a human being.
CONCLUSION	- Therefore, Ann is mortal.

MAJOR	- Our faculty are intelligent.
MINOR	- Kerry is one of our faculty.
CONCLUSION	- Therefore, Kerry is intelligent.

This diagram below summarizes the parts of the syllogism discussed in this section.

```
                        (middle term)
                    does not appear in conclusion

MAJOR               - All human beings are mortal.
                                              (major term)
                                   appears as predicate in conclusion
                    (minor term)
                  is subject in conclusion

MINOR               - Ann is human being.
                        (middle term)
                    does not appear in conclusion


CONCLUSION          - Therefore, Ann is mortal.
                              (subject)  (predicate)
```

Three Kinds of Propositions

You may have noticed by now that some of the premises refer to *all members* of a class, as in "All humans are mortal." These kinds of propositions are called *universal propositions*. They may also take the obverse form, "No humans are immortal" or simply "Humans are mortal," when the statement implies "all humans." All syllogisms must have at least one universal premise. The syllogisms above have only one universal premise, but two universals are also allowed:

All whales are mammals.
All mammals breathe by means of lungs.
Therefore: all whales breathe by means of lungs.

It is important to note that in modern logic, universal propositions do not imply that the subject actually exists – only that if the subject exists, it would have the characteristics of the predicate. Thus, "All unicorns are white" does not imply that unicorns exist, but only that if they do, they would be white. Of course, in our everyday use of logic, we usually know that at least one member of the subject exists, as in "All faculty are human beings."

The other two kinds of propositions are particular and singular. *Particular propositions* refer to *some members* of a class, as in "Some faculties are female." In logic, some means "at least one."

Four Figures

There are *four possible variations*, or figures, of the *categorical syllogism*. The figure depends on the placements of the major, minor, and middle terms:

Figure

#1	#2	#3	#4
M P	P M	M P	P M
S M	S M	M S	M S
S P	S P	S P	S P

Validity of Categorical Syllogism

By valid we mean that the argument, which is the reasoning from premises to a conclusion, is accurate. Argument can be valid or invalid, but not true or false (only premises and conclusions are true or false). An argument can be valid even if it contains false premises and a false conclusion. Conversely, it is possible to have an invalid argument with true premises and a true conclusion.

The goal of a good thinker is to develop syllogisms that have both true premises and validity. When we have a valid syllogism with true premises we have what is called a sound argument. In sound arguments the conclusion must be true – and therein lies the beauty and usefulness of the syllogism (Kirby, 1999).

Reasoning in Everyday Life

We interpret events, information, data, and arguments all the time. When we wake up in the morning and look to see what time it is, we interpret the numbers on the clock in order to tell whether it's time to get up. As we walk, we interpret the speed of an approaching car in order to decide whether the driver is going to stop at a crosswalk and allow us to cross the street. When we read an article or essay, we try to determine what information we get from it. As we perform each of these tasks, our interpretation of these texts is often accompanied by another important activity. In each case, we have to decide between two or more possible actions. When we wake up, we have to decide either to get up and go to work or go back to sleep. As we look at approaching car, we have to decide whether we should start to cross the street or wait until the car stops or drives by. Each of these decisions involves weighing the possibilities and then deciding which one is in our best interest.

The decision-making process requires us to make an informal argument, a case for one action or another based on the available evidence. If we would rather stay in bed or go to class. Several factors might influence our decision. The instructor's attendance policy, our attitude to the subject taught, our current average in the class, the number of times we have missed class before, the weather, and our state of health might all be factors that help us decide.

While we are present with such informal situations all the time, we are also often required to present our decision-making process to others on a more formal level. For example, let's say that, after waking late with a cold on a rainy day, you decide not go to work and when you return a couple of days later you find out that your boss refused to pay you for those days. Now you have to try to persuade your boss to pay your absence. The process that you use to convince this boss is similar to the one you used to decide to stay in bed.

This section discusses the basic elements in making the kinds of argument.

The Rules of Validity

Negation

1. No valid syllogism can have two negative premises.

2. If the conclusion is negative at least one premise must be negative and vice versa.

Distribution

3. The middle term in at least one premise must be distributed.

4. If a term is distributed in the conclusion it must be distributed in the premise in which it occurs.

Particularity

5. If the conclusion is particular at least one premise must be particular.

Argument 101

At most fundamental level, an argument is a claim supported by one or more reasons. By "claim" we mean a statement that you believe to be true but whose validity might be questioned by others. For example, if you missed a couple of days, you might argue that you should be paid. In this case, your claim would be:

I should be paid.

You believe that this statement is true, but your boss might not. However, a claim by itself is not an argument. To be an argument, you also need at least one reason why your boss should also believe this claim. In this case, your reason might be:

I was sick and unable to come to work.

Taken together, these two sentences compose a basic argument:

I should be paid.
I was sick and unable to come to work.

Reasons

After you check to make sure that an argument's claim is debatable, it is important to make sure that it also has at least one logical reason to support its validity. Many factors influence whether a reason offers valid support for the argument's claim. These include the reason's logical connection to the claim and the rhetorical situation in which the argument is being made.

Checking the Connections

Common sense tells us that every claim must have some reason to support it and that every reason must have some legitimate connection to that claim. For example, the following argument immediately evokes our opposition:

I should be paid because I'm smart.

This argument immediately raises the question of what being smart has to do with being allowed to be paid. It might also lead the boss to ask, "If you're so smart, why didn't you make it to work?" In this case, being smart does not rationally connect to being allowed to be paid. One might as well say that I should be allowed to be paid because I'm pretty or because I'm a man. These are all biological factors that have nothing to do with whether the boss should allow you to be paid.

Rhetorical Situation

The second factor that influences whether a reason adequately supports a claim is the rhetorical situation in which the argument is made. This rhetorical situation is the contextual situation surrounding the argument. Every argument is made within some rhetorical situation, sometimes it's classroom, at other times it might be a job situation or a conversation with your parents or friends. To support your claim, you must always choose reasons that make sense in the particular situation in which your argument is being made. For example, going back to the instance where an employee is arguing to be allowed to be paid, which of the following argument is more likely to convince that employee's boss?

I should be paid because having the flu prevented me from coming to work.

I should be paid because having hangover prevented me from coming to work.

The Enthymeme

People use categorical syllogisms all the time, but often they are in a shortened form called an enthymeme.
While using common sense logic is a good first step in making sure that an argument "works," the next step is to see if the claim and reason make logical sense more formally. One way to check the logic of an argument is to evaluate it as an enthymeme.
An enthymeme is a formal structure that has been taken from classical Greek philosophers and rhetoricians to expose how p reason with language; it is based on a syllogism. An enthymeme is a syllogism with an implied premise or conclusion, one that is not explicitly stated.

Consider the following: "I am an immigrant, so I'll never get this job." We have one premise (I am an immigrant) and one conclusion (I'll never get this job). The missing premise is "No immigrant will get this job." The implied syllogism looks like this:

> No immigrant will be a person who will get this job.
> I am an immigrant.
> Therefore, I am not a person who will get this job.

When enthymemes and their missing premise are laid out in a formal syllogism, we can more clearly see any thinking errors that may be occurring.

Using enthymemes is common. And if they are stated in the order of premise and then conclusion, the implied syllogism is not difficult to see. But in colloquial speech our premises are often hidden, and we sometimes state conclusion first, and then we state our premise or premises. This can make the underlying syllogism more difficult to find.

Ethos, Pathos, and Logos

Because arguments depend on probable rather than factual proof, the thinker's reputation and credibility also influence the audience's acceptance of his or her claim. Likewise, because one's audience changes in different rhetorical situations, writers often appeal to one audience differently than they might appeal to another one. Classical Greek writers had names for each of these appeals: logos, ethos, and pathos.

Philosophers such as Aristotle used the word logos to describe arguments that depended on logical proof to sway their audience. Such proof might take the form of a syllogism or an enthymeme. These arguments are grounded in "facts," evidence that is used to convince the audience of the claim's probable truth.

But logic alone is not always convincing. For example, let's say that the student who missed class and quiz because he was ill has already missed 5 other class meetings due to "illness." All of these "illnesses" seem to have struck him only on Fridays. At some point teacher is likely to begin to suspect that truthfulness of his excuse. At this point, the student's credibility is affecting the persuasiveness of his argument.

Let's say that another student, who has never missed class and who has an A average, misses the same quiz. Because she has earned a reputation for being a good student, the teacher might allow her to make up the same quiz.

This use of reputation and credibility to affect the outcome of an argument is called ethos.

The third factor that might influence the effectiveness of an argument is the use of emotion (pathos) to appeal to an audience. For example, if a student approaches his teacher to ask to make up some work and begins crying in the middle of his request, whether he intends it or not, his crying appeals to the instructor's emotions. Most arguments are strengthened by keeping all three of these factors in mind.

Hypothetical Syllogisms and Hypothetical (Scientific) Reasoning

Much of our thinking in everyday life is hypothetical (Kirby, 1999). This kind of thinking has the "if-then" form. The pure hypothetical syllogism is one in which the two premises and the conclusion are hypothetical, or conditional. They have the form of "if-then" statements. The "if" statement is called the antecedent, and the "then" statement is called the consequent:

> If you play with fire, you will get burned.
> You played with fire.
> You got burned

The hypothetical syllogism has the following form:

> If P, then Q
> P
> Q

CHAPTER 7

Hypothetical reasoning is used most explicitly in philosophical and scientific inquiry. Every scientific theory can be viewed as a hypothesis for unifying and rationalizing events in nature. The Ptolemic and Copernican theories about the sun and planets, Einstein's theory of relativity, Darwin's theory of evolution are all hypotheses for making sense of the data of observation. The problem for the scientist is that the underlying structure of nature is hidden from view, and the data of observation by themselves are not sufficient to reveal this structure. In response, the scientist constructs hypothesis that provide ways of conceptualizing the data and that suggest specific questions to be answered through the design of controlled experiments (Hurley, 2000).

Every philosophical system can be viewed as a grand hypothesis for interpreting the content of experience. Plato's theory of forms, Aristotle's theory of substance, Leibniz's monads, Kant's theory about the mind, Marx's theory of alienation, are all hypotheses aimed at illuminating various aspects of experience. Just as the structure of nature is hidden from the scientist, the meaning of experience is hidden from the philosopher, and ordinary common sense will not provide the answer. In response, the philosopher constructs hypothesis that can be used to shed light on the content of experience and to provide suggestions for further analysis.

Whether it is applied in philosophy, science, or ordinary life, the hypothetical method involves four basic stages:
1. Occurrence of a problem;
2. Formulating a hypothesis;
3. Drawing implications from the hypothesis;
4. Testing the implications.

These four stages may be illustrated through the two scientific discoveries.

1. In 1781 the planet Uranus was discovered by William Herschel, but the production of a table giving the motion of the new planet had to wait until the gravitational interaction between Uranus, Jupiter, and Saturn had been worked out mathematically. The latter task was accomplished by Pierre Laplace in his Mechanique Celeste, and in 1820 Alexis Bouvard used this work to construct tables for all three planets. These tables predicted the orbital motions of Jupiter and Saturn very accurately, but within a few years Uranus was found to have deviated from its predicted path. A problem thus emerged: why did the tables work for Jupiter and Saturn but not for Uranus?

In response to this problem a number of astronomers entertained the hypothesis that an eighth planet existed beyond the orbit of Uranus and that the gravitational interaction between these two planets caused Uranus to deviate from its predicted position. It was not until 1843, however, that John Couch Adams, a recent graduate of Cambridge, undertook the task of working out the mathematical implications of this hypothesis. After two years' work Adams produced a table of motions and orbital elements that predicted the location of the hypothetical planet, and his computations were so accurate that if anyone with a telescope had bothered to look, they would have found the new planet within two degrees of its predicted position.

2. The theory of spontaneous generation holds that living beings arise spontaneously from lifeless matter. The roots of the theory extend into ancient times. Aristotle held that worms, the larvae of bees and wasps, ticks, fireflies, and other insects developed continually from the morning dew and from dry wood and hair.

The first systemic effort to abolish the belief in spontaneous generation was made by the Italian physician Francesco Redi. In response to the commonly held idea that worms were spontaneously generated in rotting meat, Redi hypothesized that the worms were caused by flies. An immediate implication was that if flies were kept away from the meat, the worms would not develop. To test this hypothesis Redi cut up a piece of meat and put part of it in sealed glass flasks and the other part in flasks open to the air. Flies were attracted to the open flasks, and in a short time worms appeared; but no worms developed in the flasks that were sealed.

When Redi published his findings in 1668, they had an immediate impact on the theory of spontaneous generation.

By middle of the nineteenth century the theory had received considerable refinement. It was thought that spontaneous generation resulted from the direct action of oxygen on lifeless organic nutrients.

One of the defenders of spontaneous generation at that time was John Needham. He conducted an experiment in which flagons containing oxygen and a vegetable solution were buried in hot coals. The coals would have been expected to kill any life in the solution, but several days later the flagons were opened and the contents were found to be alive with microbes. Needham concluded that the oxygen acting alone on the nutrient solution caused the generation of the microbes.

To settle the issue once and for all, the French Academy of Science offered a prize for an experimental endeavor that would shed light on the question of spontaneous generation.

Louise Pasteur adopted hypothesis that life forms are carried by dust particles in the air. To test this hypothesis Pasteur took a wad of cotton and drew air through it, trapping dust particles in the fibers.

208

Then he washed the cotton in a mixture of alcohol and examined drops of the fluid under a microscope. He discovered microbes in the fluid.

Pasteur prepared a nutrient solution and boiled it in a narrow-necked flask. As the solution boiled, the air in the neck of the flask was forced out by water vapor, and as it cooled the water vapor was slowly replaced by sterilized air drawn through a heated platinum tube. The neck of the flask was then closed off with a flame and blowpipe. The contents of the flask thus consisted of a sterilized nutrient solution and unpolluted sterilized air – all that was supposedly needed for the production of life. With the passage of time, however, no life developed in the flask. This experiment posed a serious threat to the theory of spontaneous generation.

Pasteur now posed the hypothesis that sterile nutrient solutions exposed to the air normally developed life forms precisely because these forms were deposited by dust particles. To test this third hypothesis Pasteur reopened the flask containing the nutrient solution, and, using a special arrangement of tubes that ensured that only sterilized air would contact the solution, he deposited a piece of cotton in which dust particles had been trapped. The flask was then resealed, and in due course microbes developed in the solution. This experiment proved not only that dust particles were responsible for the life but that the "vegetative force" of the nutrient solution had not been destroyed by boiling.

Pasteur anticipated one further objection from the proponents of spontaneous generation: Perhaps the capacity of oxygen to generate life was destroyed by drawing it through a heated tube. To dispel any such notions Pasteur devised yet another experiment. He boiled a nutrient solution in a flask with a long, narrow gooseneck. As the solution boiled, the air was forced out, and as it cooled, the air returned very slowly through the long neck, trapping the dust particles on the moist inside surface. No microbes developed in the solution. Then, after a prolonged wait, Pasteur sealed the flask and shook it vigorously, dislodging the particles that had settled in the neck. In a short time the solution was alive with microbes.

When Pasteur reported these experiments to the Academy of Science in 1860, he was awarded the prize that had been offered a year earlier. The experiments dealt a mortal blow to the theory of spontaneous generation.

The Proof of Hypotheses

The examples of **hypothetical reasoning** in science that we have investigated illustrate the use of two different kinds of hypotheses. The hypothesis involved in the discovery of Neptune is called empirical hypothesis, and that relating to spontaneous generation is called theoretical hypothesis.

Empirical hypothesis concerns the production of some thing or the occurrence of some event that can be observed. When Neptune was finally sighted through the telescope, it had been observed.

Theoretical hypothesis, on the other hand, concerns how something should be conceptualized. When Needham observed life emerging in a sterile nutrient solution, he conceived it as being spontaneously generated by the action of oxygen. But when Pasteur observed it, he conceived it as being implanted there by dust particles in the air.

The ***distinction between empirical and theoretical hypotheses*** has certain difficulties, which we will turn to shortly, but it sheds some light on the problem of the verification or confirmation of hypotheses.

The Tentative Acceptance of Hypotheses

A certain amount of time is required for a hypothesis to be proved or disproved. The hypothesis relating to the discovery of Neptune required more than a year to prove. Theoretical hypotheses in science often take much longer, and theoretical hypotheses in philosophy may never be confirmed to the satisfaction of the majority of philosophers. During the period that intervenes between the proposal of a hypothesis and its proof, confirmation, or disproof the question arises as to its tentative acceptability. Four criteria that bear upon this question are:

1. Adequacy;
2. Internal coherence;
3. External consistency;
4. Fruitfulness.

A hypothesis is adequate to the extent that it fits the facts it is intended to unify or explain. A hypothesis is said to "fit" the facts when each fact can be interpreted as an instance of some idea or term

---

Empirical hypotheses are for all practical purposes proved when the thing or event hypothesized is observed. Today practically all of us would agree that the hypothesis relating to Neptune has been established. Theoretical hypotheses, on the other hand, are never proved but are only confirmed to varying degree. The greater the number of implications that are found to be correct, the more certain we can be of the hypothesis. If an implications that are found to be incorrect, however, a theoretical hypothesis can be disproved. For example, if it should happen some day that life is produced in a test tube from inorganic materials, Pasteur's hypothesis that life comes only from life might be considered to be disproved.

CHAPTER 7

in the hypothesis. For example, before the Neptune hypothesis was confirmed, every fluctuation in the position of Uranus could be interpreted as an instance of gravitational interaction with an unknown planet.

A hypothesis is inadequate to the extent that facts exist that the hypothesis cannot account for. The principle that life is generated by the direct action of oxygen on nutrient solutions was inadequate to account for the fact that life would not develop in Pasteur's flask containing a sterilized nutrient solution and sterilized oxygen.

In scientific hypotheses a second kind of adequacy is the accuracy with which a hypothesis accounts for the data. If one hypothesis accounts for a set of data with greater accuracy than another, than that hypothesis is more adequate than the other. For example, Einstein's theory of relativity accounted for the precise time of certain eclipses with greater accuracy than Newton's theory. For these reasons Einstein's theory was more adequate than the competing theory.

A hypothesis is internally coherent to the extent that its component ideas are rationally interconnected. The purpose of a hypothesis is to unify and interconnect a set of data and by so doing to explain the data, Obviously, if the hypothesis itself is not internally connected, there is no way that it can interconnect the data. After the mathematical details of the Neptune hypothesis had been worked out by Adams and Leverrier, it exhibited a great deal of internal coherence. The hypothesis showed how all the fluctuations in the position of Uranus could be rationally linked in terms of the gravitational interaction of an eighth planet.

An example of incoherence in science is provided by the theoretical interpretation of light, electricity, and magnetism that prevailed during the first half of the nineteenth century. During that period each of these phenomena was understood separately, but the interconnections between them were unknown. Toward the end of the century the English physicist James Clerk Maxwell showed how these three phenomena were interconnected in terms of his theory of the electromagnetic field. Maxwell's theory was thus more coherent than the ones that preceded it.

A hypothesis is externally consistent when it does not disagree with other, well-confirmed hypothesis. Adams's and Leverrier's hypothesis of an eighth planet was perfectly consistent with the nineteenth-century theory of the solar system, and it was rendered even more attractive by the fact that the seventh planet, Uranus, had been discovered only a few years earlier.

A hypothesis is fruitful to the extent that it suggests new ideas for future analysis and confirmation. Pasteur's hypothesis suggested changes in the procedures used to maintain sterile conditions in hospitals. After these changes were implemented, the death rate from surgical operations decreased dramatically. The procedure of pasteurization, used to preserve milk, was another outgrowth of the hypothesis that life comes only from life.

PRACTICING DEDUCTIVE THINKING

IDENTIFYING CATEGORICAL PROPOSITIONS

    1) Identify the form of the sentence.

A - universal affirmative categorical proposition

E - universal negative categorical proposition

I - particular affirmative categorical proposition

O - particular negative categorical proposition

NCP - not a categorical proposition

_____ 1. Some cars are not four-wheeled vehicles.

_____ 2. Close the door!

Modes of Thinking

_____ 3. All trees are deciduous.

_____ 4. Sometimes I sleep late and feel groggy all day.

_____ 5. No philosophers are bald-headed.

_____ 6. All bachelors are unmarried men.

_____ 7. If I were king, Pepsi Cola would be banned.

_____ 8. Some panthers are Carolina football players.

_____ 9. No green ideas sleep furiously.

_____ 10. Some philosophers are not boring.

_____ 11. Do not use no double negatives!

2) Analyzing Categorical Syllogisms

> Some mathematicians are philosophers.
> Some philosophers are set-theorists.
> _____
> Some set-theorists are mathematicians.

NOTE: The line divides the premises from the conclusion. Or one may distinguish the conclusion from the premises by using "thus" or "therefore."

USING the above standard form categorical syllogism, IDENTIFY the following syllogism parts by writing the appropriate term of proposition to the right.

    major premise:
    minor premise:
    conclusion:
    predicate term of the major premise:
    predicate term of the syllogism:
    middle term of the syllogism:
    subject term of the minor premise:
    subject term of the syllogism:

3) Arrange the following propositions into two standard form categorical syllogisms, identifying the mood and figure of each:

Some four-sided figures are not squares; all squares are rectangles; some four-sided figures are not rectangles.

4) Testing Categorical Syllogisms
The refutation by logical analogy or counter example method for testing syllogisms has four steps:

   1. Test a syllogism with true premises and true conclusion.
   2. Assume that the syllogism is valid.
   3. Attempt to discover an analogous syllogism (one with an identical mood and figure) with true premises and a false conclusion.
   4. If none can be found, treat the syllogism as valid; if one can be found, then declare the syllogism invalid.

Here are some categorical syllogisms that have true premises and a true conclusion:

No rabbits are cats.
No turtles are rabbits.
Thus no turtles are cats.

All dogs are canines.
No dogs are felines.
Thus no felines are canines.

16. INDUCTIVE THINKING

Inductive argument moves from a particular premise to a universal conclusion. Inductive reasoning begins with a set of evidence or observations about some members of a class. From this evidence or observation we draw a conclusion about all members of a class. Because of this move from the particular to the general, the conclusions of good inductive reasoning likely or probably follow from the observation; they do not absolutely follow. By moving from the particular to the general, the conclusions of inductive reasoning are not logically contained in the premises.

When done well, inductive thinking gives you reasonable, although not absolute, conclusions that we live by. Unfortunately, considerable unsound inductive thinking also occurs. Below we look at some of the major kinds of inductive reasoning fallacies. If we can learn to avoid them, we will think more competently.

Inductive Logic

The first part of this chapter dealt with deductive arguments. In deductive logic arguments were said to be valid or invalid. In the domain of deductive logic we had a great deal of certainty.

Fallacies in deductive logic when a person violates one of the rules of validity are said to be *formal fallacies* such as an argument with two negative premises. In deductive logic when you were doing truth tables or Venn diagrams the class had more of a mathematical flavor.

Now we have crossed over into the area of inductive logic. In the area of inductive logic arguments are said to be stronger or weaker. There is less certainty.

Fallacies in inductive logic are said to be *informal fallacies*. Informal Fallacies have names. Anyone who has played chess is familiar with openings. The Benoni counter gambit, the Stone Wall, King's Indian, Queen's Indian and so on. These fallacies are like chess openings they can become easy to recognize with some practice. They are used on us everyday by our employers, children, spouses, coworkers, politicians, advertisers or anyone who is trying to persuade us to do something.

Informal Fallacies

Argumentum ad hominem (circumstantial) or the argument against the person.

How can Bill Clinton know anything about health care. He went to law school not to medical school. Here instead of attacking the president's health care plan the person attacks the person's circumstances.

How can Bill Clinton be smart? Everybody that I have ever met who grew up in Arkansas is totally stupid.

Immigrants are not very smart. They don't speak good English.

Bill Clinton can't be a good president because he cheated on his wife.

A better argument might be that he is a bad husband because he cheated on his wife or that he is setting a bad example for his daughter because he cheated on his spouse.

Argumentum ad hominem (abusive) or the argument against the person, in this case by being abusive. Essentially name calling.

George Bush is a murderer. He signed off on 125 executions.

Murder is the unjust killing of an innocent person. Some would argue that Bush did not kill anyone. Just as Bill Clinton did not kill anyone in Yugoslavia. He just gave the order. Is it fair to call it murder if it is during war?

Anytime that a participant in an argument resorts to name calling it is the abusive form of argumentum ad hominem. Unless it is true. Jeffrey Dahmer was a serial killer. It would not be abusive to call him a murderer. John Wilkes both was an assassin. It would not be inappropriate to call him an assassin. Benedict Arnold was a traitor. It would not be inappropriate to call him a traitor.

Modes of Thinking

Argumentum ad baculum [to war (threat)] is any argument that contains a threat. The threat can be explicit (spelled out) such as, "If you say that about my mother's apple pie again, I am going to punch you in the nose." Or, the threat can be implicit such as when a parent says to their child, "Clean up your room or else" (implied). The child does not know if it is going to be a spanking, loss of allowance or privileges: but they know that they have been threatened.

Argumentum ad populum (bandwagon) this is the everybody is doing it argument. Politicians frequently use it. Everybody else is taking soft money. Teenagers also use it. All of the other kids have their own car. All of the other kids are buying $500 class rings. All of the other kids can stay out until 3:00 a.m. All of the other kids smoke marijuana.

Argumentum ad ignorantum (argument from ignorance) is frequently used in business. I have never seen it work before. I have never seen God so he must not exist. I have never seen a UFO so they must not exist. I have never met an honest man.

Complex Question (wife beating question) usually illustrated by the question when did you stop beating your wife? When did you stop copying Dave's homework? It is complex because there are two questions. No matter what you say you are trapped into admitting something. There is an assertion in side the question that accuses you of doing something wrong.

Argumentum ad vericundiam [appeal to authority (expertise)] frequently used in advertising. Four out of five doctors who smoke, smoke Camels. Nine out of ten dentists who chew gum, chew Trident. Tiger Woods uses Titleist golf balls. Michael Jordan wears Nike sneakers. Caution authority in this fallacy means expertise not authority like a judge or a policeman.

Argumentum ad misercordiam (pity) I should have a higher grade even though I didn't do well on the exam because I had the flu. School is hard because I am a single mother. I don't do well at work because I am an alcoholic. I don't do well in school because my parents are divorced. Maybe you didn't do well because you didn't study. Maybe you didn't do well because you didn't come to class. Maybe you didn't do well because you don't have an aptitude for the subject. But don't blame your parents.

Post hoc ergo propter hoc (after this therefore because of this) involves confusion about cause and effect. I lost money at the casino because I forgot to bring my lucky rabbit's foot. Every time I wash my car it rains. My spouse (boyfriend or girlfriend) always starts a fight with me during final exams week. Male student frequently think that middle-aged male professors give female students higher grades because they are female. Male students also think that female teachers give higher grades to female students because they are of the same gender. It may be the case that females are just better students. Or, it may be the case that the distribution of good grades is about the same regardless of gender.

Hasty generalization. This fallacy usually takes the form of prejudice. This is taking one example and applying it to an entire category of people. When a woman cuts Jim off in traffic - he shouts, "Women drivers." Blondes are dumb. Blondes have more fun. Chinese are clever and deceptive. Scottish people are thrifty. My husband is Scottish, and he is definitely not thrifty. Irishmen are drunkards. I have an Irish friend and he does not drink at all.

PRACTICING INDUCTIVE THINKING

Indentify the informal fallacies:

1. Einstein became a great physicist because his parents and his teachers left him alone to dream. Had they badgered him to study, he never would have gotten beyond the Swiss patent office.

2. As I drove to school this morning, not one car which was turning had its turn signal on. Thus, I conclude that the drivers in this state are not well trained since they never use their turn signals.

3. The best definition distinguishing man from other animals is that man is a rational animal. Therefore, you, as a person, should spend more time studying and using your brain than you should spend for partying.

4. I can see that you are greatly impressed by the power of logic and argument. Therefore, are you going to sign up for Philosophy 102: Introduction to Philosophic Inquiry this semester or next semester? It's got to be one or the other.

5. The Smithson Foundation is investigating whether or not police officers are using excessive force in traffic arrests of minorities. Hence, it is quite reasonable to conclude that *some* police officers, at least, use excessive force in that kind of arrest.

6. The testimony of the defendant accused of manslaughter in this indictment should be disallowed because she has been arrested for shoplifting on many occasions.

7. Why haven't you written to your Mother as often as you should? You would feel much better about yourself if you would attend to the details of life which are this important.

8. It should be no surprise to you that the state is, again, headed into either a recession or a deep economic downturn. After all, a Republican has just been elected governor.

9. When I was shopping at Bess's Fine Clothing, not one person gave me the time of day. I guess Bess's is not a very friendly place to work.

10. John Bardeen, a professor at the Advanced Institute of Physics, has gone on record to say that the American Medical Association needs to raise its standards for physicians. The opinion of a man of that brilliance should not be disregarded.

11. If we took a poll right now, almost every American would agree that a vaccine for AIDS will soon be found. Therefore, there can be little doubt that AIDS will be practically wiped out in the near future.

12. I made low grades on my first tests in math and English. I must really be dumb.

13. As a daughter when I was four, my father taught me the beauty of numbers, and I have excelled at mathematics ever since. My conclusion as to why females do not score as high on math tests? The males with a high aptitude for mathematics are not spending enough time with their daughters.

14. I think that the tests given in this class were more than fair, and I think you will agree with me because, if you do not, your grade in this course will certainly be in jeopardy.

15. The result of my doing well in economics is very simple. I eat Post Toasties for breakfast every morning for breakfast, and this breakfast helps my ability to analyze in great depth. I think it must be all those complex carbohydrates.

16. Oriental Philosophy is the best course taught at Lander University. I know this because all of my friends say so.

17. Look Mr. IRS examiner, of course I owe taxes—I'm not denying that. However, I was unable to file on time because my wife was sick and my two children need my attention. Surely the IRS is not opposed to keeping the family together.

18. Mr. Smith, maybe there is some truth in what you say about me being rude to sales people, but I have certainly heard may sales people complain about your manners, so you are certainly not the person to point this out to me.

19. Sir, don't you want to look more closely at our aluminum siding for your new home? When we put this up, your home will take on the glow of beauty, and you will be admired by others as someone who cares. Not only that, but your life will be richer as you proudly invite others to your home to share the better way of life.

20. It is easy to see that goodness is in the world and not just in our minds, because as we look at the world, some things are obviously not evil or indifferent in themselves.

21. Mr. Watkins has clearly and concisely detailed his arguments concerning the relative safety of tobacco products for Third World countries. But, let me remind you that we could hardly expect him to say anything else because he has worked in the tobacco industry for the last twenty years.

22. All persons act in order that they might get pleasure. Even so-called altruistic persons who help others so much that they do almost nothing for themselves must get pleasure out of giving. Otherwise, they wouldn't do it. Suppose a person hits himself over the head with a hammer. He must get pleasure from it, because why else would he do it if he didn't get pleasure from it?

23. The Roper Organization says that more persons watch CBS's *60 Minutes* that any other news program on television. Therefore, it must be the best news programming on TV.

24. Hilda Robinson, an old backwoods, ignorant lady who never got past the fourth grade in school, claims that chicken soup is good for a cold. What does she know? She is ignorant of the scientific evidence.

25. Watch the Business Report at 7:00 on channel 6. It's the best report on current dealings on Wall Street because no comparative study of business reposts has ever proved to our satisfaction that there is any better.

Answers

1. Einstein became a great physicist because his parents and his teachers left him alone to dream. Had they badgered him to study, he never would have gotten beyond the Swiss patent office.

Answer: Since there is no causal connection between "leaving someone alone to dream" and "becoming a great physicist," the fallacy of false cause occurs.

2. As I drove to school this morning, not one car which was turning had its turn signal on. Thus, I conclude that the drivers in this state are not well trained since they do not ever use their turn signals.

Answer: The number of examples and the method of selection are not reliable methods of generalization; hence, the fallacy of converse accident occurs

3. The best definition distinguishing man from the other animals is that man is a rational animal. Therefore, you, as a person, should spend more time studying and using your brain than you should spend for having a good time.

Answer: Although all persons, as human beings, have rational capacities, it does not follow that in this specific case one should necessarily be rational more often--fallacy of accident is committed.

4. I can see that you are greatly impressed by the power of logic and argument. Therefore, are you going to sign up for Philosophy 102: Introduction to Philosophic Inquiry this semester or next semester? It's got to be one or the other.

CHAPTER 7

Answer: The question presupposes that the listener will sign up for a logic course; hence, the fallacy of complex question occurs.

5. The Smithson Foundation is investigating whether or not police officers are using excessive force in traffic arrests of minorities. Hence, we may conclude that some police officers, at least, use excessive force in that kind of arrest.

Answer: An investigation does not entail that any evidence has been forthcoming so far. Since no evidence is adduced, one cannot justifiably come to a conclusion. The fallacy of *ad ignorantiam* occurs in this passage.

6. The testimony of the defendant accused of manslaughter in this indictment should be disallowed because she has been arrested for shoplifting on many occasions.

Answer: Strictly speaking, one should evaluate the cogency of the testimony and evaluate it on its own merit. Fallacy of *ad hominem* occurs because being a shoplifter does not entail not telling the truth.

7. Why haven't you written to your Mother often as you should? You would feel much better about yourself if you would attend to the details of life which are this important.

Answer: The supposition that the Mother is not written to sufficiently often is assumed without evidence and is used as the evidence for drawing another conclusion; hence, the fallacy of complex question is committed.

8. It should be no surprise to you that the state is, again, headed into either a recession or perhaps a deep economic downturn. After all, a Republican has just been elected governor.

Answer: The locutor assumes, without evidence, that the election of a Republican will cause a slowing down of the economy. The fallacy of false cause occurs.

9. When I was shopping at Bess's Fine Clothing, not one person gave me the time of day. I guess Bess's is not a very friendly place to work.

Answer: The speaker is generalizing from one experience. More evidence would be necessary to reach the conclusion that Bess's is not a good place to work. The speaker commits the fallacy of converse accident.

10. John Bardeen, a professor at the Advanced Institute of Physics, has gone on record to say that the American Medical Association needs to raise its standards for physicians. The opinion of a man of that brilliance should not be disregarded.

Answer: An authority in physics is being cited outside of his field of expertise. The *ad verecundiam* fallacy occurs11. Simply from the fact that most persons believe a statement is true, it does not follow logically that the statement is true--*ad populum* fallacy.

11. If we took a poll right now, almost every American would agree that a vaccine for AIDS will soon be found. Therefore there can be little doubt that AIDS will be practically wiped out in the near future.

Answer: Simply from the fact that most persons believe a statement is true, it does not follow logically that the statement is true--*ad populum* fallacy.

12. I made low grades on my first tests in math and English. I must really be dumb.

Answer: Too few examples are used to justify such a conclusion; fallacy of converse accident is committed.

13. As a daughter when I was four, my father taught me the beauty of numbers, and I have excelled at mathematics ever since. My conclusion on why females do not score as high on math tests? The males with a high aptitude for mathematics are not spending enough time with their daughters.

Answer: The author of this example assumes that her case would be typical of all or most other daughters if they had had similar experiences. The fallacy of converse accident occurs.

Modes of Thinking

14. I think that the tests given in this class were more than fair, and I think you will agree with me because, if you do not, your grade in this course will certainly be in jeopardy.

Answer: The threat of a poor grade is logically unrelated to the fairness of tests; hence the *ad baculum* fallacy is committed.

15. The result of my doing well in economics is very simple. I eat Post Toasties for breakfast every morning for breakfast, and this breakfast helps my ability to analyze in great depth. I think it must be all those complex carbohydrates.

Answer: No causal evidence is given for the relation between eating a breakfast cereal and ability to analyze, so the fallacy of false cause occurs.

16. Oriental Philosophy is the best course taught at Lander University. I know this because all of my friends say so.
Answer: Although most friends think so, that doesn't make it so. *Ad populum* fallacy occurs.

17. Look Mr. IRS examiner, of course I owe taxes--I'm not denying that. However, I was unable to file on time because my wife was sick and my two children need my attention. Surely the IRS is not opposed to keeping the family together.

Answer: The unfortunate circumstances of the taxpayer are logically independent of his responsibility to pay his taxes--*ad misericordiam* fallacy.

18. Mr. Smith, maybe there is some truth in what you say about me being rude to sales people, but I have certainly heard may sales people complain about your manners, so you are certainly not the person to point this out to me.

Answer: The *ad hominem* variation of "you're another" or *tu quoque* is offered.

19. Sir, don't you want to look more closely at our aluminum siding for your new home? When we put this up your home will take on the glow of beauty, and you will be admired by others as someone who cares. Not only that, but your life will be richer as you invite with pride others to your home to share the better way of life.

Answer: Some logicians would classify this passage of an instance of the *ad populum* fallacy. However, the passage is regarded here as "rhetoric and persuasion."

20. It is easy to see that goodness is in the world and not just in our minds, because as we look at the world, some things are obviously not evil in themselves.

Answer: Although "good" and "evil" are not complementary classes, this passage can be analyzed as *petitio principii*, since *ceteris paribus* the meanings are similar enough to be circular reasoning. If this analysis is acceptable then, in a sense, this fallacy turns of the fallacy of false dichotomy.

21. Mr. Watkins has clearly and concisely detailed his arguments concerning the relative safety of tobacco products for third world countries. But, let me remind you that we could hardly expect him to say anything else because he has worked in the tobacco industry for the last twenty years.

Answer: Although Mr. Watkins worked for the tobacco industry, it does not follow necessarily that he does not speak the truth. One might even offer the argument that his expertise is actually relevant to the subject of the argument. Fallacy of *ad hominem* is committed.

22. All persons act in order that they might get pleasure. Even so-called altruistic persons who help others so much that they do almost nothing for themselves get pleasure out of giving. Otherwise, they wouldn't do it. Suppose a person hits himself over the head with a hammer. He must get pleasure from it, because why else would he do it if he didn't get pleasure from it?

Answer: The fallacy is *petitio principii* or circular argument. The premiss that all persons act from the motive of pleasure is the same statement as the conclusion.

CHAPTER 7

23. The Roper Organization says that more persons watch CBS's 60 Minutes that any other news program on television. Therefore, it must be the best news programming on TV.

Answer: Simply because a program is popular, the conclusion doesn't logically follow that the program is the best--unless, of course, one defines "best" as "the most popular" as is sometimes done in marketing. Logically speaking, the fallacy of *ad populum* occurs.

24. Hilda Robinson, an old backwoods, ignorant lady who never got past the fourth grade in school, claims that chicken soup is good for a cold. What does she know? She is ignorant of the scientific evidence.

Answer: The attack on character and circumstances is characteristic of the *ad hominem* fallacy.

25. Watch the Business Report at 7:00 on channel 6. It's the best report on current dealings on Wall Street because no comparative study of business reposts has ever proved to our satisfaction that there is any better.

Answer: From the fact that a conclusion has not been proved, no other conclusion can be drawn. This passage illustrates one common version of the *ad ignorantiam* fallacy.

17. ABDUCTIVE THINKING

Abductive thinking reasons from the result and a generalization to propose a specific case. It is more closely aligned with deductive than with inductive thinking. It involves both at times and tends to be used in finding causes, as well as in fields of inquiry such as artificial intelligence. For example, because the children on my block are tall (result) and tall parents have tall children (generalization), then the children of my tall neighbors will most likely be tall.

Abduction is a method of logical inference introduced by Charles Sanders Peirce which comes prior to induction and deduction for which the colloquial name is guessing. ***Abductive reasoning starts when an inquirer considers of a set of seemingly unrelated facts, armed with the hunch that they are somehow connected.*** The term abduction is commonly presumed to mean the same thing *as hypothesis*, however, an abduction is actually the process of inference that produces a hypothesis as its end result. Used in both philosophy and computing.

Abductive Thinking – A Foundation for Creativity … No it's not about aliens, but the concept is alien to many. Up until now we've talked about Deductive and Inductive Logic. There's another "thinking" mechanism that many believe is part of the foundation of Creativity. It is called Abductive Reasoning. Here's the short version.

Deduction goes like this; All marbles in your bucket are red. If you pick a marble from your bucket, it will be red. If the premise is true, the conclusion must be true.

Induction goes like this; You have pulled 10 marbles from a bucket, and they have all been red. You plan to pull out another marble. It will probably be red. The outcome has a probability associated with it. Almost all of our thinking is based on Induction.

Abduction works sort of the other way around. You find a red marble. You observe that there is a bucket of red marbles on the other side of the room. You conclude that the red marble probably came from the bucket with red marbles. It's a guess, but not based on either deductive or inductive logic. There is no direct evidence, no set of experiments, no direct cause and effect, but a hunch, a guess, a feeling, a "relationship" that is "seen". In HeadScratching we call this process "Association".

Deduction allows deriving b as a consequence of a. In other words, deduction is the process of deriving the consequences of what is assumed. Given the truth of the assumptions, a valid deduction guarantees the truth of the conclusion. It is true by definition and is independent of sense experience. For example, if it is true (given) that the sum of the angles is 180° in all triangles, and if a certain triangle has angles of 90° and 30°, then it can be deduced that the third angle is 60°. Induction allows inferring a entails b from multiple instantiations of a and b at the same time.

Induction is the process of inferring probable antecedents as a result of observing multiple consequents. An inductive statement requires empirical evidence for it to be true. For example, the statement 'it is snowing outside' is invalid until one looks or goes outside to see whether it is true or not. Induction requires sense experience. Abduction allows inferring a as an explanation of b. Because of this, abduction allows the precondition a to be inferred from the consequence b. Deduction and abduction thus differ in the direction in which a rule like "a entails b" is used for inference. As such abduction is formally equivalent to the logical fallacy affirming the consequent or Post hoc ergo propter hoc, because there are multiple possible explanations for b.

Abductive Reasoning is best explained as the development of a hypothesis which, if true, would best explain the presented evidence.

Because it infers cause and effect, abduction is a form of the logical fallacy Post hoc ergo propter hoc (after this, on account of this).

Charles Pierce First introduced abductive thinking to modern logic, using it in his pre 1900s work to describe the use of a known rule to explain an observation.

Also called reasoning through successive approximation, this is validation ones hypothesis through abductive reasoning. According to abductive validation, an explanation is valid if it gives the "best" explanation for the data (best being defined in terms of elegance and simplicity, i.e. Occam's razor). In science, abductive validation is common practice for hypothesis formation.

18. THE "DOUBTING GAME"

This approach to problem solving emphasizes **argument and a rigidly reductive method of rationality**: problem **definition**, problem **analysis, presentation** and **evaluation of alternatives, detailing of solutions**. The doubting game forces one to poke holes in ideas, tear apart assertions, probe continually, and be analytical. Careful development of generalizations in research requires an emphasis on the doubting game. Its view of rationality makes a person feel "rigorous, disciplined, tough minded." Conversely, if a person refrains from playing the doubting game, he or she feels "unintellectual, irrational, sloppy."

In his book Writing Without Teachers, Peter Elbow introduces the concept of the "believing" and "doubting" games--complementary methods of approaching texts which he claims are both vital to the "intellectual enterprise."

Elbow says that most academics or intellectuals are obsessed with one method of approaching new texts and ideas--the doubting game--at the expense of the other. The doubting game allows you to approach a text "critically," to look for errors and contradictions; it is a game of "self-extrication" from a text's underlying assumptions and conclusions, which you flush out into the open with your hard-headed, scientific skepticism. In Elbow's words, "The truer it seems, the harder you have to doubt it". By playing the "doubting game," you can come to realize your own opinions and positions by reacting against those of another writer, by engaging in what Elbow calls a "dialectic of propositions."

Elbow's article is a plea for a more balanced approach that also includes the "believing game.""Rather than extricating yourself from the text the believing game allows you to project yourself into a writer's point of view, to try it on for size, to "try to have that experience of meaning." You intentionally believe everything--taking in a text as Elbow says, the way an owl eats a mouse--and trust your "organism" eventually to sort out the useful from the unuseful.

Ultimately, the philosophy of the believing game sees ideas not as inherently true or false, but as tools: "By believing an assertion," writes Elbow, "we can get farther and farther into it, see more and more things in terms of it or "through" it, use it as a hypothesis to climb higher and higher to a point from which more can be seen and understood."

19. THE "BELIEVING GAME"

In this approach to problem solving, the first rule is to refrain from doubting. It initially believes all assertions, on an to see further into them. Effective planning and design require the believing game, in order to engender "breakthrough" solutions. The believing game is complementary, not contradictory, to the doubting game. That is, successful solution finding requires use of both approaches. Yet the believing and doubting games cannot be played simultaneously. Each must be employed at different times in the solution-finding process.

The Believing Game is based on the concept of **methodological belief** developed by educator Peter Elbow asserts that the emphasis on critical, deductive thinking reinforces doubt and promotes the one right answer, on "true" conclusion.

CHAPTER 7

The Believing Game is a methodology of thinking that entails **believing everything** about a given idea or object, even if the parts seemingly or actually contradict. If it somehow does not work, a way must be found to **MAKE it work.**

Don Quixote says he admires Sancho Panza because he doubts everything and he believes everything.

Imagine that you see something in it that interests and pleases you - but your colleagues or classmates don't see what you see. In fact they think you are crazy or disturbed for seeing it. What would you do if you wanted to convince them that your interpretation makes sense?

If it were a matter of geometry, you could prove you are right (or wrong!). But with inkblots, you don't have logic's leverage. Your only hope is to get them to enter into your way of seeing - to have the experience you are having. You need to get them to say the magic words: "Oh now I see what you see."

This means getting them to exercise the ability to see something differently (i.e., seeing the same thing in multiple ways), and also the willingness to risk doing so (not knowing where it will lead). In short, you need them to be flexible both cognitively and emotionally. You can't make people enter into a new way of seeing, even if they are capable of it. Perhaps your colleagues or classmates are bothered by what you see in the inkblot. Perhaps they think it's aberrant or psychotic. If you want them to take the risk, your only option is to set a good example and show that you are willing to see it the way they see it.

From Inkblots to Arguments

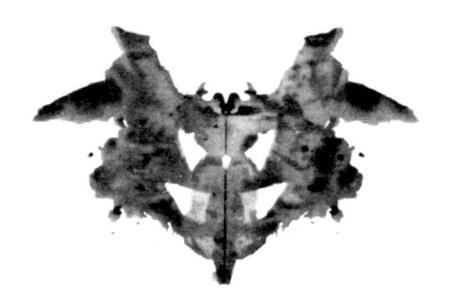

What do you see on this picture?

Interpreting inkblots or any ambiguous stimuli is highly subjective, but the process serves to highlight how arguments also have a subjective dimension. Few arguments are settled by logic. Should we invade countries that might attack us? Should we torture prisoners who might know what we need to know? Should we drop a nuclear bomb on a country that did attack us? And by the way, what grade is fair for this paper or this student? Should we use grades at all?

There is a significant force in logic. Logic can uncover a genuine error in someone's argument. But logic cannot uncover an error in someone's position. If we could have proven that Iraq had no weapons of mass destruction, that wouldn't have proven that it was wrong to invade Iraq. "We should invade Iraq" is a claim that is impossible to prove or disprove. We can use logic to strengthen arguments for or against the claim, but we cannot prove or disprove it. Over and over we see illogical arguments for good ideas and logical arguments for bad ideas. We can never prove that an opinion or position is wrong - or right. No wonder people so change their minds when someone finds bad reasoning in their argument. (By the same token - or at least a very similar token - it is impossible to prove or disprove the interpretation of a text.)

This explains a lot about how most people deal with differences of opinion:

- ***Some people love to argue and disagree***, and they do it for fun in a friendly way. They enjoy the disagreement and the give-and-take and they let criticisms and even attacks roll right off their backs. It's good intellectual sport for them.
- ***Some people look like they enjoy the sport of argument***. They stay friendly and rational---they're "cool"---because they've been trained well. "Don't let your feelings cloud your thinking." But inside they feel hurt when others attack ideas they care about. They hunker down into their ideas behind hidden walls.
- ***Some people actually get mad***, raise their voices, dig in, stop listening, and even call each other names. Perhaps they realize that language and logic have no power to make their listeners change their minds---so they give in to shouting or anger.
- And ***some people*** - seeing that nothing can be proven with words - ***just give up on argument***. They retreat. "Let's just not argue. You see it your way, I'll see it my way. That's the end of it. There's no

220

use talking." They sidestep arguments and take a relativist position: any opinion is as good as any other opinion. (It's worth pondering why so many students fall into this attitude.)

But sometimes people actually listen to each other, come to really see the merit in opinions they started off fighting. Through listening to someone else's views, they do something amazing: they actually change their thinking. Sometimes strong differences of opinion are resolved---even heated arguments.

When this happens people demonstrate the *two inkblot skills*: the ability and the willingness to see something differently - or in this case to think or understand something differently. (People often say "I see" when they "understand" something differently). These are precious skills, cognitive and psychological. You won't have much luck encouraging them in other people unless you develop them in yourself.

With inkblots, the risk seems small. If you manage to see a blot the way a classmate or colleague sees it, you don't have to say, "Stupid me. I was wrong." It's "live and let live" when you are dealing with inkblots. With arguments, however, it feels like win or lose. You often want people not just to understand your position; you often want them to give up their ("wrong, stupid") position.

Inkblots was used earlier to look for the subjective dimension in most arguments (given that logic cannot prove or destroy a position). Now inkblots can teach you something else. They can teach you that there's actually a "live-and-let-live" dimension in many arguments - probably most. But people often feel arguments as win/lose situations because they so naturally focus on how their side of an argument differs from the other person's side. They assume that one person has to say, "Stupid me. I was wrong."

The believing game will help you understand ideas you disagree with, and thereby help you see that one needs to lose or give up his or her central idea. The believing game can help you see that both sides in an argument are often right; or that both are right in a sense; or that both positions are implicitly pointing to some larger, wiser position that both arguers can agree on.

What is the Believing Game?

In a sense it was already explained with the analogy between inkblots and arguments. Now, contrasting it with the doubting game.

The **doubting game** represents the kind of thinking most widely honored and taught. It's the disciplined practice of trying to be as skeptical and analytic as possible with every idea we encounter. By doubting well, we can discover hidden contradictions, bad reasoning, or other weaknesses in ideas that look true or attractive. We scrutinize with the tool of doubt. This is the tradition that Walter Lippman invokes:

The opposition is indispensable. A good statesman, like any other sensible human being, always learns more from his opponents than from his fervent supporters. For his supporters will push him to disaster unless his opponents show him where the dangers are. So if he is wise he will often pray to be delivered from his friends, because they will ruin him. But, though it hurts, he ought . . . to pray never to be left without opponents; for they keep him on the path of reason and good sense.

The widespread veneration of "critical thinking" illustrates how our intellectual culture venerates skepticism and doubting. ("Critical thinking" is a fuzzy, fad term, but its various meanings usually appeal to skepticism and analysis for the sake of uncovering bad thinking. When people call a movement "critical linguistics" or "critical legal studies," they are saying that the old linguistics or legal studies are flawed by being insufficiently skeptical or critical---too hospitable to something that's wrong.)

The believing game is the mirror image of the doubting game or critical thinking. It's the disciplined practice of trying to be as welcoming as possible to every idea we encounter: not just listening to views different from our own and holding back from arguing with them, but actually trying to believe them. We can use the tool of believing to scrutinize not for flaws but to find hidden virtues in ideas that are unfashionable or repellent. Often we cannot see what's good in someone else's idea (or in our own!) till we work at believing it. When an idea goes against current assumptions and beliefs-- or seems alien, weird, dangerous---or if it's poorly formulated---we often cannot see any merit in it.

"Believing" is a Scary Word

Many people get nervous when they hear 'believing.' They point to an asymmetry between our sense of what "doubting" and "believing" mean. Believing seems to entail commitment, where doubting does not. It commonly feels as though we can doubt something without committing ourselves to rejecting it---but that we cannot believe something without committing ourselves to accepting it and even living by it. Thus it feels as though we can doubt and remain unscathed, but believing will scathe us. Indeed believing can feel hopelessly bound up with religion. ("Do you BELIEVE? Yes, Lord, I BELIEVE!")

CHAPTER 7

This contrast in meanings is a fairly valid picture of natural, individual acts of doubting and believing. (Though I wonder if doubting leaves us fully unchanged.) But it's not a picture of doubting and believing as methodological disciplines or unnatural games. Let me explain the distinction.

Natural individual acts of doubting happen when someone tells us something that seems dubious or hard to believe. ("You say the earth is spinning? I doubt it. I feel it steady under my feet.") But our culture has learned to go way beyond natural individual acts of doubting. We humans had to struggle for a long time to learn how to doubt unnaturally as a methodological discipline. We now know that for good thinking, we must doubt everything, not just what's dubious; indeed the whole point of critical thinking is to try to doubt what we find most obvious or true or right (as Lippman advises).

In order to develop systematic doubting, we had to overcome believing: the natural pull to believe what's easy to believe, what we want to believe, or what powerful people tell us to believe. (It's easy to believe that the earth is stationary.) As a culture, we learned systematic doubting through the growth of philosophical thinking (Greek thinkers developing logic, Renaissance thinkers developing science, and Enlightenment thinkers pulling away from established religion). And we each had to learn to be skeptical as individuals, too - for example learning not to believe that if we are very good, Santa Claus/God will bring us everything we want. As children, we begin to notice that naïve belief leads us astray. As adults we begin to notice the dreadful things that belief leads humans to do - like torturing alleged witches/prisoners till they "confess."

Now that you have finally learned systematic doubting with its tools of logic and strict reasoning and its attitude of systematic skepticism - critical thinking - you are likely to end up afraid of believing itself. You had to learn to distrust natural believing ("My parents/country/God will take care of me whenever I am in need."). So believing can seem a scary word because our culture has not yet learned to go beyond natural acts of naïve believing to develop unnatural believing as a methodological discipline. In short, the believing game is not much honored or even known (though it's not new).

The methodology of the doubting game gives you a model for the methodology of the believing game. When the doubting game asks you to doubt an idea, it doesn't ask you to throw it away forever. You couldn't do that because the game teaches you to doubt all ideas, and you'll learn to find weaknesses even in good ideas. You can't throw all ideas away. The scrutiny of doubt is methodological, provisional, conditional. So when a good doubter finally decides what to believe or do, this involves an additional act of judgment and commitment. The doubting game gives good evidence, but it doesn't do our judging and committing for us.

Similarly, when the believing game asks you to believe all ideas - especially those that seem most wrong - it cannot ask you to marry them or commit yourself to them. Your believing is also methodological, conditional, provisional - unnatural. (It's hard to try to believe conflicting ideas all at once, but we can try to enter into them one after another.) And so too, if you commit yourself to accepting an idea because the believing game helped you see virtues in it, this involves an additional act of judgment and commitment. The believing game gives you good evidence, but it doesn't do your deciding for you.

A Surprising Blind Spot for the Doubting Game

The flaws in your own thinking usually come from your assumptions - your ways of thinking that you accept without noticing. But it's hard to doubt what you can't see because you unconsciously take it for granted. The believing game comes to the rescue here. Your best hope for finding invisible flaws in what you can't see in your own thinking is to enter into different ideas or points of view - ideas that carry different assumptions. Only after you've managed to inhabit a different way of thinking will your currently invisible assumptions become visible to you.

This blind spot in the doubting game shows up frequently in classrooms and other meetings. When smart people are trained only in critical thinking, they get better and better at doubting and criticizing other people's ideas. They use this skill particularly well when they feel a threat to their own ideas or their unexamined assumptions. Yet they feel justified in fending-off what they disagree with because they feel that this doubting activity is "critical thinking." They take refuge in the feeling that they would be "unintellectual" if they said to an opponent what in fact they ought to say: "Wow, your idea sounds really wrong to me. It must be alien to how I think. Let me try to enter into it and see if there's something important that I'm missing. Let me see if I can get a better perspective on my own thinking." In short, if we want to be good at finding flaws in our own thinking (a goal that doubters constantly trumpet), we need the believing game.

> You must continue to resist the pull to believe what's easy to believe. But believing what's easy to believe is far different from using the disciplined effort to believe as an intellectual methodological tool in order to find hidden strengths in ideas that people want to ignore.

> The doubting and believing games have symmetrical weaknesses: the doubting game is poor at helping us find hidden virtues; the believing game is poor at helping us find hidden flaws. But many people don't realize that the doubting game is also poor at reaching one of its main goals: helping us find hidden flaws in our own thinking.

222

Modes of Thinking

The Believing Game is Not Actually New

If you look closely at the behavior of genuinely smart and productive people, you will see that many of them have exactly this skill of entering into views that conflict with their own. John Stuart Mill is a philosopher associated with the doubting game, but he also advises good thinkers to engage in the central act of the believing game:

[People who] have never thrown themselves into the mental position of those who think differently from them . . . do not, in any proper sense of the word, know the doctrine which they themselves profess. (129)

Yet this skill of sophisticated unnatural belief is not much understood or celebrated in our culture - and almost never taught.

Imagine, for example, a seminar or a meeting where lots of ideas come up. One person is quick to point out flaws in each idea as it is presented. A second person mostly listens and gets intrigued with each idea - and tends to make comments like these: "Oh I see" and "That's interesting" and "Tell me more about such and such" and "As I go with your thinking, I begin to see some things I never noticed before." This second person may be appreciated as a good listener, but the first person will tend to be considered smarter and a better thinker because of that quick skill at finding flaws.

Some people used to feel that they are unintelligent because when one person gave an argument they would feel, "Oh that's a good idea," but then when the other person argued the other way, they found themselves feeling, "Oh that sounds good, too." They may wonder what was the matter with their loose, sloppy mind to let them agree with people and ideas that are completely at odds with each other. The "smart people" tended to argue cleverly and find flaws that may be not so obvious. But ability to play the believing game is not just "niceness" or sloppy thinking; it's a crucial intellectual strength rather than a weakness - a discipline that needs to be taught and developed.

There is nothing wrong about the doubting game. You need the ability to be skeptical and find flaws. Indeed, the doubting game probably deserves the last word in any valid process of trying to work out trustworthy thinking. For even though the scrutiny of belief may lead us to choose a good idea that most people at first wanted to throw away, nevertheless, we mustn't commit ourselves to that idea before applying the scrutiny of doubt to check for hidden problems.

But it shouldn't dominate thinking. People need both disciplines.

Concrete Ways to Learn to Play the Believing Game

If you want to learn good thinking skills, it helps to notice the inner stances - the cognitive and psychological dispositions - you need for doubting and believing:

- If you want to doubt or find flaws in ideas that you are tempted to accept or believe (perhaps they are ideas that "everyone knows are true"), you need to work at extricating or distancing yourself from those ideas. There's a kind of language that helps here: clear, impersonal sentences that lay bare the logic or lack of logic in them.
- If, on the other hand, you want to believe ideas that you are tempted to reject ("Anyone can see that's a crazy idea") - if you are trying to enter in or experience or dwell in those ideas - you benefit from the language of imagination, narrative, and the personal experience.

Here are some specific practices to help you experience things from someone else's point of view.

1. If people are stuck in a disagreement, you can invoke Carl Rogers' application of "active listening." John must not try to argue his point till he has restated Mary's point to her satisfaction.

2. But what if John has trouble seeing things from Mary's point of view? His lame efforts to restate her view show that "he doesn't get it." He probably needs to stop talking and listen; keep his mouth shut. Thus, in a discussion where someone is trying to advance a view and everyone fights it, there is a simple rule of thumb: the doubters need to stop talking and simply give extended floor time to the minority view. The following three concrete activities give enormous help here:

- The three-minute or five-minute rule. Any participant who feels he or she is not being heard can make a sign and invoke the rule: no one else can talk for three or five minutes. This voice speaks, we listen; we cannot reply.
- Allies only - no objections. Others can speak---but only those who are having more success believing or entering into or assenting to the minority view. No objections allowed. (Most people are familiar with this "no-objections" rule from brainstorming.)
- "Testimony session." Participants having a hard time being heard or understood are invited to tell stories of the experiences that led them to their point of view and to describe what it's like having or living with this view. Not only must the rest of us not answer or argue or disagree while they are speaking;

we must refrain, even afterwards, from questioning their stories or experiences or feelings. We may speak only to their ideas. (This process is particularly useful when issues of race, gender, and sexual orientation are being discussed.)

- The goal here is safety. Most speakers feel unsafe if they sense we are just waiting to jump in with all our objections. But we listeners need safety, too. We are trying to enter into a view we want to quarrel with or feel threatened by. We're trying to learn the difficult skill of in-dwelling. It's safer for us if we have permission simply not to talk about it anymore for a while. We need time for the words we resist just to sink in for a while with no comment.

3. The language of story and poetry helps us experience alien ideas. Stories, metaphors, and images can often find a path around our resistance. When it's hard to enter into a new point of view, try telling a story of someone who believes it; imagine and describe someone who sees things this way; tell the story of events that might have led people to have this view of the world; what would it be like to be someone who sees things this way? Write a story or poem about the world that this view implies.

4. Step out of language. Language itself can sometimes get in the way of trying to experience or enter into a point of view different from our own. There are various productive ways to set language aside. We can draw or sketch images (rough stick figures are fine). What do you actually see when you take this position? It's also powerful to use movement, gesture, dance, sounds, and role-playing.

5. Silence. For centuries, people have made good use of silence for in-dwelling. If we're having trouble trying to believe someone's idea, sometimes it's helpful for no one to say anything for a couple of minutes. That's not much time out of a meeting or conference or class hour, but it can be surprisingly fertile.

6. Private writing. There's a kind of silence involved when everyone engages in private writing. Stop talking and do 7-10 minutes of writing for no one else's eyes. What's crucial is the invitation to language in conditions of privacy and safety.

7. Use the physical voice. When it's hard to enter into a piece of writing that feels difficult or distant, for example something written by someone very different from us---or an intricate work like a Shakespeare sonnet---it helps to try to read it aloud as well and meaningfully as possible. (When I'm teaching a longer text, I choose crux passages of a few paragraphs or a page.) The goal is not good acting; the goal is simply to say the words so that we feel every meaning in them---so that we fully mean every meaning. Get the words to "sound right" or to carry the meanings across—for example, to listeners who don't have a text. After we have three or four different readings of the same passage, we can discuss which ones manage to "sound right"---and usually these readings help us enter in or assent. (It's not fair to put students on the spot by asking them to read with no preparation time. I ask students to prepare these reading at home or practice them briefly in class in pairs.)

8. This activity illustrates something interesting about language. It's impossible simply to say words so they "sound right" without dwelling in them and thus feeling their meaning. So instead of asking students to "study carefully" this Shakespeare sonnet, I say, "Practice reading it aloud till you can say every word with meaning." This involves giving a kind of bodily assent.

9. Nonadversarial argument. Finally, the classroom is an ideal place to practice nonadversarial forms of argument. Our traditional model of argument is a zero-sum game: "If I'm right, you must be wrong." Essays and dissertations traditionally start off by trying to demolish the views of opponents. "Unless I criticize every other idea," the assumption goes, "I won't have a clear space for my idea." But this approach is usually counterproductive--except with readers who already agree with you and don't need to be persuaded. This traditional argument structure says to readers: "You cannot agree with my ideas---or even hear them---until after you admit that you've been wrong or stupid."

The structure of nonadversarial argument is simple, but it takes practice and discipline: argue only for your position, not against other positions. This is easy for me here since I have no criticisms at all of the doubting game or critical thinking in itself. It's much harder if I really hate the idea I'm fighting. It's particularly hard if my essential argument is negative: "Don't invade Iraq." So yes, there are some situations in which we cannot avoid arguing why an idea is wrong. Yet even in my position on Iraq, there is, in fact, some space for nonadversarial argument. I can talk about the advantages of not invading Iraq---and not try to refute for invasion. In this way, I would increase the chances of my opponent actually hearing my arguments.

Modes of Thinking

The general principle is this: If all I have to offer are negative reasons why the other person's idea is bad, I'll probably make less progress than if I can give some positive reasons for my alternative idea---and even acknowledge why the other person might favor her idea.

Look back at the inkblots. Arguments that look conflicting might both be somehow valid or right. They might need to be articulated better or seen from a larger view - a view the disputants haven't yet figured out. I may be convinced that someone else's idea is dead wrong, but if I'm willing to play the believing game with it, I will not only set a good example, I may even be able to see how we are both on the right track. Nonadversarial argument and the believing game help us work out larger frames of reference and better ideas.

PRACTICING BELIEVING / DOUBTING GAME

List 'pro' and 'cons' for the following issues:

	Pros	Cons
Death penalty		
Abortion		
Euthanasia		

20. AUTOMATIC THINKING

Definition: Automatic thoughts are just what the name implies. They are the thoughts that occur constantly as our minds seek to narrate what is going on around us.

Automatic thinking occurs without conscious thought. It enables people to act swiftly and effectively in a wide variety of situations, on the basis of relatively permanent cognitive structures known variously as mental maps, scripts, schemata, belief structures, or theories of action.

It includes:

- Reflexes
- Involuntary bodily actions
- Assumptions
- Stereotypes
- Labeling
- Actions that have become "2nd nature" over time.

Everything we think is an automatic thought. A problem arises when our automatic thoughts manifest as cognitive distortions. Cognitive distortions are automatic thoughts that are based on deeply ingrained core beliefs, and they are irrational reactions we habitually have to situations. We often don't even know that we see the world in terms of these cognitive distortions. Just as the name implies, they are based on faulty reasoning. There are several types of common cognitive distortions:

Assumptions: An assumption is a proposition that is taken for granted, as if it were true based upon presupposition without preponderance of the facts.

The natural thing to do is the thing you have always done. Every time you approach a problem you bring your accumulated experience, knowledge and training to bear on it. But this includes you accumulated assumptions and biases – conscious and unconscious. The more experienced and expert you are, the more likely you are to assume outcomes by extrapolating from the known facts and experiences to predict a result. This mental baggage can prevent you from accepting innovative ideas.

225

CHAPTER 7

Sometimes the way you frame a problem contains an assumption that prevents you from solving it. In Middle Ages the definition of astronomy was the 'study of how the heavenly bodies move around the Earth', i.e. the Earth was considered to be the centre of universe which resulted in the chain of wrong explanations of various phenomena.

Overgeneralization: As we go through life, we learn from our experiences. It is a natural process of trial and error. Problems arise when we lump all similar experiences together and decide that all experiences of a certain nature will always turn out the same way. See the uses of the words "all" and "always" in that last sentence? That's a hint at overgeneralization.

Stereotypes: a fixed set of characteristics people tend to attribute to all members of certain groups. This is one way to simplify things is to organize people into groups. Stereotypes enable you to make quick judgments, but these are often wrong.

Examples:

- Ethnic stereotypes. They may have changed or they may just have gone underground. Substantial changes in stereotypes have been reported between 1932 and 1967. Compared with 1932 undergraduates, few 1967 undergrads characterized Americans as industrious or intelligent, Italians as artistic or impulsive, blacks as superstitious or lazy, and Jews as shrewd or mercenary. However, the idea that negative stereotyping is bigoted and socially undesirable has increased, so reports may be biased by attempts to hide bigotry.
- Gender stereotypes. Males are considered more independent, dominant, aggressive, scientific, and stable in handling crises. Females are seen as more emotional, sensitive, gentle, helpful, and patient. People also have stereotypes of feminists - one study showed feminists were assumed to be less attractive, even though that was not the case.

Labeling: It can take the form of making sweeping overgeneralizations about a group of people based on the actions of only a few of them. It can also manifest as self-labeling. Self-labeling can have extremely negative effects. If a person gets a bad grade on a math test and automatically says, "I'm a bad math student," they won't take the steps necessary to improve their math skills. "Bad math student" is a label that they've applied to themselves, and it most likely is not true.

Other examples: Mind Reading: "They Must Think I'm an Idiot!"

Fortune Telling: "There's no way they'll consider me for this job."

Emotional Reasoning: "I must not be very well prepared. Otherwise I wouldn't be so nervous. I'm going to make a fool out of myself!"

Shoulding: "I should be doing this instead of doing THIS."

Blame: "Its my fault that the world exploded and fifty billion people died." Blaming yourself for something that is beyond your control.

Automatic thinking is ***like the experience of learning to drive*** a stick-shift car. Did you learn to drive a standard transmission? Do you remember what it was like? You had to concentrate very hard on coordinating your hands and your feet. With one hand on the steering wheel and one on the gearshift, you had to use your foot to press the clutch at just the right moment to change gears. If it was not done smoothly then you did either choked down or did the "bunny hop" of starting and stopping down the street. With practice you improved and today can drive across town, play a CD, talk on the phone, and arrive alive without really knowing how you did it. You don't have to think about it anymore because it is automatic. Changing gears and steering happen out of your awareness. You only pay close attention in an emergency.

Your thinking is the same. You ***have practiced certain thoughts and reactions*** so many times that they are automatic. You make a mistake and immediately think, "I can't do anything right." A coworker is rude and you say to yourself, "She's out to get me again." Someone cuts you off in traffic, and you think, "What an idiot." These automatic responses produce a mood, influence your behavior, and create your reality. You never stop and challenge what you think because you are not aware of the process. What you tell yourself just seems to be the truth. You do always mess up, your coworker is out to get you, or the world is full of jerks. There are other possibilities. If you learn to pay attention to what you say to yourself then you can challenge it. You can make different choices. Is it true that you always make a mistake? Could the boss have just criticized your coworker and that is why she was upset? Was the other driver rushing to the hospital? If you see another possibility then you get another reality and a different experience. Automatic thinking can create trouble that you don't need. It can create a distressing reality that is based upon your habitual thinking.

Yet the very *advantages of automatic thinking* for dealing with routine situations are likely to become *disadvantages in the face of change* and uncertainty. Automatic thinking leads people to see only what they already know, to ignore crucial information, and rely on standard behavioral repertoires when change is necessary. Learning from experience requires switching to a more conscious, reflective mode; yet researchers have noted that people often resist making this switch, precisely when it is most called for. Reflective thinking is quite useful under condition of ambiguity and threat.

Automatic thinking means *mastering certain skills*. After they become automatic you may perfect them in your creative way.

Automatic thinking means 'thinking inside of the box.' Before you start thinking 'out of the box' you need to know what is inside of the box. If you want to become an artist you need to practice drawing, painting, or computer graphics until it becomes automatic.

What you can do *to overcome negative sides of automatic thinking*:
- Learn to pay more attention to what you say to yourself.
- Look for other explanations for what happened.
- Consider the possibility that your first thought may not be right.
- Challenge your thinking and give life the best meaning that you can.
- Enliven life by looking for fresh possibilities and don't fall back on old, automatic habits.

21. REVERSAL THINKING

Testing assumptions is probably the second most important creative thinking principle, because it is the basis for all creative perceptions. You see only what you think you see. Whenever you look at something, you make assumptions about reality. Optical illusions - one form of creative perception - depend on this phenomenon.

Every day we act before thinking through what we are doing or the possible consequences. In fact, we make so many daily decisions that it is impossible to test all the potential assumptions.

For instance, the simple act of talking with someone else involves many assumptions. You must assume that the other person actually heard what you said and understood you, that the person's nonverbal reactions indicate what you think they indicate, and that you can figure out any hidden meanings or purposes.

Testing assumptions can help you shift perspectives and view problems in a new light.

There is an old joke that illustrates this point:

Two men were camping in the wilderness when they were awakened one morning by a large bear rummaging through their food supply. The bear noticed the men and started lumbering toward them. The men still were in their sleeping bags and didn't have time to put on their boots, so they picked up their boots and began running away from the bear. The terrain was very rough, however, and they couldn't make much progress. The bear was gaining on them.

Suddenly, one of the men sat down and began pulling on his boots. His friend couldn't believe what he was seeing and said, "Are you nuts? Can't you see that the bear is almost here? Let's go!"

The man on the ground continued putting on his boots. As he did this, he looked up at the other man and said, "Well, Charlie, the way I look at it, I don't have to outrun the bear - I only have to outrun you!"

And so, another problem is resolved by testing assumptions. In this case, both men originally assumed the problem was how to outrun the bear. When one of the men tested this assumption, a creative solution popped out. This single act provided that man with one critical extra opinion. His spontaneous creative thinking enabled him to gain an edge over his "competitor."

For years, bankers assumed that their customers preferred human tellers. In the early 1980s, Citibank concluded that installing automatic tellers would help them cut costs. However, the Citibank executives did not imagine that customers would prefer dealing with machines, so they reserved human tellers for people with more than $5,000 in their accounts and relegated modest despositors to the machines. The machines were unpopular, and Citibank stopped using them in 1983. Bank executives took this as proof of their assumption about people and machines.

Months later, another banker challenged this assumption and looked at the situation from the customer's perspective. He discovered that small depositors refused to use the machines because they resented being treated as second-class customers. He reinstituted the automatic tellers with no "class distinctions," and they were an instant success. Today, even Citibank reports that 70 percent of their transactions are handled by machine.

The banker challenged the dominant assumption by looking at it from the customer's perspective. A good way to challenge *any* assumption is by looking at it from someone else's perspective.

Reverse assumptions. Reversing your assumptions broadens your thinking. You may often find yourself looking at the same thing as everybody else, yet seeing something different. Many creative thinkers get their most original ideas when they challenge and reverse the obvious.

Consider Henry Ford. Instead of answering the usual question, "How can we get the workers to the material?" Ford asked, "How can we get the work to the people?" With this reversal of a basic assumption, the assembly line was born.

Alfred Sloan took over General Motors when it was on the verge of bankrupcy and turned it around. His genius was to take an assumption and reverse it into a "breakthrough idea." For instance, it had always been assumed that you had to buy a car before you drove it. Sloan reversed this to mean you could buy it while driving it, pioneering the concept of installment buying for car dealers.

He also changed the American corporate structure by challenging the conventional assumptions about how organizations were run. He quickly realized that GM's haphazard growth was stifling its potential. So he reversed the basic assumption that major companies are run by an all-powerful individual, creating a new theory that allowed for entrepreneurial decision-making, while still maintaining ultimate control. Under Sloan, GM grew into one of the world's biggest companies, and his reversal became the blueprint for the modern American corporation.

Reverse some of your basic assumptions about business. For instance, you might start with the idea that "A salesperson organizes the sales territory," then reverse it to "The sales territory organizes (controls) the salesperson."

This reversal would lead you to consider the demand for new salespeople as territories become more complex. A salesperson with a large territory may be too well "controlled" by it to react to new accounts and sales possibilities.

Another reversal might be: "A salesperson *dis*organizes the sales territory." This would lead to consideration of how to make salespeople more efficient. You could add telemarketing support personnel, in-office follow-up systems, and so on, to organize the territories for salespeople.

Harry Seifert, CEO of Winter Gardens Salads, used reversal to cook up a winning recipe for productivity. Instead of giving employees a bonus *after* the busy times of the year, he gives them their bonus *before* the busiest time of the year.

Just before Memorial Day, when they have the largest demand for coleslaw and potato salad, Siefert dishes out $50 to each of his 140 employees to arouse their enthusiasm for filling all of the holiday orders as efficiently as possible. "Because employees are trying to achieve a goal," he observes, "they don't feel like they are being taken advantage of during the intense periods." Production has risen 50 percent during the bonus period.

Once an assumption is reversed and a breakthrough idea achieved, you may be startled by how obvious the idea seems. The reversal need not be a 180-degree turn - just a different angle on a problem. Years ago, shopkeepers assumed they had to serve customers. Someone changed that to shoppers serving themselves and the supermarket was born.

Suppose my challenge is: "In what ways might I create a new business for airports and train stations?"

My basic assumptions are:
- Airports and train stations are for people who are travelling from one point to another;
- Planes and trains are constantly arriving and departing;
- People depart rapidly.

I reverse these assumptions to:
- Airports and train stations are for people who are *not* travelling;
- Planes and trains are *not* arriving and departing;
- People are *not* departing rapidly.

I now have a new perspective on the challenge. Perhaps I could create a business to serve people caught by bad weather, strikes, missed trains or planes, or those who have long delays or layovers and want to rest - people who, for some reason, are not able to travel. They would need lodging, but would not want or be able to leave the terminal.

Modes of Thinking

The idea: A capsule hotel that would provide basic amenities in modular, Pullman-style sleeping compartments that could be stacked two or three high. Each capsule would come with a TV, radio, alarm clock, and reading light. A community shower would be available to all guests. The front desk would be staffed twenty-four hours a day and would carry razors, soap, toothpaste, toothbrushes, and so on. The price for a twenty-four-hour stay would be 50 percent cheaper than airport hotels and would also have low hourly rates, perhaps $10 an hour. Such hotels are already in use in Japan, and are quite popular.

The capsules would be easy to clean and maintain. Because they are modular, they could be easily moved between locations. They could also be leased to cities as temporary lodging for the homeless or for people who are forced out of their homes by fires and floods.

Assumption reversal **enables you to:**
1. Escape from looking at a challenge in the traditional way;
2. Free up information so that it can come together in new ways;
3. Think provocatively. You can take a novel position and then work out its implications;
4. Look for a breakthrough.

Reversal. The reversal method for examining a problem or generating new ideas takes a situation as it is and turns it around, inside out, backwards, or upside down. A given situation can be "reversed" in several ways; there is no one formulaic way.

For example, the situation, "a teacher instructing students" could be reversed as

- *students instructing the teacher*
- *the teacher uninstructing students*
- *students instructing themselves*
- *students instructing each other*
- *teacher instructing himself*
- *students uninstructing (correcting?) the teacher*

Example problem: *a motorist came up behind a flock of sheep in the middle of the road and told the shepherd to move the sheep to the side so that he could drive through. The shepherd knew that on such a narrow roadside, he could not easily keep all his sheep off the road at once. Reversal: Instead of "drive around the sheep," drive the sheep around the car: have the car stop and drive the sheep around and in back of it.*

Example: *going on vacation: bring vacation home, stay on vacation most of year and then "go on work" for two weeks, make work into a vacation, send someone on vacation for you to bring back photos and souvenirs, etc.*

Example: *how can management improve the store?*

- *how can the store improve management?*
- *how can the store improve itself?*
- *how can management make the store worse?*
- *how can the store make itself worse?*
- *how can the store hinder management?*

Note that in some reversals, ideas are generated which then can be reversed into an idea applicable to the original problem. Example from reversal, "How can management hurt the store?" Hurt it by charging high prices on low quality goods, dirty the floors, be rude to customers, hire careless employees, encourage shoplifting, don't put prices on anything and charge what you feel like, or have to ask for a price check on every item. These bad things can then be reversed, as in, be nice and helpful to customers, make sure all items are priced, etc., and supply a good number of ideas. Sometimes it's easier to think negatively first and then reverse the negatives.

Example: *What can I do to make my relationship with my boss or spouse better? Reversal: what can I do to make it worse? Have temper tantrums, use insults, pretend not to hear, etc. Reverse: control temper, use compliments, be solicitous to needs and requests.*

In another example, a variety store chain was being hurt by the competition. Some possible reversals include these:

- *how can the store hurt competition?*
- *how can competition help the store?*
- *how can the competition hurt itself?*
- *how can the store help itself?*

The second reversal, "How can competition help the store?" was chosen and was implemented by sending employees to competing stores every week to examine displays, sales, floor plans, goods quality and selection, anything that appeared to be effective or useful. The employees brought these ideas back to company, compared, and implemented the best in the store. Result: competition helped the store.

The value of reversal is its "provocative rearrangement of information" (de Bono's term). Looking at a familiar problem or situation in a fresh way can suggest new solutions or approaches. It doesn't matter whether the reversal makes sense or not.

Ask nonexperts

Sometimes it seems that the test of a truly brilliant idea is whether or not the "experts" discount it. Often these are the ideas that later seem obvious - even to the experts.

Charles Duell, director of the U. S. Patent Office, in 1899: "Everything that can be invented has been invented."

Grover Cleveland in 1905: "Sensible and responsible women do not want to vote."

Robert Millikan, Nobel prizewinner in physics, in 1923: "There is no likelihood man can ever tap the power of the atom."

Lord Kelvin, president of Royal Society, in 1895: "Heavier-than-air flying machines are impossible."

The King of Prussia who predicted the failure of railroad because: "No one will pay good money to get from Berlin to Potsdam in one hour when he can ride his horse in one day for free."

There are as many stories about experts failing to understand new ideas as there are keys on a piano. In 1861, Philip Reis, a German inventor, built an instrument that could transmit music and was very close to transmitting speech. Experts told him there was no need for such an instrument, as "the telegraph is good enough." He discontinued his work, and it was not until fifteen years later that Alexander Graham Bell patented the telephone.

Some social scientists believe that the more expert you become in your field, the more difficult it is to create innovative new ideas - or even obvious ones. This is because becoming an expert means you tend to specialize your thinking. Specializing is like brushing one tooth. You get to know that one tooth extremely well, but you lose the rest of them in the process.

When experts specialize their thinking, they put borders around subjects and search for ideas only within the borders of their expertise. Nonexperts do not have enough expertise to draw borders. As a result, they look everywhere for ideas. This is why breakthrough ideas are usually found by nonexperts.

This is the principle that prevented the "experts" at Univac from seeing the huge business market for computers. The computer, they said, was designed for science, not business. The same thinking, in 1905, led the German manufacturer of Novocain to wage a furious national campaign to prevent dentists from using it because their company "experts" developed the drug for doctors, not dentists. And the same borders explain why virtually every "delivery expert," including the U. S. Postal Service, unanimously declared Fred Smith's concept for Federal Express unworkable, as people would not pay a fancy price for speed and reliability.

Very much aware of how experts think, Sir Clive Sinclair, the British inventor of the pocket calculator and the flat-screen television, has said that when he enters a new field, he reads "just enough to get a base, just enough to get the idiom" of the field. Anything more and he would start drawing borders.

Chester Carlson invented xerography in 1938, but more than twenty major U. S. corporations, including IBM and Kodak, showed an "enthusiastic lack of interest" in his system, as Carlson put it. No major corporation or office-supply expert saw a market for xerography. After all, who would buy a copy machine when carbon paper was so cheap and so plentiful?

To get ideas, talk to people (nonexperts) outside your field:

1. Talk to someone who is outside your field and from an entirely different background. The more casual the relationship, the more likely he or she will give you a unique perspective. If you're looking for ways to increase sales, as a priest, teacher, doctor, bartender, or Girl Scout for ideas.

Frank Perdue (the "it takes a tough man to make a tender chicken" man) was told by the chicken experts that a chicken is a chicken - consumers bought by price and price alone. Perdue went to work as a

Modes of Thinking

clerk in a supermarket and talked to housewives about chicken. He discovered what the experts and their market research did not - that the color of a chicken and unplucked feathers were more important than price.

Recently, a gynecologist developed a new birth control device. He perfected the new design in a casual discussion before a dental exam. The dentist came up with the new shape and form almost immediately after the gynecologist described his challenge.

2. Seek out idea-oriented people. Surround yourself with people who love ideas and use them in their businesses and lives. They will fire up your imagination. Surround yourself with people:

- Who are creatively alert - people who are always offering alternatives, ideas, and suggestions about anything and everything;
- Who have a keen interest in life and are excited about being alive;
- Are naive about your business, but not stupid or ignorant;
- Who have a great wit and see the absurdity in things;
- Who have different value systems than yours;
- Who travel and pay attention to what they observe;
- Who are voracious readers.

A steel company executive was finding it harder and harder to locate people to work in his plant. He discussed the challenge with his minister, who suggested recruiting at local churches. They formed a network of three local churches to search for qualified parishioners, and the executive has hired every candidate the ministers have sent his way. He's thrilled with the results. "The ministers sift out the best candidates," he observes. "They don't send loafers or drifters, just solid citizens with strong families and work ethic."

3. Draw out the creativity in strangers you meet casually. Everyone has at least one idea that might be useful to you. H. J. Lawson got his revolutionary idea for using a chain to power the bicycle from a waiter at his favorite restaurant.

An executive of a major motel chain was talking casually with his garbage man about the motel business when the garbage man said, "If I were you, I'd sell pizza in my motels. You can't believe the number of pizza boxes we pick up in the trash at motels and hotels." The executive installed pizza ovens in his chain with great results. Once the garbage man said "pizza," the executive realized that they were missing out on a big market.

4. Listen. Joseph Kennedy withdrew his money from the stock market before the 1929 crash after listening to numerous strangers (including his bootblack) on the street warn about stock speculation. At the same time, the experts, including leading Yale economist Irving Fisher, were saying that stocks had hit a "permanently high plateau."

Frieda Caplan listens. She is the chairperson and founder of Frieda's Finest, a celebrated and thriving produce company. In a field dominated by generic products and devoid a new ideas, she's created a brand idetity and persuaded millions of Americans to buy fruits and vegetables they never heard of. How? By listening. Her cardinal rule: "Always have an open door; always listen to what anyone has to offer."

She listened one day when a stranger asked if she had ever heard of a fruit called the Chinese goosberry. She had never seen one, but promised to keep as eye out. Six months later, by sheer coincidence, a broker stopped by and offered a load of Chinese gooseberries. The gooseberries were fuzzy, green, wholly unappealing little fruit.

What the fruit needed was some good PR. She gave the fruit a new name, one suggested by another stranger: Kiwifruit, derived from the kiwi bird of New Zealand. She convinced local restaurants to serve kiwi desserts and developed posters that explained to shoppers what a kiwi was and how it could be used.

By listening to a stranger, Frieda changed American cuisine.

Exercise 1. Reversals.
Choose one of the following situations and suggest at least five reversals for it.

1. street cleaner cleaning streets _____
2. workers striking against the company __ _____
3. clerk helping customer _____
4. how can a student improve his ability to write? _____
5. how can society solve the drug problem? _____

Exercise 2. Create the ugliest, the worst, or the most stupid thing.

CHAPTER 7

Pablo Picasso in the beginning of his career was known as a realistic artist. In some point of his life he decided to create an 'ugly pictures.' He tried to draw like a child. The new style called 'cubism' was born.

1. Try to write something **badly**. Create **the ugliest** story possible.
   _____

2. Try to draw something **badly**. Create **the ugliest** picture possible.
   _____

3. Try to develop a stupid theory. _____

SUMMARY

Modes of Thinking

DEFINITION/BASIC FEATURES	LEARNING STRATEGY	APPLICATIONS
Analogical Thinking		
Definition: Analogical Thinking is the transfer of an idea from one context to a new one.	⦿ A target problem (new situation) needs to be solved. ⦿ Retrieval of a source problem (familiar situation) from memory. ⦿ Comparison of the similar features of the target problem and the source problem. ⦿ Adapting the source problem to produce a solution to the target problem.	**Examples:** ⦿ Parables. ⦿ Case-based reasoning. ⦿ Legal reasoning. ⦿ Politics. ⦿ Mind as a computer. ⦿ Metaphor in language. ⦿ Inventions such as Velcro, the telephone, and Windows.
Basic Features: ⦿ Foundation for invention/discovery. ⦿ Unknown explained by known. ⦿ Requires fluency (lots of ideas). ⦿ Provides predictions, explanations, and knowledge restructuring. ⦿ Flexible pattern recognition. ⦿ A transfer of idea/concepts/object from one field to another one.		**Questions:** ⦿ What else is like this? ⦿ What have others done? ⦿ Where can I find an idea? ⦿ What ideas can I modify to fit my problem? ⦿ What can be done to this concept/idea/procedure? Put to other uses? New ways to use as is? Other uses if modified? Modify? New twist? Change meaning, color, motion, sound, form? Other changes? Magnify? What to add? Greater frequency? Longer? Extra value? Duplicate? Multiply? Exaggerate? Minify? What to subtract? Condensed? Miniature? Lighter? Split up? Understate? Rearrange? Interchange components? Other sequence? Change schedule? Combine? How about a blend, an assortment? Combine units? Combine purposes? Combine appeals?
Symbolic Thinking		
Definition:	⦿ Subtract. Simplify. Omit, or remove certain parts or	**Examples:** ⦿ Interpretation of symbols.

Modes of Thinking

A symbol is any kind of percept that stands for or represents something else.	elements. ⊙ Take something away from your subject. ⊙ Compress it or make it smaller. ⊙ Stylize it. ⊙ Visualize it. ⊙ Create a picture of a concept taught. ⊙ Learn symbols of the subject taught.	⊙ Visualization of a concept taught.
Basic Features: ⊙ Foundation for abstract thinking. ⊙ Represents visualization of concepts. ⊙ Enables symbols to be in place of words/thoughts. ⊙ Language. ⊙ Mathematics. ⊙ Chemistry. ⊙ Physics. ⊙ Allows for the translation of a feeling by some means.		**Questions:** ⊙ What can be eliminated, reduced, disposed of? ⊙ What rules can you break? ⊙ How can you simplify, abstract, stylize or abbreviate?

Analysis

Definition: The ability to break down a situation, issue, or problem into its intricate pieces in a systematic way, or trace its implications, in order to achieve a higher level of understanding and meaning.	⊙ Look beneath the surface. ⊙ Establish the validity of any assumptions surrounding the main issues. ⊙ Investigate the credibility of those advancing certain arguments if required. ⊙ Are emotional or subjective factors at play? ⊙ What are the strengths and weaknesses of the points of view being expressed?	**Examples:** ⊙ Figuring out how each part works independently. ⊙ Good for simple mechanisms. ⊙ Narrows the focus into smaller pieces. ⊙ Solves individual problems. ⊙ Seeing patterns. ⊙ Organization of parts. ⊙ Recognition of hidden meanings. ⊙ Identification of components.
Basic Features: ⊙ The ability to scrutinize and break down facts and thoughts into their strengths and weaknesses. ⊙ Developing the capacity to think in a thoughtful, discerning way, to solve problems, analyze data, and recall and use information. ⊙ Analytical thinking is focused, sharp, linear, deals with one thing at a time, is deconstructive, contains no perspective, is subject to disorientation, is brain centered, and tends to the abstract. ⊙ Analytical thinking is efficient in the following conditions – sufficient time, relatively static conditions, and a clear differentiation between the observer and the observed. ⊙ It is best suited for dealing with complexities, and works best where there are established criteria for the analysis (for example, rules of law). It is necessary when an explanation is required, seeks the best option, and can be taught in the classroom to beginners.	⊙ Would these apply in all situations and if not, what allowances would have to be made? ⊙ Leave no stone unturned. ⊙ Isolate. ⊙ Separate, crop, set apart, detach: Use only a part of your subject. ⊙ In composing a picture, use a viewfinder to crop the image or visual field selectively. ⊙ "Crop" your ideas, too, with a "mental" viewfinder. ⊙ Fragment. Separate, split, divide: Take your subject or idea apart. Dissect it. Chop it up or otherwise disassemble it.	**Questions:** ⊙ Who, what, when, where, why, how? ⊙ Analyze, separate, order, explain, connect, classify, arrange, divide, compare, select, explain, infer. ⊙ What element can you detach or focus on? ⊙ What devices can you use to divide it into smaller increments or make it appear discontinuous?

Synthesis

Definition: Synthesis thinking is a method of thinking which relies on taking existing concepts and ideas and then	⊙ Combine ideas/concepts in a complex whole ⊙ Put together parts into a whole. ⊙ Achieve a construct that	**Examples:** ⊙ Use old ideas to create new ones. ⊙ Generalize from given facts. ⊙ Relate knowledge from several areas. ⊙ Predict, draw conclusions.

creating new notions or understanding from by combining them in new or unique ways.	satisfy a goal. ⊙ Design a new artifact. ⊙ Integrate. ⊙ Modify.	
Basic Features: ⊙ Follows analytical thinking ⊙ Puts things together (creative thinking). ⊙ Allows further understanding with topics that are unfamiliar to a person. ⊙ Permits taking existing concepts and ideas and then creating new notions or understanding by combining them in new or unique ways.	⊙ Rearrange, substitute, plan, create, adapt. ⊙ Compose, formulate, prepare, generalize, rewrite. ⊙ Invent, incorporate, generalize. ⊙ Switch, exchange or replace. ⊙ Overlap, cover, place over, overlay: Superimpose dissimilar images, subjects, or ideas. Overlay elements to produce new meanings, images, or ideas. Superimpose different elements from different perspectives, disciplines or time periods on your subject. Combine sensory perceptions (sounds, color, etc.).	**Questions:** ⊙ What if? ⊙ How can we improve? ⊙ What parts can be combined together? Ideas from other disciplines? ⊙ What other idea, material, image or ingredient can you substitute for all or part of your subject? ⊙ What alternative or supplementary plan can be employed? ⊙ Think syncronistically: What elements or images from different frames of reference can be combined in a single view? Notice, for example, how Cubist painters superimposed several views of a single object in order to show many different moments at the same time simultaneously.
	**Holistic Thinking**
Definition: Holism (from ὅλος holos, a Greek word meaning all, entire, total) is the idea that all the properties of a given system (biological, chemical, social, economic, mental, linguistic, etc.) cannot be determined or explained by the sum of its component parts alone. Instead, the system as a whole determines in an important way how the parts behave.	⊙ Applies knowledge from disparate categories to resolve a problem. ⊙ Ability to provide long term solutions to large scale problems and projects. ⊙ Utilized by designers to implement design methods and new overall ideas ⊙ Aides in coping with large complexities and bewilderment associated with rapid changes.	**Examples:** ⊙ Philosophy. ⊙ Puzzles. ⊙ The human, animal, plant cells (e.g. somatic, etc.). ⊙ Most aspects of democratic government. ⊙ Military company (groups and branches of people working together to therefore complete a mission). ⊙ Society as a whole. ⊙ Economics as a whole. ⊙ Health as a whole. ⊙ Science as a whole. ⊙ Psychology as a whole. ⊙ Education as a whole. ⊙ Arts as a whole.
Basic Features: ⊙ Commonly used for analyzing and managing economics, science and politics. ⊙ The most useful while discussing extremely complex systems. ⊙ Hosts of various forms of knowledge ⊙ The whole is more than the sum of the parts. ⊙ The whole determines the nature of the parts. ⊙ The parts cannot be understood if considered in isolation from the whole. ⊙ The parts are dynamically interrelated or interdependent. ⊙ Any subject is a composite of all other subjects.		**Questions:** ⊙ What is the long term solution to a large scale problems and projects? ⊙ What is the history of a large scale problems and projects?
	**Systems Thinking**

Modes of Thinking

Definition: Systems thinking is a way of understanding reality that emphasizes the relationships among a system's parts, rather than the parts themselves. Based on a field of study known as system dynamics, systems thinking has a practical value that rests on a solid theoretical foundation.	⦿ Recognize a broader pattern. ⦿ Create direction or give guidance. ⦿ Resolve a recurring problem. ⦿ Takes away the individual worker. ⦿ Explain past as a possible chaotic situation.	**Examples:** ⦿ Create Models to represent a system. ⦿ Visual representation of a complex system. ⦿ Build a Simulation. ⦿ - Gives foresight to a system's behavior ⦿ - Is not always accurate ⦿ - Doesn't eliminate risk ⦿ - Helps understand potential risks *[fishbone diagram: Event, Problem, Situation]*
Basic Features: ⦿ Gives a more accurate picture of reality. ⦿ It is founded on some basic, universal principles. ⦿ Every system has a purpose within a larger system. Example: The purpose of the R&D department in your organization is to generate new product ideas and features for the organization. ⦿ All of a system's parts must be present for the system to carry out its purpose optimally. Example: The R&D system in organization consists of people, equipment, and processes. A system's parts must be arranged in a specific way for the system to carry out its purpose. Example: If you rearranged the reporting relationships in your R&D department so that the head of new-product development reported to the entry-level lab technician, the department would likely have trouble carrying out its purpose. ⦿ Systems change in response to feedback. The word feedback plays a central role in systems thinking. Feedback is information that returns to its original transmitter such that it influences that transmitter's subsequent actions. Example: Suppose you turn too sharply while driving your car around a curve. Visual cues (you see a mailbox rushing toward you) would tell you that you were turning too sharply. These cues constitute feedback that prompts you to change what you're doing (jerk the steering wheel in the other direction somewhat) so you can put your car back on course. ⦿ Systems maintain their stability by making adjustments based on feedback. Example: Your body		**Questions:** ⦿ If you remove any one of components, could this system function? ⦿ Which components are crucial for a system? ⦿ Which components could be removed from a system? ⦿ What is a Butterfly Effect as a sensitive dependence?

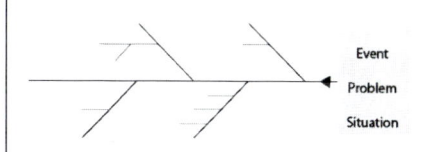

temperature generally hovers around 98.6 degrees Fahrenheit. If you get too hot, your body produces sweat, which cools you back down.
- It emphasizes wholes rather than parts, and stresses the role of interconnections—including the role we each play in the systems at work in our lives.
- It emphasizes circular feedback (for example, A leads to B, which leads to C, which leads back to A) rather than linear cause and effect (A leads to B, which leads to C, which leads to D, . . . and so on).
- It contains special terminology that describes system behavior, such as reinforcing process (a feedback flow that generates exponential growth or collapse) and balancing process (a feedback flow that controls change and helps a system maintain stability).

Dialectical Thinking

Definition:

Dialectical thinking places all the emphasis on change. Instead of talking about static structures, it talks about process and movement.

Broadly defined, Dialectic (Greek: διαλεκτική) is an exchange of propositions (theses) and counter-propositions (antitheses) resulting in a synthesis of the opposing assertions, or at least a qualitative transformation in the direction of the dialogue.

Basic Features:
- It emphasizes smooth continuous change or progress
- It states that the way change takes place is through conflict and opposition.
- Dialectics is always looking for the contradictions within people or situations as the main guide to what is going on and what is likely to happen.
- There are three main propositions which are put forward about opposites and contradictions.
- Interdependence of opposites: Opposites depend on each other, light needs darkness, up needs down, protons need electrons and so on so forth. Everything has an opposite that keeps it in balance.
- Interpenetration of opposites: There is one within the other, There is some light in darkness.

- Instead of looking at the standard structure of things, look at change and movement.
- Find contradictions in ideas until a true solution is found.
- Use opposites to make the solution.

Examples:
- Researching in writing.
- Dialectical logic in interpretation of data.
- Interpretation of self.
- Philosophical thinking.
- Epistemology in particular.
- The direct opposite of light is darkness and vice versa.
- One cannot exist without the other; without a concept of what darkness is, there can be no concept of light.
- Each is not absolute; there is darkness in light and light in darkness because if either was pure then it would leave you blind to what's really there.

Questions:

Reject normal logic and use a different concept. Instead of this object being just an object, what could it be or what it can't be?

Modes of Thinking

- Unity of opposites: dialectics goes on to say that if we take an opposite to its very ultimate extreme, and make it absolute, it actually turns into its opposite. Thus if we make darkness absolute, we are blind - we can't see anything.
- Change.
- Gradual changes lead to turning points. The two opposing forces in a process of change push against each other. As long as one side is stronger than the other side, change is gradual. But when the other side becomes stronger, there is a turning point--an avalanche, a birth, a collapse, a discovery, . . .
- Change moves in spirals, not circles. Many changes are cyclical--first one side dominates, then the other--as in day/night, breathing in/breathing out, one opposite then another. Dialectics argues that these cycles do not come back exactly to where they started; they don't make a perfect circle. Instead, change is evolutionary, moving in a spiral.

Integrative Thinking

Definition:

Integrative Thinking is the ability to constructively face the tensions of opposing models.

Instead of choosing one at the expense of the other a thinker generates a creative resolution of the tension in the form of a new model that contains elements of the individual models, but is superior to each.

- Hybridize.
- Cross-fertilize: Wed your subject with an improbable mate.
- Ask yourself: What would you get if you crossed a x-subject with an y-subject? Creative thinking is a form of "mental hybridization" in that ideas are produced by cross-linking subjects from different realms.
- Transfer the hybridization mechanism to the use of color, form, and structure; cross-fertilize organic and inorganic elements, as well as ideas and perceptions.

Examples:
- Build a model using smilingly incompatible subjects.
- Hybridize. Cross-fertilize: Wed your subject with an improbable mate.
- Transfer the hybridization mechanism to the use of color, form, and structure; cross-fertilize organic and inorganic elements, as well as ideas and perceptions.

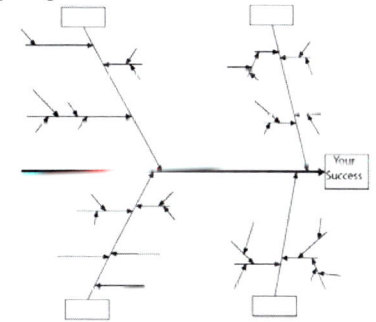

Basic Features:

Integrative thinking is a form of "mental hybridization" in that ideas are produced by cross-linking subjects from different realms.

Questions:
What would you get if you crossed an x-subject with an y-subject?

Heuristic Thinking

Definition:
A heuristic is a rule of thumb that often helps in solving a certain class of problems, but makes no guarantees.

Describing an approach to learning by trying without necessarily having an organized hypothesis or way of proving that the results proved or disproved the

Examples:
- If students are having difficulty understanding a problem, they need to try drawing a picture.
- If they can't find a solution, they need to try assuming that they have a solution

Heuristic are intuitive responses, based on past experience.

It is a process of approximation starting with an initial pattern of thought and gradually assimilating to a target pattern that constitutes an insight into the subject matter at hand. The whole process leads to a holistic or interlaced knowledge.

hypothesis. That is, "seat-of-the-pants" or "trial-by-error" learning.
- Try it before you learn how to use it.
- Guess what it is.
- What do you think about this subject?

and seeing what they can derive from that ("working backward").
- If the problem is abstract, they need to try examining a concrete example.
- Solving a more general problem first (the "inventor's paradox": the more ambitious plan may have more chances of success).

Basic Features:
- Feature List - Examining the features one by one and considering how it might be changed.
- Analogy - The use of analogies might help imagine new features.
- Search - Sometimes solving a problem is a matter of searching through a long list of possible solutions.
- Perspective Shift - When dealing with a problem that involves people, one might consider the problem from the different perspectives of the parties involved.

Questions:
- There are many types of rules that have been created to help in the process of heuristic thinking:
- When creative ideas needed, attention, escape, and movement help.
- A habit to purposefully pause and notice things is useful.
- Creating a feature list relating to the problem or question.
- Searching though a list of possible solutions to the problem

Critical Thinking

Definition:
The ability to challenge your personal believes.
...the ability to analyze facts, generate and organize ideas, defend opinions, make comparisons, draw inferences, evaluate arguments and solve problems (Chance,1986, p. 6);
...a way of reasoning that demands adequate support for one's beliefs and an unwillingness to be persuaded unless support is forthcoming (Tama, 1989, p. 64);
...a conscious and deliberate process which is used to interpret or evaluate information and experiences with a set of reflective attitudes and abilities that guide thoughtful beliefs and actions (Mertes,1991, p.24);
...active, systematic process of understanding and evaluating arguments. An argument provides an assertion about the properties of some object or the relationship between two or more objects and evidence to support or refute the assertion. Critical thinkers acknowledge that there is no single correct way to understand and evaluate arguments and that all attempts are not necessarily successful (Mayer & Goodchild, 1990, p. 4);
...the intellectually disciplined process of actively and skillfully

- Ask pertinent questions
- assess statements and arguments
- be able to admit a lack of understanding or information
- have a sense of curiosity
- is interested in finding new solutions
- be able to clearly define a set of criteria for analyzing ideas
- be willing to examine beliefs, assumptions, and opinions and weigh them against facts
- listen carefully to others and be able to give feedback
- see that critical thinking is a lifelong process of self-assessment
- suspend judgment until all facts have been gathered and considered
- look for evidence to support assumption and beliefs
- be able to adjust opinions when new facts are found
- look for proof
- examine problems closely
- be able to reject information that is incorrect or irrelevant.

Examples:
Critical thinker

- uses evidence skillfully and impartially
- organizes thoughts and articulates them concisely and coherently
- distinguishes between logically valid and invalid inferences
- suspends judgment in the absence of sufficient evidence to support a decision
- understands the difference between reasoning and rationalizing
- attempts to anticipate the probable consequences of alternative actions
- understands the idea of degrees of belief
- sees similarities and analogies that are not superficially apparent
- can learn independently and has an abiding interest in doing so
- applies problem-solving techniques in domains other than those in which learned
- can structure informally represented problems in such a way that formal techniques, such as mathematics, can be used to solve them
- can strip a verbal argument of irrelevancies and phrase it in its essential terms
- habitually questions one's own views and attempts to understand both the assumptions that are critical to those views and the implications of the views
- is sensitive to the difference between the validity of a belief and the intensity with which it is held

Modes of Thinking

conceptualizing, applying, analyzing, synthesizing, and/or evaluating information gathered from, or generated by, observation, experience, reflection, reasoning, or communication, as a guide to belief and action (Scriven & Paul, 1992); reasonable reflective thinking focused on deciding what to believe or do (Ennis, 1992).	⊙ Critical thinkers must be able to distinguish among these three types of communication:. ⊙ FACT: reports information that can be directly observed or can be verified or checked for accuracy. ⊙ OPINION: expresses an evaluation based on a personal judgment or belief which may or may not be verifiable. ⊙ INFERENCE: a logical conclusion or a legitimate implication based on factual information.	⊙ is aware of the fact that one's understanding is always limited, often much more so than would be apparent to one with a noninquiring attitude ⊙ recognizes the fallibility of one's own opinions, the probability of bias in those opinions, and the danger of weighting evidence according to personal preferences.
Basic Features: Critical thinking is the intellectually disciplined process of actively and skillfully ⊙ conceptualizing, ⊙ applying, ⊙ analyzing, ⊙ synthesizing, and/or ⊙ evaluating information gathered from, or generated by, ⊙ observation, ⊙ experience, ⊙ reflection, ⊙ reasoning, or ⊙ communication, as a guide to belief and action.		**Questions:** Handling difficult material with confidence. ⊙ Annotating: Fundamental to each of these strategies is annotating directly on the page: underlining key words, phrases, or sentences; writing comments or questions in the margins; bracketing important sections of the text; constructing ideas with lines or arrows; numbering related points in sequence; and making note of anything that strikes you as interesting, important, or questionable. ⊙ Previewing: Learning about a text before really reading it. Previewing enables readers to get a sense of what the text is about and how it is organized before reading it closely. This simple strategy includes seeing what you can learn from the headnotes or other introductory material, skimming to get an overview of the content and organization, and identifying the rhetorical situation. ⊙ Contextualizing: Placing a text in its historical, biographical, and cultural contexts. When student reads a text, he/she reads it through the lens of his/her own experience. ⊙ Questioning to understand and remember: Asking questions about the content. ⊙ Reflecting on challenges to personal beliefs and values: Examining personal responses. The reading that students do for the class might challenge they attitudes, unconsciously held beliefs, or positions on current issues. ⊙ Outlining and summarizing: Identifying the main ideas and restating them in your own words. Outlining the main ideas helps you to discover this structure. ⊙ Summarizing begins with outlining, but instead of merely listing the main ideas, a summary recomposes them to form a new text. Whereas outlining depends on a close analysis of each paragraph, summarizing also requires creative synthesis. Putting ideas together again -- in someone own words and in a condensed form -- shows how reading critically can lead to deeper understanding of any text. ⊙ Evaluating an argument means testing the logic of a text as well as its credibility

CHAPTER 7

		and emotional impact. All writers make assertions that want you to accept as true. An argument has two essential parts: a claim and support. The claim asserts a conclusion -- an idea, an opinion, a judgment, or a point of view - that the writer wants you to accept. The support includes reasons (shared beliefs, assumptions, and values) and evidence (facts, examples, statistics, and authorities) that give readers the basis for accepting the conclusion. When you assess an argument, you are concerned with the process of reasoning as well as its truthfulness (these are not the same thing). At the most basic level, in order for an argument to be acceptable, the support must be appropriate to the claim and the statements must be consistent with one another. ⊙ Comparing and contrasting related readings: Exploring likenesses and differences between texts to understand them better.
	**Divergent Thinking**
Definition: Divergent thinking is the ability to find as many possible answers to a particular problem. Divergent thinking produces one or more novel ideas relevant to the problem to which there is no correct solution therefore it works better for open ended problems.	Fantasize. Fantasize your subject. Use it to trigger surreal, outlandish, preposterous, bizarre thoughts. Topple mental and sensory expectations. How far can you extend your imagination?	**Examples:** ⊙ Brainstorming. Brainstorming is a technique which involves generating a list of ideas in a creative, unstructured manner. It separates the idea generation process from the idea evaluation process. ⊙ Reverse Brainstorming. This process involves listing ways of achieving a goal opposite of the one actually desired. What is most interesting about this process is that the ideas proposed using this technique are very often the ones currently in practice. ⊙ Keeping a Journal. Journals are an effective way to record ideas that one thinks of spontaneously. ⊙ Freewriting ⊙ Mind and subject mapping ⊙ Great thinking ⊙ Taking time to think ⊙ Art work
Basic Features: ⊙ Thinking 'outside the box.' ⊙ Opposite of Convergent thinking ⊙ Way of thinking abstractly ⊙ Random generation of ideas ⊙ Normally followed by convergent thinking to put ideas in order.		**Questions:** ⊙ What if…? ⊙ What if automobiles were made of brick? What if alligators played pool? What if insects grew larger than elephant? ⊙ What if night and day occurred simultaneously? ⊙ What happens if…? ⊙ What else could we do? Divergent thinking questions are those which represent intellectual operations wherein students are free to generate independently their own ideas or to take a new direction or perspective on a given topic. Thought processes involved while asking and answering these questions are predicting, hypothesizing, inferring, or

Modes of Thinking

		reconstructing. Divergent thinking questions usually begin with these words or phrases: ⦿ Imagine... ⦿ Suppose... ⦿ Predict... ⦿ If..., then... ⦿ Can you create... Examples of divergent thinking questions: ⦿ Can you imagine ways that professional soccer has changed American sports culture? ⦿ Suppose that Caesar never returned to Rome from Gaul. Would the Empire have existed? ⦿ What predictions can you make regarding the voting process in Ohio? ⦿ How might life in the year 2100 differ from today? ⦿ If computers correct spelling, then is it necessary for third graders to take spelling tests?
Convergent Thinking		
Definition: Thinking that brings together information focused on solving a problem (especially solving problems that have a single correct solution). Convergent thinking is the ability to find the best single answer to a problem. Allows people to gain a good education with having the correct knowledge to be able to have successful jobs in their future.	Convergent thinking is usually used when one "best" solution is being sought to the current problem. ⦿ Mathematics ⦿ Science ⦿ Software Design ⦿ Test Taking ⦿ Most of the "Hard" sciences in general	**Examples:** ⦿ Bringing in several pieces of information from several different common sources can help non-biased thinking. ⦿ Convergent thinking helps to find the "right answer," to a question seeking one particular answer (what is 2 + 2, etc.), helping to locate a logically concluding solution. ⦿ Convergent thinking vs. divergent proves to be better in a sense of accomplishment of putting pieces of information back together rather than taking them apart to study them pars whole. ⦿ Locate a problem at the "center" of our focus and then gather peripheral resources to bear down on the problem. So then our resources "converge" on the problem. ⦿ The test-taker brings knowledge from outside of the problem (perhaps learned in a course) and converges it all onto the problem in order to choose the correct answer.
Basic Features: ⦿ Thinking 'inside the box.' ⦿ Data and facts can be gathered and combined to find or approach solutions to problems, equations, or creative brain storming. ⦿ It emphasizes speed, accuracy, logic, and the like, and focuses on accumulating information, recognizing the familiar, reapplying set techniques, and preserving the already known. ⦿ It is based on familiarity with what is already known (i.e.,		**Questions:** ⦿ What is it? ⦿ What's going on? ⦿ What is happening?

CHAPTER 7

knowledge), and is most effective in situations where a ready-made answer exists and needs simply to be recalled from stored information, or worked out from what is already known by applying conventional and logical search, recognition and decision-making strategies.		
Conscious Thinking		
Definition: Consciousness deals with the state of being self aware. Conscious Thinking involves an individual's stream of surface thoughts and processes that make up the chatter in our heads. Consciousness may involve thoughts, sensations, perceptions, moods, emotions, dreams, and self-awareness. It has been defined from a biological and causal perspective as the act of yourself altering attention and calculation effort, usually with the goal of obtaining, retaining, or maximizing specific constraint, such as food, a safe environment, family, or mates.	Awareness of ⊙ Physical world (sensing and acting), ⊙ Social world (largely unconscious emotions and body language). These first two are centered in the present) ⊙ Past and future (the self conscious self, with it linguistic narrative mind that lets us talk both to ourselves and to others.) ⊙ Cognition ⊙ Free will	**Examples:** ⊙ Information gathering ⊙ Basic understanding ⊙ Making an informed decision based on subconscious thoughts from similar or past experiences. ⊙ Grants a person the ability to maneuver the body with typical motor skill functions. ⊙ Used for perspective of one's reality along with being self aware and having interests. ⊙ Picture Puzzles ⊙ Strategy Games ⊙ Crossword Puzzles ⊙ Card Games ⊙ Deduction Games (such as Clue) ⊙ Visualization Puzzles ⊙ Optical Illusions
Basic Features: ⊙ Thinking about thinking – metacognition ⊙ Depends on working memory ⊙ The conscious mind is sequential. It likes logical order. ⊙ The conscious mind is linear thinking. It thinks in terms of cause-effect. ⊙ The conscious mind is logical. It likes things to make sense – have a reason. ⊙ The conscious mind does intellectual thinking. Is responsible for self-talk. ⊙ The conscious mind is associated with the waking, thinking state. ⊙ The conscious can voluntarily move parts of one's body. ⊙ The conscious mind is only aware of the now. ⊙ The conscious mind is deliberate. ⊙ The conscious mind is verbal (including self-talk). ⊙ The conscious mind is the place of cognitive learnings and understandings ⊙ The conscious mind uses intellect to come up with logical solutions for problems. ⊙ The conscious mind seeks understanding of problems and reasons that if it understands them, it can make them go away. ⊙ Consciousness may involve thoughts, sensations, perceptions,		**Questions:** ⊙ Who? ⊙ What? ⊙ Where? ⊙ How? ⊙ Why?

moods, emotions, dreams, and self-awareness.
- It has been defined from a biological and causal perspective as the act of yourself altering attention and calculation effort, usually with the goal of obtaining, retaining, or maximizing specific constraint, such as food, a safe environment, family, or mates.
- Conscious thinking over a complex problem will lead to the right decision than making a snap decision, according to a new study.
- Categories of Consciousness:
- Awareness of the external environment -- Person knows of and monitors the existence of environmental stimuli, which are anything (objects, action, sounds, smells, etc.) in the environment.
- Reflection on environment stimuli -- Person can mentally consider aspects of your environment and process information. This involves symbolic thought, because the mind can consider and reflect on the environmental stimuli even in their absence.
- Awareness of oneself -- This can be compared to #1, because just as person is aware of concrete objects in his/her environment, he/she recognizes him/herself as one of these concrete objects.
- Just as person is aware of action in the environment, he/she is aware of his/her own internal processes like breathing and heart beating.
- Awareness of one's thoughts -- This can be compared to #2, because it is more abstract. Person is aware of thoughts and feelings and importantly, he/she connects them to oneself.
- Conscious thought is possible due to knowledge and language. Without the use of language "inner speak" would not be possible when trying to consciously solve a problem.
- Action without thought is instinct (or subconscious thinking) whereas action with thought is conscious thinking.
- Conscious thinking was developed through evolutionary development in humans.
- The capacity to think consciously is unique to humans and is born from an understanding of

CHAPTER 7

environment beyond our immediate senses. ⊙ Emotions influence both conscious and unconscious behavior ⊙ Emotion is always consciously experienced ⊙ Conscious thinking is the basis for almost all behavior and emotions.		
	**Unconscious Thinking**	

Definition:
    Unconscious thinking is thinking that takes place when a person is in an altered state of conscious. Such as sleeping.
    The unconscious mind operates well below the perception of the conscious mind as defined by Sigmund Freud and others.
	Random association	**Examples:**
		    "Sleep on it".
		    Meditate and think (music may illicit the altered state of consciousness)

Basic Features: ⊙ The unconscious mind processes simultaneously. It multitasks. ⊙ The unconscious mind makes associations and connections between many thoughts, ideas and feelings. ⊙ The unconscious mind is intuitive and can make associations of information easily. ⊙ The unconscious mind does your perceiving and feeling. ⊙ The unconscious mind is associated with the dreaming ⊙ (including day dreaming), reflecting, meditating and sleeping state. ⊙ The unconscious can involuntarily move parts of your body. ⊙ The unconscious mind is unlimited in time and space. It holds all your memories and future constructs. ⊙ The unconscious mind is automatic. ⊙ The unconscious mind is nonverbal (feeling). ⊙ The unconscious mind is the place of experiential learnings. ⊙ The unconscious mind can access internal resources from memories of experiences, linking them all together - creating a resourceful state. ⊙ The unconscious mind will tell you when you are right because it will feel right. ⊙ The unconscious mind decides what it will do about it. It can forget (amnesia), distort (make false associations) or break connections (get over it).		**Questions:**
	**Deductive Thinking**	

Modes of Thinking

Definition: Deductive thinking is compared to logic driven assumption - drawing conclusions based on valid or invalid answers to valid or invalid premises. Deductive reasoning is one of the two basic forms of valid reasoning. While inductive reasoning argues from the particular to the general, deductive reasoning argues from the general to a specific instance. The basic idea is that if something is true of a class of things in general, this truth applies to all legitimate members of that class. The key, then, is to be able to properly identify members of the class. Miscategorizing will result in invalid conclusions. Formal logic is primarily based on abstract rules whereas its counterpart, informal logic, or critical thinking, is based on analyzing verbal arguments to see if they are true -- or an even weaker goal -- to see if they are probably true. Generally, formal logic is a necessary precursor to informal logic.	⦿ Deduction starts with an assumed hypothesis or theory, which is why it has been called 'hypothetico-deduction'. This assumption may be well-accepted or it may be rather more shaky -- nevertheless, for the argument it is not questioned. ⦿ Prove a general law for a particular case and then do many deductive experiments ⦿ Deduction can also be used to test an induction by applying it elsewhere, although in this case the initial theory is assumed to be true only temporarily. ⦿ A general statement is made about an entire class of things, and then one specific example is given.	**Examples:** ⦿ If A then B; ⦿ If B then C; ⦿ Therefore, If A then C ⦿ If the premise is true; the conclusion must also be true. ⦿ All cups are green. ⦿ Socrates is a cup. ⦿ Therefore, Socrates is green. ⦿ Not even close to true, but if the premise is valid, then the conclusion has to be valid as well. ⦿
Basic Features: ⦿ Conclusions based on previously known facts ⦿ Deductive thinking is used to make general theories or predict specific instances. The premises do not have to necessarily be true- deductive reasoning does not work on a true or false system. ⦿ Deductive thinking works on a in/valid system. ⦿ Deduction is used by scientists who take a general scientific law and apply it to a certain case, as they assume that the law is true.		**Questions:** ⦿ What is the conclusion? ⦿ Is a particular argument valid? ⦿ Is a particular conclusion right? ⦿ What is wrong in one's reasoning?

Inductive Thinking

Definition: Inductive thinking, is a special reasoning technique in where one may go from specific observations to broader generalizations and theories. Also sometimes called the "bottom up" approach to thinking	⦿ Observation: collect facts, without bias. ⦿ Analysis: classify the facts, identifying patterns of regularity. ⦿ Inference: From the patterns, infer generalizations about the relations between the facts.	**Examples:** ⦿ This ice is cold... Thus all ice must be cold ⦿ When you drop something, it falls... Thus all things must fall when dropped ⦿ A light bulb will burn you if touched... Thus all light bulbs will burn you if touched ⦿ Stereotypes ⦿ Prejudices.
Basic Features: ⦿ Detect patterns and regularities, ⦿ Formulate some tentative hypotheses that can be explored, and finally ⦿ End up developing some general conclusions or theories.	⦿ Confirmation: Testing the inference through further observation. ⦿ Informal Fallacies: ⦿ Ad Hominem is a general category of fallacies in which a claim or argument	**Questions:** ⦿ Is this inductive argument valid? ⦿ Is this an informal fallacy? ⦿ A fallacy is, very generally, an error in reasoning. A fallacy is an "argument" in which the premises given for the conclusion do not provide the needed

CHAPTER 7

⦿ Conclusions arrived at by inductive reasoning do not have the same degree of certainty as the initial premises. ⦿ Our everyday reasoning depends on patterns of repeated experience rather than deductively valid arguments	is rejected on the basis of some irrelevant fact about the author of or the person presenting the claim or argument (changing object and attacking the person). ⦿ Ad Hominem Tu Quoque This fallacy is committed when it is concluded that a person's claim is false because 1) it is inconsistent with something else a person has said or 2) what a person says is inconsistent with her actions. Also, the fact that a person's claims are not consistent with his actions might indicate that the person is a hypocrite but this does not prove his claims are false. ⦿ Appeal to Authority This fallacy is committed when the person in question is not a legitimate authority on the subject. More formally, if person A is not qualified to make reliable claims in subject S, then the argument will be fallacious. ⦿ Appeal to Belief This line of "reasoning" is fallacious because the fact that many people believe a claim does not, in general, serve as evidence that the claim is true. ⦿ Appeal to Common Practice The fact that most people do X is used as "evidence" to support the action or practice. It is a fallacy because the mere fact that most people do something does not make it correct, moral, justified, or reasonable. ⦿ Bandwagon The Bandwagon is a fallacy in which a threat of rejection by one's peers (or peer pressure) is substituted for evidence in an "argument." ⦿ Begging the Question The premises include the claim that the conclusion is true or (directly or indirectly) assume that the conclusion is true. ⦿ Biased Sample A person draws a conclusion about a population based on a	degree of support.

sample that is biased or prejudiced in some manner.
- ⦿ Burden of Proof Burden of Proof is a fallacy in which the burden of proof is placed on the wrong side. Another version occurs when a lack of evidence for side A is taken to be evidence for side B in cases in which the burden of proof actually rests on side B. A common name for this is an Appeal to Ignorance.
- ⦿ Confusing Cause and Effect A person assumes that one event must cause another just because the events occur together. More formally, this fallacy involves drawing the conclusion that A is the cause of B simply because A and B are in regular conjunction (and there is not a common cause that is actually the cause of A and B). The mistake being made is that the causal conclusion is being drawn without adequate justification.
- ⦿ Division A person infers that what is true of a whole must also be true of its constituents and justification for that inference is not provided.
- ⦿ Hasty Generalization A person draws a conclusion about a population based on a sample that is not large enough.
- ⦿ Post Hoc It is evident in many cases that the mere fact that A occurs before B in no way indicates a causal relationship.
- ⦿ Straw Man A person simply ignores a person's actual position and substitutes a distorted, exaggerated or misrepresented version of that position.
- ⦿ Two Wrongs Make A Right A person "justifies" an action against a person by asserting that the person would do the same thing to him/her, when the action is not necessary to prevent B from doing X to

CHAPTER 7

	A.	
\multicolumn{3}{c}{**Abductive Thinking**}
Definition: Abductive reasoning starts when an inquirer considers of a set of seemingly unrelated facts, armed with the hunch that they are somehow connected. The term abduction is commonly presumed to mean the same thing as hypothesis, however, an abduction is actually the process of inference that produces a hypothesis as its end result. Used in both philosophy and computing.	⊙ Computing ⊙ Artificial Intelligence	**Examples:** ⊙ Jesus' parables. ⊙ Milton Erickson's analogies and therapeutic metaphors.
		Questions:
Basic Features: ⊙ A Foundation for Creativity ⊙ Also called "abduction." ⊙ Involves reasoning by analogy. ⊙ The basis of creating similes and metaphors. ⊙ Involves looking for the similarities between objects and phenomena. ⊙ More closely aligned with deductive thinking than inductive. ⊙ Abductive Reasoning is best explained as the development of a hypothesis which, if true, would best explain the presented evidence. ⊙ Because it infers cause and effect, abduction is a form of the logical fallacy Post hoc ergo propter hoc (after this, on account of this) ⊙ Also called reasoning through successive approximation, this is validation ones hypothesis through abductive reasoning. ⊙ According to abductive validation, an explanation is valid if it gives the "best" explanation for the data (best being defined in terms of elegance and simplicity, i.e. Occam's razor). ⊙ In science, abductive validation is common practice for hypothesis formation.		
\multicolumn{3}{c}{**The "Doubting Game"** **Effective in combination with "Believing Game"**}
Definition: This approach to problem solving emphasizes argument and rigidly reductive method of rationality: problem definition, problem analysis, presentation and evaluation of alternatives, detailing of solutions. The doubting game forces on to poke holes in ideas, tear apart assertions, probe continually, and be	⊙ Write opposition to the idea or concept. ⊙ Effective teaching strategy when trying to get discussion going in the classroom	**Examples:** ⊙ Challenge your personal beliefs. ⊙ Find out what is wrong with the design/structure/process/text. ⊙ Take your favorite design/structure/process/text and find out what is wrong with it.

248

analytical.

Basic Features:
Rules:
- Truth by seeking error
- Question every overt and hidden assumption and assertion
- To play this game is to be rigorous, rational, and tough minded
- Detach oneself; gain perspective
- Take things literally
- Be aggressive, stubborn, and adversarial

Questions:
- Should we invade countries that might attack us?
- Should we torture prisoners who might know what we need to know?
- Should we drop a nuclear bomb on a country that did attack us?
- Should instructors grade the assignments?

The "Believing Game"

Definition:
The Believing Game is a methodology of thinking that entails believing everything about a given idea or object, even if the parts seemingly or actually contradict. If it somehow does not work, a way must be found to MAKE it work.

- Effective teaching strategy when trying to get discussion going in the classroom
- Writing- Our current model for academic or essayist writing tends to be adversarial. When people write an essay arguing for a position, especially in the academy, they are usually expected start off trying to show that other points of view are wrong. There are epistemological problems with this ritual.
- Discussion- Because of the dominance of critical thinking, especially in the academy, academics and students tend to feel that the best way to show they are smart is by pointing out flaws in the views of others. Discussions can take an adversarial tone. People tend to feel not smart if they don't see the flaws that "smart" people point out--or if they don't criticize but rather say something like, "Tell me more about that. I'm trying to see things as you see them."
- Reading-The believing game helps us enter more fully into texts that we find difficult or alien--and also helps us discover and understand a wider range of interpretations.

Examples:
- Children believe everything a parent tells them even if it is not true.
- Religion
- Politics.

Basic Features:
- Promotes positive thinking on an idea
- Generates constructive ideas to debate with the "doubting game"
- Difficult to get the hang of
- Not natural since it does not point out the flaws in a statement
- This method of thinking promotes discussion
- If discussion dives into a debate, the Believing Game is no longer being played.
- Stay away from debate
- Using the Believing Game, good, thoughtful questions and points are developed and brought into the discussion
- "Put yourself in another's shoes"
- "Do not toss the baby out with the bathwater"
- The believing game involves people who cannot make their own opinions based on the facts that are given to them.
- Rules:
- "Believe all the assertions" – even if they are contradicting.
- Settle for the Truth mixed with error.
- Never argue, and believe everything.
- Make the idea work, and find ways to make it work.

Questions:
- Should we invade countries that might attack us?
- Should we torture prisoners who might know what we need to know?
- Should we drop a nuclear bomb on a country that did attack us?
- Should instructors grade the assignments?

Automatic Thinking

Definition:
Automatic Thinking is the brains ability to create meaning from the environment. In a way, Automatic Thinking is more

Arts/writing/programming – practice basic skills until they become automatic.

Examples:
- A good physical example of automatic thinking is stick-shift driving.
- Conditioning of responses based on salient consequence and memory.

appropriately called "Reactionary Thinking." The key aspect of Automatic Thinking is that it automated thoughts are not necessarily conscious ones. These reactionary thoughts establish moods based on our perceptions of others or events.		⦿ ANTS or Automatic Negative Thinking which causes instant negative thoughts when using words such as "always" and "never".
Basic Features: ⦿ This type of thinking is used in split second decisions, and quick choices. ⦿ Since it uses what person has experienced in the past and quickly analyzes it, he/she can get some of the best (or worst) decisions of your life.		**Questions:** ⦿ Do you like/dislike it? ⦿ Why?

Thinking Process and Related Skills

Thinking Process	Examples of Teaching/Learning Strategies
Perception and recognition of problem or issue	• Recognize a problem. • Recall prior related experience. • Define the goal. • Define terms important for context studied. • Generate appropriate questions. • Analyze alternatives. • Devise solution plan. • Plan experiment.

Storage and retrieval of data	• Determine sources for relevant data.
	    - Devise strategies to locate data.
	    - Define key terms and elements for search.
	 • Judge credibility of sources.

Organization and transformation of data	• Organize data in multiple formats. • Interpret data. • Distinguish between fact and opinion. • Distinguish relevant from irrelevant information. • Determine accuracy. • Determine credibility.

CHAPTER 8

Creative Thinking

What is creativity? A talent? A gift? What you can do to make yourself creative? What stops creativity? What is the most effective way to reduce obstacles to creativity?

LEARNING OBJECTIVES

After reading this chapter, you will be able to

1. Define creativity
2. Compare and contrast theories of creativity
3. Identify and apply stages of creative process
4. Describe and discuss obstacles to creativity
5. Apply various techniques for creativity stimulation.

THINK ABOUT THIS.

Using Your Imagination:

In today's world, it is no longer enough to do the same thing as the competition. As the boundaries between countries and industries crumble, everyone is facing a plethora of competition. In order to stand out from the crowd, one must be able to see something distinctly new and better than what others are seeing and then, of course, put this new insight into action.

That is exactly what Japanese manufacturers of toilets have done! Known for their constant pursuit of innovation, Japanese manufacturers, such as Toto, Matsushita, and Inax, have put their imaginations to work in reinventing the common place toilet. Gone are the days of plain and basic toilets. The Japanese manufacturers have included many exotic features, such as:

- A toilet that glows in the dark
- A talking toilet that plays back pre-recorded messages or soundtracks of relaxing music
- A toilet that blasts cool air in the summer or warm air in the winter to cool or heat the bathroom
- A lid that opens when a sensor detects a human being
- A toilet with numerous jet sprays, and
- A toilet with electrodes in the seat to measures weight, body fat ratios, blood pressure, and which can also measure sugar levels in the urine and other health care measures.

Tribute to Arthur Melin:

Let's pay tribute to great innovator. Arthur Melin is a co-founder of the toy company, Wham-O. During his lifetime, Arthur demonstrated an insatiable appetite for inventing or marketing new toys, such as the Superball, Frisbee, Hula Hoop, Slip N Slide, and Silly String. Of these, the Frisbee and Hula Hoop are the most well known.

Arthur Melin first introduced the Frisbee flying disc to the world in 1955. It was first named the Pluto Platter to tap into the public's fascination with UFOs at the time. The flying disc toy was later renamed the Frisbee, after the Frisbee Baking Company, whose pie tins were the actual inspiration for the toy. Interestingly, Arthur did not invest a lot in advertising the new toy; he simply marketed it on college campuses. Soon, through word of mouth, interest grew and sales of the Frisbee topped $100 million (USD). His other great contribution to the toy world was the Hula Hoop. An inventor from Australia showed Arthur the rattan hoop and soon Arthur was marketing plastic hoops and organizing Hula Hoop competitions across America. The Hula Hoop became a national craze, selling over 25 million in the first few months it was introduced!

And now let's lower our voice and be a bit wary! For we want to enter the realm of creativity.... This space does not permit a direct approach. It does not respond to concrete demands. It does not yet know the structure, it knows neither name nor number. It does not want to yield to anything, it does not heed commands. It is the space of creative readiness and is a sanctuary....

Creative ability belongs to the sphere of reality as much as to the realm of fantasy. And there are always two currents, two circles of tension, which magnetically attract one another, flash up and oscillate together until, completely attuned, they penetrate one another: on the one hand, the creative readiness which evokes the image; on the other hand, the will to act whipped up to a point of obsession, that will which takes possession of the image and transforms its yet fleeting matter into malleable working substance in order to give its final form in the crucible of molding.

Mary Wigman (1963)

Creativity means a person's capacity to produce new or original ideas, insights, restructurings, inventions, or artistic objects, that are accepted by experts as being of scientific, aesthetic, social, or technological value; the acceptability or appropriateness of the creative product, even though this valuation may change with the passage of time.

Men and women one of these days will have the courage to be eccentric. They will do as they like – just as the great ones have always done. The word 'eccentric' is a terms of reproach and mild contempt and amusement today, because we live under a system which hates real originality.

Holbrook Jackson

CREATIVE THINKING

Critical Thinking Questions about Creativity and Innovations

Question	Possible Answer
Are there any achievements that are completely original?	There is nothing new under the sun – Aristotle said 2300 years ago Creativity is the ability to change the old into the new.
Can a person be creative without a product?	Erich Fromm (1959) considered two possible meanings: 1. Creativity in the sense of creating something new, something which can be seen or heard by others, such as a painting, a sculpture, a symphony, a poem, a novel, etc.; 2. Creativity as an attitude, which is the condition of any creation in the former sense but which can exist even though nothing new is created in the world of things.
Am I creative? How do I know if I am, or could be, creative?	Every living, breathing human being has the potential to be creative. Each of us is a unique individual capable of creating...it comes with the human territory. We are, simply, quite a creative species. All people can be creative but those who are recognized as being creative have an awareness that others don't. Creative people seem to be able to tune in more to their thought patterns and glean great ideas. People who do not use their creative potential don't know how to do this or aren't even aware it is possible. Creative people can start thinking about something, then forget it. Meanwhile, their brains are still thinking about it. Later on, the person will start thinking about whatever it was again and their brain will say, "Excuse me, I've been thinking about this while you were off doing other things and I have a few ideas. Care to hear them?" Non- creative people don't know that their brains are working for them off- shift -- they don't know what they don't know! There are many components that influence the creativity of individuals. This is not to say that people tremendously fluctuate in their creativity day to day and hour to hour; the opposite is often believed - that some individuals are generally more

Creative Thinking

	creative most of the time than others. The reasons why some people are more creative, however, are many. a) Without the abilities needed to do the creative act, it is highly unlikely the individual will do the act. Just because a person has the ability to do something, however, does not necessarily mean that the person will do it. This is why researchers examine people's motives. b) Without the motivation to do so, it is unlikely that a person would complete an act, regardless of the person's abilities. c) Lastly, opportunities in the environment can affect the creativeness of individuals and groups of individuals. d) If you've ever generated a novel response to a problem or challenge then congratulate yourself as being creative. If you do this on a regular basis, say every day, then put the "creative person" badge on yourself. With, practice, your ability to generate novel and useful responses to problems and challenges will greatly improve. One aspect of a creative personality is the fluency with which he/she generates a number of new ideas. Not only does the creative person think of good ideas, but he/she can think of many ideas, explore them, and record them. If you feel a need to quantify your creative ability, go to a local psychologist and ask about taking a test to measure your creative ability. If you live near a college or university approach their psychology department with this request. But recognize that creative ability can be learned, improved upon, and increased over time.
Isn't creativity found in a few people, like inventors or artists?	Most (if not all) people are creative to various extents. It's just that some people act on their ideas and others ignore them. Inventors and artists take action on their ideas. How may people have said "I could have done that". The response to that is "Well, why didn't you?" or "Too late...someone else thought of it first". That is the whole purpose of creativity training...to develop one's ability to generate and implement new ideas. Different people have different levels and abilities of creativity, much like anything else that is a skill However, everyone can be creative if they want to be. And like other skills, creativity can be developed. Often people will think they aren't creative because they are basing their opinion on a skill they don't have, e.g. "I am a lousy painter." But that doesn't mean I can't be creative as a painter even though I make horrid stuff. A lack of creativity is not what is limiting my output as a painter. Creativity, the ability to generate novel responses to problems and challenges, is a basic human ability. Some people are encouraged to express their creative ability more than others and may even get rewarded for doing so. Artists, in addition to expressing their creativity, also have traits like manual dexterity, good eye-hand coordination and other skills than enable them to more fully express their creative thoughts. Similarly, athletes, teachers, scientists and auto mechanics have special skill sets that enable them to express their creative ideas. In western societies people seem to assign certain universal human abilities, like creativity, to only a subset of all people (usually artists, musicians and architects) making it more difficult for all members of society to see themselves as creative people. This is a Western myth that we must be aware of and work to overcome. Some people have extraordinary talents in fields that have been recognized as "creative." When they combine these extraordinary talents with the determination and persistence that it takes to achieve skill mastery, they are recognized as creative

> artists. Inventors are generally better than average at channeling their creativity towards practical ends, whereas artists are better at expressing themselves creatively.
>
> There are, however, many ways of being creative. Each of us can be creative if we recognize our unique talents and develop mastery in those areas. That is no guarantee that the world will recognize us... but it does provide the soul satisfaction that comes with living a creative life.

I. Briefly stated, creativity is often thought to exist on at least five levels:
   1. a higher level versus a lower level
   2. grand versus modest
   3. big "C" versus little c
   4. paradigm-shifting versus garden-variety
   5. eminent versus everyday

II. Some researchers claim other categories of creativity as well:
   1. expressive versus productive
   2. expressive versus inventive
   3. expressive versus innovative
   4. invention versus discovery
   5. theory versus invention versus discovery
   6. accommodative versus assimilative
   7. personal versus public

You would expect **differences between different types or areas of creativity**. But the sciences – physical or biological, mathematical, psychological and social, and also engineering – do show a good deal in common. Likewise there are **some resemblances**, and also **some differences** between scientific and artistic creativity, as, for example, in literary, philosophical, musical, visual or decorative artistic, and sculptural creativity (Vernon, 1989).

DEFINITIONS OF CREATIVITY

Creativity can best be thought of in terms of accomplishments, "…achievements that are original and make a meaningful contribution to culture" (Nicholls, 1972, p. 717).

People differ in the extent to which they can be said to be creative, and these differences can be thought of as a function of the interactive influence of antecedent conditions, cognitive factors, personality, and surrounding contextual and social influences.

Piirto (1998) believes that **creativity is in the personality, the process, and the product within a domain in interaction with genetic influences and with optimal environmental influences of home, school, community and culture, gender, and chance.**

Creativity is a basic human instinct to make that which is new.

Thompson (1992) suggests that **creativity is not a trait monopolized by a few fortunate persons**. Every individual is creative, because creativity is the trait that makes us human. *Creativity* is just another way to describe *intelligence*. According to Thompson (1992), **to be creative is to be able to perceive and recognize the world around us, to understand what we need or wish to do in response to it, and to set about changing it. To be creative is to find a way, a thought, an expression, a human manifestation no one else has found and to bring newly discovered possibilities into reality.**

Creativity means a person's capacity to produce **new or original** ideas, insights, restructurings, inventions, or artistic objects, **that are accepted by experts** as being of scientific, aesthetic, social, or technological value; the acceptability or appropriateness of the creative product, even though **this valuation may change with the passage of time.**

Scientific creativity always involves some addition to our previous knowledge, either an improved theory or a new object or procedure, whereas **artistic creation** may give some new representation of life (e.g., a painting or poem) or feeling, but not usually a progression from previous representations. Another possible type of creativity might be termed social or spiritual (e.g., Martin Luther King).

You are more creative than you think

Everything comes to he who hustles, while he waits.

Thomas Edison

In a vital sense, the creative process can be considered as movement: from the amorphous, dimly perceived idea toward an intelligible structure; from obscure inwardness toward tangible clarity; from the implicit toward the explicit; from the chaotic toward the organized.

Unfortunately, this romantic notion of complete vision has become firmly rooted among contemporary investigators of, and writers on, creativity. Its perpetuation only serves to convince those who have failed to experience such inspired visions that they really do not have creative talent, when, in fact, they may possess it to a considerable degree. This notion has dissuaded many promising creative men and women from wholeheartedly applying their talents.

Scrutiny shows that what does occur during the creative process is a slow, selective construction of an idea that is at first only imperfectly grasped, and that follows the dictates of intuition as to what does and does not belong, what is and what is not proper.

Imagine yourself standing on a shore on a foggy day. A ship sailing in the distance is enshrouded by fog. You alternately catch a glimpse of part of its sail, the top of its mast, its prow. Although you never get a full view, you know the ship is there, and you eventually do construct an image of it in its entirety.

Similarly, at the beginning of the creative process you sense the total structure of your idea even though you have perceived only a limited number of its details. You start elaborating on these few details, and this process of elaboration and shaping helps other details to emerge. If you withhold critical judgment, these additional details often fall into place spontaneously.

Thus, the initial idea – rather than being comprehensive of the whole conception – is often only a fragment of what is still to emerge.

Although this is so, the total idea nevertheless controls the entire creative process – so much so in fact it is impossible for the creative person to put elements into the evolving idea that do not fit its predominant configuration. Intuitive sensing, therefore (and not an all-embracing insight), serves as the vital measure of which elements are to be incorporated into the creation.

William J.J. Gordon, of Synectics, Inc., observed this process of intuition in his invention-design group: "Intuition is an inner judgment made by the individual about a concept relative to a problem on which he is working.... The individual with good intuition is the one who, beyond what could be expected from mere probability alone, repeatedly selects the viewpoint which turns out to lead, for instance, to a great painting or an important invention."

Creativity depends on suspending judgment

Nothing *inhibits the creative process* more than *critical judgment* of an emerging idea. On this there is unanimous agreement among creative persons and investigators of creativity. One must resist the mounting pressure to criticize the progressively articulated portions of an idea.

One of the primary reasons why judiciousness and creativity make uncomfortable bedfellows is that criticism is based on what has already been accepted. Critical judgment must have recourse to precedent and facts – everything that is past.

This being so, judgment is essentially opposed to the untried, the original. For creative advancement, the past serves as a guidepost only to a limited degree. By itself, however, judgment is incapable of either bringing forth a new idea or of predicting what would happen if it were developed.

The knowledge of what already exists also involves stereotyped orientation. None of the unexpectedly new combinations of elements in a creative idea, in its formative stage, meet the requirements of established facts or logic. A new idea is of course based on available knowledge, but it does not issue from it by any direct rational process.

Failure to suspend judgment and consider a range of alternatives frequently results in early commitment to an approach that may contain a "restrictive error" or an "incorrigible strategy." For example, subjects in a perceptual laboratory who made an early, incorrect interpretation of a picture on an "ambigu-meter" (a device that gradually brings a blurred picture into focus) tended to retain the wrong perception. They failed to "see" even after the picture had been fully and clearly exposed.

This idea not mean that critical judgment has no place in the production of a new idea. On the contrary, it serves a useful purpose – but only at the end of the process, when an objective assessment of the idea should be attempted.

Critical attitude destroys creativity in others

That critical and evaluative attitudes can stifle creativity in others has been noted by many researchers. As psychologist A.R. Wight points out: "A person will submit ideas with increasing reluctance if these are pounced upon immediately and subjected to critical and often merciless evaluation. It is difficult for a new idea to survive this kind of treatment. The effect on the individual suggesting the idea is equally devastating. Attacking his idea is felt to be, and often is, an attack on him personally. The individual feels hostility toward and often loses respect for the person initiating the attack. He soon refrains from suggesting anything at all. Or he resorts to second-guessing in an attempt to suggest something that will be accepted and approved."

One way to lessen the harmful effects of criticism is by learning to be tactful when we have to criticize. We should be receptive to ideas and suggestions by becoming understanding listeners. We should learn to evaluate ideas without resorting to external evaluation – that is, we should *react* to ideas rather than *judge* them.

The ability to remain coolly objective in the face of criticism comes only with time. It is founded on successes in creative problem-solving. No matter how tough the individual, ridicule, criticism, or even indifference by others to his ideas can destroy his creativity.

The emotional concomitants

Among the observable characteristics of an emerging new idea is the sharp sense of value attached to it. It arrives brimming with positiveness, giving the creative thinker a sense of certainty about its relevance to the problem.

The idea alone is too often believed to be all there is to the creative process. Yet almost everyone has known of idea men who could figuratively shakes ideas from their sleeves, but who rarely accomplished much because they failed to work their ideas out into something practical. Nevertheless, for most creative men and women the conviction as to the importance of their idea, and the exaltation it instills in them, are largely the reason for starting the creative process. Additionally, this positive feeling provides the creative person with the staying power to conquer every deficiency or temporary blockage that may occur, and drives him or her to understand the idea in its smallest detail.

The intuitive moment is also frequently accompanied by a sense of compulsion that drives the creative person to do something immediately with the idea. It recurrently invades his consciousness, charging his thoughts to further develop the idea. This compulsion may even obstruct the emergence of other ideas if it is not satisfied.

The positiveness that infuses the idea undoubtedly lies at the root of many great achievements; still, it is not everything, for the difficult process of shaping it into something workable lies ahead.

How to handle ideas

Creative ideas are often notoriously evanescent and elusive. At the moment when the idea appears, the person feels that it would be impossible to forget it. Yet, only moments later, the impression becomes blurred or fades away altogether. If the creative individual fails to capture ideas when they occur, fails to fix them in some form for later reference, they vanish and seldom return.

There are creative individuals, however, who prefer not to make a notation of their ideas until they become more fully structured. They allow glimmerings of an idea to occur to them a number of times without committing them to daylight. The reason for this is that some ideas take time to mature, and with each successive emergence of them into consciousness, they become more firmly developed.

It is imperative, however, that novice creators fix the unexpected ideas in some form as soon as they emerge. As we all have experienced time and again, some ideas appear to us brimming with important meaning at the time of their intrusion into consciousness, yet a later recall of them often fails to occur.

As a general rule, the more complex idea, the more advisable it is to postpone a commitment to paper. Otherwise there is the real danger to forcing the original implicit idea irretrievably into a restrictive scheme, the limitations of which can straitjacket any subsequent development.

In the final analysis, the dilemma of whether to immediately capture or to incubate an idea has to be solved by each individual alone. A prevalent notion among many investigators of creativity seems to be that initial ideas – those that occur when a person is first aced with finding a solution to a problem – are valueless. This may be true when the problem is relatively unfamiliar and when conscious effort has not been previously spent on it. However, when a problem has been through a period of unconscious cerebration, the first ideas that follow are frequently the best. Consequently, it is advisable to pay closer attention to the first ideas that occur during a productive mood even though the effortless fashion in which they often appear may make them suspect.

An accomplished creative person learns from long practice and frequents disappointments that proper technique for handling ideas. He leans, for example, that some ideas should be jotted down immediately, as soon as they occur, while others should be kept fluid and outside conscious focus until the last possible instant. Still others should be dropped back into the unconscious for further development and incubation.

The primacy of the whole

The creative process begins with the *intuitive moment*. This is when the creative individual first grasps the overall essence of an idea that might solve the problem. This intimation of the wholeness of the idea comes in to being during the creative process through the channel of feeling or intuition. This intuition also directs the shaping of the idea's details during its progressive articulation.

This intimation of the whole has to persevere through every phase of the progressive molding of the idea, until the person finally feels that he can give his approval to the outcome. A sense of completion accompanies this act, which signifies that the original concept has been more or less fully exploited.

> The criterion for the process of elaboration remains the immediate feeling of whether or not particular details do or do not contribute to the emerging configuration. This intuitive feeling continues until the moment when the person finds that he cannot add or change anything about his product to improve it.

The original overall grasp of the idea furnishes both the end and the means for achieving the end. It guides the elaboration of the idea safely through the shifting chaos of an enormous number of either unconsciously or consciously perceived alternatives and details, to its unique terminus. The intimation of an idea's totality controls its details: rejecting some possibilities, accepting others, molding the latter into the elements of the final outcome.

It occasionally happens that many of the elements and details that are first incorporated into a creation may later be dropped, when seen to be irrelevant, and others may take their place. But this does not argue against the theory that it is the implicit whole that determines what is and what is not admitted into the evolving idea. Only when the individual has firmly grasped the intimated whole can be burrow to the appropriate data in his memory and assemble the elements that contribute toward the development of the idea. Only then can be possible properly elaborating the idea, selecting from past observations, restructuring, combining, and transforming the details.

Distractions impair creativity

One chief reason why the creative process almost invariably produces a strain is because the intimation of the implicit idea and its developmental direction must be maintained at all costs – throughout unwelcome distractions (whether external or internal), momentary inhibitions, periods of fatigue or flagging interest, times of doubt about the idea's value, and remembered other obligations and concerns that make up the creative individual's environment.

Of course, the process of creation occurs quite differently when a person can become totally absorbed in the task. He then attends to the work unhampered by the strain of having to sift an excess of consciously perceived alternatives at each successive step in the idea's development. He does whatever his unconscious promptings lead him to do, and ultimately find as that his idea has grown effortlessly and spontaneously.

As a rule, ideas developed in this fashion need very little revision. However, this mode of creative, although coveted, occurs rarely or cannot be maintained for too long a period. Constraint, mounting effort, and tension inevitable set in.

As tension mounts beyond an optimum point, the creative individual senses that he is being forced to spend more effort for less results, finds that errors start to pile up, and that his direction becomes rambling and confused.

This is when most creative people quit. More obstinate ones may stick to their work, taking recourse to their richly stocked bag of past methods or continuing to consciously elaborate as much as possible in tune with the initial concept.

Numerous rough drafts attest however that it is almost impossible for the creative individual to consciously assume conformity with the intimated end of his new idea when the hum of the mood has stopped and when he finds himself no longer tuned in to the unconscious. The firmer his anticipation of the initial totality, the easier it is for him to shape its emerging derivatives, ward off adventitious conscious choices, and arrive at a satisfactory creative product.

The end is also the means

Many scientists have noted that an intuitive moment indicates the arrival of a passive solution. Albert Einstein, for example, is said to have had the capacity to feel the direction of a possible solution for his problem before he actually knew what the solution was. He always trusted and acted upon his hunches.

When a person starts to research a particular problem, he is usually already under the sway of an intuitive hunch that imputes relevance to the facts he so assiduously collects. No person ever has a hunch, nor can he pose a problem, if he is wholly in the dark about a possible solution and what data he needs to arrive at a solution. If he does not arrive at a satisfactory explanation, the trouble may lie in the complexity of the problem, but seldom in the genuineness of the original hunch.

Selectivity in the creative process

The best evidence that there is an intimation of an implicit wholeness at the intuitive moment is the highly selective activity that occurs throughout the creative process. Selectivity works through the intuitive feeling of moment-to-moment appropriateness of the details and elements being incorporated into the evolving idea, guiding their choice and the way they are to be used.

Selectivity operates during the total spectrum of the creative endeavor, starting with the choice of the problem to be undertaken. In addition to the compelling preference exhibited toward a problem, there is the selection of specific data to be collected to form the groundwork for solving the problem and developing an idea. During the process of developing the idea itself, selectivity operates to admit elements and details that belong and to suppress those that do not. Thus selectivity cuts across all the facets of the creative process.

In the beginning stages, the structure of intimated wholeness is only vaguely left. Many of the details, their balances and correspondences, although tending toward the implicit wholeness, are not quite consistent or congruent with it. Consequently, much restructuring is necessary before the requirements of the implicit configuration are satisfied. But so pervasive and insistent is the established sense of the idea's whole, so unifying is its pull, that it imposes the conditions for its realization and inexorably demands the proper transformations and rearrangements.

Conditions that contribute to creativity

The appearance of new ideas cannot easily be foretold (except, possibly, a feeling of peculiar restlessness just before the advent of one), and it is quite impossible to induce at will. Creative ideas are not under our voluntary control, and as a consequence cannot be governed by planning, schedules, or sheer enforcement.

But once the creative current is running strongly and the organic development of the idea is under way, one can assume an attitude that resembles will and that does help to maintain creativity at a desirable intensity. This may be a wish, a challenging urge on the part of the creative individual to give his or her utmost while submitting to the creative act.

A genuinely creative person desires to transcend his past performance, to give his best on every new occasion o problem solving, and thus achieve more than was aspired to before. This urgent wish toward fuller self-realization helps the creative individual to sustain the intensity of the creative mood and to keep the avenues of the unconscious free from both internal and external interruptions, as well as from the habit patterns of consciousness.

Choose your best time for creating

Although it is impossible to induce creative ideas at will, there are nevertheless certain conditions that are propitious for the evocation of ideas. For example, for many people the night is most conducive of the creative mood. This is the time when many creative individuals begin (as one person put it) "a blind date with their deeper selves." Night, with its pervading peacefulness and mystery, brings to them a sense of isolation conductive to creation.

Daytime, on the other hand, with its predominantly practical orientation, its bustle and noise, can block creativity and prevent the flow from the unconscious.

There are of course people who prefer the early-morning hours, the freshness of a newly born day.

Again, others need high-powered activity around them in order to find release for their ideas. They have to be in the whirlwind of restless activity to receive the stimulus. Many such men and women have the knack of closing out the external world at will, of being able to detach themselves whenever necessary to set ideas into motion.

Many creative individuals can tune in to their private selves in the noisiest of environments. The condition of inward isolation, however, is a primary requirement for significant creative work. Indeed, such moments of detachment from one's external environment can be more productive than hours of merely physical isolation.

The power of eccentric rituals

Many of the apparently trivial idiosyncrasies of creative men and women that provide entertaining anecdotes for biographers actually helped to evoke and then to sustain the creative mood.

Debussy often gazed at the Seine and the reflections of the setting sun on its waves to establish an atmosphere for composing. Schiller kept rotten apples in his desk drawer because their aroma helped him to evoke a creative mood. Dostoevsky found that he could best dream up stories and characters while doodling.

It seems that there is hardly a creative individual who does not have a ritual, an eccentricity for provoking free-floating concentration and an uncensored alertness to the implications of an idea.

Such idiosyncrasies seem also necessary for keeping the overactive thought-patterns of consciousness in abeyance, and for shutting out all distractions. Anchoring oneself so singly mutes outward distractions. This is essential, for the shrill ringing of the telephone in a neighboring room, a conversation down the hall, s rumbling noise in the distance, even momentary bodily discomfitures, can shatter the protective bubble of the creative mood. By channeling one's attention into a ritual, all distractions lose their power to disrupt.

Many creative individuals pace the floor endlessly, and biographers are replete with instances of ideas occurring to creative individuals when they were walking or traveling. That physical motion animates the imagination; that our legs are the wheels of thought, has long been known.

Many creative workers frequently claim that the ideas they value most occur to them during passive, relaxed, or even fatigued states of half-waking. It is well known that Newton solved many of his problems when his attention was waylaid by complete relaxation. Similarly, Edison knew the value of half-waking states, and, whenever confronted with a seemingly insurmountable barrier that defied all his efforts, he would stretch out on a couch in his workshop – brought there for just this reason – and try to fall asleep.

Insignificant incidents may stimulate

The creative mood seizes an individual without any detectable reason or stimulus. It apparently can be catalyzed by insignificant and wayward incidents. Because intuitive moments cannot be voluntarily controlled, creative ideas may, and do, appear at any hour and under the strangest of circumstances.

For example, there is a story about Vivaldi being overcome by inspiration while celebrating Mass. As soon as the "divine afflatus" had struck him, he rushed away from the altar into the sacristy, where he wrote down his theme. It was only after he had carefully marked down the melody and assured himself of its retention that he returned to the altar to resume the Mass. Needless to say, the officials of the church, ignorant of the waywardness of the creative process, summarily dismissed him from his office.

An incident that has been reported about Newton was that, during the course of a dinner for guests, he left the table to get some wine from the cellar. On his way, he was overcome by an idea, forgot his errand and company, and was soon hard at work in his study.

Many seasoned creative individuals have an unreasoned, intuitive sense for such preparatory cues and the external conditions necessary for evoking a creative mood. Although it is impossible to summon creative ideas at will, many such men and women have mastered the trick of exposing themselves to stimuli that make the occurrence of the creative mood possible. Experience eventually shows every creative person which conditions are personally propitious.

There are of course long stretches of barren periods in every creative individual's life. There are periods when the incipient mood for productive activity serves only to arouse conflicts instead of ideas, with the result that people may lapse into a state of lassitude in which excuses are found to postpone creative work, sometimes for months or years. The creative person should establish regular habits of work. He should regulate and coordinate the acquisition of fresh information and impressions, allow time for their digestion and the incubation of ideas, and note how long it takes for an insight to emerge and to elaborate it into reality. He is likely to be most creative when adhering to his individual rhythm for these phases. Violations of this rhythm because of undue haste, or even of tardiness, can retard creative efficiency.

Achieving Extraordinary Results

What would you attempt if you knew you could not fail? You'd be unstoppable! What would you add or change in your life? Would you pursue a new career opportunity, a new relationship or start a new business? Whatever it is you want to achieve, believe you can do it!

Write down five desires that you would like to accomplish. Describe them with details. Visualize, verbalize and vigorously pursue your dreams to turn them into reality.

1)
2)
3)
4)
5)

People created our civilization. Just ordinary people created it; people who achieved extraordinary results.

Maybe you were raised to believe that good things come to those who are out there hustling. You decide what you want and go for it! That's what this is all about, how to make your dreams come true.

Your Personal Definition of Success

1. If I were living a successful life what would that look like?
2. What would my successful life look like 5 years from now?
3. What would my successful life look like 100 years from now?
4. What would my successful life look like 20 years from now?
5. What would my successful life look like when I retire?

Reconsidering Difficult Ideas

You have a vivacious idea. But you also have a large doubt about it. You notice yourself saying, "No, this idea is just too difficult (or stupid, or just crazy)."

This "too difficult" can mean many things. It can mean that the idea feels too slippery, too dark, too ambitious, too dangerous, too self-revealing. It can also mean that the idea, even if splendidly realized, will have little or no chance in the marketplace, that it is "too difficult" for the average reader, collector, movie-goer, listener.
Now answer the following questions:

1. What has been your habit with respect to "difficult" ideas?
2. Do you actually stop to analyze which "too difficult" it might be or whether it really is too difficult to tackle?
3. Do you relegate the idea to the scrap heap and breathe a sign of relief?
4. Rather than reject the idea outright, do you alter it to make it easier?

Deep creativity often means dangerous creativity. The idea that presents itself as you hush and hold arises from a place that knows perfectly well that animal paintings sell, that adolescent boys and men are the market for action movies, that millions of women are insatiably hungry for romance novels. The top of your mind knows many such things.
Will you choose to work on the idea that is dangerous?
Which ideas have you rejected in the past as too difficult to deal with? Can you name a few?
Pick one. Grab it. Write about it a little, discuss it with yourself, think about it. What exactly is too difficult about it? Is it too ambitious? Too disturbing? Too self-revealing? Too technically difficult?
What, as you think about it now, are the good reasons for entertaining it? What are the good reasons for rejecting it? Make a list of the pros and cons.

Pros   **Cons**

Give this difficult idea a fair airing. Try to decide if it is or isn't an idea worth choosing to work on.

> The Discipline of the writer is to learn to be still and listen to what his subject has to tell him.
>
> Rachel Carson

Concentration

There is no creative life without this ability to concentrate.

To create you must quiet your mind. You need a quiet mind so that ideas will have the chance of connecting. You are hushing your mind so that you can use your mind. But much too often our mind is on autoscan, darting from one thought, usually a negative one, to another.

The following exercise is very important. Do it frequently.

You must stop your mind from operating on autoscan. Maintaining an autoscan mind is no way to live and no way to think.

Find a quiet place. If there is no quiet place in your environment, that's your first task, to make a haven in which silence is available. Enter that quiet place affirmatively by whispering, "I am hushing." Gently hush your thoughts, just as if you were comforting a baby. Work to grow quiet inside. Thoughts will come, but hush them away. Work to hush your thought until you have no thoughts, until you are just empty and breathing. This will take some time. Don't despair if you can't do it easily, quickly, or even at all. Just try.   Hush and hush again.

Feel your breathing deepen, feel yourself descending. You will want to close your eyes. So silently into the darkness.

You are entrancing yourself. What do you see? Ideas will come to you, melodies, lyrics, images. The very darkness will acquire a tone, the very silence a music.

Something that passes by in that hushed stillness may seem especially important. That is an idea with vivacity. Hush again and hold it. Give it a chance to grow more distinct. Hold it and nurture it until you can capture it. Then write it down, draw it, play it on the piano.

Whether you've been creating for decades or are just now starting, this is an exercise to return to again and again.

> The ideas is like a blueprint; it creates an image of the form, which then magnetizes and guides the physical energy to flow into that form and eventually manifests it on the physical plane.
>
> Shakti Gawain

Thoughts

Pick a familiar subject and come up with new thoughts about it.
List your most pleasant experience in the last 24 hours.
List your impressive ideas or thought in the past 24 hours.
List your most unusual observation of the last two days.

Fantasies

Fantasies, or day dreaming, are a normal part of our thought patterns. Fantasies are where you can create any experience you choose. List some positive and productive situations you regularly create in your fantasies.

What results would you create for yourself, your family, your friends, your business and others if you brought some of these positive aspects into reality?

Which results are you willing to create into reality?
When are willing to begin creating them?
Who will you enlist to support you in shifting fantasy into reality?
When will you start causing the shift to take place?

Overcoming Block to Creativity
Our tears prepare the ground for our future growth. Without this
creative moistening, we may remain barren. We must allow the bolt
of pain to strike us. Remember, this is useful pain; lightning illuminates.
Julia Cameron

How do you know if you are creatively blocked? Jealousy is an excellent clue. Are there artists whom you resent? Do you tell yourself, "I could do that, if only…" Do you tell yourself that if only you took your creative potential seriously, you might:

- Stop telling yourself, "it's too late;"

- Stop waiting until you make enough money to do something you'd really love;
- Stop telling yourself, "It'd just my ego" whenever you yearn for a more creative life;
- Stop telling yourself that dreams don't matter, that they are only dreams and that you should be more sensible;
- Stop telling yourself that creativity is a luxury and that you should be grateful for what you've got;
- Stop fearing that your family and friends would think you crazy.

As you learn to recognize, nurture, and protect your inner artist, you will be able to move beyond pain and creative constriction. You will learn ways to recognize and resolve fear, remove emotional scar tissue, and strengthen your confidence.

THE ENEMIES OF IDEAS

No idea is any good until someone does something with it or to it. Someone has to accept it, adopt it, run with it, put it into action. Implementing ideas requires a team effort. So you must tell somebody about your idea. And if you've ever tried to bring up new ideas to other people, you know that although your idea could be met with thunderous applause, it may just as easily elicit derisive laughter, or perhaps just a shrug.

What do you know will happen to your great idea as soon as you suggest it to your boss, colleague, spouse, or other important person in your life? Somebody, somewhere, at some time, will come up, gun loaded, aim, and say:

"It's not in the budget."
"We don't do it that way."
"We've tried it before."

Idea Generators must learn all about Killer Phrases

Psychologists have said that the human reaction to a new idea unfolds something like this:
1. It's irrelevant to this situation.
2. It's relevant, but it's unproven.
3. It's proven, but it's dangerous.
4. It's safe, but it's not sellable.
5. It'll sell, what a great idea!

At home, parents utter 18 negative statements for every positive one – usually to an inquisitive child who wants to know how something works.

Killer Phrases are part of our culture, part of our upbringing. One study showed that negative *no-can-do* statements are all around us, outweighing positive *can-do* statements by substantial margins.

Toyota now implements an average of forty suggestions per employee per year.

Killer Phrases do perform some **useful** functions:
- preventing precipitous, mindless change;
- protecting us from potential danger.

They also **squelch** good ideas:
- retard progress;
- inhibit innovation.

They come from society's tendency to cling to the known and to fear the unknown, the untried, the new.

Internalized Killer Phrases

1. **Self-Doubt Killer Phrases:**
   - I'll look stupid

- I am not old enough
- I am not experienced enough
- I am not good (tall, fast, smart, forceful, young, creative, etc.) enough

Remember the words of Eleanor Roosevelt: **"No one can make you feel inferior without your consent."**

> There are always twenty excellent reasons for doing nothing for every one reason for starting anything - especially if it has never been done before.
>
> Prince Phillip

2. Excuse Killer Phrases:
- Somebody has already done it
- I don't have time
- I need special equipment.

3. Procrastination Killer Phrases:
- I'll wait until tomorrow
- It's better to wait and see what happens tomorrow.

4. Fear Killer Phrases:
- I don't want to offend anybody
- They won't like my idea

The Idea Generator needs to divert and neutralize Killer Phrases before they do lasting damage.

Killer Phrases

Most of us feel we are open-minded, encouraging, and supportive of new ideas. This attitude, however, is seldom demonstrated. Indeed, it is safe to say that most people have a trigger-ready tendency to be overly critical when confronted with a new idea. They automatically feel a need to point out its shortcomings rather than its benefits or ways to make it work. Premature critical attitudes have caused the demise of countless valuable ideas.

This exercise is designed to make you aware of the negative reactions a creative notion frequently evokes. This awareness will enable you to formulate new, ingenious strategies for overcoming the many roadblocks your idea may encounter.

Part 1

List as many idea-squelching "Killer-phrases" as you can. Write down those you have heard or personally experienced as well as those that might be used.

Examples

It won't work...
We haven't the time...
We've tried that before...

Now list your own.

Part 2

List as many idea-squelching "self-killer-phrases" as you can. List those you might have used yourself, or others have used, or might use.

Examples

This may not work, but...
It isn't clear we need this, but...
Would it hurt if we did...

Now it's your turn.

Answers

Killer Phrases

Part 1

Examples

We've never done it that way before.
We haven't the manpower.
It's not in the budget.
All right in theory but can you put it into practice?
Too academic.
What will the customers think.
Somebody would have suggested it before if it were any good.
Too modern.
Too old-fashioned.
Let's discuss it some other time.
You don't understand our problem.
We're too small for that.
We're too big for that.
We have too many projects now.
Let's make a market research test first.

What bubblehead thought that up?
Let's form a committee.
Let's think it over for a while and watch developments.
That's not our problem.
Production won't accept it.
They'll think we're long-haired.
Engineering can't do it.
Won't work in my territory.
Customers won't stand for it.
You'll never sell that to management.
Don't move too fast.
The union will scream.
Here we go again.
No adolescent is going to tell *me* how to run my business!

Part 2
Examples

This may not be applicable, but…
While we have only made a few preliminary tests…
This approach is screwy, but…
I don't know if the money can be appropriated, but…
It might be a dead end, but…
Do you suppose it would be possible to…
It make take a long time, but…
It may sound harebrained, but…
I don't know just what you want, but…
You probably have ideas about this too, but…
You aren't know just what you want, but…
This is contrary to policy, but…
This may not be the right time, but…

You can probably do this better, but…
If I were younger and had my health…
I suppose our competitors have already tried this, but…
I'm not too familiar with this, but…
This may be too expensive, but…
I don't know what is in the literature on this, but…
This is not exactly on this subject, but…
I haven't thought this one through, but…
You'll probably laugh, but…
My opinions are not worth much, but…
I'm no genius, but…
I don't get enthused over this idea myself, but…
It may not be important, but…
If you'll take the suggestion of a novice…

Now here's a sketchy idea of what I have in mind, for you to kick holes in…

Kick that block

Lack of creative receptivity and performance is not so much due to the absence of creative potential as it is to the various perceptual, cognitive, emotional, and environmental blocks and barriers. Once the inhibitors have been identified and removed, the immediate upsurge of creative output can be considerable.

Effort and achievement would exceed all expectations if the energies and imaginations of men could be freed of restrictions and restraints.

Crawford H. Greenewalt

This exercise is good to do in a group. When all participants have completed listing the blocks, each person takes turns verbalizing and discussing how and why each block inhibits creative problem-solving and what can be done to overcome it. The purpose of this is to provide everyone with a kind of *self-reclamation* journey that would open and release their creativity.

List the blocks and barriers that inhibit and stifle creative production in yourself and others.

Examples

Lack of confidence in the ability to be creative
Lack of motivation
Lack of self-discipline
Fear that idea will be stolen
Fear of risk-taking

Answer

Kick That Block

Examples

Fear of failure
Fear of making a mistake or for criticism
Tendency to prematurely judge ideas
Need to conform
Intolerance of ambiguity
Inability to perceive what the real problem is
Lack of frustration-tolerance
Using wrong approaches to solve problems
Insistence on being logical
Distrust of intuitive thinking
Inability to utilize all one's abilities
Laziness
Pathological desire for security
Lack of endurance and perseverance
Lack of inner quietude
Jumping to conclusions
Disinterest, indifference, lack of desire to create

Belief that indulging in fantasy is useless
Lack of curiosity
Faulty observation and insensitivity to clues
Superficiality, shallowness, incompleteness, and hastiness of thought
Difficulty in seeing remote relationships
Inhibited inquisitiveness
Lack of knowledge of one's field
Fear of making a fool of oneself
Lack of flexibility
Over-motivation to succeed
Being overwhelmed by the immensity of a problem
Incorrect problem statement
Tendency to cling to habitual, routine ways of thinking
Concrete or practical mindedness
Fear of being a pioneer
Fear of being too aggressive

> If you are not having problems, you are missing an opportunity for growth.
>
> Thomas Blandi

Make a "Bug list"

All of us have problems, annoyances, peeves, and complaints of various kinds. Although we can do little or nothing about some of our problems, many of them can be solved creatively. There is a wonderful prayer that goes like this:

**God grant me the serenity to accept the things I cannot change,
The courage to change the things I can,
And the wisdom to know the difference.**

Unfortunately, most people not only lack courage and wisdom, but they have never specifically thought about what precisely in life bother them. And even if they are aware of a few things that cause discomfort or frustration, rare indeed are those men or women who do something effective or creative about them. You can be different.

This exercise is in two parts. First, take paper and pencil and list everything that bothers, annoys, or "bugs" you – specific problems and personal annoyances at home and at work, involving persons, objects, and events. The list should include those bugs that are common and shared by many, as well as far-out ones you consider to be your own. If you run out of problems and bugs in less that ten minutes, you're either a saint or extremely insensitive.

As the next step, list the problems or bugs you feel are most in need of creative solutions and write out the problem or problems you would like to tackle first. Writing down your problems enables you to crystallize your thoughts. It also commits you to do something about them and provides the needed motivational push.

Answer

Make a "Bug List"

Examples

Poor TV programs	Pets that aren't housebroken
Window shades that won't go down or up	Cleaning Kitty Litter
Telephone ringing and no one answers	Overripe bananas
Paperless toilets	Broken Shoelaces
Drippy faucets	Dog dropping on lawn
Defective mirrors	Drawers that stick
Dusty furniture	Car horns
Roaches in food	Cigar smoke
Burn toast	Wobbly chairs
Electric fixtures interfering with TV	Crowded beaches
Dull knives	

How Ob(li)vious

Although the creative person likes the challenge of the complex, chaotic, difficult, and disorderly, he or she doesn't overlook the obvious and simple. If a problem can be solved in a simple, elegant, or economical way, he is not inclined to overcomplicate matters to achieve a complex solution.

The general tendency, however, is to frequently search for the complicated when a simple solution would be sufficient. We are so over-conditioned to look for, and develop, complex processes that we have become almost blind to what is frequently "obvious."

The following set of several mini-problems has been designed to test and develop your capacity to extract the obvious solutions from situations that at first glance seem somewhat complicated. Although you should figure out the problem quickly, try to inhibit your tendency to form snap judgments of what is involved.

> Genius is a perception of the obvious which nobody else sees.
>
> Ronald Weiss

1. You go to bed at 8 o'clock in the evening and set the alarm to get up at 9 in the morning. How many hours of sleep would this allow you?
2. One month has 28 days. Of the remaining 11 months, how many have 30 days?
3. A woman gave a beggar 50 cents. The woman is the beggar's sister, but the beggar is not the woman's brother. What is their relationship?
4. Why can't a man living in New York, N.Y., be buried west of the Mississippi?
5. Do they have a fourth of July in England?
6. How can you throw a tennis ball with all your might and have it stop and come right back to you without hitting and wall, net, or any other obstruction?
7. If you stand on a hard marble floor, how can you drop a raw egg five feet without breaking its shell?
8. Two fathers and two sons shot three deer. Yet each took home one deer. How was that possible?
9. How many times can you subtract the numeral 2 from the numeral 24?

10. A farmer has 47/9 haystacks in one corner of the field and 5 2/9 haystacks in another corner of his field. If he puts them all together, how many haystacks will he have?

11. Seven gas-guzzling cars were lined up in a dealer's showroom bumper-to-bumper. How many bumpers were actually touching each other?

12. Would it be cheaper for you to take one girlfriend to the movies twice or two girlfriends at the same time?

13. Take 5 apples from 7 apples and what have you got?

14. Was the old coin-dealer who said he had a silver coin marked 459 B. C. either lying or trying to put one over on the customer? If "Yes," why?

15. You won a prize in a contest and could choose either a truckload of nickels or half a truckload of dimes. Which would you choose? (Both trucks are identical in size and shape.)

16. Visualize four horizontal lines, one inch apart, one above the other. Now visualize four vertical lines, one inch apart, each cutting through the horizontal lines. How many squares did you form? (Do not use paper or pencil.)

17. Six robbers rode in a Chevette for over 150 miles to their hideout. The trip took exactly two hours, yet no one in the car noticed that they had a flat tire all this time. How was this possible?

18. The attempt to commit a certain crime is punishable. What crime is involved?

19. You are sitting in a room with 12 friends. Can any of them seat themselves in any particular place in this room where it would be impossible for you to do so?

20. After a woman was blindfolded, a man hung up her hat. She walked 50 meters, turned around, and shot a bullet through her hat. How was she able to do this?

Answers

1. One hour. The alarm would go off at 9 that night.
2. All 11 months.
3. The beggar is the woman's sister.
4. He is still living.
5. Yes.
6. If you throw it straight up in the air.
7. Hold the egg up and drop it from a height of 6 feet. It will drop 5 feet without breaking. After that you will need to clean up the mess.
8. The 2 fathers and 2 sons were: a son, his father, and his father's father.
9. Only once. After the first time, you're subtracting from 22, then 20, and so on.
10. One sizable haystack.
11. 12
12. Two girlfriends at the same time: 3 admission tickets. One girlfriend twice: 4 tickets.
13. Five apples, naturally.
14. He was lying. No one knew Christ was coming in 459 years.
15. If you're governed by the profit motive, you'd choose half a truckload of dimes, since they're smaller and worth twice as much.
16. 9.
17. The spare tire was flat.
18. Suicide.
19. They all could take turns and sit on your lap. You certainly couldn't accomplish that.
20. Her hat was hung over the end of the gun.

> Genius is the capacity for seeing relationships where lesser men see none.
>
> William James

Close Associates

Creativity is that process which results in a new combination or association of attributes, elements, or images, giving rise to new patterns, arrangements, or products that better solve a need. This is a condensation of several hundred definitions of the process of creative thinking, and the noteworthy element of almost all the definitions is that they emphasize the associative or combinational aspect of the creative process.

Creative men and women have described their creative thought-processes in associative terms. Albert Einstein said, "The psychical entities which seem to serve as elements of thought are certain signs and more or less clear images which can be combined.... This combinatory play seems to be the essential feature in productive thought." Samuel Taylor Coleridge, reflecting upon his own creative process, stated, "Facts which sank at intervals out of conscious recollection drew together beneath the surface through the almost chemical affinities of common elements." Similarly, Andre Breton remarked: "Creativity is a marvelous capacity to grasp two mutually distinct realities, without going beyond the field of our experience, and to draw a spark from their juxtaposition."

Most lucid and explicit is the statement by the mathematician Jules Poincare, who said, "To create consists of making new combinations of associative elements which are useful. The mathematical facts worthy of being studied... are those which reveal to us unsuspected kinships between other facts well known but wrongly believed to be strangers to one another." And Jacob Bronowski added, "The discoveries of science, the works of art, are explorations – more, are explosions – of a hidden likeness."

This exercise is designed to stimulate this all-important ability to form associative elements. Take all the time you need to complete it.

Part 1
Think of a word that precedes those in the first two columns and follows those in the last two. (You can form compounds, hyphenated words, commonly used expressions, colloquial usage, or slang in some cases.)

Examples

| Break | strings | heart | purple | take |
| Sell | rock | hard | work | hit |

Rate	account	------	savings	left
Salad	head	____	lay	rotten
Corner	rope	____	sit	hold
Opera	house	____	flash	flood
Artist	clause	____	narrow	fire
Jacket	changer	____	world	off
Dog	skin	____	herds	count
In	ugly	____	spark	drain
Ox	bunny	____	deaf	strike
Backer	drawing	____	fishing	telephone
Shooting	door	____	shut	tourist
Ware	foot	____	fall	a
Step	flesh	____	wild	cook
Up	guy	____	penny	side

Creative Thinking

Park	life	____	daily	play
Pie	cart	____	good	Christmas
Air	tub	____	get	boiling
Off	toe	____	hot	finger
Rage	look	____	wash	reach
Day	theory	____	magnetic	playing
Finger	leader	____	bathtub	key
Pay	throw	____	all	stay
Out	pan	____	czar	saint

Part 2
Think of a word that may be inserted in the blanks below to form new words.

Example

___ba, ___mage, ____my, ____or, ____pus, ____runner

Answer: RUM

1. ____al, ____rabbit, ____et, ____frost, ____knife, ____pot
2. ____acid, ____arctic, ____elope, ____ler, ____hology, ____hem
3. ____an, ____bug, ____id, ____bled, ____or, ____us
4. ____cat, ____al, ____uity, ____head, ____igue, ____ten
5. ____alyst, ____atonia, ____ch, ____ty, ____nip, ____skill
6. ____ad, ____ast, ____itics, ____oon, ____ot, ____point
7. ____ace, ____ate, ____ette, ____lor, ____sy, ____try
8. ____er, ____beat, ____ice, ____end, ____hand, ____key

Answers
Part 1

1. Bank
2. Egg
3. Tight
4. Light
5. Escape
6. Record
7. Sheep
8. Plug
9. Dumb

Creative Thinking

10.	Line	16.	Apple	22.	Field
11.	Trap	17.	Night	23.	Ring
12.	Flat	18.	Hot	24.	Over
13.	Goose	19.	Tip	25.	Peter
14.	Wise	20.	Check		
15.	Double	21.	Out		

Part 2

1.	Jack	4.	Fat	7.	Pal
2.	Ant	5.	Cat	8.	Off
3.	Hum	6.	Ball		

Successful inventors often demonstrate one of the major attributes that are the ability to see correspondences or similarities not immediately apparent to others. What inventors generally do is to bring the operating principles, or associative elements, of a device form one field into contiguity with an entirely different one.

Although there have been innumerable examples of associative combinations over the centuries, a very contemporary example will serve; it's a very popular child's stroller. Formerly, baby strollers were built on the baby carriage principle. They were almost invariably heavy, awkward, and impossible to load into buses, planes, and subcompact automobiles. Not long ago a team of inventors took note of the problems and redesigned the baby stroller, using as models "things that fold for carrying" like the umbrella and the tubular aluminum lawn chair. Both of these are, after all, nothing more than fabric on a frame that becomes rigid when unfolded. The end result was a folding stroller with umbrella handles light enough to be transported hanging on a person's arm. The name was well chosen to reflect the synthesis. They called it "The Umbroller."

Different Circles

Effective learning means arriving at new power, and the consciousness of new power
Is one of the most stimulating things in life.
Janet Erskine Stuart

This exercise will increase your visual-figural acuity and your verbal fluency.

Add vertical lines to the circles and create as many words as you can. Copy as many circles on a piece of paper as you need to form.

o   o   o   o   ∩   o   ∪   o   o   o   o   o

Examples

b   o   o   b

Answers

pop	pap	pad	gag	goop
god	papa	do	gob	add
dad	boa	poop	gogo	gab
bad	ago	boo	good	gad
dab	ado	boo-boo	goo	pago pago

271

Creative Thinking

Matter of Semantics

The dictionary is a great book; it hasn't
Much plot, but the author's vocabulary
Is wonderful!
Bill Nye

Creative people not only have rich vocabularies, but they also know how to handle words effectively. This effectiveness is due to their knowledge of the precise meaning of words, which contributes to conceptual clarity.

Clear and firm concepts are the building blocks to further creative learning and problem solving.

From the four possibilities, select the one that most closely approximates the meaning for each word at the left.

1. felicitous	-	neat, elegant, congruous, appropriate
2. jovial	-	blithe, hearty, merry, sunny
3. tenacity	-	cohesion, firmness, activity, readiness
4. alacrity	-	energy, briskness, activity, strength
5. simulate	-	mimic, reflect, counterfeit, feign
6. recondite	-	tortuous, occult, furtive, abstruse
7. frustrate	-	hinder, thwart, spoil, outwit
8. emanate	-	appear, exude, issue, proceed
9. bombastic	-	turgid, explosive, high-flown, swollen
10. palliate	-	soften, mitigate, smooth, relieve
11. theory	-	postulate, hypothesis, conjecture, principle
12. stricture	-	compression, narrowing, obloquy, criticism
13. expound	-	preach, instruct, edify, interpret
14. equivocal	-	perplexing, ambiguous, mysterious, obscure
15. mien	-	attitude, bearing, conduct, action
16. fidelity	-	equality, probity, uniformity, loyalty
17. sagacious	-	shrewd, penetrating, sensible, rational
18. refractory	-	tenacious, stubborn, firm, sullen
19. obdurate	-	unfeeling, stubborn, firm, stern
20. tentative	-	fortuitous, empirical, experimental, makeshift
21. esoteric	-	unusual, bookish, profound, erudite
22. relegate	-	banish, consign, transpose, promote
23. ephemeral	-	elusive, fugitive, passing, transitory
24. cynical	-	arrogant, sneering, sarcastic, haughty
25. sentient	-	quick, keen, sensitive, emotional
26. explicit	-	definite, positive, manifest, open
27. amorphous	-	formless, misshapen, unshapely, malformed
28. dissident	-	dissonant, improper, discordant, differing
29. perspicacity	-	shrewdness, intelligence, wisdom, discernment
30. fortitude	-	bravery, courage, firmness, valor

Answers

1. felicitous – appropriate
2. jovial – hearty
3. tenacity – persistence
4. alacrity – briskness
5. simulate – feign
6. recondite – abstruse

Creative Thinking

7. frustrate – thwart
8. emanate – issue
9. bombastic – high-flown
10. palliate – mitigate
11. theory – hypothesis
12. stricture – criticism
13. expound – interpret
14. equivocal – ambiguous
15. mien – bearing
16. fidelity – loyalty
17. sagacious – shrewd
18. refractory – stubborn
19. obdurate – unfeeling
20. tentative – experimental
21. esoteric – profound
22. relegate – consign
23. ephemeral – transitory
24. cynical – sneering
25. sentient – sensitive
26. explicit – definite
27. amorphous – formless
28. dissident – differing
29. perspicacity – discernment
30. fortitude – courage

Future Headlines

Most of us are so deeply mired in here-and-now problems that we rarely think about the future, or if we do, the possible scenarios we project are laden with even greater dangers than we're experiencing at present.

The purpose of this game is to pull you out of the present and put into a future free of mind. It is an exercise of "imaginative realism" with a *positive* stance. Forecasting the future, verbalizing and discussing the possible *positive* developments, constitutes the first step toward influencing the days to come in a manner that would produce a less threatening and more desirable state of affairs.

Create future headlines to stories you would like to read about in your newspapers within the next thirty years.

This is good game to [play with others. After the participants have listed their headlines, you can have a stimulating discussion about whether or not each headline can indeed be anticipated within the thirty-year time frame. Since this is a game of exploration rather than competition, there are no winners or losers. The purpose is to focus attention on the future, and thus enable everyone to become more pro-actively future oriented.

> The pace of events is so fast that unless we can find some way to keep our sights on tomorrow, we cannot expect to be in touch with today.
>
> Dean Rusk

Answer
Future Headlines
Examples

World Attains Zero Population Growth
Weather Forecast Now Reliable
All Forms of Cancer Defeated
Average Work Week Now Twenty Hours
Forced Retirement Abolished
Inaugurating Weekly Flights to the Moon
Breakthrough in Ocean Farming Techniques

Immunization Against All Viral Infections
Life-long Learning Curriculums Established
Full Control of Multi-National Corporations
Tedium at Work Eliminated
Creative Leisure Programs For Everyone
Violence on Television Eliminated

GROUP ACTIVITIES

Exercises
Warm-Up

Each participant picks up an envelope. Open the envelope and read the name of object. Think about this object.

Through your posture, facial expressions and movements demonstrate to the censor your subject. The Censor needs to guess what subject is presented. The best performer presents his or her subject to the rest of participants in the theater.

Sculpture of Creativity

For many people, a sculpture is a place for pigeons to light; for others, a sculpture may demonstrate a sublime representation of the agonies of displaced human frailties (or some other equally esoteric line of art babble). Sculpture represents different interpretations of reality. As such, they also are stimuli capable of promoting different perspectives.

Instruction

Read and carefully follow these instructions.

The main goal of this exercise is to discover an individual's creative potential.

In order to discover an individual's creative potential, several members work together as a team performing this exercise and preparing a short presentation that will be provided at the conclusion of this task to the rest of participants.

Distribution of the Roles

Each member of the group is required to play a particular role:

1. **Sculptor**
2. **Supportive Staff** (3-8 members)
3. **Evaluator**
4. **Speaker**

Responsibilities

1. **Sculptor**

The Sculptor is responsible for the proper completion of the entire task. This activity includes creating a "sculpture" that represents or symbolizes creativity. The Sculptor needs to direct the process of creating the "sculpture" of *Creativity*. He or she uses the supportive staff for creating the "sculpture" of his or her own personal creativity. So, the creative team becomes the "glue," "marble," or "stone" for the Sculptor.

Process of creation:

The Sculptor assigns roles among the team members. The first member becomes the Sculptor's *creative thinking*, the second member becomes the Sculptor's *inspiration*, the third member becomes the Sculptor's *imagination*, the fourth member – the Sculptor's *dreams*, the fifth member – the Sculptor's *creative emotions*.

After roles are assigned, the Sculptor gives each member precise instructions about the nature of the activities that they are to perform in order to express the Sculptor's *creative potential*. For example, the first member needs to express the Sculptor's *creative thinking*. The sculptor explains to *creative thinking person* what he or she has to do in order to exhibit through movements, posture, facial expressions the *creative thinking process*. The same is true for the rest of the team members:

They are told what they need to do in order to express the Sculptor's *inspiration, imagination, dreams, creative feelings* and so on.

2. Staff. Perform all instructions that the Sculptor gives to them. Staff and Sculptor exchange their roles so that each and every participants eventually becomes the Sculptor.

3. The Evaluator. The main objective for the Evaluator is to ask provocative questions, to be friendly, to provide constructive criticism, to objectively evaluate, and make an assessment of the outcome. For example, the Evaluator may ask *creative thinking person*, "How he or she feels in his or her role?" He may ask the Sculptor, "Why he or she gave such and such instruction to the staff?" The Evaluator can express his or her personal opinion about the "sculpture." He or she can make suggestions about possible improvements to the sculpture itself and so on. The Evaluator chooses the best sculpture that will be the one presented to the rest of participants in the theater.

4. The Speaker. The Speaker supervises the whole exercise and prepares short presentation about it. After the task is performed completely, the Speaker provides a teach-back. In his or her presentation, he or she briefly describes the assignment to his or her team assignment. Then he or she provides a short explanation of the discoveries unearthed or detected while performing their tasks:
- What is creativity?
- What components of creative potential that they discovered through this exercise?
- How different components of creativity influence one another?

Stimulation and Suppression of Creativity
Instruction

Read and carefully follow these instructions.

The main goal of this exercise is to discover what can stimulate and what can block an individual's creative potential.

Several members will work together as a team to complete this exercise and prepare a short presentation that will be provided at the end of this task to the rest of participants.
Participants:
1. **The Creators – each participant in turn performs the role of the Creator**
2. **Evaluator**
3. **Speaker**

1. **Creator**

The Creator uses 2 chairs:
- **The first chair** is designed for the highly successful Creator, who has already achieved fame and appreciation from society for his or her work in the area of visual arts, music, science, business, or leadership.
- **The second chair** is designed for a "loser," a person who has never succeeded in his or her life. This person has tried different activities in his or her life and has always failed. Failure has become a way of life for this person.

The Creator sits in the first chair. This chair is designed for a highly successful Creator (see description of the first chair). The Creator recalls his or her highest achievements. The Creator describes his or her accomplishments, and how he or she feels about it. The Creator describes his or her success using as many details as possible. After completion of the first part, the Creator moves to the second chair that is designed for a "loser." The Creator then describes his or her failures and how he or she feels about them. After completion of this part, the Creator moves again to the first chair trying to recall as much as possible about his or her success. After completion of this part, the Creator moves again to the second chair trying to recall more of his or her failures.

2. The Evaluator. The main goal of the Evaluator is to ask questions, to be friendly, to offer constructive criticism, to provide evaluation, and to draw conclusions. For example, the Evaluator may ask *the successful Creator,* "How he or she feels in his or her role?" He may ask the Creator, "Why he or she feels that they were able to achieve such results?" Then when the Creator moves to the chair designed for the "loser", the Evaluator may ask questions such as: "Why the Creator did not achieve what he or she planned to achieve? What he or she needs for creativity improvement?" The Evaluator can express his or her personal opinion about the Creator's achievements and make suggestions about stimuli and blocks of the Creator's.

4. **The Speaker.** The Speaker supervises the whole exercise and prepares short presentation about it using input and opinions from the rest of the team members. After the task is performed completely, the Speaker provides a teach-back. In his or her presentation, they briefly describe their team's assignment. Then he or she provides short explanation of the discoveries or insights that took place while performing the exercise:
- What is creativity?
- What components of creative potential did they discover through this exercise?
- How different components of creativity influence one another?
- What blocks creativity?
- What stimulates creativity?

Participants work together and create **the Map of Creativity Stimulation and Suppression.**

Warm-Up

Each participant picks up the envelope with the name of the subject. Working in pairs each participant creatively describes the characteristics of his or her subject and his or her partner needs to guess what the subject is.

Instruction

Read and carefully follow these instructions.

The main goal, purpose or learning objective of this exercise is to discover things that can stimulate as well as block an individual's creative potential.

Modern technology is beginning to provide various devices to assist the most difficult part of creative process: the start. There is an old saying (I believe that its origin is Native American) that the journey of 1000 miles starts with the first step. What can be a more intimidating for an artist than to face a new, all-white canvas or for a writer to see a blank page, or for any creator to simply get started. Today technology offers software with ready-to-be-used samples of artistic images, or software for architects, designers, and other creators.

In this exercise we provide a "start" or a new list of ideas to increase the profitability of the private university.

Several members work together as a team performing this exercise and preparing a short presentation that will be provided at the end of this task to the rest of participants.

Participants:
1. **Evaluator**
2. **Speaker**
3. **Creators** (1-20 members)

2. **The Evaluator.** The main goal of the Evaluator is to ask questions, to be friendly, to constructively criticize, to objectively evaluate, and to make an assessment of the results. For example, the censor may ask the Creator, "How he or she feels in his or her role?" The Evaluator may express his personal opinion about the Creator's performance.

3. **The Speaker.** The Speaker supervises the whole exercise and prepares a short presentation about input and suggestions from the rest of the members of the team. After the task is performed completely, the Speaker provides a teach-back. In his or her presentation, he or she briefly describes his or her team assignments. Then he or she reveals creative works completed by the

individual team members as well as provides short explanation of discoveries made while performing the exercise:
- What is creativity?
- What components of creative potential that they discovered through this exercise?
- How different components of creativity influence one another?

4. **Creators**

The Creators individually describe new ideas for making more profit at University of Advancing Computer Technology. The Censor uses the mapping technique to create a map of the strategy for increasing profit at university.

After completion of the task, the speaker provides a teach-back.

Samples of Ideas

Here is a short list of new ideas for making the university more profitable
1. Develop software for sale to industry;
2. Develop e-course materials for sale to other learning institutions;
3. Provide professional development courses on-line.

Samples of the new ideas for students retention
1. Front end loading of tuition so that the longer the student is in school the less he or she pays
2. Find grants for students
3. Create new foundation for University of Advancing Computer Technology students
4. Get them a social life, many of them are lonely.

Samples of Ideas for Marketing
1. The University opens an art gallery for the creative products of employees and students in downtown Tempe.
2. The University develops 3 new study programs (the statistics demonstrate that the more courses and programs university offers, the more profitable it becomes):
3. Some new programs might be:
    - E-education;
    - E-counseling;
    - E-management.

Some new courses might be:
- Foreign Languages;
- E-counseling;
- E-management.

Greeting Cards

Greeting Cards is a hand-on technique that allows group members to express themselves in an environment conducive to creative thinking. The steps are as follows:
1. Each group needs to prepare two greeting cards designed for
    - Students and
    - Instructors.
2. Each group receives the materials needed to create greeting cards, including such items as magazines and catalogs (for pictures), scissors, colored construction paper, glue sticks, markers, crayons, pens, and adhesive tape.
3. Group members look through the catalogs and magazines and cut out about ten pictures that look interesting.

Group members paste the pictures onto folded sheets of paper and write catchy text that is designed to help students and instructors to improve their performance.

Improbable Idea

Each participant needs to develop the most improbable idea. The least probable idea wins the game.

Instruction
1. Each group member get numbered card from a facilitator.
2. Each participant write the most improbable idea he or she can imagine.
3. All ideas are displayed for the entire group to read.

4. Participants study each idea and try to think of ways to make it more practical to reduce the idea owner's chances of winning.
5. Facilitator writes down all suggestions about each idea.
6. Idea that obtained the least number of suggestions is the winner.

Warm-Up: Collective Mirror

One of the participant demonstrates some of gesture, posture and face expression in front of the group. The rest of participants repeat/mirror his or her movement. Each participant needs to repeat the same procedure.

Assignment 3

The first team using the hand-outs creates list of killer phrases, provides their classification (self-doubt, excuse, procrastination, fear and so on) and presents them to the second team.
The second team prepares counter-phrases that kill the killers.
Both teams create a mind map of the Killer Phrases and present it for the rest of participants.

Warm-Up

This exercise needs to be performed in pairs. Looking into each others eyes, participants apply their creative imaginations and attempt to read the mind of his or her partner.

Assignment 3

Analogies

This technique is based on general analogical thinking that relies on the direct comparison of one thing or action to another. Some research suggests that analogies are more likely than other direct stimulation methods to yield unique ideas. Analogies also seem to work especially well for mechanical problems. For instance, analogies have been used to design a new type of thermos bottle closure and a way to attach spacesuit helmets.

Instructions

Participants seek comparisons that might spark ideas. Once the similarities are identified, participants then elaborate on them and use them to stimulate ideas.

1. Each participant thinks of the major principle underlying the problem and uses it to generate a list of thing similar to the problem. To help generate this list, they may say, "This problem is like…."
2. Each participant selects one of the analogies and describes it in detail. He or she elaborates as much as possible, listing parts, functions, or uses. It is suggested to include many action-oriented phrases.
3. Each participant reviews each description and uses it to stimulate ideas.

Example

Suppose participants decide to use analogies to help to increase a students' enrollment. The major principle in this case is getting more of something. Thus, they might think of analogies prompted by the phrase "This problem is like…"

- Trying to seduce my coworker's spouse;
- Asking my parents for an increase in my allowance;
- Asking my boss for a raise;
- Asking a cook for more food;
- Asking for more time to complete a project;
- An employee trying to get more power over another employee;
- A football team trying to win more games;
- Calling people to sell more magazines.

Participants select one on these analogies and elaborate it.
Trying to seduce my coworker's spouse involves the following things:

- Looking as presentable as possible: dress, make-up, hair style, and so on;
- Being more interesting: read more, gather humorous stories, interesting facts;
- Be available: trying to be around;
- Trying to attract her or his attention.

Finally, using the elaborations participants suggest **ideas for students' enrollment**:
- Work on image of the university;
- Make the image more attractive in comparison with the other universities;
- Gather facts from the history of university showing its success;
- Advertise more.

Roll Call

Although we have been taught to think before we speak, this advice may sometimes be counterproductive. If we think too much before we talk during idea generation, we may judge our ideas prematurely and restrict our creativity. Self-censors are the enemies of all creative thought.

Unlike many situations in life, this technique works best when participants talk before they think. Its major strength is that it encourages spontaneity and helps eliminate judgmental thinking. Group members are forced to leap to conclusions instead of leaping to ideas. Thus, they have little choice but to defer judgment. Hall (1994) describes the steps as follows:

1. The group breaks up into two groups.
2. Each member of the first group call out one word. The words would be whatever pops into their heads. Group members shouldn't think very long about what word to say, and the words should be unrelated to the problem.
3. All members of the second group have two minutes to create a practical idea based on combining the words or using the individual words for stimulation.
4. Groups exchange their roles.

Associations

This exercise uses a reminding chain or memory probe. Holding up, for instance, a Granny Smith apple, remind participants that this apple first came to the United States from New Zealand, on the other side of the world, and then tell a story about its voyage, talking about how it is winter here but summer down there, and eventually you turn your perception topsy-turvy. Then complete this line:

"The Granny Smith apple reminds me of..." Someone might write, "...of a green spring day," then continue, "...a green spring day reminds me of..."

Go through the first few lines, then write using concrete images from your associational memories and not abstractions like love, peace, happiness or sadness. Many are able to associate all the way back to very early emotional experiences.

Have a Ball!

The very idea that there is another idea is something gained.

Richard Jeffries

Flexibility and *fluency* are the most important attributes for creative problem solving and for coping with the rapid change-dynamics of the present time.

The creative person is both flexible and fluent. Capable of producing ideas in volume, he or she has a better chance of developing significant alternative when confronting a problem or when seeking improvements in existing situations. The creative person is able to choose and investigate a wide variety of approaches to solve his or her problems. He or she is resourceful in the ability to shift gears, to discard one frame of reference for another, to change approaches and to adapt quickly to new developments. He or she constantly asks himself or herself, "What else?" or "What would happen if I viewed my problem from a different perspective?"

This exercise is designed to enhance your facility to think up a large number of different ideas when confronting a problem. It can be done solo or in-group. A group usually generates a lot of excitement and a blizzard of ideas. When playing this game with others, agree to a 4-minute time limit. The winner is the person who produces the largest number of alternative or different ideas:

Now list all possible uses for a ball or balls (ping-pong, tennis, basketball, baseball, soccer, football, and so on.

Answer:

These are only several examples of the uses for balls. You probably came up with many others not listed here.

1. Head for finger puppet
2. Christmas tree ornaments (when painted and decorated
3. Hang in fringe for low clearances
4. Clown nose
5. Target for slingshot, BB guns
6. Juggle them
7. Gearshift knob
8. Roll down hill
9. Train dogs to retrieve
10. Wheels on toy automobile
11. Fish lure for big fish
12. Plug a hole
13. Hang on trees to frighten birds
14. Collect as a hobby
15. Make rattle for babies
16. Pulley for window-shade
17. Fill with lead and use for diving and retrieving
18. Window display
19. Stop up sink
20. Put on string for cat to play with
21. Cut up and cover eyes when sunbathing
22. Teach children to count
23. Construct mobile
24. False mumps
25. Hide narcotics
26. String as beads
27. Demonstrate structure
28. Costume for strippers
29. Decorate garden
30. Astronomical display.

Devising alternative uses for common objects is not merely an academic exercise; it is continually demonstrated by those concerned about our environment. For example, among the countless varieties of manmade pollutants are the approximately 20 million discarded automobile and truck tires that litter our landscapes, highways, and dumps.

Many excellent and innovative ideas and solutions to this problem have already been developed. There is no doubt that we can generate new and novel ideas to meet most of the challenges we are now facing and will face in the future. It is in the department of action and implementation that most of us fall short of the mark.

Pairing up

We can have facts without thinking, but we cannot have thinking without facts.
John Dewey

Creative people usually form good, clear, sharp impressions of thing they observe around them. As a result, the accumulated information in their memory storage is substantial. And they can easily retrieve the needed information when called upon to do so. Readily recallable information is essential for creative functioning.

This exercise, which you can play either solo or with others, helps you to increase your facility of recall.

List all the things you can think of that can come in pairs.

_____
_____
_____

Examples
Eyeglasses, earmuffs, lovebirds

Answers
Legs, stockings, arms, bookend, stereo speakers, dumbbells, turn signals, running lights, twin-beds, bedside tables, ping pong paddles, skis, skates, swim fins, falsies, breasts, nipples, eyes, ears, nostrils, hands, feet, lungs, siames twins, twins, oars, crutches, handcuffs, married couples, yoke of oxen, eyebrows, lips, buttocks, testicles, candlesticks, doorknobs.

Creative Thinking

Aphoristic Definitions

Dictionary definitions lean more toward the conceptual and abstract. They often convey only desiccated meaning from which all but a pinpointing precision has been eliminated. Consequently they often seem rather inconsequential and leave a feeling of incompleteness in the mind of the reader.

Good aphoristic definitions, on the other hand, pack a force that ineluctably turn the reader to the experiential, to the immediately felt unique quality and flavor of life: experiences and happenings. By giving us a different and vivid slice of reality, they appeal to our imagination, interests, and values. They also come closer to capturing and conveying the real meaning of a word or situation, and are more provocative of thoughts than designed to train your ability to add your own idiosyncratic quality and flavor to your observations of life experiences. It is an excellent and stimulating game to play with others, but choose partners who are not afraid to express their individuality.

Pick five words from the following list and write your own original, concise definitions for each word.

1. Advertising _____
2. Argument _____
3. Block _____
4. A bore _____
5. Conceit _____
6. A cynic _____
7. Depression _____
8. Doctor _____
9. Envy _____
10. Executive _____
11. Failure _____
12. A friend _____
13. Gratitude _____
14. Happiness _____
15. Initiative _____
16. Life _____
17. Luxury _____
18. Marriage _____
19. A pessimist _____
20. A politician _____
21. Procrastination _____
22. Progress _____
23. Reality _____
24. Self-evident _____
25. Self-respect _____
26. Storyteller _____

Examples

Marriage: A lottery in which men stake their liberty and women their happiness. (Madame De Rieux) One long conversation, chequered by disputes. (Robert Louis Stevenson)

Answers

1. Advertising   The science of arresting the human intelligence long enough to get money from it. (Stephen Leacock)
2. Argument   A sure sign of conversation gone sour. (Dagobert D. Runes)
3. Block   The distance between some people's ears
4. Bore   A person who talks when you with him to listen. (Ambrose Bierce)
    A fellow who opens his mouth and puts his feats in it. (Henry Ford)
    A man who deprives you of solitude without providing you with company. (Gian Vincenzo Gravino)
5. Conceit   Self-respect in one whom we dislike. (Ambrose Bierce)

Creative Thinking

6. Cynic — A man who knows the price of everything, and the value of nothing. (Oscar Wilde)
7. Depression — A period when you can't spend money you don't have.
8. Doctor — Someone who acts like a humanitarian and charges like a TV repairman. (Henry D. Spalding)
9. Envy — The sincerest form of flattery. (Churton Collins)
10. Executive — A person who can, without the facts, make quick decision that occasionally are right.
11. Failure — The path of least persistence (Lames M. Barrie)
12. Friend — One who dislike the same people that you do. (Oscar Wild)
13. Gratitude — A strong and secret hope of greater favors. (La Rochefoucauld)
14. Happiness — A delicate balance between what one is and what one has. (L.H. Denison)
15. Initiative — Doing the right thing without being told. (Elbert Hubbard)
16. Life — One long process of getting tired. (Samuel Butler)
17. Luxury — Something you don't really need and can't do without.
18. Marriage — A noose often endured around the neck, but seldom endured around the feet. (Henry S. Haskins)
19. Pissimist — One who, when he has the choice of two evils, chooses both. (Oscar Wild)
20. Politician — A fellow who shakes your hand before the election and shakes you after the election.
21. Procratination — The art of keeping up with yesterday. (Don Marquis)
22. Progress — The exchange of one nuisance for another nuisance. (Havelock Ellis)
23. Reality — A poor substitute for imagination. (Dagobert D. Runes)
24. Self-Evident — Evident to one's self and top nobody else. (Ambrose Bierce)
25. Self-Respect — The secure feeling that no one, as yet, is suspicious. (H.L. Mencken)
26. Stiryteller — A person who has a good memory and hopes other people haven't. (Irwin S. Cobb).

Chapter 9

Problem Solving

What is the problem with the problem-solving process? Is there a recipe, a formula, a good instruction for the right way to do it? Is there a difference between individual and group decision-making?

LEARNING OBJECTIVES

After reading this chapter, you will be able to

1. Define problem
2. Compare and contrast problem-solving and decision-making processes
3. Identify and apply various techniques for successful problem-solving
4. Compare and contrast programmed and non-programmed decisions
5. Describe and discuss group decision-making process
6. Apply various problem-solving techniques.

What great thinkers say about creativity?

An idea can turn to dust or magic, depending on the talent that rubs against it.

- Bill Bernbach

Trust in yourself. Your perceptions are often far more accurate than you are willing to believe.

- Claudia Black

I must create a system or be enslaved by another man's. I will not reason and compare; My business is to create.

- William Blake

The analysis of data will not by itself produce new ideas

- Edward de Bono

Life is "trying things to see if they work"

- Ray Bradbury

We have to understand that the world can only be grasped by action, not by contemplation. The hand is more important than the eye... The hand is the cutting edge of the mind

- Jacob Bronowski

The only truly happy people are children and the creative minority.

- Jean Caldwell

You can observe a lot by watching.

- Yogi Berra

When you're through changing, you're through.

- Bruce Barton

Imagination rules the world

- Napoleon Bonaparte

The essential conditions of everything you do must be choice, love, passion.

- Nadia Boulanger

How many of you do your best thinking and get your most creative ideas at work? When we ask people in our groups this question, no one ever raises their hand. (from "Sacred Cows Make the Best Burgers")

- Robert Kriegel and David Brandt

Live and work but do not forget to play, to have fun in life and really enjoy it.

- Eileen Caddy

Leap and the net will appear.

- Julia Cameron

PROBLEMS

A problem is a gap between existing and desirable situation. A problem is usually some difficulty or thing that people want to overcome or be rid of. The term "problem" can also be used when people are trying to achieve some task, though in many cases "design" or "task achieving" are more appropriate.

When the course of action toward a desired objective is not easy or routine, then people have a problem.

The traditional method for problem solving is to find the cause of the problem and then to seek to remove that cause.

Problems are situations that most people find uncomfortable, if not unpalatable. When confronted with a dilemma, the natural inclination is to seek, as quickly as possible, the simplest solution, and then move on to something else. People often jump to conclusion even before they have a full understanding of the situation. A poorly analyzed problem, however, invariably results in an inadequate or wrong response.

When a problem fails to yield a quick answer, many people doggedly stick to the one way of approach they have chosen and are unable to let go of it. A good problem-solver, on the other hand, turns the problem over on all sides, restates it several times, inhibits the tendency to persist in one direction, and deliberately experiments with a multitude of one direction, and deliberately experiments to one approach, he keeps his mind and his options open.

Problem Finding as Creativity

Gestalt psychologists (Henle, 1962, 1974; Wertheimer, 1959) have emphasized the importance of posing the correct question. Henle (1974) argued that the perception of "dynamic gaps" incites the creative process: "And yet posing the right question may be the most creative part of the whole process."

James Stephens pointed that "a well-packed question carries its answer on its back as a snail carries its shell" (1920, p.68)" Henle described six conditions leading to the perception of gaps:

1. Contradictions of all kinds;
2. Unexpected similarities between one phenomenon and an apparently unrelated one;
3. Strange, new phenomena;
4. In science, a hypothesis derived from theory;
5. Again in science, difficulties with prevailing explanation, and of great importance;
6. The presence of a "welcoming mind," actively looking for those gaps.

Related to Guilford's (1950) notion of "sensitivity to problems" and the everyday meaning of actively refers to their looking for discrepancies or something they do not understand.

Gestalt psychologists (Henle, 1962, 1974; Wertheimer, 1959) have emphasized the importance of posing the correct question. Henle (1974) argue that the perception of "dynamic gaps" incites the creative process: "And yet posing the right question may be the most creative part of the whole process."

James Stephens pointed that "a well-packed question carries its answer on its back as a snail carries its shell" (1920, p.68) Henle described six conditions leading to the perception of gaps: (1) contradictions of all kinds; (2) unexpected similarities between one phenomenon and an apparently unrelated one; (3) strange, new phenomena; (4) in science, a hypothesis derived from theory; (5) again in science, difficulties with prevailing explanation, and of great importance; and (6) the presence of a "welcoming mind," actively looking for those gaps.

PROBLEM SOLVING AND DECISION MAKING

According to Simon (1960) there are two types of decisions:

1. **Programmed decisions.** If a **particular situation occurs often**, a routine procedure usually will be worked out for solving it. Decisions are programmed to the extent that they are repetitive and routine and a definite procedure has been developed for handling them.

"Creativity is looking at a problem or a situation in a different way from everybody else and seeing something that they have missed. The trail can be cultivated by refusing to accept the obvious."

Yurjio Yanamoto

Rossman (1931) sees creativity as:

Need or difficulty observed;

Analysis; problem defined;

Information surveyed; possible occurrence of incubation;

Many possible solutions formulated;

Critical evaluation of solutions, sustained and ongoing incubation, particularly in complex problems;

Formulation and refinement of most promising solution; acceptance of final solution.

Less than two out, with a man on first, a ground ball is hit to you – the throw is to first base.

2. **Non-programmed decisions.** Decisions are non-programmed when they are novel and unstructured. There is no established procedure for handling the problem, either because it has not arisen in exactly the same manner before or because it is complex or extremely important. Such decisions deserve special treatment.

Types of Decisions

Type of a Problem	Programmed Decisions	Non-Programmed Decisions
Procedure	Frequent, repetitive, routine, much certainty regarding cause-and-effect relationships	Novel, unstructured, much uncertainty regarding cause-and-effect relationships
	Dependence on policies, rules, and definite procedures	Necessity for creativity, intuition, tolerance for ambiguity, creative problem solving
Examples *University:*	Necessary grade-point average for good academic standing	Construction of new classroom facilities
Business firm:	Periodic reorders of inventory	Diversification into new products and markets
Government:	Merit system for promotion of State employees	Reorganization of state government agencies

Traditionally, **programmed decisions** have been handled through
1. rules,
2. standard operating procedures, and
3. **the structure of the society, organization or group that develops specific procedures for handling them.** Operations researchers – through the development of mathematical models – have facilitated the handling of these types of decisions.

On the other hand, **non-programmed decisions** usually have been handled by
1. general problem-solving processes,
2. judgment,
3. intuition, and
4. creativity.

Ideally, the main concern of **creative individual** should be **non-programmed decisions.**

THE DECISION-MAKING PROCESS

Decisions should be thought of as **a means rather than ends**. They are the mechanisms through which an attempt is made **to achieve a desired state**. They are, in fact, **a response to a problem**. Every decision is the outcome of a dynamic process that is influenced by a multitude of forces.

This process consists from the following **stages**:
1. Establishing specific goals and objectives and measuring results
2. Problem identification
3. Establishing priorities

4. Consideration of causes
5. Development of alternative solutions
6. Evaluation of alternative solution
7. Solution selection
8. Implementation
9. Follow-up.

Establishing specific goals and objectives and measuring results

Goals and objective are needed in each area where performance influences the effectiveness of the organization and individual. If goals and objectives are adequately established, they will dictate **what results must** be achieved and the measures that indicate **whether or not they have been achieved.**

Problem identification

A necessary condition for a decision is a **problem** – if problems did not exist, there would be no need for decisions. Problems typically result from a determination that a **discrepancy exists between a desired state and current reality.**

This underscores the importance of establishing **goals and objectives.** How critical a problem is for the individual or group is measured **by the gap** between the levels of performance attained.

It is easy to understand that a **problem exists when a gap occurs between desired results and actual results.** However, certain factors often lead to **difficulties** in identifying exactly what the problem is. These factors are:

1. **Perceptual problems.**

    - **Individual feelings** may act in such a way as to protect or defend us from unpleasant perceptions.
    - **Negative information** may be **selectively perceived** in such a way as to distort its true meaning or it may be totally ignored. For example, a college dean may fail to identify increasing class sizes as a problem while at the same time being sensitive to problems faced by the president of the university in raising funds for the school.

2. **Defining problems in terms of solutions.** This is really a form of **jumping to conclusions.** For example, a sales manager may say, "The decrease in profits is due to our poor product quality." The sales manager's definition of the problem **suggests a particular solution** – the improvement of product quality in the production department. Certainly, other solutions may be possible. Perhaps the sales force has been inadequately selected or trained. Perhaps competitors have a superior product.

    Wright Brothers is a perfect example. They very specifically defined their problem as **heavier than air controlled flight.** If they had not had such a clear definition of the problem they may have been successful anyhow, but it would have taken a lot longer.

3. **Identifying symptoms as problems.** "Our problem is a 20 percent decline in students' detention." While it is certainly true that students' detention have declined, the decline in detention is really **a symptom of the real problem.** When school's administration identifies the **real** problem, the cause of the decline in retention will be found.

Establishing Priorities

All problems **are not created equal.**

The process of decision making and solution implementation requires **resources.** Unless the resources are unlimited, it is necessary to establish priorities for dealing with problems. This, in turn, means being able to make a determination of the significance level of the problem.

Problems usually are of three types:

1. **opportunity,**
2. **crisis,** or
3. **routine.**

Crisis and routine problems present themselves and must be attended to by the managers of an organization or just by individual.

Opportunities, on the other hand, usually must be found. They await discovery, and they often go unnoticed and eventually are lost by an inattentive manager or individual. This is because, by their very nature, most crises and routine problems demand immediate attention. Thus, a person may spend more time in handling problems than in pursuing important new opportunities.

Determining problem significance involves consideration of three issues:

1. urgency,
2. impact, and
3. growth tendency.

Urgency relates **to time**. How critical is the time pressure? Putting out a fire in the building is probably more urgent than buying new canvas or paint. On the other hand, buying new canvas and paint is likely to be more urgent than fixing the previously created painting.

Impact describes **the seriousness of the problem's effects**. Effects may be on public image, people, equipment, or important relationship. Whether problem effects are short term or long term, and whether the problem is likely to create other problems are also questions related to impact.

Growth tendency addresses **future considerations**. Even though problem may currently be of low urgency and have little impact, if allowed to go unattended it may grow. The decision to cut back on routine preventive maintenance of plant equipment as a cost-cutting measure may not create a significant problem immediately. Over time, however, major difficulties may arise.

Consideration of Causes

While not impossible, it is ordinarily difficult and ill-advised to determine a solution to a problem **when the problem cause is unknown**.

The practice of blood-letting and the use of leeches are examples of solutions that formerly were applied to a variety of medical problems. If the causes of the medical conditions had been known, other solutions would have been implemented.

Frequently, the search for problem causes leads to a better definition of the real problem. **Causes can be turned into new – and better – problem statements.**

Development of Alternative Solutions

Before a decision is made, feasible **alternatives** should be developed (actually these are potential solutions to the problem), and the potential consequences of each alternative should be considered. This is really a search process in which the relevant internal and external factors are investigated to provide information that can be developed into possible alternatives. Obviously, this search is conducted within certain time and cost constraints, since only so much effort can be devoted to developing alternatives.

Evaluation of alternative solutions

Once alternatives have been developed, they must be evaluated and compared.

1. Certainty. The decision maker has **complete knowledge** of the probability of the outcome of each alternative.

2. Uncertainty. The decision maker has **absolutely no knowledge** of the probability of the outcome of each alternative.

3. Risk. The decision maker has **some probabilistic estimate** of the outcomes of each alternative.

Solution selection

The purpose of selecting a particular solution is **to solve a problem** in order to achieve a predetermined objective.

Unfortunately, situations **rarely** exist in which **one alternative** achieves the desired objective without having some positive or negative impact on another objective. Situations often exist where two objectives cannot be optimized simultaneously. If one objective is optimized, the other is sub-optimized.

A situation could also exist where attainment of **a group or individual objective** would be **at the expense** of a societal objective. The reality of such situation is seen clearly in the rise of ecology groups, environmentalists, and the consumerist movement.

> **In process of creativity**, for example, if ideas are optimized, the economic resources may be sub-optimized, or vice versa.

Implementation

Any decision is little more than an abstraction if it is not implemented, and it must be **effectively implemented** in order to achieve the objective for which it was made. It is entirely possible for a "good" decision to be hurt by poor implementation. In this sense, implementation may be more important than the actual choice of the alternative.

Follow-up

Effective creative process involves **periodic measurements of results**.

Actual results are **compared** with planned results (the objective), and if deviations exist, **changes must be made**. Here again, we see the importance of **measurable objectives**.

If such objectives do not exist, then there is no way to judge performance.

If actual results do not match planned results, changes must be made in the solution chosen, in its implementation, or in the original objective if it is deemed unattainable.

If the original objective must be revised, then the entire decision-making process will be reactivated.

The important point is that once a decision is implemented, individual cannot assume that the outcome will meet the original objective. Some **system of control and evaluation** is necessary to make sure the actual results are consistent with the results planned for when the decision was made.

Sometimes the result or outcome of a decision is **unexpected** or is perceived differently by different people, and dealing with this possibility is an important part of the following-up phase in the decision process.

Heuristics

"You can't there from here." Or so it may seem when you face a problem. Solving problems often requires a strategy. If the number of alternatives is small, a **random search strategy** might work. This is another example of trial-and-error thinking in which *all possibilities are tried more or less randomly*. Imagine, for example, that you are traveling and decide to look up an old friend, John Brown, in a city you are visiting. You open the phone book and find 57 J. Brown listed. Of course, you could dial each number until you find the right one. "Forget it," you say to yourself. "Is there any way I can narrow the search?" "Oh, yeah! I remember hearing that John lives by the beach." Then you take out a map and call only the numbers with addresses near the waterfront.

The approach used in this example is a **heuristic**: a strategy for identifying and evaluating problem solutions). Typically, a heuristic is a "rule of thumb" that reduces the number of alternatives thinkers must consider. This raises the odds of success, although it does not guarantee a solution. Here are some heuristic strategies that often work:

- Try to identify **how the current state of affairs differs from the desired goal**. Then find steps that will reduce the difference.
- Try **working backward from the desired goal to the starting point** or current state.
- If you can't reach the goal directly, try to **identify an intermediate goal or sub-problem** that at least gets you closer.
- **Represent the problem in other ways**, with graphs, diagrams, or analogies, for instance.
- **Generate a possible solution and test it**. Doing so may eliminate many alternatives, or it may clarify what is needed for a solution.

Insightful Solutions

During problem solving, we say that **insight** has occurred when an **answer appears suddenly**. Insights are usually so rapid and clear that we wonder why we didn't see the solution sooner. Insight is usually based on **reorganizing the elements of a problem**. Seeing the problem in a new way is what makes its solution seem obvious.

Fixation

One of the most important **barriers** to problem solving is **fixation**, the tendency to get "hung up" on wrong solutions or to become blind to alternatives. Usually this occurs when we place unnecessary restrictions on our thinking.

A prime example of restricted thinking is **functional fixedness**. This is an inability to see new uses (functions) for familiar objects or for things that were used in a particular way. If you have ever used a dime as a screwdriver, you've overcome functional fixedness.

Mechanical Problem's Solutions

A mechanical solution may be achieved by **trial and error** or by **rote**. If I forget the combination to my bike lock, I may be able to discover it by trial and error. In an era of high-speed computers, many trial-and-error solutions are best left to machines. A computer could generate all possible combinations of the five numbers on my lock in a split second.

When a problem is solved *by rote*, thinking is guided by a **learned set of rules**. If you have a good background in math, you may have solved the math's problem by rote.

Solutions by Understanding

Many problems cannot be solved mechanically or by habitual modes of thought. In that case, **understanding** (deeper comprehension of a problem) is necessary.

There are **two phases** to successful problem solving. First, it is necessary to discover the *general properties* of a correct solution.

1. A **general solution** states the requirements for success, but not in enough detail for further action.

2. In the second phase a number of **functional solutions** are proposed and the best one is selected.

BEHAVIORAL INFLUENCE ON DECISION MAKING

A number of *behavioral factors* influence the decision-making process

Values

Values pervade the decision-making process. As one example, consider the **issue of ethics** in decision making. An ethical decision can be viewed as one that is **legal and morally acceptable** to society; an unethical decision is either illegal or morally unacceptable.

Propensity for Risk

From personal experience, you are aware that decision makers vary greatly in their propensity for taking risks.

Potential for Dissonance

Much attention has been focused on the forces and influences affecting the decision maker before a decision is made and on the decision itself. But only recently has attention been given to what happens *after* a decision has been made. Specifically, behavioral scientists have focused attention on the occurrence of **post-decision anxiety**.

Such anxiety is related to what Festinger calls cognitive dissonance. Festinger's **cognitive dissonance** theory states that there is often a lack of consistency or **harmony** among an individual's various conditions (**attitudes, beliefs,** and so on) after a decision has been made. That is, there will be a conflict between what the decision maker knows and believes and what was done, and as a result the decision maker will have **doubts and second thoughts** about the choice that was made. In addition, there is a likelihood that the intensity of the anxiety will be greater when any of the following conditions exist:

1. The decision is an important one psychologically or financially;
2. There are a number of foregone alternatives;
3. The forgone alternatives have many favorable features.

When dissonance occurs, it can be **reduced by admitting that a mistake has been made.** Unfortunately, many individuals are reluctant to admit they have made a wrong decision and will be more likely to use one or more of the following methods to reduce their dissonance:

1. Seek information that **supports the wisdom of their decision**.
2. **Selectively perceive (distort) information** in a way that supports their decision.
3. **Adopt a less favorable view** of the forgone alternatives.
4. **Minimize the importance of the negative aspects** of the decision and exaggerate the importance of the positive aspect.

The potential of dissonance is influenced heavily by one's personality, specifically one's **self-confidence and persuasibility**.

Escalation of Commitment

Gamblers who place larger and larger wagers in an effort to recoup earlier losses are displaying a decision-making behavior called escalation of commitment. **Escalation of commitment** refers to an increasing commitment to a previous decision when a "rational" decision maker would withdraw. The **gambler's fallacy** may also be fueling this commitment. It typically results from a need to turn a losing or poor decision into a winning or good decision.

Escalation of commitment can result from becoming too ego-involved in a decision process. Because failure is threatening to an individual's self-esteem, people tend to **ignore negative information**.

STAGES OF CREATIVE PROCESS

Stage 1. The Engagement

By deciding to create something new, you've made a commitment to express your contemporary life, experience, and environment. Depending of field where you are going to create, you have different medium: language, if you are a writer, sounds, if you are a musician, paint, if you are an artist, research, if you are a scientist, project, if you are a manager and so on. Content is achieved through the words, sounds, colors, or actions. In the true creative process, medium and content become one; keep this foremost in your mind. This is your goal. Creating is a worthwhile experience for its own sake. Worthwhile experience, however, does not come easily. There are risks. This fact will not deter you. You have responded to the attraction, the lure of inspiration. It will not abandon you unless you default on your pledge.

Who will become the great artist, musician, writer, or entrepreneur? No one can predict exactly who among the present practitioners of the art will represent our era to generations of the future. To become an achiever takes a combination of talent, sensitivity, pride and humility, knowledge and insight, and a fascination with the process of creation as a living phenomenon.

Whether or not you become a great artist or businessman, you will – given the least spark of insight into the meaning and beauty of the creation - experience moments of joy and deep satisfaction when a particular idea flashes through your mind or grows step by painstaking step on the canvas or paper, nurtures your effort and increasing skills. Many of us are happy to settle for such moments.

Be cautioned, however, that if dissatisfaction with your work goes too far, nothing will ever be finished. Learn to recognize when revision after revision is actually helping you to achieve its greatest potential. But learn as well when the time to stop revising comes. Keep in mind that your goal is to complete the project.

The other kind of doubt you would contend with concerns the potential relationship between your work and audience they envision for it – actually the contribution they see themselves making to the creation in general.

At times, you will not be able to refrain from asking yourself: Is what I'm attempting worth doing at all? Isn't it merely ego serving to try to express in your work what others already have expressed better than I shall ever be able to do? Why should anyone be interested in what I have to do?

These recurring doubts are natural. Don't let them frighten you. Your personal devil stands at your left shoulder, but your personal angel stands at your right.

Stage 2. Uniqueness

One of the splendid attributes of human nature is that each of us is endowed with an individual set of perceptions; the mode and character of your perceptions are different from those of anyone else. In the creative acts, this proves to be one of the creator's most valuable strengths. You are you, and there is only one you in the entire universe. Your ways of hearing, seeing, feeling, thinking, absorbing, experiencing, planning, and expressing yourself are not like the ways of any other individual. Depending on how well you are for your work, your contribution will be valuable because of these differences, this uniqueness that only you can offer as your personal vision.

Stage 3. Motives

Examining your motives for wanting to create may enable you to work with more confidence and clarity. Why the urge to express yourself in this fashion? What is your goal? Do you feel the need to be noticed, to perform, to obtain publicity? Is it important for you to live the life of an artist, a writer, a musician, an entrepreneur? Do you look upon creative act as therapy? Have you something important to do that you believe you alone can create? Are you unable to resist imagining, daydreaming, inventing, turning the blank page into meaningful one? Do you need challenges to exploit and experiment with language, to exhort it to expanded perimeters? Creative act results from a combination of these motives plus many others.

Stage 4. Perspective and Objectivity

Your unique way of thinking enables you to achieve an individual perspective. This results in a personal vision of life unlike that of anyone else. Your work should exhibit, along with a sense of spontaneity, the shape and direction of such personal vision. Try to understand the sources of your "intuitions," your private symbols and their meanings, the developmental logic of your expressions.

Having achieved an understanding of your aims and impulses, you should be able to take a more objective view of your work. If you find it difficult to encourage this view initially you will have to practice being objective for the first few times. Imagine yourself as a consumer of your creative product (painting, essay, music, or service) and the product itself. Your task is to review the work critically, taking into account all the things a consumer might. After you've tried this awhile, you'll be able to detect weaknesses and faults in your creative product and thereby will be in a position to correct them. It may help you further to make a list of things for improvement: interest factor, universality, theme, emotional content, diction, tone, form, visual presentation, sound, logic, order, and so on.

To do anything well takes training and practice. Gaining objectivity about your creative product is no exception.

Stage 5. Mystery

However much we may analyze or dissect a creative product, there remains, at times, a quality that defies investigation. This is one of the mysteries of creativity and one of the mysteries in creative process. Analysis can never be truly complete in a real life.

Another mystery is involved in the product's conception: Where does the idea come from? What made the author select this particular form? Where have his or her illustrating images originated? The answers to these and similar questions remain elusive.

We can look at the completed product and arrive at the author's intent and meaning, and we are able to appreciate the product's shape and sound, the success of its style, diction, and mood; but the remaining mystery is in the very act of creation itself. Of course, we are considering the author's real piece of art, those that start inside the self, and not those executed merely as assignments to improve personal skills or to fit a particular occasion.

These mysteries are part of the natural evolution of the creative product; unfortunately, they sometimes become associated with certain pitfalls of which the beginner should be aware. Moody vagueness, superficial philosophic musings, profundity without depth (a paradox too often encountered), and deliberate obscurity do not add mystery – they only detract from it. The true mystery of a creation is rarely evident to the creator until he or she has completed the work.

There will evolve from a wide range of your efforts a series of related symbols and the development of certain themes that are especially important to you – your personal mythology. This further outlines your private terms. If, because of your methods of expression and your ability to convince, your readers or listeners are compelled to accept such a world, you have succeeded in an important aspect of the relationship between poetry and audience. Gaining the consumer's acceptance, in spite of the fact that they find elements of logic or reality eluding them, reveals that you have captured the essence of art: mystery, myth, and magic.

> *Stage 6. Studying Other's Creative Work*
> This is an important part of your life as a creator. Read and study in your domain as much as you can, both past and contemporary. It cannot harm you (as some beginners fear it will), and it may help you considerably. Do not read to "copy" except as an exercise. Read and study to see how other prominent people express themselves, how they achieve their effects, how they put the elements of their work together – in other words, how they make their creative product.
>
> You may ask yourself why you really don't like some of famous works of art that have been revered throughout time and are included in anthology after anthology. Can I really create something, if I don't understand or appreciate as others do? It is natural to dislike certain pieces of art and to feel misgivings about such dislike. Liking is a subjective affair. We don't all like the same things; there's no reason why all of us should like the same things. It is more honest to admit not liking something than to pretend to like it because everyone else seems to like it. It would be naive to accept all famous works indiscriminately. As your own critical skills develop, you will detect faults in many favorite works.
>
> In most areas there exists a community of your domain. Become a part of it. You can benefit from such association; the interchanges among specialists are both stimulating and challenging. Discuss with your colleagues, friend, and family members your ideas.

GROUP DECISION MAKING

In most organizations a great deal of decision making is achieved **through committees, teams, task forces, and other kinds of groups.** This is especially true for **non-programmed problems**, which are novel and have much uncertainty regarding the outcome. In most organizations, it is unusual to find decisions on such problems being made by one individual on a regular basis.

The increased complexity of many non-programmed decisions requires **specialized knowledge** in numerous fields, usually not possessed by one person.

Individual versus Group Decision Making

Considerable debate has occurred over the relative effectiveness of **individual versus group** decision making. Groups usually **take more time** to reach a decision that individuals do. But bringing together individual specialists and experts has its **benefits** since the mutually reinforcing impact of their interaction results in better decisions. In fact, a great deal of research gas shown that consensus decisions with **five or more participants** are superior to individual decision making, majority vote, and leader decisions.

Certain decisions appear to be better made by groups, while others appear better suited to individual decision making. **Non-programmed decisions appear to be better suited to group** decision making. Usually calling for pooled talent, the decisions are so important that they are frequently made by top management and, to a somewhat lesser extent, by middle managers.

In terms of the decision making process itself, the following points concerning group processes for non-programmed decisions can be made:

1. In **establishing goals and objectives**, **groups** probably are superior to individuals because of the greater amount of knowledge available to groups.

2. In **identifying causes** and developing alternative solutions, **the individual efforts** of group members are necessary to ensure a broad search in the various functional areas of the organization.

3. In **evaluating alternative solutions**, the **collective judgment** of the group, with its wider range of viewpoint, seems superior to that of the individual decision maker.

4. In **solution selection**, it has been shown that **group interaction** and the achievement of consensus usually results in the acceptance of **more risk** than would be accepted by an individual decision maker. In any event, the group decision is more likely to be accepted as a result of the participation of those affected by its consequences.

Problem-Solving

5. **Implementation** and follow-up of a decision, whether or not made by a group, usually is accomplished by **individual managers**. Thus, since a group ordinarily is not responsible, the responsibility for implementation and follow-up necessarily rests with the individual manager.

Creativity in Group Decision Making

If groups are better suited to non-programmed decisions than individuals are, then **an atmosphere fostering group creativity must be created**. In this respect, group decision making may be similar to brainstorming in that discussion must be **free-flowing and spontaneous**.

Techniques for Stimulating Creativity

It seems safe to say that, in many instances, group decision making is preferable to individual decision making. But we have all heard the statement, **"A camel is a racehorse designed by a committee."**

Brainstorming In many situations, groups are expected to produce creative or imaginative solutions to organizational problems. In such instances, brainstorming often has been found to enhance the creative output of the group. The technique of brainstorming includes a strict series of rules. The purpose of the rules is to promote the generation of ideas while, at the same time, avoiding the inhibitions of members that usually are caused by face-to-face groups. The basic rules are:

1. **No ideas are too ridiculous**. Group members are encouraged to state any extreme or outlandish idea.
2. **Each idea presented belongs to the group**, not to the person stating it. In this way, it is hoped that group members will utilize and build on the ideas of others.
3. **No idea can be criticized**. The purpose of the session is to generate, not evaluate, ideas.

The Delphi Technique This technique involves the solicitation and comparison of anonymous judgments on the topic of interest through a set of sequential questionnaires that are interspersed with summarized information and feedback of opinions from earlier responses.

The Delphi process retains the advantage of having several judges while removing the biasing effects that might occur during face-to-face interaction. The basic approach has been **to collect anonymous judgments by mail questionnaires.** For example, the members independently generate their ideas to answer the first questionnaire and return it. The **staff members summarize the responses as the group consensus and feed this summary back along with a second questionnaire for reassessment.** Based on this feedback, the respondents independently evaluate their earlier responses. The underlying belief is that the consensus estimate will result in a better decision after **several rounds of anonymous group judgment**. While it is possible to continue the procedure for several rounds, studies have shown essentially no significant change after the second round of estimation.

The Nominal Group Technique (NGT) NGT has gained increasing recognition in health, social service, education, industry, and government organizations. The term *nominal group technique* was adopted by earlier researchers to refer to processes that bring people together but **do not allow them to communicate verbally.** Thus, the collection of people is a group "nominally," or in name only. You will see, however, that NGT in its present form combines both verbal and nonverbal stages.

Basically, NGT is a structured group meeting that proceeds as follows: A group of individuals (7 to 10) sit around a table but do not speak to one another. Rather, **each person writes ideas on a pad of paper.** After five minutes, a structured sharing of ideas takes place. **Each person around the table presents one idea.** A person designated as recorder writes the ideas on a flip chart in full view of the entire group. This continues until all of the participants indicate that they have no further ideas to share. There is still no discussion.

The output of this phase is **a list of ideas** (usually between 18 and 25). The next phase involves **structured discussion** in which each idea receives attention before a vote is taken. This is achieved by asking for clarification or stating the degree of support for each idea listed on the flip hart. The next stage

---

Increasing Creativity in Decision Making

As knowledge/information-based organizations become the norm, it has become clear that creativity is a competence that these organizations need.

1. Get out of the office. A walk in the park or a trip to a toy store may be more productive than sitting at your desk with pencil and pad.

2. Be childlike. Some believe this is the most important tip because creativity seems to be connected with age.

3. Be a maverick. The best ideas and decisions often come from those who don't care what others are thinking or how they are doing things.

4. Sit on the other side of the room. Break your routine, drive to work a different way.

5. Ask "what if...?" This question can stimulate thought for you and plenty of discussion in a group.

6. Listen. No one has monopoly on good ideas. Ask others, and listen.

involves **independent voting** in which each participant, in private, selects priorities by ranking or voting. The group decision is the mathematically pooled outcome of the individual votes.

Both Delphi technique and NGT have had an excellent record of successes. Basic differences between them are:

    1. Delphi participants typically are anonymous to one another, while NGT participants become acquainted.

    2. NGT participants meet face-to-face around the table, while Delphi participants are physically distant and never meet face-to-face.

    3. In the Delphi process, all communication between participants is by way of written questionnaires and feedback from the monitoring staff. In NGT, communication is direct between participants.

Einhorn and Hogarth (1978) have added insight to understanding the problems of learning in decision making, characteristic of the right side of the previous table, by addressing the role of feedback in the typical **decision-making problem**. Feedback is critical for nearly any form of learning or skill acquisition. Yet several characteristics of decision making prevent it from offering its usual assistance.

    1. Feedback is often **ambiguous**, in a probabilistic or uncertain world. That is, sometimes a decision process will clearly be **poorly executed** but, because of **good luck**, will produce **a positive outcome**; at other times, a decision process can follow all of the best procedures, but bad luck produces a negative outcome. In the first case, the positive reinforcement will increase reliance on the bad process, whereas in the second case, the punishment realized by the bad outcome, will extinguish the effective processing that went into the decision.

    2. **Feedback is often delayed.** In many decisions, such as those made in investment, or even prescribing treatment in medicine, the outcome may not be realized for some time. Added delay in feedback beyond a few minutes is rarely of benefit. When the feedback finally arrives, the decision maker may have forgotten the processes and strategies used to make the decision in the first place, and therefore may fail to either reinforce those processes (if the feedback was good), or correct them (if the feedback was bad).

    3. **Feedback is processed selectively**. The learning of a decision maker who is classifying applicants as either acceptable to or rejected from a program and is learning from feedback regarding the outcome of those who were selected.

COMMON BARRIERS TO PROBLEM SOLVING

People think; it is our nature to do so. But much of our thinking, left to itself, is **biased, distorted, partial, uninformed or down-right prejudiced.**

    1. **Emotional barriers:** Inhibition and fear of making a fool of oneself, fear of making a mistake, inability to tolerate ambiguity, excessive self-criticism.

Example: An architect is afraid to try an unconventional design because she fears that other architects will think it is frivolous.

    2. **Cultural barriers:** Values that hold that fantasy is a waste of time; that playfulness is for children only; that reason, logic, and numbers are good; that feelings, intuitions, pleasure, and humor are bad or have no value in the serious business of problem solving.

Example: A corporate manager wants to solve a business problem but becomes stern and angry when members of his marketing team joke playful about possible solutions.

3. Learned barriers: Conventions about uses (functional fixedness), meanings, possibilities, taboos.

Example: A cook doesn't have any clean mixing bowls and fails to see that he could use a frying pan as a bowl.

4. Perceptual barriers: Habits leading to a failure to identify important elements of a problem.

Example: A beginning artist concentrates on drawing a vase of flowers without seeing that the "empty" spaces around the vase are part of the composition, too.

Much of what we know about thinking comes from direct studies of how people solve problems. Yet, surprisingly, much can also be learned from machines. Computerized problem solving provides a fascinating "laboratory" for testing ideas about how you and I think.

How Solve Problems?

(**Modified from** *How to Be Twice as Smart* **by S. Witt (1993)**)

Eliminate the Two Barriers that Confuse Most People:

1. **Misinformation**
2. **Incorrect Focus**

What people often don't realize is that if you go about trying to solve tough problems using conventional methods, the odds are stacked against you.

Rule Number 1 in problem solving is this: Recheck the facts to (a) determine if the problem really does exist, and (b) provide a solid foundation for solving it.

Eliminate the first barrier: correct the misinformation and solve the unsolvable. Most people wouldn't dream of solving an arithmetic problem by majority vote – but it's amazing how many other problems they try to solve that way. If you needed to know the sum of a column of figures, and four people told you it was 4,397 while another person claimed it was 4,398, you probably wouldn't accept either answer as correct. Instead, you'd add the figure yourself.

But when it comes to other types of problems, we happily swallow information handed us by other people without checking the facts – and then wonder why we aren't making much headway. When your facts aren't correct, you either can't solve the problem or it's going to take you a lot longer.

Three Problem-Solving Examples. When people say something is impossible, they are basing their assumption on whatever information they have at hand. Some or all of that information may be incorrect. The person who comes along with the right information may easily accomplish what others thought impossible.

The ability to solve difficult or even "unsolvable" problems by replacing misinformation with facts has been a big boost in the lives and careers of many people.

Know the sources of misinformation:

- "Facts" from people who have a personal stake in the matter;
- Observations of people who have little training or experience in that particular field;
- Hastily prepared data that may have typographical and numerical errors;
- Superficial reports that don't go thoroughly into the subject;
- Preconceived notions that were never right in the first place.

Problem-Solving

Eliminate the second barrier: focus on the desired outcome. When a problem suddenly crops up, it's human nature to become so concerned with the problem itself that you forget it was merely an obstacle in the path toward a goal. You start paying so much attention to the obstacle that you lose sight of the goal it's preventing you from achieving.

When successful problem solver are faced with an obstacle, they look beyond it to the goal they are seeking – and then examine various ways of achieving that goal. Often they find that there really isn't much of a problem at all, because it can easily be bypassed.

Just think, for example, of the great many excellent business ideas that must have gone down the drain because their originators couldn't find adequate financing. It's an obstacle that has nipped many a potential wealth-building idea in the bud.

The usual source of financial backing for a business is, of course, the local bank. Unfortunately, thousands of people have discovered just how unfriendly a bank can be when they seek a business loan to finance their money-making schemes.

Bankers, it seems, frown on lending money for unproven ideas. If you can show that your plan has already been tried and proven, you may get the loan. But without cash to get your plan rolling, how can you prove it works? For many people it's a vicious cycle, and eventually many of them give up.

But Witt (1993) mentioned Pamela S. who in the beginning was concentrating so much on getting a business loan she had made THAT her goal instead of realizing that her real goal was to get hold of $20,000 to finance a business. Realizing this Pamela decided to increase the mortgage on her home. The bank holding the mortgage was more than willing to increase it by the $20,000 she needed.

Set your sights on the long-range goal and examine alternative ways of reaching it. This may seem as if you're avoiding the immediate problem, but why not? The world's most successful people have found that the easiest way to solve a problem is to find a means of getting around it.

Psychologists have discovered (and so have business problem solvers) that the human mind is much more orderly when it has something tangible to work with. Your mind can wander in a thousand different directions as you puzzle over a problem, but if you must put the problem on paper, you are forced to concentrate on that one item alone. And as you follow the path the orderly reasoning process will become even more efficient.

People who must frequently face problems find that carrying a tiny micro-cassette recorder can be a great help.

Tools that strengthen your conscious reasoning skills:

Mull it over in your mind;

Discuss it with associates;

Use trial and error to find solution.

How your subconscious helps solve problems. When you start to chart a problem, you are not only putting it on paper, you're also sending a message to your subconscious mind. You are, in effect, telling it to get busy with the problem even after your conscious mind has turned to other matters.

Because it is indeed subconscious, we're not aware of all that is going on in this "hidden" mind that each of us has. Nor are we aware of its great power to help resolve our problems. And certainly most people don't know how to tap this tremendous mental resource.

Here are some things you should know about subconscious:

- It is subject to suggestions. This means it will accept almost any thought you give it. Unlike your conscious mind, it is not controlled by reason, so it doesn't argue with what you tell it. If, for example, you repeatedly say to yourself, "I am a multimillionaire," your subconscious will believe it even though your conscious mind knows it's not true;
- Your brain stores enough information to fill 90,000,000 books. Somewhere, buried in all that information, are the solutions to nearly every problem you are likely to face. Unfortunately, only a small portion of this data is readily available to your conscious mind;
- When you are stumped by a problem, you can "tell" your subconscious that somewhere within the depths of your mind there are ideas that will lead to a workable solution. Then, as you go about your other business, your subconscious will search through your memory for ideas and events matching the current circumstances. It will present to your conscious mind information that you would never recalled otherwise.

Ask nonexperts

Sometimes it seems that the test of a truly brilliant idea is whether or not the "experts" discount it. Often these are the ideas that later seem obvious - even to the experts.

Charles Duell, director of the U. S. Patent Office, in 1899: "Everything that can be invented has been invented."

Grover Cleveland in 1905: "Sensible and responsible women do not want to vote."

Robert Millikan, Nobel prizewinner in physics, in 1923: "There is no likelihood man can ever tap the power of the atom."

Lord Kelvin, president of Royal Society, in 1895: "Heavier-than-air flying machines are impossible."

The King of Prussia who predicted the failure of railroad because: "No one will pay good money to get from Berlin to Potsdam in one hour when he can ride his horse in one day for free."

There are as many stories about experts failing to understand new ideas as there are keys on a piano. In 1861, Philip Reis, a German inventor, built an instrument that could transmit music and was very close to transmitting speech. Experts told him there was no need for such an instrument, as "the telegraph is good enough." He discontinued his work, and it was not until fifteen years later that Alexander Graham Bell patented the telephone.

Some social scientists believe that the more expert you become in your field, the more difficult it is to create innovative new ideas - or even obvious ones. This is because becoming an expert means you tend to specialize your thinking. Specializing is like brushing one tooth. You get to know that one tooth extremely well, but you lose the rest of them in the process.

When experts specialize their thinking, they put borders around subjects and search for ideas only within the borders of their expertise. Nonexperts do not have enough expertise to draw borders. As a result, they look everywhere for ideas. This is why breakthrough ideas are usually found by nonexperts.

This is the principle that prevented the "experts" at Univac from seeing the huge business market for computers. The computer, they said, was designed for science, not business. The same thinking, in 1905, led the German manufacturer of Novocain to wage a furious national campaign to prevent dentists from using it because their company "experts" developed the drug for doctors, not dentists. And the same borders explain why virtually every "delivery expert," including the U. S. Postal Service, unanimously declared Fred Smith's concept for Federal Express unworkable, as people would not pay a fancy price for speed and reliability.

Very much aware of how experts think, Sir Clive Sinclair, the British inventor of the pocket calculator and the flat-screen television, has said that when he enters a new field, he reads "just enough to get a base, just enough to get the idiom" of the field. Anything more and he would start drawing borders.

Chester Carlson invented xerography in 1938, but more than twenty major U. S. corporations, including IBM and Kodak, showed an "enthusiastic lack of interest" in his system, as Carlson put it. No major corporation or office-supply expert saw a market for xerography. After all, who would buy a copy machine when carbon paper was so cheap and so plentiful?

To get ideas, talk to people (nonexperts) outside your field:

1. Talk to someone who is outside your field and from an entirely different background. The more casual the relationship, the more likely he or she will give you a unique perspective. If you're looking for ways to increase sales, as a priest, teacher, doctor, bartender, or Girl Scout for ideas.

Frank Perdue (the "it takes a tough man to make a tender chicken" man) was told by the chicken experts that a chicken is a chicken - consumers bought by price and price alone. Perdue went to work as a clerk in a supermarket and talked to housewives about chicken. He discovered what the experts and their market research did not - that the color of a chicken and unplucked feathers were more important than price.

Recently, a gynecologist developed a new birth control device. He perfected the new design in a casual discussion before a dental exam. The dentist came up with the new shape and form almost immediately after the gynecologist described his challenge.

2. Seek out idea-oriented people. Surround yourself with people who love ideas and use them in their businesses and lives. They will fire up your imagination. Surround yourself with people:

- Who are creatively alert - people who are always offering alternatives, ideas, and suggestions about anything and everything;
  - Who have a keen interest in life and are excited about being alive;

Problem-Solving

- Are naive about your business, but not stupid or ignorant;
- Who have a great wit and see the absurdity in things;
- Who have different value systems than yours;
- Who travel and pay attention to what they observe;
- Who are voracious readers.

A steel company executive was finding it harder and harder to locate people to work in his plant. He discussed the challenge with his minister, who suggested recruiting at local churches. They formed a network of three local churches to search for qualified parishioners, and the executive has hired every candidate the ministers have sent his way. He's thrilled with the results. "The ministers sift out the best candidates," he observes. "They don't send loafers or drifters, just solid citizens with strong families and work ethic."

3. Draw out the creativity in strangers you meet casually. Everyone has at least one idea that might be useful to you. H. J. Lawson got his revolutionary idea for using a chain to power the bicycle from a waiter at his favorite restaurant.

An executive of a major motel chain was talking casually with his garbage man about the motel business when the garbage man said, "If I were you, I'd sell pizza in my motels. You can't believe the number of pizza boxes we pick up in the trash at motels and hotels." The executive installed pizza ovens in his chain with great results. Once the garbage man said "pizza," the executive realized that they were missing out on a big market.

4. Listen. Joseph Kennedy withdrew his money from the stock market before the 1929 crash after listening to numerous strangers (including his bootblack) on the street warn about stock speculation. At the same time, the experts, including leading Yale economist Irving Fisher, were saying that stocks had hit a "permanently high plateau."

Frieda Caplan listens. She is the chairperson and founder of Frieda's Finest, a celebrated and thriving produce company. In a field dominated by generic products and devoid a new ideas, she's created a brand identity and persuaded millions of Americans to buy fruits and vegetables they never heard of. How? By listening. Her cardinal rule: "Always have an open door; always listen to what anyone has to offer."

She listened one day when a stranger asked if she had ever heard of a fruit called the Chinese gooseberry. She had never seen one, but promised to keep as eye out. Six months later, by sheer coincidence, a broker stopped by and offered a load of Chinese gooseberries. The gooseberries were fuzzy, green, wholly unappealing little fruit.

What the fruit needed was some good PR. She gave the fruit a new name, one suggested by another stranger: Kiwifruit, derived from the kiwi bird of New Zealand. She convinced local restaurants to serve kiwi desserts and developed posters that explained to shoppers what a kiwi was and how it could be used.

By listening to a stranger, Frieda changed American cuisine.

SUMMARY

1. A problem is a gap between existing and desirable situation. A problem is usually some difficulty or thing that people want to overcome or be rid of. The term "problem" can also be used when people are trying to achieve some task, though in many cases "design" or "task achieving" are more appropriate.

2. Gestalt psychologists (Henle, 1962, 1974; Wertheimer, 1959) have emphasized the importance of posing the correct question. Henle (1974) argued that the perception of "dynamic gaps" incites the creative process: "And yet posing the right question may be the most creative part of the whole process."

3. Problem-Solving stages:
- Establishing specific goals and objectives and measuring results

299

- Problem identification
- Establishing priorities
- Consideration of causes
- Development of alternative solutions
- Evaluation of alternative solution
- Solution selection
- Implementation
- Follow-up.
4. Common barriers to problem-solving;

- **Emotional barriers:** Inhibition and fear of making a fool of oneself, fear of making a mistake, inability to tolerate ambiguity, excessive self-criticism.
- **Cultural barriers:** Values that hold that fantasy is a waste of time; that playfulness is for children only; that reason, logic, and numbers are good; that feelings, intuitions, pleasure, and humor are bad or have no value in the serious business of problem solving.
- **Learned barriers:** Conventions about uses (functional fixedness), meanings, possibilities, taboos.
- **Perceptual barriers:** Habits leading to a failure to identify important elements of a problem.

PRACTICING PROBLEM SOLVING TECHNIQUES

The Synectic Trigger Mechanisms

Using the following Synectic Trigger Mechanisms create new design. images, ideas, melodies and more...

"Manipulation is the brother of creativity. When your imagination is as blank as a waiter's stare, take an existing item and manipulate it into a new idea. Remember that everything new is just an addition or modification to something that already existed."

Michalko M.

Do Something to It

One of the print ads was done in the 1960's by Charles Piccirillo and Monte Ghertler (both of Doyle Dane Bernbach) to promote National Library Week. The headline consisted of the alphabet in lower case letters like so: abcdefghijklmnopqrstuvwxyz followed by this copy: "At your public library they've got these arranged in ways that can make you cry, giggle, love, hate, wonder, ponder and understand.

It's astonishing what those twenty-six little marks can do.

In Shakespeare's hands they become *Hamlet*. Mark Twain wound them into *Huckleberry Finn*. James Joyce twisted them into *Ulysses*.Gibbon pounded them in *The Decline and Fall of the Roman Empire*. Milton shaped them into *Paradise Lost*. Einstein added some numbers and signs (to save time and space) and they formed *The General Theory of Relativity*...

Creative ideas come from manipulating and transforming your resources – no matter how few and simple they are.

Roger von Oech

Problem-Solving

Exercise. Select any image or idea and play with it following 21 synectic's steps.

1. Subtract. Simplify. Omit, or remove certain parts or elements. Take something away from your subject. Compress it or make it smaller. Ask yourself: What can be eliminated, reduced, disposed of? What rules can you break? How can you simplify, abstract, stylize or abbreviate?

Henry David Thoreau: "Our life is frittered by detail... Simplify, simplify!"

Albert Einstein once said, "Any intelligent fool can make things bigger and more complex. It takes a genius and a lot of courage to move in the opposite direction." So often we tend to complicate things, perhaps thinking that the more complicated the analysis and eventual solution, the higher is the value of the solution. In truth, it is often the simple solutions that harbor more value.

How often have we asked ourselves,
"What does the consumer really want?"
"What is really most important to communicate in this next meeting?"
"What are the numbers really saying?"
Organizations like Starbucks, Federal Express, and Dell Computers have been able to win in the marketplace because they went right back to the basics and offered the consumer a simple solution.

So look for the simpler things in work and life. Eliminate those things that you do not **really need. Free yourself from excess baggage! Clear the way for a simpler view of work and everyday life.**

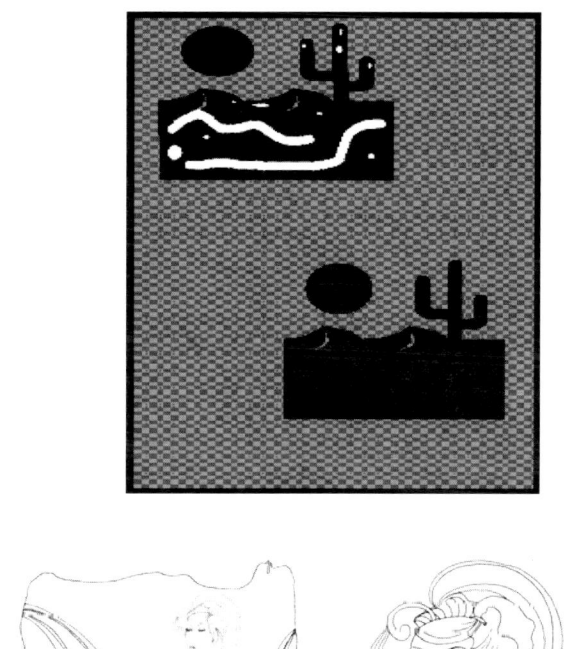

2. Repeat. Repeat a shape, color, form, image or idea. Reiterate, echo, restate or duplicate your reference subject in some way.

Repeat action, performance, production, or presentation. Create a reproduction, copy, or replica. Repetition is a major rhetorical strategy for producing emphasis, clarity, amplification, or emotional effect. Within the history of rhetoric terms have been developed to name both general and very specific sorts of repetition. Repetition, or consistency, means that you should repeat some aspect of the design throughout the entire document. Repetition acts as a visual key that ties your piece together--in other words, it unifies it. Repetition controls the reader's eye and helps you keep their attention on the piece as long as possible. Repeat elements such as a graphic, font style or size. To get started, repeat elements that you're already using.

Ask yourself: How can you control the factors of occurrence, repercussion, sequence and progression?

Sully: "Every feeling tends to a certain extent to become deeper by repetition."

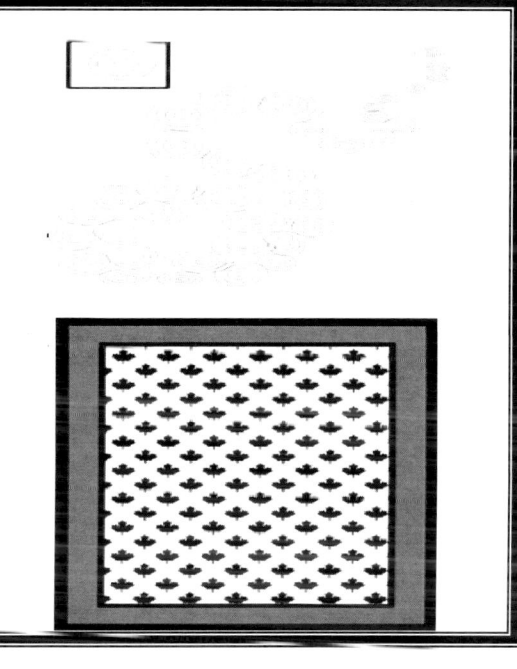

3. Combine. Bring things together. Connect, arrange, link, unify, mix, rearrange, merge, wed. Combine ideas. Combine materials, ideas, and techniques. Bring together dissimilar things to produce synergistic integration. Ask yourself: What else can you connect to your subject? What kind of connections can you make from different sensory modes, subject disciplines or frames of reference?

A popular new variety of sandwich is rocket salad and curry. Purists in Italy or India might be horrified but for consumers it is an exciting new combination. A great way to generate original ideas for your business is to look for weird combinations. Most new ideas are really combinations of other ideas. So look to see how you could mix your products or services with those from completely different sources.

A weird combination that worked for the BBC is their celebrity stock exchange, Celebdaq. On this site you can take a future option on the media coverage for your chosen celebrity and then watch your option rise or fall in value. By marrying celebrity gossip and financial spread betting the BBC has created a radical innovation that is proving very popular. Marrying ideas has been around a long time. What is the greatest invention of all? One contender is Johannes Gutenberg's printing press. Before Gutenberg, all books had been laboriously copied out by hand or stamped out with woodblocks. Around 1450 in Strasbourg, Gutenberg combined two ideas to invent a od of printing with moveable type. He coupled the flexibility of a coin punch with the power of a wine press. His invention enabled the production of books and the spread of knowledge and ideas throughout the Western World. In terms of revolutionizing communication only the invention of the Internet comes close.

2 + 2 = 5 or more!

When you combine two ideas to make a third then two plus two can equal five. In the ancient world one of the great discoveries was that by combining two soft metals – iron and tin – you could create a strong alloy – bronze. In a similar way combining two minor inventions – the coin punch and the wine press – gave birth to the mighty printing press.

How can a concert violinist create an innovation? The acclaimed Finnish violinist Linda Brava has performed with many leading symphony orchestras. She posed for Playboy magazine and appeared on the US TV series, Baywatch. By combining glamour with virtuosity in classical music she has established a unique brand for herself.

Consider absurd combinations.

Take a product and think of an absurd way to make it work. Trevor Bayliss is the English inventor who conceived the clockwork radio. What a strange combination! Radios need electricity and clockwork is a mechanical od. Surely batteries or mains electricity are better ways to power a radio. However, in the developing world batteries are expensive and mains electricity is unreliable. Bayliss built a reliable radio that people could wind up by hand. It has transformed the availability of information in many of the poorest regions of the Earth.

Combine geometrical forms.

Now you try it!
Remember that:
• Someone put a trolley and a suitcase together and got a suitcase with wheels.
• Someone put an igloo with a hotel and got an ice palace.
• Someone put copier and a telephone together and got a fax machine.
• Someone put a bell and a clock together and got an alarm clock.
• Someone put a coin punch and a wine press together and we got books.

So the next time you wheel your suitcase or read a fax or a book you are benefiting from someone's ingenuity in putting together a combination of ideas. Why not try it with your own products to drive innovation in your business?

Ralph Caplan: "All art, and most knowledge, entails either seeing connections or making them. Until it is hooked up with what you already know, nothing can ever be learned or assimilated."

4. Add. Magnify it: Make it bigger. Expand, extend, or otherwise develop your reference subject. Augment it, supplement, annex or advance it. Ask yourself: What else can be added to your image, idea, object, or material?

Exaggerate: make your subject to seem more important than it really is. Enlarge it. Use a photographic print that has been enlarged.

Accelerate the growth or progress. Raise your idea to a higher rank

Bring it forward in time. Raise it in rate, in rank, position, or importance.

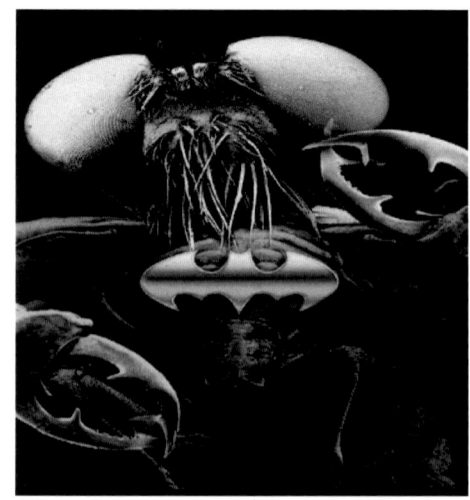

Use microscopic images for inspiration

Problem-Solving

5. Transfer. Move your subject into a new situation, context or environment. Transpose, adapt, relocate, or dislocate. Move your subject out of its normal environment; transpose it to a different social, historical, geographical, psychological, or political setting or time. Adapt the subject to a new and different frame of reference. Look at it from a different point of view.

Adapt an engineering principle, design quality, or other special quality of your subject to that of another. (The structure of a bird's wing, for example, has served as a model for designing bridges).

Change (by rotation or mapping) one configuration or expression into another in accordance with a mathematical, physical, chemical rule. Change variables or coordinates in which a function of new variables or coordinates is substituted for each original variable or coordinate. Converts by insertion, deletion, or permutation.

Transfer can also denote *transformation*. Ask yourself: How can your subjects be translated, converted, or transfigured?

Move your subject into new surroundings. The square in the center of the first figure has the same size as the second one.

6. Animate. Mobilize psychological, visual or physical tension in your creative product. Apply factors of repetition, progression, serialization or narration. Bring life to inanimate subjects by thinking of them as having human qualities.

7. Empathize. Relate yourself to your subject. Put yourself in its "shoes." If the subject is inorganic or inanimate, think of it as having human qualities. How can you relate to it emotionally or subjectively?
Emphasize the size of something or compare the size to make a point. Enlarge the details you want to emphasize.

Offering helpful insight to an art student, the eighteenth century German painter Henry Fuseli once advised, "Transpose yourself into your subject."

8. Superimpose. Overlap, cover, place over, overlay: Superimpose dissimilar images, subjects, or ideas. Overlay elements to produce new meanings, images, or ideas. Superimpose different elements from different perspectives, disciplines or time periods on your subject. Combine sensory perceptions (sounds/color, etc.).

Think syncronistically: What elements or images from different frames of reference can be combined in a single view? Notice, for example, how Cubist painters superimposed several views of a single object to show many different moments in time simultaneously.

9. Substitute. Switch, exchange or replace. Ask yourself: What other idea, material, image or ingredient can you substitute for all or part of your subject? What alternate or supplementary plan can be employed?

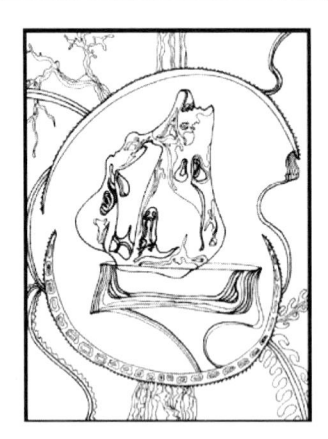

10. Change Scale. Make your subject smaller or bigger. Change proportion, relative size, dimensions, ration or normal graduated series.

Americans tend to believe that bigger is better. People often perceive objects they value highly as being larger than objects they value less. Bruner and Goldman, in 1947, did a study that demonstrated that poor children perceived coins as being much larger than rich children did.

Which figure on the right attracts your attention? Notice how your attention is automatically attracted to the large figure. This is why magnification is often used in advertising and equipment design. Search for ways to magnify, add to, or multiply your idea, product, or service.

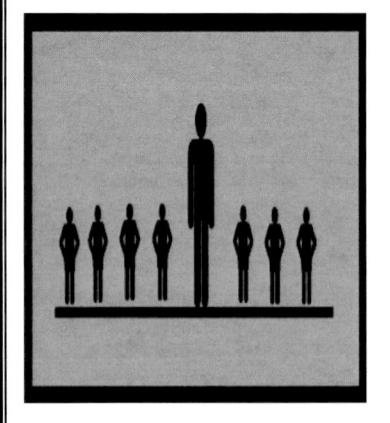

Create an unusual image by presenting an element far out of its normal size or scale. Changing the scale of the product not only establishes a strong focal point, but adds humor to the message.

Problem-Solving

11. **Fragment.** Separate, split, divide: Take your subject or idea apart. Dissect it. Chop it up or otherwise disassemble it. What devices can you use to divide it into smaller increments or make it appear discontinuous?

12. **Isolate.** Separate, crop, set apart, detach: Use only a part of your subject. In composing a picture, use a viewfinder to crop the image or visual field selectively. "Crop" your ideas, too, with a "mental" viewfinder.

    Ask yourself: What element can you detach of focus on?

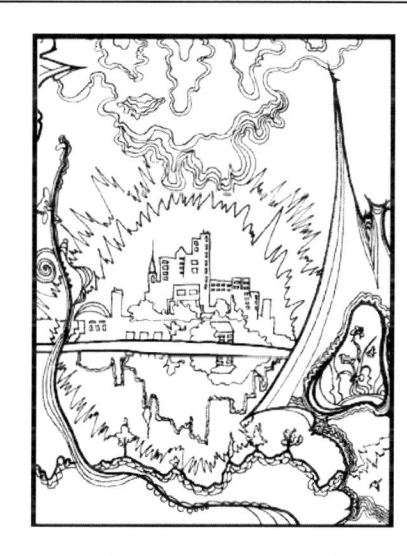

13. **Distort.** Twist your subject out of its true shape, meaning or proportion. Ask yourself: What kind of imagined or actual distortions can you effect? How can you misshape it? Can you make it longer, wider, fatter, narrower? Can you maintain or produce a unique metaphoric and aesthetic quality when you misshape it? Can you melt it, burn it, split something on it, crush it, bury it, tear it, crack it or subject it to yet other "tortures"?

Problem-Solving

14. **Contradict.** Contradict the subject's original function. Contravene, deny, disaffirm, reverse: Many great works of art and science are visual or intellectual contradictions. They may contain opposite, antithetical, antipodal or converse elements which are integrated in their aesthetic and structural form. Contradict laws of nature such as gravity, time, etc. Ask yourself: How can you visualize your subject in connection with the reversal of laws of nature, magnetic fields, gravity, growth cycles, proportions; mechanical and human functions, procedures, rituals, games or social conventions?

Optical illusions and "flip-flop" designs are equivocal configurations that contradict optical and perceptual harmony. Satirical art is based on the observation of social hypocrisy and contradictory behavior. Ask yourself: How can you use contradiction or reversal to change your subject?

George Orwell: "Doublethink means the power of holding two contradictory beliefs in one's mind simultaneously, and accepting both of them."

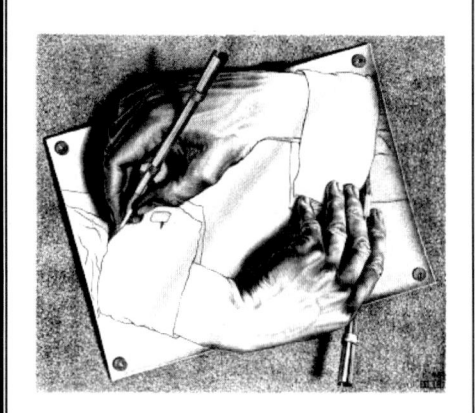

15. **Disguise.** Camouflage, deceive, conceal or encrypt: How can you hide, mask or "implant" your subject into another frame of reference? In nature, for example, chameleons and certain other species conceal themselves by mimicry: Their figure imitates the ground. How can you apply this to your subject?

Visualize subliminal imagery: How can you create a latent image that will communicate subconsciously, below the threshold of conscious awareness?

16. **Parody.** Mimic, ridicule, mock, burlesque or caricature: Make fun of your subject. Lampoon it, "roast" it. Transform it into a visual joke or pun. Exploit the humor factor. Make zany, comic or ludicrous references. Create a visual oxymoron or conundrum.

Tom Paine: "The sublime and the ridiculous are often so nearly related, that it is difficult to class them separately. One step above the sublime, makes the ridiculous; and one step above the ridiculous, makes the sublime again."

George Orwell: "Every joke is ultimately a custard pie."

Problem-Solving

17. Prevaricate. Equivocate. Fictionalize, falsify, fantasize. Although telling fibs is not considered acceptable social conduct, it is the stuff that legends and myths are made of. Ask yourself: How can you use your subject as a theme to present ersatz information?

Equivocate: Present equivocal information that is subject to two or more interpretations and used to mislead or confuse.

William Shakespeare: "Faith, here's an equivocator, that could swear in both the scales against either scale."

18. Metamorphose. Convert, transform, transmutate: Depict your subject in a state of change. It can be a simple transformation (an object changing its color, for example) or a more radical change in which the subject changes its configuration. Think of "cocoon-to-butterfly" types of transformations, aging, structural progressions, as well as radical and surreal metamorphosis such as "Jekyll and Hyde" transmutations.

Mutation is a radical hereditary change brought about by a change in chromosome structure or a biochemical change in the codons that make up genes. Ask yourself: How can you apply metamorphosis or mutation to your subject?

Ovid: "Nothing in the entire universe ever perishes, believe me, but the things vary, and adopt a new form."

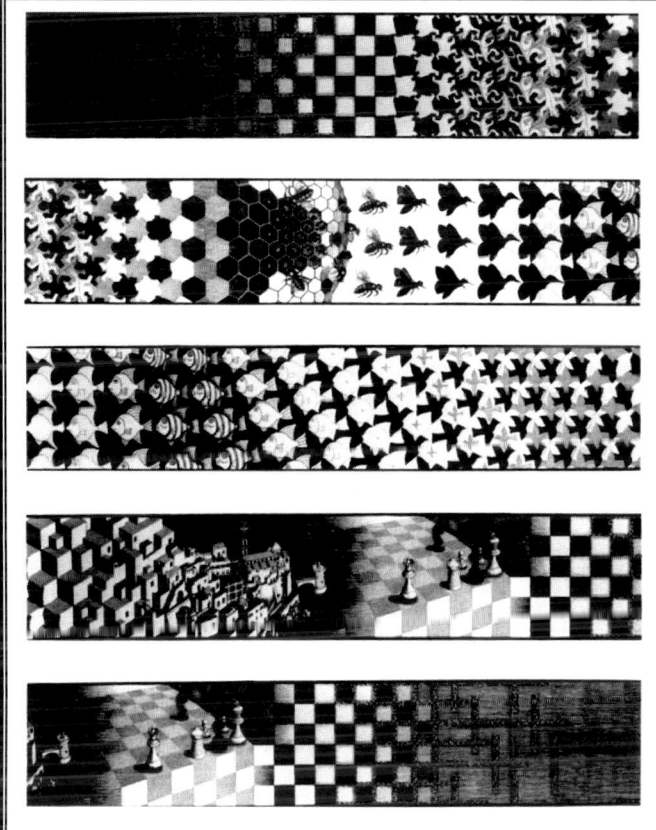

19. **Hybridize.** Cross-fertilize: Wed your subject with an improbable mate. Ask yourself: What would you get if you crossed a x-subject with an y-subject? Creative thinking is a form of "mental hybridization" in that ideas are produced by cross-linking subjects from different realms. Transfer the hybridization mechanism to the use of color, form, and structure; cross-fertilize organic and inorganic elements, as well as ideas and perceptions.

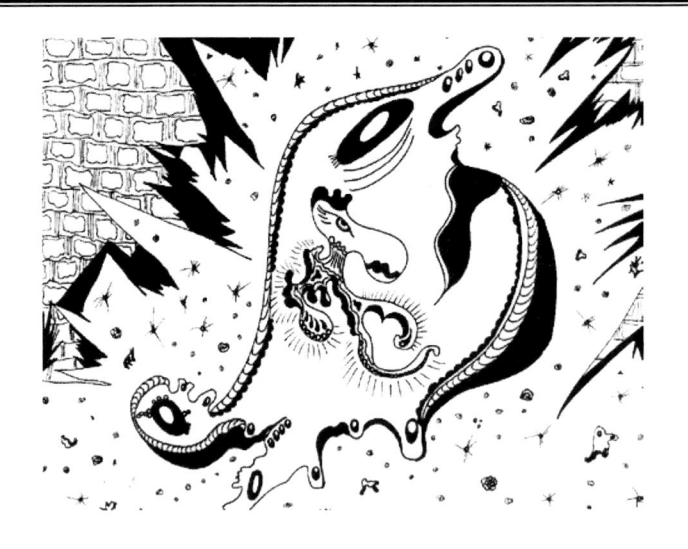

20. **Mythologize.** Build a myth around your subject. In the 60's Pop artists "mythologized" common objects. The Coca0Cola bottle, Brillo Pads, comic strip characters, movie stars, mass media images, hot rods, hamburgers and French fries and other such frivolous subjects became the visual icons of twentieth century art. Ask yourself: How can you transform your subject into an iconic object?

Claude Levi-Strauss: "The message of the myth is conveyed by the amalgam of its relationships and its mediations."

21. **Fantasize.** Fantasize your subject. Use it to trigger surreal, outlandish, preposterous, bizarre thoughts. Topple mental and sensory expectations. How far can you extend your imagination? Ask yourself: What if automobiles were made of brick? What if alligators played pool? What if insects grew larger than humans? What if night and day occurred simultaneously?

Jean Jacques Rousseau: "The world of reality has its limits; the world of imagination is boundless."

CHAPTER 10

What Can We Learn from Great People?

Who are those bright people that created exceptional art, stunning discoveries and inventions? What characteristics they have in common? Can you learn from their experience? This chapter explores the lives of highly creative people.

LEARNING OBJECTIVES

After reading this chapter, you will be able to

1. Define talent
2. Define genius
3. Describe and discuss histories of highly creative people
4. Compare and contrast primary traits related to creativity
5. Compare and contrast various approaches to giftedness
6. Describe and discuss Maslow's theory of creativity
7. Determine your personal creativeness.

What great people say about greatness?

The whole difference between construction and creation is exactly this: that a thing constructed can only be loved after it is constructed; but a thing created is loved before it exists.

- Charles Dickens

Creativity is the ability to see relationships where none exist.

- Thomas Disch

Genius is (1%) one percent inspiration, and (99%) ninety-nine percent perspiration.

- Thomas Edison

Everything comes to him who hustles while he waits

- Thomas Edison

Opportunity is missed by most people because it is dressed in overalls and it looks like work.

- Thomas Edison

The most beautiful and profound emotion we can experience is the sensation of the mystical. It is the sower of all true science. He to whom this emotion is a stranger, who can no longer wonder and stand rapt in awe, is good as dead.

- Albert Einstein

The world we have made as a result of the level of thinking we have done thus far creates problems we cannot solve at the same level of thinking at which we created them.

- Albert Einstein

The mere formulation of a problem is far more often essential than its solution, which may be merely a matter of mathematical or experimental skill. To raise new questions, new possibilities, to regard old problems from a new angle requires creative imagination and marks real advances in science.

- Albert Einstein

1. **Out of clutter, find simplicity.**
2. **From discord, find harmony.**
3. **In the middle of difficulty lies opportunity**
(Three rules of work)
- Albert Einstein
Ideas must work through the brains and the arms of good and brave men, or they are no better than dreams.
- Ralph Waldo Emerson

Write as if you are dying.
- Annie Dillard

The best way to predict the future is to create it

- Peter Drucker

I'll try anything...I'll even try Limburger cheese!

- Thomas Edison

There's a way to do it better...find it

- Thomas Edison

Nearly every man who develops an idea works it up to the point where it looks impossible, and then he gets discouraged. That's not the place to become discouraged.

- Thomas Edison

If we knew what we were doing, it would not be called research would it?

- Albert Einstein

Common sense is the collection of prejudices acquired by the age of eighteen.

- Albert Einstein

Great spirits have always encountered violent opposition from mediocre minds

- Albert Einstein

Everything should be made as simple as possible, but not simpler.

- Albert Einstein

The creation of a thousand forests is in one acorn.

- Ralph Waldo Emerson

What We Can Learn from Great Thinkers?

Who are those bright people that created exceptional art, stunning discoveries and inventions? What characteristics they have in common? Can you learn from their experience? This chapter explores the lives of highly creative people.

- Be curious. Adopt an "insight outlook."
- Create a map for yourself. Have an idea of what you are looking for.
- Leave your own turf. Look in outside fields, disciplines, and industries.
- Too much is not enough. Look for lots of ideas.
- Don't be afraid to be led astray. You'll find what you weren't looking for.
- Break up your routine. Use obstacles to get out of ruts.
- Shift your focus. Pay attention to a variety of information.
- Don't overlook the obvious. What is right in front of you?
- Get out your magnifying glass. Big things come in small packages.
- What does it all really mean? Stand back and look at the Big Picture.
- Slay a dragon. Look for ideas in a place you've been avoiding.
- Remember where you've been. Trigger the ideas you already have.
- Stake your claim to the new territory. Write your idea down when you find it.

Roger von Oech

FAILURE AND GREATNESS

If there is one word that the best characterizes all 'over-achievers' it would be ***persistence.***' All great people went through failures and rejections. But their strong self-efficacy helped them to fulfill their goals.

> Nothing in the world can take the place of persistence,
> Talent will not,
> Nothing is more common than unsuccessful men with talent.
> Genius will not, unrewarded genius is almost a proverb.
> Education will not, the world is full of educated derelicts.
> Persistence and determination are omnipotent.
> The slogan "press on" has solved and always will
> solve the problems of the human race.
>
> Calvin Coolidge

Conditions for creativity:

1) The ability to be puzzled
2) The ability to concentrate
3) The ability to accept conflict and tension
4) The willingness to be born everyday (courage and faith)
5) To feel a sense of self.

Erich Fromm (1959)

In his delightful book, titled, Rejection, John White provides vivid testimony, that the striking characteristic of people who have achieved eminence in their fields is an ***inextinguishable sense of personal efficacy*** and a firm belief in the worth of what they are doing. This resilient self-belief system enabled them to override repeated early rejections of their work.

Many of our literary classics brought their authors countless rejections. James Joyce's, the Dubliners, was rejected by 22 publishers. Gertrude Stein continued to submit poems to editors for 20 years before one was finally accepted. Over a dozen publishers rejected a manuscript by e. e. cummings. When he finally got it published, by his mother, the dedication read, in upper case: With no thanks to . . . followed by the list of 16 publishers who had rejected his manuscript.

Early rejection is the rule, rather than the exception, in other creative endeavors. The Impressionists had to arrange their own exhibitions because their works were routinely rejected by the Paris Salon. Van Gogh sold only one painting during his lifetime. Rodin was rejected three times for admission to the 'cole des Beaux-Arts.

The musical works of most renowned composers, were initially greeted with derision. Stravinsky was run out of town by enraged Parisians and critics when he first served them the Rite of Spring. Entertainers in the contemporary pop culture have not fared any better. Decca records rejected a recording contract with the Beatles with the non-prophetic evaluation, "We don't like their sound. Groups of guitars are on the way out." Columbia records was next to turn them down.

Abraham Harold Maslow is one of the founders of humanistic psychology, the third (after psychoanalysis and behaviorism) and most recent perspective on personality, offered a radically different picture of the human nature. According to his view, it is human nature to **move consistently in the direction of personal growth**, creativity, and self-sufficiency, unless there are extremely strong environmental conditions to the contrary. Proponents of humanistic psychology also maintain that people are largely conscious and rational beings who are not dominated by unconscious needs and conflicts. In general, humanistic personologists view people as active shapers of their own lives, with freedom to choose and develop a life-style limited only by physical or social constraints.

CREATIVE LIFE

Csikszentmichalyi (1996) recommended some ideas about how to experience life more creatively, about strategies creative people use to increase the likelihood that they will accomplish original work. He stressed that his suggestions hold no promise for great creative achievement. To move from personal to cultural creativity one needs **talent, training, and an enormous dose of good luck**.

In order to get in the root of the problem, Thompson (1992) suggests the procedure of asking several times again and again "Why it happened?"

We can add several suggestions like:

Without access to a domain, and without the support of a field, a person has no chance of recognition. Even though personal creativity may not lead to fame and fortune, it can do something that from the individual's point of view is even more important: make day-to-day experiences more vivid, more enjoyable, more rewarding.

Calvin Coolidge, the former President of the United States wrote, "Nothing in the world can take the place of persistence. Talent will not. Nothing is more common than unsuccessful men with talent. Genius will not, un-rewarded genius is almost a proverb. Education will not, the world is full of educated derelicts. ***Persistence and determination are omnipotent.*** The slogan 'press on' has solved and always will solve the problems of the human race."

1. Approach your creative encounter the way you once explored a new world ***as a little child*** when you were most interested in finding out how it felt to try a new experience. Support the little child still residing within. As Jung (1972) pointed: "In every adult there lurks a child – an eternal child, something that is always becoming, is never completed, and calls for unceasing care, attention, and education. That is the part of the human personality which wants to develop and become whole."

2. Give yourself permission to approach each encounter as something you will ***enjoy***. With this freedom, you have a lot to gain and nothing to lose. Approach the encounter in the spirit of fun, humor and entertainment. Laughter is encouraged.

3. ***Avoid expectations***. Just allow the coaching to support you. Take the attitude that whatever happens, happens. There is no right or wrong. This position keeps you open to possibilities rather than limiting you to preconceives options. If remain open, positively or negatively surprising results will show up.

4. ***Be persistent***. People often fail when they set goals or resolutions because they give up too quickly. You've heard that it takes 21 or more repetitions to develop a new habit. Unfortunately, many people lack the discipline or the willpower to persist until the goal is achieved.

5. ***Never give up.*** "If there is one common denominator of men whom the world calls successful it is this: they get up when they fall down" (Paul Harvey).

THE KEY ELEMENTS OF MASLOW'S HUMANISTIC PERSPECTIVE

Human Creative Potential

The primacy of human creative potential is perhaps the most significant concept of humanistic psychology. Maslow (1950) merits the distinction of being the first to point out that ***creativeness is the most universal chara***cteristic of the people he studied or observed. Describing it as an attribute common to human nature, Maslow (1987) viewed creativity as potentially present in all people at birth. It is natural

– trees sprout leaves, birds fly, humans create. However, he also recognized that most human beings lose it as they become "enculturated" (formal education stamps out a lot of it). Fortunately, a few individuals hold onto this fresh, naïve, and direct way of looking at things or, if they number among the majority who lose it, are able to recover it later in life. Maslow theorized that since creativity is potential in anyone, it requires no special talents or capacities. We need not write books, compose music, or produce art objects to be creative. Comparatively few people do. Creativity is a universal human function and leads to all forms of self-expression. Thus, for example, there can be creative disc jockeys, computer programmers, business executives, sales clerks, and even college professors!

Emphasis of Psychological Health

Maslow argued that none of the available psychological approaches to the study of behavior does justice to the healthy human being's functioning, mode of living, or life goals. In particular, he strongly criticized Freud's preoccupation with the study of sickness, pathology, and maladjustment. Quite simply, Maslow considered psychoanalytic theory to be one-sided and lacking in comprehensiveness since it was grounded in the abnormal or "sick" part of human nature.

To correct this deficiency, Maslow focused attention on the ***psychologically healthy person*** and the understanding of such a person in terms other than comparison with the mentally ill. It was his belief that we cannot understand mental illness until we first understand mental health. Stated more baldly, Maslow (1987) argued that the study of crippled, immature, and unhealthy specimens can yield only a "crippled" psychology. He strongly urged the study of self-actualizing, psychologically healthy persons as the basis for a more universal science of psychology. Accordingly, humanistic psychology considers self-fulfillment to be the main theme in human life – a theme never revealed by studying disturbed individuals alone.

Prerequisites for Creativity

If creativity involves new combinations of mental elements, then the more mental elements a person had, the more creative he or she should be. Besides having a lot of mental elements, they should also be distributed across a wide spectrum of domains. Remote associations are most likely to give rise to creative ideas. Being an expert in a given specialty does not guarantee that one will be creative in that area.

We might guess that intelligence should be a good predictor of creativity, because the more intelligent one is, the more mental elements one should be able to acquire. However, this may not be the case. Beyond an IQ level 120 or so, intelligence and creativity are often held not to be closely related (Barron, 1955). A minimal IQ of 120 or so is necessary for one to be creative in any meaningful sense of the term. However, beyond that level, intelligence does not doubt, however, that an ***IQ of 120 would be sufficient for creative work in all disciplines***. Different areas of endeavor most certainly required different minimal levels of intelligence. Once this minimum level is reached, however, creativity and intelligence are not highly correlated. By elimination, then, it must be the type of cognition, a particular method of combining mental elements. In order to understand creativity, we need to discover what this type of thought is.

Domain-Relevant Skills

A necessary but not sufficient condition for creativity is that ***one has certain skills*** or knowledge ***relevant to the area*** in which one is working. It is clear enough that one cannot think of a creative idea about physics if one does not know anything about physics. You cannot very well combine mental elements in a new way if the elements are not known to you in the first place. It is also fairly clear that certain aptitudes or special abilities not directly connected with creativity are necessary. For example, to be a creative composer, one needs not only ability fro creative thinking but also musical talent. Although there are certainly many notable exceptions, ***creativity is generally confined to a single domain***. Michelangelo and Dante Gabriel Rossetti were both poets and visual artists, but they are exceptional. In general, poets are not good painters and painters are not good poets. Many visual artists are rather deficient in their verbal skills. Even though it should be kept in mind that such skills are probably crucial in creative achievement.

Motivational and Personality Factors

Thomas Alva Edison remarked that genius is 1% inspiration and 99% perspiration. Because inspiration is more interesting than perspiration, it has been studied much more intensively (Martindale, 1989). However, the 1% versus 99% partitioning of the "variance" in creativity is probably close to the mark.

Creative people might also be expected to have **high levels of self-confidence** if we consider the most likely reaction to creative ideas. This reaction is often extremely negative. Without a good deal of self-confidence, one would hardly be expected to venture toward a goal (production of a creative idea) that if reached would quite likely result in derision, hostility, and so on. Most people simply do not like novelty. It must be the case that creative people do like it, otherwise they would take no pleasure in producing creative ideas and would produce none. Except under rather unusual circumstances, people do not do things that bring them displeasure.

Situational Variables

Situation is often as good a predictor of behavior as are personality traits it would seem that more attention should be paid to situational factors affecting creativity. Certain situations are more conductive to creativity than others. It is difficult to imagine creative thought in a situation in which such thought is severely punished or in which, by dint of circumstances, the mental elements one thinks about are not ***susceptible to creative combinations***. If the task at hand were burying one's grandmother, one could think of novel methods, but they would likely be inappropriate, given that funeral ceremonies are tightly constrained by social and legal restrictions.

Everyone knows that the chance visit of "a person from Porlock" considerably shortened one of the greatest poems ("Kubla Khan") in the English language. Interruption is one of the lethal enemies of creativity (compare Tchaikovsky, 1878/1906). At least some minimal amount of time for solitary contemplation must be a necessary factor in creativity.

The Creative Personality

Creative people must **be able to combine mental elements in a different way** than uncreative people. They do have this ability. Can the necessary traits exist in an otherwise "normal" personality or are they linked to other traits or personality configurations that are not, in a logical sense, necessary for creativity. They linked to other traits. Creative geniuses are ***eccentric and bizarre creatures***. It is impossible to picture the mad, sad, and thoroughly bad Lord Byron trying to earn a living as an insurance salesman. But Wallance Stevens, whose immense creativity cannot be questioned, did in fact earn his keep as an insurance company executive and, so far is known, led a thoroughly normal life. Thus, the question comes down to one of probabilities. Are the Stevens or the Byrons more likely?

Cognitive Traits

Creative geniuses often exhibit an amazing ***lack of interest in or concern with the mundane details*** that constitute virtually the entire fabric of the ordinary person's mental life. Indeed, creative people, in general, tend to be uninterested in details or facts for their own sake. To tale an example of another sort, no matter how much a person knows about linguistics, he or she will not be able to explain the historical sound changes that seem to occur constantly in all languages unless that person has mental elements drawn from other domains. The reason is that modern linguistics consists almost wholly of statements of rules, and none of these rules pertain to or could cause changes in the phonetic realization of the elements of speech. To solve the problem, our hypothetical linguist would have to know something about psychology, sociology, or physiology, because these neighboring disciplines do have constructs that could explain phonetic change. In short, the more diverse and general a person's store of ideas, the greater is the chance that a creative idea will emerge.

As a rule, creative people do have a ***very wide range of interests***. Among the eminently creative, diversity of interests is rather astounding. For example, geneticist Theodosius Dobzhansky interests included music, history, anthropology, philosophy, religion, natural science, and linguistics. Edgar Allan Poe believed that his lasting fame would rest not upon his literary works but upon his contributions to cosmological theory.

Creative people consistently describe themselves as having a wide range of interests. It is very common for creative ideas to arise from combining ideas from different disciplines. Hardinh (1965) formulated her "law" of creative thought: an idea will eventually be applied to everything that it is applicable to.

Cross-Sexual Interests

Creative people have *more cross-sexual or androgynous interests and traits* than less creative people; that is, they have interests generally held by members of the opposite sex. They hold these interests in addition to, rather than in place of, interests stereotypically associated with members of their own sex. Thus, a creative woman might be interested in both carpentry and cooking. This pattern of wide-ranging interests has been found for both creative men and creative women. Because of this wider range of interests, creative people may respond in an unusual manner to problem as compared with less creative members of their sex.

There is some evidence that creative people *tend to have less clear-cut sex-role identities* than uncreative people. Besdine (1968) examined the biographies of a number of highly creative men. He found evidence for what he called "Oedipal victory" in a large number of these people. By Oedipal victory he means a situation where the son has replaced the father in the affections of the mother. Freud held that the normal pattern of development involves Oedipal rivalry; for example, around the age of five, the son wants to replace the father in the eyes of his mother. Most children lose this struggle and this leads, as Freud argued, to the establishment of male sex-role identity based upon identification with the father. Identification with the father is also hypothetically the basis for the development of the superego. In the case of Oedipal victory, this would not occur, and we should expect the child to maintain his initial infantile identification with his mother and not to develop a normal superego. The disinhibition or lack of control often found in creative people would be consistent with weak superego functioning. Another way that a male child can fail to establish a firm masculine sex-role identity is if the father is absent from the home during this crucial period. This would lead to a sort of de facto Oedipal victory. In a sample of eminent French and English poets Martindale (1989) found a father-absence rate of 30% - far higher than would be expected for the general population.

Homosexual subjects are not more creative than heterosexual subjects. In fact, several studies have found trends in the opposite direction. Thus cross-sexual interests and cross-sexual identification may be related to creativity but homosexuality is not. It seems to be cognitive orientation rather than sexual orientation that is crucial.

Creative people also *categorize ideas in a different way* than do less creative people. It would appear that their categorizations are both broader and more idiosyncratic than those of the uncreative. On object-sorting tasks, the categorizations of creative people are as "bizarre" as those of schizophrenics. Broader categories would allow one to see more items as similar. Perception of similarity where none had been seen before is the basis of creative insight. It should be noted that broad, diffuse, or hazy categories are an attribute of primary process states of consciousness.

Second-Language Learning and Creativity

In a study of creativity in women mathematicians, Helson (1971) found that more of the creative ones were *foreign born.* Landry (1972) produced evidence that just learning a foreign language enhances creativity. In that study, grammar school children signed up to learn a foreign language. One group began instruction immediately, whereas another group (comparable in terms of intelligence and other possible confounding variables) had to wait. After a period of time, the children taught a second language scored higher on several paper-and-pencil tests of creative ability.

"Balanced" bilingual children (i.e., those who had learned two languages about equally well) were more creative than monolingual children. Learning a second language also involves learning associative hierarchies that are "deviant" as compared to those learned for the first language; that is, the connotations of words in different languages are not exactly the same. This factor apparently enhances creativity. But it hardly seems likely that learning a second language would induce very large increases in creativity. However, these results are of interest because they imply that even factors that only lightly increase a person's store of mental elements and associations are positively related to creativity.

Creativity, Age, and Expertise

Creativity exhibits a *curvilinear relationship to age*. In general, a person's most creative work is done *at a fairly early age,* and this age of peak productivity varies from field to field. It is early in lyric poetry, mathematics, physics, and chemistry (ages 25 – 35) and somewhat later in psychology and the social sciences (ages 30 – 40). Only a few specialties, such as architecture and novel writing show peak performance at later ages (40 – 45). Not only the best work but the most work is produced at these ages. Output rises rather abruptly to this peak and then declines throughout the rest of a person's career.

Although age per se may be a crucial factor in creativity, "age-within-specialty" is also important: One's most creative work may be done relatively early in one's career within a given specialty, regardless of actual age. A person cannot have any creative ideas until at least some of the elements relevant to a field have been learned. But it would seem that one's best ideas come early – before one becomes an "expert." Once you have become an expert, you may be less likely to be creative. Why? Because being an expert means knowing which elements are important and (the potentially disastrous part) which elements are irrelevant and inappropriate. In other words, the expert may be less likely to make "inappropriate" responses and is consequently less likely to make creative ones. If this line of reasoning is correct, then the way to maintain one's creativity with increasing age is to shift fields. Many consistently creative people do just this. The chemist, Linus Pauling, provides us with a good example of this strategy.

Another example would be the psychologist, Leon Festinger. After formulating and testing several important theories in social psychology, Festinger gave up his work in this area completely and began research on visual perception. There is no empirical research on the question of whether age per se or age-within-specialty is the main determinant of creativity. Now that mid-life career changes are more common, such a research project is possible.

Even the expertise involved in formal education is important for creativity. In a study of 301 geniuses in various fields, Simonton (1976) found an inverted-U relationship between creativity and amount of education. Those with a moderate amount of education were most creative. This was the case even in the sciences. Now a Ph.D. is more or less required for work in most areas of science, it seems unlikely that an inverted-U relationship would be found. Success in school or college does not seem to be related to creative achievement. However, Simonton (1984) gave a number of examples of eminently creative people whose scholastic work was mediocre or poor. Time devoted to achieving scholastic excellence may be time made unavailable for acquiring the "irrelevant" knowledge necessary for creativity. Extremely creative people often dislike formal education and prefer self-education.

Motivational Traits

Creative people appear to have the ***motivational factors*** that would seem necessary. It is interesting that these factors are often present in an exacerbated or extreme form. Creative people are self-confident. When asked to describe themselves, creative people pick adjectives, such as confident, egotistical, and self-confident.

Creative people also describe themselves with adjectives, such as ambitious, curious, and enthusiastic. At high levels of creativity, interest sometimes takes on an almost obsessive quality. For example, Newton occasionally left his lodgings having forgotten to get dressed. We may presume that his intense interest in some intellectual problem left no time for such trivial details as putting in his clothes.

Although creative people often describe themselves as energetic, this contrasts with findings that they tend to be physically inactive and with a number of well-documented self-reports. Indeed, Lombroso (1901) held that abulia, apathy, and lack of will are among the most common traits shared by creative artists alternates between erethism and atony – that is, between excitement and inspiration on the one hand and exhaustion and apathy on the other. The reports of Charles Baudelaire and Gustav Flaubert are filled with remarks of extreme lack of energy to the point that getting out of bed or beginning to write were seen as almost Herculean tasks. Flaubert's behavior is especially enlightening. When he was in bed, he did not have the energy to get up. Once he began writing, he persisted hour after hour – often on the same sentence. Other examples could readily be adduced. Creative people have a tendency to persist in whatever state they are in. If they are doing nothing, they find it difficult to begin a task; but if they are performing a task, they find it difficult to stop doing it; they either perseverate. One wonders whether creative people are capable of sustaining attention on a topic for a long period of time or incapable of shifting it away from the topic. There is no systematic research on these questions.

There is also some confusion concerning the relationship between creativity and preference for simplicity versus complexity. If asked to chose between pairs of visual designs, creative people are generally found to prefer the more complex, asymmetric, or ambiguous design. On the other hand, creative people have a high need for order and prefer consonant over dissonant tone pairs.

Almost all aestheticians agree that beauty arises when both unity and variety are maximal. That is, a beautiful object is one that unifies a set of diverse elements. It would seem that the goal of the creative person is to produce such an object. For example, a creative scientific theory is beautiful, because it unifies elements that, on the surface, are diverse and unrelated. As the poet Samuel Taylor Coleridge

(1817-1907) noted, creativity required the ability to "exist in ambiguity" or to tolerate disorder. However, the ultimate goal is to arrive at an overall synthesis or order.

Intrinsic motivation is important for creativity. Intrinsic rewards are those that arise from performing a task; that is, the task is interesting and pleasurable in itself. Extrinsic rewards are those that come from beyond the domain of the task; for example, being paid or praised for working on the task. It would seem that creativity is enhanced by intrinsic rewards and decreased by extrinsic rewards.

In one of her studies, Amabile (1985) had poets compose poems under two conditions. In one condition, poets were first led to think about extrinsic rewards that could be important in writing. In the other condition, they were led to ponder the intrinsic rewards of writing. Rated creativity of poems written in the extrinsic-reward condition was significantly lower.

These findings fit with some of what we know about creativity in the real world. Creative scientists tend to prefer "pure" science and are often reluctant to undertake, or even disdainful of, practical projects that might yield a good deal of financial remuneration.

However, these findings should not be generalized too far. A poet wants to create a beautiful poem (an intrinsic reward), but this act of creation very often occurs in the context of seeking fame or immortality (extrinsic rewards). A scientist aims to solve important problems not only for their own sake but also in order to obtain some extrinsic reward. Indeed, if intrinsic rewards alone were important to creative people, it would be difficult to explain why scientists would bother to publish their findings and why artists would exhibit and sell their paintings.

Creative Environment

As we mentioned before, several theorists have argued that *freedom from external pressure or control* and a *warm, supportive environment* are necessary or at least quite helpful for creativity. There are empirical evidence that child-rearing practices producing such an environment are correlated with creative potential in both preschool children and adolescents. Amabile's (1983) contention that extrinsic reward decreases creativity is related to this notion. She also mentions surveillance and externally imposed deadlines as being detrimental to creativity.

Epocs characterized by political fragmentation produce more creative individuals. It would seem that any sort of control emanating from the environment has negative effects. Given that creative people tend to be dis-inhibited, one would expect that environmental control of any sort should be especially noxious to them. If a creative person is stuck in such an environment, one would expect lessened creativity. One would also suppose that, if possible, creative people would avoid such environments. There are other reasons to expect that creative people may tend to minimize environmental inputs of all sorts – not merely those of a constraining or controlling sort.

One is more likely to be creative if there are *creative role models* to emulate or compete with. Simonton (1984) provided strong quantitative evidence for this point of view. There is a very high correlation between the number of eminently creative people in a given generation and the number in the prior generation. Over half of the people who win Nobel prizes had previously studied under another Nobel laureate. It seems likely that these findings are due to the provision of role models for already potentially creative people.

Over-Sensitivity and Withdrawal

The stereotype that creative people are *oversensitive at both sensory and the emotional level*, would seem to be no stereotype at all.

This the Belgian poet Emile Verhaeren disconnected his doorbell because its ringing caused him physical pain. Marcel Proust withdraw into his cork-libed room because normal levels of light and sound were, he said, painful to him. Lombroso (1901) collected a number of similar self-reports. Creative people are physiologically over reactive to stimuli. For example, Martindale and Armstrong (1974) found more electroencephalogram (EEG) blocking to onset to a tone in more creative as compared with less creative subjects. The other authors found much large skin potential responses to noise in more as compared with less creative people. The more creative a subject is, the lower the intensity of his maximally preferred tone. Creativity is also correlated with augmentation ("amplification" of the intensity of stimulation) on the kinesthetic aftereffect task.

We know that sensory deprivation causes decreases in cortical arousal and increases in primary process thinking. Thus, it should facilitate creative inspiration. Although creative people do not seem generally to have low levels of arousal, their over-sensitivity may drive them to withdraw or to restrict sensory input. This would put them in the low-arousal state necessary for creative inspiration.

APPROACHES TO GIFTEDNESS

Certain personal traits contribute to the requisite developmental history. An individual who would be great needs to be daring, *able to take risks, willing to confront the unknown*. But even that is not enough. If his contributions are to be sustained, the individual must also display staying power: he must have the fiber to transcend an early triumph (or disaster) and continue to deepen. The presence of sensitive models and teachers, the existence of an audience to appreciate his inventions, and a healthy injection of luck – all these are at a premium.

Guilford (1978) believed that individuals differ markedly from one another in the extent to which they can negotiate their way through a domain. In all likelihood, hereditary factors play their part: certain people seem specially "prepared" to grasp the regularities in specific domains of knowledge, as prepared as all of us are to grasp the rules that operate in the realm of language.

But individual gifts and tenacity are not the only variables. In order to understand the origins and ultimate fate of prodigious behaviors, one must take into account other factors as well. First, there is the nature of the domain itself. Some domains require very little interaction with the outside world, little knowledge about one's own psychology or about other individuals

Personalities: they are relatively ***self-contained***. It is in these domains – such as chess or mathematics, and also certain aspects of music – that an individual can progress very quickly with relatively little direct tutelage. In contrast, in such domains of knowledge as literature, philosophy, or history, one is much more dependent upon years of experience in the world. Not infrequently, supreme achievements in these fields do not emerge until one's mature years, as happened, for example, in the cases of the philosopher Kant and the poet Yeats.

Another factor of importance, one often overlooked, is the ***maturity of the domain itself*** within a given society. Sometimes a domain, like mathematics, has been highly developed, in which case progress are a rapid rate becomes possible. Moreover, the fact that a domain is situated in a locale which cares about that field can engender prodigious behaviors. Upwards of 50 percent of the chess prodigies in the United States come from three metropolitan areas – New York, San Francisco, and Los Angeles – which, taken together, have but 10 percent of the population. One can find similarly high percentages of youthful violinists in families of Russian-Jewish extraction. But when a domain may have developed only to a slight degree in a society, or perhaps not have been invented at all, there can be poignant results. The potentially greatest chess player in the world cannot even become a "hack" if the game has not yet spread to his locale. And even the most gifted mathematician cannot make genuine innovations if he lives in a culture where mathematics has been little developed. What is innovative within his culture will be "old hat" elsewhere.

This fate in fact befell the Indian mathematician Ramanujan, said to be the most talented natural mathematician of this century. Working virtually on his own in India, Ramanujan matched the accomplishments of several centuries of mathematics. However, this work had already been performed in the West, and so when he finally arrived in England it was too late for him to join the forefront of his profession. Mozart's musical talent might have shone through in any age and culture: yet there may have been a special fit between his particular flair and the style of classical music he heard in his home and which he was later to recast in such innovative ways.

We occasionally hear of the "omnibus" prodigy – the individual, like the young Goethe or John Stuart Mill, who is reputed to excel "across the board." But such individuals, who sprint simultaneously along multiple tracks of excellence, must be exceedingly rare. For example, in the six youngsters whom Feldman has studied intensively, and in the dozen or so others that he has heard about, there is little evidence for such "transfer of prodigiousness." These youngsters, who include gifted artist, writers, and a young scientifically oriented child, are certainly bright and often very appealing personalities. But when Feldman gave three of them batteries of tests, including measures of operational intelligence, moral reasoning, social perspective-taking, individuals who were "off the scale." Nor do the few case studies that have been published support the notion that a prodigy is a prodigy in everything. Brightness may cut across domains, but prodigiousness does not.

According to Guilford (1950) at least eight primary abilities underlay creativity.
- ***Sensitivity to problem.*** Creative people see problems where others so not, an ability possibly related to curiosity. Test: List things that are wrong with, or could be improved in, common household appliances.

318

- *Fluency.* Those people who produce large numbers of ideas are more likely to have significant ideas. Test: State as many consequences as possible to a hypothetical situation, such as: "A new invention makes it unnecessary for people to eat" (p. 452).
- *Novel ideas.* Creative people have unusual but appropriate ideas. Test: Note the frequency of remote verbal items (only those indirectly linked by mediators to the original item) in a word-association test.
- *Flexibility.* Creative people should be able easily to change set. Test: Note the variety of types of answers to completion questions.
- *Synthesizing and analyzing abilities.* Creative thinking requires the organizing of ideas into large, more inclusive patterns and symbolic structures must often be broken down before new ones can be built.
- *Complexity.* Possibly related to synthesizing complexity refers to the "numbers of interrelated ideas an individual can manipulate at once.
- *Evaluation*. At some point, the value of new ideas must be determined. Test: Rank in order of excellence several correct solutions to a problem.

Genius, defined as supreme creative achievement, socially recognized over the centuries, is the product of many different components acting synergistically, i.e. multiplying with each other, rather than simply adding one to the other. Among these components are

- high intelligence,
- persistence, and
- creativity, regarded as a trait.

We define genius as the proven ability to produce artistic, scientific, or other intellectual work that is considered supremely valuable during or after the lifetime of the producer.

- Certain qualifications must be met in order to achieve recognition of the work done. The candidate for genius must produce, perform, discover, or invent something that is highly valued.
- If this work is too far ahead of its time, it will be ignored or derided; unless the work can be preserved to be appreciated later, recognition may never come.

Genius, therefore, is not an attribute: it is a dynamic relationship between its possessor and society. It indicates, in a general way, what society expects of the genius and how it responds to that person. There are always geniuses in potentia; but there are no unrecognized geniuses.

Eysenck's Genius Principal Traits:

- All cognitive endeavors require **new association to be made**, or **old ones to be reviewed**;
- There are marked differences between individuals in the **speed with which associations are formed**;
- **Speed** in the formation of associations is *the foundation of individual differences in intelligence*;
- Only a **sub-sample of associations** is relevant in a **given problem**;
- Individuals **differ** in the **range of associations** considered in problem-solving;
- **Wideness of range** is the foundation of individual differences in **creativity**;
- **Wideness of range** is in principle *independent* of speed of forming associations, suggesting that *intelligence and creativity are essentially independent*;
- However, **speed** of forming associations leads to **faster learning**, and hence to a **greater number of elements** with which to form associations;
- **The range** of associations considered for problem-solving is so wide that a **critical evaluation** is needed (comparator) to eliminate unsuitable associations.

Genuine creativity requires
(1) a large pool of elements to form associations:
(2) speed in producing associations, and
(3) well-functioning comparator to eliminate false solutions.

PRIMARY TRAITS RELATED TO CREATIVITY

In 1950 (Guilford, 1950) it was predicted that we should find a factor characterized as an *ability to see problems*; a generalized *sensitivity to problems*. Such a trait was found, and it is best indicated by tests asking examinees to state defects or deficiencies in common implements or in social institutions or to state problems created by common objects or actions. The factor has been identified logically as belonging in the general category of evaluative abilities (Guilford, 1957).

The reason is that the act involved is essentially a judgment that things are not all right; that goals have not been reached; or that not everything to be desired has been achieved. Such a decision would play no constructive part in productive thinking, but without this step productive thinking would not get started.

It was hypothesized that fluency of thinking would be an important aspect of creativity. This is a quantitative aspect that has to do with fertility of ideas. Four fluency factors were discovered:

1. *The word fluency* (Thurstone, 1938; Guilford, 1959). This is an ability to produce words each containing a specified letter or combination of letters. It is not easy to see where this ability would have much importance in creative work in everyday life, but Drevdahl (1956) has found it to be related in both science and arts students.

2. A factor of *associational fluency* is indicated best in a test that requires the examinee to produce as many synonyms as he can for a given words in limited time. In contrast to word fluency, where only letter requirements are to be observed, associational fluency involves a requirement of meaning for the words given. One would expect such an ability to be important to the average writer who wants to find a word to satisfy a particular meaning he has in mind and a quick running over of words in that area is an advantage.

3. A factor of *expressional fluency* is best measured by a test calling for the production of phrases or sentences. The need for rapid juxtaposition of words to meet the requirements of sentence structure seems to be the unique characteristic of tests of this ability. Whether the same ability pertains to oral speech we do not know, but there is some reasonable presumption of at least a moderate correlation between corresponding performances in writing and in oral speech. Although in writing one does not ordinarily work under pressure of time, the facility for framing sentences must be an important asset. In oral speech it should be of even greater importance, particularly for oratorical talents. It can be said that the possession of a high degree of expressional fluency, as measured by written test, can apparently lead observers to the conclusion that the expressionally fluent person has a high degree of creativity. In one study ratings of men in several different traits of creativity tended to be correlated positively with scores for the factor of expressional fluency.

4. A trait of probably much wider usefulness if fluency in the production of ideas, or the factor of *ideational fluency.* This is the ability to produce ideas to fulfill certain requirements in limited time. A test of this factor may ask examinees to name objects that are hard, white, and adible or to give various uses for a common brick, or to write appropriate titles for a given story plot. In scoring for this factor, sheer quantity is the important consideration; quality need not be considered so long as responses are appropriate.

There are certain stages in most problem-solving where there must be a searching for answers. The problem as structured or defined provides the specifications for the solutions that are sought. Unless the specifications point to a unique solution, some searching and testing of alternative solutions is likely to occur. The scanning process is more likely to arrive at suitable solutions if it can elicit a greater number of possibilities. Thus ideational fluency probably plays an important role in problem-solving and many problems require novel solutions, which means creative thinking.

Creative thinkers are *flexible thinkers*. They readily desert old ways of thinking and strike out in new directions. A factor of flexibility of thinking was therefore predicted. Guilford (1959) found two abilities, both of which seem to fit into this general category.

One of these factors has been called *spontaneous flexibility*. It is defined as the ability or disposition to produce a great variety of ideas, with freedom from inertia or from perseveration. In tests of this factor, the examinee shows his freedom to roam about in his thinking even when it is not necessary for him to do so. In naming uses of a common brick, he jumps readily from one category of response to another – the brick used as building material, as a weight, as a missile, or as a source of red powder, and so on. Rigid thinkers, on the other hand, tend to stay within one or two categories of response. Another example of spontaneously flexible thinkers in dealing with concrete material are those who see rapid fluctuations in ambiguous figures, such as the Necker's outline cube or the staircase figure.

The other type of flexibility of thinking is called *adaptive flexibility* for the reason that it facilitates the solution of problems. This is shown best in a type of problem that requires a most unusual type of solution. The problem may appear to be soluble by means of more familiar or conventional methods, but these methods will not work. One task that calls for this kind of solution is based upon the familiar game involving matchsticks. The examinee is given a set of contiguous squares, each side formed by a match, and is told that he is to take away a certain number of matches, leaving a certain number of squares. He is not told that the squares must be all of the same size, but if he adopts this obvious assumption he cannot solve one or more problems, for the only satisfactory and result is a number of squares that differ in size. Persistence in wrong but inviting directions of thinking means low status on the factor of *adaptive flexibility*.

In the art of creativity there is such a trait as *originality*. It is indicated by the scores of some tests in which the keyed responses are weighted in proportion to their infrequency of occurrence in the population of examinees. Unusualness of responses, in a statistical sense, is one principle of measurement of originality.

The factor is also indicated by tests in which items call for *remote associations* or relationships; remote either in time or in a logical sense. If we ask examinees to list all the consequences they can think of in the event that a new discovery makes eating unnecessary, the number of remote consequences they give indicates originality, whereas the number of obvious consequences indicates ideational fluency. This means that it takes a quality criterion to indicate the extent of originality of which a person is characteristically capable.

A third way of indicating degree of originality in taking tests is the *number of responses* an examinee can give that are judged as being clever. The titles given for short-story plots, for example, can be rated as clever or not clever. The number of clever responses indicates originality.

There are opinions that what is called originality is actually a case of adaptive flexibility when dealing with verbally meaningful material, parallel to the factor of adaptive flexibility as now known, which pertains to tasks dealing with nonverbal material. In either case one must get away from the obvious, the ordinary, or the conventional in order to make a good score.

The next factor is so called *redefinition*, which called for an *ability to give up old interpretations* of familiar objects in order to use them or their parts in some new way. Which of the following objects, or their parts, could best be adapted to making a needle: pencil, radish, shoe, fish, or carnation? The keyed (correct) response is "fish", since a bone from a typical fish seems to be most readily adaptable for the purpose of making a needle. Improvising, in general, probably reflects the ability of redefinition. It has been suggested that a low status on this factor means the condition of "functional fixity" or "functional fixedness," which has been gaining in use to describe failure to solve problems in which improvising must occur, such as making a pendulum out of a string and pliers.

Another factor, which was predicted and found in a study of planning abilities is a factor called *elaboration*. It was indicated by a test in which the examinee is given one or two simple lines and told to construct on this foundation a more complex object. The score is the amount of elaboration demonstrated. It is also indicated by a test in which the bare outline of a plan is given, the examinee to list all the minor steps needed to make the plan work. It is possible that two abilities are involved, one pertaining to elaboration of figural material and one pertaining to elaboration of meaningful material. If so, the two abilities are probably positively correlated.

HISTORIES OF CREATIVE PEOPLE

Csikzentmihalyi (1996) studied creativity, based on histories of contemporary people who know about creativity firsthand. Between 1990 and 1995 he and his students at the University of Chicago videotaped interview with a group of ninety-nine exceptional individuals. The in-depth analysis of these interviews helped him illustrate what creative people are like, how the creative process works, and what conditions encourage or hinder the generation of original ideas.

Csikzentmihalyi (1996) provided the following characteristics of creative people:

1. ***Creative individuals have a great deal of physical energy, but they are also often quiet and at rest.*** They work long hours, with great concentration, while projecting an aura of freshness and enthusiasm. This suggests a superior physical endowment, a genetic advantage. Yet it is surprising how often individuals who in their seventies and eighties exude energy and health remember a childhood plagued by illness. This does not mean that creative persons are hyperactive, always "on," constantly churning away. In fact, they often take rests and sleep a lot. The important thing is that the energy is under their own control – it is not controlled by the calendar, the clock, an external schedule. When necessary they can focus it like a laser beam; when it is not, they immediately start recharging their batteries. They consider the rhythm of activity followed by idleness or reflection very important for the success of their work. And this is not biorhythm they inherited with their genes; it was learned by trial and error, as a strategy for achieving their goal.

One manifestation of energy is sexuality. Creative people are paradoxical in this respect also. They seem to have quite a strong dose of eros, or generalized libidinal energy, which some express directly into sexuality. At the same time, a certain Spartan celibacy is also a part of their makeup; continence tends to accompany superior achievement. Without eros, it would be difficult to take life on with vigor; without restraint, the energy could easily dissipate.

2. ***Creative individuals tend to be smart, yet also naïve at the same time.*** How smart they actually are is open to question. It is probably true that what psychologists cal the g factor – meaning a core of general intelligence – is high among people who make important creative contributions. But we should not take seriously the lists that used to be printed on the sidebars of psychology textbooks, according to which John Stuart Mills must have had an IQ of 170 and Mozart an IQ of 135. Had they been tested at the time, perhaps they would have scored high. Perhaps not. And how many children in the eighteenth century would have scored even higher but never did anything memorable?

The earliest longitudinal study of superior mental abilities initiated at Stanford University by the psychologist Lewis Terman in 1921, shows rather conclusively that children with very high IQs do well in life, but after a certain point IQ does not seem to be correlated any longer with superior performance in real life. Later studies suggest that the cutoff point is around 120; it might be difficult to do creative work with a lower IQ, but beyond 120 an increment in IQ does not necessarily imply higher creativity.

Why a low intelligence interferes with creative accomplishment is quite obvious. But being intellectually brilliant can also be detrimental to creativity. Some people with high IQs get complacent, and, secure in their mental superiority, they lose the curiosity essential to achieving anything new. Learning facts, playing by the existing rules of domains, may come so easily to a high-IQ person that he or she never has any incentive to question, doubt, and improve of existing knowledge. This is probably why Goethe, among others, said that naivete is the most important attribute of genius.

Another way of expressing this dialectic is by the contrasting poles of wisdom and childishness. As Howard Gardner remarked in his study of the major creative geniuses of this century, a certain immaturity, both emotional and mental, can go hand in hand with deepest insight. Mozart comes immediately to mind.

Furthermore, people who bring about an acceptable novelty in a domain seem able to use well two opposite ways of thinking: the convergent and the divergent. Convergent thinking is measured by IQ tests, and it involves solving well-defined, rational problems that have one correct answer. Divergent thinking leads to no agreed-upon solution. It involves fluency, or the ability to generate a great quantity of ideas. These are the dimensions of thinking that most creativity tests measure and that most workshops try to enhance.

It is probably true that in a system that is conducive to creativity, a person whose thinking is fluent, flexible, and original is more likely to come up with novel ideas. Therefore, it makes sense to cultivate divergent thinking in laboratories and corporations – especially if management is able to pick out and implement the most appropriate ideas from the many that are generated. Yet there remains the nagging suspicion that at the highest levels of creative achievement the generation of novelty is not the main issue. Galileo or Darwin did not have that many new ideas, but the ones they fastened upon were so central that they changed the entire culture. Similarly, the individuals in the Scikszentmihalyi's study often claimed to have had only two or three good ideas in their entire career, but each idea was so generative that it kept them busy for a lifetime of testing, filling out, elaborating, and applying.

Divergent thinking is not much use without the ability to tell a good idea from a bad one – and this selectivity involves convergent thinking. Manfred Eigen is one of several scientists who claim that the only difference between them and their less creative colleagues is that they can tell whether a problem is soluble or not, and this saves enormous amounts of time and many false starts. George Stigler stresses the importance of fluidity, that is, divergent thinking on the one hand, and good judgment in recognizing a viable problem on the other:

"I consider that I have good intuition and good judgment on what problems are worth pursuing and what lines of work are worth doing. I used to say (and I think this was bragging) that whereas most scholars have ideas that do not pan out more than, say, 4 percent of the time, mine come through maybe 80 percent of the time."

3. ***A third paradoxical trait refers to the related combination of playfulness and discipline, or responsibility and irresponsibility.*** There is no question that a playfully light attitude is typical of creative individuals. John Wheeler says that the most important thing in a young physicist is "this bounce, which I always associate with fun in science, kicking things around. It's not quite joking, but it has some of the lightness of joking. It's exploring ideas." David Riesman, in describing the attitude of "detached attachment" that makes him an astute observer of the social scene, stresses the fact that he always "wanted at the same time to be irresponsible and responsible."

But this playfulness doesn't go very far without its antithesis, a quality of doggedness, endurance, perseverance. Much hard work is necessary to bring a novel idea to completion and to surmount the obstacles a creative person inevitably encounters. When asked what enable him to solve the physics problems that made him famous, Hans Bethe answered with a smile: "Two things are required. One is brain. And second is the willingness to spend long times in thinking, with a definite possibility that you come out with nothing."

Nina Holton, whose playfully wild germs of ideas are the genesis of her sculpture, is very firm about the importance of hard work:

"Tell anybody you're a sculptor and they'll say, "Oh, how exciting, how wonderful." And I tend to say, "What's so wonderful?" I mean, it's like being a mason, or being a carpenter, half the time. But they don't wish to hear that because they really only imagine the first part, the exciting part. But, as Khrushchev once said, that doesn't fry pancakes, you see. That germ of an idea does not make a sculpture which stands up. It just sits there. So the next stage, of course, is the hard work. Can you really translate it into a piece of sculpture? Or will it be a wild thing which only seemed exciting while you were witting in the studio alone? Will it look like something? Can you actually do it physically? Can you personally, do it physically? What do you have by way of materials? So the second part is a lot of hard work. And sculpture is that, you see. It is the combination of wonderful wild ideas and then a lot of hard work."

Jacob Rabinov uses an interesting mental technique to slow himself down when work on an invention requires more endurance than intuition:

"Yeah, there's a trick I pull for this. When I have a job to do like that, where you have to do something that takes a lot of effort, slowly, I pretend I'm in jail. Don't laugh. And if I'm in jail, time is of no consequence. In other words, if it takes a week to cut this, it'll take a week. What else have I got to do? I'm going to be here for twenty years. See? This is a kind of mental trick. Because otherwise you say, "My God, it's not working," and then you make mistakes. But the other way, you say time is of absolutely no consequence. People start saying how much will it cost me in time? If I work with somebody else it's fifty bucks an hour, a hundred dollars an hour. Nonsense. You just forget doing this. I work fast, normally. But if something will take a day gluing and then next day I glue the other side – it'll take two days – it doesn't bother me at all."

Despite the carefree air that many creative people affect, most of them work late into the night and persist when less driven individuals would not. Vasari wrote in 1550 that when the Renaissance painter Paolo Uccello was working out the laws of visual perspective, he would walk back and forth all night, muttering to himself: "What a beautiful thing is this perspective!" while his wife kept calling him back to bed with no success. Close to five hundred years later, physicist and inventor Frank Offner describes the time he was trying to understand how the membrane of the ear works:

"Ah, the answer may come to me in the middle of the night. My wife, when I was first into this membrane stuff, would kick me in the middle of the night and say, "Now get your mind off of membranes and get to sleep."

    4. ***Creative individuals alternate between imagination and fantasy at one end, and a rooted sense of reality at the other.*** Both are needed to break away from the present without losing touch with the past. Albert Einstein once wrote that art and science are two of the greatest forms of escape from reality that humans have devised. In a sense he was right: Great art and great science involve a leap of imagination into a world that is different from the present. The rest of society often views these new ideas as fantasies without relevance to current reality. And they are right. But the whole point of art and science is to go beyond what we now consider real, and create a new reality. At the same time, this "escape" is not into a never-never land. What makes a novel idea creative is that once we see it, sooner or later we recognize that, strange as it is, it is true.

This dialectic is reflected by the way that, many years ego, the artists responded to so-called projective tests, like the Rorschach or the Thematic Apperception Test. These require you to make up a story about some ambiguous stimuli, such as inkblots or drawings, that could represent almost anything. The more creative artists gave responses that were definitely more original, with unusual, colorful, detailed elements. But they never gave "bizarre" responses, which normal people occasionally do. A bizarre response is one that, with all the goodwill in the world, one could not see in the stimulus. For instance if an inkblot looks vaguely like a butterfly, and you say that it looks like a submarine without being able to give a sensible clue as to what in the inkblot made you say so, the response would be scored as bizarre. Normal people are rarely original, but they are sometimes bizarre. Creative people, it seems, are original without being bizarre. The novelty they see is rooted in reality.

Most of us assume that artists – musicians, writer, poets, painters – are strong on the fantasy side. This may be true in terms of day-to-day routine activities. But when a person begins to work creatively, all bets are off – the artist may be as much a realist as the physicist, and the physicist as imaginative as the artist.

We certainly think of bankers, for example, as having a rather pedestrian, commonsense view of what is real and what is not. Yet a financial leader such as John Reed has much to say that dispels that notion. In his interview, he returns again and again to the theme that reality is relative and constantly changing, a perspective that he thinks is essential to conforming the future creatively:

"I don't think there is such a thing as reality. There are widely varying descriptions of reality, and you've got to be alert to when they change and what's really going on. No one is going to truly grasp it, but you have to stay truly active on that end. That implies you have to have a multifaceted perspective.

There is a set of realities that exist at any moment in time. I always have some kind of a model in my mind as to what I think is going on in the world. I'm always tuning that [model] and trying to get different insights as I look at things, and I try to relate it back to what it means to our business, to how one behaves, if you will.

I don't mean to say there isn't anything in the center. I just think we can look at it [reality] in so many different ways. Right now, in my business, banks are deemed to be successful based on capital ratios. Ten years ago there was no concept of the "capital ratio." I failed totally to understand the impact of the savings and loan crisis on Congress, the regulators, and the industry. The world I'm living in today bears little resemblance to the world I lived in ten years ago, with regard to what was thought to be important. So we have defined a reality, which as I say is not empty, but it's close to being empty.

Like anybody else, I was slow to recognize the new reality. Knowing these kinds of things turns out to be awfully relevant, because your degrees of freedom get taken away of you're off base. I went through a massive adjustment to play a game that was different from the one you saw before. But it's a changing reality. I know goddamn well that these capital ratios are not sufficiently robust to be long-term, decent leading indicators of things, and five years from now the people who worry about how to price bank stocks are not going to be focusing on those. I describe success as evolutionary success."

What Einstein implied about art and science reappears in this account of banking: It is an evolutionary process, where current reality becomes rapidly obsolete, and one must be on the alert for the shape of things to come. At the same time, the emerging reality is not a fanciful conceit but something inherent in the here and now. It would be easy to dismiss Reed's visionary view as the comancing of a businessman who has had one too many encounters with reality. But apparently his unorthodox approach works: A recent issue of Newsweek announced: "John Reed might be excused a little gloating.... Since his darkest days three years ago he's quietly produced a stunning 425 percent return for investors who bought Citicorp shares." And one commentator adds that the overseas investments Reed made were considered junk five years ago, whereas now they are seen as a hot stock. "Nothing's changed but the perception," the financial expert says, echoing Reed's take on the reality of the market.

5. ***Creative people seem to harbor opposite tendencies on the continuum between extroversion and introversion.*** Usually each of us tends to be one or the other, wether preferring to be in the thick of crowds or sitting on the sidelines and observing the passing show. In fact, in current psychological research, extroversion and introversion are considered the most stable personality traits that differentiate people from each other and that can be reliably measured. Creative individuals, on the other hand, seem to express both traits at the same time.

The stereotype of the "solitary genius" is strong and gets ample support also from Scikszentmihalyi's interviews. One must generally be alone in order to write, paint, or do experiments in a laboratory. As we know from studies of young talented people, teenagers who cannot stand being alone tend not to develop their skills because practicing music or studying math requires solitude they dread. Only those teens who can tolerate being alone are able to master the symbolic content of a domain.

Yet over and over again, the importance of seeing people, hearing people, exchanging ideas, and getting to know another person's work and mind are stressed by creative individuals. The physicist John Wheeler expresses this point with his usual directness: "If you don't kick things around with people, you are out of it. Nobody, I always say, can be anybody without somebody being around."

Physicist Freeman Dyson expresses with a fine nuance the opposite phases of this dichotomy in his work. He points to the door of his office and says:

"Science is a very gregarious business. It is essentially the difference between having this door open and having it shut. When I am doing science I have the door open. I mean, that is kind of symbolic, but it is true. You want to be, all the time, talking with people. Up to a point you welcome being interrupted because it is only by interacting with other people that you get anything interesting done. It is essentially a communal enterprise. There are new things happening all the time, and you should keep abreast and keep yourself aware of what is going on. You must be constantly talking. But, of course, writing is different. When I am writing I have the door shut, and even then too much sound comes through, so very often when I am writing I go and hide in the library. It is a solitary game. So, I suppose that is the main difference. But then, afterward, of course the feedback is very strong, and you get a tremendous enrichment of contacts as a result. Lots and lots of people write me letters simply because I have written books which address a general public, so I get into touch with a much wider circle of friends. It's broadened my horizons very much. But that is only after the writing is finished and not while it is going on."

John Reed builds the alternation between inner-directed reflection and intense social interaction into his daily routine:

"I'm an early morning guy. I get up at five always, get out of the shower about 5:30, and I typically try to work either at home or at the office, and that's when I do a good bit of my thinking and priority setting. I'm a great lister. I have twenty lists of things to do all the time. If I ever have five free minutes I sit and make lists of things that I should be worrying about or doing. Typically I get to the office about 6:30 or 10:00. Then you get involved in lots of transactions. If you are chairman of the company it's like being a tribal chieftain. People come into your office and talk to you."

Even in the very private realm of the arts the ability to interact is essential. Nina Holton describes well the role of sociability in art:

"You really can't work entirely alone in your place. You want to have a fellow artist come and talk things over with you – "How does that strike you?" You have to have some sort of feedback. You can't be sitting there entirely by yourself and never show it. And then eventually, you know, when you begin to show, you have to have a whole network. You have to get to know gallery people, you have to get to know people who work in your field who are involved. And you may want to find out whether you wish to be part of it or not be part of it, but you cannot help being part of fellowship, you know?"

Jacob Rabinow again puts into clear words the dilemma that many creative individuals face:

"I remember once we had a big party and Gladys [his wife] said that I sometimes walk to a different drummer. In other words, I'm so involved in an idea I'm working on, I get so carried away, that I'm all by myself. I'm not listening to what anybody says. This sometimes happens. That you've got a new idea and you feel that it's very good and you're so involved that you're not paying attention to anybody. And you tend to drift away people. It's very hard for me to be objective. I don't know. I'm social, I like people, I like to tell jokes, I like to go to the theater. But it's probably true that there are times when Gladys would have liked me to pay more attention to her and to the family. I love my children, they love me, and we have a wonderful relationship. But it could be that if I were not an inventor but had a routine job. I'd spend more time at home and I'd pay more attention to them, and the job would be something that I wouldn't like to do. So maybe people who don't like their jobs love their home more. It's quite possible."

6. *Creative individuals are also remarkably humble and proud at the same time.* It is remarkable to meet a famous person whom you expect to be arrogant or supercilious, only to encounter self-deprecation and shyness instead. Yet there are good reasons why this should be so. In the first place, these individuals are well aware that they stand, in Newton's words, "on the shoulders of giants." Their respect for the domain in which they work makes them aware of the long line of previous contributions to it, which puts their own into perspective. Second, they also are aware of the role that luck played in their own achievements. And third, they are usually so focused on future projects and current challenges that their past accomplishments, no matter how outstanding, are no longer very interesting to them. Elisabeth Noelle-Neumann's answer to the question "Looking back on all your accomplishments, which one would you say you are most proud of?" is typical:

" I never think of what I am proud about. I never look back, except to find out about mistakes. Because mistakes are hard to remember and to draw conclusions from. But I only see danger in thinking back about things you are proud of. When people ask me if I am proud of something, I just shrug and hope to get away as soon as possible. I should explain that my way is always to look ahead, all my pleasant thoughts are about the future. It has been this way since I was twenty years old. I start every day fresh. The most important thing for me is to keep up the research institute, to keep up empirical research.

Despite her great accomplishments and reputation in the field neuro-psychologist Brenda Milner tells of being very self-critical and of having enormous self-doubts about being creative. The Canadian artist Michael Snow attributes the restless experimentation that led him to so many successes to a sense of confusion and insecurity he has been trying to dispel.

Another indication of modesty is how often this question was answered in terms of the family rather than the accomplishments that made a person famous. For instance, Freeman Dyson's answer was: "I suppose it is just to have raised six kids, and brought them up, as far as one can see, all to be interesting people. I think that's what I am most proud of, really." And John Reed's: "Oh, God. That's real... I suppose being a parent. I have four kids. If you had to say what has both surprised and given you a lot of pleasure, I'd say that I'm close to my kids and I enjoy them, and I never would have guessed that that would be as much fun as it's turned out to be."

At the same time, of course, no matter how modest these individuals are, they know that in comparison with others they have accomplished a great deal. And this knowledge provides a sense of security, even pride. This is often expressed as a sense of self-assurance. For instance, medical physicist Rosalyn Yalow mentioned repeatedly that all through her life she never had any doubts about succeeding in what she started out to do. Jacob Rabinow concurs: "There's one other thing that you do when you invent. And that is what I call the Existence Proof. This means that you have to assume that it can be done. If you don't assume that, you won't even try. And I always assume that the only it can be done, but I can do it." Some individuals stress humility, others self-assurance, but in actually all of the people interviewed by Csikzentmihalyi (1996) seemed to have a good dose of both.

Another way of expressing this duality is to see it as a contrast between ambition and selflessness, or competition and cooperation. It is often necessary for creative individuals to be ambitious and aggressive. Yet at the same time, they are often willing to subordinate their own personal comfort and advancement to the success of whatever project they are working on. Aggressiveness is required especially in fields where competition is acute, or in domains where it is difficult to introduce novelty. In George Stidler's words:

"Every scholar, I think, is aggressive in some sense. He has to be aggressive if he wants to change his discipline. Now, if you get a Keynes or a Friedman, they are also aggressive in that they want to change the world, and so they become splendid public figures as well. But that's a very hard game to play."

Brenda Milner claims that she has always been very aggressive verbally. John Gardner, statesman and founder of several national grassroots political organizations, describes well both the peaceful and aggressive instincts that coexist within the same person:

"I was the president of the Carnegie Corporation. I had a very interesting life, but not a lot of new challenges, not a tumultuous life. I was well protected. When I went to Washington I discovered a lot of things about myself that I didn't know. I discovered that I liked politicians. I got along well with them. I enjoyed dealing with the press, as much as anyone can enjoy dealing with the press. And then I discovered that I enjoyed a political fight, which was about as far away from my self-image as you can get. I'm a very peaceful person. But these things come out. Life pulls them out of you, and as I say, I'm a slow learner, but in my mid-fifties I learned some interesting things."

Several persons mentioned that in the course of their careers motivation has shifted from self-centered goals to more altruistic interests. For instance, Sarah Le Vine, who started out as an anthropologist and then became a fiction writer, has this to say:

"Up until quite recently, I used to think of production only for the greater glory of myself, really. I don't see it that way at all anymore. I mean, it's nice if one gets recognition for what one people can learn about, and I suppose that comes with middle age."

7. In all cultures, men are brought up to be "masculine" and to disregard and repress those aspects of their temperament that the culture regards as "feminine," whereas women are expected to do the opposite. Creative individuals to a certain extent escape this rigid gender role stereotyping. When tests of masculinity/femininity are given to young people, over and over one finds that creative and talented girls are more dominant and tough than other girls, and creative boys are more sensitive and less aggressive than their male peers.

This tendency toward androgyny is sometimes understood in purely sexual terms, and therefore it gets confused with homosexuality. But psychological androgyny is a much wider concept, referring to a person's ability to be at the same time aggressive and nurturant, sensitive and rigid, dominant and submissive, regardless of gender. A psychologically androgynous person in effect doubles his or her repertoire of responses and can interact with the world in terms of a much richer and varied spectrum of opportunities. It is not surprising that creative individuals are more likely to have not only the strengths of their own gender but those of the other one, too.

Among the people interviewed by Csikzentmihalyi (1996) this form of androgyny was difficult to detect – no doubt in part because he did not use any standard test to measure its presence. Nevertheless, it was obvious that the women artists and scientists tended to be much more assertive, self-confident, and openly aggressive than women are generally brought up to be in our society. Perhaps the most noticeable evidence for the "femininity" of the men in the sample was their great preoccupation with their family and their sensitivity to subtle aspects of the environment that other men are inclined to dismiss as unimportant. But despite having these traits that are not usual to their gender, they retained the usual gender-specific traits as well. In general, the women were perfectly "feminine" and the men thoroughly "masculine," in addition to having cross-gender traits.

8. Generally, creative people are thought to be rebellious and independent. Yet it is impossible to be creative without having first internalized a domain of culture. And a person must believe in the importance of such a domain in order to learn its rules; hence, he or she must be to a certain extent a traditionalist. So it is difficult to see how a person can be creative without being both traditional and conservative and at the same time rebellious and iconoclastic. Being only traditional leaves the domain unchanged; constantly taking chances without regard to what has been valued in the past rarely leads to novelty that is accepted as an improvement. The artist Eva Zeisel, who says that the folk tradition in which she works is "her home," nevertheless produces ceramics that were recognized by the Museum of Modern Art as masterpieces of contemporary design. This is what she says about innovation for its own sake:

"This idea to create something different is not my aim, and shouldn't be anybody's aim. Because, first of all, if you are a designer or a playful person in any of these crafts, you have to be able to function a long life, and you can't always try to be different. I mean different from different from different. Secondly, wanting to be different can't be the motive of your work. Besides – if I talk too much let me know – to be different is a negative motive, and no creative thought or created thing grows out of a negative impulse. A negative impulse is always frustrating. And to be different means not like this and not like that. And the "not like" – that's why postmodernism, with the prefix of "post" couldn't work. No negative impulse can work, can produce any happy creation. Only a positive one."

But the willingness to take risks, to break with the safety of tradition, is also necessary. The economist George Stigler is very emphatic in this regard:

"I'd say one of the most common failures of able people is a lack of nerve. They'll play safe games. They'll take whatever the literature's doing and add a little bit to it. In our field, for example, we study duopoly, which is a situation in which there are two sellers. Then why not try three and see what that does. So there's a safe game to play. In innovation, you have to play a less safe game, if it's going to be interesting. It's not predictable that it'll go well."

9. ***Most creative persons are very passionate about their work, yet they can be extremely objective about it as well.*** The energy generated by this conflict between attachment and detachment has been mentioned by many as being an important part of their work. Why this is the case is relatively clear. Without the passion, we soon lose interest in a difficult task. Yet without being objective about it, our work is not very good and lacks creadibility. So the creative process tends to be what some respondents called a yin-yang alternation between these two extremes. Here is how the historian Natalie Davis puts it:

"I am sometimes like a mother trying to bring the past to life again. I love what I am doing and I love to write. I just have a great deal of affect invented in bringing these people to life again, in some way. It doesn't mean that I love my characters, necessarily, these people from the past. But I love to find out about them and re-create them or their situation. I think it is very important to find a way to be detached from what you write, so that you can't be so identified with your work that you can't accept criticism and response, and that is the danger of having as much affect as I do. But I an aware of that and of when I think it is particularly important to detach oneself from the work, and that is something where age really does help."

10. ***Finally, the openness and sensitivity of creative individuals often exposes them to suffering and pain yet also a great deal of enjoyment.*** The suffering is easy to understand. The greater sensitivity can cause slights and anxieties that are nor usually felt by the rest of us. Most would agree with Rabinow's words: "Inventors have a low threshold of pain. Thing bother them." A badly designed machine causes pain to an inventive engineer, just as the creative writer is hurt when reading bad prose. Being alone at the forefront of a discipline also makes you exposed and vulnerable. Eminence invites criticism and often vicious attacks. When an artist has invested years in making a sculpture, or a scientist in developing a theory, it is devastating if nobody cares.

Weisberg (1992) believes, that creative scientists are different from non-creative scientists in their need to be free of rules (flexibility), in their need for recognition by their peers, and by the possession of strong aesthetic feelings about their work. Creative scientists consistently talk about their desire to produce theories or to design experiments that are simple, elegant, and beautiful, which is taken to be evidence for an aesthetic component in scientific judgment. Creative scientists have also been found to differ from the non-creative in their sensitivity or in their ability to be open to new experiences. This latter characteristic is particularly important because it makes creative scientists more sensitive to scientific problems than are their non-creative colleagues. Artistic genius includes the ability to move others emotionally through one's work, and those who can do so are more sensitive and open to feelings.

Ever since the Romantic movement gained ascendance a few centuries ego, artists have been expected to suffer in order to demonstrate the sensitivity of their souls. In fact, research shows that artists and writer do have unusually high rates of psychopathology and addictions. But what is the cause, what is the affect? The poet Mark Strand comments:

"There have been a lot of unfortunate cases of writers, painters, who have been melancholic, depressed, taken their own lives. I don't think it goes with the territory. I think those people would have been depressed, or alcoholic, suicidal, whatever, even if they weren't writing. I just think it's their characterological makeup. Whether that characterological makeup drove them to write or to paint, as well as to alcohol or to suicide, I don't know. I know there are an awful lot of healthy writers and painters who have no thoughts of suicide. I think it's a myth, by and large. It creates a special aura, a frailty, around the artist to say that he lives so close to the edge. He's so responsive to the world around him, so sensitive, so driven to respond to it, it's almost unbearable. That he must escape either through drugs or alcohol, finally suicide, the burden of consciousness is so great. But the burden of consciousness is great for people who don't – you know – want to kill themselves."

It is also true that deep interest and involvement in obscure subjects often goes un-rewarded, or even brings on ridicule. Divergent thinking is often perceived as deviant by the majority, and so the creative person may feel isolated and misunderstood. These occupational hazards do come with the territory, so to speak, and it is difficult to see how a person could be creative and at the same time insensitive to them.

Perhaps the most difficult thing for a creative individual to bear is the sense of loss and emptiness experienced when, for some reason or another, he or she cannot work. This is especially painful when a person feels one's creativity drying out; then the whole self-concept is jeopardized, as Mark Strand suggests:

"Yeah, there's a momentary sereneness, a sense of satisfaction, when you come up with an idea that you think is worth pursuing. Another form of that is when you have completed, where you've done as much as you can with an idea that you thought was worth working on. Then you sort of bask in the glow or two more of wine at night because you don't feel you have to go upstairs and look at anything again.

And then you're beginning again. You hope. Sometimes the hiatus will last not overnight but for weeks, months, and years. And the longer the hiatus is between books that you're committed to finishing, the more painful and frustrating life becomes. When I say "painful," that's probably too grandiose a term for the pretty frustration one feels. But if it goes on, and on, and you develop what people call a writer's block, it's painful, because your identity's at stake. If you're not writing, and you're a writer and known as a writer, what are you?"

Yet when the person is working in the area of his or her expertise, worries and cares fall away, replaced by a sense of bliss. Perhaps the most important quality, the one that is most consistently present in all creative individuals, is the ability to enjoy the process of creation for its own sake. Without this traits poets would give up striving for perfection and would write commercial jungles, economists would work for banks where they would earn at least twice as much as they do at the university, physicists would stop doing basic research and join industrial laboratories where the conditions are better and the expectations more predictable. In fact, enjoyment is very important part of creativity.

Margaret Butler is a computer scientist and mathematician, the first woman elected a fellow of the American Nuclear Society. In describing her work, like most of our respondents, she keeps stressing this element of fun, of enjoyment. In answer to the question "Of your accomplishments at work, what are you most proud of?" She answers:

"Well, in my work I think that the most interesting and exciting things that I have done were in the early days at Argonne when we were building computers. We worked on a team to design one of the first computers. We developed image analysis software with the people in the biology division for scanning chromosomes and trying to do automatic karyotyping, and I think that was the most fun that I had in all of my forty-plus years at the lab."

It is interesting that this response, stressing fun and excitement, came in answer to a question about what she is most proud of in her work. Later on, she says:

"I worked and worked. You work hard. You try to do your best. When we were working on the chromosome project, Jim [her husband] and I spent sometimes the whole night over there working. We would come out in the morning and the sun would be coming up. Science is very much fun. And I think women should have the opportunity to have fun."

These ten pairs of contrasting personality traits might be the most telling characteristics of creative people. Of course, this list is to a certain extent arbitrary. It could be argued that many other important traits have been left out. But what is important to keep in mind is that these conflicting traits – or any conflicting traits – are usually difficult to find in the same person. Yet without the second pole, new ideas will not be recognized. And without the first, they will not be survives to change a domain is usually the work of someone who can operate at both ends of these polarities – and that is the kind of person we call "creative."

GENIUS PRODUCTIVITY AND ERRORS

One characteristic believed to be associated with scientific genius is a **greater sensitivity to potentially solvable problems** of great import. The non-genius may waste time on problems that have no solution or, if solvable, are not important in the long run. Studies of the lives of successful people, however, including Leonardo da Vinci and Isaac Newton, provide much evidence that many of them

Our society tends to view great people in heroic light, that leads to the belief that such individuals can do no wrong in their professional judgments (Weisberg, 1992). Contrary to this assumption, there are great fluctuations in the "genius" of a given individual, that indicates that attempting to measure the personality characteristics that form the basis for genius is a mistaken enterprise, because the same characteristics are related to both genius and non-genius production.

spent significant portions of their careers working on problems that similarly turned out to be of little import, and which may have not had solutions.

Leonardo da Vinci is the classic example of the type of individual as living "a lifetime of original thinking" (Barron, 1981). The common version of Leonardo's life centers on his wide-ranging investigations and insightful commentary on all areas of human study.

This view of Leonardo has recently come under revision based on modern analyses of his notebooks and their relations to the works of others. Many ideas in Leonardo's notebooks he copied or paraphrased from others, sometimes without acknowledgment. In addition, the breadth of interests revealed in his notebooks, ranging from painting to military engineering and anatomy, were subjects that trained artists of the time often studied and were not peculiar to Leonardo. Furthermore, many of the projects described in his notebooks were never put into practice, a parallel to his tendency not to complete artistic works.

Leonardo also made his share of mistakes, some of them major. In his speculations on human flight, for example, he spent years considering a flying machine that flew by flapping its wings, a design that was not successful. In addition, he developed a new method of painting on plaster that allowed him to paint his fresco of the Last Supper at a more leisurely pace, but unfortunately this method resulted in the paint's fading prematurely, so that the Last Supper is in relatively poor condition today. Examples of this sort simply indicate that even the greatest scientists and inventors among is are nonetheless human, and as such are fallible.

In Chrales Hope's opinion (Weisberg, 1992), Leonardo's chief claim as a theorist of art was the idea that the artists should strive to reproduce as accurately as possible the external world. In Leonardo's view, painters were unique in their ability to move the audience because of the vividness with which they could depict scenes, that places painting above poetry in effectiveness. Leonardo was not the first Italian artist to attempt to represent the world as realistically as possible, but he did so at a high level of energy and commitment. This indicates that one of the unique aspects of Leonardo's personality may have been a commitment to his work, which is important characteristic of genius.

Isaac Newton is acknowledged to be one of the greatest scientists who ever lived. He developed the laws of physics that bear his name, produced seminal work on light, and invented the calculus, among other accomplishments. In addition, however, Newton also spent twenty-five years in the study of alchemy, searching in secret for mysterious elixirs and forces to influence nature. This alchemical work led to no outcome of value, although Newton wrote thousands of pages on it.

There thousands examples about creative people failures and errors. Artists of the highest levels of accomplishment also do not exhibit constancy of genius throughout their careers: no artist produces only masterpieces. Wayne Dennis's analysis of the careers of well-known composers reveals an essentially constant relationship between the production of major and minor works, classified on the basis of their being discussed in music reference works. This has been formulated by Simonton as the constant-probability-of-success model. In the periods in which composers produced relatively large numbers of major works, or works of genius, they also produced large numbers of minor works.

This findings raises a question about the alleged sensitivities of genius. If a genius makes public a piece of work, presumably he or she would believe it to be worthy, and not simply a quick way to earn some money (although the latter may also be the case). If posterity deems the work a minor work, however, then the artist's judgment is mistaken. This raises the possibility that the artist of genius, contrary to our culture's beliefs, is not always particularly sensitive to the responsiveness of the audience.

The Relative Nature of Genius

As Weisberg (1992) stressed in his book Creativity, one of the unarticulated assumptions motivating the genius view is that "genius" is a psychological characteristic of an individual that can be measured as can any other. However, a number of recent theorists have come to the conclusion that ***genius is not a psychological characteristic***, and therefore ***one cannot measure genius***. The genius view assumes that the greatness of an individual (that is, the ability to produce works of great value and influence) is ***the result of cognitive and personality characteristics***, but if genius is not a psychological characteristic, then the greatness of an individual does not reside in that individual. The genius view also assumes that ***a product becomes great*** (that is, valued and influential) because of the ***extraordinary characteristics of the individual who produced it***. If, however, the creator does not possess extraordinary characteristics, it follow that the greatness of a product does not reside in the product, either. Finally, these two conclusions imply that "greatness" is not something that is "put into" the product by its creator.

Although it is hard to overstate geniuses brilliance, recent scientific research reveals that *people usually underestimated their potential for learning and creativity* (Gelb, 1998). Ninety-five percent of what we know about the capabilities of the human brain has been learned in the last twenty years. Schools, universities, and corporations are only beginning to apply this emerging understanding of human potential.

In *The Book of Genius* Tony Buzan and Raymond Keene make the world's first objective attempt to rank the greatest geniuses of history. Rating their subjects in categories including "Originality," "Versatility," "Dominance-in-Field," "Universality-of-Vision," and "Strength and Energy," they offer the following as their "top ten":

10. Albert Einstein
9. Phidias (architect of Athens)
8. Alexander the Great
7. Thomas Jefferson
6. Sir Issac Newton
5. Michelangelo
4. Johann Wolfgang von Goethe
3. The Great Pyramid Builders
2. William Shakespeare
1. Leonardo da Vinci

The Seven Da Vincian Principles of creativity are:

Curiosita – An insatiably curious approach to life and an unrelenting quest for continouos learning

Dimostrazione – A commitment to test knowledge through experience, persistence, and a willingness to learn from mistakes.

Sensazione – The continual refinement of the senses, especially sight, as the means to enliven experience

Sfumato (literally "Going up in Smoke") – A willingness to embrace ambiguity, paradox, and uncertainty.

Arte/Scienza – The development of grace, ambidexterity, fitness, and poise.

Connessione – A recognition of and appreciation for the interconnectedness of all things and phenomena. Systems thinking.

Improving Creativity

1. ***Brainwriting*** – solo brainstorming, is arriving at creative ideas by jotting them down yourself. It is often best to edit the ideas a few hours or even a day later.
2. ***Forced-association technique***. A widely used method of releasing creativity is to make forced associations between the properties of two objects in order to solve a problem. The method works in this way. You select a word at random from a dictionary. Next you list al the properties and attributes of this word. You then force-fit these properties and attributes to the problem you are trying to solve. The properties of the random object are related to the properties

of the object involved in your problem. A new way of delivering medicine was supposedly developed by listing the properties of a time bomb. One key property was "slow release," leading to medicine that goes to work several hours after it was taken – a time capsule.

3. ***Develop a synergy between both sides of the brain.*** Logical people are "left brained" and creative people are "right brained." The left hemisphere tends to be analytical and logical and concerned with words. The right hemisphere is more holistic and intuitive and concerned with spatial relations. Because of this, creativity involves contributions from the integrated activity of both hemispheres. The message for creativity improvement is that both logical and intuitive thinking are required. Synergy: a phenomenon of group effort whereby the whole is greater that the sum of the parts.

4. ***The Raudsepp exercise and principles.*** Eugene Raudsepp has developed a set of 12 exercises and principles as a guide to creative growth. Many of his suggestions have been incorporated into current creativity training programs.

- *Keep track of your ideas at all times*. Keeping an idea notebook at hand will help you to capture a permanent record of flashes of insights and good ideas borrowed from others.
- *Pose new questions every day.* If your mind is questioning and inquiring it will be creatively active. It is also a mind that constantly enlarges the circumference of its awareness. Have fun, and enjoy your creative probings and experiences.
- *Maintain competence in your field.* The information explosion makes knowledge become obsolete quickly. Having current facts in mind gives you the raw material to form creative links from one bit of information to another.
- *Read widely in fields that are not directly related to your field of interest.* Look for the relationship between what you read and what you already know. Once you learn how to cross-index the pieces of information you gather, you will be able to cross-fertilize seemingly unrelated ideas.
- *Avoid rigid patterns of doing things.* Strive to overcome fixed ideas and look for new viewpoints. Experiment and always generate several alternative solutions to your problems. Develop the ability to let go of one idea in favor of another.
- *Be open and receptive to your own as well as to others' ideas.* Seize on tentative, half-formed ideas and hunches. A new idea seldom arrives in finished form. Entertain and generate your own fantastic or silly ideas. If you are interested to the ideas of others, you will learn new things that can help you behave creatively.
- *Be alert in observation.* Search for the similarities, differences, and unique features of things and ideas. The greater the number of new associations and relationships you form, the greater your chances of arriving at creative and original combinations and solutions.
- *Engage in creative hobbies.* Develop hobbies that allow you to produce something with your hands. You can also keep your brain tuned up by playing games and doing puzzles and exercises. Creative growth is possible only through constant and active use of your mind.
- *Improve your sense of humor and laugh easily.* Humor helps to relieve tension, and most people are more productively creative when they are relaxed. Also, humor is an everyday expression of creativity.
- *Adopt a risk-taking attitude.* The fear of failure suppresses creativity, so be willing to fail on occasion.
- *Have courage and self-confidence.* Move ahead on the assumption that you can solve your problems or achieve your goals. Many people surrender just when they are on the brink of a solution, so persist when you are seeking a creative solution to a problem.
- *Learn to know and understand yourself.* Creativity is an expression of one's uniqueness. To be creative, then, is to oneself.

5. Be an explorer, artist, judge, and lawyer. Adopt four roles in your thinking.

- ***Explorer.*** *Speak to people in different fields and get ideas that you can use.*
- ***Artist.*** *Stretch your imagination. Spend about 5 percent of your day asking "what if" questions.*
- ***Judge.*** *After developing some wild ideas, evaluate these ideas.*
- ***Lawyer.*** *Negotiate and find ways to implement your ideas within your field or place of work.*

What We Can Learn from Great Thinkers?

Thomas Edison

Genius is one percent inspiration and ninety-nine percent perspiration.

Thomas Edison

Thomas Alva Edison was born on February 11, 1847, in Milan, Ohio, the youngest of seven children born to Samuel and Nancy Elliott Edison. His parents had no special mechanical background. He began to lose his hearing after having scarlet fever as a young child. As he grew older his deafness increased until finally he was totally deaf in his left ear and had only 10% hearing in his right ear. Edison did not consider this a "handicap" and said that it was rather an advantage as it gave him more time to think because he did not have to listen to foolish "small talk."

By 1862 young "Al," as his father called him, was printing, publishing and selling The Weekly Herald on a train of the Grand Trunk Railroad out of Port Huron, Michigan. This was the first newspaper printed on a moving train. Later he learned to be a telegraph operator and worked at that trade throughout the Central Western states as well as Canada, always studying and experimenting to improve the equipment.

In 1868 Edison made his first patented invention, the Electrical Vote Recorder. Congress was apparently not interested in purchasing this as it counted votes too quickly. Edison vowed he would never again invent anything unless there was a "commercial demand" for it.

At age 23 Edison made his first sale of an invention, a Universal Stock Tickler, to General Lefferts, the head of the Gold and Stock Telegraph Co. Edison had decided that the invention was worth $5000 but was ready to accept $3000 when Lefferts said, "How would $40,000 strike you?" In later years Edison reported that he had almost fainted, but managed to stammer that the offer seemed fair enough. That money was used to set up Edison's first business.

Edison created the world's first "invention factory". He and his partners invented, built and shipped the product - all in the same complex. This was a new way to do business. Today many businesses have copied Edison's invention factory design.

A business friend once asked Edison about the secret to his success. Edison replied, "Genius is hard work, stick-to-itiveness, and common sense". But his "common sense" was very uncommon. More patents were issued to Edison than have been issued to any other single person in U.S. history: 1,093. A patent is something that says no one can copy your idea.

Thomas Edison's interests varied widely and he received patents in many areas. For example, in 1876 he patented his Electric Pen which was later used in mimeograph systems and in 1877 he applied for a patent on a Carbon Telephone Transmitter that led to a commercial telephone and later, radio broadcasting.

Considered his most original invention, the Phonograph was patented in 1878. Edison sketched out this new and different idea he had, handed it down to two men who worked in his shop, John Kruesi and Charles Batchelor, and they made the machine. Edison took tin foil, wrapped it around the cylinder and casually said, "This machine is going to talk." He recited "Mary had a little lamb" into the strange device and to everyone's amazement (even Edison's) the machine repeated the words exactly.

Why was Edison a Genius?

- Edison believed in hard work and determination.
- Work habits: Edison sometimes worked twenty hours a day.
- He was very good at bringing people together to make an inventing team.
- He was able to reason with many different people.
- He encouraged creativity in his employees.
- He knew a lot about what his competitors were working on.
- He almost never worked on any invention that wasn't already being worked on by several other people.

SUMMARY

1. We all possess the thought processes underlying creativity. Actual production of creative works, on the other hand, involves much more than cognitive processes – among other things, very high degrees of persistence and motivation, which we do not all possess (Weisberg, 1992).
2. Once a creative work is produced, other factors, mostly out of the creator's control, determine whether or not the creator will be considered to possess genius.
3. Creative and successful at the same time people have several features in common:
4. Knowledge. Creative thinking requires a broad background of information including facts and observations.
5. Intellectual abilities. Creative people tend to be bright rather than brilliant.
6. Personality factors:

- Intense preoccupation with a field of creative expression of discovery. They can pursue their creative interests for long stretches of time without becoming bored or restless.
- They are frequently nonconformists who place a high value on their own independence and originality. They do not have a strong need to gain approval from the group.
- Well-developed sense of humor, manifesting itself in witty comments, practical jokes, and other forms of playfulness.
- Tend to have a positive self-image. They feel good about themselves.
- They have ability to tolerate isolation. Isolation is useful because it helps put a person into a receptive mood for ideas.
- Type T personality. Their thrill-seeking tendencies often lead to outstanding creativity because finding imaginative solutions to problems is thrilling.
- Creative people are persistent. Finding creative solutions to problems is hard work and requires intense concentration.
- They are resistant to frustration in the sense that they have a high toleration fro ambiguity and chaos.

ABRAHAM MASLOW'S SELF-ACTUALIZING PEOPLE

Listed below are a series of 16 characteristics of a self-actualizing individual as described by Abraham Maslow. Self-actualizing here is defined as a person who is in the process of fulfilling their potential. After slowly and thoroughly reading each characteristic, rate yourself on the scale listed below that characteristic from 1 to 10. Your results will give you both a linear and intuitive representation of your strength and weaknesses in moving towards being a self-actualizing person. Spend some time focusing on why you are stronger in some characteristics than others. What is it that has given you a higher score? What might you do to make your score higher on any given characteristic. The highest total you can receive is 160 points. How close are you? What you need to improve to get closer to those great people that possess such characteristics?

From his informal study Maslow concluded that **self-actualizing people** manifest the following characteristics.

1. More efficient perception of reality. Self-actualizers are able to perceive the world around them, including other people, correctly and efficiently. They see reality exactly as it is, not as they might want or need it to be. They are less emotional and more objective about their perceptions; they do not allow their hopes and fears to distort their perceptions. Because of their superior perception, self-actualizers can more easily detect phoniness and dishonesty in others. Maslow discovered that this ability to see more efficiently extended to many other areas of life, including art, music, science, politics and philosophy.

The self-actualized person's perception is also less distorted by expectations, anxiety, stereotypes, false optimism, or pessimism. Maslow called this non-biased kind of perception "being or B-cognition." Related to this highly objective perception is the finding that self-actualizing people have a greater tolerance of ambiguity and uncertainty than do most people. They feel comfortable with problems and puzzles that have no definite right or wrong solutions. They welcome doubt, indefiniteness, and uncharted paths.
   1 2 3 4 5 6 7 8 9 10   _____

2. Acceptance of self, others, and nature. Self-actualizers can accept themselves the way they are. They are not overly critical of their own shortcomings, frailties, and weaknesses. They are not burdened by undue guilt, shame, and anxiety – emotional states which are so prevalent in the general population.

Self-acceptance is also vividly expressed at the physiological level. Self-actualizers accept their own animal nature with a kind of gusto or *joie de vivre*. They have hearty appetites, sleep well, and enjoy their sex lives without unnecessary inhibition. Basic biological processes (e.g., urination, pregnancy, menstruation, growing old) are considered part of human nature and are graciously accepted.

In similar fashion, they are accepting of others and of humankind in general. They have no compelling need to instruct, inform, or control. They can tolerate weakness in others and are not threatened by their strengths. They realize that people suffer, grow old, and eventually die.
   1 2 3 4 5 6 7 8 9 10   _____

3. Spontaneity, simplicity, and naturalness. The behavior of self-actualizing people is marked by spontaneity and simplicity, by an absence of artificiality or straining for effect. This does not imply consistently unconventional, natural, and spontaneous. Their unconventionality is not intended to impress others and may even be suppressed in order not to distress others, so that they may even abide by ceremonies and rituals. Thus, they may conform if it means protecting themselves or others from pain or injustice. For this reason, if it suits their purposes, self-actualizers may tolerate practices within educational institutions that they regard as foolish, repetitive, or mind-debilitating. However, when the situation warrants it, they can be uncompromising even at the price of ostracism and censure. In short, they do not hesitate to defy social rules when it is deemed necessary to do so.
   1 2 3 4 5 6 7 8 9 10   _____

4. Problem-centered. Without exception, Maslow found his subjects to be committed to some task, duty, vocation, or beloved job which they regard as important. That is, they are not ego-centered but rather oriented toward problems beyond their immediate needs, problems to which they are dedicated like a mission in life. In this sense, they live to work rather than work to live; their work is subjectively experienced as a defining characteristic of themselves. Maslow portrayed the self-actualizer's commitment to and absorption in work as analogous to a love affair: the job and person seem "meant for each other.... the person and (the) job fit together and belong together perfectly like a key and a lock" (1971, pp. 301 – 302).

Self-actualizers are also deeply concerned with philosophical and ethical issues. Accordingly, they live and work within the widest frame of reference, tending to devote themselves to non-personal "missions" or tasks. Such a lifestyle denotes a lack of concern for the trivial and petty, thus enabling them to clearly distinguish between the important and the unimportant issues in the world.
   1 2 3 4 5 6 7 8 9 10   _____

5. Detachment: need for privacy. They are described by Maslow as having an intense need for privacy and solitude. Because they do not have a clinging relationship with others, they can enjoy the richness and fullness of other's friendship.

Unfortunately, this quality of detachment is not always understood or accepted by others. In social encounters they are often viewed by "normal" people as aloof, reserved, snobbish, and cold. This is particularly the case for those people who have not had their love and belongingness needs adequately satisfied. But in self-actualizing people, these deficiency needs have been met, and , thus, they do not need other people in the usual sense of friendship. As a result, there is a need for another level of encounter – with the self. As one of Maslow's subjects put it, "When I'm alone, I'm with my best friend." This comment could be constructed as the height of narcissism. Maslow's point is simply that self-actualizers can be alone without being lonely.

The need for privacy and self-reliance encompasses other aspects of behavior as well. For instance, they remain calm and serene during periods of personal misfortune or setback. Maslow explained that this comes in part from the self-actualizer's tendency to stand by his or her own interpretation of situations instead of relying upon what other people think or feel about matters. In effect, they are self-movers, resisting society's attempts to make them adhere to social convention.

1   2   3   4   5   6   7   8   9   10   _____

6. *Autonomy:* independence of culture and environment. Self-actualizers are free to act independently of their physical and social environment. This autonomy enables them to rely on their own potentialities and latent resources for growth and development. Thus, for example, truly self-actualizing college students do not really need the "right" academic atmosphere on campus to learn. They can learn anywhere because they have themselves. In this sense, they are a "self-contained" entity.

Healthy people also have a high degree of self-direction and "free will." They regard themselves as self-governed, active, responsible, and self-disciplined agents in determining their own destinies. They are strong enough to be oblivious to others' opinions and affection; thus, they shun honors, status, prestige, and popularity. Such extrinsic satisfactions are perceived as less significant than self-development and inner growth. Of course, attaining this point of relative independence depends upon having receiving love and security from others in the past.

1   2   3   4   5   6   7   8   9   10   _____

7. *Continued freshness of appreciation.* They possess the capacity to appreciate even the most ordinary events in their lives with a sense of newness, awe, pleasure, and even ecstasy. Thus, for instance, the hundredth rainbow is as lovely and majestic as the first; a ride through the woods never ceases to be a joyful experience; watching a child a play uplifts the spirit. Unlike others who take their blessings for granted, self-actualizers have an appreciation of their good fortune, health, friends, and political freedom. They seldom complain about a boring, uninteresting experience.

A key aspect of this quality of open responsiveness to new experience is that self-actualizers avoid lumping experiences into categories and then dismissing them. Rather, their subjective experience is very rich, and the day-to-day business of living and working remains thrilling and exciting to them.

1   2   3   4   5   6   7   8   9   10   _____

8. *Peak of mystic experiences.* Many of these people commonly had what Maslow called *peak experience*. These are moments of intense excitement and high tension as well as those of relaxation, peacefulness, blissfulness, and stillness. Representing the most ecstatic moments of life, such occurrences usually come from love and sexual climax, bursts of creativity, insight, discovery, and fusion with nature. These people can "turn on" without artificial stimulants. Just being alive turns them on.

For Maslow, peak or mystic experiences are not theological or supernatural in nature, though they are religious at their core. He found that "peakers" feel more in harmony with the world, lose their self-awareness or transcend it, feel simultaneously more powerful and more helpless than before, and become less conscious of time and space. According to Maslow, the peak experiences that really change a person come about when they are earned: "The person comes to some glorious insight as the result of a year of sweating on a psychoanalytic couch; or a philosopher who has been working for fifteen years at some problem comes to an illumination" (Hardeman, 1979, p.24).

1   2   3   4   5   6   7   8   9   10   _____

9. *Social interest.* Even though self-actualizers are sometimes troubled, saddened, and even enraged by the shortcomings of the human race, they nevertheless possess a deep feeling of kinship for humanity. Consequently, they have a genuine desire to help improve the lot of their fellow mortals. This nurturant attitude is evidenced by a feeling of compassion, sympathy, and affection for all humanity.

Oftentimes this is a special kind of brotherhood, like the attitude of an older brother or sister toward younger siblings.
1 2 3 4 5 6 7 8 9 10 _____

10. Profound interpersonal relations. Self-actualizing people tend to form deeper and closer personal relationships than those of the "average" adult. For the most part, those with whom they associate are likely to be healthier and closer to self-actualization than the average person. That is, self-actualizers are more inclined to associate intimately with others of similar character, talent, and capacity ("birds of a feather"), though their social interest allows them to have a special feeling of empathy for less healthy people. Usually their circle of intimate friends is small, since befriending in the self-actualizing style demands a great deal of time and effort. They also have especially tender feelings for children and are easily touched by them.
1 2 3 4 5 6 7 8 9 10 _____

11. Democratic character structure. Maslow described self-actualizers as being "democratic" in the deepest sense. Since they are free of prejudice, they show respect for other people regardless of their class, race, religion, sex, age, occupation, or other group membership traits. Moreover, they are willing to learn from anybody without adopting a superior or authoritarian attitude. The self-actualizing musician, for example, is genuinely respectful toward the skilled mechanic because the mechanic possesses skills and knowledge that the musician does not possess. At the same time, Maslow discovered that self-actualizers do not indiscriminately equalize all human beings: "These individuals, themselves elite, select for their friends elite, but this is an elite of character, capacity, and talent, rather than of birth, race, blood, name, family, age, youth, fame, or power" (1987, p. 139).
1 2 3 4 5 6 7 8 9 10 _____

12. Discrimination between means and ends. In their day-to-day living, self-actualizing people show less confusion, inconsistency, and conflict than the average person about what is right or wrong, good or bad. They have definite moral and ethical standard, although very few of them are religious in the orthodox sense of the term. Maslow's subjects also showed an unusually keen ability to discriminate between ends (goals) and the means for accomplishing those ends. On the other hand, they often enjoy the means, or instrumental behavior leading to a goal, which more impatient persons would dislike. That is, they are more likely to appreciate doing something for its own sake (e.g., exercising) and not just because it is a means to some other end (e.g., fitness).
1 2 3 4 5 6 7 8 9 10 _____

13. Philosophical sense of humor. Another distinguishing characteristic of self-actualizing people is their distinct preference for philosophical, non-hostile humor. Whereas the average person may enjoy humor that pokes fun at another's inferiority, that hurt or degrades someone, or that is "off-color," the healthy person typically finds humor expressing the foolishness of humanity in general most appealing. Abraham Lincoln's humor serves as a relevant example. His jokes always had something to convey, a purpose beyond just producing a laugh. They often dealt with a parable or fable. Maslow noted that philosophical humor usually elicit a smile rather than a laugh. This attitude toward humor often makes the self-actualizer appear rather sober and serious.
1 2 3 4 5 6 7 8 9 10 _____

14. Creativeness. Maslow found that, without exception, self-actualizing people were creative in some sense of the word. However, the creativeness manifested by his subjects was different from unusual talent or genius as reflected in poetry, art, music, or science. Maslow likened it to the natural and spontaneous creativeness found in unspoiled children. This kind of self-actualizing creativity appears in everyday life as an expression of a personality that is perceptive, innovative, and refreshingly simple.

The self-actualizing person need not write books, compose music, or produce art objects to be creative. In speaking of his mother-in-law, whom he regarded as self-actualizing, Maslow vividly emphasized this fact. He said that while his mother-in-law had no special talents as a writer or artist, she was highly creative in preparing home-made soup. Maslow remarked that first-rate soup was more creative than second-rate poetry any day!
1 2 3 4 5 6 7 8 9 10 _____

15. Resistance to enculturation. Finally, self-actualizers are in harmony with their culture and yet maintain a certain inner detachment from it. Being essentially autonomous and self-reliant, they are free to resist social and cultural pressures to think and behave along certain lines. This resistance to enculturation does not mean that self-actualizers are unconventional or antisocial in all realms of behavior. For instance, they remain well within the limits of conformity concerning choice of clothes, speech, food, and the manner of doing things, which are not really important enough to prompt objection. Similarly, they do not waste energy fighting against insignificant social rituals and regulations of society. However, they can become extremely independent and unconventional when they feel basic issues are involved. For this reason, they are sometimes considered as rebellious and eccentric by those who do not take the time to know and appreciate them. Self-actualizers also manifest a calm, long-term commitment to cultural improvement. Although cognizant of society's imperfections, they accept the fact that social change can be slow and painstaking but is best achieved by working within the system.

    1 2 3 4 5 6 7 8 9 10   _____

Annotated Bibliography

Basadur, M. & Thompson, R. (1986) Usefulness of the ideation principle of extended effort in real world professional and managerial creative problem solving. Journal of Creative Behavior, 20 (1), 23-34.

"These results lead the authors to conclude that the belief that extended effort is useful in creative problem solving is supported for real world managerial and technical problem solving in this study. While it does not appear that the most preferred ideas are more likely to come more often at the very end than at the very beginning of the idea series, nevertheless, it does appear that they are more likely to occur after the first early burst of ideas". (p.31)

Brockman, J. (Ed.) (1993) Creativity. New York: Touchstone. (153.35/B864c)

Includes contributions from Teresa Amabile, 'Questions of creativity', Howard Gardner, 'Seven creators of the modern era', Richard Restak, 'The creative brain', and dean Simonton, 'Genius and chance: A Darwinian perspective'.

Brown, M. (1983) The Inventive 'I': Innovation to Ingenuity. La Habra: Foxtail Press.

Includes chapters on 'The character of invention', 'Innovation applies imagination to reality', 'Resourceful thinking produces ingenuity', 'The process of inventing' and 'The patent system registers invention'.

Brown, A.E. & Jeffcott, H.A. (1970) Absolutely Mad Inventions. New York: Dover Publications. (608.773/B877B) An illustrated compilation of proposed inventions from the records of the United States Patent Office.

Castiglione, L.V. (1986) Creativity: Concept to measurement to educational goal. Design for Arts in Education, 88 (1), 27-32.

Attempts to clarify what is meant by creativity. Warns that "there is no substantial evidence that creativity training actually generalizes far beyond the classroom door to everyday behavior." (p.32)

Chislett, L.M. (1994) Integrating the CPS and Schoolwide Enrichment Models to enhance creative productivity. Roeper Review, 17 (1), 4-7.

"This article compares the components of Creative Problem Solving (CPS) to the investigative procedure of Type III enrichment in the Schoolwide Enrichment Model to show that the two models are complimentary. Training in and use of the CPS heuristic with Type III enrichment is offered an integrated approach for authenticating problem solving activity and enhancing student creative productivity." (p.4)

Craft, A. (2000) Creativity Across the Primary Curriculum. London: Routledge. (370.157/C885c)

'This book draws on empirical research and philosophical thinking from both sides of the Atlantic to explore the nature of the creative mind. The role of play is investigated and distinctions made between play and creativity. ... The personal and professional identities of teachers are explored and ways of analyzing and describing creative practice are considered.' (p.i)

Davis, G.A. & Scott, J.A. (1978) Training Creative Thinking. New York: Robert E. Krieger. (153.35/D261T)

Contains 23 papers covering synectics, creative thinking techniques, creativity training, and examples and rationales of test tasks for assessing creative abilities.

Davis, G.A. (1986) Creativity Is Forever. Dubuque: Kendall/Hunt. (153.42/D261c, 1986)

"This book was prepared for any adult reader interested in understanding the topic of creativity, becoming a more creative person, or teaching others to think more creatively." (p.xi)

Davis, G.A. (1987) What to teach when you teach creativity. Gifted Child Today, 10 (1), 7-10.

"The present recommendations to 1) teach creativity consciousness, 2) reinforce creative traits, 3) help students understand creativity, 4) teach principles of creativity and problem solving, 5) teach idea- finding techniques, 6) exercise creative abilities, and 7) involve students in creative activities should help make creativity training more sensible, comprehensible, organized and effective." (p.10)

Davis, G.A. (1989) Objectives and activities for teaching creative thinking. Gifted Child Quarterly, 33 (2), 81-84. Outlines five objectives and lists activities and materials designed to help achieve these.

de Bono. E. (1986) CoRT Thinking. Chicago: SRA. (CR153.42/D287c/1986)

Comprises five packs of student workcards, each of which may be used, and borrowed, separately. CoRT 1, 'Breadth', is the most commonly used but see also CoRT 2, 'Organization', CoRT 3, 'Interaction', CoRT 4, 'Creativity' and CoRT 5, 'Information and Feeling'.

de Bono. E. (1986) CoRT Thinking: Teacher's Notes New York: Pergamon. (CR153.42/D287c, 1986)

There is one of these booklets for each of the sets of workcards (see above), with parallel numbering and subtitles, e.g., '1: Breadth'. Each booklet provides lesson notes and background information.

de Bono, E. (1992) Six Thinking Hats for Schools. Melbourne: Hawker Brownlow Education. (CR153.42/D287s) [v.1 - v.4, see below]
The six hats are explained and for each there is provided a set of 'Teacher notes' and set of 'Student activities'. If borrowing please note that there are four versions of this resource book:

Book 1 (Lower primary - v.1), Book 2 (middle/upper primary - v.2), Book 3 (Lower secondary - v.3) and Book 4 (Middle/upper secondary - v.4).

de Bono, E. (1994) Parallel Thinking. London: Viking. (153.42/D287p)

Subtitled 'from Socratic to de Bono thinking'. "Traditional thinking uses adversarial argument and refutation to explore a subject. Parallel thinking uses cooperative 'parallel' thinking. ... The essence of parallel thinking is to move forward from possibilities, in contrast to exercising judgment at every moment." (p.x.)

Delcourt, M.A.B. (1993) Creative productivity among secondary school students: Combining energy, interest, and imagination. Gifted Child Quarterly, 37 (1), 23-31.

"This study identified 18 secondary school students who exhibited creative productive behavior by engaging in first-hand investigations of self-selected topics both in and out of school. (p.30) "When students know that they can make significant contributions through their projects, they derive a sense of pride from their actions and are more likely to exhibit these types of behaviors in the future." (p.31)

Duffy, B. (1998) Supporting Creativity and Imagination in the Early Years. Buckingham: Open University Press. (370.157/D858s) [See under Early Childhood]

Eberle, B. (1990) Scamper On. Melbourne: Hawker Brownlow. (371.397/E16s)

A set of activities and ideas associated with the SCAMPER technique.

Eriksson, G.I. (1989) Developing creative thinking through an integrated arts program for talented children. Gifted Education International, 6 (1), 8-15.

"This paper discusses the nature and development of creative thinking in relation to expression and communication in the arts based on the results of an evaluation study of an Integrated Arts Program." (p.8)

Feldhusen, J.F. & Clinkenbeard, P.R. (1986) Creativity instructional materials: A review of research. Journal of Creative Behavior, 20 (3), 153-182.

"Fostering creativity in the classroom involves the establishment of conditions for new, complex kinds of student behavior, which lead to extended involvement of the schools in real problems,, not merely 'exercises and activities.'" (p.178) Reviews various materials and approaches to teaching creativity.

Feldhusen, J.F. & Treffinger, D.J. (1977) Teaching Creative Thinking and Problem Solving. Dubuque: Kendall/Hunt. (370.152/F312T)
Covers 'Teaching children to think', 'Special needs of disadvantaged children', 'Methods of teaching creativity and problem solving', 'How to get a project started in your classroom', and a major section of 'Reviews of instructional material and books for teaching creativity and problem solving'.

Feldhusen, J.F. & Treffinger, D.J. (1980) Creative Thinking and Problem Solving in Gifted Education. Dubuque: Kendall/Hunt. (370.152/F312T, 1980)

Includes 'Teaching creative thinking and problem solving to the gifted, creative and talented', 'Methods of teaching creativity and problem solving', 'How to get a project started in your classroom', and an extensive set of reviews of commercially available material in the U.S.A.

Ferguson, V. (1987) Five reasons for a daffodil: One way of coping with creative children in the classroom. Primary Education, 18 (1), 5-9.

Describes the operation of an Inventor's Club for "bright and creative" primary school children - how they were selected, how it was organized, examples of activities undertaken and examples of children's responses to some of these.

Flack, J.D. (1989) Inventing, Inventions and Inventors. Englewood: Teacher Ideas Press. (608/F571i)

This 'teaching resource book' includes sections on the past, present and future of inventing, with a section on the humorous side of inventing and an introduction to numerous techniques such as CPS, SCAMPER, Synectics, forced relationships, futures wheels, Delphi polls, scenario writing and imagineering.

Flaherty, M.A. (1992) The effects of a holistic creativity program on the self-concept and creativity of third graders. The Journal of Creative Behavior, 26 (3), 165-171.

"The study predicted that a twelve week intervention of creative, multimodal activities would increase self-concept, and cognitive and affective creativity in third graders. The data show that subjects in the experimental group performed significantly higher than the control group on measures of self-concept, and the elaboration dimension of cognitive creativity." (p.169)

Gnezda-Smith, N. (1994) The internal forces of creativity: When hearts start to flutter. Roeper Review, 17 (2), 138-143.
"Four artistic people were interviewed, including an eleven year old, a high school student, a college student, and an adult with a well-established career. ... The people in the study described conscious and unconscious thought which alternated throughout their creative processes, emotions which precipitated creative activity and intermingled with cognition, and intrinsic motivators and rewards." (p.138)

Gudeman, J. (1984) Creative Encounters with Creative People. Carthage: Good Apple.

Includes brief biographical sketches followed by various activities associated with the lives and ideas of such people as Hans Christian Anderson, Walt Disney, Thomas Edison, Henry Ford, Helen Keller, David Livingstone, Wolfgang Mozart and Isaac Newton.

Gunter, M. (1987) Developing creative thinking. TalentEd, 19, 5-11.

A review of the de Bono's CoRT material, based on a trial with a Year 9 English class.

Hunsaker, S.L. & Callahan, C.M. (1995) Creativity and giftedness: Published instrument uses and abuses. Gifted Child Quarterly, 39 (2), 110-114.

"This article reports a study of [USA] schools' assessment of creativity as part of their identification procedures for gifted programs. ... Districts often select instruments for assessment of creativity without attending to the definition of the construct." (p.110)

Kegley, J.F. & Siggers, W.W. (1989) The creative child in an orderly environment: The parents' challenge. The Gifted Child Today, 12 (4), 2-5.

"Parents need to balance the requirements of structure with the initiative of creativity. Of the two, structure is more easily understood. Structure is clearly delineated by the rules of institutions. What is less clear are the obstacles that impede creativity." (p. 4) Nine obstacles are discussed: insecurity, fear of uncertainty, ritualistic problem solving, dogmatic dichotomous thinking, inner resourcelessness, lack of playfulness, restricted affect, forcing premature solutions to problems, and lack of self-assertiveness.

Khatena, J. (1978) The Creativity Gifted Child: Suggestions for Parents and Teachers. New York: Vantage Press. (371.95/K63c)

Discusses changing concepts of intelligence, measures of creativity, activities to stimulate creative thinking, and problems of creative children.

Kohn, A. (1987) Art for art's sake. Psychology Today, 21 (9), 52-57.

Summarises Teresa Amabile's research on creativity. "People will be most creative when they feel motivated primarily by the interest, enjoyment, satisfaction and challenge of the work itself - and not by external pressures." (p.55)

Landau, E. (1991) The Courage to be Gifted. Melbourne: Hawker Brownlow Education. (649.155/L253c) "I am strengthened in my belief that the creative approach is the basis for all self-actualization, the actualization of a person's gifts and talents. Therefore, for me creativity and giftedness are tightly interwoven. Both of these, creativity as well as talent, require the courage to be different from the average." (p.1) The fifteen short chapters include 'The creative attitude', 'The creative approach to education of the gifted', 'Aggression as creative energy', 'Parents and their gifted child', Problems parents see in the gifted children', 'Creative questions for the future', and four case studies.

Lewis, G. (1991) The need to create: Constructive and destructive behavior in creatively gifted children. Gifted Education International, 7 (2), 62-68.

"The article explores the relationship of 'creation' and 'destruction' in the creative process, however it argues that the destructive element can be transformed into a constructive element. This is achieved where creativity is rewarded and accepted in an atmosphere of tolerance. The writer discusses the negative effects of the repression of creativity and suggests that supported creative expression leads to mental health. She reports the findings of a research study to substantiate her hypotheses and makes suggestions for improved educational practice." (p.62)

Lytton, H. (1971) Creativity and Education. London: Routledge & Kegan Paul. (370.152/L998C)

Covers the creative process, convergent and divergent thinking, nurturing creativity, and the creative child at school. Includes a short appendix containing creativity test items.

Mason, B. (1989) It's in our CoRT now. Support for Learning, 4 (3), 175-180.

Discusses some of de Bono's CoRT materials, with examples from his own trianing of them at Heathfield Senior High School.

McAuliff, J.H. & Stoskin, L. (1987) Synectics: The creative connection. Gifted Child Today, 10 (4), 18-20. "The three phases of synectics (direct analogy, personal analogy, and symbolic analogy) give students an opportunity to see the familiar in strange new ways." (p.20)

Meador, K.S. (1994) The effect of synectics training on gifted and nongifted kindergarten students. Journal for the Education of the Gifted, 18 (1), 55-73.

"The current study confirmed that training in synectics, which is seldom used with young children, is an effective strategy for use in kindergarten. Although it revealed no significant differences between the experimental and control group in measured self-concept or verbal skills, it did demonstrate the positive effect of the training on student creativity. The training was beneficial for both gifted and non-gifted students." (p.69)

Milgram, R.M. & Hong, E. (1993) Creative thinking and creative performance in adolescents as predictors of creative attainments in adults: A follow-up study after 18 years. Roeper Review, 15 (3), 135-139.

"The findings suggest that creative thinking and creative performance are better predictors of adult life accomplishment than intelligence or school grades. ... As might be expected, school grades in adolescence predicted academic achievement in adults. However, grades in school were unrelated to any accomplishments in adult life outside the academic area. Intelligence test scores did not predict adult life accomplishment in a single life area." (p.138)

Monson, J.A. (1994) Getting serious about humor. Gifted Child Today, 17 (5), 14-17, 40-41.

Discusses the link between humor and creativity and suggests ways of using humor with gifted students: e.g., 'Tom Swifties', 'Boners', 'How's business' jokes, hunting for headlines, create a laugh centre.

Morgan, S.R. (1992) An analysis of behavioral differences of emotionally disturbed children assessed high on creativity. Psychology in the Schools, 29 (4), 301-306. [See under Social/Emotional Development]

Necka, E. (1989) Stimulating curiosity. Gifted Education International, 6 (1), 25-27.

"The article discusses the development and nurturing of curiosity and suggests the following principles: The rewarding of questioning, the use of open questions, delaying answers, accepting that knowledge is not finite and that our vision of the world is incomplete. The writer also suggests various teaching techniques: brainquestioning, role playing, hypothesizing and pursuing curiosity." (p. 25)

Perkins, D.N. (1984) Creativity by design. Educational Leadership, 42 (1), 18-25.

"Schools can promote creative thinking by focusing on aesthetics, purpose, mobility, objectivity, and intrinsic motivation, and by encouraging students to work at the edge of their competence." (p.18)

Perry, F. (1995) Exploring and developing creativity in young people. In J. Edwards (Ed.) Thinking: International Interdisciplinary Perspectives. Highett: Hawker Brownlow Education. pp.277-285. (153.42/T443, 1994)

Explains strategies for developing the inner voice and the inner eye - e.g., Moon art, Doodlebreak, Mapping, Brain photocopier, Mind walking, Improvisation, and Shifting perspective.

Renzulli, J.S. (1979) New Directions in Creativity: Mark 1/2/3. New York: Harper & Row. (372.8/R424N, Vol. 1/2/3) "The creativity training program described in this manual represents one attempt to provide both teachers and students with a set of materials that will help them learn a variety of ways for expressing their creative potential. Creativity is a dynamic process that involves 'a way of looking at things'; therefore the activities included in this program are designed to broaden the way that youngsters look at their world." (p.1, Vol.1) Based on part of Guilford's Structure of the Intellect model.

Rimm, S.B. (1987) Marching to the beat of a different drummer. Gifted Child Today, 10 (1), 2-6.

Discusses characteristics of creative underachievers and what parents and teachers can do to help them. "Creative children often feel so internally pressured to be creative that they define their personal creativity only as determined nonconformity." (p.6)

Rimm, S., Davis, G.A. & Bien, Y. (1982) Identifying creativity: A characteristics approach. Gifted Child Quarterly, 26 (4), 165-171.

Four inventories are discussed - GIFT, GIFFI I and II, and PRIDE. "The characteristics approach as measured by self-report inventories appear to be an efficient and effective method of selecting creative students ... when combined with at least one other method." (p.171)

Rose, L.H. & Lin, H. (1984) A meta-analysis of long-term creativity training programs. Journal of Creative Behavior, 18 (1), 11-22.

"The overall results of the meta-analysis suggest that training does affect creativity." (p.22)

Runco, M.A. (1993) Creativity as an Educational Objective for Disadvantaged Students Storrs: National Research Center on the Gifted and Talented. (CR371.9043/R939c) [See under Underachievers/Special Populations - General]

Runco, M.A. (1993) Divergent thinking, creativity and giftedness. Gifted Child Quarterly, 37 (1), 16-22. "This article reviews the most recent research on divergent thinking. Several new assessment techniques are reviewed, including those using either lenient or stringent solution standards, those relying on ideational pools (examinees' total output of ideas), and those involving qualitative aspects of ideation." (p.16)

Runco, M.A. & Nemiro, J. (1994) Problem finding, creativity, and giftedness. Roeper Review, 16 (4), 235-241.

"This article reviews the research showing problem finding to be distinct from problem solving, as well as the research supporting its role in intrinsically motivated creative performances. ... Specific educational implications and suggestions for developing the problem finding skills of gifted children are discussed." (p.235)

Smith, N. & Ainsworth, M. (1985) Ideas Unlimited. Melbourne: Nelson. (658.314/S655I) Concerned with promoting creative and innovative management but outlines many techniques of general applicability - e.g. slip writing, brainstorming, semantic processes, matrices.

Stanish, B. (1990) Mindanderings: Creative Classroom Approaches to Thinking, Writing and Problem Solving. Carthage: Good Apple. (CR370.157/S786m)

Provides examples of classroom uses for morphological synthesis, attribute listing, and analogies and metaphorical associations.

Stanish, B. (1986) Mindglow. Carthage: Good Apple. (153.4207/S786M)

Subtitled 'Classroom Encounters with Creative Thinking'. Contains activities for promoting creativity - e.g. 'Different ways of giving a book report', 'Ambiguities', 'Mind food', 'Improving', 'Seashells or how to organize a topic for creative expression'.

Starko, A.J. (1995) Creativity in the Classroom. White Plains: Longman. (370.157/S795c)

In particular see chapter 4, 'Creativity and talent development', chapter 5, 'Creativity in the content areas', chapter 6, 'Teaching creative thinking skills and habits' (which covers SCAMPER, attribute listing, synectics, visualization, CPS), and chapter 7, 'Motivation, creativity, and classroom organization'.

Sternberg, R.J. & Lubart, T.I. (1993) Creative giftedness: A multivariate investment approach. Gifted Child Quarterly, 37 (1), 7-15.

"This article presents an 'investment' view of creative giftedness. Creatively gifted individuals 'buy low and sell high.' In other words, they propose ideas that initially seem odd, out of sync with the ideas of others. ... In order to buy low and sell high, one needs a combination of six resources that function interactively: intelligence, knowledge, styles of thinking, personality, motivation, and environment. Each of these resources and its role in creative giftedness is described." (p.7)

Torrance, E.P. (1977) Encouraging Creativity in the Classroom. Dubuque: Wm. C. Brown. (371.3/T688E)

Discusses principles and specific ideas for encouraging creativity in children - e.g. the 'magic net' for creating and acting out stories (pp.3-5), 'going beyond textbooks' (pp.81-90), 'a poetry project in a Baltimore slum' (pp.111-112) and 'what happens when teachers are respectful of unusual questions and ideas' (pp.117-119).

Torrance, E.P. (1984) The role of creativity in identification of the gifted and talented. Gifted Child Quarterly, 28 (4), 153-156.
Suggests five policies and procedures regarding the identification of the gifted/talented, e.g. "Creativity should almost always be one of the criteria, though not the sole criterion." (p.155)

Treffinger, D.J. (1986) Research on creativity. Gifted Child Quarterly, 30 (1), 15 19.

"What is the relationship of creativity to gifted behavior? The author raises key questions relative to previous research in the field. He builds and defends a model for weaving creativity into the fabric of exceptional performance in any arena of endeavor." (p.15)

Wallace, B. (1986) Creativity: some definitions: The creative personality; the creative process; the creative classroom. Gifted Education International, 4 (2), 68-73.

An overview of creativity and how to foster it.

Wallace, D.B. & Gruber, H.E. (1989) Creative People at Work. New York: Oxford University Press. (153.35/W188c)

"Our book is about how creative people do what they do. It has three main aspects: we present a unifying theoretical approach to creative work, one that welcomes and takes account of the natural diversity of creators and their products; we grapple with the problem of simultaneously insisting on the uniqueness of each creative person and remaining true to the goal of contributing to the scientific understanding of creativity; and we provide a set of case studies of creative people at work, illustrating both the unity of our approach and the diversity of creative people." (p.v.)

Wassermann, S. (1992) Serious play in the classroom: How messing around can win you the Nobel Prize. Childhood Education. 68 (3), 133-139.

"The creation of new ideas does not come from minds trained to follow doggedly what is already known. Creation comes from tinkering and playing around, from which new forms emerge." (p.134) Cites the case of Richard Feynman as an example of the link between play and significant outcomes and discusses 'building curriculum based on serious play'.

Williams, F.E. (1972) A Total Creativity Program for Individualizing and Humanizing the Learning Process: Identifying and Measuring Creative Potential. (Vols 1 and 3) Englewood Cliffs: Educational Technology Publications. (371.3/W723t)

Includes a volume on 'Identifying and measuring creative potential', another on 'Encouraging creative potential', a teachers handbook, demonstration cassettes and a teaching strategies packet.

REFERENCES

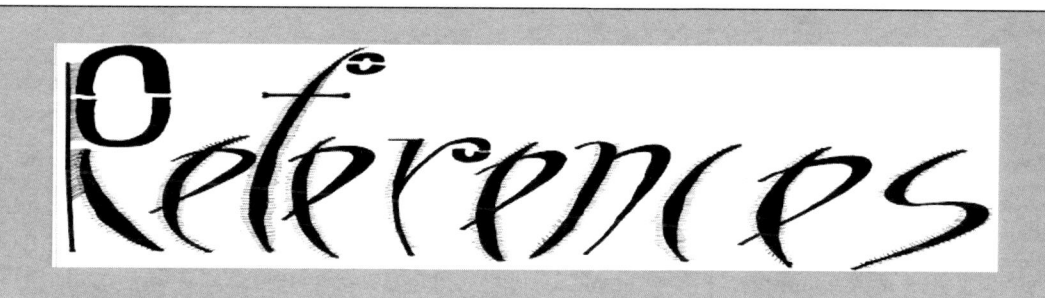

Albrecht, K. (1987). *Brain Building*. New Jersey: Prentice Hall.

Amend, Victor E. and Hendrick, Leo T. (1964). *Ten Contemporary Thinkers*. Toronto: The Free Press of Glencoe.

Aptheker, Herbert (1965). *Marxism and Alienation*. New York: Humanities Press:

Arendt, Hannah (1958). *The Human Condition*. Chicago: The University of Chicago Press.

Aristotle (1943). *On Man in the Universe*. New York: Walter J. Black.

Avey, Albert E. (1952). *Handbook in the History of Philosophy*. New York: Barnes & Noble, Inc.

Ayer, A. J. (1968). *Language, Truth and Logic*. New York: Dover Publications, Inc.

Baird, Forrest E. (2000). *Nineteenth-Century Philosophy*. New Jersey: Prentice Hall.

Ballard, Keith Emerson (1972). *Study Guide for Copy: Introduction to Logic* New York: The MacMillan Company.

Beardsley, Monroe C. (1960). *The European Philosophers from Descartes to Nietzsche*. New York: The Modern Library.

Berkeley (1968). *A Treatise Concerning the Principles of Human Knowledge*. New York: The Bobbs-Merrill Company, Inc.

Berkman, Alexander (1970). *Prison Memoirs of an Anarchis*. New York: Schocken Books.

Becker, Carl L. (1970). *The Heavenly City of the Eighteenth-century Philosophers. Based on the Storrs Lectures Delivered at Yale University*. London: New Haven.

Beckett, Samuel (1954). *Waiting for Godot*. New York: Evergreen.

Bierman, Arthur K. and Assali, Robin N. (1996). *The Critical Thinking Handbook*. New Jersey: Prentice Hall.

Biffle, Christopher (1999) *Landscape of Wisdom. A Guided Tour of Western Philosophy,* Mayfield Publishing Company: Mountain View, CA, London, Toronto.

Birsch, Douglas (2000). *Ethical Insights. A Brief Introduction,* Mayfield Publishing Company: Mountain View, CA.

Borges, Jorge L. (1969). *The Book of Imaginary Beings,* Discus Books: New York.

Borges, Jorge L. (1988). *The Book of Fantasy,* Viking: New York.

Boethius (1966). *The Consolation of Philosophy,* The Bobbs-Merrill Company, Inc.: New York.

Bressert, S. (2005). What is Emotional Intelligence? Retrieved 8/12/2009 from http://psychcentral.com/lib/2007/what-is-emotional-intelligence-eq/

Burhardt Du Bois, W.E. (1968). *Dusk of Dawn,* Schocken Books: New York

Burr, John R. and Goldinger, Milton (2000). *Philosophy and Contemporary Issues*. New Jersey: Prentice Hall.

Burt, Edwin A. (1939). *The English Philosophers from Bacon to Mill. The Golden Age of English Philosophy*. New York: The Modern Library.

Camus, Albert (1946). *The Stranger*. New York: Vintage Books.

Camus, Albert (1946). *The Rebel*. New York: Vintage Books.

Camus, Albert (1955). *The Myth of Sisyphus*. New York: Vintage Books.

Camus, Albert (1956). *The Fall*. New York: Vintage Books.

Camus, Albert (1973). *A Happy Death*. New York: Vintage Books.

Capouya, Emila and Tompkins, Keitha (1975). *The Essential Kropotkin: A general selection from the writings of the great Russian anarchist thinker*. New York: Liveright.

Capra, Fritjof (1991) *The Tao of Physics*. Boston: Shambhala.

Carnap, Rudolf (1967). *Meaning and Necessity*. Chicago: The University of Chicago Press.

Carney, James D. (1974). *Fundamentals of Logic*. New York: Macmillan Publishing Company, Inc..

Cassirer, Ernst (1973). *The Philosophy of Symbolic Forms*. New Haven: Yale University Press.

Chappell, V.C. (1966). *Hume: A Collection of Critical Essays*. New York: Doubleday & Company, Inc.

Chomsky, Noam (1968). *Language and Mind*. : New York: Harcourt, Brace & World, Inc.

Cleary, Thomas (1993). *The Essential Koran: The Heart of Islam*. New York: Castle Books.

REFERENCES

Cohen, Elliot D. (1999). *Philosophers at Work: The Issues and Practice of Philosophy*. New York: Harcourt College Publishers.

Coleman, Francis J. (1968). *Aesthetics: Contemporary Studies in Aesthetics*. New York: McGraw-Hill Book Company.

Cooper, Lane (1967). *Aristotle on the Art of Poetry*. New York: Cornell University Press:

Copi, Irving M. and Gould, James A. (1968). *Contemporary Readings in Logical Theory*. New York: The Macmillan Company:

Copi, Irving M. (1969). *Symbolic Logic*. New York: The Macmillan Company:

Copi, Irving M. (1994). *Introduction to Logic*. New York: The Macmillan Company:

Copi, I. M. and Carl Cohen (1994). *Introduction to Logic*. New York: The Macmillan Company.

Copi, Irving M. (1990). *Solutions to Exercises. Introduction to Logic*. New York: The Macmillan Company.

Copleston, Frederick (1964). *A History of Philosophy. 17 Volumes*. New York: Garden City Pub.

Cornford, Donald (1964). *The Republic of Plato*. New York: Oxford University Press.

Danto, Arthur (1969). *Philosophy of Science*, A Merilian Book: New York.

Derrida, Jacques (1986). *Margins of Philosophy*. Chicago: The University of Chicago Press:

Dewey, John (1957). *Reconstruction in Philosophy*, The Beacon Press: Boston.

Dewey, John (1979). *The Middle Works 1899-1924*. Carbondale: Southern Illinois University Press.

Drennen, D.A. (1962). *A Modern Introduction to Metaphysics*. New York: The Free Press:

Drinnon, Richard (1961). *Rebel in Paradise: A Biography of Emma Goldman*. Chicago: University of Chicago Press.

Easton, Loyd D. (1964). *Writings of the Young Marx on Philosophy and Society*. New York: A Doubleday Anchor Book.

Edman, Irwin (1939). *Arts and the Man*. New York: W.W. Norton & Co.

Edwards, Paul and Pap, Arthur (1966). *A Modern Introduction to Philosophy*. New York: The Free Press.

Elbow, P. (1986). *Embracing Contraries: Explorations in Learning and Teaching*. New York: Oxford University Press.

Elwes, R.H. (1955). *The Chief Works of Benedict de Spinoza*. New York: Dover Publications, Inc.

Euthyphro, Apology, Crito (1956). *Plato*. New York: The Bobbs-Merrill Company, Inc.

Feldman, Richard (1999). *Reason and Argument*. New Jersey: Prentice Hall.

Feynman, Richard P. (1989). *What Do You Care What Other People Think? Further Adventures of a Curious Character*. New York: Bantam Books.

Feynman, Richard P. (1989). *"Surely You're Joking, Mr. Feynman!" Adventures of a Curious Character*. New York: Bantam Books:

Feynman, Richard P. (1995). *Six Pieces. Essentials of Physics Explained by Its Most Brilliant Teacher*. New York: Helix Books.

Finch, H.L. (1995). *Wittgenstein*. Rockport, MA: Element.

Finer, S.E. (1979). *Five Constitutions*. New York: Penguin Books.

Flage, Daniel E. (1995). *Understanding Logic*. New Jersey: Prentice Hall.

Flage, Daniel E. (1995). *Instructional Manual. Understanding Logic*. New Jersey: Prentice Hall: New Jersey.

Fletcher, Joseph (1962). *Situation Ethics: The New Morality*. Philadelphia.

Frankfort, Henri (1968). *Before Philosophy*. Baltimore, Maryland: Penguin Books.

Kaufmann, Walter (1966). *Neitzsche*. New York: The Viking Press.

Freuer, Lewis (1959). *Marx and Engels: Basic Writings on Politics and Philosophy*. New York: Anchor Books.

Fromm, Eric (1971). *Marx's Concept of Man*. New York: Frederick Ungar Publishing Co.

Fuller, Lon L. (1964). *The Morality of Law*. New Haven: Yale University Press:

Gaarder, Jostein (1997). *Sophie's World. A Novel About the History of Philisiphy*. New York: Berkley Books.

Girvetz, Harry K. (1964). *Contemporary Moral Issues*. Belmont, CA: Wadsworth Publishing Company:

Goodstein, David L. and Goodstein, Judith R. (1992). *Feynman's Lost Lectures*. New York: Norton.

Great Dialogues of Plato (1956). New York: A Mentor Book.

Grene, David and Richamond Lattimore Editors (1960). *Greek Tragedies*. Chicago: The University of Chicago Press.

Gribbin, John (1984). *In Search of Schrodinger's Cat: Quantum Physics and Reality*. New York: Bantam Books.

Hampshire, Stuart (1967). *Spinoza*. Baltimore, Maryland: Penguin Books.

Harman, Gilbert (1974). *On Noam Chomsky Critical Essays*. Boston: The University of Massachusetts Press.

Hartshorne, Charles (1962). *The Logic of Perfection*. Illinois: Open Court.

Hartshorne, Charles (1967). *A Natural Theology for Our Time*. Illinois: Open Court.

REFERENCES

Hartshorne, Charles (1967). *The Divine Relativity: A Social Conception of God.* Illinois: Open Court.

Hartshorne, Charles (1969). *Creative Synthesis and Philosophic Method.* La Salle, Illinois: The Open Court Publishing Co.

Hayakawa, S. I. (1941). *Language in Action.* New York: Harcourt, Brace and Company:

Hayman, Ronald (1980). *Nietzsche: A Critical Life.* New York: Penguin Books.

Heidegger, Martin (1971). *Poetry, Language and Thought.* New York: Harper Colophon Books.

Heilbroner, Robert (1992). *The Worldly Philosophers. The Lives, Times and Ideas of the Great Economic Thinkers.* New York: A Touchstone Book.

Hicks, Stephen R. (1994). *The Art of Reasoning: Readings for Logical Analysis.* New York: W.W. Norton & Company:

Hobbes, Thomas (1958). *Leviathan; Parts One and Two.* New York: The Library of Liberal Arts.

Hoffer, Eric (1966). *The Temper of Our Time.* New York: Perennial Library:

Homer (1989). *The Odyssey.* New York: Everyman's Library.

Honderich, Ted (1995). *The Oxford Companion to Philosophy.* New York: Oxford University Press.

Hunnex, Milton D. (1986). *Chronological and Thematic Charts of Philosophies and Philosophers.* Academia: Michigan.

Lames, King (1992). *The Full Life Study Bible.* Zondervan Publishing House: Grand Rapids, Michigan.

James, William (1964). *Essays in Pragmatism.* Harper Tourchbooks: New York.

James, William (1971). *The Essential Writings.* Harper Tourchbooks: New York.

James, William (1997). *Selected Writings.* Book-of-the-Month Club: New York.

Jaspers, Karl (1962). *Kant. From the Great Philosophers.* A Harvest Book: New York.

Jaspers, Karl (1966). *Way to Wisdom.* Yale University Press: New Haven and London.

Jaspers, Karl (1972). *Philosophy of Existence.* University of Pennsylvania Press: Philadelphia.

Jaspers, Karl (1989). *Pholisophy and the World. Selected Essays.* Gateway Editions: Washington, D.C.

Johnson, Robert M. (1992). *A Logic Book.* Wadsworth Publishing Company: New York.

Jones, W.T. (1952). *The Classical Mind.* Harcourt, Brace: New York.

Jones, W.T. (1969). *Hobbes to Hume.* Harcourt, Brace: New York.

Jones, W.T. (1969). *The Medieval Mind.* Harcourt, Brace: New York.

Jones, W.T. (1969). *Kant to Wittgenstein and Sartre.* Harcourt, Brace: New York

Kafka, Franz (1964). *The Castle.* The Modern Library: New York.

Kafka, Franz (1964). *The Trial.* Schocken Books: New York.

Kafka, Franz (1964). *The Great Wall of China.* Schocken Books: New York.

Kahane, Howard and Cavender, Nancy (1998). *Logic and Contemporary Rhetoric: The Use of Reason in Everyday Life.* Wadsworth Publishing Company: Belmont, CA, London, Toronto, Tokyo, New York.

Kant, Immanuel (1951). *Critique of Judgement.* Hafner Publishing Company: New York and London.

Kant, Immanuel (1951). *Critique of Practical Reason.* Hafner Publishing Company: New York and London.

Kant, Immanuel (1958). *Critique of Pure Reason.* The Modern Library: New York.

Kaufmann, Walter (1972). *Existentialism from Dostoevsky to Sartre.* A Meridian Book: New York.

Kaufmann, Walter (1974). *Nietzsche: Philosopher, Psychologist, and Antichrist.* Princeton: New Jersey.

Kierkegaard, Soren (1956). *Purity of Heart.* Harper & Row, Publishers: New York.

Kierkegaard, Soren (1959). *Either/Or.* Harper & Row, Publishers: New York.

Kierkegaard, Soren (1962). *The Point of View for My Work as an Author.* Harper & Row, Publishers: New York.

Kierkegaard, Soren (1964). *Stages on Life's Way,* Schocken Books: New York.

Kirby, Gary R. and Goodpaster, Jeffery R. (1999). *Thinking,* Prentice Hall: New Jersey.

Kloss, Jethro (1992). *Back to Eden,* Back to Eden Publishing: New York.

Krimerman, Leonard I. (1966). *Patterns of Anarchy. A Collection of Writings on the Anarchist Tradition,* Anchor Books: New York.

Lavrin, Janko (1971). *Nietzsche. A biographical Introduction.* Charles Scribner's Sons: New York.

Lawhead, William (2000). *The Philosophical Journey: An Interactive Approach.* Mayfield Publishing Company: Mountain View, CA, London.

Layman, Stephen C. (1999). *The Power of Logic:* Mayfield Publishing Company: Mountain View, CA, London, Toronto.

Leiser, Burtin M. (1973). *Liberty, Justice, and Morals: Contemporary Value Conflicts.* The MacMillan Company: New York.

Lillie, William (1957). *An Introduction to Ethics.* Barnes & Noble: New York.

REFERENCES

Lippman, Walter (1960). *A Preface to Morals*. Beacon Press: Boston.

Livraga, Giorgio A. (1989). *Thebes*. New Acropolis, Publisher: Valencia, Spain.

Lowenthal, Marvin (1935). *The Autobiography of Michel de Montaigne*. Vintage Book: New York.

Macintyre, Alasdair (1965). *Hume's Ethical Writings*. Collier Books: New York.

Macintyre, Alasdair (1971). *Herbert Marcuse: An Exposition and a Polemis*. The Viking Press: New York.

Mann, Heinrich (1962). The Living Thoughts of *Nietzsche*. David McKay Company: Washington Square, Philadelphia.

Marcus Aurelius and His Time. The Transition from Paganism to Christianity. Walter J. Black, Inc.: New York.

Marcuse, Herbert (1962). *Eros and Civilization: A Philosophical Inquiry into Freud*. Vintage Books: New York.

Marcuse, Herbert (1964). *One-Dimensional Man*. Vintage Books: New York.

Marcuse, Herbert (1969). *An Essay on Liberation*. New York: Vintage Books.

Martin, C.B. and Armstrong D.M. (1968). *Locke and Berkeley*. New York: Anchor Books.

Marx, Karl (1986). *The Essential Writings*. London: Westview Press.

Marx, Karl (1987). *Capita*. London: Westview Press.

Marx, Karl and Engels, Friedrich (1992). *The Communist Manifesto*. New York: Bantam Books.

Matthews, Anne (1992). *Where the Buffalo Roam: The Storm over the Revolutionary Plan to Restore America's Great Plains*. New York: Grove Press.

McGinn, Marie (1997). *Wittgenstein and Philosophical Investigation*. New York: Marie McGinn.

Meszaros, Istvan (1970). *Marx's Theory of Alienation*. New York: Harper Torchbooks.

Meyerhoff, Hans (1958). *The Philosophy of History in Our Time: An Anthology*. New York: Doubleday & Company, Inc.

Michod, Richard E. (1995). *Eros and Evolution: A Natural Philosophy of Sex*. New York: Helix Books.

Mill, John S. (1961). *The Utilitarians*. New York: Dolphin Books.

Mill, John S. (1956). *On Liberty*. New York: The Bobbs-Merrill Company, Inc.

Millman, Dan (1989). *Way of the Peaceful Warrior*. Tiburon, CA: H.J. Kramer, Inc.

Miura, Isshu and Sasaki, Ruth Fuller (1965). *The Zen Koan*. New York: A Harvest Book.

Molina, Fernando R. (1969). *The Sources of Existentialism as Philosophy*. New Jersey: Prentice-Hall.

Montaigne, Michel (1943). *Selected Essays*. New York: Walter J. Black.

Montaigne, Michel (1968). *In Defense of Raymond Sebond*. New York: Frederick Ungar Publishing Co..

Moore, G.E. (1971). *Principia Ethica*. Cambridge at the University Press.

Moore, Walter (1994). *Schrodinger Life and Though*. New York: Cambridge University Press.

Morgan, George A. (1965). *What Nietzsche Means*. New York: Harper Torchbooks.

Neibuhr, Reinhold (1964). *Marx & Engels on Reigion*. New York: Schocken Books.

Neihardt, John G. (1961). *Black Elk Speaks. Being the Life Story of a Holy Man of the Oglala Sioux*. University of Nebraska Press: Lincoln.

Nietzsche, Friedrich (1967). *The Will to Power*. New York: Vintage Books.

Nietzsche, Friedrich (1967). *Ecce Homo and The Birth of Tragedy*. New York: The Modern Library.

Nietzsche, Friedrich (1982). Volumes One, Two, Three. Four. San Francisco: Harper.

Nietzsche, Friedrich (1966). *Beyond Good and Evil*. New York: Vintage Books.

Nietzsche, Friedrich (1956). *The Birth of Tragedy and The Genealogy of Morals*. New York: Doubleday & Company, Inc.

Ortega, Jose (1941). *History as a System and Other Essay Toward a Philosophy of History*. New York: W.W. Norton & Company, Inc.

Ouspensky, P.D. (1957). *The Fourth Way*. New York: Vintage Books.

Ouspensky, P.D. (1957). *Tertium Oganum: A Key to the Enigmas of the World*. New York: Vintage Books.

Paine, Thomas (1986). *Common Sense*. New York: Penguin Books.

Parker, Dewitt H. (1931). *Human Values. In Interpretation of Ethics Based on a Study of Values*. New York: Harper & Brothers Publishers.

Pascal (1993). *Pensee*. Paris: Bordas.

Peck, Abe (1991). *Uncovering the Sixties: The Life and Times of the Underground Press*. New York: Citadel Press.

Pech, James (1987). *The Chomsky Reader*. New York: Pantheon Books.

Peterfreund, Sheldon P. (1959). *An Introduction to American Philosophy*. New York: The Odyssey Press, Inc.

Peters, Eugene H. (1970). *Hartshorne and Neoclassical Metaphysics; An Interpretation*. University of Nebraska Press: Lincoln.

REFERENCES

Philosophy in Context: An Experiment in Teaching. Cleveland, OH: Cleveland State University Department of Philosophy.

Piper, Thomas R., Gentile, Mary C. and Sharon D. Parks (1993). *Can Ethics Be Taught? Perspectives, Challenges, and Approaches at Harvard Business School.* Boston: Harvard Business School.

Plato (1949). *Meno.* New York: The Bobbs-Merrill Company, Inc.

Plato (1949). *Timaeus.* Borges, Jorge L.

Plato (1952). *Gorgias.* New York: The Bobbs-Merrill Company, Inc.

Plato's Phaedo (1955). New York: The Bobbs-Merrill Company, Inc.

Plato (1965) *The Plato Dictionary.* New Jersey: Littlefield, Adams and Co.

Plato (1971) *Timaeus and Critias.* London: Penguin Books.

Plato (1972). *The Last Days of Socrates.* New York: Penguin Books.

Plato (1994). *The Collected Dialogues Including the Letters.* Princeton: Bollingen Series.

Pojman, Louis P. (2000). *Philosophical Traditions: A Text with Readings.* New York: Wadsworth Publishing Company.

Popkin, Richard H. (1964). *The History of Skepticism from Erasmus to Descartes.* New York: Harper Torch books.

Potter, J. (2005). *Becoming a Strategic Thinker: Developing Skills for Success.* New Jersey: Prentice Hall.

Potter, J. (2005). *Becoming a Strategic Thinker: Developing Skills for Success.* New Jersey: Prentice Hall

Price, Joan A. (2000). *Philosophy through the Ages.* Wadsworth: Australia, Canada, South Africa, United States.

Pyziur, Eugene (1968). *The Doctrine of Anarchism of Michael A. Bakunin.* Chicago: A Gateway Edition.

Quine, Willard Van Orman (1960). *Word and Object.* Cambridge, MA: The M.I.T. Press.

Ratner, Joseph (1954). *The Philosophy of Spinoza.* New York: Modern Library Book.

Rawl, John (1971). *A Theory of Justice.* Boston: Harvard University Press.

Read, Herbert (1969). *Icon and Idea. The Function of Art in the Development of Human Consciousness.* New York: Schocken Books.

Read, Herbert (1971). *Anarchy & Order: Essays in Politics.* Boston: Beacon Press.

Reck, Andrew J. (1976). *Introduction to William James.* London: Indiana University Press.

Regis, Ed (1990). *Great Mambo Chicken & The Transhuman Condition. Science Slightly over the Edge.* Ontario: Addison-Wesley Publishing Company, Inc.

Reichenbach, Hans (1958). *Space and Time.* New York: Dover Publications, Inc.

Roeder, Ralph (1958). *The Man of the Renaissance.* New York: Meridian Books, Inc.

Rosenberg, Jay F. (1971). *Readings in the Philosophy of Language.* Prentice Hall: New Jersey.

Rousseau, Jean-Jacques (1950). *Emile.* New York: Great Neck.

Rousseau, Jean-Jacques (1990). *The Social Contract and Discourses.* London: Everyman's Library.

Rude, George (1964). *Revolutionary Europe 1783-1815.* New York: Harper Torchbooks.

Ruggiero, Ryan (1989). *Critical Thinking.* College Survival Inc.: Rapid City, SD.

Runes, Dagobert D. (1972). *Dictionary of Philosophy.* New York: Philosophical Library.

Russell, Bertrand (1956). *The Autobiography of Bertrand Russell.* Boston: Little, Brown and Company

Russell, Bertrand (1959). *My Philosophical Development.* New York: Simon and Schuster.

Russell, Bertrand (1959). *The Problem of Philosophy.* London: Oxford University Press.

Russell, Bertrand (1951). *Skeptical Essays.* New York: Barnes & Noble Books.

Russell, Bertrand (1957). *Mysticism and Logic.* New York: Anchor Books.

Russell, Bertrand (1967). *Why I Am not a Christian.* New York: Clarion Books

Russell, Bertrand (1969). *Philosophical Essays.* New York: Simon and Schuster.

Russell, Bertrand (1972). *A Collection of Critical Essays.* New York: Anchor Books.

Sahakian, William S. (1968). *History of Philosophy.* New York: Barnes & Noble Books.

Salmon, Wesley C. (1973). *Logic.* New Jersey: Prentice-Hall, Inc.

Santayana, George (1952). *Scepticism and Animal Faith: Introduction to a System of Philosophy.* New York: Charles Scribner's Sons.

Sartre, Jean-Paul (1967). *Essays in Existentialism.* New York: The Citadel Press.

Schaff, Adam (1973). *Language and Cognition.* New York: McGraw-Hill Book Company.

Scheler, Max (1972). *Ressentiment.* New York: Schocken Books.

Shulman, Alix K. (1972). *Red Emma Speaks: Selected Writings and Speeches by Emma Goldman.* New York: Vintage Books.

Selected Stories of Franz Kafka (1952). New York: Modern Library.

REFERENCES

Skinner, B.F. (1990). *Beyond Freedom and Dignity*. New York: Bantam Books.

Smith, T.V. and Marjorie Green (1957). *Philosophers Speak for Themselves from Descartes to Locke*. Chicago: The University of Chicago Press.

Sophocles (1952). *The Theban Plays: King Oedipus. Oedipus at Colonus. Antigone*. New York: Penguin Books.

Sophocles (1952). *Electra and Other Plays*. New York: Penguin Books.

Smith, T.V. (editor) (1969). *Berkley, Hume, and Kant*. Chicago: The University of Chicago Press.

Spinoza, Benedictus (1961). *The Principles of Descartes' Philosophy*. Illinois: The Open Court Publishing Company.

Stebbing, Susan L. (1950). *A Modern Introduction to Logic*. New York: Harper Torchbooks.

Stirner, Max (1972). *The Ego and His Own: The Case of the Individual Against Authority*. New York: Dover Publications, Inc.

Stott, John R. (1971). *Basic Christianity*. Illinois: Intervarsity Press.

Stuhr, John J. (1987). *Classical American Philosophy. Essential Readings and Interpretive Essays*. New York: Oxford University Press.

Stumpf, Samuel E. (1999). *Socrates to Sartre: A History of Philosophy*. New York: McGraw Hill Company.

Taylor, Richard (1974). *Metaphysics*. New Jersey: Prentice-Hall, Inc.

The Age of Analysis: Basic Writings of: Bergson, Peirce, Whitehead and Others (1962). New York: A Mentor Book.

The Age of Belief: Basic Writings of: St. Augustine, Boethius Abelard, St. Bernard, St. Thomas Aquinas, Duns Scotus, William of Ockham. (1962). New York: A Mentor Book.

The Age of Reason: Basic Writings of: Bacon, Pascal, Hobbes, Galileo, Descartes, Spinoza, and Leibniz (1963). New York: A Mentor Book.

The Basic Writings of Bertrand Russell. New York: Simon and Schuster.

The Encyclopedia of Philosophy. 8 Volumes. New York: Macmillan Publishing Company.

The Rationalists: Descartes, Spinoza & Leibniz. (1974). New York: Anchor Books.

Tivnan, Edward (1995). *The Moral Imagination: Confronting the Ethical Issues of Our Day*. New York: A Touchstone Book.

Tucker, Robert (1971). *The Marxian Revolutionary Idea*. New York: W.W. Norton & Company, Inc.

Tucker, Robert (1972). *The Marx-Engels Reader*. New York: W.W. Norton & Company. Inc.

Venable, Vernon (1966). *Human Nature. The Marxian View*. Meridian Cleveland, OH: Meridian Books.

Walsh, Jill P. (1998). *Knowledge of Angels*. London: Black Swan.

Weisskopf, Walter A. (1973). *Alienation and Economics*. A Delta Book: New York.

White, Thomas I. (1988). *Right and Wrong: A brief Guide to Understanding Ethics*. New Jersey: Prentice Hall.

White, Thomas I. (1989). *Right and Wrong: A brief Guide to Understanding Ethics*. New Jersey: Prentice Hall.

Warnock, G.J. (1966). *English Philosophy since 1900*. New York: Oxford University Press.

Whitehead, Alfred N. (1938). *Modes of Thought*. New York: The Free Press.

Whitehead, Alfred N. (1952). *Symbolism, Its Meaning and Effect*. New York: The Free Press.

Whitehead, Alfred N. (1961). *Adventures of Ideas*. New York: The Free Press.

Wilson, Colin (1974). *The Philosopher's Stone*. Warner Books: New York: Warner Books.

Wippel, John F. (1969). *Medieval Philosophy*. New York: The Free Press.

Wittgenstein, Ludwig (1975). *Philosophical Remarks*. Chicago: The University of Chicago Press.

Wittgenstein, Ludwig (1997). *Tractatus Logico-Philosophius*. London: Poutledge.

Wolff, Robert P. (1998). *In Defense of Anarchism*. New York: Harper Torchbooks.

Wolff, Robert P. (1998). *About Philosophy*. New Jersey: Prentice Hall.

Yutang, Lin (1938). *The Wisdom of Confucius*. New York: The Modern Library.

Index

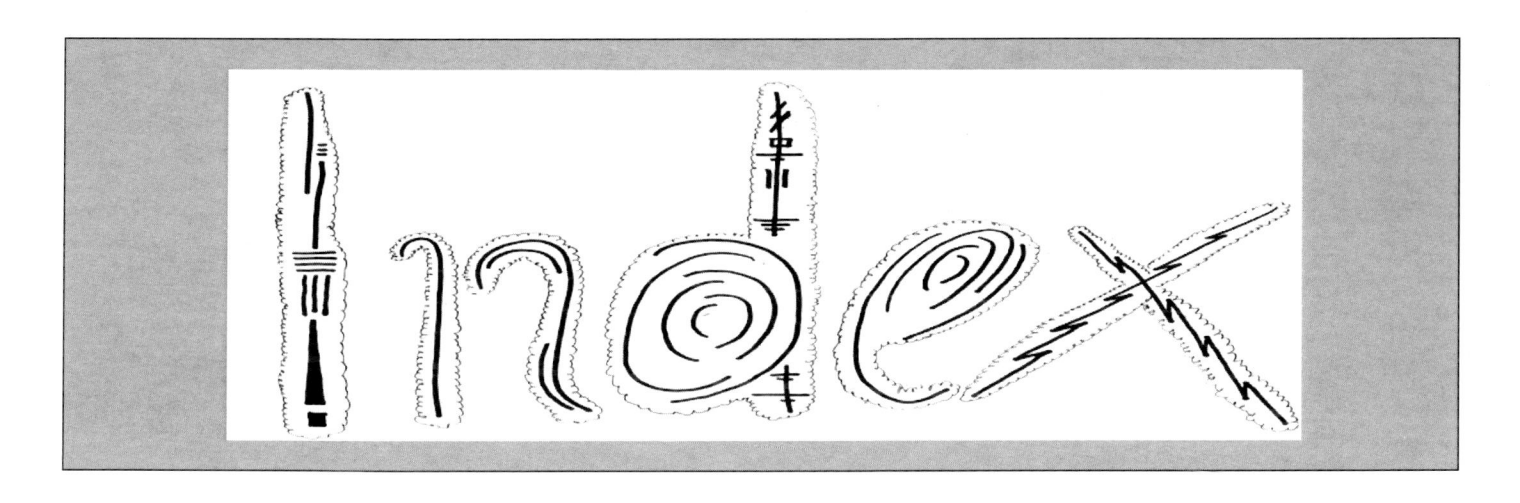

Brain, 2-16
    cerebral cortex, 9
    functions, 3-16
    interesting fact, 10
    glial cells, 7-9
    neurons, 7,
    neurotransmission, 8
    structure, 2-16
    synapses, 9 – 10

Creativity
    blocks, 262-264
    Da Vinci principles, 331
    definitions, 253
    enemies of ideas, 263
    environment, 53-56, 317
    improving, 331
    killer phrases, 262-265
    motivation, 316
    personal, 255
    self and creativity, 78
    stages of creative process, 291
    techniques, 263-273

Development
    early brain development, 44
    children creativity, 49
    genetic theory, 51
    gifted children, 51
    parental influence, 50
    predictability, 52
    sensitive period, 45
    stages of thinking development, 46

Intelligence, 87-101
    components, 93
    crystallized intelligence, 36
    emotional, 37, 38
    fluid intelligence, 36
    Gardner's Multiple Intelligences Theory, 91
    genius, 89
    history of study, 89
    interesting facts, 96
    IQ, 89
    range, 89
    Sternberg's theory, 93

Learning
    cognitive learning, 27
    conditioned stimuli, 19
    conditioned response, 19
    classical conditioning, 19-22
    learning enhancement, 29
    operant conditioning, 22-23
    social learning theory, 23-25
    unconditioned response, 19
    unconditioned stimuli, 19
    'What-Is-It?' Reaction, 25-26

Modes of thinking, 121- 250
    abductive thinking, 218, 248
        definition, 218
    analogical thinking, 123-133, 232
        Archimides' principle, 126
        definition, 123
        metaphors, 128, 131
        organizer, 126
        stages, 127
    analysis, 147-150, 233
        Aristotle's categories, 152
        attribution, 148
        definition, 147
        morphological, 151
        skills, 147
    automatic thinking, 225, 249
        assumptions, 225
        definition, 225
    conscious thinking, 189, 242
        definition, 189
    convergent thinking, 189, 241

definition, 189
critical thinking, 191, 238
    definition, 191
    elements, 192
    standards, 193
    traits, 194
deductive thinking, 202
    categorical syllogism, 203
    definition, 202
    four figures, 204
    hypothetical syllogism, 207-208
    rhetoric's, 206
    validity, 205
dialectical thinking, 169, 233
    definition, 169
    Hegel, 169
    history of study, 169-170
    laws, 170-172
    technique, 173
divergent thinking, 181, 240
    definition, 181
    strategies, 181
    techniques, 185
heuristic thinking, 178
    definition, 178
    intuition, 179, 181
holistic thinking, 158-160, 234
    definition, 158
    technique, 160
inductive thinking, 212, 245
    definition, 212
    informal fallacies, 212-213
    technique, 213-214
integrative thinking, 173, 237
    cause and effect, 174
    definition, 173
    interpretation, 175
    irrational believes, 176-177
    steps, 173
    technique, 178
reversal thinking, 227
    definition, 227
symbolic thinking, 138-146, 232
    definition, 138
    historical review, 138
    language, 139
    relation to creativity, 141
    semiotics, 142-144
synthesis, 156
    definition, 156
    question cues, 156
    skills, 156
systems thinking, 161
    components, 161
    definition, 161
    modularity, 164-165
    types, 162
the "Believing Game," 219, 249
    definition, 219
the "Doubting Game," 219, 248
    definition, 219
unconscious thinking, 189, 244
    definition, 189

Thinking, 101-122
    concepts, 104, 112
    conceptual differentiation, 37
    definition, 101
    judgment, 118
    lateral, 37
    memory, 106
    problem-solving, 119
    reasoning, 103
    recognition, 112
    technique, 210-212
    vertical, 37

Problem-Solving
    barriers, 295
    behavioral influence, 290
    common barriers, 295
    decision making, 285
        definition, 285
        group decision making, 293
        process, 286
        programmed, 285
    problem's definition, 285
    problem's solutions, 296

Problem-Solving Techniques
    analogical thinking, 133
    CIA technique, 153-155
    content analysis, 153-155
    creative, 268-273
    critical thinking (Da Vinci), 195-197
    Da Vinci's technique, 168-169
    deductive thinking, 210-212
    divergent thinking, 185
    group activities, 274-280
    holistic thinking, 160
    idea quota, 16
    informal fallacies, 212-213
    integrative thinking, 173
    mindmaping, 12-15
    symbolic thinking, 146
    synectic, 299-308
    synthesis, 156-157
    system thinking, 167

Prominent Thinkers
    failure and greatness, 311
    genius, 329
        csikzentmihalyi's theory, 322-324
        Eysenck's principles, 319
        Guilford's theory, 318
        Maslow's theory, 312
    giftedness, 318
    histories of creative people, 322
    Maslow's humanistic perspective, 312
    primary traits, 319